ADVANCED ENGINE PERFORMANCE DIAGNOSIS

SEVENTH EDITION

James D. Halderman
Curt Ward

Vice President, Portfolio Management: Andrew Gilfillan

Executive Portfolio Manager: Jenifer Niles

Portfolio Management Assistant: Lara Dimmick

Senior Vice President, Marketing: David Gesell

Marketing Coordinator: Elizabeth MacKenzie-Lamb

Director, Digital Studio and Content Production: Brian Hyland

Digital Studio Producer: Allison Longley

Managing Producer: Cynthia Zonneveld

Managing Producer: Jennifer Sargunar

Content Producer: Holly Shufeldt

Content Producer: Faraz Sharique Ali

Manager, Rights Management: Johanna Burke

Operations Specialist: Deidra Smith

Cover Design: Pearson CSC

Cover Credit: Henrik5000/Getty Images

Full-Service Management and Composition: Integra Software Service Pvt. Ltd.

Printer/Binder: LSC Communications, Inc.

Cover Printer: LSC Communications

Text Font: Times LT Pro

Library of Congress Cataloging-in-Publication Data

Names: Halderman, James D., author.

Title: Advanced engine performance diagnosis / James D. Halderman.

Description: Seventh edition. | Boston : Pearson, [2018] | Includes index.

Identifiers: LCCN 2018034149| ISBN 9780134893495 | ISBN 0134893492

Subjects: LCSH: Automobiles—Motors—Maintenance and repair. | Automobiles—Performance.

Classification: LCC TL210 .H287 2018 | DDC 629.25/040288—dc23

LC record available at *https://lccn.loc.gov/2018034149*

6 2021

ISBN 10:   0-13-489349-2

ISBN 13: 978-0-13-489349-5

BRIEF CONTENTS

CONTENTS

chapter 5
GASOLINE ENGINE SYSTEMS 79

chapter 6
IN-VEHICLE ENGINE SERVICE 89

chapter 7
VALVE TRAIN AND VARIABLE VALVE TIMING DIAGNOSIS 101

chapter 8
ENGINE AND MISFIRE DIAGNOSIS 117

chapter 9
CAN AND NETWORK COMMUNICATIONS 137

PREFACE

Advanced Engine Performance Diagnosis combines topics in engine performance (ASE A8) and the advanced engine performance (ASE L1) topics into one practical, comprehensive textbook that is easy for instructors to teach with, and an affordable option for students.

This hands-on introduction to the diagnosis and troubleshooting of automotive engine control systems serves students as a single source for information on digital storage, oscilloscopes, fuel injection and ignition system diagnoses, five-gas exhaust analysis, emission testing, and more.

The book is formatted to appeal to today's technical trade students with a a technical, but easy-to-read and understand presentation that uses helpful real-world tips and visuals to bring concepts to life and guide students through the procedures they'll use on the job.

UPDATES TO THE SEVENTH EDITION

The following changes and updates have been made to the new seventh edition based on requests from instructors and reviewers from throughout North America:

- The content was reorganized to make it flow smoothly form beginning to the end.
- The chapters have been rewritten to be more concise.
- Over 75 new full color line drawings and photos have been added to the new edition to help bring the subject to life.
- Case studies have been added to many chapters that include the "three Cs" (Complaint, Cause, and Correction).
- Updated throughout and correlated to the latest ASE tasks.

- A new chapter title **Oscilloscopes and DSOs** (Chapter 4) has been greatly enhanced.
- The chapter **Valve and Variable Valve Timing Diagnosis** (Chapter 7) has been rewritten and updated to include Fiat-Chrysler Multiair systems and additional diagnosis procedures.
- Chapter 20, **Fuel Trim Diagnosis**, has been expanded and enhanced.
- The new Tier 3 emission standards have been added to Chapter 26 (**Vehicle Emissions Standards and Testing**).
- **Module Programming** (Chapter 28) has been added to the new edition.

SAFETY TIP

Never Disconnect a Spark Plug Wire When the Engine Is Running!

Ignition systems produce a high-voltage pulse necessary to ignite a lean air–fuel mixture. If you disconnect a spark plug wire when the engine is running, this high-voltage spark could cause personal injury or damage to the ignition coil and/or ignition module.

SAFETY TIPS alert students to possible hazards on the job and how to avoid them.

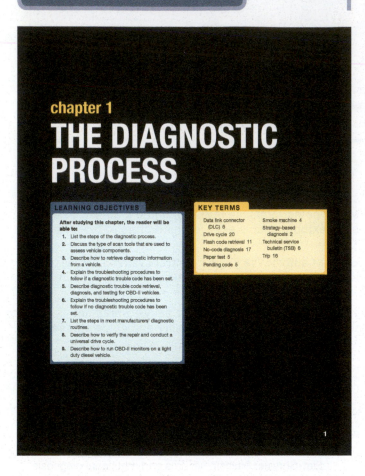

chapter 1
THE DIAGNOSTIC PROCESS

LEARNING OBJECTIVES

After studying this chapter, the reader will be able to:

1. List the steps of the diagnostic process.
2. Discuss the type of scan tools that are used to assess vehicle components.
3. Describe how to retrieve diagnostic information from a vehicle.
4. Explain the troubleshooting procedures to follow if a diagnostic trouble code has been set.
5. Describe diagnostic trouble code retrieval, diagnosis, and testing for OBD-II vehicles.
6. Explain the troubleshooting procedures to follow if no diagnostic trouble code has been set.
7. List the steps in most manufacturers' diagnostic routines.
8. Describe how to verify the repair and conduct a universal drive cycle.
9. Describe how to run OBD-II monitors on a light duty diesel vehicle.

KEY TERMS

Data link connector (DLC) 6
Drive cycle 20
Flash code retrieval 11
No-code diagnosis 17
Paper test 5
Pending code 5
Smoke machine 4
Strategy-based diagnosis 2
Technical service bulletin (TSB) 6
Trip 16

1

OBJECTIVES AND KEY TERMS appear at the beginning of each chapter to help students and instructors focus on the most important material in each chapter. The chapter objectives are based on specific ASE and NATEF tasks.

CASE STUDY

The Chevrolet Pickup Truck Story

The owner of a Chevrolet pickup truck complained that the engine ran terribly. It would hesitate and surge, yet there were no diagnostic trouble codes (DTCs). After hours of troubleshooting, the technician discovered while talking to the owner that the problem started after the transmission had been repaired. However, the transmission shop said that the problem was an engine problem and not related to the transmission.

A thorough visual inspection revealed that the front and rear oxygen sensor connectors had been switched. The PCM was trying to compensate for an air–fuel mixture condition that did not exist. Reversing the O2S connectors restored proper operation of the truck.

Summary:

- **Complaint**—Vehicle owner complained that the pickup truck ran terribly.
- **Cause**—During a previous repair, the upstream and downstream oxygen sensor connectors were reversed.
- **Correction**—The connectors were moved to their correct locations which restored proper engine operation.

REAL WORLD FIXES present students with actual automotive service scenarios and show how these common (and sometimes uncommon) problems were diagnosed and repaired.

TECH TIP

Smoke Machine Testing

Vacuum (air) leaks can cause a variety of driveability problems and are often difficult to locate. One good method is to use a machine that generates a stream of smoke. Connecting the outlet of the **smoke machine** to the hose that was removed from the vacuum brake booster allows smoke to enter the intake manifold. Any vacuum leaks will be spotted by observing smoke coming out of the leak. ● **SEE FIGURE 1–6**.

TECH TIPS feature real-world advice and "tricks of the trade" from ASE-certified master technicians.

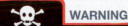

? FREQUENTLY ASKED QUESTION

What Happens When the Engine Stops?

When the engine stops, the oil pressure drops to zero and a spring-loaded locking pin is used to keep the camshaft locked, preventing noise at engine start. When the engine starts, oil pressure releases the locking pin.

☠ WARNING

Check the coolant level in the radiator only when the radiator is cool. If the radiator is hot and the radiator cap is removed, the drop in pressure above the coolant will cause the coolant to boil immediately and as the coolant explosively expands upward and outward from the radiator opening, it can cause severe burns and personal injury.

FREQUENTLY ASKED QUESTIONS are based on the author's own experience and provide answers to many of the most common questions asked by students and beginning service technicians.

NOTE: A cam-within-a-cam is used on the 2008 + Viper V-10 OHV engine. This design allows the exhaust lobes to be moved up to 36° to improve idle quality and reduction of exhaust emissions.

NOTES provide students with additional technical information to give them a greater understanding of a task or procedure.

CAUTION: Do not use more than three squirts oil from a hand-operated oil squirt can. Too much oil can cause a hydrostatic lock, which can damage or break pistons or connecting rods or even crack a cylinder head.

CAUTIONS alert students about potential to the vehicle that can occur during a specific task or service procedure.

WARNINGS alert students to potential dangers to themselves during a specific task or service procedure.

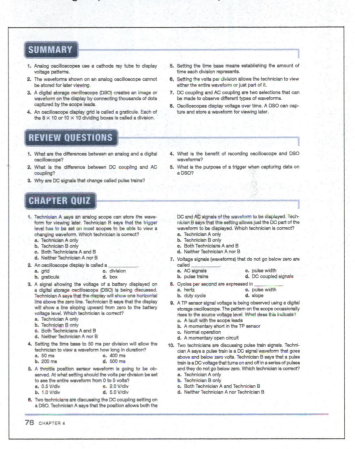

THE SUMMARY, REVIEW QUESTIONS, AND CHAPTER QUIZ at the end of each chapter help students review the material presented in the chapter and test themselves to see how much they've learned.

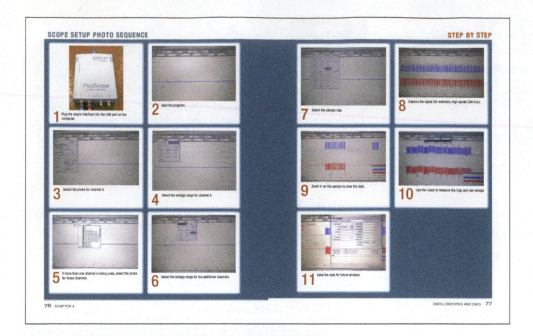

STEP-BY-STEP photo sequences show in detail the steps involved in performing a specific task or service procedure.

INSTRUCTOR RESOURCES

These resources are provided to help you teach your course, and can be found at pearsonhighered.com/automotive Search for this title there.

RESOURCES IN PRINT AND ONLINE				
Advanced Engine Performance Diagnosis				
NAME OF SUPPLEMENT	PRINT	ONLINE	AUDIENCE	DESCRIPTION
Instructor Resource Manual 0134985788		✔	Instructors	NEW! The Ultimate teaching aid: Chapter summaries, key terms, chapter learning objectives, lecture resources, discuss/demonstrate classroom activities, and answers to the in text review and quiz questions.
TestGen 0134985761		✔	Instructors	Test generation software and test bank for the text.
PowerPoint Presentation 0134985737		✔	Instructors	Slides include chapter learning objectives, lecture outline of the text, and graphics from the book.
Image Bank 0134985745		✔	Instructors	All of the images and graphs from the textbook to create customized lecture slides.
ASE Correlated Task Sheets – for instructors 0134985729		✔	Instructors	Downloadable ASE task sheets for easy customization and development of unique task sheets.
ASE Correlated Task Sheets – for Students 0134985796	✔		Students	Study activity manual that correlates ASE Automobile Standards to chapters and page numbers in the text. Available to students at a discounted price when packaged with the text.
VitalSource eBook 0133515214		✔	Students	An alternative to purchasing the print textbook, students can subscribe to the same content online and save up to 50% off the suggested list price of the print text. Visit **www.vitalsource.com**

All online resources can be downloaded from the Instructor's Resource Center: **www.pearsonhighered.com/irc**

ACKNOWLEDGMENTS

A large number of people and organizations have cooperated in providing the reference material and technical information used in this text. The author wishes to express sincere thanks to the following individuals for their special contributions:

Randy Briggs, Car Quest Technical Institute

Randy Dillman

Rick Escalambre, Skyline College

Bill Fulton, Ohio Automotive Technology

Jim Linder, Linder Technical Services

Scot Manna

Dan Marinucci, Communique'

Albin Moore

Jim Morton, Automotive Training Center (ATC)

Dr. Norman Nall

Dave Scaler, Mechanic's Education Association

John Thornton, Autotrain

Mark Warren

TECHNICAL AND CONTENT REVIEWERS

The following people reviewed the manuscript before production and checked it for technical accuracy and clarity of presentation. Their suggestions and recommendations were included in the final draft of the manuscript. Their input helped make this textbook clear and technically accurate while maintaining the easy-to-read style that has made other books from the same author so popular.

Jim Anderson
Greenville High School

Victor Bridges
Umpqua Community College

Dr. Roger Donovan
Illinois Central College

A. C. Durdin
Moraine Park Technical College

Al Engledahl
College of Dupage

Larry Hagelberger
Upper Valley Joint Vocational School

Oldrick Hajzler
Red River College

Betsy Hoffman
Vermont Technical College

Richard Krieger
Michigan Institute of Technology

Steven T. Lee
Lincoln Technical Institute

Carlton H. Mabe, Sr.
Virginia Western Community College

Roy Marks
Owens Community College

Tony Martin
University of Alaska Southeast

Kerry Meier
San Juan College

Fritz Peacock
Indiana Vocational Technical College

Dennis Peter
NAIT (Canada)

Greg Pfahl
Miami-Jacobs Career College

Kenneth Redick
Hudson Valley Community College

Jeff Rehkopf
Florida State College

Mitchell Walker
St. Louis Community College at Forest Park

Jennifer Wise
Sinclair Community College

SPECIAL THANKS

The author wishes to thank Chuck Taylor of Sinclair Community College in Dayton, Ohio, who helped with many of the photos. A special thanks to Tom Birch, and Jeff Rehkopf for their detailed and thorough review of the manuscript before publication. Most of all, I wish to thank Michelle Halderman for her assistance in all phases of manuscript preparation.

James D. Halderman

Curt Ward

JIM HALDERMAN brings a world of experience, knowledge, and talent to his work. His automotive service experience includes working as a flat-rate technician, a business owner, and a professor of automotive technology at a leading U.S. community college.

He has a Bachelor of Science degree from Ohio Northern University and a master's degree from Miami University in Oxford, Ohio. Jim also holds a U.S. patent for an electronic transmission control device. He is an ASE certified Master Automotive Technician and is also Advanced Engine Performance (L1) ASE certified. Jim is the author of many automotive textbooks, all published by Pearson Education. Jim has presented numerous technical seminars to national audiences, including the California Automotive Teachers (CAT) and the Illinois College Automotive Instructor Association (ICAIA). He is also a member and presenter at the North American Council of Automotive Teachers (NACAT). Jim was also named Regional Teacher of the Year by General Motors Corporation and a member of the advisory committee for the department of technology at Ohio Northern University. Jim and his wife, Michelle, live in Dayton, Ohio. They have two children. You can reach Jim at

jim@jameshalderman.com

CURT WARD Prior to his years at Chrysler, he has worked as a technician, shop foreman, and service manager in the retail sector of the automotive industry for 13 years. During this time, Curt became a Chrysler Master Technician. Curt has an Associates of Applied Science in Automotive Service Technology from Southern Illinois University. He has a Bachelor of Fine Arts in Organizational Communications from North Central College. He earned his master's degree in Adult Education at the University of Phoenix.

Curt is an ASE Master Automotive Technician. Curt has presented technical seminars at numerous conferences around the country. He has presented for the Illinois College Automotive Instructor Association (ICAIA), the California Automotive Teachers (CAT), and the North American Council of Automotive Teachers (NACAT). Curt is an active member in the ICAIA and the NACAT. He has served as the secretary and president of the NACAT organization and was the conference host for the 2015 NACAT Conference. In 2015, Curt was named the NACAT MVP award winner for his outstanding contribution to the NACAT organization. Curt and his wife Tammy have five children and five grandchildren.

Together they enjoy traveling and exploring historical sites. In his spare time, Curt enjoys modeling 3-rail O-gauge railroads. You can reach Curt at: curt@curtward.net

THE DIAGNOSTIC PROCESS

LEARNING OBJECTIVES

After studying this chapter, the reader should be able to:

1. List the steps of the diagnostic process.
2. Discuss the type of scan tools that are used to assess vehicle components.
3. Describe how to retrieve diagnostic information from a vehicle.
4. Explain the troubleshooting procedures to follow if a diagnostic trouble code has been set.
5. Describe diagnostic trouble code retrieval, diagnosis, and testing for OBD-II vehicles.
6. Explain the troubleshooting procedures to follow if no diagnostic trouble code has been set.
7. List the steps in most manufacturers' diagnostic routines.
8. Describe how to verify the repair and conduct a universal drive cycle.
9. Describe how to run OBD-II monitors on a light duty diesel vehicle.

KEY TERMS

Data link connector (DLC) 7
Drive cycle 20
Flash code retrieval 11
No-code diagnosis 17
Paper test 5
Pending code 6

Smoke machine 5
Strategy-based diagnosis 2
Technical service bulletin (TSB) 7
Trip 16

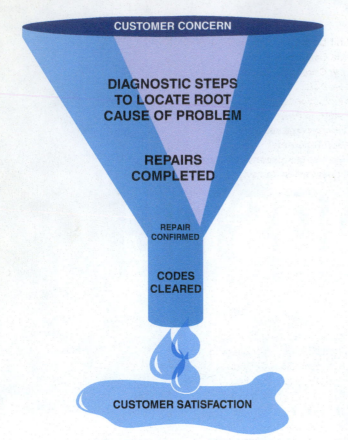

FIGURE 1–1 A funnel is one way to visualize the diagnostic process. The purpose is to narrow the possible causes of a concern until the root cause is determined and corrected.

THE EIGHT-STEP DIAGNOSTIC PROCEDURE

STRATEGY-BASED DIAGNOSIS Successful diagnose depends on using the same process for all problems and customer concerns to arrive at the root cause of the problem. The process is called **strategy-based diagnosis**.

Many different things can cause an engine performance problem or concern. The service technician has to narrow the possibilities to find the cause of the problem and correct it. A funnel is a way of visualizing a diagnostic procedure. ● **SEE FIGURE 1–1**. At the wide top are the symptoms of the problem; the funnel narrows as possible causes are eliminated until the root cause is found and corrected at the bottom of the funnel.

All problem diagnosis deals with symptoms that could be the result of many different causes. The wide range of possible solutions must be narrowed to the most likely and these must eventually be further narrowed to the actual cause. The following section describes eight steps the service technician can take to narrow the possibilities to one cause.

STEP 1 VERIFY THE PROBLEM (CONCERN)
Before a minute is spent on diagnosis, be certain that a problem exists.

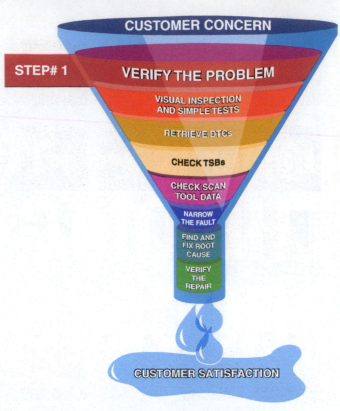

FIGURE 1–2 Step #1 is to verify the customer concern or problem. If the problem cannot be verified, then the repair cannot be verified.

If the problem cannot be verified, it cannot be solved or tested to verify that the repair was complete. ● **SEE FIGURE 1–2**.

The driver of the vehicle knows much about the vehicle and how it is driven. *Before* diagnosis, always ask the following questions:

- Is the malfunction indicator light (check engine) on?
- What was the temperature outside?
- Was the engine warm or cold?
- Was the problem during starting, acceleration, cruise, or some other condition?
- How far had the vehicle been driven?
- Were any dash warning lights on? If so, which one(s)? ● **SEE FIGURE 1–3**.
- Has there been any service or repair work performed on the vehicle lately?

NOTE: This last question is very important. Many engine performance faults are often the result of something being knocked loose or a hose falling off during repair work. Knowing that the vehicle was just serviced before the problem began may be an indicator as to where to look for the solution to a problem.

After the nature and scope of the problem are determined, the complaint should be verified before further diagnostic tests are performed. A sample form that customers could fill out with details of the problem is shown in ● **FIGURE 1–4**.

1. Anit-Lock Brake System Warning
2. Gas Cap Loose
3. Low Coolant Level Detected
4. Low Fuel
5. Malfunction Indicator Lamp (MIL)
6. Reduced Power
7. Service Required
8. Theft Deterrent
9. Time for Maintenance Indicator
10. Transmission Warning

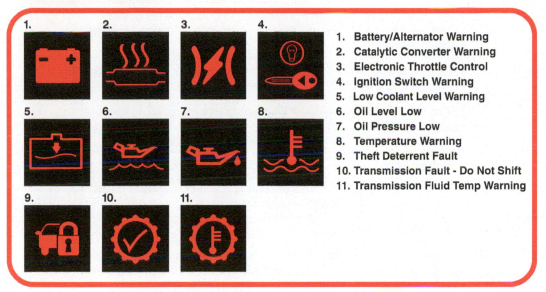

1. Battery/Alternator Warning
2. Catalytic Converter Warning
3. Electronic Throttle Control
4. Ignition Switch Warning
5. Low Coolant Level Warning
6. Oil Level Low
7. Oil Pressure Low
8. Temperature Warning
9. Theft Deterrent Fault
10. Transmission Fault - Do Not Shift
11. Transmission Fluid Temp Warning

FIGURE 1–3 The amber dash warning symbols indicate that a fault has been detected. A red dash warning light indicates that a major fault has been detected requiring action by the driver as soon as possible.

NOTE: Because drivers differ, it is sometimes the best policy to take the customer on the test-drive to verify the concern.

STEP 2 PERFORM A THOROUGH VISUAL INSPECTION AND BASIC TESTS

The visual inspection is the most important aspect of diagnosis! Most experts agree that between 10% and 30% of all engine performance problems can be found simply by performing a *thorough* visual inspection. The inspection should include the following:

- **Check for obvious problems (basics, basics, basics).**
  Fuel leaks
  Vacuum hoses that are disconnected or split
  Corroded connectors
  Unusual noises, smoke, or smell

  Check the air cleaner and air duct (squirrels and other small animals can build nests or store dog food in them). ● **SEE FIGURE 1–5**.

- **Check everything that does and does not work.** This step involves turning things on and observing that everything is working properly.

- **Look for evidence of previous repairs.** Any time work is performed on a vehicle, there is always a risk that something will be disturbed, knocked off, or left disconnected.

- **Check oil level and condition.** Another area for visual inspection is oil level and condition.

  Oil level. Oil should be to the proper level.

  Oil condition. Using a match or lighter, try to light the oil on the dipstick; if the oil flames up, gasoline is present

ENGINE PERFORMANCE DIAGNOSIS WORKSHEET

(To Be Filled Out By the Vehicle Owner)

Name: _____ Mileage: _____ Date: _____

Make: _____ Model: _____ Year: _____ Engine: _____

(Please Circle All That Apply in All Categories)	
Describe Problem:	
When Did the Problem First Occur?	• Just Started • Last Week • Last Month • Other _____
List Previous Repairs in the Last 6 Months:	
Starting Problems	• Will Not Crank • Cranks, but Will Not Start • Starts, but Takes a Long Time
Engine Quits or Stalls	• Right after Starting • When Put into Gear • During Steady Speed Driving • Right after Vehicle Comes to a Stop • While Idling • During Acceleration • When Parking
Poor Idling Conditions	• Is Too Slow at All Times • Is Too Fast • Intermittently Too Fast or Too Slow • Is Rough or Uneven • Fluctuates Up and Down
Poor Running Conditions	• Runs Rough • Lacks Power • Bucks and Jerks • Poor Fuel Economy • Hesitates or Stumbles on Acceleration • Backfires • Misfires or Cuts Out • Engine Knocks, Pings, Rattles • Surges • Dieseling or Run-On
Automatic Transmission Problems	• Improper Shifting (Early/Late) • Changes Gear Incorrectly • Vehicle Does Not Move when in Gear • Jerks or Bucks
Usually Occurs	• Morning • Afternoon • Anytime
Engine Temperature	• Cold • Warm • Hot
Driving Conditions During Occurrence	• Short—Less Than 2 Miles • 2–10 Miles • Long—More Than 10 Miles • Stop and Go • While Turning • While Braking • At Gear Engagement • With A/C Operating • With Headlights On • During Acceleration • During Deceleration • Mostly Downhill • Mostly Uphill • Mostly Level • Mostly Curvy • Rough Road
Driving Habits	• Mostly City Driving • Highway • Park Vehicle Inside • Park Vehicle Outside **Drive Per Day:** • Less Than 10 Miles • 10–50 • More Than 50
Gasoline Used	**Fuel Octane:** • 87 • 89 • 91 • More Than 91 **Brand:** _____
Temperature when Problem Occurs	• 32–55° F • Below Freezing (32° F) • Above 55° F
Check Engine Light/ Dash Warning Light	• Light on Sometimes • Light on Always • Light Never On
Smells	• "Hot" • Gasoline • Oil Burning • Electrical
Noises	• Rattle • Knock • Squeak • Other

FIGURE 1–4 A form that the customer should fill out if there is a driveability concern to help the service technician more quickly find the root cause.

FIGURE 1–5 This is what was found when removing an air filter from a vehicle that had a lack-of-power concern. Obviously the nuts were deposited by squirrels or some other animal, blocking a lot of the airflow into the engine.

FIGURE 1–6 Using a bright light makes seeing where the smoke is coming from easier. In this case, smoke was added to the intake manifold with the inlet blocked with a yellow plastic cap and smoke was seen escaping past a gasket at the idle air control.

TECH TIP

"Original Equipment" Is Not a Four-Letter Word

To many service technicians, an original equipment (OE) part is considered to be only marginal and to get the really "good stuff" an aftermarket (renewal market) part has to be purchased. However, many problems can be traced to the use of an aftermarket part that has failed early in its service life. Technicians who work at dealerships usually begin their diagnosis with an aftermarket part identified during a visual inspection. It has been their experience that simply replacing the aftermarket part with the factory OE part often solves the problem.

OE parts are *required* to pass quality and durability standards and tests at a level not required of aftermarket parts. The technician should be aware that the presence of a new part does not necessarily mean that the part is good.

TECH TIP

Smoke Machine Testing

Vacuum (air) leaks can cause a variety of driveability problems and are often difficult to locate. One good method is to use a machine that generates a stream of smoke. Connecting the outlet of the **smoke machine** to the hose that was removed from the vacuum brake booster allows smoke to enter the intake manifold. Any vacuum leaks will be spotted by observing smoke coming out of the leak. ● **SEE FIGURE 1–6.**

in the engine oil. Drip some engine oil from the dipstick onto the hot exhaust manifold. If the oil bubbles or boils, coolant (water) is present in the oil. Check for grittiness by rubbing the oil between your fingers.

NOTE: Gasoline in the oil will cause the engine to run rich by drawing fuel through the positive crankcase ventilation (PCV) system.

■ **Check coolant level and condition.** Many mechanical engine problems are caused by overheating. The proper operation of the cooling system is critical to the life of any engine.

NOTE: Check the coolant level in the radiator only if the radiator is cool. If the radiator is hot and the radiator cap is removed, the drop in pressure above the coolant will cause the coolant to boil immediately, which can cause severe burns because the coolant expands explosively upward and outward from the radiator opening.

■ **Use the paper test.** even and steady exhaust flow at the tailpipe when running. For the **paper test,** hold a piece of paper (even a dollar bill works) or a 3-by-5-inch card within 1 inch (2.5 m) of the tailpipe with the engine running at idle. The paper should blow evenly away from the end of the tailpipe without "puffing" or being drawn inward toward the end of the tailpipe. If the paper is at times drawn *toward* the tailpipe, the valves in one or more cylinders could be burned. Other reasons why the paper might be drawn toward the tailpipe include the following:

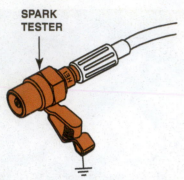

SPARK
TESTER

FIGURE 1–7 A spark tester connected to a spark plug wire or coil output. A typical spark tester will only fire if at least 25,000 volts are available from the coil, making a spark tester a very useful tool. Do not use one that just lights when a spark is present, because they do not require more than about 2,000 volts to light.

1. The engine could be misfiring because of a lean condition that could occur normally when the engine is cold.

2. Pulsing of the paper toward the tailpipe could also be caused by a hole in the exhaust system. If exhaust escapes through a hole in the exhaust system, air could be drawn—in the intervals between the exhaust puffs—from the tailpipe to the hole in the exhaust, causing the paper to be drawn toward the tailpipe.

■ **Ensure adequate fuel level.** Make certain that the fuel tank is at least one-fourth to one-half full; if the fuel level is low, it is possible that any water or alcohol at the bottom of the fuel tank is more concentrated and can be drawn into the fuel system.

■ **Check the battery voltage.** The voltage of the battery should be at least 12.4 volts and the charging voltage (engine running) should be 13.5 to 15.0 volts at 2000 RPM. Low battery voltage can cause a variety of problems, including reduced fuel economy and incorrect (usually too high) idle speed. Higher-than-normal battery voltage can also cause powertrain control module (PCM) problems and could cause damage to electronic modules.

■ **Check the spark using a spark tester.** Remove one spark plug wire and attach the removed plug wire to the spark tester. Attach the grounding clip of the spark tester to a good clean engine ground, start or crank the engine, and observe the spark tester. ● **SEE FIGURE 1–7.** The spark at the spark tester should be steady and consistent. If an intermittent spark occurs, then this condition should be treated as a no-spark condition. If this test does not show satisfactory spark, carefully inspect and test all components of the primary and secondary ignition systems.

NOTE: Do not use a standard spark plug to check for proper ignition system voltage. An electronic ignition spark tester is designed to force the spark to jump about 0.75 inch (19 mm). This amount of gap requires between 25,000 and 30,000 volts (25 and

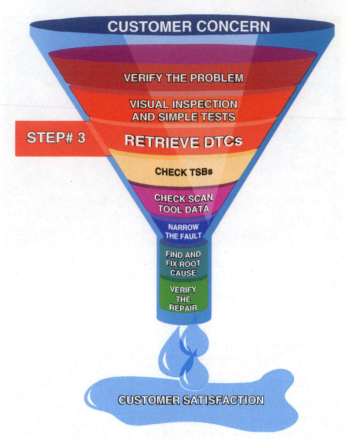

CUSTOMER CONCERN

VERIFY THE PROBLEM

VISUAL INSPECTION AND SIMPLE TESTS

STEP# 3   RETRIEVE DTCs

CHECK TSBs

CHECK SCAN TOOL DATA

NARROW THE FAULT

FIND AND FIX ROOT CAUSE

VERIFY THE REPAIR

CUSTOMER SATISFACTION

FIGURE 1–8 Step 3 in the diagnostic process is to retrieve any stored diagnostic trouble codes.

30 kV) at atmospheric pressure, which is enough voltage to ensure that a spark can occur under compression inside an engine.

■ **Check the fuel-pump pressure.** Checking the fuel-pump pressure is relatively easy on many port-fuel-injected engines. Often the cause of intermittent engine performance is due to a weak electric fuel pump or clogged fuel filter. Checking fuel-pump pressure early in the diagnostic process eliminates low fuel pressure as a possibility.

STEP 3 RETRIEVE THE DIAGNOSTIC TROUBLE CODES (DTCs) If a DTC is present in the computer memory, it may be signaled by illuminating a malfunction indicator lamp (MIL), commonly labeled "check engine" or "service engine soon." ● **SEE FIGURE 1–8.** Any code(s) that is displayed on a scan tool when the MIL is *not* on is called a **pending code.** Because the MIL is not on, this indicates that the fault has not repeated to cause the PCM to turn on the MIL. Although this pending code is helpful to the technician to know that a fault has, in the past, been detected, further testing will be needed to find the root cause of the problem. Check and record the freeze-frame information. This indicates when the DTC was set, and this not only will help the technician determine what may have caused the code to set but also helps to verify the repair by operating the vehicle under the same or similar conditions.

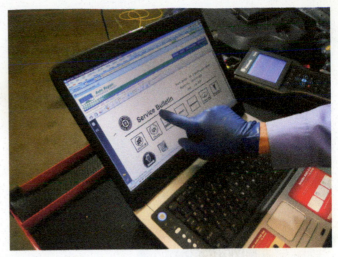

FIGURE 1–9 After checking for stored diagnostic trouble codes (DTCs), the wise technician checks service information for any technical service bulletins that may relate to the vehicle being serviced.

Perform Both a Pre-Scan and a Post-Scan

Many experts advise shops to make a pre-scan of all the vehicle's computer modules as well as a scan after the vehicle has been repaired to be a part of their standard operation procedure (SOP). Not only is this good business practice, but it really helps communications with the customer about possible faults with the vehicle that may not be part of the original customer concern.

- **Pre-scan:** This involves accessing all of the modules in the vehicle and retrieving any or all of the stored diagnostic trouble codes (DTCs), including pending codes. Any stored DTCs are recorded on the work order, and if related to the customer concern, the customer may need to be notified to get their approval before proceeding with the repairs.

- **Post-scan:** After the vehicle has been repaired and before it is released to the customer, a total module scan is performed again to not only verify the repair but also to ensure that another DTC was not set during the repair process. The results of this post-scan should also be documented on the repair order so it becomes a part of the documentation for the vehicle history.

STEP 4 CHECK FOR TECHNICAL SERVICE BULLETINS (TSBS) Check for corrections or repair procedures in **technical service bulletins (TSBs)** that match the symptoms. ● **SEE FIGURE 1–9.** According to studies performed by automobile manufacturers, as many as 30% of vehicles can be repaired following the information, suggestions, or replacement parts found in a service bulletin. DTCs must be known before searching for service bulletins, because bulletins often include information on solving problems that involve a stored diagnostic trouble code.

STEP 5 LOOK CAREFULLY AT SCAN TOOL DATA Vehicle manufacturers have been giving the technician more and more data on a scan tool connected to the **data link connector (DLC).** ● **SEE FIGURE 1–10.** Beginning technicians are often observed scrolling through scan data without a real clue about what they are looking for. When asked, they usually reply that they are looking for something unusual, as if the screen will flash a big message "LOOK HERE—THIS IS NOT CORRECT." That statement does not appear on scan tool displays. The best way to look at scan data is in a definite sequence and with specific, selected bits of data that can tell the most about the operation of the engine, such as the following:

- Engine coolant temperature (ECT) is the same as intake air temperature (IAT) after the vehicle sits for several hours.
- Idle air control (IAC) valve is being commanded to an acceptable range.
- Oxygen sensor (O2S) is operating properly.

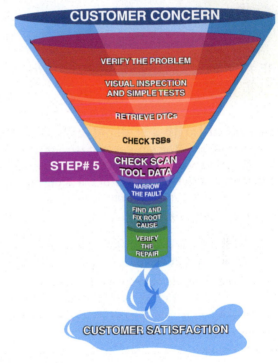

FIGURE 1–10 Looking carefully at the scan tool data is very helpful in locating the source of a problem.

1. Readings below 200 mV at times
2. Readings above 800 mV at times
3. Rapid transitions between rich and lean

STEP 6 NARROW THE PROBLEM TO A SYSTEM OR CYLINDER Narrowing the focus to a system or individual cylinder is the hardest part of the entire diagnostic process. For example:

- Perform a cylinder power balance test.
- If a weak cylinder is detected, perform a compression and a cylinder leakage test to determine the probable cause.

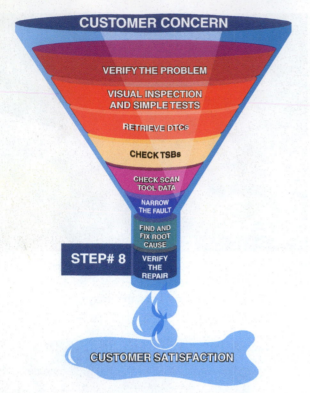

FIGURE 1–11 Step 8 is very important. Be sure that the customer's concern has been corrected.

STEP 7 REPAIR THE PROBLEM AND DETERMINE THE ROOT CAUSE

The repair or part replacement must be performed following vehicle manufacturer's recommendations and be certain that the root cause of the problem has been found. Also follow the manufacturer's recommended repair procedures and methods.

STEP 8 VERIFY THE REPAIR AND CLEAR ANY STORED DTCS ● SEE FIGURE 1–11.

- Test-drive to verify that the original problem (concern) is fixed.
- Verify that no additional problems have occurred during the repair process.
- Check for and then clear all diagnostic trouble codes. (This step ensures that the computer will not make any changes based on a stored DTC, but should not be performed if the vehicle is going to be tested for emissions because all of the monitors will need to be run and pass.)
- Return the vehicle to the customer and double check the following:
  1. The vehicle is clean.
  2. The radio is turned off.
  3. The clock is set to the right time and the radio stations have been restored if the battery was disconnected during the repair procedure.

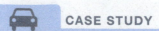 **CASE STUDY**

The Case of the No-Start Lexus

The owner of a Lexus IS250 had the car towed to a shop as a no-start. The technician discovered that the "check engine" light would not come on even with key on, engine off (KOEO). A scan tool would not communicate either. Checking the resources on www.iatn. net, the technician read of a similar case where the fuel pressure sensor was shorted, which disabled all serial data communications. The technician disconnected the fuel pressure sensor located on the backside of the engine and the communications were restored and the engine started. The fuel pressure sensor was replaced and the vehicle returned to the happy owner.

Summary:

- **Complaint**—The vehicle owner stated that the engine would not start.
- **Cause**—A shorted fuel pressure sensor was found as per a previous similar case.
- **Correction**—The fuel pressure sensor was replaced and this corrected the serial data fault that caused the no-start condition.

SCAN TOOLS

Scan tools are the workhorse for any diagnostic work on all vehicles. Scan tools can be divided into two basic groups:

1. **Factory scan tools.** These are the scan tools required by all dealers that sell and service the brand of vehicle. Examples of factory scan tools include:
   - **General Motors**—Tech 2 or GM MDI ● **SEE FIGURE 1–12.**
   - **Ford**—New Generation Star (NGS) and IDS (Integrated Diagnostic Software).

 **TECH TIP**

One Test Is Worth 1,000 "Expert" Opinions

Whenever any vehicle has an engine performance or driveability concern, certain people always say:

"Sounds like it's a bad injector."
"I'll bet you it's a bad computer."
"I had a problem just like yours yesterday and it was a bad EGR valve."

Regardless of the skills and talents of those people, it is still more accurate to perform tests on the vehicle than to rely on feelings or opinions of others who have not even seen the vehicle. Even your own opinion should not sway your thinking. Follow a plan, perform tests, and the test results will lead to the root cause.

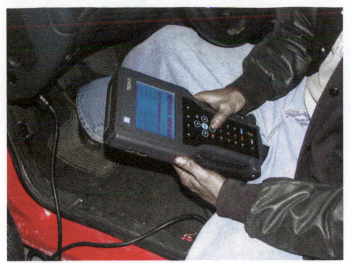

FIGURE 1–12 A TECH 2 scan tool is the factory scan tool used on General Motors vehicles.

FIGURE 1–13 What the technician discovered after removing the valve cover was the root cause of the misfire.

The Case of the Rough-Running Impala

A customer with a Chevrolet Impala equipped with a 3.4 liter engine is complaining of a running-rough condition and the MIL is illuminated. The customer commented the condition first occurred after a hard acceleration.

The technician was able to verify the customer concern.

The technician retrieved the codes from the engine control module and found a P0306 and a P0300 to be present.

Using the graphic misfire counter on the scan tool, the technician was able to confirm that cylinder #6 was consistently misfiring.

The technician was able to confirm that both the injector and the ignition coil were operating normally.

A compression test of the cylinder #6 revealed compression readings below specifications. A cylinder leakage test of cylinder #six showed leakage percentage to be at an acceptable level.

The technician removed the valve cover to discover the bolt that held the #6 intake valve rocker arm had pulled out of the cylinder head. ● **SEE FIGURE 1–13**.

The technician was able to repair the bolt hole in the cylinder head with a thread repair kit and reinstall the rocker arm. The technician completed a drive cycle and confirmed the misfire condition was repaired.

Summary:
- **Complaint**—The owner complained of a running-rough condition and an illuminated MIL.
- **Cause**—Following the correct diagnostic procedure it was determined that the rocker arm bolt had pulled out of the cylinder head.
- **Correction**—The cylinder head was repaired and the rocker arm was reinstalled, which corrected the rough-running concern and turned off the MIL.

- **Chrysler**—DRB-III or Star Scan, wiTECH
- **Honda**—HDS or Master Tech
- **Toyota**—Master Tech or Tech Stream

All factory scan tools are designed to provide bidirectional capability, which allows the service technician the opportunity to operate components using the scan tool, thereby confirming that the component is able to work when commanded. Also, all factory scan tools are capable of displaying all factory parameters.

2. **Aftermarket scan tools.** These scan tools are designed to function on more than one brand of vehicle while many aftermarket scan tools can display most, if not all, of the parameters of the factory scan tool, there can be a difference when trying to troubleshoot some faults. Examples of aftermarket scan tools include:

- **Snap-on** (various models including the MT2500 and Modis)
- **OTC** (various models including Pegasus, Genisys, and Task Master)
- **AutoEnginuity** and other programs that use a laptop or handheld computer for the display

3. **Global (generic) scan tools.** Scan tools that read and display just global data are capable of only displaying emission-related information. While global only data is helpful at times, generic scan tools are not usually considered to be suitable for use by professional service technicians. ● **SEE FIGURE 1–14**.

RETRIEVAL OF DIAGNOSTIC INFORMATION

To retrieve diagnostic information from the PCM, a scan tool is needed. If a factory or factory-level scan tool is used, then all of the data can be retrieved. If a global (generic)-only-type scan tool is used, only the emissions-related data can be retrieved. To retrieve diagnostic information from the PCM, use the following steps:

FIGURE 1–14 A Bluetooth adapter that plugs into the DLC and transmits global OBD II information to a smart phone that has a scan tool app installed.

STEP 1 Locate and gain access to the data link connector (DLC).

STEP 2 Connect the scan tool to the DLC and establish communication.

NOTE: If no communication is established, follow the vehicle manufacturer's specified instructions.

STEP 3 Follow the on-screen instructions of the scan tool to correctly identify the vehicle.

STEP 4 Observe the scan data, as well as any diagnostic trouble codes.

STEP 5 Follow vehicle manufacturer's instructions if any DTCs are stored. If no DTCs are stored, compare all sensor values with a factory-acceptable range chart to see if any sensor values are out of range.

Parameter Identification (PID)		
Scan Tool Parameter	**Units Displayed**	**Typical Data Value**
Engine Idling/Radiator Hose Hot/Closed Throttle/ Park or Neutral/Closed Loop/Accessories Off/ Brake Pedal Released		
3X Crank Sensor	RPM	Varies
24X Crank Sensor	RPM	Varies
Actual EGR Position	Percent	0
BARO	kPa/Volts	65–110 kPa/ 3.5–4.5 Volts
CMP Sensor Signal Present	Yes/No	Yes
Commanded Fuel Pump	On/Off	On

Parameter Identification (PID)		
Scan Tool Parameter	**Units Displayed**	**Typical Data Value**
Cycles of Misfire Data	Counts	0–99
Desired EGR Position	Percent	0
ECT	°C/°F	Varies
EGR Duty Cycle	Percent	0
Engine Run Time	Hr: Min: Sec	Varies
EVAP Canister Purge	Percent	Low and Varying
EVAP Fault History	No Fault/Excess Vacuum/Purge Valve Leak/ Small Leak/Weak Vacuum	No Fault
Fuel Tank Pressure	Inches of H_2O/ Volts	Varies
HO2S Sensor 1	Ready/Not Ready	Ready
HO2S Sensor 1	Millivolts	0–1,000 and Varying
HO2S Sensor 2	Millivolts	0–1,000 and Varying
HO2S X Counts	Counts	Varies
IAC Position	Counts	15–25 preferred
IAT	°C/°F	Varies
Knock Retard	Degrees	0
Long-term FT	Percent	0–10
MAF	Grams per second	3–7
MAF Frequency	Hz	1,200–3,000 (depends on altitude and engine load)
MAP	kPa/Volts	20–48 kPa/0.75–2 Volts (depends on altitude)
Misfire Current Cyl. 1–10	Counts	0
Misfire History Cyl. 1–10	Counts	0
Short-term FT	Percent	0–10
Start Up ECT	°C/°F	Varies
Start Up IAT	°C/°F	Varies
Total Misfire Current Count	Counts	0
Total Misfire Failures	Counts	0

Parameter Identification (PID)		
Scan Tool Parameter	Units Displayed	Typical Data Value
Total Misfire Passes	Counts	0
TP Angle	Percent	0
TP Sensor	Volts	0.20–0.74
Vehicle Speed	MPH/Km/h	0

Note: Viewing the PID screen on the scanner is useful in determining if a problem is occurring at the present time

FIGURE 1–15 Diagnostic trouble codes (DTCs) from Chrysler and Dodge vehicles can be retrieved by turning the ignition switch to on and then off three times.

TROUBLESHOOTING USING DIAGNOSTIC TROUBLE CODES

Pinning down causes of the actual problem can be accomplished by trying to set the opposite code. For example, if a code indicates an open throttle position (TP) sensor (high resistance), clear the code and create a shorted (low-resistance) condition. This can be accomplished by using a jumper wire and connecting the signal terminal to the 5-volt reference terminal. This should set a diagnostic trouble code.

- **If the opposite code sets,** this indicates that the wiring and connector for the sensor is okay and the sensor itself is defective (open).

- **If the same code sets,** this indicates that the wiring or electrical connection is open (has high resistance) and is the cause of the setting of the DTC.

METHODS FOR CLEARING DIAGNOSTIC TROUBLE CODES
Clearing diagnostic trouble codes from a vehicle computer sometimes needs to be performed. There are three methods that can be used to clear stored diagnostic trouble codes.

CAUTION: Clearing diagnostic trouble codes (DTCs) also will clear all of the noncontinuous monitors.

- **Clearing codes—Method 1.** The preferred method of clearing codes is by using a scan tool. This is the method recommended by most vehicle manufacturers if the procedure can be performed on the vehicle. The computer of some vehicles cannot be cleared with a scan tool.

- **Clearing codes—Method 2.** If a scan tool is not available or a scan tool cannot be used on the vehicle being serviced, the power to the computer can be disconnected.

1. Disconnect the fusible link (if so equipped) that feeds the computer.

2. Disconnect the fuse or fuses that feed the computer.

NOTE: The fuse may not be labeled as a computer fuse. For example, many Toyotas can be cleared

by disconnecting the fuel-injection fuse. Some vehicles require that two fuses be disconnected to clear any stored codes.

- **Clearing codes—Method 3.** If the other two methods cannot be used, the negative battery cable can be disconnected to clear stored diagnostic trouble codes.

NOTE: Because of the adaptive learning capacity of the computer, a vehicle may fail an exhaust emissions test

TECH TIP

Do Not Lie to a Scan Tool!

Because computer calibration may vary from year to year, using the incorrect year for the vehicle while using a scan tool can cause the data retrieved to be incorrect or inaccurate.

TECH TIP

Quick and Easy Chrysler Code Retrieval

Most Chrysler-made vehicles (Dodge, Ram, and Chrysler) can display the diagnostic trouble code on the dash by turning the ignition switch on and then off and then on three times with the last time being on. This makes it easy for anyone to see if there are any stored trouble codes without having to use a scan tool. ● SEE FIGURE 1–15.

NEAR CENTER OF DASH

BEHIND ASHTRAY

LEFT CORNER OF DASH

if the vehicle is not driven enough to allow the computer to run all of the monitors.

CAUTION: By disconnecting the battery, the radio presets will be lost. They should be reset before returning the vehicle to the customer. If the radio has a security code, the code must be entered before the radio will function. Before disconnecting the battery, always check with the vehicle owner to be sure that the code is available.

DLC LOCATIONS

The data link connector (DLC) is a standardized 16-cavity connector where a scan tool can be connected to retrieve diagnostic information from the vehicle's computers.

The normal location is under the dash on the driver's side but it can be located within 12 inches (30 cm) of the center of the vehicle. It can be covered, but if it is, then the cover has to be able to be removed without the use of a tool, such as when it is located underneath the ash tray. ● SEE FIGURE 1–16.

OBD-II DIAGNOSIS

Starting with the 1996 model year, all vehicles sold in the United States must use the same type of 16-pin data link connector (DLC) and must monitor emission-related components. ● SEE FIGURE 1–17.

FIGURE 1–17 A typical OBD-II data link connector (DLC). The location varies with make and model and may even be covered, but a tool is not needed to gain access. Check service information for the exact location if needed.

RETRIEVING OBD-II CODES A scan tool is required to retrieve diagnostic trouble codes from most OBD-II vehicles. Every OBD-II scan tool will be able to read all generic Society of Automotive Engineers (SAE) DTCs from any vehicle.

Fuel and Air Metering System

P0100	Mass or Volume Airflow Circuit Problem
P0101	Mass or Volume Airflow Circuit Range or Performance Problem
P0102	Mass or Volume Airflow Circuit Low Input
P0103	Mass or Volume Airflow Circuit High Input
P0105	Manifold Absolute Pressure or Barometric Pressure Circuit Problem

P0106	Manifold Absolute Pressure or Barometric Pressure Circuit Range or Performance Problem
P0107	Manifold Absolute Pressure or Barometric Pressure Circuit Low Input
P0108	Manifold Absolute Pressure or Barometric Pressure Circuit High Input
P0110	Intake Air Temperature Circuit Problem
P0111	Intake Air Temperature Circuit Range or Performance Problem
P0112	Intake Air Temperature Circuit Low Input
P0113	Intake Air Temperature Circuit High Input
P0115	Engine Coolant Temperature Circuit Problem
P0116	Engine Coolant Temperature Circuit Range or Performance Problem
P0117	Engine Coolant Temperature Circuit Low Input
P0118	Engine Coolant Temperature Circuit High Input
P0120	Throttle Position Circuit Problem
P0121	Throttle Position Circuit Range or Performance Problem
P0122	Throttle Position Circuit Low Input
P0123	Throttle Position Circuit High Input
P0125	Excessive Time to Enter Closed-Loop Fuel Control
P0128	Coolant Temperature Below Thermostat Regulating Temperature
P0130	O2 Sensor Circuit Problem (Bank 1* Sensor 1)
P0131	O2 Sensor Circuit Low Voltage (Bank 1* Sensor 1)
P0132	O2 Sensor Circuit High Voltage (Bank 1* Sensor 1)
P0133	O2 Sensor Circuit Slow Response (Bank 1* Sensor 1)
P0134	O2 Sensor Circuit No Activity Detected (Bank 1* Sensor 1)
P0135	O2 Sensor Heater Circuit Problem (Bank 1* Sensor 1)
P0136	O2 Sensor Circuit Problem (Bank 1* Sensor 2)
P0137	O2 Sensor Circuit Low Voltage (Bank 1* Sensor 2)
P0138	O2 Sensor Circuit High Voltage (Bank 1* Sensor 2)
P0139	O2 Sensor Circuit Slow Response (Bank 1* Sensor 2)
P0140	O2 Sensor Circuit No Activity Detected (Bank 1* Sensor 2)
P0141	O2 Sensor Heater Circuit Problem (Bank 1* Sensor 2)
P0142	O2 Sensor Circuit Problem (Bank 1* Sensor 3)
P0143	O2 Sensor Circuit Low Voltage (Bank 1* Sensor 3)
P0144	O2 Sensor Circuit High Voltage (Bank 1* Sensor 3)
P0145	O2 Sensor Circuit Slow Response (Bank 1* Sensor 3)
P0146	O2 Sensor Circuit No Activity Detected (Bank 1* Sensor 3)
P0147	O2 Sensor Heater Circuit Problem (Bank 1* Sensor 3)
P0150	O2 Sensor Circuit Problem (Bank 2 Sensor 1)
P0151	O2 Sensor Circuit Low Voltage (Bank 2 Sensor 1)
P0152	O2 Sensor Circuit High Voltage (Bank 2 Sensor 1)
P0153	O2 Sensor Circuit Slow Response (Bank 2 Sensor 1)
P0154	O2 Sensor Circuit No Activity Detected (Bank 2 Sensor 1)
P0155	O2 Sensor Heater Circuit Problem (Bank 2 Sensor 1)
P0156	O2 Sensor Circuit Problem (Bank 2 Sensor 2)
P0157	O2 Sensor Circuit Low Voltage (Bank 2 Sensor 2)
P0158	O2 Sensor Circuit High Voltage (Bank 2 Sensor 2)
P0159	O2 Sensor Circuit Slow Response (Bank 2 Sensor 2)
P0160	O2 Sensor Circuit No Activity Detected (Bank 2 Sensor 2)
P0161	O2 Sensor Heater Circuit Problem (Bank 2 Sensor 2)
P0162	O2 Sensor Circuit Problem (Bank 2 Sensor 3)
P0163	O2 Sensor Circuit Low Voltage (Bank 2 Sensor 3)
P0164	O2 Sensor Circuit High Voltage (Bank 2 Sensor 3)
P0165	O2 Sensor Circuit Slow Response (Bank 2 Sensor 3)
P0166	O2 Sensor Circuit No Activity Detected (Bank 2 Sensor 3)
P0167	O2 Sensor Heater Circuit Problem (Bank 2 Sensor 3)
P0170	Fuel Trim Problem (Bank 1*)
P0171	System Too Lean (Bank 1*)
P0172	System Too Rich (Bank 1*)

(continued)

P0173   Fuel Trim Problem (Bank 2)

P0174   System Too Lean (Bank 2)

P0175   System Too Rich (Bank 2)

P0176   Fuel Composition Sensor Circuit Problem

P0177   Fuel Composition Sensor Circuit Range or Performance

P0178   Fuel Composition Sensor Circuit Low Input

P0179   Fuel Composition Sensor Circuit High Input

P0180   Fuel Temperature Sensor Problem

P0181   Fuel Temperature Sensor Circuit Range or Performance

P0182   Fuel Temperature Sensor Circuit Low Input

P0183   Fuel Temperature Sensor Circuit High Input

Fuel and Air Metering (Injector Circuit)

P0201   Injector Circuit Problem—Cylinder 1

P0202   Injector Circuit Problem—Cylinder 2

P0203   Injector Circuit Problem—Cylinder 3

P0204   Injector Circuit Problem—Cylinder 4

P0205   Injector Circuit Problem—Cylinder 5

P0206   Injector Circuit Problem—Cylinder 6

P0207   Injector Circuit Problem—Cylinder 7

P0208   Injector Circuit Problem—Cylinder 8

P0209   Injector Circuit Problem—Cylinder 9

P0210   Injector Circuit Problem—Cylinder 10

P0211   Injector Circuit Problem—Cylinder 11

P0212   Injector Circuit Problem—Cylinder 12

P0213   Cold Start Injector 1 Problem

P0214   Cold Start Injector 2 Problem

Ignition System or Misfire

P0300   Random Misfire Detected

P0301   Cylinder 1 Misfire Detected

P0302   Cylinder 2 Misfire Detected

P0303   Cylinder 3 Misfire Detected

P0304   Cylinder 4 Misfire Detected

P0305   Cylinder 5 Misfire Detected

P0306   Cylinder 6 Misfire Detected

P0307   Cylinder 7 Misfire Detected

P0308   Cylinder 8 Misfire Detected

P0309   Cylinder 9 Misfire Detected

P0310   Cylinder 10 Misfire Detected

P0311   Cylinder 11 Misfire Detected

P0312   Cylinder 12 Misfire Detected

P0320   Ignition or Distributor Engine Speed Input Circuit Problem

P0321   Ignition or Distributor Engine Speed Input Circuit Range or Performance

P0322   Ignition or Distributor Engine Speed Input Circuit No Signal

P0325   Knock Sensor 1 Circuit Problem

P0326   Knock Sensor 1 Circuit Range or Performance

P0327   Knock Sensor 1 Circuit Low Input

P0328   Knock Sensor 1 Circuit High Input

P0330   Knock Sensor 2 Circuit Problem

P0331   Knock Sensor 2 Circuit Range or Performance

P0332   Knock Sensor 2 Circuit Low Input

P0333   Knock Sensor 2 Circuit High Input

P0335   Crankshaft Position Sensor Circuit Problem

P0336   Crankshaft Position Sensor Circuit Range or Performance

P0337   Crankshaft Position Sensor Circuit Low Input

P0338   Crankshaft Position Sensor Circuit High Input

Auxiliary Emission Controls

P0400   Exhaust Gas Recirculation Flow Problem

P0401   Exhaust Gas Recirculation Flow Insufficient Detected

P0402   Exhaust Gas Recirculation Flow Excessive Detected

P0405   Air Conditioner Refrigerant Charge Loss

P0410   Secondary Air Injection System Problem

P0411   Secondary Air Injection System Insufficient Flow Detected

P0412   Secondary Air Injection System Switching Valve or Circuit Problem

P0413   Secondary Air Injection System Switching Valve or Circuit Open

P0414   Secondary Air Injection System Switching Valve or Circuit Shorted

P0420   Catalyst System Efficiency below Threshold (Bank 1*)

P0421   Warm Up Catalyst Efficiency below Threshold (Bank 1*)

P0422   Main Catalyst Efficiency below Threshold (Bank 1*)

P0423   Heated Catalyst Efficiency below Threshold (Bank 1*)

P0424   Heated Catalyst Temperature below Threshold (Bank 1*)

P0430   Catalyst System Efficiency below Threshold (Bank 2)

P0431   Warm Up Catalyst Efficiency below Threshold (Bank 2)

P0432	Main Catalyst Efficiency below Threshold (Bank 2)
P0433	Heated Catalyst Efficiency below Threshold (Bank 2)
P0434	Heated Catalyst Temperature below Threshold (Bank 2)
P0440	Evaporative Emission Control System Problem
P0441	Evaporative Emission Control System Insufficient Purge Flow
P0442	Evaporative Emission Control System Leak Detected
P0443	Evaporative Emission Control System Purge Control Valve Circuit Problem
P0444	Evaporative Emission Control System Purge Control Valve Circuit Open
P0445	Evaporative Emission Control System Purge Control Valve Circuit Shorted
P0446	Evaporative Emission Control System Vent Control Problem
P0447	Evaporative Emission Control System Vent Control Open
P0448	Evaporative Emission Control System Vent Control Shorted
P0450	Evaporative Emission Control System Pressure Sensor Problem
P0451	Evaporative Emission Control System Pressure Sensor Range or Performance
P0452	Evaporative Emission Control System Pressure Sensor Low Input
P0453	Evaporative Emission Control System Pressure Sensor High Input

Vehicle Speed Control and Idle Control

P0500	Vehicle Speed Sensor Problem
P0501	Vehicle Speed Sensor Range or Performance
P0502	Vehicle Speed Sensor Low Input
P0505	Idle Control System Problem
P0506	Idle Control System RPM Lower Than Expected
P0507	Idle Control System RPM Higher Than Expected
P0510	Closed Throttle Position Switch Problem

Computer Output Circuit

P0600	Serial Communication Link Problem
P0605	Internal Control Module (Module Identification Defined by J1979)

Transmission

P0703	Brake Switch Input Problem
P0705	Transmission Range Sensor Circuit Problem (PRNDL Input)
P0706	Transmission Range Sensor Circuit Range or Performance
P0707	Transmission Range Sensor Circuit Low Input
P0708	Transmission Range Sensor Circuit High Input
P0710	Transmission Fluid Temperature Sensor Problem
P0711	Transmission Fluid Temperature Sensor Range or Performance
P0712	Transmission Fluid Temperature Sensor Low Input
P0713	Transmission Fluid Temperature Sensor High Input
P0715	Input or Turbine Speed Sensor Circuit Problem
P0716	Input or Turbine Speed Sensor Circuit Range or Performance
P0717	Input or Turbine Speed Sensor Circuit No Signal
P0720	Output Speed Sensor Circuit Problem
P0721	Output Speed Sensor Circuit Range or Performance
P0722	Output Speed Sensor Circuit No Signal
P0725	Engine Speed Input Circuit Problem
P0726	Engine Speed Input Circuit Range or Performance
P0727	Engine Speed Input Circuit No Signal
P0730	Incorrect Gear Ratio
P0731	Gear 1 Incorrect Ratio
P0732	Gear 2 Incorrect Ratio
P0733	Gear 3 Incorrect Ratio
P0734	Gear 4 Incorrect Ratio
P0735	Gear 5 Incorrect Ratio
P0736	Reverse Incorrect Ratio
P0740	Torque Converter Clutch System Problem
P0741	Torque Converter Clutch System Performance or Stuck Off
P0742	Torque Converter Clutch System Stuck On
P0743	Torque Converter Clutch System Electrical
P0745	Pressure Control Solenoid Problem
P0746	Pressure Control Solenoid Performance or Stuck Off
P0747	Pressure Control Solenoid Stuck On
P0748	Pressure Control Solenoid Electrical
P0750	Shift Solenoid A Problem
P0751	Shift Solenoid A Performance or Stuck Off
P0752	Shift Solenoid A Stuck On
P0753	Shift Solenoid A Electrical

(continued)

P0755	Shift Solenoid B Problem
P0756	Shift Solenoid B Performance or Stuck Off
P0757	Shift Solenoid B Stuck On
P0758	Shift Solenoid B Electrical
P0760	Shift Solenoid C Problem
P0761	Shift Solenoid C Performance or Stuck Off
P0762	Shift Solenoid C Stuck On
P0763	Shift Solenoid C Electrical
P0765	Shift Solenoid D Problem
P0766	Shift Solenoid D Performance or Stuck Off
P0767	Shift Solenoid D Stuck On
P0768	Shift Solenoid D Electrical
P0770	Shift Solenoid E Problem
P0771	Shift Solenoid E Performance or Stuck Off
P0772	Shift Solenoid E Stuck On
P0773	Shift Solenoid E Electrical

* The side of the engine where number one cylinder is located.

OBD-II ACTIVE TESTS

The vehicle computer must run tests on the various emission-related components and turn on the malfunction indicator lamp (MIL) if faults are detected. OBD II is an *active* computer analysis system because it actually tests the operation of the oxygen sensors, exhaust gas recirculation system, and so forth whenever conditions permit. It is the purpose and function of the powertrain control module (PCM) to monitor these components and perform these active tests.

For example, the PCM may open the EGR valve momentarily to check its operation while the vehicle is decelerating. A change in the manifold absolute pressure (MAP) sensor signal will indicate to the computer that the exhaust gas is, in fact, being introduced into the engine. Because these tests are active and certain conditions must be present before these tests can be run, the computer uses its internal diagnostic program to keep track of all the various conditions and to schedule active tests so that they will not interfere with each other.

OBD-II DRIVE CYCLE The vehicle must be driven under a variety of operating conditions for all active tests to be performed. A **trip** is defined as an engine-operating drive cycle that contains the necessary conditions for a particular test to be performed. For example, for the EGR test to be performed, the engine has to be at normal operating temperature and decelerating for a minimum amount of time. Some tests are performed when the engine is cold, whereas others require that the vehicle be cruising at a steady highway speed.

TYPES OF OBD-II CODES Not all OBD-II diagnostic trouble codes are of the same importance for exhaust emissions.

Each type of DTC has different requirements for it to set, and the computer will only turn on the MIL for emissions-related DTCs.

TYPE A CODES. A type A diagnostic trouble code is emission related and will cause the MIL to be turned on at the *first trip* if the computer has detected a problem. Engine misfire or a very rich or lean air–fuel ratio, for example, would cause a type A diagnostic trouble code. These codes alert the driver to an emissions problem that may cause damage to the catalytic converter.

TYPE B CODES. A type B code will be stored as a pending code in the PCM and the MIL will be turned on only after the second consecutive trip, alerting the driver to the fact that a diagnostic test was performed and failed.

NOTE: Type A and Type B codes are emission related and will cause the lighting of the malfunction indicator lamp, usually labeled "check engine" or "service engine soon."

TYPE C AND D CODES. Type C and type D codes are for use with non-emission-related diagnostic tests. They will cause the lighting of a "service" lamp (if the vehicle is so equipped).

OBD-II FREEZE-FRAME To assist the service technician, OBD II requires the computer to take a "snapshot" or freeze-frame of all data at the instant an emission-related DTC is set. A scan tool is required to retrieve this data. CARB and EPA regulations require that the controller store specific freeze-frame (engine-related) data when the first emission-related fault is detected. The data stored in freeze-frame can only be replaced by data from a trouble code with a higher priority such as a problem related to a fuel system or misfire monitor fault.

NOTE: Although OBD II requires that just one freeze-frame of data be stored, the instant an emission-related DTC is set, vehicle manufacturers usually provide expanded data about the DTC beyond that required. However, retrieving enhanced data usually requires the use of an enhanced or factory-level scan tool.

The freeze-frame has to contain data values that occurred at the time the code was set (these values are provided in standard units of measurement). Freeze-frame data are recorded during the first trip on a two-trip fault. As a result, OBD-II systems record the data present at the time an emission-related code is recorded and the MIL activated. These data can be accessed and displayed on a scan tool. Freeze-frame data are one frame or one instant in time. They are not updated (refreshed) if the same monitor test fails a second time.

REQUIRED FREEZE-FRAME DATA ITEMS.
- Code that triggered the freeze-frame
- A/F ratio, airflow rate, and calculated engine load
- Base fuel injector pulse width
- ECT, IAT, MAF, MAP, TP, and VS sensor data
- Engine speed and amount of ignition spark advance
- Open- or closed-loop status

- Short-term and long-term fuel trim values
- For misfire codes—identify the cylinder that misfired

NOTE: All freeze-frame data will be lost if the battery is disconnected, power to the PCM is removed, or the scan tool is used to erase or clear trouble codes.

DIAGNOSING INTERMITTENT MALFUNCTIONS Of all the different types of conditions that you will see, the hardest to accurately diagnose and repair are intermittent malfunctions. These conditions may be temperature related (only occur when the vehicle is hot or cold), or humidity related (only occur when it is raining). Regardless of the conditions that will cause the malfunction to occur, you must diagnose and correct the condition.

When dealing with an intermittent concern, you should determine the conditions when the malfunction occurs, and then try to duplicate those conditions. If a cause is not readily apparent to you, ask the customer when the symptom occurs. Ask if there are any conditions that seem to be related to, or cause the concern.

Another consideration when working on an OBD-II-equipped vehicle is whether a concern is intermittent, or if it only occurs when a specific diagnostic test is performed by the PCM. Since OBD-II systems conduct diagnostic tests only under very precise conditions, some tests may be run only once during an ignition cycle. Additionally, if the requirements needed to perform the test are not met, the test will not run during an ignition cycle. This type of onboard diagnostics could be mistaken as "intermittent" when, in fact, the tests are only infrequent (depending on how the vehicle is driven). Examples of this type of diagnostic test are HO2S heaters, evaporative canister purge, catalyst efficiency, and EGR flow. When diagnosing intermittent concerns on an OBD-II-equipped vehicle, a logical diagnostic strategy is essential. The use of stored freeze-frame information can also be very useful when diagnosing an intermittent malfunction if a code has been stored.

NO-CODE DIAGNOSIS

POSSIBLE CAUSES No-code diagnosis is what the service technician needs to perform when there is a customer concern but there are no stored diagnostic trouble codes (DTCs). This type of customer complaint often results in a potential long process to locate the root cause. There are many possible causes of a problem such as a hesitation, stalling of poor performance that will not cause a DTC to set. Some of the possible causes include:

- Alcohol (ethanol) in high concentrations in the fuel
- Contaminated fuel that has water or diesel fuel mixed with the fuel
- Clogged air intake systems due to an animal nest of road debris caught in the air intake system
- Partially clogged or restricted exhaust system
- Engine mechanical fault such as recessed valves into the cylinder head resulting in reduced valve lift, thereby reducing engine power.

- Incorrect oil level or viscosity
- Incorrectly timed timing belt or chain causing valve timing to off but not enough to cause a crank/cam correlation DTC to be set.

NO-CODE DIAGNOSTIC STRATEGY If there are no stored DTCs, diagnostic strategy the wise service technician follows includes the following steps:

STEP #1: After verifying the customer concern, check vehicle service history and perform a thorough visual inspection checking for the following:

- Evidence of a previous repair or recent body work that may be an indication of an accident (collision).
- Check the fuel for contamination or excessive alcohol content
- Check that all of the tire sizes are the same, because if they are not, this can cause a vibration that is often confused as being a misfire, especially in four-wheel-drive and all-wheel-drive vehicles.
- Check for evidence of previous service work if the vehicle history is not available that may include engine work such as a timing belt or water pump replacement.
- Check for technical service bulletins (TSBs) that relate to the customer's concern.

STEP #2: Check scan tool data and look at fuel trim numbers. A preferred fuel trim is less than 5% whereas anything less than 10% is considered to be acceptable. A diagnostic trouble code for a rich or lean air–fuel ratio is usually set when the fuel number exceeds 25%. Sometimes driveability issues can be experienced by the driver when the exhaust is lean but not lean enough to set a DTC.

STEP #3: Perform a test drive using a scan tool set to record the major high-authority sensors in movie mode. The high-authority sensors that should be selected include:

- MAP/MAF
- ECT/IAT
- TP sensor
- O_2 sensors

The TP and MAF sensor should track each other, and when shown using the graphing capability on the scan tool, they show a direct relationship to each other as the vehicle is accelerated. Any sensor that shows to be not responding during engine load test needs to be checked more thoroughly.

STEP #4: If the root cause has not been located, perform a five-gas analysis of the exhaust gases. See Chapter 26 for details regarding what the results may indicate.

STEP #5: Using all available resources, including vehicle manufacturer's recommended testing procedures, determine the root cause of the problem. After making the repair,

The Case of the No-Power Kia

A customer had a Kia Sorento towed to a shop because it would not accelerate and the engine would not increase in speed higher than 1000 RPM. No diagnostic trouble codes were found and no technical service bulletins were found that pertained to this condition either. The data display on the scan tool did not show anything out of range and a through visual inspection found that the engine appeared to well maintain without any obvious or visible faults. Then another technician in the shop told the technician working on the vehicle that the brake lights were on whenever the engine was running even though no one was in the vehicle. This led to a closer examination of the brake switch, and when it was moved the engine was then able to be accelerated normally. A replacement brake switch was installed and the problem of a lack of acceleration was solved, and after replacement, the vehicle performed normally. The customer was pleased that a simple and low-cost solution was found.

Summary:

- **Complaint**—The vehicle owner complained that the engine would not accelerate and the engine speed would not increase higher than 1000 RPM.
- **Cause**—A defective brake switch caused the PCM to sense that the brake was applied and limited engine speed.
- **Correction**—A replacement brake switch fixed the problem and allowed the vehicle to accelerate normally.

verify the repair by performing a test-drive under similar conditions that caused the customer concern to make sure that the cause has been successfully repaired.

DETERMINING ROOT CAUSE OF REPEATED COMPONENT FAILURES

THE FIVE WHYS Typically when a component or system fails multiple times, the root cause of the failure was not corrected. When diagnosing the root cause of repeated component or system failure, the wise technician asks why five times. For example, for a case where the PCM set repeated P0017 (CKP/CMP correlation) DTCs, the oil control valve was replaced and the DTC cleared. According to the repair forums, this was a common repair for this condition. The engine

appeared to be operating correctly; however, the check engine light with the same code occurred again after a week? Why?

Why #1: The technician did not complete a thorough diagnosis, instead relying on a silver bullet in a repair forum. On the second attempt to repair the vehicle the technician followed the diagnostic procedure for the code. The resistance of the new oil control valve was found to be within specifications. The camshaft position (CMP) sensor was tested based on the advice from another technician. The sensor passed all the diagnostic tests and appeared to be generating a normal signal.

Why #2: If the oil control valve and the sensor are both good, why did the code reset? The technician checked all of the wiring and the electrical connectors and found them to be okay. Why was the problem still occurring?

Why #3: During a subsequent test drive, the code set again. This time the technician tested the crankshaft sensor and verified the condition of the timing belt. Each of the components tested normally.

Why #4: The technician thought that the recurring problem was related to the OCV because when these were replaced, it fixed the vehicle for some time. The technician then noticed the engine oil was low and very dirty. Why was this important?

Why #5: Understanding that clean oil was needed for the system to operate properly, the engine oil and filter were replaced making sure to use the oil recommended by the manufacturer and an oil filter that met original equipment specifications. The code was cleared and on subsequent test drives the failure did not reoccur.

On the second repair attempt the technician followed the diagnostic process to a logical end. No assumptions were made, but instead decisions were made based on the test results. In the end, the root cause of the problem was actually very simple and the repair was relatively inexpensive.

MULTIPLE COMPONENT FAILURE DIAGNOSIS If more than one component is found to be defective, the root cause has to be found. If the components are electrical, use a wiring diagram and check for the following:

- Do the components share a common ground connection? If so, this could be the most likely cause and the first place to check.

 TECH TIP

The Brake Pedal Trick

If the vehicle manufacturer recommends that battery power be disconnected, first disconnect the negative battery cable and then depress the brake pedal. Because the brake lights are connected to battery power, depressing the brake pedal causes all of the capacitors in the electrical system and computer(s) to discharge through the brake lights.

- Do the components share the same power? If so, then this could be the source of common component failure.
- Are the components or wiring near a heat source such as the exhaust system or EGR system components? Heat can cause electrical issues and often cause issues with more than one component.
- Are the components or wiring near something that is moved such as a door, hood, or trunk (tailgate) opening? The movement can cause electrical issues and often cause issues with more than one component.
- Follow the diagnostic strategy to find and correct the root cause, then verify the repair has solved the customer concern before returning the vehicle.

MANUFACTURER'S DIAGNOSTIC ROUTINES

Each vehicle manufacturer has established their own diagnostic routines and they should be followed. Most include the following steps:

STEP 1 Retrieve diagnostic trouble codes.

STEP 2 Check for all technical service bulletins that could be related to the stored DTC.

STEP 3 If there are multiple DTCs, the diagnostic routine may include checking different components or systems instead of when only one DTC was stored.

STEP 4 Perform system checks.

STEP 5 Perform the necessary service or repair

STEP 6 Perform a road test matching the parameters recorded in the freeze-frame to check that the repair has corrected the malfunction.

STEP 7 Repeat the road test to cause the MIL to be extinguished.

NOTE: Do not clear codes (DTCs) unless instructed by the service information.

Following the vehicle manufacturer's specific diagnostic routines will ensure that the root cause is found and the repair verified. This is important for customer satisfaction.

VERIFYING THE REPAIR

PROCEDURE After the repair has been successfully completed, the vehicle should be driven under similar conditions that caused the original concern in order to verify that the problem has been corrected. To perform this test drive, it is helpful to have a copy of the freeze-frame parameters that

were present when the DTC was set. By driving under similar conditions, the PCM may perform a test of the system and automatically extinguish the malfunction indicator light (MIL). This is the method preferred by many vehicle manufacturers.

OBD MONITORS FOR REPAIR VERIFICATION All 1996 and newer vehicles perform enhanced diagnostic checks of specific emission control components such as engine, transmission, fuel systems, and other emissions controls. Each diagnostic check communicates with the powertrain control module's (PCM) diagnostic executive to record the data in the *readiness monitor*. These diagnostic checks are generally performed while the vehicle is driven in a specific manner and are a great way to prove the repair was successful. If the diagnostic checks have been performed and passed, the PCM marks them as "ready." Technicians in a non-emissions test area are able to use the data to ensure the vehicle is repaired and that no other codes are set prior to returning the vehicle to the customer.

For technicians who work on vehicles in an emission test area this is an important step in the repair process. If diagnostic data has been erased during vehicle repairs or through battery disconnection, the PCM will flag the monitors as "incomplete" or "not ready." Vehicles are rejected from emission testing when these diagnostic checks are not completed. The number of monitors allowed to be not complete depends on the year of the vehicle and the emission testing area requirements.

The vehicle performs the self-diagnostic tests when the vehicle is driven, referred to as a "drive cycle." Therefore, after the repair is complete the vehicle will need to be driven through a drive cycle. If the check engine light does not turn off, then additional repair(s) may be required. If the repairs require the DTCs to be cleared or a battery disconnect (which also clears DTCs), then the vehicle needs to be driven to get the monitors to run and pass.

ROAD TEST (DRIVE CYCLE)

Use the freeze-frame data and test-drive the vehicle so that the vehicle is driven to match the conditions displayed on the freeze-frame. If the battery has been disconnected, then the vehicle may have to be driven under conditions that allow the PCM to conduct monitor tests. This drive pattern is called a **drive cycle.** The drive cycle is different for each vehicle manufacturer but a universal drive cycle may work in many cases. In many cases performing a universal drive cycle will reset most monitors in most vehicles.

UNIVERSAL DRIVE CYCLE

PRECONDITIONING: Phase I.

MIL must be off.

No DTCs present.

Fuel fill between 15% and 85%.

Cold start – Preferred = 8 – hour soak at 68°F to 86°F.

Alternative: ECT = IAT.

1. With the ignition off, connect scan tool.
2. Start engine and drive between 20 and 30 mph for 22 minutes, allowing speed to vary.
3. Stop and idle for 40 seconds, gradually accelerate to 55 mph.
4. Maintain 55 mph for 4 minutes using a steady throttle input.
5. Stop and idle for 30 seconds, then accelerate to 30 mph.
6. Maintain 30 mph for 12 minutes.
7. Repeat steps 4 and 5 four times.

Using scan tool, check readiness. If insufficient readiness set, continue to universal drive trace phase II.

Important: (Do not shut off engine between phases).

Phase II:

1. Vehicle at a stop and idle for 45 seconds, then accelerate to 30 mph.
2. Maintain 30 mph for 22 minutes.
3. Repeat steps 1 and 2 three times.
4. Bring vehicle to a stop and idle for 45 seconds, then accelerate to 35 mph.
5. Maintain speed between 30 and 35 mph for 4 minutes.
6. Bring vehicle to a stop and idle for 45 seconds, then accelerate to 30 mph.
7. Maintain 30 mph for 22 minutes.

8. Repeat steps 6 and 7 five times.
9. Using scan tool, check readiness.

DIESEL OBDII MONITOR READINESS

PRIOR TO START

- Fuel level greater than 25%.
- Coolant temperature below 140°F (60°C)
- Battery voltage must be between 11 and 16 volts. PTO is not engaged

TO RUN THE MONITORS

1. Allow the engine to idle for a minimum of two minutes and warm the engine to greater than 140 degrees. (Vehicle must be stationary and the accelerator must not be depressed during this time.)
2. Drive for 5 minutes at speeds above 25 mph and less than 45 mph (in-town driving).
3. Drive the vehicle at highway speeds and perform 10–15 zero fueling events (decelerate for 10 seconds with foot off of accelerator).
4. Drive the vehicle at highway speeds and perform 15–20 boost events (sudden depression of the accelerator pedal to provide turbocharger boost to the system).
5. Drive the vehicle at highway speeds in a steady state for 12–15 minutes.
6. Return to the shop and let vehicle idle for 30 seconds.
7. With the vehicle in park increase the engine speed to 1200–1300 RPM for 2–3 minutes (repeat 3–4 times).
8. Let idle for 30 seconds.
9. Shut off vehicle.
10. Cycle key back on and check readiness status.

SUMMARY

1. Funnel diagnostics—Visual approach to a diagnostic procedure:

    Step 1 Verify the problem (concern)

    Step 2 Perform a thorough visual inspection and basic tests

    Step 3 Retrieve the diagnostic trouble codes (DTCs)

    Step 4 Check for technical service bulletins (TSBs)

    Step 5 Look carefully at scan tool data

    Step 6 Narrow the problem to a system or cylinder

    Step 7 Repair the problem and determine the root cause

    Step 8 Verify the repair and check for any stored DTCs

2. A thorough visual inspection is important during the diagnosis and troubleshooting of any engine performance problem or electrical malfunction.

3. If the MIL is on, retrieve the DTC and follow the manufacturer's recommended procedure to find the root cause of the problem.

4. OBD-II vehicles use a 16-pin DLC and common DTCs.

1. Why should TSBs be checked after retrieving diagnostic trouble codes?

2. Why does the customer concern need to verified?

3. What is the difference between an aftermarket scan tool and a factory-level scan tool?

4. What is the preferred method to use to clear DTCs?

5. What is the definition of a trip?

CHAPTER QUIZ

1. Technician A says that the first step in the diagnostic process is to verify the problem (concern). Technician B says the second step is to perform a thorough visual inspection. Which technician is correct?
   a. Technician A only
   b. Technician B only
   c. Both Technicians A and B
   d. Neither Technician A nor B

2. Which item is *not* important to know before starting the diagnosis of an engine performance problem?
   a. List of previous repairs
   b. The brand of engine oil used
   c. The type of gasoline used
   d. The temperature of the engine when the problem occurs

3. A generic (global)-type scan tool can retrieve _____ data.
   a. emissions-related
   b. HVAC
   c. ABS brake system
   d. All of the above

4. The steps in a manufacturer-specific diagnostic routine are being discussed. Technician A says that after recording any DTCs, the codes should be erased. Technician B says to road test the vehicle twice to turn off the MIL. Which technician is correct?
   a. Technician A only
   b. Technician B only
   c. Both technicians are correct
   d. Neither technician is correct

5. Technician A says that if the opposite DTC can be set, the problem is the component itself. Technician B says if the opposite DTC cannot be set, the problem is with the wiring or grounds. Which technician is correct?
   a. Technician A only
   b. Technician B only
   c. Both Technicians A and B
   d. Neither Technician A nor B

6. The preferred method to clear diagnostic trouble codes (DTCs) is to _____.
   a. disconnect the negative battery cable for 10 seconds
   b. use a scan tool
   c. remove the computer (PCM) power feed fuse
   d. cycle the ignition key on and off 40 times

7. Which is the factory scan tool for Chrysler brand vehicles equipped with CAN?
   a. wiTECH
   b. Tech 2
   c. NGS
   d. Master Tech

8. What fault could occur that can cause a driveability issue and not set a diagnostic trouble code (DTC)?
   a. Alcohol (ethanol) in high concentrations in the fuel
   b. Contaminated fuel that has water or diesel fuel mixed with the fuel.
   c. Clogged air intake systems due to an animal nest of road debris caught in the air intake system
   d. Any of the above

9. Technician A says that knowing if there are any stored diagnostic trouble codes may be helpful when checking for related technical service bulletins. Technician B says that only a factory scan tool should be used to retrieve DTCs. Which technician is correct?
   a. Technician A only
   b. Technician B only
   c. Both Technicians A and B
   d. Neither Technician A nor B

10. A drive cycle is designed to reset all the OBD-II monitors. Before starting the drive cycle the engine should be _____.
   a. fully warmed up (cooling fans cycled on and off two times)
   b. have a full tank of fuel
   c. cold (ECT = IAT)
   d. operated at idle for two minutes

ALTERNATIVE FUELS, AND DIESEL FUELS

LEARNING OBJECTIVES

After studying this chapter, the reader should be able to:

1. Discuss the characteristics of gasoline, refining of gasoline, and volatility of gasoline.
2. Explain air–fuel ratios, normal and abnormal combustion, and octane rating.
3. Discuss gasoline additives, gasoline blending, and testing gasoline for alcohol content.
4. Discuss general gasoline recommendations.
5. Explain alternative fuel vehicles, and discuss the safety procedures when working with alternative fuels.
6. Discuss E85, methanol, and propane fuel.
7. Discuss compressed natural gas, liquefied natural gas, and P-series fuels.
8. Discuss synthetic fuels.
9. Compare diesel fuel, biodiesel, and E-diesel fuel.

KEY TERMS

AFV 33
Air–fuel ratio 25
Antiknock index (AKI) 27
API gravity 41
ASTM 23
B5 42
B20 42
Biodiesel 42
Biomass 35
Catalytic cracking 23
Cetane number 41
Cloud point 40
Coal to liquid (CTL) 39
Compressed natural gas (CNG) 35
Cracking 23
Detonation 26
Diesohol 43
Distillation 23
E10 28
E85 32
E-diesel 43
Ethanol 28
Ethyl alcohol 32
FFV 33
Fischer–Tropsch 38
Flex fuel 33
FTD 39
Fuel compensation sensor 33
Fungible 23
Gasoline 23
Grain alcohol 32

GTL 39
Hydrocracking 23
Liquefied petroleum gas (LPG) 35
LP gas 35
M85 35
Methanol 34
Methanol to gasoline (MTG) 40
NGV 35
Octane rating 26
Oxygenated fuels 28
Petrodiesel 42
Ping 26
PPO 43
Propane 35
Reid vapor pressure (RVP) 23
Spark knock 26
Stoichiometric 25
SVO 43
Syncrude 40
Syn-gas 35
UCO 43
ULSD 41
Underground coal gasification (UCG) 40
Variable fuel sensor 33
V-FFV 34
Volatility 23
WVO 43
WWFC 31

INTRODUCTION

Using the proper fuel is important for the proper operation of any engine. Although gasoline is the most commonly used fuel today, there are several alternative fuels that can be used in some vehicles. Diesel fuel contains much lower amounts of sulfur than before 2007 and this allows the introduction of many new clean burning diesel engines.

GASOLINE

Gasoline is a term used to describe a complex mixture of various hydrocarbons refined from crude petroleum oil for use as a fuel in engines. Gasoline and air burn in the cylinder of the engine and produce heat and pressure, which is transferred to rotary motion inside the engine and eventually powers the drive wheels of a vehicle. When the combustion process in the engine is perfect, all of the fuel and air are consumed and only carbon dioxide and water are produced.

REFINING

DISTILLATION   In the late 1800s, crude was separated into different products by boiling in a process called **distillation**. Distillation works because crude oil is composed of hydrocarbons with a broad range of boiling points.

In a distillation column, the vapor of the lowest boiling hydrocarbons, propane and butane, rises to the top. The straight-run gasoline (also called naphtha), kerosene, and diesel fuel cuts are drawn off at successively lower positions in the column.

CRACKING   **Cracking** is the process during which hydrocarbons with higher boiling points can be broken down (cracked) into lower boiling hydrocarbons by treating them to very high temperatures. This process, called *thermal cracking*, was used to increase gasoline production starting in 1913.

Today, instead of high heat, cracking is performed using a catalyst and is called **catalytic cracking**. A catalyst is a material that speeds up or otherwise facilitates a chemical reaction without undergoing a permanent chemical change itself. Catalytic cracking produces gasoline of higher quality than thermal cracking.

Hydrocracking is similar to catalytic cracking in that it uses a catalyst, but the catalyst is in a hydrogen atmosphere. Hydrocracking can break down hydrocarbons that are resistant to catalytic cracking alone and it is used to produce diesel fuel rather than gasoline.

Other types of refining processes include:

- Reforming
- Alkylation
- Isomerization
- Hydrotreating
- Desulfurization
  - ● **SEE FIGURE 2–1.**

SHIPPING   The gasoline is transported to regional storage facilities by tank railway car or by pipeline. In the pipeline method, all gasoline from many refiners is often sent through the same pipeline and can become mixed. All gasoline is said to be **fungible**, meaning that it is capable of being interchanged because each grade is created to specification so there is no reason to keep the different gasoline brands separated except for grade. Regular grade, midgrade, and premium grades are separated by using a device, called a *pig*, in the pipeline and sent to regional storage facilities. ● **SEE FIGURE 2–2.**

It is at these regional or local storage facilities where the additives and dye (if any) are added and then shipped by truck to individual gas stations.

VOLATILITY

DEFINITION   **Volatility** describes how easily the gasoline evaporates (forms a vapor). The definition of volatility assumes that the vapors will remain in the fuel tank or fuel line and will cause a certain pressure based on the temperature of the fuel.

REID VAPOR PRESSURE   **Reid vapor pressure (RVP)** is the pressure of the vapor above the fuel when the fuel is at 100°F (38°C). Increased vapor pressure permits the engine to start in cold weather. Gasoline without air will not burn. Gasoline must be vaporized (mixed with air) to burn in an engine. ● **SEE FIGURE 2–3.**

SEASONAL BLENDING   Cold temperatures reduce the normal vaporization of gasoline; therefore, winter-blended gasoline is specially formulated to vaporize at lower temperatures for proper starting and driveability at low ambient temperatures.

- **Winter blend.** The **American Society for Testing and Materials (ASTM)** standards for winter-blend gasoline allow volatility of up to 15 pounds per square inch (PSI) RVP.
- **Summer blend.** At warm ambient temperatures, gasoline vaporizes easily. However, the fuel system (fuel pump, fuel-injector nozzles, etc.) is designed to operate with liquid gasoline. The volatility of summer-grade gasoline should be about 7 PSI RVP. According to ASTM standards, the maximum RVP should be 10.5 PSI for summer-blend gasoline.

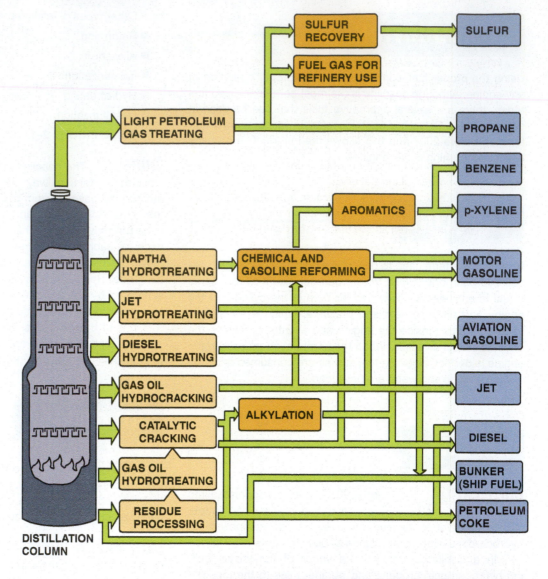

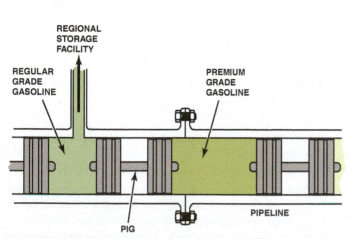

FIGURE 2–2 A pig is a plug-like device that is placed in a pipeline to separate two types or grades of fuel.

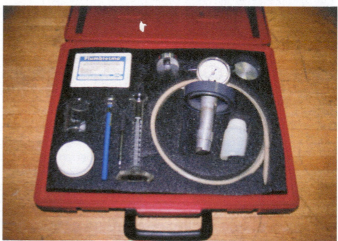

FIGURE 2–3 A gasoline testing kit, including an insulated container where water at 100°F is used to heat a container holding a small sample of gasoline. The reading on the pressure gauge is the Reid vapor pressure (RVP).

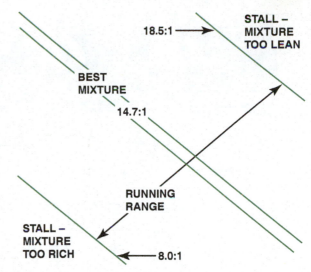

FIGURE 2–4 An engine will not run if the air–fuel mixture is either too rich or too lean.

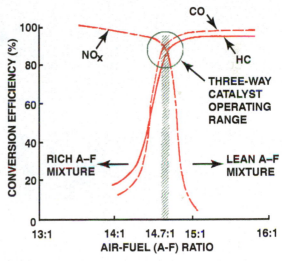

FIGURE 2–5 With a three-way catalytic converter, emission control is most efficient with an air–fuel ratio between 14.65:1 and 14.75:1.

FREQUENTLY ASKED QUESTION

Why Do I Get Lower Gas Mileage in the Winter?

Several factors cause the engine to use more fuel in the winter than in the summer.

- Gasoline that is blended for use in cold climates is designed for ease of starting and contains fewer heavy molecules, which contribute to fuel economy. The heat content of winter gasoline is lower than summer-blend gasoline.
- In cold temperatures, all lubricants are stiff, causing more resistance. These lubricants include the engine oil, as well as the transmission and differential gear lubricants.
- Heat from the engine is radiated into the outside air more rapidly when the temperature is cold, resulting in longer run time until the engine has reached normal operating temperature.
- Road conditions, such as ice and snow, can cause tire slippage or additional drag on the vehicle.

VOLATILITY-RELATED PROBLEMS If using winter-grade fuel during warm weather, the following may occur:

- Heat causes some fuel to evaporate, thereby causing bubbles.
- When the fuel is full of bubbles (sometimes called *vapor lock*), the engine is not being supplied with enough fuel and the engine runs lean. A lean engine will lead to the following:

1. Rough idle
2. Stalling
3. Hesitation on acceleration
4. Surging

If using summer-grade fuel in cold temperatures, then the engine will be hard to start (long cranking before starting) due to the lack of volatility to allow the engine to start easily.

AIR–FUEL RATIOS

DEFINITION The **air–fuel ratio** is the proportion by weight of air and gasoline that the injection system mixes as needed for engine combustion. Air–fuel ratios in which a gasoline engine can operate without stalling range from 8:1 to 18.5:1. ● **SEE FIGURE 2–4.**

The following ratios are usually stated by weight:

- 8 parts of air by weight combined with 1 part of gasoline by weight (8:1), which is the richest mixture that an engine can tolerate and still fire reliably

- 18.5 parts of air mixed with 1 part of gasoline (18.5:1), which is the leanest practical ratio

Richer or leaner air–fuel ratios cause the engine to misfire badly or not run at all.

STOICHIOMETRIC AIR–FUEL RATIO The ideal mixture or ratio at which all of the fuel combines with all of the oxygen in the air and burns completely is called the **stoichiometric** ratio, a chemically perfect combination. In theory, this ratio for gasoline is an air–fuel mixture of 14.7:1. The stoichiometric ratio is a compromise between maximum power and maximum economy. ● **SEE FIGURE 2–5.**

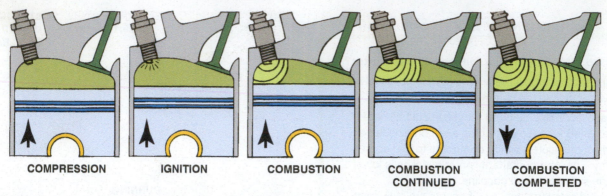

COMPRESSION   **IGNITION**   **COMBUSTION**   **COMBUSTION CONTINUED**   **COMBUSTION COMPLETED**

FIGURE 2–6 Normal combustion is a smooth, controlled burning of the air–fuel mixture.

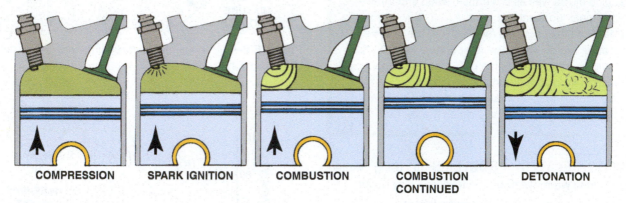

COMPRESSION   **SPARK IGNITION**   **COMBUSTION**   **COMBUSTION CONTINUED**   **DETONATION**

FIGURE 2–7 Detonation is a secondary ignition of the air–fuel mixture. It is also called spark knock or pinging.

NORMAL AND ABNORMAL COMBUSTION

TERMINOLOGY The **octane rating** of gasoline is the measure of its antiknock properties. **Spark knock** (also called **detonation** or **ping**) is a metallic noise an engine makes, usually during acceleration, resulting from abnormal or uncontrolled combustion inside the cylinder. Normal combustion occurs smoothly and progresses across the combustion chamber from the point of ignition.
● **SEE FIGURE 2–6**.

Normal flame-front combustion travels between 45 and 90 mph (72 and 145 km/h). The speed of the flame front depends on air–fuel ratio, combustion chamber design (determining amount of turbulence), and temperature.

ABNORMAL COMBUSTION During periods of abnormal combustion, called spark knock or detonation, the combustion speed increases by up to 10 times to near the speed of sound. The increased combustion speed also causes increased temperatures and pressures, which can damage pistons, gaskets, and cylinder heads. ● **SEE FIGURE 2–7**.

CONTROLLING SPARK KNOCK Spark knock was commonly heard in older engines especially when under load and in warm weather temperatures. Most engines built since the 1990s are equipped with a knock sensor that is used to signal the powertrain control module (PCM) to retard the ignition timing if knock is detected. Using the proper octane fuel helps to ensure that spark knock does not occur.

OCTANE RATING

RATING METHODS The two basic methods used to rate gasoline for antiknock properties (octane rating) include the *Research method* and the *Motor method.*

Each uses a model of the special *cooperative fuel research* (CFR) single-cylinder engine to test the octane of a fuel sample, and the two methods use different engine settings. The research method typically results in readings that are 6 to 10 points higher than those of the motor method. For example, a fuel with a research octane number (RON) of 93 might have a motor octane number (MON) of 85.

GASOLINE GRADES The octane rating posted on pumps in the United States is the average of the two methods and is referred to as R + M ÷ 2, meaning that, for the fuel used in the previous example, the rating posted on the pumps would be:

$$\frac{RON + MON}{2} = \frac{93 + 85}{2} = 89$$

FIGURE 2–8 A pump showing regular with a pump octane of 87, plus rated at 89, and premium rated at 93. These ratings can vary with brand as well as in different parts of the country.

FIGURE 2–9 The posted octane rating in most high-altitude areas shows regular at 85 instead of the usual 87.

GRADES	OCTANE RATING
Regular	87
Midgrade (also called Plus)	89
Premium	91 or higher

CHART 2–1

The octane rating displayed on the fuel pumps can vary depending on climate.

? **FREQUENTLY ASKED QUESTION**

What Grade of Gasoline Does the EPA Use When Testing Engines?

Due to the various grades and additives used in commercial fuel, the government (EPA) uses a liquid called indolene, which has a research method octane number of 96.5 and a motor method octane rating of 88, resulting in a (R + M) ÷ 2 rating of 92.25.

This pump octane rating is often called the **antiknock index (AKI)**.
- **SEE FIGURE 2–8.**
- **SEE CHART 2–1** for the grades and octane ratings.

OCTANE EFFECTS OF ALTITUDE As the altitude increases, atmospheric pressure drops. The air is less dense because a pound of air takes more volume. The octane rating of fuel does not need to be as high because the engine cannot take in as much air. This process will reduce the combustion (compression) pressures inside the engine. In mountainous areas, gasoline (R + M) ÷ 2 octane ratings are two or more numbers lower than normal (according to the SAE, about one octane number lower per 1,000 ft (300 m) in altitude). **SEE FIGURE 2–9.**

A second reason for the lowered octane requirement of engines running at higher altitudes is the normal enrichment of the air–fuel ratio and lower engine vacuum with the decreased air density. Some problems, therefore, may occur when driving out of high-altitude areas into lower areas where the octane rating must be higher. Most electronic fuel injection systems can compensate for changes in altitude and modify air–fuel ratio and ignition timing for best operation.

TECH TIP

Horsepower and Fuel Flow

To produce 1 hp, the engine must be supplied with 0.50 lb of fuel per hour (lb/hr). Fuel injectors are rated in pounds per hour. For example, a V-8 engine equipped with 25 lb/hr fuel injectors could produce 50 hp per cylinder (per injector) or 400 hp. Even if the cylinder head or block is modified to produce more horsepower, the limiting factor may be the injector flow rate.

The following are flow rates and resulting horsepower for a V-8 engine.

- 30 lb/hr: 60 hp per cylinder, or 480 hp
- 35 lb/hr: 70 hp per cylinder, or 560 hp
- 40 lb/hr: 80 hp per cylinder, or 640 hp

Of course, injector flow rate is only one of many variables that affect power output. Installing larger injectors without other major engine modifications could decrease engine output and drastically increase exhaust emissions.

Because the combustion burn rate slows at high altitude, the ignition (spark) timing can be advanced to improve power. The amount of timing advance can be about 1 degree per 1,000 ft over 5,000 ft. Therefore, if driving at 8,000 ft of altitude, the ignition timing can be advanced 3 degrees.

VOLATILITY EFFECTS OF ALTITUDE High altitude also allows fuel to evaporate more easily. The volatility of fuel should be reduced at higher altitudes to prevent vapor from forming in sections of the fuel system, which can cause driveability and stalling problems. The extra heat generated in climbing to higher altitudes plus the lower atmospheric pressure at higher altitudes combine to cause possible driveability problems as the vehicle goes to higher altitudes.

GASOLINE ADDITIVES

DYE Dye is usually added to gasoline at the distributor to help identify the grade and/or brand of fuel. Fuels are required to be colored using a fuel soluble dye in many countries. In the United States and Canada, diesel fuel used for off-road use and not taxed is required to be dyed red for identification. Gasoline sold for off-road use in Canada is dyed purple.

OXYGENATED FUEL ADDITIVES Oxygenated fuels contain oxygen in the molecule of the fuel itself. Examples of oxygenated fuels include:

- **Methyl tertiary butyl ether (MTBE).** This fuel is manufactured by means of the chemical reaction of methanol and isobutylene. Unlike methanol, MTBE does not increase the volatility of the fuel, and is not as sensitive to water as are other alcohols. The maximum allowable volume level, according to the EPA, is 15% but is currently being phased out due to health concerns, as well as MTBE contamination of drinking water if spilled from storage tanks.
- **Tertiary-amyl methyl ether (TAME).** This fuel contains an oxygen atom bonded to two carbon atoms, and is added to gasoline to provide oxygen to the fuel. It is slightly soluble in water, very soluble in ethers and alcohol, and soluble in most organic solvents including hydrocarbons.
- **Ethyl tertiary butyl ether (ETBE).** This fuel is derived from ethanol. The maximum allowable volume level is 17.2%. The use of ETBE is the cause of much of the odor from the exhaust of vehicles if using reformulated gasoline, as mandated for use in some parts of the country.
- **Ethanol.** Also called *ethyl alcohol,* **ethanol** is drinkable alcohol and is usually made from grain. Adding 10% ethanol (ethyl alcohol or grain alcohol) increases the $(R + M) \div 2$ octane rating by three points.

FIGURE 2–10 This fuel pump indicates that the gasoline is blended with 10% ethanol (ethyl alcohol) and can be used in any gasoline vehicle. E85 contains 85% ethanol and can only be used in vehicles specifically designed to use it.

The alcohol added to the base gasoline, however, also raises the volatility of the fuel about 0.5 PSI. Most automobile manufacturers permit up to 10% ethanol if driveability problems are not experienced.

The oxygen content of a 10% blend of ethanol in gasoline, called **E10**, is 3.5% oxygen by weight. ● **SEE FIGURE 2–10.**

GASOLINE BLENDING

Gasoline additives, such as ethanol and dyes, are usually added to the fuel at the distributor. Adding ethanol to gasoline is a way to add oxygen to the fuel itself. There are three basic methods used to blend ethanol with gasoline to create E10 (10% ethanol, 90% gasoline).

 FREQUENTLY ASKED QUESTION

What Is Meant by "Phase Separation"?
All alcohols absorb water, and the alcohol-water mixture can separate from the gasoline and sink to the bottom of the fuel tank. This process is called phase separation. To help avoid engine performance problems, try to keep at least a quarter tank of fuel at all times, especially during seasons when there is a wide temperature span between daytime highs and nighttime lows. These conditions can cause moisture to accumulate in the fuel tank as a result of condensation of the moisture in the air. Keeping the fuel tank full reduces the amount of air and moisture in the tank. ● **SEE FIGURE 2–11.**

FIGURE 2–11 A container with gasoline containing water and alcohol. Notice the separation line where the alcohol-water mixture separated from the gasoline and sank to the bottom.

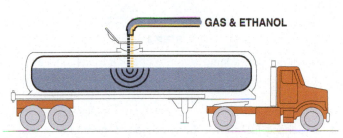

FIGURE 2–12 In-line blending is the most accurate method for blending ethanol with gasoline because computers are used to calculate the correct ratio.

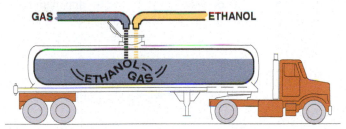

FIGURE 2–13 Sequential blending uses a computer to calculate the correct ratio as well as the prescribed order that the products are loaded.

1. **In-line blending.** Gasoline and ethanol are mixed in a storage tank or in the tank of a transport truck while it is being filled. Because the quantities of each can be accurately measured, this method is most likely to produce a well-mixed blend of ethanol and gasoline. ● **SEE FIGURE 2–12.**

2. **Sequential blending.** This method is usually performed at the wholesale terminal and involves adding a measured amount of ethanol to a tank truck followed by a measured amount of gasoline. ● **SEE FIGURE 2–13.**

3. **Splash blending.** This method can be done at the retail outlet or distributor and involves separate purchases of ethanol and gasoline. In a typical case, a distributor can purchase gasoline, and then drive to another supplier and

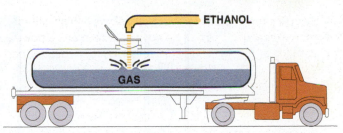

FIGURE 2–14 Splash blending occurs when the ethanol is added to a tanker with gasoline and is mixed as the truck travels to the retail outlet.

? FREQUENTLY ASKED QUESTION

Is Water Heavier than Gasoline?

Yes. Water weighs about 8 lb per gallon, whereas gasoline weighs about 6 lb per gallon. The density as measured by specific gravity includes:

Water = 1.000 (the baseline for specific gravity)
Gasoline = 0.730 to 0.760

This means that any water that gets into the fuel tank will sink to the bottom.

purchase ethanol. The ethanol is then added (splashed) into the tank of gasoline. This method is the least accurate method of blending and can result in ethanol concentration for E10 that should be 10%, and ranges from 5% to over 20% in some cases. ● **SEE FIGURE 2–14.**

TESTING GASOLINE FOR ALCOHOL CONTENT

Take the following steps when testing gasoline for alcohol content:

☠ WARNING

Do not smoke or run the test around sources of ignition!

1. Pour suspect gasoline into a graduated cylinder.
2. Carefully fill the graduated cylinder to the 90 mL mark.
3. Add 10 mL of water to the graduated cylinder by counting the number of drops from an eyedropper.

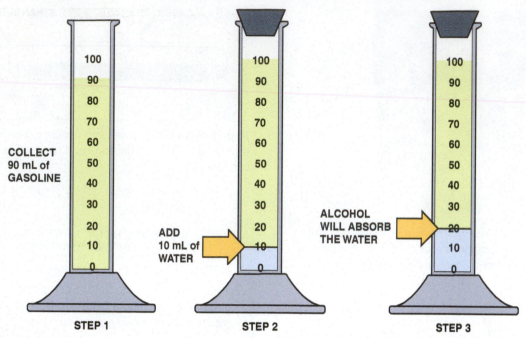

COLLECT 90 mL of GASOLINE

ADD 10 mL of WATER

ALCOHOL WILL ABSORB THE WATER

STEP 1　　　　STEP 2　　　　STEP 3

FIGURE 2–15 Checking gasoline for alcohol involves using a graduated cylinder and adding water to check if the alcohol absorbs the water.

4. Put the stopper in the cylinder and shake vigorously for one minute. Relieve built-up pressure by occasionally removing the stopper. Alcohol dissolves in water and will drop to the bottom of the cylinder.

5. Place the cylinder on a flat surface and let it stand for two minutes.

6. Take a reading near the bottom of the cylinder at the boundary between the two liquids.

7. For percentage of alcohol in gasoline, subtract 10 to get the percentage.

For example,
The reading is 20 mL: 20 − 10 = 10% alcohol

If the increase in volume is 0.2% or less, it may be assumed that the test gasoline contains no alcohol. ● **SEE FIGURE 2–15.**

Alcohol content can also be checked using an electronic tester. See the photo sequence at the end of the chapter.

GENERAL GASOLINE RECOMMENDATIONS

The fuel used by an engine is a major expense in the operation cost of the vehicle. The proper operation of the engine depends on clean fuel of the proper octane rating and vapor pressure for the atmospheric conditions.

To help ensure proper engine operation and keep fuel costs to a minimum, follow these guidelines:

1. Purchase fuel from a busy station to help ensure that it is fresh and less likely to be contaminated with water or moisture.

2. Keep the fuel tank above one-quarter full, especially during seasons in which the temperature rises and falls by more than 20°F between daytime highs and nighttime lows. This helps to reduce condensed moisture in the fuel tank and could prevent gas line freeze-up in cold weather.

NOTE: Gas line freeze-up occurs when the water in the gasoline freezes and forms an ice blockage in the fuel line.

3. Do not purchase fuel with a higher octane rating than is necessary. Try using premium high-octane fuel to check for operating differences. Most newer engines are equipped with a detonation (knock) sensor that signals the vehicle computer to retard the ignition timing when spark knock occurs. Therefore, an operating difference may not be noticeable to the driver when using a low-octane fuel, except for a decrease in power and fuel economy. In other words, the engine with a knock sensor will tend to operate knock free on regular fuel, even if premium, higher octane fuel is specified. Using premium fuel may result in more power and greater fuel economy. The increase in fuel economy, however, would have to be substantial to justify the increased cost of high-octane premium fuel. Some drivers find a good compromise by using midgrade (plus) fuel to benefit from the engine power and fuel economy gains without the cost of using premium fuel all the time.

FIGURE 2–16 Not all top-tier gas stations mention that they are top-tier like this station. For more information and the list of top-tier gasoline stations, visit *www.toptiergas.com*.

FIGURE 2–17 Many service stations have signs posted warning customers to place plastic fuel containers on the ground while filling. If placed in a trunk or pickup truck bed equipped with a plastic liner, static electricity could build up during fueling and discharge from the container to the metal nozzle, creating a spark and possible explosion. Some service stations have warning signs not to use cell phones while fueling to help avoid the possibility of an accidental spark creating a fire hazard.

 FREQUENTLY ASKED QUESTION

What Is "Top-Tier" Gasoline?

Top-tier gasoline has specific standards for quality, including enough detergent to keep all intake valves clean. Four automobile manufacturers (BMW, General Motors, Honda, and Toyota) developed the standards. Top-tier gasoline exceeds the quality standards developed by the **World Wide Fuel Charter (WWFC)** in 2002 by vehicle and engine manufacturers. The gasoline companies that agreed to make fuel that matches or exceeds the standards as a top-tier fuel include ChevronTexaco, Shell, and ConocoPhillips. ● **SEE FIGURE 2–16**.

4. Try to avoid using gasoline with alcohol in warm weather, even though many alcohol blends do not affect engine driveability. If warm-engine stumble, stalling, or rough idle occurs, change brands of gasoline.

5. Do not purchase fuel from a retail outlet when a tanker truck is filling the underground tanks. During the refilling procedure, dirt, rust, and water may be stirred up in the underground tanks. This undesirable material may be pumped into your vehicle's fuel tank.

6. Do not overfill the gas tank. After the nozzle clicks off, add just enough fuel to round up to the next dime. Adding additional gasoline will cause the excess to be drawn into the charcoal canister. This can lead to engine flooding and excessive exhaust emissions.

 TECH TIP

The Sniff Test

Problems can occur with stale gasoline from which the lighter parts of the gasoline have evaporated. Stale gasoline usually results in a no-start situation. If stale gasoline is suspected, sniff it. If it smells rancid, replace it with fresh gasoline.

NOTE: If storing a vehicle, boat, or lawnmower over the winter, put some gasoline stabilizer into the gasoline to reduce the evaporation and separation that can occur during storage. Gasoline stabilizer is frequently available at most automotive parts stores.

7. Be careful when filling gasoline containers. Always fill a gas can on the ground to help prevent the possibility of static electricity buildup during the refueling process. ● **SEE FIGURE 2–17**.

Why Should I Keep the Fuel Gauge above One-Quarter Tank?

The fuel pickup inside the fuel tank can help keep water from being drawn into the fuel system unless water is all that is left at the bottom of the tank. Over time, moisture in the air inside the fuel tank can condense, causing liquid water to drop to the bottom of the fuel tank. (Recall that water is heavier than gasoline–about 8 pound per gallon for water and about 6 pound per gallon for gasoline.) If alcohol-blended gasoline is used, the alcohol can absorb the water and the alcohol-water combination can be burned inside the engine. However, when water combines with alcohol, a separation layer occurs between the gasoline at the top of the tank and the alcohol-water combination at the bottom. When the fuel level is low, the fuel pump will draw from this concentrated level of alcohol and water. Because alcohol and water do not burn as well as pure gasoline, severe driveability problems can occur such as stalling, rough idle, hard starting, and missing.

 TECH TIP

Do Not Overfill the Fuel Tank

Gasoline fuel tanks have an expansion volume area at the top. The volume of this expansion area is equal to 10% to 15% of the volume of the tank. This area is normally not filled with gasoline, but rather is designed to provide a place for the gasoline to expand into, if the vehicle is parked in the hot sun and the gasoline expands. This prevents raw gasoline from escaping from the fuel system. A small restriction is usually present to control the amount of air and vapors that can escape the tank and flow to the charcoal canister.

This volume area could be filled with gasoline if the fuel is slowly pumped into the tank. Since it can hold an extra 10% (2 gallons in a 20 gallon tank), some people deliberately try to fill the tank completely. When this expansion volume is filled, liquid fuel (rather than vapors) can be drawn into the charcoal canister. When the purge valve opens, liquid fuel can be drawn into the engine, causing an excessively rich air–fuel mixture. Not only can this liquid fuel harm vapor recovery parts, but overfilling the gas tank could also cause the vehicle to fail an exhaust emission test, particularly during an enhanced test when the tank could be purged while on the rollers.

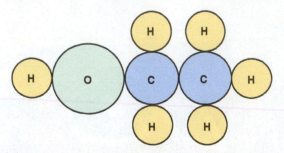

FIGURE 2–18 The ethanol molecule showing two carbon atoms, six hydrogen atoms, and one oxygen atom.

FIGURE 2–19 E85 has 85% ethanol mixed with 15% gasoline.

E85

WHAT IS E85? Vehicle manufacturers have available vehicles that are capable of operating on gasoline plus ethanol or a combination of gasoline and ethanol called **E85**, composed of 85% ethanol and 15% gasoline. Ethanol is also called **ethyl alcohol** or **grain alcohol**, because it is usually made from grain and is the type of alcohol found in alcoholic drinks such as beer, wine, and distilled spirits like whiskey. Ethanol is composed of two carbon atoms and six hydrogen atoms with one added oxygen atom. ● **SEE FIGURE 2–18.**

Pure ethanol has an octane rating of about 113. E85, which contains 35% oxygen by weight, has an octane rating of 100 to 105. This compares to a regular unleaded gasoline which has a rating of 87. ● **SEE FIGURE 2–19.**

NOTE: The octane rating of E85 depends on the exact percentage of ethanol used, which can vary from 81% to 85%. It also depends on the octane rating of the gasoline used to make E85.

HEAT ENERGY OF E85 E85 has less heat energy than gasoline.

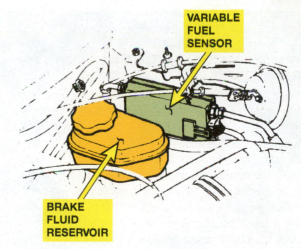

FIGURE 2–20 The location of the variable fuel sensor can vary, depending on the make and model of vehicle, but it is always in the fuel line between the fuel tank and the fuel injectors.

Purchase a Flex Fuel Vehicle

If purchasing a new or used vehicle, try to find a flex fuel vehicle. Even though you may not want to use E85, a flex fuel vehicle has a more robust fuel system than a conventional fuel system designed for gasoline or E10. The enhanced fuel system components and materials usually include:

- Stainless steel fuel rail
- Graphite commutator bars instead of copper in the fuel pump motor (ethanol can oxidize into acetic acid, which can corrode copper)
- Diamondlike carbon (DLC) corrosion-resistant fuel injectors
- Alcohol resistant O-rings and hoses

  The cost of a flex fuel vehicle compared with the same vehicle designed to operate on gasoline is a no-cost or a low-cost option.

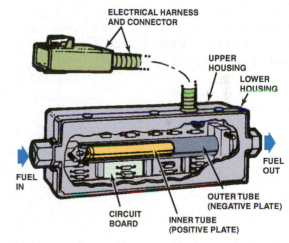

FIGURE 2–21 A cutaway view of a typical variable fuel sensor.

Gasoline: 114,000 BTUs per gallon

E85: 87,000 BTUs per gallon

This means that the fuel economy is reduced by 20% to 30% if E85 is used instead of gasoline.

Example: A Chevrolet Tahoe 5.3 liter V-8 with an automatic transmission has an EPA rating using gasoline of 15 mpg in the city and 20 mpg on the highway. If this same vehicle is fueled with E85, the EPA fuel economy rating drops to 11 mpg in the city and 15 mpg on the highway.

ALTERNATIVE FUEL VEHICLES

The 15% gasoline in the E85 blend helps the engine start, especially in cold weather. Vehicles equipped with this capability are commonly referred to as:

- **Alternative fuel vehicles (AFVs)**
- **Flex fuels**
- **Flexible fuel vehicles (FFVs)**

Using E85 in a flex fuel vehicle can result in a power increase of about 5%. For example, an engine rated at 200 hp using gasoline or E10 could produce 210 hp if using E85.

NOTE: E85 may test as containing less than 85% ethanol if tested because it is often blended according to outside temperature. A lower percentage of ethanol with a slightly higher percentage of gasoline helps engines start in cold climates.

These vehicles are equipped with an electronic sensor in the fuel supply line that detects the presence and percentage of ethanol. The PCM then adjusts the fuel injector on-time and ignition timing to match the needs of the fuel being used.

E85 contains less heat energy, and therefore will use more fuel, but the benefits include a lower cost of the fuel and less environmental impact associated with using an oxygenated fuel.

General Motors, Ford, Chrysler, and Mazda are a few of the manufacturers offering E85 compatible vehicles. E85 vehicles use fuel system parts designed to withstand the additional alcohol content, modified driveability programs that adjust fuel delivery and timing to compensate for the various percentages of ethanol fuel, and a **fuel compensation sensor** that measures both the percentage of ethanol blend and the temperature of the fuel. This sensor is also called a **variable fuel sensor**. ● SEE FIGURES 2–20 AND 2–21.

E85 FUEL SYSTEM REQUIREMENTS Most E85 vehicles are very similar to non-E85 vehicles. Fuel system components may be redesigned to withstand the effects of higher

How Does a Sensorless Flex Fuel System Work?

Many General Motors flex fuel vehicles do not use a fuel compensation sensor and instead use the oxygen sensor to detect the presence of the lean mixture and the extra oxygen in the fuel.

The powertrain control module (PCM) then adjusts the injector pulse width and the ignition timing to optimize engine operation to the use of E85. This type of vehicle is called a **virtual flexible fuel vehicle (V-FFV)**. It can operate on pure gasoline or blends up to 85% ethanol.

FIGURE 2–22 A flex fuel vehicle often has a yellow gas cap, which is labeled E85/gasoline.

How Long Can Oxygenated Fuel Be Stored before All of the Oxygen Escapes?

The oxygen in oxygenated fuels, such as E10 and E85, is not in a gaseous state like the CO_2 in soft drinks. The oxygen is part of the molecule of ethanol or other oxygenates and does not bubble out of the fuel. Oxygenated fuels, like any fuel, have a shelf life of about 90 days.

FIGURE 2–23 This flexible fuel vehicle (FFV) vehicle emission control information (VECI) sticker located under the hood indicates that is can operate on either gasoline or ethanol.

NOTE: For additional information on E85 and for the location of E85 stations in your area, go to www.e85fuel.com.

concentrations of ethanol. In addition, since the stoichiometric point for ethanol is 9:1 instead of 14.7:1 as for gasoline, the air-fuel mixture has to be adjusted for the percentage of ethanol present in the fuel tank.

The benefits of E85 vehicles include:

- Reduced pollution
- Less CO_2 production
- Less dependence on imported oil

FLEX FUEL VEHICLE IDENTIFICATION
Flexible fuel vehicles (FFVs) can be identified by:

- Emblems on the side, front, and/or rear of the vehicle
- Yellow fuel cap showing E85/gasoline (● **SEE FIGURE 2–22.**)
- Vehicle emission control information (VECI) label under the hood (● **SEE FIGURE 2–23.**)
- Vehicle identification number (VIN)

METHANOL

METHANOL TERMINOLOGY Methanol, also known as *methyl alcohol*, *wood alcohol*, or *methyl hydrate*, is a chemical compound formula that includes one carbon atom, four hydrogen atoms, and one oxygen atom. ● **SEE FIGURE 2–24.**

Methanol is a light, volatile, colorless, tasteless, flammable, poisonous liquid with a very faint odor. Methanol can be used in the following ways:

- As an antifreeze, a solvent, or a fuel
- To denature ethanol (to make undrinkable)

Methanol burns in air, forming CO_2 (carbon dioxide) and H_2O (water). A methanol flame is almost colorless. Methanol is often called wood alcohol because it was once produced chiefly as a by-product of the destructive distillation of wood. ● **SEE FIGURE 2–25.**

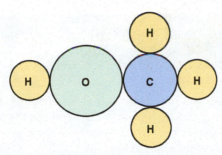

FIGURE 2–24 The molecular structure of methanol showing the one carbon atom, four hydrogen atoms, and one oxygen atom.

FIGURE 2–25 Sign on methanol pump shows that methyl alcohol is a poison and can cause skin irritation and other personal injury. Methanol is used in industry as well as being a fuel.

PRODUCTION OF METHANOL The biggest source of methanol in the United States is coal. Using a simple reaction between coal and steam, a gas mixture called **syn-gas** (synthesis gas) is formed. The components of this mixture are carbon monoxide and hydrogen, which, through an additional chemical reaction, are converted to methanol.

Natural gas can also be used to create methanol and is reformed or converted to synthesis gas, which is later made into methanol.

Biomass can be converted to synthesis gas by a process called partial oxidation, and later converted to methanol. Biomass is organic material, and includes:

- Urban wood wastes
- Primary mill residues
- Forest residues
- Agricultural residues
- Dedicated energy crops (e.g., sugarcane and sugar beets) that can be made into fuel

Electricity can be used to convert water into hydrogen, which is then reacted with carbon dioxide to produce methanol.

Methanol is toxic and can cause blindness and death. It can enter the body by ingestion, inhalation, or absorption through the skin. Dangerous doses will build up if a person is regularly exposed to fumes or handles liquid without skin protection. If methanol has been ingested, a doctor should be contacted immediately. The usual fatal dose is 4 fl oz (100 to 125 mL).

M85 Some flexible fuel vehicles are designed to operate on 85% methanol and 15% gasoline, called **M85**. Methanol is very corrosive and requires that the fuel system components be constructed of stainless steel and other alcohol-resistant rubber and plastic components. The heat content of M85 is about 60% of that of gasoline.

PROPANE

Propane is the most widely used of all the alternative fuels mainly because of its use in fleets, which utilize a central refueling station. Propane is normally a gas but is easily compressed into a liquid and stored in inexpensive containers. When sold as a fuel, it is also known as **liquefied petroleum gas (LPG)** or **LP gas**, because the propane is often mixed with about 10% of other gases, including:

- Butane
- Propylene
- Butylenes
- Mercaptan, to give the colorless and odorless propane a smell

Propane is nontoxic, but if inhaled can cause asphyxiation through lack of oxygen. Propane is heavier than air and lays near the floor if released into the atmosphere. Propane is commonly used in forklifts and other equipment located inside warehouses and factories, because the exhaust from the engine using propane is not harmful. Propane is a by-product of petroleum refining of natural gas. In order to liquefy the fuel, it is stored in strong tanks at about 300 PSI (2,000 kPa). The heating value of propane is less than that of gasoline; therefore, more is required, which reduces the fuel economy. ● **SEE FIGURE 2–26.**

COMPRESSED NATURAL GAS

CNG VEHICLE DESIGN Another alternative fuel that is often used in fleet vehicles is **compressed natural gas (CNG)**. Vehicles using this fuel are often referred to as **natural gas vehicles (NGVs)**. Look for the blue CNG label on vehicles designed to operate on compressed natural gas. ● **SEE FIGURE 2–27.**

FIGURE 2–26 Propane fuel storage tank in the trunk of a Ford taxi.

FIGURE 2–28 A CNG storage tank from a Honda Civic GX shown with the fixture used to support it while it is being removed or installed in the vehicle. Honda specifies that three technicians be used to remove or install the tank through the rear door of the vehicle due to the size and weight of the tank.

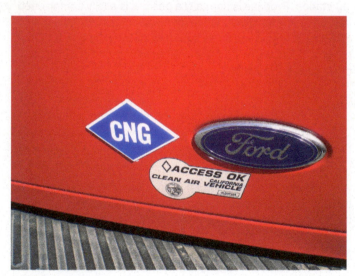

FIGURE 2–27 The blue sticker on the rear of this vehicle indicates that it is designed to use compressed natural gas. This Ford truck also has a sticker that allows it to be driven in the high occupancy vehicle (HOV) lane, even if there is just the driver, because it is a CNG vehicle.

Because natural gas must be compressed to 3,000 PSI (20,000 kPa) or more, the weight and cost of the storage container are major factors when it comes to preparing a vehicle to run on CNG. The tanks needed for CNG are typically constructed of 0.5 inch (3 mm) thick aluminum reinforced with fiberglass. ● **SEE FIGURE 2–28**.

The octane rating of CNG is about 130 and the cost per gallon is roughly half of the cost of gasoline. However, the heat value of CNG is also less, and therefore more is required to produce the same power; and the miles per gallon is less.

? **FREQUENTLY ASKED QUESTION**

What Is the Amount of CNG Equal to in Gasoline?

To achieve the amount of energy of 1 gallon of gasoline, 122 ft^3 of compressed natural gas (CNG) is needed. While the octane rating of CNG is much higher than gasoline (130 octane), using CNG instead of gasoline in the same engine would result in a 10%–20% reduction of power due to the lower heat energy that is released when CNG is burned in the engine.

CNG COMPOSITION Compressed natural gas is a blend of the following:

- Methane
- Propane
- Ethane
- N-butane
- Carbon dioxide
- Nitrogen

Once it is processed, compressed natural gas is at least 93% methane. Natural gas is nontoxic, odorless, and colorless in its natural state. It is odorized during processing, using ethyl mercaptan ("skunk"), to allow for easy leak detection. Natural gas is lighter than air and will rise when released into the air. Since CNG is already a vapor, it does not need heat to vaporize before it will burn, which improves cold start-up and results

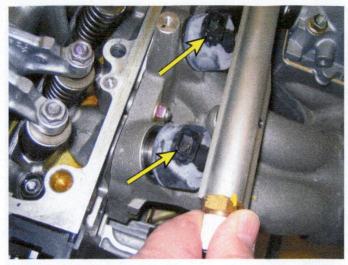

FIGURE 2–29 The fuel injectors used on this Honda Civic GX CNG engine are designed to flow gaseous fuel instead of liquid fuel and cannot be interchanged with any other type of injector.

FIGURE 2–30 This CNG pump is capable of supplying compressed natural gas at either 3,000 PSI or 3,600 PSI. The price per gallon is higher for the higher pressure.

in lower emissions during cold operation. However, because it is already in a gaseous state, it displaces some of the air charge in the intake manifold, leading to a 10% reduction in engine power as compared to an engine operating on gasoline. Natural gas also burns slower than gasoline; therefore, the ignition timing must be advanced more when the vehicle operates on natural gas. The stoichiometric ratio, the point at which all the air and fuel is used or burned, is 16.5:1 compared to 14.7:1 for gasoline. This means that more air is required to burn 1 pound of natural gas than is required to burn 1 pound of gasoline. ● **SEE FIGURE 2–29**.

The CNG engine is designed to include:

- Increased compression ratio
- Strong pistons and connecting rods
- Heat-resistant valves
- Fuel injectors designed for gaseous fuel instead of liquid fuel

CNG FUEL SYSTEMS When completely filled, the CNG tank has 3,600 PSI of pressure in the tank. When the ignition is turned on, the alternate fuel electronic control unit activates the high-pressure lock-off, which allows high-pressure gas to pass to the high-pressure regulator.

- The high-pressure regulator reduces the high-pressure CNG to approximately 150 to 170 PSI and sends it to the low-pressure lock-off. The low-pressure lock-off is also controlled by the alternate fuel electronic control unit and is activated at the same time as the high-pressure lock-off.
- From the low-pressure lock-off, the CNG is directed to the low-pressure regulator. This is a two-stage regulator that first reduces the pressure to approximately 4 to 6 PSI in the first stage and then to about 0.5 PSI in the second stage.

- From here, the low-pressure gas is delivered to the gas mass sensor/mixture control valve. This valve controls the air–fuel mixture. The CNG gas distributor adapter then delivers the gas to the intake stream.

CNG vehicles are designed for fleet use that usually have their own refueling capabilities. One of the drawbacks to using CNG is the time that it takes to refuel a vehicle. The ideal method of refueling is the slow-fill method. The slow filling method compresses the natural gas as the tank is being fueled. This method ensures that the tank will receive a full charge of CNG; however, this method can take three to five hours to accomplish. If more than one vehicle needs filling, the facility will need multiple CNG compressors to refuel the vehicles.

There are three commonly used CNG refilling station pressures:

P24: 2,400 PSI

P30: 3,000 PSI

P36: 3,600 PSI

Try to find and use a station with the highest refilling pressure. Filling at lower pressures will result in less compressed natural gas being installed in the storage tank, thereby reducing the driving range. ● **SEE FIGURE 2–30**.

The fast-fill method uses CNG that is already compressed. However, as the CNG tank is filled rapidly, the internal temperature of the tank will rise, which causes a rise in tank pressure. Once the temperature drops in the CNG tank, the pressure in the tank also drops, resulting in an incomplete charge in the CNG tank. This refueling method may take only about five minutes, but it will result in an incomplete charge to the CNG tank, reducing the driving range. ● **SEE CHART 2–2** for a comparison of the most frequently used alternative fuels.

ALTERNATE FUEL COMPARISON CHART

CHARACTERISTIC	PROPANE	CNG	METHANOL	ETHANOL	REGULAR UNLEADED GAS
Octane	104	130	100	100	87–93
BTU per gallon	91,000	NA	70,000	83,000	114,000–125,000
Gallon equivalent	1.15	122 ft^3–1 gallon of gasoline	1.8	1.5	1
Onboard fuel storage	Liquid	Gas	Liquid	Liquid	Liquid
Miles/gallon as compared to gas	85%	Varies with pressure	55%	70%	100%
Relative tank size required to yield driving range equivalent to gas	Tank is 1.25 times larger	Tank is 3.5 times larger	Tank is 1.8 times larger	Tank is 1.5 times larger	
Pressure	200 PSI	3,000–3,600 PSI	NA	NA	NA
Cold weather capability	Good	Good	Poor	Poor	Good
Vehicle power	5%–10% power loss	10%–20% power loss	4% power increase	5% power increase	Standard
Toxicity	Nontoxic	Nontoxic	Highly toxic	Toxic	Toxic
Corrosiveness	Noncorrosive	Noncorrosive	Corrosive	Corrosive	Minimally corrosive
Source	Natural gas/ petroleum refining	Natural gas/ crude oil	Natural gas/coal	Sugar and starch crops/biomass	Crude oil

CHART 2–2

The characteristics of alternative fuels compared to regular unleaded gasoline show that all have advantages and disadvantages.

LIQUEFIED NATURAL GAS

Natural gas can be turned into a liquid if cooled to below −260°F (−127°C). The natural gas condenses into a liquid at normal atmospheric pressure and the volume is reduced by about 600 times. This means that the natural gas can be more efficiently transported over long distances where no pipelines are present when liquefied.

Because the temperature of liquefied natural gas (LNG) must be kept low, it is best used for fleets where a central LPG station can be used to refuel the vehicles.

P-SERIES FUELS

P-series alternative fuel is patented by Princeton University and is a nonpetroleum or natural gas based fuel suitable for use in flexible fuel vehicles or any vehicle designed to operate on E85 (85% ethanol, 15% gasoline). P-series fuel is recognized by the U.S. Department of Energy as being an alternative fuel, but is not yet available to the public. P-series fuels are blends of the following:

- Ethanol (ethyl alcohol)
- Methyltetrahydrofuran (MTHF)
- Natural gas liquids, such as pentanes
- Butane

The ethanol and MTHF are produced from renewable feedstocks, such as corn, waste paper, biomass, agricultural waste, and wood waste (scraps and sawdust). The components used in P-series fuel can be varied to produce regular grade, premium grade, or fuel suitable for cold climates. ● **SEE CHART 2–3** for the percentages of the ingredients based on fuel grade.

SYNTHETIC FUELS

INTRODUCTION Synthetic fuels can be made from a variety of products, using several different processes. Synthetic fuel must, however, make these alternatives practical only when conventional petroleum products are either very expensive or not available.

FISCHER–TROPSCH Synthetic fuels were first developed using the **Fischer–Tropsch** method, and have been in use since the 1920s to convert coal, natural gas, and other fossil

COMPOSITION OF P-SERIES FUELS (BY VOLUME)			
COMPONENT	REGULAR GRADE (%)	PREMIUM GRADE (%)	COLD WEATHER (%)
Pentanes plus	32.5	27.5	16
MTHF	32.5	17.5	26
Ethanol	35	55	47
Butane	0	0	11

CHART 2–3

P-series fuel varies in composition, depending on the octane rating and temperature.

 FREQUENTLY ASKED QUESTION

What Is a Tri-Fuel Vehicle?

In Brazil, most vehicles are designed to operate on ethanol or gasoline, or any combination of the two. In this South American country, ethanol is made from sugarcane, is commonly available, and is lower in price than gasoline. Compressed natural gas (CNG) is also being made available so many vehicle manufacturers in Brazil, such as General Motors and Ford, are equipping vehicles to be capable of using gasoline, ethanol, or CNG. These vehicles are called tri-fuel vehicles.

fuel products into a fuel that is high in quality and clean burning. The process for producing Fischer–Tropsch fuels was patented by two German scientists, Franz Fischer and Hans Tropsch, during World War I. The Fischer–Tropsch method uses carbon monoxide and hydrogen (the same synthesis gas used to produce hydrogen fuel) to convert coal and other hydrocarbons to liquid fuels in a process similar to hydrogenation, another method for hydrocarbon conversion. The process using natural gas, also called **gas-to-liquid (GTL)** technology, uses a catalyst, usually iron or cobalt, and incorporates steam reforming to give off the by-products of carbon dioxide, hydrogen, and carbon monoxide. ● **SEE FIGURE 2–31**.

Whereas traditional fuels emit environmentally harmful particulates and chemicals, namely sulfur compounds, Fischer–Tropsch fuels combust with no soot or odors and emit only low levels of toxins. Fischer–Tropsch fuels can also be blended with traditional transportation fuels with little equipment modification, as they use the same engine and equipment technology as traditional fuels.

The fuels contain a very low sulfur and aromatic content and they produce virtually no particulate emissions. Researchers also expect reductions in hydrocarbon and carbon monoxide emissions. Fischer–Tropsch fuels do not differ in fuel performance from gasoline and diesel. At present,

Fischer–Tropsch fuels are very expensive to produce on a large scale, although research is under way to lower processing costs. Diesel fuel created using the **Fischer–Tropsch diesel (FTD)** process is often called *GTL diesel*. GTL diesel can also be combined with petroleum diesel to produce a GTL blend. This fuel product is currently being sold in Europe and plans are in place to introduce it in North America.

COAL TO LIQUID Coal is very abundant in the United States and can be converted to a liquid fuel through a process called **coal to liquid (CTL)**. The huge cost of processing is the main obstacle to this type of fuel. The need to invest $1.4 billion per plant before it can make product is the reason no one has built a CTL plant yet in the United States. Investors need to be convinced that the cost of oil is going to remain high in order to get them to commit this kind of money.

A large plant might be able to produce 120,000 barrels of liquid fuel a day and would consume about 50,000 tons of coal per day. However, such a plant would create about 6,000 tons of CO_2 per day, which could contribute to global warming. With this factor and with the costs involved, CTL technology is not likely to expand.

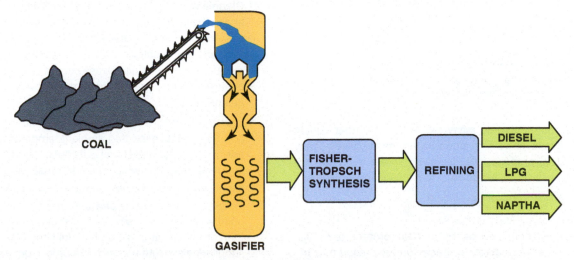

FIGURE 2–31 A Fischer–Tropsch processing plant is able to produce a variety of fuels from coal.

Despite the limitations, two procedures can be used to convert CTL fuel:

1. **Direct method.** In the direct method, coal is broken down to create liquid products. First the coal is reacted with hydrogen (H_2) at high temperatures and pressure with a catalyst. This process creates a synthetic crude, called **syncrude**, which is then refined to produce gasoline or diesel fuel.

2. **Indirect method.** In the indirect method, coal is first turned into a gas and the molecules are reassembled to create the desired product. This process involves turning coal into syngas, which is then converted into liquid, using the Fischer–Tropsch diesel (FTD) process.

Russia has been using CTL by injecting air into the underground coal seams. Ignition is provided and the resulting gases are trapped and converted to liquid gasoline and diesel fuel through the Fischer–Tropsch process. This underground method is called **underground coal gasification (UCG)**.

METHANOL TO GASOLINE Exxon Mobil has developed a process for converting methanol (methyl alcohol) into gasoline in a process called **methanol to gasoline (MTG)**. The MTG process was discovered by accident when a gasoline additive made from methanol was being created. The process instead created olefins, paraffins (alkenes), and aromatic compounds, which in combination are known as gasoline. The process uses a catalyst and is currently being produced in New Zealand.

FUTURE OF SYNTHETIC FUELS Producing gasoline and diesel fuels by other methods besides refining from crude oil has usually been more expensive. With the increasing cost of crude oil, alternative methods are now becoming economically feasible. Whether the diesel fuel or gasoline is created from coal, natural gas, or methanol, or created by refining crude oil, the transportation and service pumps are already in place. Compared to using compressed natural gas or other similar alternative fuels, synthetic fuels represent the lowest cost.

SAFETY PROCEDURES WHEN WORKING WITH ALTERNATIVE FUELS

All fuels are flammable and many are explosive under certain conditions. Whenever working around compressed gases of any kind (CNG, LNG, propane, or LPG), always wear personal protective equipment (PPE), including at least the following items:

1. Safety glasses and/or face shield
2. Protective gloves
3. Long-sleeve shirt and pants, to help protect bare skin from the freezing effects of gases under pressure in the event that the pressure is lost

WARNING

Do not smoke or have an open flame in the area when working around or refueling any vehicle.

If a spill should occur, take the following actions:

1. If any fuel gets on the skin, the area should be washed immediately.

2. If fuel spills on clothing, change into clean clothing as soon as possible.

3. If fuel spills on a painted surface, flush the surface with water and air-dry. If simply wiped off with a dry cloth, the paint surface could be permanently damaged.

4. As with any fuel-burning vehicle, always vent the exhaust to the outside. If methanol fuel is used, the exhaust contains *formaldehyde*, which has a sharp odor and can cause severe burning of the eyes, nose, and throat.

DIESEL FUEL

FEATURES OF DIESEL FUEL Diesel fuel must meet an entirely different set of standards than gasoline. Diesel fuel contains 12% more heat energy than the same amount of gasoline. The fuel in a diesel engine is not ignited with a spark, but is ignited by the heat generated by high compression. The pressure of compression (400 to 700 PSI, or 2,800 to 4,800 kPa) generates temperatures of 1,200°F to 1,600°F (700°C to 900°C), which speeds the preflame reaction to start the ignition of fuel injected into the cylinder.

DIESEL FUEL REQUIREMENTS All diesel fuel must have the following characteristics:

- **Cleanliness.** It is imperative that the fuel used in a diesel engine be clean and free from water. Unlike the case with gasoline engines, the fuel is the lubricant and coolant for the diesel injector pump and injectors. Good-quality diesel fuel contains additives such as oxidation inhibitors, detergents, dispersants, rust preventatives, and metal deactivators.

- **Low-temperature fluidity.** Diesel fuel must be able to flow freely at all expected ambient temperatures. One specification for diesel fuel is its "pour point," which is the temperature below which the fuel would stop flowing.

- **Cloud point.** Another concern with diesel fuel at lower temperatures concerns **cloud point**, the low-temperature point when the waxes present in most diesel fuels tend to form crystals that can clog the fuel filter. Most diesel fuel suppliers distribute fuel with the proper pour point and cloud point for the climate conditions of the area.

CETANE NUMBER The cetane number for diesel fuel is the opposite of the octane number for gasoline. The **cetane number** is a measure of the ease with which the fuel can be ignited. The cetane rating of the fuel determines, to a great extent, its ability to start the engine at low temperatures and to provide smooth warmup and even combustion. The cetane rating of diesel fuel should be between 45 and 50. The higher the cetane rating, the more easily the fuel is ignited.

SULFUR CONTENT The sulfur content of diesel fuel is very important to the life of the engine. Sulfur in the fuel creates sulfuric acid during the combustion process, which can damage engine components and cause piston ring wear. Federal regulations are getting extremely tight on sulfur content to less than 15 parts per million (ppm). High-sulfur fuel contributes to acid rain.

DIESEL FUEL COLOR Diesel fuel intended for use on the streets and highways is either clear or green. Diesel fuel to be used on farms and off-road use is dyed red. ● **SEE FIGURE 2–32.**

GRADES OF DIESEL FUEL ASTM also classifies diesel fuel by volatility (boiling range) into the following grades:

Grade 1	This grade of diesel fuel has the lowest boiling point and the lowest cloud and pour points, as well as a lower BTU content (less heat per pound of fuel). As a result, grade 1 is suitable for use during low-temperature (winter) operation. Grade 1 produces less heat per pound of fuel compared to grade 2, and may be specified for use in diesel engines involved in frequent changes in load and speed, such as those found in city buses and delivery trucks.
Grade 2	This grade has a higher boiling point, cloud point, and pour point as compared with grade 1. It is usually specified where constant speed and high loads are encountered, such as in long-haul trucking and automotive diesel applications.

DIESEL FUEL SPECIFIC GRAVITY TESTING The density of diesel fuel should be tested whenever there is a driveability concern. The density or specific gravity of diesel fuel is measured in units of **API gravity**, which is an arbitrary scale expressing the gravity or density of liquid petroleum products devised jointly by the American Petroleum Institute and the National Bureau of Standards. The measuring scale is calibrated in terms of degrees API. Oil with the least specific gravity has the highest API gravity. The formula for determining API gravity is as follows:

$$\text{Degrees API gravity} = (141.5 \div \text{Specific gravity at } 60°F) - 131.5$$

The normal API gravity for grade 1 diesel fuel is 39 to 44 (typically 40). The normal API gravity for grade 2 diesel fuel is 30 to 39 (typically 35). A hydrometer calibrated in API gravity units should be used to test diesel fuel. ● **SEE FIGURE 2–33.**

ULTRA-LOW-SULFUR DIESEL FUEL Diesel fuel is used in diesel engines and is usually readily available throughout the United States, Canada, and Europe, where many more cars are equipped with diesel engines. Diesel engines manufactured to 2007 or newer standards must use **ultra-low-sulfur diesel (ULSD)** fuel containing less than 15 PPM of sulfur compared to the older, low-sulfur specification of 500 PPM. The purpose of the lower sulfur amount in diesel fuel is to reduce emissions of sulfur oxides (SOx) and particulate matter (PM) from heavy-duty highway engines and vehicles that use diesel fuel. The emission controls used on 2007 and newer diesel engines require the use of ULSD for reliable operation.

DIESEL FUEL ADDITIVES These types of additives include:

Winter Conditioners—Winter conditioners are designed to reduce the **Cold Filter Plugging Point (CFPP)**. CFPP is lowest temperature at that a specified volume of diesel type of fuel can pass through a standardized filtration device in a specified time when cooled under certain conditions.

(a)

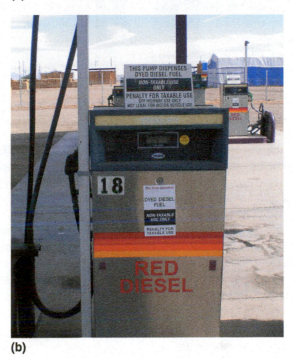

(b)

FIGURE 2–32 (a) Regular diesel fuel on the left has a clear or greenish tint, whereas fuel for off-road use is tinted red for identification. (b) This fuel pump in a farming area clearly states the red diesel fuel is for off-road use only.

FIGURE 2–33 Testing the API viscosity of a diesel fuel sample using a hydrometer.

Multifunctional Conditioners—Many multifunctional additives increase the cetane rating of the fuel and helps keep injectors clean. By raising the cetane rating of the diesel fuel engine power and fuel economy is improved. This type of additive is designed to be used year-round.

Microbicide—Microbes can grow in diesel fuel at the junction between the water and the diesel. Water is heavier than the diesel fuel and is near the bottom of the tank. Water in the fuel can be caused by condensation of moist air in the fuel tank and during transport and storage. A microbicide is designed to kill microorganisms including bacteria and fungi.

BIODIESEL

DEFINITION OF BIODIESEL **Biodiesel** is a domestically produced, renewable fuel that can be manufactured from vegetable oils, animal fats, or recycled restaurant greases. Biodiesel is safe, biodegradable, and reduces serious air pollutants such as particulate matter (PM), carbon monoxide, and hydrocarbons. Biodiesel is defined as mono-alkyl esters of long-chain fatty acids derived from vegetable oils or animal fats which conform to ASTM D6751 specifications for use in diesel engines. Biodiesel refers to the pure fuel before blending with diesel fuel. ● SEE FIGURE 2–34.

Biodiesel blends are denoted as BXX, with the "XX" representing the percentage of biodiesel contained in the blend (i.e., **B20** is 20% biodiesel, 80% petroleum diesel). Blends of 5% biodiesel with 95% petroleum diesel, called **B5**, can generally be used in unmodified diesel engines. Some diesel-powered vehicles can use B20 (20% biodiesel). Dodge, for example, allows the use of B5 in all diesel vehicles and B20 only if the optional additional fuel filter is installed. Biodiesel can also be used in its pure form (B100), but it may require certain engine modifications to avoid maintenance and

FIGURE 2–34 A biodiesel pump decal indicating that the diesel fuel is ultra-low-sulfur diesel (ULSD) and must be used in 2007 and newer diesel vehicles.

performance problems and may not be suitable for wintertime use. Users should consult their engine warranty statement for more information on fuel blends of greater than 20% biodiesel.

In general, B20 costs 30 to 40 cents more per gallon than conventional diesel. Although biodiesel costs more than regular diesel fuel, often called **petrodiesel**, fleet managers can make the switch to alternative fuels without purchasing new vehicles, acquiring new spare parts inventories, rebuilding refueling stations, or hiring new service technicians.

FEATURES OF BIODIESEL Biodiesel has the following characteristics:

1. Purchasing biodiesel in bulk quantities decreases the cost of fuel.

2. Biodiesel maintains similar horsepower, torque, and fuel economy.

3. Biodiesel has a higher cetane number than conventional diesel, which increases the engine's performance.

4. Biodiesel has a high flash point and low volatility so it does not ignite as easily as petrodiesel, which increases the margin of safety in fuel handling. In fact, it degrades four times faster than petrodiesel and is not particularly soluble in water.

5. It is nontoxic, which makes it safe to handle, transport, and store. Maintenance requirements for B20 vehicles and petrodiesel vehicles are the same.

6. Biodiesel acts as a lubricant, which can add to the life of the fuel system components.

NOTE: For additional information on biodiesel and the locations where it can be purchased, visit www.biodiesel.org.

I Thought Biodiesel Was Vegetable Oil?

Biodiesel is vegetable oil with the glycerin component removed by means of reacting the vegetable oil with a catalyst. The resulting hydrocarbon esters are 16 to 18 carbon atoms in length, almost identical to the petroleum diesel fuel atoms. This allows the use of biodiesel fuel in a diesel engine with no modifications needed. Biodiesel-powered vehicles do not need a second fuel tank, whereas vehicles powered with vegetable oil do.

There are three main types of fuel used in diesel engines:

- Petroleum diesel, a fossil hydrocarbon with a carbon chain length of about 16 carbon atoms
- Biodiesel, a hydrocarbon with a carbon chain length of 16 to 18 carbon atoms
- Vegetable oil, a triglyceride with a glycerin component joining three hydrocarbon chains of 16 to 18 carbon atoms each, called **straight vegetable oil (SVO)**

Other terms used when describing vegetable oil include:

- **Pure plant oil (PPO)**, a term most often used in Europe to describe SVO
- **Waste vegetable oil (WVO)**, which could include animal or fish oils from cooking
- **Used cooking oil (UCO)**, a term used when the oil may or may not be pure vegetable oil

Vegetable oil is not liquid enough at common ambient temperatures for use in a diesel engine fuel delivery system designed for the lower viscosity petroleum diesel fuel. Vegetable oil needs to be heated to obtain a similar viscosity to biodiesel and petroleum diesel. This means that a heat source needs to be provided before the fuel can be used in a diesel engine. This is achieved by starting on petroleum diesel or biodiesel fuel until the engine heat can be used to sufficiently warm a tank containing the vegetable oil. It also requires purging the fuel system of vegetable oil with petroleum diesel or biodiesel fuel prior to stopping the engine to avoid the vegetable oil thickening and solidifying in the fuel system away from the heated tank. The use of vegetable oil in its natural state does, however, eliminate the need to remove the glycerin component.

Many vehicle and diesel engine fuel system suppliers permit the use of biodiesel fuel that is certified as meeting testing standards. None permit the use of vegetable oil in its natural state.

E-DIESEL FUEL

DEFINITION E-diesel, also called **diesohol** outside of the United States, is standard No. 2 diesel fuel that contains up to 15% ethanol. While E-diesel can have up to 15% ethanol by volume, typical blend levels are from 8% to 10%.

CETANE RATING OF E-DIESEL The higher the cetane number, the shorter the delay between injection and ignition. Normal diesel fuel has a cetane number of about 50. Adding 15% ethanol lowers the cetane number. To increase the cetane number back to that of conventional diesel fuel, a cetane-enhancing additive is added to E-diesel. The additive used to increase the cetane rating of E-diesel is ethylhexyl nitrate or ditertbutyl peroxide.

E-diesel has better cold-flow properties than conventional diesel. The heat content of E-diesel is about 6% less than conventional diesel, but the particulate matter (PM) emissions are reduced by as much as 40%, carbon monoxide by 20%, and oxides of nitrogen (NO_x) by 5%.

Currently, E-diesel is considered to be experimental and can be used legally in off-road applications or in mass–transit buses with EPA approval. For additional information, visit www.e-diesel.org.

FUEL	NOZZLE DIAMETER	PUMP HANDLE COLOR (VARIES— NO ESTABLISHED STANDARD)
Gasoline	13/16 inch (21 mm)	Black, red, white, green, or blue
E10	13/16 inch (21 mm)	Black, red, white, green, or blue
E85	13/16 inch (21 mm)	Yellow or black
Diesel fuel	15/16 inch (24 mm)	Yellow, green, or black
Biodiesel	15/16 inch (24 mm)	Green
Truckstop diesel	1 1/4 or 1 1/2 inch (32 or 38 mm)	Varies

CHART 2–4

Fuel pump nozzle size is standardized except for use by over-the-road truckstops where high fuel volumes and speedy refills require larger nozzle sizes compared to passenger vehicle filling station nozzles.

What Are the Pump Nozzle Sizes?

Unleaded gasoline nozzles are smaller than those used for diesel fuel to help prevent fueling errors. However, it is still possible to fuel a diesel vehicle with gasoline.

 SEE CHART 2–4 for the sizes and colors used for fuel pump nozzles.

TESTING FOR ALCOHOL CONTENT IN GASOLINE

1 A fuel composition tester (SPX Kent-Moore J-44175) is the recommended tool to use to test the alcohol content of gasoline.

2 This battery-powered tester uses light-emitting diodes (LEDs), meter lead terminals, and two small openings for the fuel sample.

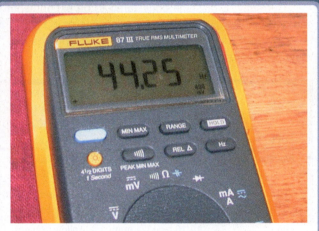

3 The first step is to verify the proper operation of the tester by measuring the air frequency by selecting AC hertz on the meter. The air frequency should be between 35 Hz and 48 Hz.

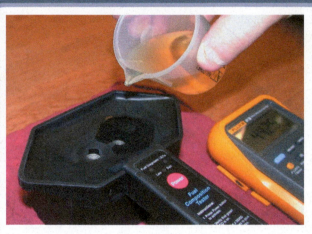

4 After verifying that the tester is capable of correctly reading the air frequency, gasoline is poured into the testing cell of the tool.

5 Record the AC frequency as shown on the meter and subtract 50 from the reading (e.g., 60.50 − 50.00 = 10.5). This number (10.5) is the percentage of alcohol in the gasoline sample.

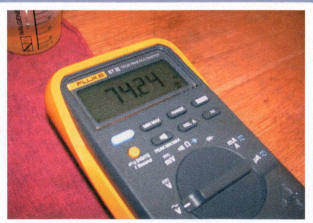

6 Adding additional amounts of ethyl alcohol (ethanol) increases the frequency reading.

SUMMARY

1. Gasoline is a complex blend of hydrocarbons. Gasoline is blended for seasonal usage to achieve the correct volatility for easy starting and maximum fuel economy under all driving conditions.

2. Winter-blend fuel used in a vehicle during warm weather can cause a rough idle and stalling because of its higher Reid vapor pressure (RVP).

3. Abnormal combustion (also called detonation or spark knock) increases both the temperature and the pressure inside the combustion chamber.

4. Most regular grade gasoline today, using the (R + M) ÷ 2 rating method, is 87 octane; midgrade (plus) is 89 and premium grade is 91 or higher.

5. Oxygenated fuels contain oxygen to lower CO exhaust emissions.

6. Flexible fuel vehicles (FFVs) are designed to operate on gasoline or gasoline-ethanol blends up to 85% ethanol (E85).

7. E85 has fewer BTUs of energy per gallon compared with gasoline and will therefore provide lower fuel economy.

8. Methanol is also called methyl alcohol or wood alcohol and, while it can be made from wood, it is mostly made from natural gas.

9. Propane is the most widely used alternative fuel. Propane is also called liquefied petroleum gas (LPG).

10. Compressed natural gas (CNG) is available for refilling in several pressures, including 2,400 PSI, 3,000 PSI, and 3,600 PSI.

11. Safety procedures when working around alternative fuel include wearing the necessary personal protective equipment (PPE), including safety glasses and protective gloves.

12. Diesel fuel requirements include cleanliness, low-temperature fluidity, and proper cetane rating.

13. Emission control devices used on 2007 and newer engines require the use of ultra-low-sulfur diesel (ULSD) that has less than 15 parts per million (ppm) of sulfur.

14. Biodiesel is the blend of vegetable-based liquid with regular diesel fuel. Most diesel engine manufacturers allow the use of a 5% blend, called B5, without any changes to the fuel system or engine.

REVIEW QUESTIONS

1. What is the difference between summer-blend and winter-blend gasoline?

2. What is Reid vapor pressure?

3. What does the (R + M) ÷ 2 gasoline pump octane rating indicate?

4. What is stoichiometry?

5. How is a flexible fuel vehicle identified?

CHAPTER QUIZ

1. Winter-blend gasoline _____.
   a. vaporizes more easily than summer-blend gasoline
   b. has a higher RVP
   c. can cause engine driveability problems if used during warm weather
   d. All of the above

2. Technician A says that spark knock, ping, and detonation are different names for abnormal combustion. Technician B says that any abnormal combustion raises the temperature and pressure inside the combustion chamber and can cause severe engine damage. Which technician is correct?
   a. Technician A only
   b. Technician B only
   c. Both Technicians A and B
   d. Neither Technician A nor B

3. Technician A says that the research octane number is higher than the motor octane number. Technician B says that the octane rating posted on fuel pumps is an average of the two ratings. Which technician is correct?
   a. Technician A only
   b. Technician B only
   c. Both Technicians A and B
   d. Neither Technician A nor B

4. What personal protective equipment should be used when working around alternative fuels?
   a. Safety glasses
   b. Long-sleeve shirt and long pants
   c. Protective gloves
   d. All of the above

5. Which of the following is considered to be a synthetic or man-made fuel?
   a. Fischer–Tropsch
   b. P-series
   c. E-diesel
   d. Both a and b

6. What can be used to measure the alcohol content in gasoline?
   a. Graduated cylinder
   b. Electronic tester
   c. Scan tool
   d. Both a and b

7. E85 means that the fuel is made from _____.
   a. 85% gasoline and 15% ethanol
   b. 85% ethanol and 15% gasoline
   c. ethanol that has 15% water
   d. pure ethyl alcohol

8. Overfilling the fuel tank can damage which component?
   a. Fuel pump
   b. Charcoal cannister
   c. Gas cap
   d. Fuel injectors

9. A flex fuel vehicle can be identified by _____.
   a. emblems on the side, front, and/or rear of the vehicle
   b. VECI
   c. VIN
   d. All of the above

10. When refueling a CNG vehicle, why is it recommended that the tank be filled to a high pressure?
    a. The range of the vehicle is increased.
    b. The cost of the fuel is lower.
    c. Less of the fuel is lost to evaporation.
    d. Both a and c.

chapter 3

CIRCUIT TESTERS AND DIGITAL METERS

LEARNING OBJECTIVES

After studying this chapter, the reader should be able to:

1. Discuss how to safely set up and use a fused jumper wire, a test light, and a logic probe.
2. Explain how to safely and properly use a digital meter to read voltage, resistance, and current.
3. Describe the purpose and function of inductive ammeters.
4. Describe diode check, duty cycle, and frequency.
5. List the electrical unit prefixes used by digital multimeters.
6. Explain the procedure for safely using and reading a digital multimeter.

This chapter will help you prepare for the ASE Electrical/Electronic Systems (A6) certification test content area "A" (General Electrical/Electronic System Diagnosis).

KEY TERMS

AC/DC clamp-on DMM 53
DMM 50
DVOM 50
High-impedance test meter 50
IEC 60
Inductive ammeter 53
Kilo (k) 55
LED test light 49
Logic probe 49
Mega (M) 55
Meter accuracy 59
Meter resolution 58
Milli (m) 55
OL 51
RMS 58
Test light 48

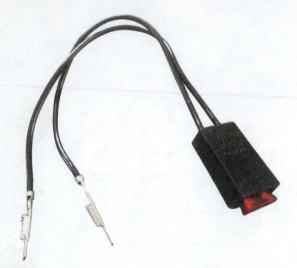

FIGURE 3–1 A technician-made fused jumper lead, which is equipped with a red 10 ampere fuse. This fused jumper wire uses terminals for testing circuits at a connector instead of alligator clips.

FUSED JUMPER WIRE

DEFINITION A fused jumper wire is used to check a circuit by bypassing the switch or to provide a power or ground to a component. A fused jumper wire, also called a test lead, can be purchased or made by the service technician. ● **SEE FIGURE 3–1.**

It should include the following features:

- **Fuse.** A typical fused jumper wire has a blade-type fuse that can be easily replaced. A 10 ampere fuse (red color) is often the value used.

- **Alligator clip ends.** Alligator clips at the ends allow the fused jumper wire to be clipped to a ground or power source while the other end is attached to the power side or ground side of the unit being tested.

- **Good-quality insulated wire.** Most purchased jumper wire is about 14 gauge stranded copper wire with a flexible rubberized insulation to allow it to move easily even in cold weather.

USES OF A FUSED JUMPER WIRE A fused jumper wire can be used to help diagnose a component or circuit by performing the following procedures:

- **Supply power or ground.** If a component, such as a horn, does not work, a fused jumper wire can be used to supply a temporary power and/or ground. Start by unplugging the electrical connector from the device and connect a fused jumper lead to the power terminal. Another fused jumper wire may be needed to provide the ground. If the unit works, the problem is in the power side or ground side circuit.

CAUTION: Never use a fused jumper wire to bypass any resistance or load in the circuit. The increased current flow could damage the wiring and could blow the fuse on the jumper lead.

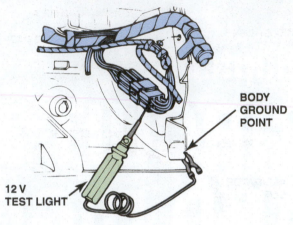

FIGURE 3–2 A 12 volt test light is attached to a good ground while probing for power.

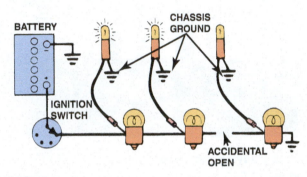

FIGURE 3–3 A test light can be used to locate an open in a circuit. Note that the test light is grounded at a different location than the circuit itself.

TEST LIGHTS

NONPOWERED TEST LIGHT A 12 volt test light is one of the simplest testers that can be used to detect electricity. A **test light** is simply a lightbulb with a probe and a ground wire attached. ● **SEE FIGURE 3–2.**

It is used to detect battery voltage potential at various test points. Battery voltage cannot be seen or felt and can be detected only with test equipment.

The ground clip is connected to a clean ground on either the negative terminal of the battery or a clean metal part of the body and the probe touched to terminals or components. If the test light comes on, this indicates that voltage is available. ● **SEE FIGURE 3–3.**

A purchased test light could be labeled a "12 volt test light." Do not purchase a test light designed for household current (110 or 220 volts), as it will not light with 12 to 14 volts.

USES OF A 12 VOLT TEST LIGHT A 12 volt test light can be used to check the following:

- **Electrical power.** If the test light comes on, then there is power available. It will not, however, indicate the voltage level or if there is enough current available to operate an

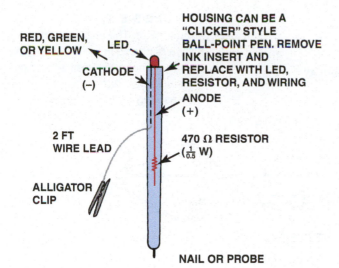

FIGURE 3–4 An LED test light can be easily made using low cost components and an old ink pen. With the 470 ohm resistor in series with the LED, this tester only draws 0.025 ampere (25 milliamperes) from the circuit being tested. This low current draw helps assure the technician that the circuit or component being tested will not be damaged by excessive current flow.

electrical load. This only indicates that there is enough voltage and current to light the test light (about 0.25 A).

- **Grounds.** A test light can be used to check for grounds by attaching the clip of the test light to the positive terminal of the battery or to any 12 volt electrical terminal. The tip of the test light can then be used to touch the ground wire. If there is a ground connection, the test light will come on.

HIGH-IMPEDANCE TEST LIGHT
A high-impedance test light has a high internal resistance and therefore draws very low current in order to light. High-impedance test lights are safe to use on computer circuits because they will not affect the circuit current in the same way as conventional 12 volt test lights when connected to a circuit. There are two types of high-impedance test lights.

- Some test lights use an electronic circuit to limit the current flow to avoid causing damage to electronic devices.
- An **LED test light** uses a light-emitting diode (LED) instead of a standard automotive bulb for a visual indication of voltage. An LED test light requires only about 25 milliamperes (0.025 A) to light; therefore, it can be used on electronic circuits as well as on standard circuits.
  ● **SEE FIGURE 3–4** for construction details for a home-made LED test light.

LOGIC PROBE

PURPOSE AND FUNCTION
A **logic probe** is an electronic device that lights up a red (usually) LED if the probe is touched to battery voltage. If the probe is touched to ground, a green (usually) LED lights. ● **SEE FIGURE 3–5.**

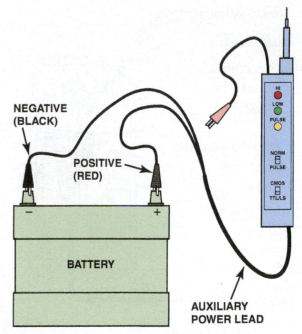

FIGURE 3–5 A logic probe connected to the vehicle battery. When the tip probe is connected to a circuit, it can check for power, ground, or a pulse.

A logic probe can "sense" the difference between high- and low-voltage levels, which explains the name *logic*.

- A typical logic probe can also light another light (often amber color) when a change in voltage occurs.
- Some logic probes will flash the red light when a pulsing voltage signal is detected.
- Some will flash the green light when a pulsing ground signal is detected.

This feature is helpful when checking for a variable voltage output from a computer or ignition sensor.

USING A LOGIC PROBE
A logic probe must first be connected to a power and ground source such as the vehicle battery. This connection powers the probe and gives it a reference low (ground).

Most logic probes also make a distinctive sound for each high- and low-voltage level. This makes troubleshooting easier when probing connectors or component terminals. A sound (usually a beep) is heard when the probe tip is touched to a changing voltage source. The changing voltage also usually lights the pulse light on the logic probe. Therefore, the probe can be used to check components such as:

- Pickup coils
- Hall-effect sensors
- Magnetic sensors

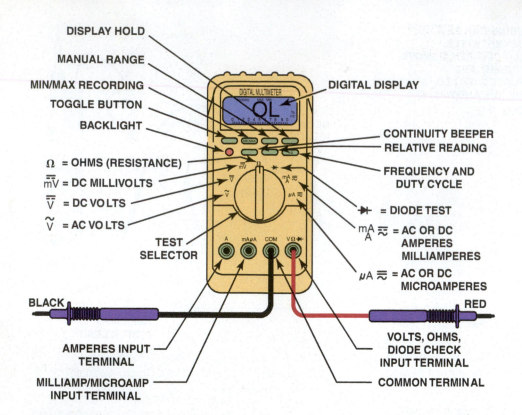

DISPLAY HOLD

MANUAL RANGE

MIN/MAX RECORDING

TOGGLE BUTTON

BACKLIGHT

DIGITAL DISPLAY

CONTINUITY BEEPER
RELATIVE READING

Ω = OHMS (RESISTANCE)

$\overline{mV}$ = DC MILLIVOLTS

$\overline{V}$ = DC VOLTS

$\widetilde{V}$ = AC VOLTS

FREQUENCY AND
DUTY CYCLE

➤ = DIODE TEST

mA ⇌ = AC OR DC
AMPERES
MILLIAMPERES

μA ⇌ = AC OR DC
MICROAMPERES

TEST
SELECTOR

BLACK

RED

VOLTS, OHMS,
DIODE CHECK
INPUT TERMINAL

AMPERES INPUT
TERMINAL

COMMON TERMINAL

MILLIAMP/MICROAMP
INPUT TERMINAL

FIGURE 3–6 Typical digital multimeter. The black meter lead is always placed in the COM terminal. The red meter test lead should be in the volt-ohm terminal except when measuring current in amperes.

DIGITAL MULTIMETERS

TERMINOLOGY **Digital multimeter (DMM)** and **digital volt-ohm-meter (DVOM)** are terms commonly used for electronic **high-impedance test meters**. *High impedance* means that the electronic internal resistance of the meter is high enough to prevent excessive current draw from any circuit being tested. Most meters today have a minimum of 10 million ohms (10 megohms) of resistance. This high internal resistance between the meter leads is present only when measuring volts. The high resistance in the meter itself reduces the amount of current flowing through the meter when it is being used to measure voltage, leading to more accurate test results because the meter does not change the load on the circuit. High-impedance meters are required for measuring computer circuits.

CAUTION: Analog (needle-type) meters are almost always lower than 10 megohms and should not be used to measure any computer or electronic circuit. Connecting an analog meter to a computer circuit could damage the computer or other electronic modules.

A high-impedance meter can be used to measure any automotive circuit within the ranges of the meter. ● **SEE FIGURE 3–6**.

The common abbreviations for the units that many meters can measure are often confusing. ● **SEE CHART 3–1** for the most commonly used symbols and their meanings.

MEASURING VOLTAGE A voltmeter measures the *pressure* or potential of electricity in units of volts. A voltmeter is connected to a circuit in parallel. Voltage can be measured by selecting either AC or DC volts.

SYMBOL	MEANING
AC	Alternating current or voltage
DC	Direct current or voltage
V	Volts
mV	Millivolts (1/1,000 volts)
A	Ampere (amps), current
mA	Milliampere (1/1,000 amps)
%	Percent (for duty cycle readings only)
Ṽ	Ohms, resistance
kΩ	Kilohm (1,000 ohms), resistance
MΩ	Megohm (1,000,000 ohms), resistance
Hz	Hertz (cycles per second), frequency
kHz	Kilohertz (1,000 cycles/sec.), frequency
ms	Milliseconds (1/1,000 sec.) for pulse width measurements

CHART 3–1

Common symbols and abbreviations used on digital meters.

■ **DC volts (DCV).** This setting is the most common for automotive use. Use this setting to measure battery voltage and voltage to all lighting and accessory circuits.

■ **AC volts (ACV).** This setting is used to check for unwanted AC voltage from alternators and some sensors.

■ **Range.** The range is automatically set for most meters but can be manually ranged if needed.

● **SEE FIGURES 3–7 AND 3–8**.

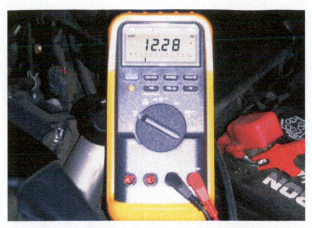

FIGURE 3–7 Typical digital multimeter (DMM) set to read DC volts.

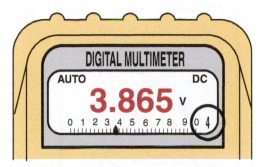

BECAUSE THE SIGNAL READING IS BELOW 4 VOLTS, THE METER AUTORANGES TO THE 4 VOLT SCALE. IN THE 4 VOLT SCALE, THIS METER PROVIDES THREE DECIMAL PLACES.

(a)

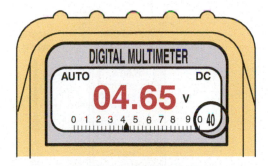

WHEN THE VOLTAGE EXCEEDS 4 VOLTS, THE METER AUTORANGES INTO THE 40 VOLT SCALE. THE DECIMAL POINT MOVES ONE PLACE TO THE RIGHT LEAVING ONLY TWO DECIMAL PLACES.

(b)

FIGURE 3–8 A typical autoranging digital multimeter automatically selects the proper scale to read the voltage being tested. The scale selected is usually displayed on the meter face. (a) Note that the display indicates "4," meaning that this range can read up to 4 volts. (b) The range is now set to the 40 volt scale, meaning that the meter can read up to 40 volts on the scale. Any reading above this level will cause the meter to reset to a higher scale. If not set on autoranging, the meter display would indicate OL if a reading exceeds the limit of the scale selected.

FIGURE 3–9 Using a digital multimeter set to read ohms Ω to test this lightbulb. The meter reads the resistance of the filament.

MEASURING RESISTANCE An ohmmeter measures the resistance in ohms of a component or circuit section when no current is flowing through the circuit. An ohmmeter contains a battery (or other power source) and is connected in series with the component or wire being measured. When the leads are connected to a component, current flows through the test leads and the difference in voltage (voltage drop) between the leads is measured as resistance. Note the following facts about using an ohmmeter.

- Zero ohms on the scale means that there is no resistance between the test leads, thus indicating continuity or a continuous path for the current to flow in a closed circuit.

- Infinity means no connection, as in an open circuit.

- Ohmmeters have no required polarity even though red and black test leads are used for resistance measurement.

CAUTION: The circuit must be electrically open with no current flowing when using an ohmmeter. If current is flowing when an ohmmeter is connected, the reading will be incorrect and the meter can be destroyed.

Different meters have different ways of indicating infinite resistance, or a reading higher than the scale allows. Examples of an over-limit display include:

- **OL,** meaning **over limit** or overload

- Flashing or solid number 1

- Flashing or solid number 3 on the left side of the display

Check the meter instructions for the exact display used to indicate an open circuit or over range reading. ● **SEE FIGURES 3–9 AND 3–10.**

To summarize, open and zero readings are as follows:

$0.00 \, \Omega$ = Zero resistance (component or circuit has continuity)

OL = An open circuit or reading is higher than the scale selected (no current flows)

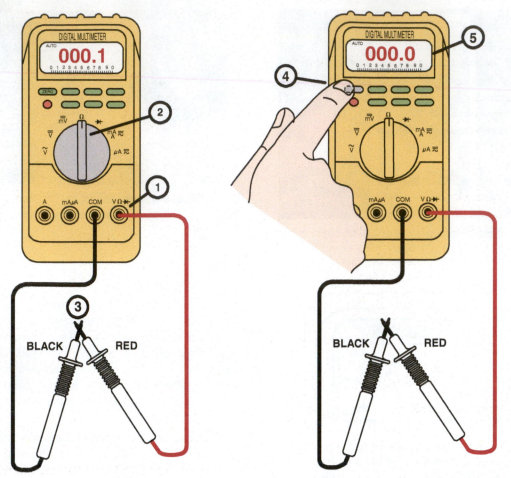

FIGURE 3–10 Many digital multimeters can have the display indicate zero to compensate for test lead resistance. (1) Connect leads in the Ω and COM meter terminals. (2) Select the Ω scale. (3) Touch the two meter leads together. (4) Push the "zero" or "relative" button on the meter. (5) The meter display will now indicate zero ohms of resistance.

MEASURING AMPERES An ammeter measures the flow of *current* through a complete circuit in units of amperes. The ammeter has to be installed in the circuit (in series) so that it can measure all the current flow in that circuit, just as a water flow meter would measure the amount of water flow (cubic feet per minute, for example). ● **SEE FIGURE 3–11.**

CAUTION: An ammeter must be installed in series with the circuit to measure the current flow in the circuit. If a meter set to read amperes is connected in parallel, such as across a battery, the meter or the leads may be destroyed, or the fuse will blow, by the current available across the battery. Some digital multimeters (DMMs) beep if the unit selection does not match the test lead connection on the meter. However, in a noisy shop, this beep sound may be inaudible.

Digital meters require that the meter leads be moved to the ammeter terminals. Most digital meters have an ampere scale that can accommodate a maximum of 10 amperes. See the Tech Tip "Fuse Your Meter Leads!"

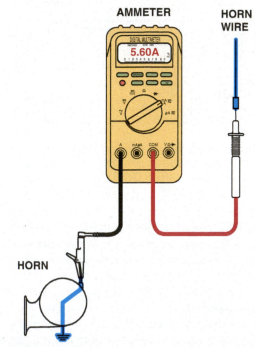

FIGURE 3–11 Measuring the current flow required by a horn requires that the ammeter be connected to the circuit in series and the horn button be depressed by an assistant.

How Much Voltage Does an Ohmmeter Apply?

Most digital meters that are set to measure ohms (resistance) apply 0.3 to 1 volt to the component being measured. The voltage comes from the meter itself to measure the resistance. Two things are important to remember about an ohmmeter.

1. The component or circuit must be disconnected from any electrical circuit while the resistance is being measured.
2. Because the meter itself applies a voltage (even though it is relatively low), a meter set to measure ohms can damage electronic circuits. Computer or electronic chips can be easily damaged if subjected to only a few milliamperes of current, similar to the amount an ohmmeter applies when a resistance measurement is being performed.

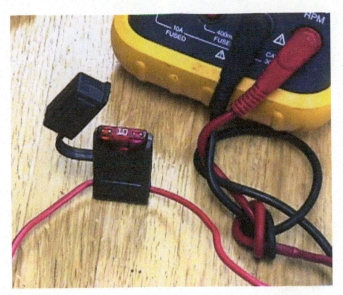

FIGURE 3–12 Note the blade-type fuse holder soldered in series with one of the meter leads. A 10 ampere fuse helps protect the internal meter fuse (if equipped) and the meter itself from damage that may result from excessive current flow if accidentally used incorrectly.

 **TECH TIP**

Fuse Your Meter Leads!

Most digital meters include an ammeter capability. When reading amperes, the leads of the meter must be changed from volts or ohms (V or Ω) to amperes (A), milliamperes (mA), or microamperes (μA).

A common problem may then occur the next time voltage is measured. Although the technician may switch the selector to read volts, often the leads are not switched back to the volt or ohm position. Because the ammeter lead position results in zero ohms of resistance to current flow through the meter, the meter or the fuse inside the meter will be destroyed if the meter is connected to a battery. Many meter fuses are expensive and difficult to find.

To avoid this problem, simply solder an inline 10 ampere blade-fuse holder into one meter lead. ● **SEE FIGURE 3–12**.

Do not think that this technique is for beginners only. Experienced technicians often get in a hurry and forget to switch the lead. A blade fuse is faster, easier, and less expensive to replace than a meter fuse or the meter itself. Also, if the soldering is done properly, the addition of an inline fuse holder and fuse does not increase the resistance of the meter leads. All meter leads have some resistance. If the meter is measuring very low resistance, touch the two leads together and read the resistance (usually no more than 0.2 ohm). Simply subtract the resistance of the leads from the resistance of the component being measured.

What Does "CE" Mean on Many Meters?

The "CE" means that the meter meets the newest European Standards and the CE mark stands for *Conformité Europeenne*, which is French for "European Conformity."

INDUCTIVE AMMETERS

OPERATION **Inductive ammeters** do not make physical contact with the circuit. They measure the strength of the magnetic field surrounding the wire carrying the current, and use a Hall-effect sensor to measure current. The Hall-effect sensor detects the strength of the magnetic field that surrounds the wire carrying an electrical current. ● **SEE FIGURE 3–13**.

This means that the meter probe surrounds the wire(s) carrying the current and measures the strength of the magnetic field that surrounds any conductor carrying a current.

AC/DC CLAMP-ON DIGITAL MULTIMETERS An **AC/DC clamp-on digital multimeter (DMM)** is a useful meter for automotive diagnostic work. ● **SEE FIGURE 3–14**.

The major advantage of the clamp-on-type meter is that there is no need to break the circuit to measure current (amperes). Simply clamp the jaws of the meter around the

FIGURE 3–13 An inductive ammeter clamp is used with all starting and charging testers to measure the current flow through the battery cables.

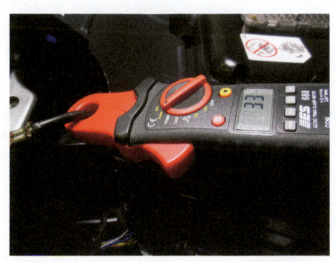

FIGURE 3–14 A typical mini clamp-on-type digital multimeter. This meter is capable of measuring alternating current (AC) and direct current (DC) without requiring that the circuit be disconnected to install the meter in series. The jaws are simply placed over the wire and current flow through the circuit is displayed.

power lead(s) or ground lead(s) of the component being measured and read the display. Most clamp-on meters can also measure alternating current, which is helpful in the diagnosis of an alternator problem. Volts, ohms, frequency, and temperature can also be measured with the typical clamp-on DMM, but use conventional meter leads. The inductive clamp is only used to measure amperes.

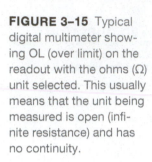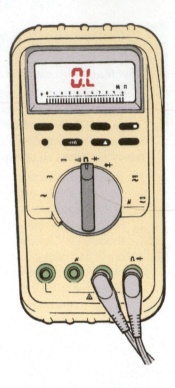

FIGURE 3–15 Typical digital multimeter showing OL (over limit) on the readout with the ohms (Ω) unit selected. This usually means that the unit being measured is open (infinite resistance) and has no continuity.

🔧 **TECH TIP**

Over Limit Display Does Not Mean the Meter Is Reading "Nothing"

The meaning of the over limit display on a digital meter often confuses beginning technicians. When asked what the meter is reading when an over limit (OL) is displayed on the meter face, the response is often, "Nothing." Many meters indicate *over limit* or *over load,* which simply means that the reading is over the maximum that can be displayed for the selected range. For example, the meter will display OL if 12 volts are being measured but the meter has been set to read a maximum of 4 volts.

Autoranging meters adjust the range to match what is being measured. Here OL means a value higher than the meter can read (unlikely on the voltage scale for automobile usage), or infinity when measuring resistance (ohms). Therefore, OL means infinity when measuring resistance or an open circuit is being indicated. The meter will read 00.0 if the resistance is zero, so "nothing" in this case indicates continuity (zero resistance), whereas OL indicates infinite resistance. Therefore, when talking with another technician about a meter reading, make sure you know exactly what the reading on the face of the meter means. Also be sure that you are connecting the meter leads correctly. ● **SEE FIGURE 3–15.**

DIODE CHECK, DUTY CYCLE, AND FREQUENCY

DIODE CHECK Diode check is a meter function that can be used to check diodes including light-emitting diodes (LEDs).

The meter is able to text diodes in the following way:

- The meter applies roughly a 3-volt DC signal to the text leads.
- The voltage is high enough to cause a diode to work and the meter will display:
  1. 0.4 to 0.7 volt when testing silicon diodes such as those found in alternators
  2. 1.5 to 2.3 volts when testing LEDs such as those found in some lighting applications

DUTY CYCLE Duty cycle is the amount of time by percentage that a signal is on compared to being off.

- 100% duty cycle indicates that a device is being commanded on all of the time.
- 50% duty cycle indicates that a device is being commanded on half of the time.
- 25% duty cycle indicates that a device is being commanded on just 25% of the time.

Pulse width is used to measure the on-time for fuel injectors and other computer-controlled solenoid and devices.

FREQUENCY Frequency is a measure of how many times per second a signal changes. Frequency is measured in a unit called hertz, formerly termed "cycles per second."

Frequency measurements are used when checking the following:

- Mass airflow (MAF) sensors for proper operation
- Ignition primary pulse signals when diagnosing a no-start condition
- Checking a wheel speed sensor

ELECTRICAL UNIT PREFIXES

DEFINITIONS Electrical units are measured in numbers such as 12 volts, 150 amperes, and 470 ohms. Large units over 1,000 may be expressed in kilo units. **Kilo (k)** means 1,000.
● **SEE FIGURE 3–16**.

4,700 ohms = 4.7 kilohms (kΩ)

If the value is over 1 million (1,000,000), then the prefix **mega (M)** is often used. For example:

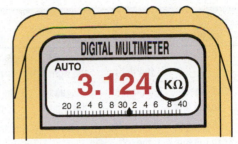

THE SYMBOL ON THE RIGHT SIDE OF THE DISPLAY INDICATES WHAT RANGE THE METER HAS BEEN SET TO READ.

Ω = OHMS
IF THE ONLY SYMBOL ON THE DISPLAY IS THE OHMS SYMBOL, THE READING ON THE DISPLAY IS EXACTLY THE RESISTANCE IN OHMS.

KΩ = KILOHMS = OHMS TIMES 1,000
A "K" IN FRONT OF THE OHMS SYMBOL MEANS "KILOHMS"; THE READING ON THE DISPLAY IS IN KILOHMS. YOU HAVE TO MULTIPLY THE READING ON THE DISPLAY BY 1,000 TO GET THE RESISTANCE IN OHMS.

MΩ = MEGOHMS = OHMS TIMES 1,000,000
AN "M" IN FRONT OF THE OHMS SYMBOL MEANS "MEGOHMS"; THE READING ON THE DISPLAY IS IN MEGOHMS. YOU HAVE TO MULTIPLY THE READING ON THE DISPLAY BY 1,000,000 TO GET THE RESISTANCE IN OHMS.

FIGURE 3–16 Always look at the meter display when a measurement is being made, especially if using an autoranging meter.

1,100,000 volts = 1.1 megavolts (MV)

4,700,000 ohms = 4.7 mega ohms (MΩ)

Sometimes a circuit conducts so little current that a smaller unit of measure is required. Small units of measure expressed in 1/1,000 are prefixed by **milli (m)**. To summarize:

mega (M) = 1,000,000 (decimal point six places to the right = 1,000,000)

kilo (k) = 1,000 (decimal point three places to the right = 1,000)

milli (m) = 1/1,000 (decimal point three places to the left = 0.001)

NOTE: Lowercase m equals a small unit (milli), whereas a capital M represents a large unit (mega).

● **SEE CHART 3–2**.

PREFIXES The prefixes can be confusing because most digital meters can express values in more than one unit, especially if the meter is autoranging. For example, an ammeter reading may show 36.7 mA on autoranging. When the scale

TO/FROM	MEGA	KILO	BASE	MILLI
Mega	0 places	3 places to the right	6 places to the right	9 places to the right
Kilo	3 places to the left	0 places	3 places to the right	6 places to the right
Base	6 places to the left	3 places to the left	0 places	3 places to the right
Milli	9 places to the left	6 places to the left	3 places to the left	0 places

CHART 3–2

A conversion chart showing the decimal point location for the various prefixes.

TECH TIP

Think of Money

Digital meter displays can often be confusing. The display for a battery measured as 12 1/2 volts would be 12.50 V, just as $12.50 is 12 dollars and 50 cents. A 1/2 volt reading on a digital meter will be displayed as 0.50 V, just as $0.50 is half of a dollar.

It is more confusing when low values are displayed. For example, if a voltage reading is 0.063 volt, an autoranging meter will display 63 millivolts (63 mV), or 63/1,000 of a volt, or $63 of $1,000. (It takes 1,000 mV to equal 1 volt.) Think of millivolts as one-tenth of a cent, with 1 volt being $1.00. Therefore, 630 millivolts are equal to $0.63 of $1.00 (630 tenths of a cent, or 63 cents).

To avoid confusion, try to manually range the meter to read base units (whole volts). If the meter is ranged to base unit volts, 63 millivolts would be displayed as 0.063 or maybe just 0.06, depending on the display capabilities of the meter.

is changed to amperes ("A" in the window of the display), the number displayed will be 0.037 A. Note that the resolution of the value is reduced.

NOTE: Always check the face of the meter display for the unit being measured. To best understand what is being displayed on the face of a digital meter, select a manual scale and move the selector until *whole units appear*, such as "A" for amperes instead of "mA" for milliamperes.

HOW TO READ DIGITAL METERS

STEPS TO FOLLOW Getting to know and use a digital meter takes time and practice. The first step is to read, understand, and follow all safety and operational instructions that come with the meter. Use of the meter usually involves the following steps.

STEP 1 **Select the proper unit of electricity for what is being measured.** This unit could be volts, ohms (resistance), or amperes (amount of current flow). If the meter is not autoranging, select the proper scale for the anticipated reading. For example, if a 12 volt battery is being measured, select a meter reading range that is higher than the voltage but not too high. A 20 or 30 volt range will accurately show the voltage of a 12 volt battery. If a 1,000 volt scale is selected, a 12 volt reading may not be accurate.

STEP 2 **Place the meter leads into the proper input terminals.**

- The black lead is inserted into the common (COM) terminal. This meter lead usually stays in this location for all meter functions.
- The red lead is inserted into the volt, ohm, or diode check terminal usually labeled "VΩ" when voltage, resistance, or diodes are being measured.
- When current flow in amperes is being measured, most digital meters require that the red test lead be inserted in the ammeter terminal, usually labeled "A" or "mA."

CAUTION: If the meter leads are inserted into ammeter terminals, even though the selector is set to volts, the meter may be damaged or an internal fuse may blow if the test leads touch both terminals of a battery.

STEP 3 Measure the component being tested. Carefully note the decimal point and the unit on the face of the meter.

- **Meter lead connections.** If the meter leads are connected to a battery backward (red to the battery negative, for example), the display will still show the correct reading, but a negative sign (−) will be displayed in front of the number. The correct polarity is not important when measuring resistance (ohms) except where indicated, such as measuring a diode.

VOLTAGE BEING MEASURED					
	0.01 V (10 mV)	0.150 V (150 mV)	1.5 V	10.0 V	12.0 V	120 V
Scale Selected	Voltmeter will display:					
200 mV	10.0	150.0	OL	OL	OL	OL
2 V	0.100	0.150	1.500	OL	OL	OL
20 V	0.1	1.50	1.50	10.00	12.00	OL
200 V	00.0	01.5	01.5	10.0	12.0	120.0
2 kV	00.00	00.00	000.1	00.10	00.12	0.120
Autorange	10.0 mV	15.0 mV	1.50	10.0	12.0	120.0

RESISTANCE BEING MEASURED					
	10 OHMS	100 OHMS	470 OHMS	1 KILOHM	220 KILOHMS	1 MEGOHM
Scale Selected	Ohmmeter will display:					
400 ohms	10.0	100.0	OL	OL	OL	OL
4 kilohms	010	100	0.470 k	1000	OL	OL
40 kilohms	00.0	0.10 k	0.47 k	1.00 k	OL	OL
400 kilohms	000.0	00.1 k	00.5 k	0.10 k	220.0 k	OL
4 megohms	00.00	0.01 M	0.05 M	00.1 M	0.22 M	1.0 M
Autorange	10.0	100.0	470.0	1.00 k	220 k	1.00 M

CURRENT BEING MEASURED					
	50 mA	150 mA	1.0 A	7.5 A	15.0 A	25.0 A
Scale Selected	Ammeter will display:					
40 mA	OL	OL	OL	OL	OL	OL
400 mA	50.0	150	OL	OL	OL	OL
4 A	0.05	0.00	1.00	OL	OL	OL
40 A	0.00	0.000	01.0	7.5	15.0	25.0
Autorange	50.0 mA	150.0 mA	1.00	7.5	15.0	25.0

CHART 3–3

Sample meter readings using manually set and autoranging selection on the digital meter control.

■ **Autorange.** Many meters automatically default to the autorange position and the meter will display the value in the most readable scale. The meter can be manually ranged to select other levels or to lock in a scale for a value that is constantly changing.

If a 12 volt battery is measured with an autoranging meter, the correct reading of 12.0 is given. "AUTO" and "V" should show on the face of the meter. For example, if a meter is manually set to the 2 kilohm scale, the highest that the meter will read is 2,000 ohms. If the reading is over 2,000 ohms, the meter will display OL. ● **SEE CHART 3–3**.

STEP 4 Interpret the reading. This is especially difficult on autoranging meters, where the meter itself selects the proper scale. The following are two examples of different readings.

Example 1: A voltage drop is being measured. The specifications indicate a maximum voltage drop of 0.2 volt. The meter reads "AUTO" and "43.6 mV." This reading means that the voltage drop is 0.0436 volt, or 43.6 mV, which is far lower than the 0.2 volt (200 mV). Because the number showing on the meter face is much larger than the specifications, many beginner technicians are led to believe that the voltage drop is excessive.

NOTE: Pay attention to the units displayed on the meter face and convert to whole units.

Example 2: A spark plug wire is being measured. The reading should be less than 10,000 ohms for each foot

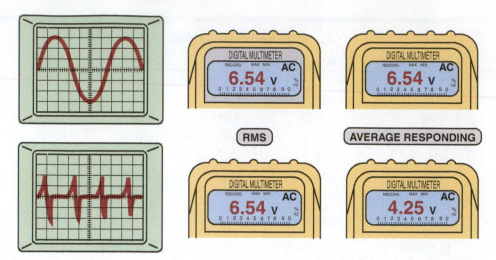

FIGURE 3–17 When reading AC voltage signals, a true RMS meter (such as a Fluke 87) provides a different reading than an average responding meter (such as a Fluke 88). The only place this difference is important is when a reading is to be compared with a specification.

in length if the wire is okay. The wire being tested is 3 ft long (maximum allowable resistance is 30,000 ohms). The meter reads "AUTO" and "14.85 kΩ." This reading is equivalent to 14,850 ohms.

NOTE: When converting from kilohms to ohms, make the decimal point a comma.

Because this reading is well below the specified maximum allowable, the spark plug wire is okay.

RMS VERSUS AVERAGE Alternating current voltage waveforms can be true sinusoidal or nonsinusoidal. A true sine wave pattern measurement will be the same for both **root-mean-square (RMS)** and average reading meters. RMS and averaging are two methods used to measure the true effective rating of a signal that is constantly changing. ● **SEE FIGURE 3–17**.

Only true RMS meters are accurate when measuring nonsinusoidal AC waveforms, which are seldom used in automotive applications.

RESOLUTION, DIGITS, AND COUNTS Meter resolution refers to how small or fine a measurement the meter can make. By knowing the resolution of a DMM, you can determine whether the meter could measure down to only 1 volt or down to 1 millivolt (1/1,000 of a volt).

The terms *digits* and *counts* are used to describe a meter's resolution. DMMs are grouped by the number of counts or digits they display.

- A 3 1/2-digit meter can display three full digits ranging from 0 to 9, and one "half" digit that displays only a 1 or is left blank. A 3 1/2-digit meter will display up to 1,999 counts of resolution.
- A 4 1/2-digit meter can display up to 19,000 counts of resolution. It is more precise to describe a meter by counts of resolution than by 3 1/2 or 4 1/2 digits. Some 3 1/2-digit meters have enhanced resolution of up to 3,200 or 4,000 counts.

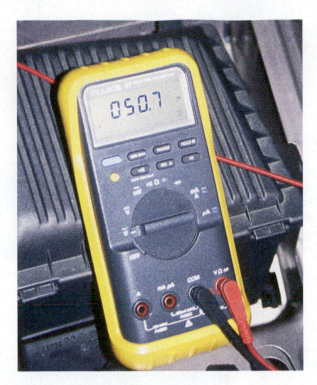

FIGURE 3–18 This meter display shows 050.7 AC volts. Notice that the zero beside the 5 indicates that the meter can read over 100 volts AC with a resolution of 0.1 volt.

Meters with more counts offer better resolution for certain measurements. For example, a 1,999 count meter will not be able to measure down to a tenth of a volt when measuring 200 volts or more. ● **SEE FIGURE 3–18.**

However, a 3,200 count meter will display a tenth of a volt up to 320 volts. Digits displayed to the far right of the display may at times flicker or constantly change. This is called *digit rattle* and represents a changing voltage being measured on the ground (COM terminal of the meter lead). High-quality meters are designed to reject this unwanted voltage.

ACCURACY **Meter accuracy** is the largest allowable error that will occur under specific operating conditions. In other words, it is an indication of how close the DMM's displayed measurement is to the actual value of the signal being measured.

Accuracy for a DMM is usually expressed as a percent of reading. An accuracy of ±1% of reading means that for a displayed reading of 100.0 V, the actual value of the voltage could be anywhere between 99.0 V and 101.0 V. Thus, the lower the percent of accuracy is, the better.

- Unacceptable = 1.00%
- Okay = 0.50% (1/2%)
- Good = 0.25% (1/4%)
- Excellent = 0.10% (1/10%)

For example, if a battery had 12.6 volts, a meter could read between the following, based on its accuracy.

±0.1%	high =	12.61
	low =	12.59
±0.25%	high =	12.63
	low =	12.57
±0.50%	high =	12.66
	low =	12.54
±1.00%	high =	12.73
	low =	12.47

Before you purchase a meter, check the accuracy. Accuracy is usually indicated on the specifications sheet for the meter.

Meter Usage on Hybrid Electric Vehicles

Many hybrid electric vehicles use system voltage as high as 650 volts DC. Be sure to follow all vehicle manufacturer's testing procedures. If a voltage measurement is needed, be sure to use a meter and test leads that are designed to insulate against high voltages. The **International Electrotechnical Commission (IEC)** has several categories of voltage standards for meter and meter leads. These categories are ratings for overvoltage protection and are rated CAT I, CAT II, CAT III, and CAT IV. The higher the category, the greater the protection against voltage spikes caused by high-energy circuits. Under each category there are various energy and voltage ratings.

CAT I   Typically a CAT I meter is used for low-energy voltage measurements such as at wall outlets in the home. Meters with a CAT I rating are usually rated at 300 to 800 volts.

CAT II   This higher rated meter would be typically used for checking higher energy level voltages at the fuse panel in the home. Meters with a CAT II rating are usually rated at 300 to 600 volts.

CAT III   This minimum rated meter should be used for hybrid vehicles. The CAT III category is designed for high-energy levels and voltage measurements at the service pole at the transformer. Meters with this rating are usually rated at 600 to 1,000 volts.

CAT IV   CAT IV meters are for clamp-on meters only. If a clamp-on meter also has meter leads for voltage measurements, that part of the meter will be rated as CAT III.

NOTE: Always use the highest CAT rating meter, especially when working with hybrid vehicles. A CAT III, 600 volt meter is safer than a CAT II, 1,000 volt meter because of the energy level of the CAT ratings.

Therefore, for best personal protection, use only meters and meter leads that are CAT III or CAT IV rated when measuring voltage on a hybrid vehicle.
● **SEE FIGURES 3–19 AND 3–20.**

FIGURE 3–19 Be sure to use only a meter that is CAT III rated when taking electrical voltage measurements on a hybrid vehicle.

FIGURE 3–20 Always use meter leads that are CAT III rated on a meter that is also CAT III rated, to maintain the protection needed when working on hybrid vehicles.

1 For most electrical measurements, the black meter lead is inserted in the terminal labeled "COM" and the red meter lead is inserted into the terminal labeled "V."

2 To use a digital meter, turn the power switch and select the unit of electricity to be measured. In this case, the rotary switch is turned to select DC volts V.

3 For most automotive electrical use, such as measuring battery voltage, select DC volts.

4 Connect the red meter lead to the positive (+) terminal of a battery and the black meter lead to the negative (−) terminal. The meter reads the voltage difference between the leads.

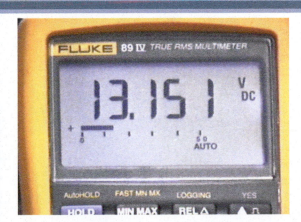

5 This jump start battery unit measures 13.151 volts with the meter set on autoranging on the DC voltage scale.

6 Another meter (Fluke 87 III) displays four digits when measuring the voltage of the battery jump start unit.

CONTINUED ▶

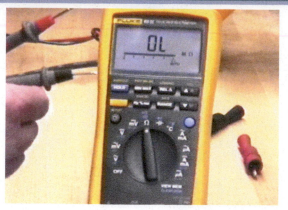

7 To measure resistance, turn the rotary dial to the ohm (Ω) symbol. With the meter leads separated, the meter display reads OL (over limit).

8 The meter can read your own body resistance if you grasp the meter lead terminals with your fingers. The reading on the display indicates 196.35 kΩ.

9 When measuring anything, be sure to read the symbol on the meter face. In this case, the meter reading is 291.10 kΩ.

10 A meter set on ohms can be used to check the resistance of a lightbulb filament. In this case, the meter reads 3.15 ohms. If the bulb were bad (filament open), the meter would display OL.

11 A digital meter set to read ohms should measure 0.00 as shown when the meter leads are touched together.

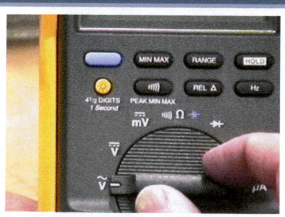

12 The large letter V means volts and the wavy symbol over the V means that the meter measures alternating current (AC) voltage if this position is selected.

13 The next symbol is a V with a dotted and a straight line overhead. This symbol stands for direct current (DC) volts. This position is most used for automotive service.

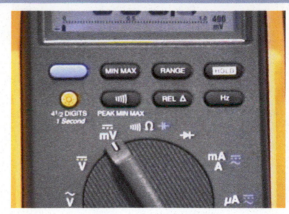

14 The symbol mV indicates millivolts or 1/1,000 of a volt (0.001). The solid and dashed line above the mV means DC mV.

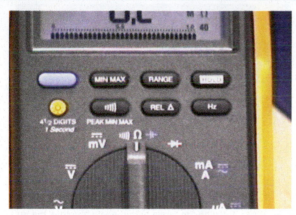

15 The rotary switch is turned to Ω (ohms) unit of resistance measure. The symbol to the left of the Ω symbol is the beeper or continuity indicator.

16 Notice that AUTO is in the upper left and the MΩ is in the lower right. MΩ means megaohms or that the meter is set to read in millions of ohms.

17 The symbol shown is that of a diode. In this position, the meter applies a voltage to a diode and the meter reads the voltage drop across the junction of a diode.

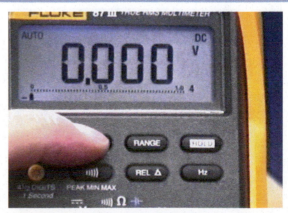

18 One of the most useful features of this meter is the MIN/MAX feature. By pushing the MIN/MAX button, the meter will be able to display the highest (MAX) and the lowest (MIN) reading.

CONTINUED ▶

19 Pushing the MIN/MAX button puts the meter into record mode. Note the 100 ms and "rec" on the display. In this position, the meter is capturing any voltage change that lasts 100 ms (0.1 sec.) or longer.

20 To increase the range of the meter, touch the range button. Now the meter is set to read voltage up to 40 volts DC.

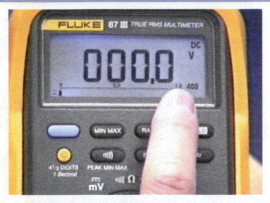

21 Pushing the range button one more time changes the meter scale to the 400 voltage range. Notice that the decimal point has moved to the right.

22 Pushing the range button again changes the meter to the 4,000 volt range. This range is not suitable to use in automotive applications.

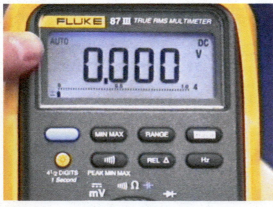

23 By pushing and holding the range button, the meter will reset to autorange. Autorange is the preferred setting for most automotive measurements except when using MIN/MAX record mode.

SUMMARY

1. Circuit testers include test lights and fused jumper leads.
2. Digital multimeter (DMM) and digital volt-ohm-meter (DVOM) are terms commonly used for electronic high-impedance test meters.
3. Use of a high-impedance digital meter is required on any computer-related circuit or component.
4. Ammeters measure current and must be connected in series in the circuit.
5. Voltmeters measure voltage and are connected in parallel.
6. Ohmmeters measure resistance of a component and must be connected in parallel, with the circuit or component disconnected from power.
7. Logic probes can indicate the presence of power, ground, or pulsed signals.

REVIEW QUESTIONS

1. Why should high-impedance meters be used when measuring voltage on computer-controlled circuits?
2. How is an ammeter connected to an electrical circuit?
3. Why must an ohmmeter be connected to a disconnected circuit or component?
4. How is a diode tested using a digital meter?
5. What is meant when a meter reads "OL" when measuring ohms?

CHAPTER QUIZ

1. Inductive ammeters work because of what principle?
   a. Magic
   b. Electrostatic electricity
   c. A magnetic field surrounds any wire carrying a current
   d. Voltage drop as it flows through a conductor

2. A meter used to measure amperes is called a(n) _____.
   a. amp meter
   b. ampmeter
   c. ammeter
   d. Coulomb meter

3. A voltmeter should be connected to the circuit being tested _____.
   a. in series
   b. in parallel
   c. only when no power is flowing
   d. Both a and c

4. An ohmmeter should be connected to the circuit or component being tested _____.
   a. with current flowing in the circuit or through the component
   b. when connected to the battery of the vehicle to power the meter
   c. only when no power is flowing (electrically open circuit)
   d. Both b and c

5. When using a test light to probe for electrical power, the alligator clip is connected to _____.
   a. the battery negative terminal
   b. a clean metal part of the vehicle body
   c. the battery positive terminal
   d. Either a nor b

6. A meter is set to read DC volts on the 4-volt scale. The meter leads are connected at a 12-volt battery. The display will read _____.
   a. 0.00
   b. OL
   c. 12 V
   d. 0.012 V

7. What could happen if the meter leads were connected to the positive and negative terminals of the battery while the meter and leads were set to read amperes?
   a. Could blow an internal fuse or damage the meter
   b. Would read volts instead of amperes
   c. Would display OL
   d. Would display 0.00

8. When testing a diode with the multimeter set on "Diode Check," a reading of 0.6 volts is obtained. This indicates that the diode being tested is a _____.
   a. shorted diode
   b. light emitting diode (LED)
   c. silicon diode
   d. open diode

9. If a digital meter face shows 0.93 when set to read kΩ, the reading means _____.
   a. 93 ohms
   b. 930 ohms
   c. 9,300 ohms
   d. 93,000 ohms

10. A reading of 432 shows on the face of the meter set to the millivolt scale. The reading means _____.
    a. 0.432 volt
    b. 4.32 volts
    c. 43.2 volts
    d. 4,320 volts

chapter 4
OSCILLOSCOPES AND DSOs

LEARNING OBJECTIVES

After studying this chapter, the reader should be able to:

1. Compare the different types of oscilloscopes.
2. Explain how to set up and adjust an oscilloscope.
3. Compare the DC coupling and AC coupling positions on a scope.
4. Describe pulse train signals.
5. Describe scope channels and triggers.
6. Explain how to use a scope and a current clamp to diagnose an electrical circuit.
7. Describe how to analyze a waveform.

KEY TERMS

AC coupling 69
Cathode ray tube (CRT) 67
Channel 69
Current clamp 72
DC coupling 69
Digital storage oscilloscope (DSO) 67
Duty cycle 69
External trigger 70
Frequency 69
Graticule 67

Hertz 69
Oscilloscope (scope) 67
Pressure transducer 73
Pulse train 69
Pulse width 69
Pulse-width modulation (PWM) 69
Time base 68
Trigger level 71
Trigger slope 71

FIGURE 4–1 A scope display allows technicians to take measurements of voltage patterns. In this example, each vertical division is 1 volt and each horizontal division is set to represent 50 milliseconds.

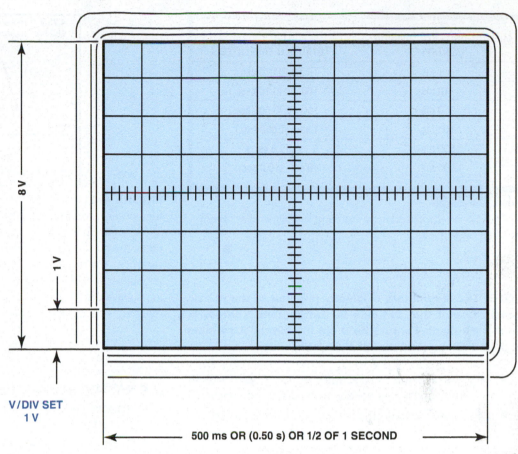

8 V

1 V

V/DIV SET 1 V

500 ms OR (0.50 s) OR 1/2 OF 1 SECOND

TIME BASE SET TO "50 ms"

TYPES OF OSCILLOSCOPES

TERMINOLOGY An **oscilloscope** (usually called a scope) is a visual voltmeter with a timer that shows when a voltage changes. Following are two types of oscilloscopes.

- An *analog scope* uses a **cathode ray tube (CRT)** similar to a television screen to display voltage patterns. The scope screen displays the electrical signal constantly.

- A *digital scope* commonly uses a liquid crystal display (LCD), but a CRT may also be used on some digital scopes. A digital scope takes samples of the signals that can be stopped or stored and is therefore called a **digital storage oscilloscope, or DSO**.

A digital scope does not capture each change in voltage, but instead captures voltage levels over time and stores them as dots. Each dot is a voltage level. Then the scope displays the waveforms using the thousands of dots (each representing a voltage level) and electrically connects the dots to create a waveform.

A DSO can be connected to a sensor output signal wire and can record the voltage signals over a long period of time. It can be replayed and a technician can see if any faults were

detected. This feature makes a DSO the perfect tool to help diagnose intermittent problems.

A digital storage scope, however, can sometimes miss faults called *glitches* that may occur between samples captured by the scope. This is why a DSO with a high "sampling rate" is preferred. Sampling rate means that a scope is capable of capturing voltage changes that occur over a very short period of time. Some digital storage scopes have a capture rate of 25 million (25,000,000) samples per second. This means that the scope can capture a glitch (fault) that lasts just 40 nano (0.00000040) seconds.

- A scope has been called "a voltmeter with a clock."
- The voltmeter part means that a scope can capture and display changing voltage levels.
- The clock part means that the scope can display these changes in voltage levels within a specific time period; and with a DSO, it can be replayed so that any faults can be seen and studied.

OSCILLOSCOPE DISPLAY GRID A typical scope face usually has eight or ten grids vertically (up and down) and ten grids horizontally (left to right). The transparent scale (grid), used for reference measurements, is called a **graticule**. This arrangement is commonly 8 × 10 or 10 × 10 divisions. ● **SEE FIGURE 4–1.**

MILLISECONDS PER DIVISION (MS/DIV)	TOTAL TIME DISPLAYED
1 ms	10 ms (0.010 sec.)
10 ms	100 ms (0.100 sec.)
50 ms	500 ms (0.500 sec.)
100 ms	1 sec. (1.000 sec.)
500 ms	5 sec. (5.0 sec.)
1,000 ms	10 sec. (10.0 sec.)

CHART 4–1

The time base is milliseconds (ms) and total time of an event that can be displayed.

NOTE: These numbers originally referred to the metric dimensions of the graticule in centimeters. Therefore, an 8 × 10 display would be 8 cm (80 mm or 3.14 inch) high and 10 cm (100 mm or 3.90 inch) wide.

- Voltage is displayed on a scope starting with zero volts at the bottom and higher voltage being displayed vertically.
- The scope illustrates time left to right. The pattern starts on the left and sweeps across the screen from left to right.

SCOPE SETUP AND ADJUSTMENT

SETTING THE TIME BASE Most scopes use 10 graticules from left to right on the display. Setting the **time base** means setting how much time will be displayed in each block called a division. For example, if the scope is set to read 2 seconds per division (referred to as *s/div*), the total time displayed would be 20 seconds (2 × 10 divisions = 20 sec.). The time base should be set to an amount of time that allows two to four events to be displayed. Milliseconds (0.001 sec.) are commonly used in scopes when adjusting the time base. Sample time is milliseconds per division (indicated as *ms/div*) and total time. ● **SEE CHART 4–1**.

NOTE: Increasing the time base reduces the number of samples per second.

The horizontal scale is divided into 10 divisions (sometimes called *grats*). If each division represents 1 second of time, the total time period displayed on the screen will be 10 seconds. The time per division is selected so that several events of the waveform are displayed. Time per division settings can vary greatly in automotive use, including:

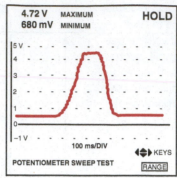

FIGURE 4–2 The digital storage oscilloscope (DSO) displays the entire waveform of the throttle position (TP) sensor from idle to wide-open and returns to idle. The display also indicates the maximum (4.72 V) and minimum (680 mV or 0.68 V) readings. The display does not show anything until the throttle is opened because the scope has been set to start displaying a waveform only after a certain voltage level has been reached. This voltage is called the trigger or trigger point.

- MAP/MAF sensors: 2 ms/div (20 ms total)
- Network (CAN) communications network: 2 ms/div (20 ms total)
- Throttle position (TP) sensor: 100 ms per division (1 sec. total)
- Fuel injector: 2 ms/div (20 ms total)
- Oxygen sensor: 1 sec. per division (10 sec. total)
- Primary ignition: 10 ms/div (100 ms total)
- Secondary ignition: 10 ms/div (100 ms total)
- Voltage measurements: 5 ms/div (50 ms total)

The total time displayed on the screen allows comparisons to see if the waveform is consistent or is changing. Multiple waveforms shown on the display at the same time also allow for measurements to be seen more easily. ● **SEE FIGURE 4–2** for an example of a throttle position sensor waveform created by measuring the voltage output as the throttle was depressed and then released.

VOLTS PER DIVISION The volts per division, abbreviated *V/div*, should be set so that the entire anticipated waveform can be viewed. Examples include:

- Throttle position (TP) sensor: 1 V/div (8 V total)
- Battery, starting and charging: 2 V/div (16 V total)
- Oxygen sensor: 200 mV/div (1.6 V total)

Notice from the examples that the total voltage to be displayed exceeds the voltage range of the component being tested. This ensures that all the waveform will be displayed. It also allows for some unexpected voltage readings. For example, an oxygen sensor should read between 0 and 1 V (1,000 mV). By setting the V/div to 200 mV, up to 1.6 V (1,600 mV) will be displayed.

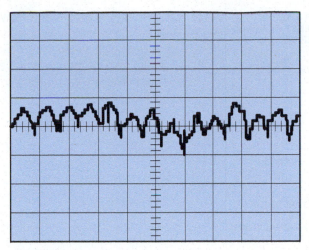

FIGURE 4–3 Ripple voltage is created from the AC voltage from an alternator. Some AC ripple voltage is normal, but if the AC portion exceeds 0.5 V, a bad diode is the most likely cause. Excessive AC ripple can cause many electrical and electronic devices to work incorrectly.

DC AND AC COUPLING

DC COUPLING **DC coupling** is the most used position on a scope because it allows the scope to display both alternating current (AC) voltage signals and direct current (DC) voltage signals present in the circuit. The AC part of the signal will ride on top of the DC component. For example, if the engine is running, and the charging voltage is 14.4 volts DC, this will be displayed as a horizontal line on the screen. Any AC ripple voltage leaking past the alternator diodes will be displayed as an AC signal on top of the horizontal DC voltage line. Therefore, both components of the signal can be observed at the same time.

AC COUPLING When the **AC coupling** position is selected, a capacitor is placed into the meter lead circuit, which effectively blocks all DC voltage signals, but allows the AC portion of the signal to pass and be displayed. AC coupling can be used to show output signal waveforms from sensors such as:

- Distributor pickup coils
- Magnetic wheel speed sensors
- Magnetic crankshaft position sensors
- Magnetic camshaft position sensors
- The AC ripple from an alternator. ● SEE FIGURE 4–3.
- Magnetic vehicle speed sensors

NOTE: Check the instructions from the scope manufacturer for the recommended settings to use. Sometimes it is necessary to switch from DC coupling to AC coupling, or from AC coupling to DC coupling, to properly see some waveforms.

PULSE TRAINS

DEFINITION Scopes can show all voltage signals. Among the most commonly found in automotive applications is a DC voltage that varies up and down and does not go below zero like an AC voltage. A DC voltage that turns on and off in a series of pulses is called a **pulse train**. Pulse trains differ from an AC signal in that they do not go below zero. An alternating voltage goes above and below zero voltage. Pulse train signals can vary in several ways. ● SEE FIGURE 4–4.

FREQUENCY **Frequency** is the number of cycles per second measured in **hertz**. The engine revolutions per minute (RPM) is an example of a signal that can occur at various frequencies. At low engine speed, the ignition pulses occur fewer times per second (lower frequency) than when the engine is operated at higher engine speeds (RPM).

DUTY CYCLE **Duty cycle** refers to the percentage of on-time of the signal during one complete cycle. As on-time increases, the amount of time the signal is off decreases and is usually measured in percentage. Duty cycle is also called **pulse-width modulation (PWM)** and can be measured in degrees. ● SEE FIGURE 4–5.

PULSE WIDTH The **pulse width** is a measure of the actual on-time measured in milliseconds. Fuel injectors are usually controlled by varying the pulse width. ● SEE FIGURE 4–6.

NUMBER OF CHANNELS

DEFINITION Scopes are available that allow the viewing of more than one sensor or event at the same time on the display. The number of events, which require leads for each, is called a **channel**. A channel is an input to a scope. Commonly available scopes include:

- **Single channel.** A single-channel scope is capable of displaying only one sensor signal waveform at a time.
- **Two channel.** A two-channel scope can display the waveform from two separate sensors or components at the same time. This feature is very helpful when testing the camshaft and crankshaft position sensors on an engine to see if they are properly timed. ● SEE FIGURE 4–7.
- **Four channel.** A four-channel scope allows the technician to view up to four different sensors or actuators on one display.
- **Eight channel.** An eight-channel scope is now available for technicians who need to view more data than can be graphed by a four-channel scope.

1. FREQUENCY—FREQUENCY IS THE NUMBER OF CYCLES THAT TAKE PLACE PER SECOND. THE MORE CYCLES THAT TAKE PLACE IN ONE SECOND, THE HIGHER THE FREQUENCY READING. FREQUENCIES ARE MEASURED IN HERTZ, WHICH IS THE NUMBER OF CYCLES PER SECOND. AN 8 HERTZ SIGNAL CYCLES EIGHT TIMES PER SECOND.

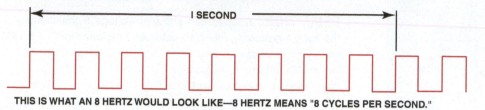

THIS IS WHAT AN 8 HERTZ WOULD LOOK LIKE—8 HERTZ MEANS "8 CYCLES PER SECOND."

2. DUTY CYCLE—DUTY CYCLE IS A MEASUREMENT COMPARING THE SIGNAL ON-TIME TO THE LENGTH OF ONE COMPLETE CYCLE. AS ON-TIME INCREASES, OFF-TIME DECREASES. DUTY CYCLE IS MEASURED IN PERCENTAGE OF ON-TIME. A 60% DUTY CYCLE IS A SIGNAL THAT'S ON 60% OF THE TIME, AND OFF 40% OF THE TIME. ANOTHER WAY TO MEASURE DUTY CYCLE IS DWELL, WHICH IS MEASURED IN DEGREES INSTEAD OF PERCENT.

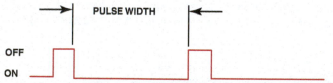

DUTY CYCLE IS THE RELATIONSHIP BETWEEN ONE COMPLETE CYCLE, AND THE SIGNAL'S ON-TIME. A SIGNAL CAN VARY IN DUTY CYCLE WITHOUT AFFECTING THE FREQUENCY.

3. PULSE WIDTH—PULSE WIDTH IS THE ACTUAL ON-TIME OF A SIGNAL, MEASURED IN MILLISECONDS. WITH PULSE WIDTH MEASUREMENTS, OFF-TIME DOESN'T REALLY MATTER—THE ONLY REAL CONCERN IS HOW LONG THE SIGNAL'S ON. THIS IS A USEFUL TEST FOR MEASURING CONVENTIONAL INJECTOR ON-TIME, TO SEE THAT THE SIGNAL VARIES WITH LOAD CHANGE.

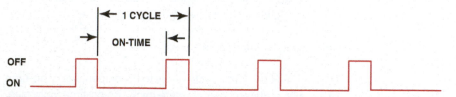

PULSE WIDTH IS THE ACTUAL TIME A SIGNAL'S ON, MEASURED IN MILLISECONDS. THE ONLY THING BEING MEASURED IS HOW LONG THE SIGNAL IS ON.

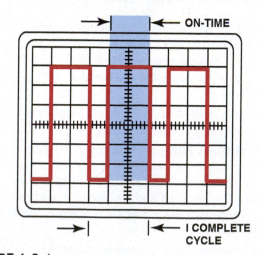

FIGURE 4–5 A scope representation of a complete cycle showing both on-time and off-time.

FIGURE 4–4 A pulse train is any electrical signal that turns on and off, or goes high and low in a series of pulses. Ignition module and fuel injector pulses are examples of a pulse train signal.

NOTE: Often the capture speed of the signals is slowed when using more than one channel.

TRIGGERS

EXTERNAL TRIGGERS An **external trigger** is when the waveform starts when a signal is received from another external source, rather than from the signal pickup lead. A common example of an external trigger comes from the probe clamp around the cylinder #1 spark plug wire to trigger the start of an ignition pattern.

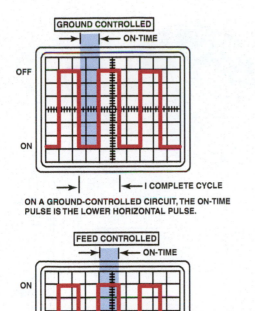

ON A GROUND-CONTROLLED CIRCUIT, THE ON-TIME
PULSE IS THE LOWER HORIZONTAL PULSE.

ON A FEED-CONTROLLED CIRCUIT, THE ON-TIME
PULSE IS THE UPPER HORIZONTAL PULSE.

FIGURE 4–6 The computer can control the device by either turning on or off the ground or power side of the component.

TRIGGER LEVEL

Trigger level is the voltage that must be detected by the scope before the pattern will be displayed. A scope will start displaying a voltage signal only when it is triggered or is told to start. The trigger level must be set to start the display. If the pattern starts at 1 volt, the trace will begin displaying on the left side of the screen *after* the trace has reached 1 volt.

TRIGGER SLOPE

The **trigger slope** is the voltage direction that a waveform must have in order to start the display. Most often, the trigger to start a waveform display is taken from the signal itself. Besides trigger voltage level, most scopes can be adjusted to trigger only when the voltage rises past the trigger level voltage. This is called a *positive slope*. When the voltage falling past the higher level activates the trigger, this is called a *negative slope*.

The scope display indicates both a positive and a negative slope symbol. For example, if a waveform, such as a magnetic sensor used for crankshaft position or wheel speed, starts moving upward, a positive slope should be selected. If a negative slope is selected, the waveform will not start showing until the voltage reaches the trigger level in a downward direction. A negative slope should be used when a fuel injector circuit is being analyzed. In this circuit, the computer provides the ground and the voltage level drops when the computer commands the injector on. Sometimes the technician needs to change from negative to positive or positive to negative trigger if a waveform is not being shown correctly. ● **SEE FIGURE 4–8.**

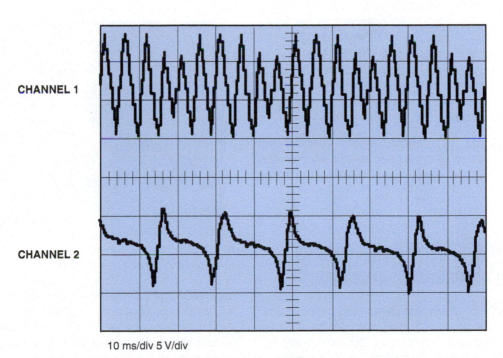

10 ms/div 5 V/div

FIGURE 4–7 A two-channel scope being used to compare the cam and crank signal.

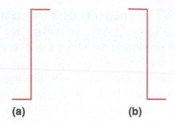

(a)   **(b)**

FIGURE 4–8 (a) A symbol for a positive trigger—a trigger occurs at a rising (positive) edge of the waveform. (b) A symbol for a negative trigger—a trigger occurs at the falling (negative) edge of the waveform.

USING A SCOPE

SCOPE LEADS Most scopes, both analog and digital, normally use the same test leads. These leads usually attach to the scope through a BNC connector, which is a miniature standard coaxial cable connector. BNC is an international standard that is used in the electronics industry. If using a BNC connector, be sure to connect one lead to a good clean metal engine ground. The probe of the scope lead attaches to the circuit or component being tested. Many scopes use one ground lead and each channel has its own signal pickup lead.

MEASURING BATTERY VOLTAGE WITH A SCOPE One of the easiest things to measure and observe on a scope is battery voltage. A lower voltage can be observed on the scope display as the engine is started, and a higher voltage should be displayed after the engine starts. ● **SEE FIGURE 4–9**.

An analog scope displays rapidly and cannot be set to show or freeze a display. Therefore, even though an analog scope shows all voltage signals, it is easy to miss a momentary glitch on an analog scope.

CAUTION: Check the instructions for the scope being used before attempting to scope household AC circuits. Some scopes are not designed to measure high-voltage AC circuits.

USING DSO ACCESSORIES

CURRENT CLAMPS A **current clamp** (also called an *amp clamp*) is an electrical probe with jaws that open to allow the clamping around an electrical conductor. The probe measures the magnetic field created by the current flow and converts it into a waveform on the scope. It can be used with a scope to

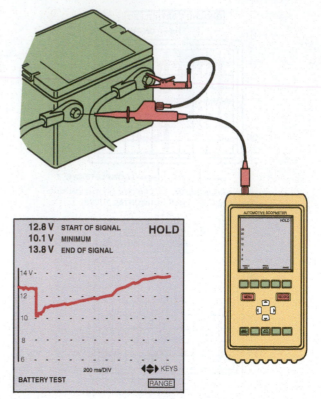

FIGURE 4–9 The battery voltage is represented by the single scope trace. The drop in voltage occurred when the vehicle was started.

FIGURE 4–10 The current clamp is being used to measure the operating current of a fuel pump.

measure AC or DC current in a circuit without disconnecting any wires or components. Current clamps, depending on their design, can measure very small current or large current flow. A current clamp can be a useful tool when diagnosing components, such as a fuel pump, a solenoid, or an electrical motor. ● **SEE FIGURE 4–10**.

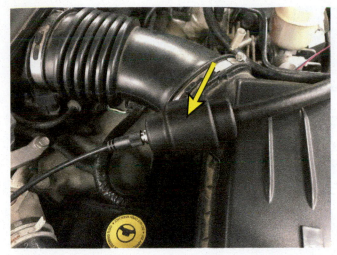

FIGURE 4–11 The relative vacuum transducer is attached to the intake manifold and is measuring the change in engine vacuum.

PRESSURE TRANSDUCERS

A **pressure transducer** is an electrical device that converts pressure into an electrical signal. Pressure transducers are divided into two categories;

1. Actual: An actual transducer measures the actual pressure of the system being tested.
2. Relative: A relative transducer measures the change in system pressure.

A pressure transducer can be used with a scope to measure operating pressures of various powertrain systems, such as fuel pressure, engine vacuum, exhaust pressure, and cylinder compression. ● SEE FIGURE 4–11.

DATA RECORDING Most oscilloscopes and DSOs have the ability to record and playback the data that is being monitored. In some cases, the recording can be saved for viewing at a later time. In a typical scenario, the technician would record the data until a malfunction was detected. The data would be saved and then reviewed in an effort to determine what failure had occurred. When looking at the data, it is important to first understand how the circuit or component is supposed to work and look for specific failures.

CAN THE CONDITION EXIST NORMALLY? When analyzing a waveform, first look to see if the condition can exist under normal operating conditions. In ● FIGURE 4–12, the coolant temperature drops from 200 degrees F to below zero and back up to almost 200 degrees F in the span of 45 seconds. There is no possible way this could happen on a normal operating engine and should therefore be a clue that something is wrong electrically. The coolant temperature voltage is at 5 volts throughout most of the graph. This is not a normal condition for a two-wire NTC thermistor circuit.

In ● FIGURE 4–13 the MAP sensor voltage is changing; however, there is not a corresponding change to the engine RPM or the MAP vacuum. On a normal operating engine, this is not possible. The change in MAP voltage would have a corresponding change in MAP vacuum and engine RPM.

LINE CHARACTERISTICS The characteristics of the line of data being recorded can be an indicator of a failure. In the example in ● FIGURE 4–14, the RPM signal is very irregular.

FIGURE 4–12 The graph shows an abnormal change in coolant temperature during the time shown.

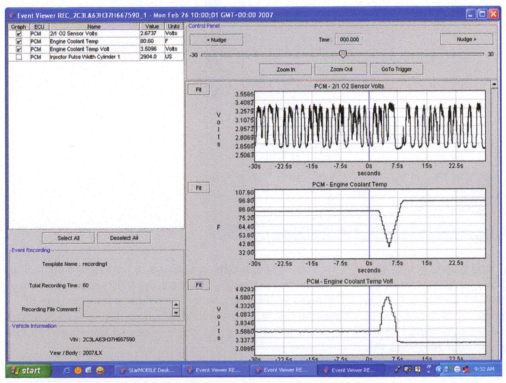

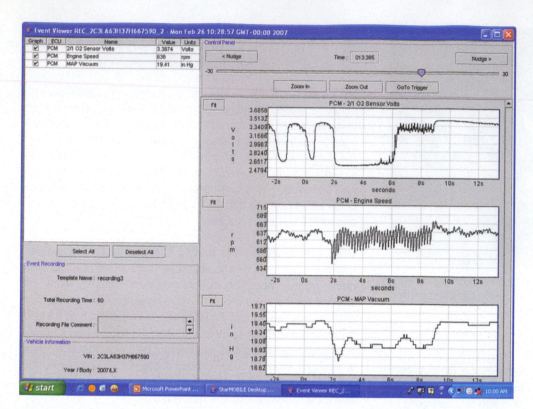

FIGURE 4–13 The change in MAP voltage without the corresponding change in MAP vacuum and engine RPM indicates a possible electrical circuit problem or a sensor failure.

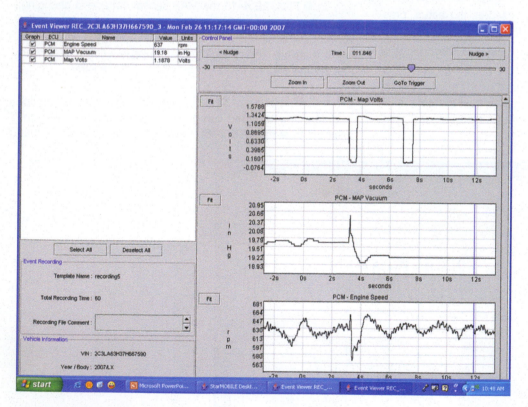

FIGURE 4–14 The sharp-toothed look of the RPM signal is an indicator of a misfire condition.

The same irregularities are also seen in the graphs of the other signals. This type of irregularity is typical of a misfire condition.

The nearly vertical change in the MAP sensor voltage in ● **FIGURE 4–15** is an indication of an electrical failure. In this case the voltage increased to source voltage, indicating an open circuit. If the voltage had dropped to near zero volts, this would have indicated a short circuit.

The RPM is dropping slowly over time before stabilizing. Note the corresponding change in the MAP vacuum and injector pulse width. The change over time is an indication of an external failure like an engine running out of fuel, as opposed to an electrical failure that would create an immediate change.

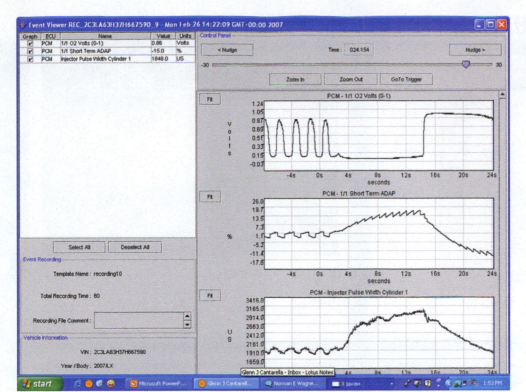

FIGURE 4–15 The increase in MAP voltage with no time change indicates an electrical malfunction.

SCOPE SETUP PHOTO SEQUENCE

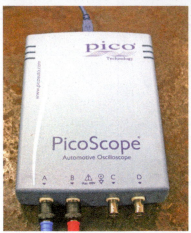

1 Plug the scope interface into the USB port on the computer.

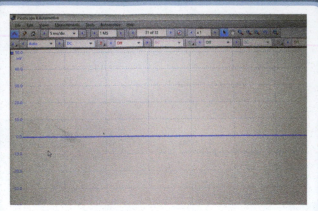

2 Start the program.

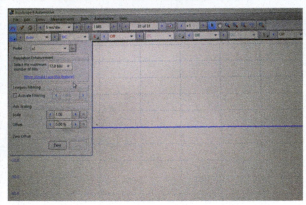

3 Select the probe for channel A.

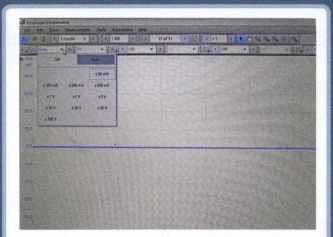

4 Select the voltage range for channel A.

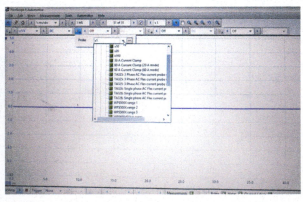

5 If more than one channel is being used, select the probe for these channels.

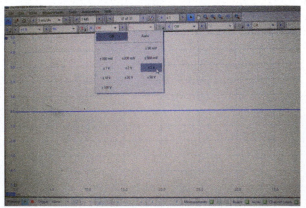

6 Select the voltage range for the additional channels.

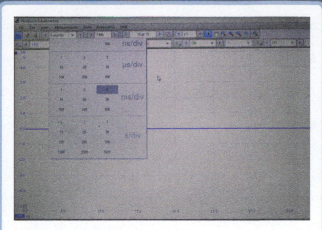

7 Select the sample rate.

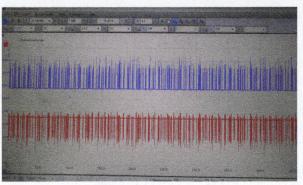

8 Capture the signal (for example, high-speed CAN bus).

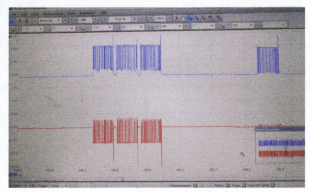

9 Zoom in on the sample to view the data.

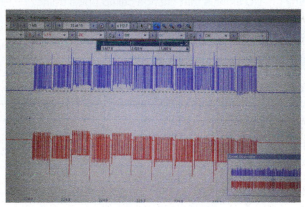

10 Use the rulers to measure the high and low voltage

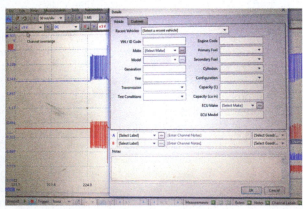

11 Save the data for future analysis.

1. Analog oscilloscopes use a cathode ray tube to display voltage patterns.

2. The waveforms shown on an analog oscilloscope cannot be stored for later viewing.

3. A digital storage oscilloscope (DSO) creates an image or waveform on the display by connecting thousands of dots captured by the scope leads.

4. An oscilloscope display grid is called a graticule. Each of the 8 × 10 or 10 × 10 dividing boxes is called a division.

5. Setting the time base means establishing the amount of time each division represents.

6. Setting the volts per division allows the technician to view either the entire waveform or just part of it.

7. DC coupling and AC coupling are two selections that can be made to observe different types of waveforms.

8. Oscilloscopes display voltage over time. A DSO can capture and store a waveform for viewing later.

REVIEW QUESTIONS

1. What are the differences between an analog and a digital oscilloscope?

2. What is the difference between DC coupling and AC coupling?

3. Why are DC signals that change called pulse trains?

4. What is the benefit of recording oscilloscope and DSO waveforms?

5. What is the purpose of a trigger when capturing data on a DSO?

CHAPTER QUIZ

1. Technician A says an analog scope can store the waveform for viewing later. Technician B says that the trigger level has to be set on most scopes to be able to view a changing waveform. Which technician is correct?
   a. Technician A only
   b. Technician B only
   c. Both Technicians A and B
   d. Neither Technician A nor B

2. An oscilloscope display is called a _____.
   a. grid
   b. graticule
   c. division
   d. box

3. A signal showing the voltage of a battery displayed on a digital storage oscilloscope (DSO) is being discussed. Technician A says that the display will show one horizontal line above the zero line. Technician B says that the display will show a line sloping upward from zero to the battery voltage level. Which technician is correct?
   a. Technician A only
   b. Technician B only
   c. Both Technicians A and B
   d. Neither Technician A nor B

4. Setting the time base to 50 ms per division will allow the technician to view a waveform how long in duration?
   a. 50 ms
   b. 200 ms
   c. 400 ms
   d. 500 ms

5. A throttle position sensor waveform is going to be observed. At what setting should the volts per division be set to see the entire waveform from 0 to 5 volts?
   a. 0.5 V/div
   b. 1.0 V/div
   c. 2.0 V/div
   d. 5.0 V/div

6. Two technicians are discussing the DC coupling setting on a DSO. Technician A says that the position allows both the DC and AC signals of the waveform to be displayed. Technician B says that this setting allows just the DC part of the waveform to be displayed. Which technician is correct?
   a. Technician A only
   b. Technician B only
   c. Both Technicians A and B
   d. Neither Technician A nor B

7. Voltage signals (waveforms) that do not go below zero are called _____.
   a. AC signals
   b. pulse trains
   c. pulse width
   d. DC coupled signals

8. Cycles per second are expressed in _____.
   a. hertz
   b. duty cycle
   c. pulse width
   d. slope

9. A TP sensor signal voltage is being observed using a digital storage oscilloscope. The pattern on the scope occasionally rises to the source voltage level. What does this indicate?
   a. A fault with the scope leads
   b. A momentary short in the TP sensor
   c. Normal operation
   d. A momentary open circuit

10. Two technicians are discussing pulse train signals. Technician A says a pulse train is a DC signal waveform that goes above and below zero volts. Technician B says that a pulse train is a DC voltage that turns on and off in a series of pulses and they do not go below zero. Which technician is correct?
    a. Technician A only
    b. Technician B only
    c. Both Technician A and Technician B
    d. Neither Technician A nor Technician B

chapter 5

GASOLINE ENGINE SYSTEMS

LEARNING OBJECTIVES

After studying this chapter, the reader should be able to:

1. Describe engine construction, parts, and systems.
2. Explain how a four-stroke cycle gasoline engine operates.
3. Describe how engine size and compression ratio are measured.
4. Define torque and horsepower.
5. Explain the purpose and function of superchargers and turbochargers.

KEY TERMS

Bore 84
Bottom dead center (BDC) 81
Cycle 81
Displacement 84
Exhaust valve 83
Four stoke cycle 81

Intake valve 81
Oil galleries 81
Piston stroke 81
Stroke 84
Top dead center (TDC) 81

FIGURE 5–1 The rotating assembly for a V-8 engine that has eight pistons and connecting rods and one crankshaft.

FIGURE 5–2 A cylinder head with four valves per cylinder, two intake valves (larger) and two exhaust valves (smaller).

ENGINE CONSTRUCTION

BLOCK All automotive and truck engines are constructed using a solid frame, called a block. A block is constructed of cast iron or aluminum and provides the foundation for most of the engine components and systems. The block is cast and then machined to very close tolerances to allow other parts to be installed.

ROTATING ASSEMBLY Pistons are installed in the block and move up and down in their respective cylinders during engine operation. Pistons are connected to **connecting rods,** which connect the pistons to the **crankshaft.** The crankshaft converts the up-and-down motion of the piston to rotary motion, which is then transmitted to the drive wheels and propels the vehicle. ● **SEE FIGURE 5–1.**

FIGURE 5–3 The coolant temperature is controlled by the thermostat, which opens and allows coolant to flow to the radiator when the temperature reaches the rating temperature of the thermostat.

CYLINDER HEADS All engines use a cylinder head to seal the top of the cylinders, which are in the engine block. The cylinder head also contains both intake valves, which allow air and fuel into the cylinder, and exhaust valves, which allow the hot gases left over to escape from the engine. Cylinder heads are constructed of cast iron or aluminum and are then machined for the valves and other valve-related components. ● **SEE FIGURE 5–2.**

ENGINE PARTS AND SYSTEMS

INTAKE AND EXHAUST MANIFOLDS Air and fuel enter the engine through the intake manifold and exit through the exhaust manifold. Intake manifolds operate cooler than exhaust manifolds and are therefore made of nylon-reinforced plastic or aluminum. Exhaust manifolds must be able to withstand hot exhaust gases, so most are constructed from cast iron or steel tubing.

COOLING SYSTEM All engines must have a cooling system to control engine temperatures. While some older engines were air cooled, all currently manufactured passenger vehicle engines are cooled by circulating antifreeze coolant through passages in the block and cylinder head. The coolant picks up the heat from the engine and after the thermostat opens, the water pump circulates the coolant through the radiator where the excess heat is released to the outside air, reducing the temperature of the coolant. The coolant is continuously circulated through the cooling system and the temperature is controlled by the thermostat. ● **SEE FIGURE 5–3.**

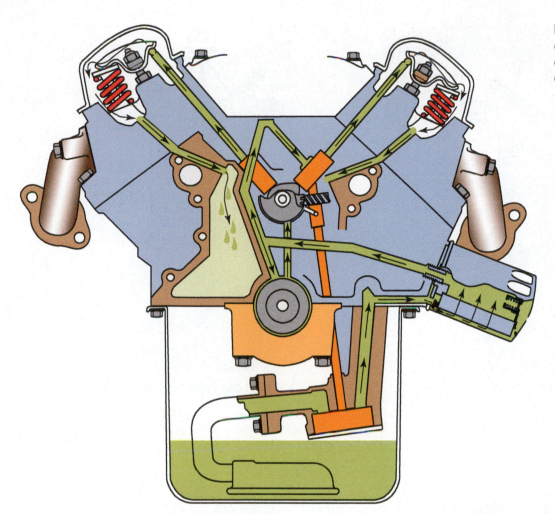

LUBRICATION SYSTEM All engines contain moving and sliding parts that must be kept lubricated to reduce wear and friction. The oil pan, bolted to the bottom of the engine block, holds 4 to 7 quarts (4 to 7 liters) of oil. An oil pump, which is driven by the engine, forces the oil through the oil filter and then into passages in the crankshaft and block to lubricate the main and rod bearings. These passages are called **oil galleries.** The oil is also forced up to the valves. The oil then moves down through openings in the cylinder head and block, and again back into the oil pan. ● **SEE FIGURE 5–4.**

FUEL SYSTEM All engines require both a fuel system to supply fuel to the cylinders and an ignition system to ignite the air–fuel mixture in the cylinders. The fuel system includes the following components:

- Fuel tank, where fuel is stored and where most fuel pumps are located
- Fuel filter and lines, which transfer the fuel for the fuel tank to the engine
- Fuel injectors, which spray fuel into the intake manifold or directly into the cylinder, depending on the type of system used.

FOUR-STROKE CYCLE OPERATION

BACKGROUND The first **four-stroke cycle** engine was developed by a German engineer, Nickolaus Otto, in 1876. Most automotive engines use the four-stroke cycle of events. The process begins by the starter motor rotating the engine until combustion takes place. The four-stroke cycle is repeated for each cylinder of the engine. ● **SEE FIGURE 5–5.**

OPERATION Engine cycles are identified by the number of piston strokes required to complete the cycle. A piston stroke is a one-way piston movement, either from top to bottom or bottom to top of the cylinder. During one stroke, the crankshaft rotates 180 degrees (1/2 revolution). A cycle is a complete series of events that continually repeats. Most automobile engines use a four-stroke cycle.

- **Intake stroke.** The **intake valve** is open and the piston inside the cylinder travels downward, drawing a mixture of air and fuel into the cylinder. The crankshaft rotates 180 degrees from **top dead center (TDC)** to **bottom dead center (BDC)** and the camshaft rotates 90 degrees.

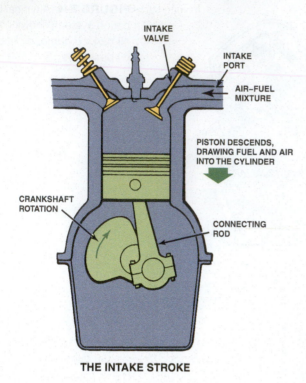

THE INTAKE STROKE

INTAKE VALVE

INTAKE PORT

AIR–FUEL MIXTURE

PISTON DESCENDS, DRAWING FUEL AND AIR INTO THE CYLINDER

CRANKSHAFT ROTATION

CONNECTING ROD

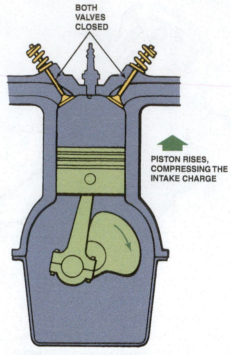

THE COMPRESSION STROKE

BOTH VALVES CLOSED

PISTON RISES, COMPRESSING THE INTAKE CHARGE

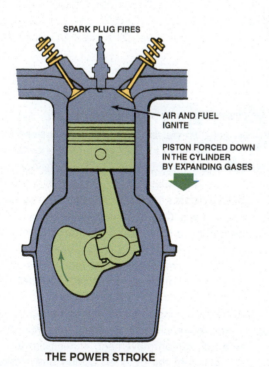

THE POWER STROKE

SPARK PLUG FIRES

AIR AND FUEL IGNITE

PISTON FORCED DOWN IN THE CYLINDER BY EXPANDING GASES

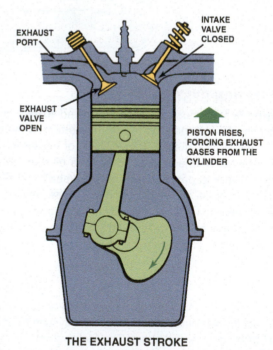

THE EXHAUST STROKE

EXHAUST PORT

INTAKE VALVE CLOSED

EXHAUST VALVE OPEN

PISTON RISES, FORCING EXHAUST GASES FROM THE CYLINDER

FIGURE 5–5 The downward movement of the piston draws the air–fuel mixture into the cylinder through the intake valve on the intake stroke. On the compression stroke, the mixture is compressed by the upward movement of the piston with both valves closed. Ignition occurs at the beginning of the power stroke, and combustion drives the piston downward to produce power. On the exhaust stroke, the upward-moving piston forces the burned gases out through the open exhaust valve.

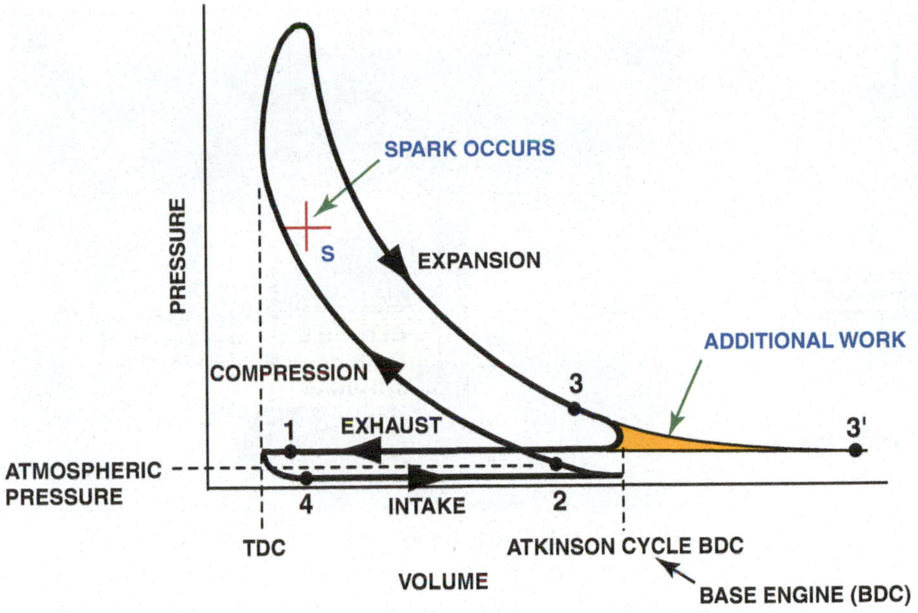

FIGURE 5–6 A pressure–volume diagram showing where additional work is generated by the delayed closing of the intake valve. Point "S" is where the spark occurs.

- **Compression stroke.** As the engine continues to rotate, the intake valve closes and the piston moves upward in the cylinder, compressing the air–fuel mixture. The crankshaft rotates 180 degrees from BDC to TDC and the camshaft rotates 90 degrees.

- **Power stroke.** When the piston gets near the top of the cylinder, the spark at the spark plug ignites the air–fuel mixture, which forces the piston downward. The crankshaft rotates 180 degrees from TDC to BDC and the camshaft rotates 90 degrees. The combustion pressure developed in the combustion chamber at the correct time will push the piston downward to rotate the crankshaft.

- **Exhaust stroke.** The engine continues to rotate, and the piston again moves upward in the cylinder. The exhaust valve opens, and the piston forces the residual burned gases out of the **exhaust valve** and into the exhaust manifold and exhaust system. The crankshaft rotates 180 degrees from BDC to TDC and the camshaft rotates 90 degrees.

This sequence repeats as the engine rotates. To stop the engine, the electricity to the ignition system is shut off by the ignition switch, which stops the spark to the spark plugs.

THE 720-DEGREE CYCLE

Each cycle (four strokes) of events requires that the engine crankshaft make two complete revolutions, or 720 degrees (360 degrees × 2 = 720 degrees). Each stroke of the cycle requires that the crankshaft rotate 180 degrees. The greater the number of cylinders, the closer together the power strokes of the individual cylinders will occur. The number of degrees that the crankshaft rotates between power strokes can be expressed as an angle. To find the angle between cylinders of an engine, divide the number of cylinders into 720 degrees.

Angle with 3 cylinders: 720/3 = 240 degrees

Angle with 4 cylinders: 720/4 = 180 degrees

Angle with 5 cylinders: 720/5 = 144 degrees

Angle with 6 cylinders: 720/6 = 120 degrees

Angle with 8 cylinders: 720/8 = 90 degrees

Angle with 10 cylinders: 720/10 = 72 degrees

This means that in a 4-cylinder engine, a power stroke occurs at every 180 degrees of the crankshaft rotation (every 1/2 rotation). A V-8 is a much smoother operating engine because a power stroke occurs twice as often (every 90 degrees of crankshaft rotation).

? FREQUENTLY ASKED QUESTION

What Is the Atkinson Cycle?

In 1882, James Atkinson, a British engineer, invented an engine that achieved a higher efficiency than the Otto cycle but produced lower power at low engine speeds. The Atkinson cycle engine was produced in limited numbers until 1890, when sales dropped, and the company that manufactured the engines finally went out of business in 1893. However, the one key feature of the Atkinson cycle that remains in use today is that the intake valve is held open longer than normal to allow a reverse flow into the intake manifold. This reduces the effective compression ratio and engine displacement and allows the expansion to exceed the compression ratio while retaining a normal compression pressure. ● **SEE FIGURE 5–6**.

This is desirable for good fuel economy because the compression ratio in a spark ignition engine is limited by the octane rating of the fuel used, while a high expansion delivers a longer power stroke and reduces the heat wasted in the exhaust. This increases the efficiency of the engine because more work is being achieved. The Atkinson cycle engine design is commonly used in hybrid electric vehicles.

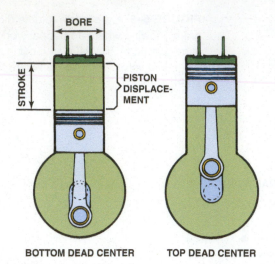

FIGURE 5–7 The bore and stroke of pistons are used to calculate an engine's displacement.

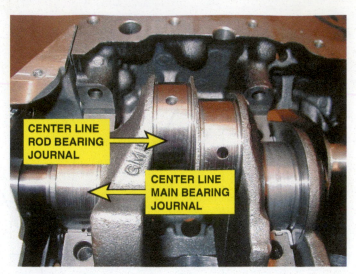

FIGURE 5–8 The distance between the centerline of the main bearing journal and the centerline of the connecting rod journal determines the stroke of the engine. This photo is a little unusual because it shows a V-6 with a splayed crankshaft used to even out the impulses on a 90-degree, V-6 engine design.

ENGINE MEASUREMENT

BORE The diameter of a cylinder is called the **bore.** The larger the bore, the greater the area on which the gases have to work. Pressure is measured in units, such as pounds per square inch (PSI). The greater the area (in square inches), the higher the force exerted by the pistons to rotate the crankshaft. ● **SEE FIGURE 5–7.**

STROKE The **stroke** of an engine is the distance the piston travels from top dead center (TDC) to bottom dead center (BDC). This distance is determined by the throw of the crankshaft. The throw is the distance from the centerline of the crankshaft to the centerline of the crankshaft rod journal. The throw is one-half of the stroke. ● **SEE FIGURE 5–8.**

The longer this distance is, the greater the amount of air–fuel mixture that can be drawn into the cylinder. The more air–fuel mixture inside the cylinder, the more force will result when the mixture is ignited.

NOTE: Changing the connecting rod length does not change the stroke of an engine. Changing the connecting rod only changes the position of the piston in the cylinder. Only the crankshaft determines the stroke of an engine.

DISPLACEMENT Engine size is described as displacement. **Displacement** is the cubic inch (cu. in.) or cubic centimeter (cc) volume displaced or how much air is moved by all of the pistons. A liter (L) is equal to 1,000 cubic centimeters; therefore, most engines today are identified by their displacement in liters.

$$1 \text{ L} = 1,000 \text{ cc}$$

$$1 \text{ L} = 61 \text{ cu. in.}$$

$$1 \text{ cu. in.} = 16.4 \text{ cc}$$

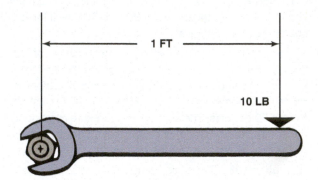

FIGURE 5–9 Torque is a twisting force equal to the distance from the pivot point times the force applied expressed in units called pound-feet (lb-ft) or newton-meters (N-m).

CONVERSION

- To convert cubic inches to liters, divide cubic inches by 61.02.
- To convert liters to cubic inches, multiply by 61.02.
- Cubic inches = Liters × 61.02

HORSEPOWER AND TORQUE

DEFINITION OF TORQUE "Torque" is the term used to describe a rotating force that may or may not result in motion.

Torque is measured as the amount of force multiplied by the length of the lever through which it acts. If you use a 1 foot long wrench to apply 10 pounds (lb) of force to the end of the wrench to turn a bolt, then you are exerting 10 pound-feet (lb-ft) of torque. ● **SEE FIGURE 5–9.**

Is Torque ft-lb or lb-ft?

Torque is a force (lb) applied to an object times the distance from that object (ft). Therefore, based on the definition of the term, "torque" should be:

- lb-ft (a force times a distance)
- Newton-meter (N-m) (a force times a distance)

However, torque is commonly labeled, even on some torque wrenches, as ft-lb.

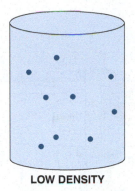

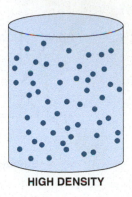

LOW DENSITY   **HIGH DENSITY**

FIGURE 5–10 The more air and fuel that can be packed in a cylinder, the greater the density of the air–fuel charge.

Torque is the twisting force measured at the end of the crankshaft and measured on a dynamometer. Engine torque is always expressed at a specific engine speed (RPM) or range of engine speeds where the torque is at the maximum. For example, an engine may be listed as producing 275 lb-ft @ 2400 RPM. The metric unit for torque is newton-meters, because the newton is the metric unit for force and the distance is expressed in meters.

1 pound-foot = 1.3558 newton-meter

1 newton-meter = 0.7376 pound-foot

DEFINITION OF POWER The term "power" means the rate of doing work. Power equals work divided by time. Work is achieved when a certain amount of mass (weight) is moved a certain distance by a force. Whether the object is moved in 10 seconds or 10 minutes, it does not make a difference in the amount of work accomplished, but it does affect the amount of power needed. Power is expressed in units of foot-pounds per minute and power also includes the engine speed (RPM) where the maximum power is achieved. For example, an engine may be listed as producing 280 HP @ 4400 RPM.

DEFINITION OF HORSEPOWER The power of one horse was determined by James Watt (1736–1819), a Scottish inventor who first calculated the power of a horse while working on a steam engine to remove water from a coal mines.

One horsepower was determined to be the power required to move 550 pounds one foot in one second or 33,000 pounds one foot in one minute (550 × 60 seconds = 33,000 pounds per minute). Engine output is measured using a dynamometer. A dynamometer measures the torque of the engine and then calculates the horsepower by the formula:

Horsepower = Torque × RPM/5252

Horsepower is always expressed with the rating and the engine speed where the maximum power was achieved. For example, an engine may be listed as producing 280 hp @ 4400 RPM.

HORSEPOWER AND ALTITUDE Because the density of air is lower at high altitude, the power that a normal engine can develop is greatly reduced at high altitude. According to SAE conversion factors, a non-supercharged or non-turbocharged engine loses about 3% of its power for every 1,000 feet (300 m) of altitude. Therefore, an engine that develops 200 brake horsepower at sea level will only produce about 116 brake horsepower at the top of Pike's Peak in Colorado at 14,110 feet (4,300 m) (3% × 14 − 42%). Supercharged and turbocharged engines are not as greatly affected by altitude as normally aspirated engines, which are those engines that breathe air at normal atmospheric pressure.

SUPERCHARGERS AND TURBOCHARGERS

PURPOSE AND FUNCTION The amount of force an air–fuel charge produces when it is ignited is largely a function of the charge density. "Charge density" is a term used to define the amount of the air–fuel charge introduced into the cylinders. Density is the mass of a substance in a given amount of space. ● **SEE FIGURE 5–10.**

What's with These Kilowatts?

A watt is the electrical unit for *power*, the capacity to do work. It is named after a Scottish inventor, James Watt (1736–1819). The symbol for power is *P*. Electrical power is calculated as amperes times volts:

P (power) = I (amperes) × E (volts)

Engine power is commonly rated in watts or kilowatts (1,000 watts equal 1 kilowatt), because 1 horsepower is equal to 746 watts. For example, a 200 horsepower engine can be rated in the metric system as having the power equal to 149,200 watts or 149.2 kilowatts (kW).

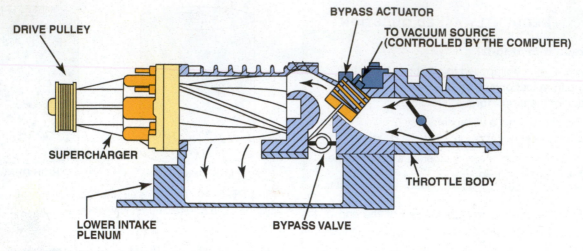

FIGURE 5–11 The bypass actuator opens the bypass valve to control boost pressure.

The greater the density of an air–fuel charge forced into a cylinder, the greater the force it produces when ignited, and the greater the engine power. An engine that uses atmospheric pressure for its intake charge is called a naturally (normally) aspirated engine. A better way to increase air density is to use some type of air pump such as a turbocharger or supercharger. When air is pumped into the cylinder, the combustion chamber receives an increase in air pressure known as boost, and can be measured in:

- Pounds per square inch (PSI)
- Atmospheres (ATM) (1 atmosphere is 14.7 PSI)
- Bars (1 bar is 14.7 PSI)

While boost pressure increases air density, friction heats air in motion and causes an increase in temperature. This increase in temperature works in the opposite direction, decreasing the air density. Because of these and other variables, an increase in pressure does not always result in greater air density.

SUPERCHARGERS

A supercharger is an engine-driven air pump that pumps more than the normal amount of air into the intake manifold and boosts engine torque and power. A supercharger provides an instantaneous increase in power without any delay. However, a supercharger, because it is driven by the engine, requires horsepower to operate and is not as efficient as a turbocharger. A supercharger is an air pump mechanically driven by the engine. Gears, shafts, chains, or belts from the crankshaft can all be used to turn the pump. This means that the air pump or supercharger pumps air in direct relation to engine speed. Many factory-installed superchargers are equipped with a bypass valve that allows intake air to flow directly into the intake manifold, bypassing the supercharger when the engine is operating at idle speed. The computer controls the bypass valve actuator. ● SEE FIGURE 5–11.

TURBOCHARGERS

A turbocharger uses the heat of the exhaust to power a turbine wheel and therefore does not directly reduce engine power. In a naturally aspirated engine,

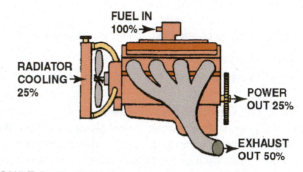

FIGURE 5–12 A turbocharger uses some of the heat energy that would normally be wasted.

about half of the heat energy contained in the fuel goes out the exhaust system. However, some engine power is lost due to the exhaust restriction. This loss in power is regained, though, to perform other work and the combustion heat energy lost in the engine exhaust (as much as 40% to 50%) can be harnessed to do useful work. Another 25% is lost through radiator cooling. Only about 25% is actually converted to mechanical power. A mechanically driven pump uses some of this mechanical output, but a turbocharger gets its energy from the exhaust gases, converting more of the fuel's heat energy into useful mechanical energy. ● SEE FIGURE 5–12.

A turbocharger turbine looks much like a typical centrifugal pump used for supercharging. Hot exhaust gases flow from the combustion chamber to the *turbine wheel*. The gases are heated and expanded as they leave the engine. It is not the force of the exhaust gases that rotates the turbine wheel, as is commonly thought, but the expansion of hot gases against the turbine wheel's blades. A turbocharger consists of two chambers connected with a center housing. The two chambers contain a turbine wheel and an *impeller* (compressor) *wheel* connected by a shaft, which passes through the center housing. ● SEE FIGURE 5–13.

To take full advantage of the exhaust heat that provides the rotating force, a turbocharger must be positioned as close as possible to the exhaust manifold. This allows the hot

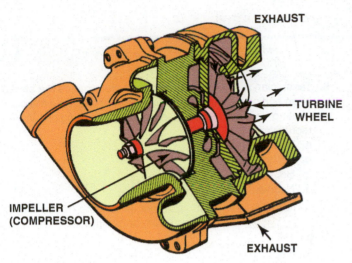

FIGURE 5–13 A turbine wheel is turned by the expanding exhaust gases.

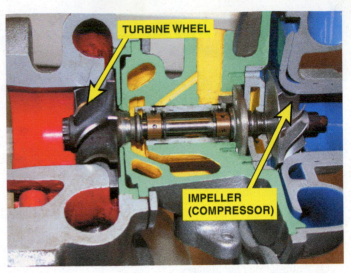

FIGURE 5–14 The exhaust drives the turbine wheel on the left, which is connected to the impeller wheel on the right through a shaft. The bushings that support the shaft are lubricated with engine oil under pressure.

exhaust to pass directly into the unit with minimal heat loss. As exhaust gas enters the turbocharger, it rotates the turbine blades. Both the turbine wheel and the compressor wheel are on the same shaft and so rotate at the same speed. Rotation of the compressor wheel draws air in through a central inlet and centrifugal force pumps it through an outlet at the edge of the housing. A pair of bearings in the center housing supports the turbine and compressor wheel shaft, and is lubricated by engine oil. ● **SEE FIGURE 5–14.**

Both the turbine and the compressor wheels must operate with extremely close clearances to minimize possible leakage around their blades. Any leakage around the turbine blades will lead to dissipation of the heat energy required for compressor rotation. Leakage around the compressor blades prevents the turbocharger from developing its full boost pressure.

SUMMARY

1. The four strokes of the four-stroke cycle are intake, compression, power, and exhaust.
2. Engine size is called displacement and represents the volume displaced by all of the pistons.
3. Engines produce torque and horsepower is then calculated from the torque, and engine speed measurements.
4. Volumetric efficiency is a comparison of the actual volume of air–fuel mixture drawn into the engine to the theoretical maximum volume that can be drawn into the cylinder.

REVIEW QUESTIONS

1. What are the strokes of a four-stroke cycle?
2. If an engine at sea level produces 100 HP, how many horsepower would it develop at an altitude of 6,000 feet?
3. What are the reasons why supercharging increases engine power?
4. What is the definition of horsepower?
5. What is the difference between a turbocharger and a supercharger?

1. What engine part converts the up and down motion of the pistons to rotary motion?
   a. Crankshaft
   b. Connecting rod
   c. Camshaft
   d. Timing gears

2. Horsepower is expressed in units of _____.
   a. pound-feet
   b. horsepower
   c. foot-pounds per minute
   d. pound-feet per second

3. One cylinder of an automotive four-stroke cycle engine completes a cycle every _____.
   a. 90 degrees
   b. 180 degrees
   c. 360 degrees
   d. 720 degrees

4. How many rotations of the crankshaft are required to complete each stroke of a four-stroke cycle engine?
   a. One-fourth
   b. One-half
   c. One
   d. Two

5. A rotating force is called _____.
   a. horsepower
   b. torque
   c. combustion pressure
   d. eccentric movement

6. Technician A says that a crankshaft determines the stroke of an engine. Technician B says that the length of the connecting rod determines the stroke of an engine. Which technician is correct?
   a. Technician A only
   b. Technician B only
   c. Both Technicians A and B
   d. Neither Technician A nor B

7. A normally aspirated automobile engine loses about _____ power per 1,000 feet of altitude.
   a. 1%
   b. 3%
   c. 5%
   d. 6%

8. Boost pressure is generally measured in _____.
   a. inch Hg
   b. PSI
   c. inch H_2O
   d. inch pound

9. At what speed does the camshaft rotate?
   a. Twice crankshaft speed
   b. Half crankshaft speed
   c. The same speed as the crankshaft
   d. One-fourth of the crankshaft speed

10. One horsepower is how many watts?
    a. 1,000
    b. 10,000
    c. 746
    d. 467

chapter 6

IN-VEHICLE ENGINE SERVICE

LEARNING OBJECTIVES

After studying this chapter, the reader should be able to:

1. Explain thermostat replacement and water pump replacement in engines.
2. Discuss intake manifold gasket inspection and replacement.
3. Describe the steps involved in timing belt replacement.
4. Explain how to inspect engine mounts.
5. Discuss hybrid engine precautions.

KEY TERMS

Engine mounts 93
EREV 93
Fretting 91

HEV 93
Idle stop 93
Skewed 90

THERMOSTAT REPLACEMENT

FAILURE PATTERNS All thermostat valves move during operation to maintain the desired coolant temperature. Thermostats can fail in the following ways:

- **Stuck open.** If a thermostat fails open or partially open, the operating temperature of the engine will be less than normal. ● **SEE FIGURE 6–1.**
- **Stuck closed.** If the thermostat fails closed or almost closed, the engine will likely overheat.
- **Stuck partially open.** This will cause the engine to warm up slowly if at all. This condition can cause the powertrain control module (PCM) to set a P0128 diagnostic trouble code (DTC), which means that the engine coolant temperature does not reach the specified temperature.
- **Skewed.** A **skewed** thermostat works, but not within the correct temperature range. Therefore, the engine could overheat or operate cooler than normal, or even do both.

REPLACEMENT PROCEDURE Before replacing the thermostat, double-check that the cooling system problem is not due to another fault, such as being low on coolant or an inoperative cooling fan. Check service information for the specified procedure to follow to replace the thermostat. Most recommended procedures include the following steps:

STEP 1 Allow the engine to cool for several hours so the engine and the coolant are at room temperature.

JIGGLE VALVE

FIGURE 6–1 If the thermostat has a jiggle valve, it should be placed toward the top to allow air to escape. If a thermostat were to become stuck open or open too soon, this can set a diagnostic trouble code P0128 (coolant temperature below thermostat regulating temperature).

STEP 2 Drain the coolant into a suitable container. Most vehicle manufacturers recommend that new coolant be used and the old coolant disposed of properly or recycled.

STEP 3 Remove any necessary components to gain access to the thermostat.

STEP 4 Remove the thermostat housing and thermostat.

STEP 5 Replace the thermostat housing gasket and thermostat. Torque all fasteners to specifications.

STEP 6 Refill the cooling system with the specified coolant and bleed any trapped air from the system.

STEP 7 Pressurize the cooling system to verify that there are no leaks around the thermostat housing.

STEP 8 Run the engine until it reaches normal operating temperature and check for leaks.

STEP 9 Verify that the engine is reaching correct operating temperature.

WATER PUMP REPLACEMENT

NEED FOR REPLACEMENT A water pump will require replacement if any of the following conditions are present:

- Coolant leaking from the weep hole
- Bearing noisy or loose
- Lack of proper coolant flow caused by worn or slipping impeller blades

REPLACEMENT GUIDELINES After diagnosis has confirmed that the water pump requires replacement, check service information for the exact procedure to follow. The steps usually include the following:

STEP 1 Allow the engine to cool to room temperature.

STEP 2 Drain the coolant and dispose of properly or recycle.

STEP 3 Remove engine components to gain access to the water pump as specified in service information.

STEP 4 Remove the water pump assembly.

STEP 5 Clean the gasket surfaces and install the new water pump, using a new gasket or seal as needed. ● **SEE FIGURE 6–2.** Torque all fasteners to factory specifications.

STEP 6 Install removed engine components.

STEP 7 Fill the cooling system with the specified coolant.

STEP 8 Run the engine, check for leaks, and verify proper operation.

FIGURE 6–2 Use caution if using a steel scraper to remove a gasket from aluminum parts. It is best to use a wood or plastic scraper.

INTAKE MANIFOLD GASKET INSPECTION

CAUSES OF FAILURE Many V-type engines leak oil and coolant, or experience an air (vacuum) leak caused by a leaking intake manifold gasket. This failure can be contributed to one or more of the following:

1. Expansion/contraction rate difference between the cast-iron head and the aluminum intake manifold can cause the intake manifold gasket to be damaged by the relative motion of the head and intake manifold. This type of failure is called **fretting**.
2. Plastic (Nylon 6.6) gasket deterioration caused by the coolant. ● **SEE FIGURE 6–3.**

DIAGNOSIS OF LEAKING INTAKE MANIFOLD GASKET Because intake manifold gaskets are used to seal oil, air, and coolant in most cases, determining that the intake manifold gasket is the root cause can be a challenge. To diagnose a possible leaking intake manifold gasket, perform the following tests:

Visual inspection. Check for evidence of oil or coolant between the intake manifold and the cylinder heads.

Coolant level. Check the coolant level and determine if the level has been dropping. A leaking intake manifold gasket can cause coolant to leak and then evaporate, leaving no evidence of the leak.

Air (vacuum) leak. If there is a stored diagnostic trouble code (DTC) for a lean exhaust (P0171, P0172, or P0174), a leaking intake manifold gasket could be the cause. Use propane to check if the engine changes

FIGURE 6–3 An intake manifold gasket that failed and allowed coolant to be drawn into the cylinder(s).

when dispensed around the intake manifold gasket. If the engine changes in speed or sound, then this test verifies that an air leak is present.

INTAKE MANIFOLD GASKET REPLACEMENT

When replacing the intake manifold gasket, always check service information for the exact procedure to follow. The steps usually include the following:

STEP 1 Be sure the engine has been off for about an hour and drain the coolant into a suitable container.

STEP 2 Remove covers and other specified parts needed to access to the retaining bolts.

STEP 3 To help ensure that the manifold does not warp when removed, loosen all fasteners in the reverse order of the tightening sequence. This means that the bolts should be loosened starting at the ends and working toward the center.

STEP 4 Remove the upper intake manifold (plenum), if equipped, and inspect for faults. ● **SEE FIGURES 6–4 AND 6–5.**

STEP 5 Remove the lower intake manifold, using the same bolt removal procedure starting at the ends and working toward the center.

STEP 6 Thoroughly clean the area and replace the intake manifold if needed. Check that the correct replacement manifold is being used, since even the current part could look different from the original. ● **SEE FIGURE 6–6.**

STEP 7 Install the intake manifold using new gaskets as specified. Some designs use gaskets that are reusable. Replace as needed.

STEP 8 Torque all fasteners to factory specifications and in the proper sequences. The tightening sequences usually start at the center and work outward to the ends.

FIGURE 6–4 The lower intake manifold attaches to the cylinder heads.

FIGURE 6–5 The upper intake manifold, often called a plenum, attaches to the lower intake manifold.

CAUTION: Double-check the torque specifications and be sure to use the correct values. Many intake manifolds use fasteners that are torqued to values expressed in pound-inches and not pound-feet.

STEP 9 Reinstall all parts needed to allow the engine to start and run, including refilling the coolant if needed.

STEP 10 Start the engine and check for leaks and proper engine operation.

STEP 11 Reset or relearn the idle if specified, using a scan tool.

STEP 12 Install all of the remaining parts and perform a test-drive to verify proper operation and no leaks.

STEP 13 Check and replace the air filter if needed.

STEP 14 Change the engine oil if the intake manifold leak could have caused coolant to leak into the engine, which would contaminate the oil.

SPRING-LOAD
PRESSURE-RELIEF VALVE

FIGURE 6–6 Some plastic intake manifolds are equipped with a pressure relief valve that would open in the event of a backfire condition to prevent the higher internal pressures from causing damage to the manifold.

TIMING BELT REPLACEMENT

NEED FOR REPLACEMENT Timing belts have a limited service and a specified replacement interval ranging from 60,000 miles (97,000 km) to about 100,000 miles (161,000 km). Timing belts are required to be replaced if any of the following conditions occur:

- Meets or exceeds the vehicle manufacturer's recommended timing belt replacement interval.
- The timing belt has been contaminated with coolant or engine oil.
- The timing belt has failed (missing belt teeth or broken).

TIMING BELT REPLACEMENT GUIDELINES Before replacing the timing belt, check service information for the recommended procedure to follow. Most timing belt replacement procedures include the following steps:

STEP 1 Allow the engine to cool before starting to remove components to help eliminate the possibility of personal injury or warpage of the parts.

STEP 2 Remove all necessary components to gain access to the timing belt and timing marks.

STEP 3 If the timing belt is not broken, rotate the engine until the camshaft and crankshaft timing marks are aligned according to the specified marks. ● **SEE FIGURE 6–7.**

STEP 4 Loosen or remove the tensioner as needed to remove the timing belt.

FIGURE 6–7 A single overhead camshaft engine with a timing belt that also rotates the water pump.

STEP 5 Replace the timing belt and any other recommended items. Components that some vehicle manufacturers recommend replacing in addition to the timing belt include:

- Tensioner assembly
- Water pump
- Camshaft oil seal(s)
- Front crankshaft seal

STEP 6 Check (verify) that the camshaft timing is correct by rotating the engine several revolutions.

STEP 7 Install enough components to allow the engine to start to verify proper operation. Check for any leaks, especially if seals have been replaced.

STEP 8 Complete the reassembly of the engine and perform a test-drive before returning the vehicle to the customer.

ENGINE MOUNT REPLACEMENT

TERMINOLOGY **Engine mounts,** also called *motor mounts* or *powertrain mounts,* are used to attach the engine (or transmission/transaxle) to the body or frame of the vehicle. They are designed to perform the following functions:

- Support the weight and torque of the engine or powertrain
- Isolate engine noise and vibrations from the body or frame of the vehicle.

CASE STUDY

The Case of the Shaking Chrysler

The owner of a Chrysler Pacifica complained that the vehicle would shake and a loud knock sound was heard when decelerating, but everything seemed to be normal if the vehicle was accelerated slowly. Everything seemed to be fine when driven in reverse. The technician was able to confirm the situation and felt that an engine mount had failed. A visual inspection confirmed that the mount was torn. Replacing the engine mount solved the vibration problem. ● **SEE FIGURE 6–8.**

Summary:

- **Complaint**—Owner complained that the vehicle would shake during rapid acceleration and a loud knock sound was heard during deceleration.
- **Cause**—The engine mount was found to be defective due to fluid leaking from the mount.
- **Correction**—The engine mount was replaced and this corrected the customer concern.

INSPECTION OF ENGINE MOUNTS Engine mounts are made from rubber attached to a steel backing on both sides. One side is attached to the engine and the other side is attached to the body or frame of the vehicle. The mounts are often fluid filled to help dampen and absorb engine vibrations. These are not transferred to the body of the vehicle. Check the mounts by carefully checking for the following:

- Obvious damage or fluid leakage
- Loose or damaged fasteners

With an assistant to help, start the engine and with the hood open, look for excessive movement of the engine when the transmission selector is moved from drive to reverse and back to drive. Excessive movement may indicate a worm engine or powertrain mount.

HYBRID ENGINE PRECAUTIONS

HYBRID VEHICLE ENGINE OPERATION Gasoline engines used in **hybrid electric vehicles (HEVs)** and in **extended range electric vehicles (EREVs)** can be a hazard to be around under some conditions. These vehicles are designed to stop the gasoline engines unless needed. This feature is called **idle stop.** This means that the engine is not running, but could start at any time if the computer detects the need to charge the hybrid batteries, or any other issue that requires the gasoline engine to start and run.

(a)

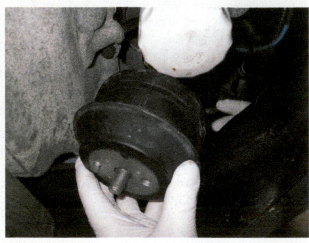

(b)

FIGURE 6–8 (a) The old front engine mount contained hydraulic fluid. The oil was leaking from a split in the mount. (b) The new original equipment (OE) mount ready to be installed.

PRECAUTIONS Always check service information for the exact procedures to follow when working around or under the hood of a hybrid electric vehicle. These precautions could include the following:

- Before working under the hood or around the engine, be sure that the ignition is off and the key is out of the ignition.
- Check that the "Ready" light is off. ● **SEE FIGURE 6–9.**
- Do not touch any circuits that have orange electrical wires or conduit. The orange color indicates dangerous high-voltage wires, which could cause serious injury or death if touched.
- Always use high-voltage linesman's gloves whenever de-powering the high-voltage system.

HYBRID ENGINE SERVICE The gasoline engine in most hybrid electric vehicles specifies low viscosity engine oil as a

FIGURE 6–9 A Toyota/Lexus hybrid electric vehicle has a ready light. If the ready light is on, the engine can start at anytime without warning.

FIGURE 10–10 Always use the viscosity of oil specified on the oil fill cap.

way to achieve maximum fuel economy. ● **SEE FIGURE 6–10.** he viscosity required is often:

- SAE 0W-16
- SAE 0W-20
- SAE 5W-20

Many shops do not keep this viscosity in stock so preparations need to be made to obtain and use the specified engine oil.

In addition to engine oil, some hybrid electric vehicles, such as the Honda Insight (1999–2004), require special spark plugs. Check service information for the specified service procedures and parts needed if a hybrid electric vehicle is being serviced.

1 Before starting the process of adjusting the valves, look up the specifications and exact procedures. The technician is checking for information.

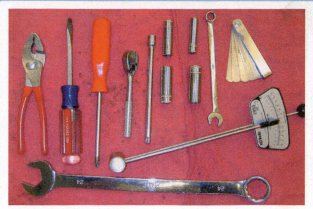

2 The tools necessary to adjust the valves on an engine with adjustable rocker arms include basic hand tools, feeler gauge, and a torque wrench.

3 An overall view of the 4-cylinder engine that is due for a scheduled valve adjustment, according to the vehicle manufacturer's recommendations.

4 Start the valve adjustment procedure by first disconnecting and labeling, if necessary, all vacuum lines that need to be removed to gain access to the valve cover.

5 The air intake tube is being removed from the throttle body.

6 With all vacuum lines and the intake tube removed, the valve cover can be removed after removing all retaining bolts.

CONTINUED ▶

7 Notice how clean the engine appears. This is a testament of proper maintenance and regular oil changes by the owner.

8 To help locate how far the engine is being rotated, the technician is removing the distributor cap to be able to observe the position of the rotor.

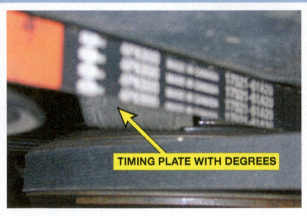

TIMING PLATE WITH DEGREES

9 The engine is rotated until the timing marks on the front of the crankshaft line up with zero degrees—top dead center (TDC)—with both valves closed on #1 cylinder.

10 With the rocker arms contacting the base circle of the cam, insert a feeler gauge of the specified thickness between the camshaft and the rocker arm. There should be a slight drag on the feeler gauge.

11 If the valve clearance (lash) is not correct, loosen the retaining nut and turn the valve adjusting screw with a screwdriver to achieve the proper clearance.

12 After adjusting the valves that are closed, rotate the engine one full rotation until the engine timing marks again align.

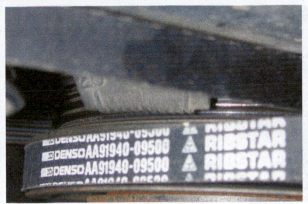

13 The engine is rotated until the timing marks again align, indicating that the companion cylinder will now be in position for valve clearance measurement.

14 On some engines, it is necessary to watch the direction the rotor is pointing to help determine how far to rotate the engine. Always follow the vehicle manufacturer's recommended procedure.

15 The technician is using a feeler gauge that is one-thousandth of an inch thinner and another one thousandth of an inch thicker than the specified clearance as a double-check that the clearance is correct.

16 Adjusting a valve takes both hands—one to hold the wrench to loosen and tighten the lock nut and another to turn the adjusting screw. Always double-check the clearance after an adjustment is made.

17 After all valves have been properly measured and adjusted as necessary, start the reassembly process by replacing all gaskets and seals as specified by the vehicle manufacturer.

18 Reinstall the valve cover being careful to not pinch a wire or vacuum hose between the cover and the cylinder head.

CONTINUED ▶

19 Use a torque wrench and torque the valve cover retaining bolts to factory specifications.

20 Reinstall the distributor cap.

21 Reinstall the spark plug wires and all brackets that were removed to gain access to the valve cover.

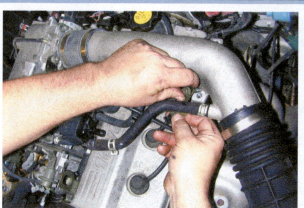

22 Reconnect all vacuum and air hoses and tubes. Replace any vacuum hoses that are brittle or swollen with new ones.

23 Be sure that the clips are properly installed. Start the engine and check for proper operation.

24 Double-check for any oil or vacuum leaks after starting the engine.

SUMMARY

1. Thermostats can fail in the following ways:
   - Stuck open
   - Stuck closed
   - Stuck partially open
   - Skewed

2. A water pump should be replaced if any of the following conditions are present:
   - Leaking from the weep hole
   - Noisy bearing
   - Loose bearing
   - Lack of normal circulation due to worn impeller blades

3. A leaking intake manifold gasket can cause coolant to get into the oil or oil into the coolant, as well as other faults, such as a poor running engine.

4. When a timing belt is replaced, most vehicle manufacturers also recommend that the following items be replaced:
   - Tensioner assembly
   - Water pump
   - Camshaft seal(s)
   - Front crankshaft seal

5. When working on a Toyota/Lexus hybrid electric vehicle (HEV), be sure that the key is off and out of the ignition and the READY light is off.

REVIEW QUESTIONS

1. How can a thermostat fail?
2. How can a water pump fail requiring replacement?
3. What will happen to the engine if the intake manifold gasket fails?
4. Why must timing belts be replaced?
5. Why is it important that the READY light be out on the dash before working under the hood of a hybrid electric vehicle?

CHAPTER QUIZ

1. A thermostat can fail in which way?
   - a. Stuck open
   - b. Stuck closed
   - c. Stuck partially open
   - d. Any of the above

2. A skewed thermostat means it is _____.
   - a. working, but not at the correct temperature
   - b. not working
   - c. missing the thermo wax in the heat sensor
   - d. contaminated with coolant

3. Coolant drained from the cooling system when replacing a thermostat or water pump should be _____.
   - a. reused
   - b. disposed of properly or recycled
   - c. filtered and reinstalled after the repair
   - d. poured down a toilet

4. A water pump can fail to provide the proper amount of flow of coolant through the cooling system if what has happened?
   - a. The coolant is leaking from the weep hole.
   - b. The bearing is noisy.
   - c. The impeller blades are worn or slipping on the shaft.
   - d. A bearing failure has caused the shaft to become loose.

5. Intake manifold gaskets on a V-type engine can fail due to what factor?
   - a. Fretting
   - b. Coolant damage
   - c. Relative movement between the intake manifold and the cylinder head
   - d. All of the above

6. A defective thermostat can cause the powertrain control module to set what diagnostic trouble code (DTC)?
   a. P0171
   b. P0172
   c. P0128
   d. P0300

7. The engine is attached to the vehicle using _____.
   a. motor mounts
   b. engine cables
   c. engine rods
   d. engine blocks

8. The torque specifications for many plastic intake manifolds are in what unit?
   a. Pound-inches
   b. Pound-feet
   c. Ft-lb per minute
   d. Lb-ft per second

9. When replacing a timing belt, many experts and vehicle manufacturers recommend that what other part(s) be replaced?
   a. Tensioner assembly
   b. Water pump
   c. Camshaft oil seal(s)
   d. All of the above

10. Hybrid electric vehicles usually require special engine oil of what viscosity?
   a. SAE 5W-30
   b. SAE 10W-30
   c. SAE 0W-20
   d. SAE 5W-40

chapter 7

VALVE TRAIN AND VARIABLE VALVE TIMING DIAGNOSIS

LEARNING OBJECTIVES

After studying this chapter, the reader should be able to:

1. Describe the purpose and function of the camshaft and camshaft design.
2. Explain how to diagnose valve train faults.
3. Explain the operation of the variable valve timing and variable lift
4. Explain how to diagnose faults with the variable valve timing system.
5. Describe the Atkinson cycle and why it is used on many hybrid electric vehicles.
6. Explain the operation of cylinder deactivation systems.
7. Explain how to diagnose faults with cylinder deactivation systems.

KEY TERMS

Atkinson cycle 109

Oil control valve (OCV) 104

Pulse-width modulation (PWM) 106

Spline phaser 106

Vane phaser 106

Variable cam timing (VCT) 104

Variable displacement system 113

Variable Valve Timing and Lift Electronic Control (VTEC) 110

Variable valve timing (VVT) 104

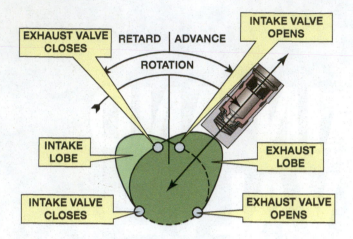

FIGURE 7–1 A camshaft uses lobes to open the valves and is timed to the crankshaft so that the opening and closing of the valves occur at the proper time.

ENGINE VALVETRAIN

PURPOSE AND FUNCTION The purpose of the valvetrain is to allow air or an air–fuel mixture to enter and exit the combustion chamber. The operation of the valvetrain involves many factors such as:

- The distance the valves open
- The timing of when the valves are opened and closed
- The duration of the opening and closing of the valves.

CAMSHAFT The major function of a camshaft is to open the valves. Camshafts have eccentric shapes called *lobes* that open the valve against the force of the valve springs. The valve spring closes the valve when the camshaft rotates off of the lobe. The camshaft lobe changes rotary motion (camshaft) to linear motion (valves). Cam shape or contour is the major factor in determining the operating characteristics of the engine. Cam lobe shape has more control over engine performance characteristics than any other single engine part. Engines identical in every way except cam lobe shape may have completely different operating characteristics and performance. ● **SEE FIGURE 7–1.**

CAMSHAFT TIMING The camshaft is driven by:

- Timing gears
- Timing chains
- Timing belts ● **SEE FIGURE 7–2.**

The gear or sprocket on the camshaft has twice as many teeth, or notches, as the one on the crankshaft. This results in two crankshaft revolutions for each revolution of the camshaft. The camshaft turns at one-half the crankshaft speed in all four-stroke cycle engines. ● **SEE FIGURE 7–3.**

NORMAL VALVE TIMING Cam timing specifications are stated in terms of the angle of the crankshaft in relation to

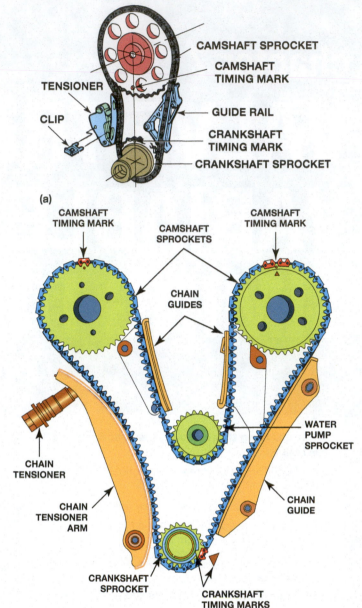

(a)

(b)

FIGURE 7–2 (a) A typical overhead valve (OHV) cam-in-block engine timing chain showing the timing marks. (b) An overhead camshaft (OHC) engine showing the water pump sprocket and hydraulic chain tensioners.

top dead center (TDC) or bottom dead center (BDC) when the valves open and close.

- **Intake valve.** The intake valves should open slightly before the piston reaches TDC and starts down on the intake stroke. This ensures that the valve is fully open when the piston travels downward on the intake stroke. The flow through a partially open valve (especially a valve ground at 45° instead of 30°) is greatly reduced as compared with that when the valve is in its fully open position. The intake valve closes after the piston reaches BDC because the air-fuel mixture has inertia, or the tendency of matter to remain in motion. Even after the piston stops traveling downward on the intake stroke and starts upward on the compression stroke, the inertia of the air–fuel mixture can still be used to

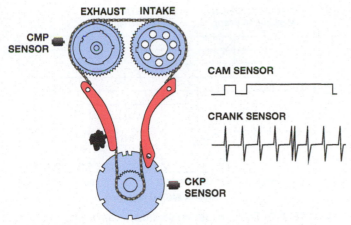

FIGURE 7–3 The crankshaft–camshaft relationship can be viewed using a scope connected to the crankshaft position (CKP), bottom trace, sensor and the camshaft (CMP) position sensor.

draw in additional charge. Typical intake valve specifications are to open at 19° before top dead center (BTDC) and close at 46° after bottom dead center (ABDC).

- **Exhaust valve.** The exhaust valve opens while the piston is traveling down on the power stroke, before the piston starts up on the exhaust stroke. Opening the exhaust valve before the piston starts up on the exhaust stroke ensures that the combustion pressure is released and the exhaust valve is mostly open when the piston starts up. The exhaust valve does not close until after the piston has traveled past TDC and is starting down on the intake stroke. Because of inertia of the exhaust, some of the burned gases continue to flow out the exhaust valve after the piston is past TDC. This can leave a partial vacuum in the combustion chamber to start pulling in the fresh charge. This partial vacuum is called scavenging and helps bring in a fresh air–fuel charge into the cylinders. Typical exhaust valve specifications are to open at 49° before bottom dead center (BBDC) and close at 22° after top dead center (ATDC). ● **SEE FIGURE 7–4.**

VALVE TRAIN PROBLEM DIAGNOSIS

SYMPTOMS A camshaft with a partially worn lobe is often difficult to diagnose. Sometimes a valve "tick, tick, tick" noise is heard if the cam lobe is worn. The ticking noise can be

FIGURE 7–5 The cause of a misfire diagnostic trouble code was discovered to be a pushrod that had worn through the rocker arm on a General Motors 3.4 liter V-6 engine.

intermittent, which makes it harder to determine the cause. If the engine has an overhead camshaft (OHC), it is usually relatively easy to remove the cam cover and make a visual inspection of all cam lobes and the rest of the valve train. In an overhead valve (OHV) engine, the camshaft is in the block, where easy visual inspection is not possible. However, it is always wise to perform a visual inspection. ● **SEE FIGURE 7–5.**

VALVE NOISE DIAGNOSIS Valve lifters are often noisy, especially at engine start-up. When the engine is off, some valves are open. The valve spring pressure forces the inner plunger to leak down (oil is forced out of the lifter). Therefore, many vehicle manufacturers consider valve ticking at one half engine speed after start-up to be normal, especially if the engine is quiet after 10 to 30 seconds. Be sure that the engine is equipped with the correct oil filter, and that the filter has an internal check valve. If in doubt, use an original equipment oil filter. If all of the valves are noisy, check the oil level. If low, the oil may have been aerated (air mixed with the oil), which would prevent proper operation of the hydraulic lifter. Aeration can be caused by:

- Low oil pressure, which can also cause all valves to be noisy
- The oil level being too high, which can also cause noisy valve lifters (The crankshaft counterweights create foam as they rotate through the oil. This foam can travel

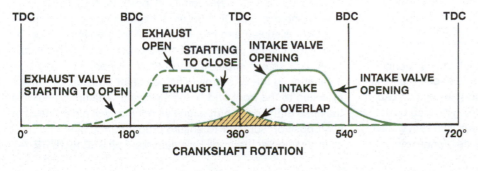

CRANKSHAFT ROTATION

FIGURE 7–4 Graphic representation of a typical camshaft showing the relationship between the intake and exhaust valves. The shaded area represents the overlap period of 100°.

through the oiling systems to the lifters. The foam in the lifters prevents normal operation and allows the valves to make noise.)

If the valves are abnormally noisy, remove the valve cover and use a stethoscope to listen or apply pressure to the rocker arms to determine which valves or valve train parts may be causing the noise. Check for all of the following items:

- Valve lash too loose
- Worn camshaft lobe
- Dirty, stuck, or worn lifters
- Worn rocker arm (if the vehicle is so equipped)
- Worn rocker arm shaft
- Worn or bent pushrods (if the vehicle is so equipped)
- Broken or weak valve springs
- Sticking or warped valves

Any of the above can cause the engine to idle roughly, misfire, or even backfire during acceleration.

VARIABLE VALVE TIMING

PURPOSE OF VARIABLE VALVE TIMING Conventional camshafts are permanently synchronized to the crankshaft so that they operate the valves at a specific point in each combustion cycle. In an engine, the intake valve opens slightly before the piston reaches the top of the cylinder and closes about 60° after the piston reaches the bottom of the stroke on every cycle, regardless of the engine speed or load.

VARIABLE VALVE TIMING SYSTEMS **Variable valve timing (VVT)** involves the use of electric and hydraulic actuators that are used to change the timing of the camshaft(s) in relation to the crankshaft. Variable valve timing, also called **variable cam timing (VCT)**, allows the valves to be operated at different points in the combustion cycle to improve performance.

There are four basic types of variable valve timing (VVT) used on engines:

- **Exhaust only** An engine that uses variable valve timing on the exhaust only is used to create an EGR affect, thereby eliminating the need for an exhaust gas recirculation (EGR) valve. In this system, the exhaust valve is retarded when the engine is operating at part throttle. This delays the closing of the exhaust valves which allows exhaust gases to be trapped in the combustion chamber. ● SEE FIGURE 7–6.
- **Intake only** Changing the intake camshaft timing results in improved engine performance. This is due to commanding the intake valve to close earlier in the compression stroke, resulting in less of the air/fuel charge being pushed back into the intake port (reversions). The result is improved low speed torque that the engine can produce. For example:

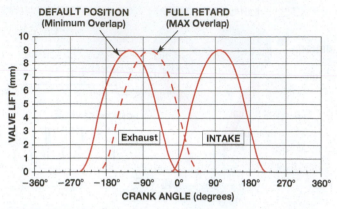

FIGURE 7–6 The exhaust only variable cam timing systems allow the overlap period where both valves are open to be changed. The at-rest position provides little valve overlap, whereas the maximum overlap allows for internal EGR needed to reduce NO_x exhaust emissions.

- Advancing the intake valve opening from 70° to 80° BTDC improves low speed engine torque.
- Retarding the intake valve opening to 65° BTDC instead of 80° BTDC helps the engine produce greater high-speed power.

- **Cam-in-block** Some overhead valve (OHV) engines that use a single camshaft to control the valves are equipped with a phaser that allows the cam to be rotated in relation to the crankshaft to achieve variable valve timing. The powertrain control module (PCM) retards the camshaft to achieve exhaust gases so an EGR valve is not needed to meet NO_x exhaust emissions. The camshaft can be changed to create a broad engine torque range and improved fuel economy.

- **Both Intake and Exhaust Cams** Many double overhead camshaft (DOHC) engines use variable valve timing on both the intake and the exhaust camshafts. By varying both camshafts, the engine torque is increased over a wide engine speed range. This allows the PCM to control the amount of exhaust gases trapped in the combustion chamber to control the formation of oxides of nitrogen (NO_x) emissions. This is achieved by allowing the intake valve(s) to open sooner or the exhaust valve(s) to stay open longer. ● SEE CHART 7–1.

PARTS AND OPERATION The camshaft position actuator **oil control valve (OCV)** directs oil from the oil feed in the head to the appropriate camshaft position actuator oil passages. There is one OCV for each camshaft position actuator. The OCV is sealed and mounted to the front cover. The ported end of the OCV is inserted into the cylinder head with a sliding fit. A filter screen protects each OCV oil port from any contamination in the oil supply. The camshaft position actuator is mounted to the front end of the camshaft. The timing notch in the nose of the camshaft aligns with the dowel pin in the camshaft position actuator to ensure proper cam timing and camshaft position actuator oil hole alignment. ● SEE FIGURE 7–7.

CAMSHAFT POSITION CHART			
DRIVING CONDITION	CHANGE IN CAMSHAFT POSITION	OBJECTIVE	RESULT
Idle	No change	Minimize valve overlap	Stabilize idle speed
Light engine load	Retard valve timing	Decrease valve overlap	Stable engine output
Medium engine load	Advance valve timing	Increase valve overlap	Better fuel economy with lower emissions
Low to medium RPM with heavy load	Advance valve timing	Advance intake valve closing	Improve low to midrange torque
High RPM with heavy load	Retard valve timing	Retard intake valve closing	Improve engine output

CHART 7–1

An overview of how variable valve timing is able to improve engine performance and reduce exhaust emissions.

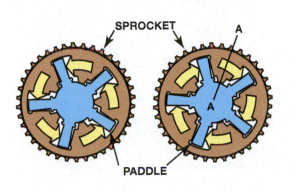

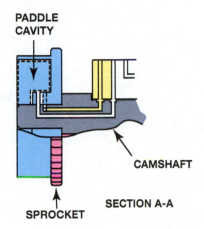

FIGURE 7–7 Camshaft rotation during advance and retard.

TERMINOLOGY USED BY MANUFACTURERS Variable valve timing systems are known by many different terms, depending on the vehicle manufacturer. These terms include:

- **BMW** VANOS (Variable Nockenwellen Steuerung)
- **Ford** VVT (Variable Valve Timing)
- **GM** DCVCP (Double Continuous Variable Cam Phasing), if used for both intake and exhaust camshafts
- **Honda** VTEC (Variable valve Timing and lift Electronic Control)
- **Hyundai** MPI CVVT (Multiport Injection Continuously Variable Valve Timing)
- **Mazda** S-VT (Sequential Valve Timing)
- **Mitsubishi** MIVECC (Mitsubishi Innovative Valve Timing Electronic Control system)
- **Nissan** N-VCTT (Nissan Variable Control Timing)
- **Nissan** VVL (Variable Valve Lift)
- **Porsche** Variocam (Variable camshaft timing)
- **Suzuki** VVT (Variable Valve Timing)
- **Subaru** AVCS (Active Valve Control System)
- **Toyota** VVT-i (Variable Valve Timing-intelligent)
- **Toyota** VVTL-i (Variable Valve Timing and Lift-intelligent)
- **Volkswagen** VVT (Variable Valve Timing)
- **Volvo** VVT (Variable Valve Timing)

OHV VARIABLE VALVE TIMING

EXAMPLES The GM 3900 V-6 engine, the Chrysler 5.7 and 6.2-liter V-8s, and the V-10 engines are an example of an overhead valve (OHV) cam-in-block engine that uses variable valve timing (VVT). The variable valve timing system uses an electronically controlled, hydraulic gear–driven cam phaser that can alter the relationship of the camshaft from 15° retard to 25° advance (40° overall) relative to the crankshaft. By using variable valve timing (VVT), engineers were able to eliminate the EGR valve and still be able to meet the standards for oxides of nitrogen (NO_x). The VVT also works in conjunction with an active manifold that gives the engine a broader torque curve. A valve in the intake manifold creates a longer path for intake air at low speeds, improving combustion efficiency and torque output. At higher speeds, the valve opens creating a shorter air path for maximum power production. Varying the exhaust and/or the intake camshaft position allows for reduced exhaust emissions and improved performance. By varying the exhaust cam phasing, vehicle manufacturers are able to meet newer NO_x reduction standards and eliminate the exhaust gas recirculation (EGR) valve. By using exhaust cam phasing, the PCM can close the exhaust valves sooner than usual, thereby trapping

Idle Valve Timing

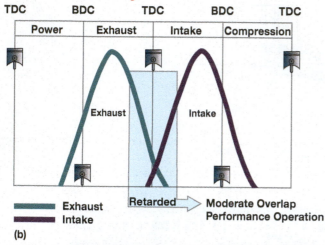

(a)

Performance Valve Timing

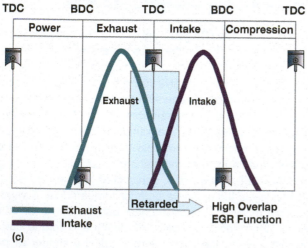

(b)

EGR Function Valve Timing

(c)

FIGURE 7–8 (a) At engine start, the camshaft timing has little valve overlap, which improves idle quality. (b) During acceleration, the valve overlap is increased to improve engine performance. (c) To reduce NO$_x$ emissions, the valve timing is changed to trap some of the exhaust gases in the combustion chamber, thereby eliminating the needs for an EGR valve.

INTAKE AND EXHAUST CAMSHAFT PHASING CHART	
CAMSHAFT PHASING CHANGED	**IMPROVES**
Exhaust cam phasing	Reduces NO$_x$ exhaust emissions
Exhaust cam phasing	Increases fuel economy (reduced pumping losses)
Intake cam phasing	Increases low-speed torque
Intake cam phasing	Increases high-speed power

CHART 7–2

By varying the intake camshaft timing, engine performance is improved. By varying the exhaust camshaft timing, the exhaust emissions and fuel consumption are reduced.

? FREQUENTLY ASKED QUESTION

What Happens When the Engine Stops?

When the engine stops, the oil pressure drops to zero and a spring-loaded locking pin is used to keep the camshaft locked, preventing noise at engine start. When the engine starts, oil pressure releases the locking pin.

some exhaust gases in the combustion chamber. General Motors uses one or two actuators that allow the camshaft piston to change up to 50° in relation to the crankshaft position. ● **SEE FIGURE 7–8 AND CHART 7–2**.

TYPES OF CAMSHAFT PHASERS There are two types of cam phasing devices used:

1. **Spline phaser** is used on overhead camshaft (OHC) engines. ● **SEE FIGURE 7–9**.
2. **Vane phaser** is used on overhead camshaft (OHC) and overhead valve (OHV) cam-in-block engines.

SPLINE PHASER SYSTEM OPERATION On a typical overhead camshaft engine, the control valve is located on the front passenger side of the cylinder head. The oil control valve is controlled using a **pulse-with modulation (PWM)** signal from the PCM. Oil pressure is regulated by the control valve and then directed to the ports in the cylinder head leading to the camshaft and cam phaser position. The cam phaser is located on the exhaust cams and is part of the exhaust cam sprocket. When the PCM commands an increase in oil pressure, the piston is moved inside the cam phaser and rides along the helical splines, which compresses the coil spring. This movement causes the cam phaser gear and the camshaft to move in an opposite direction, thereby retarding the cam timing. ● **SEE FIGURE 7–10**.

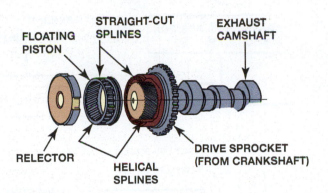

FIGURE 7–9 Spline cam phaser assembly.

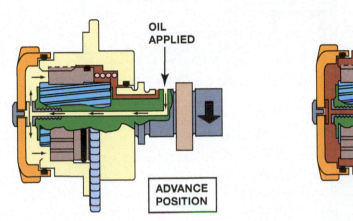

Note: A cam-within-a-cam is used on the 2008 + Viper V-10 OHV engine. This design allows the exhaust lobes to be moved up to 36° to improve idle quality and reduction of exhaust emissions.

VANE PHASER SYSTEM ON AN OVERHEAD CAMSHAFT ENGINE

The vane phaser system used on overhead camshaft (OHC) engines uses a camshaft piston (CMP) sensor on each camshaft. Each camshaft has its own actuator and its own oil control valve (OCV). Instead of using a piston along a helical spline, the vane phaser uses a rotor with four vanes, which is connected to the end of the camshaft. The rotor is located inside the stator, which is bolted to the cam sprocket. The stator and rotor are not connected. Oil pressure is controlled on both sides of the vanes of the rotor, which creates a hydraulic link between the two parts. The oil control valve varies the balance of pressure on either side of the vanes and thereby controls the position of the camshaft. A return spring is used under the reluctor of the phaser to help return it to the home or 0° position. ● **SEE FIGURE 7–11.**

MAGNETICALLY CONTROLLED VANE PHASER

A magnetically controlled vane phaser is controlled by the ECM by using a 12-volt pulse-width-modulated (PWM) signal to an electromagnet, which operates the oil control valve (OCV). A magnetically controlled vane phaser is used on many General Motors engines that use overhead camshafts on both the intake and exhaust. The OCV directs pressurized engine oil to either advance or retard chambers of the camshaft actuator

to change the camshaft position in relation to the crankshaft position. ● **SEE FIGURE 7–12.**

The following occurs when the pulse width is changed:

- **0% pulse width** The oil is directed to the advance chamber of the exhaust camshaft actuator and the retard chamber of the intake camshaft activator.

- **50% pulse width** The PCM is holding the cam in the calculated position based on engine RPM and load. At 50% pulse width, the oil flow through the phaser drops to zero. ● **SEE FIGURE 7–13.**

- **100% pulse width** The oil is directed to the retard chamber of the exhaust camshaft actuator and the advance chamber of the intake camshaft actuator.

The cam phasing is continuously variable with a range from 40° for the intake camshaft and 50° for the exhaust camshaft. The PCM uses the following sensors to determine the best position of the camshaft for maximum power and lowest possible exhaust emissions:

- Engine speed (RPM)
- MAP sensor
- Crankshaft position (CKP) sensor
- Camshaft position (CMP) sensor
- Barometric pressure (BARO) sensor

CAM-IN-BLOCK ENGINE CAM PHASER

Overhead valve engines that use a cam-in-block design use a magnetically controlled cam phaser to vary the camshaft in relation to the crankshaft. This type of phaser is not capable of changing the

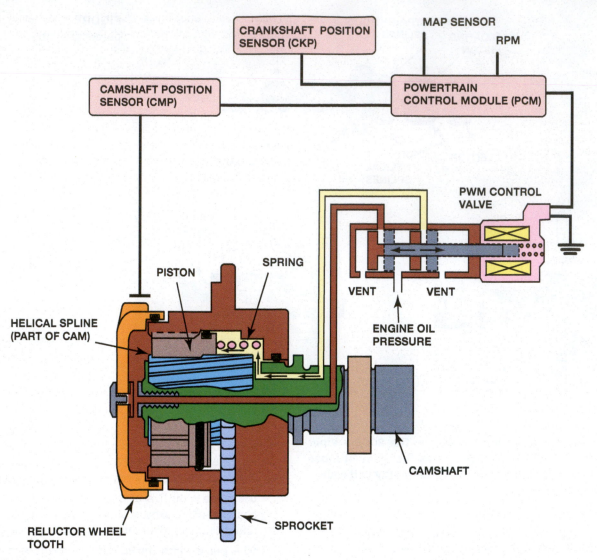

FIGURE 7–10 A spline phaser showing the control valve and how it works internally. Note that the PCM uses the engine speed (RPM), crankshaft position sensor (CKP) and the camshaft position sensor (CMP) to monitor and command the camshaft for maximum power and lowest possible exhaust emissions.

FIGURE 7–11 A vane phaser is used to move the camshaft using changes of oil pressure from the oil control valve.

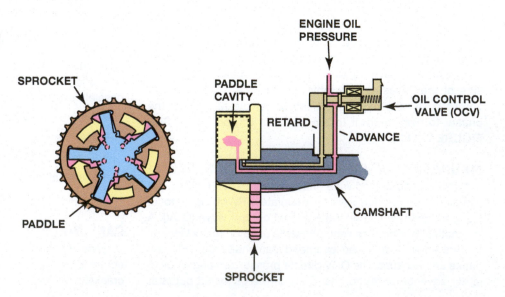

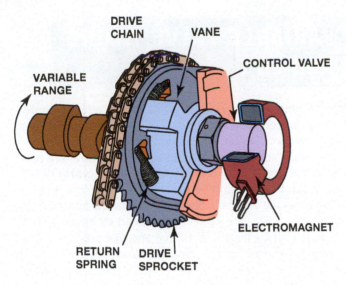

FIGURE 7–12 A magnetically controlled vane phaser.

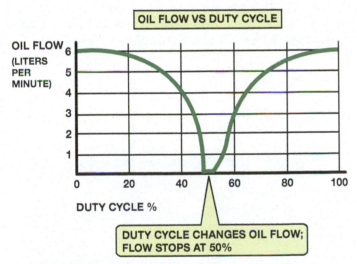

FIGURE 7–13 When the PCM commands 50% duty cycle, the oil flow through the phaser drops to zero.

duration of valve opening or valve lift. Inside the camshaft actuator is a rotor with vanes that are attached to the camshaft. Oil pressure is supplied to the vanes, which causes the camshaft to rotate in relation to the crankshaft. The camshaft actuator solenoid valve directs the flow of oil to either the advance or retard side vanes of the actuator. ● **SEE FIGURE 7–14**.

The ECM sends a pulse-width-modulated (PWM) signal to the camshaft actuator magnet. The movement of the pintle is used to direct oil flow to the actuator. The higher the duty cycle is, the greater the movement in the valve position and change in camshaft timing.

ATKINSON CYCLE VALVE TIMING

PURPOSE AND FUNCTION The purpose of using an **Atkinson cycle** valve engine is to improve engine efficiency. With a typical four-cycle engine, the intake valve opening and the exhaust valve opening are almost equal in degrees. In an Atkinson cycle engine, the following occurs:

- The intake valve is kept open longer and remains open during part of the compression stroke.
- The expansion (power) stroke is the same as conventional engine.
- The mechanical compression ratio is higher than usual, but the working compression is much lower due to the late closing of the intake valve.
- The result is a longer expansion stroke compared to the compression stroke, which improves thermal efficiency and allows the engine to produce more torque at higher engine speeds than conventional engines.
- However, an Atkinson engine produces less low-speed torque than a conventional engine so this design is usually offered in a hybrid electric vehicle (HEV) where the electric motor can be used to provide torque at low speeds. ● **SEE FIGURE 7–15**

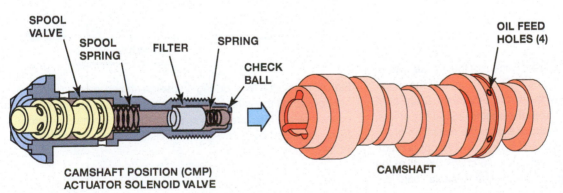

FIGURE 7–14 A camshaft position actuator used in a cam-in-block engine.

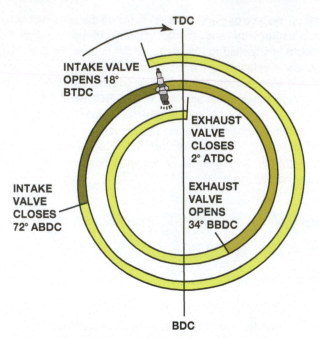

FIGURE 7–15 An Atkinson cycle engine valve timing diagram showing the intake valve remaining open well into the compression stroke. This delaying of the closing of the intake valve effectively reduces engine compression and displacement while keeping the expansion ratio high.

FIAT–CHRYSLER MULTIAIR

PARTS AND OPERATION Some Chrysler and Fiat brand vehicles use a type of variable valve timing system that includes the following unique features:

- The engine has one overhead camshaft, but only the exhaust cam lobes actually open the exhaust valves.
- The intake camshaft lobes are used to pressurize engine oil, which is then directed to a solenoid that is pulse-width modulated.
- The oil from the solenoid is sent to a piston on top of the intake valves, which are opened by the piston.
- The timing and valve lift are determined by the PCM that pulses the control solenoid to allow oil to open the valve. ● **SEE FIGURE 7–16.**

SERVICE CONSIDERATIONS Because the intake values are opened using pressured engine oil, it is critical that the specified oil be used and changed at the specified interval. Some customers complain of a "clatter" from the engine, especially at idle, which is normal for this engine and is due to the operation of the control solenoids. This is normal and before an attempt is made to diagnosis the noise, the technician should check that all of the sound deadening material is present and in serviceable condition.

VARIABLE VALVE TIMING AND LIFT

Many engines use variable valve timing in an effort to improve high-speed performance without the disadvantages of a high-performance camshaft at idle and low speeds. Variable camshafts, such as the system used by Honda/Acura, are called **Variable Valve Timing and Lift Electronic Control (VTEC).** This system uses two different camshafts for low and high RPM. When the engine is operating at idle and speeds below about 4000 RPM, the valves are opened by camshafts that are optimized by maximum torque and fuel economy. When engine speed reaches a predetermined speed, depending on the exact make and model, the computer turns on a solenoid, which opens a spool valve. When the spool valve opens, engine oil pressure pushes against pins that lock the three intake rocker arms together. With the rocker arms lashed, the valves must follow the profile of the high RPM cam lobe in the center. This process of switching from the low-speed camshaft profile to the high-speed profile takes about 100 milliseconds (0.1 sec). ● **SEE FIGURES 7–17 AND 7–18.**

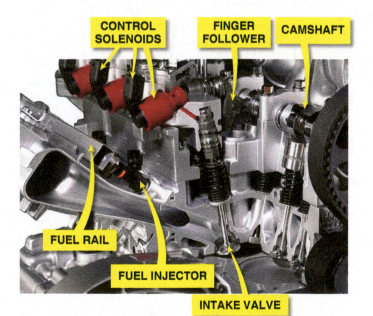

Figure 7–16 In a Multiair engine design, the exhaust valves are opened by the exhaust camshaft lobes. Intake valves are opened by the high-pressure engine oil, with the high pressure being produced by a lobe-actuated piston and controlled by PCM-controlled solenoids.

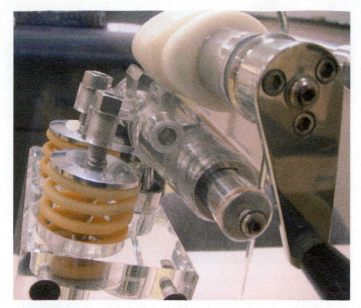

FIGURE 7–17 A plastic mock-up of a Honda VTEC system that uses two different camshaft profiles: one for low-speed engine operation and the other for high-speed operation.

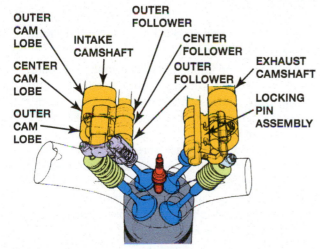

OUTER CAM LOBE
OUTER FOLLOWER
INTAKE CAMSHAFT
CENTER FOLLOWER
CENTER CAM LOBE
OUTER FOLLOWER
OUTER CAM LOBE
EXHAUST CAMSHAFT
LOCKING PIN ASSEMBLY

FIGURE 7–18 Engine oil pressure is used to switch cam lobes on a VTEC system.

PCM CONTROL OF VARIABLE VALVE TIMING

TWO DIFFERENT CIRCUIT CONTROLS Variable valve timing is controlled by the Powertrain Control Module (PCM) and can be one of two different circuits:

- Ground side switching is the most commonly used. ● **SEE FIGURE 7–19**.

The variable valve timing (VVT) solenoid usually has 3 to 6 ohms of resistance and therefore requires 2 to 4 amperes of current to operate.

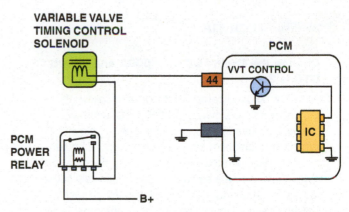

FIGURE 7–19 The schematic of a variable valve timing control circuit, showing that battery power (+), is being applied to the variable valve timing (VVT) solenoid and pulsed to ground by the PCM.

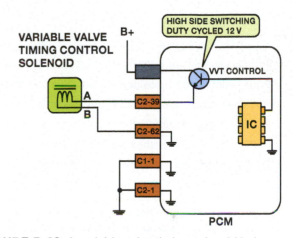

FIGURE 7–20 A variable valve timing solenoid being controlled by applying voltage from the PCM.

- Power side switching is commonly found on General Motors vehicles and the solenoid has 8 to 12 ohms of resistance requiring 1.0 to 1.5 amperes of current to operate. ● **SEE FIGURE 7–20**.

DIAGNOSIS OF VARIABLE VALVE TIMING SYSTEMS

DIAGNOSTIC STEPS The diagnostic procedure as specified by most vehicle manufacturers usually includes the following steps:

STEP 1 Verify the customer concern. This will usually be a "check engine light" (malfunction indicator light or MIL), as the engine performance effects would be minor under most operating conditions.

Change the Engine Oil If a P000A and P000B DTC Is Set

A P000A DTC indicates that the intake camshaft timing changed too slowly. A P000B DTC is set when the exhaust camshaft timing changes too slowly. While these diagnostic trouble codes could be set due to a fault with the solenoids or the electrical circuits controlling the solenoids, the most likely cause is engine oil-related. Dirty oil, oil of the incorrect viscosity, or even a low oil level is often the most likely cause. If the electrical circuits are found to be within factory specification, changing the engine oil using the specified viscosity may well be the solution to either code fault.

FIGURE 7–21 The screen(s) protects the solenoid valve from dirt and debris that can cause the valve to stick. This fault can set a P0017 diagnostic trouble code (crankshaft position–camshaft position correlation error).

STEP 2 Check for stored diagnostic trouble codes (DTCs). Typical variable valve timing–related DTCs include:

P0011—Intake cam position is over advanced bank 1

P0012—Intake cam position is over retarded bank 1

P0013—Exhaust camshaft position actuator

P0014—Exhaust camshaft too far advanced

P0021—Intake cam position is over advanced bank 2

P0022—Intake cam position is over retarded bank 2

STEP 3 Use a scan tool and check for duty cycle on the cam phase solenoid while operating the vehicle at a steady road speed. The commanded pulse width should be 50%. If the pulse width is not 50%, the PCM is trying to move the phaser to its commanded position and the phaser has not reacted properly. A PWM signal of higher or lower than 50% usually indicates a stuck phaser assembly.

STEP 4 Check the solenoid for proper resistance. If a scan tool with bidirectional control is available, connect an ammeter and measure the current as the solenoid is being commanded on by the scan tool.

STEP 5 Check for proper engine oil pressure. Low oil pressure or restricted flow to the cam phaser can be the cause of many diagnostic trouble codes.

STEP 6 Determine the root cause of the problem and clear all DTCs.

STEP 7 Road-test the vehicle to verify the fault has been corrected.

Check the Screen on the Control Valve If There Are Problems

If a NO$_x$ emission failure at a state inspection occurs or a diagnostic trouble code is set related to the cam timing, check the resistance of the control solenoid. If the measured resistance is within factory specifications, remove the control valve and check for a clogged oil screen. A lack of regular oil changes can cause the screen to become clogged, thereby preventing proper operation. A rough idle is a common complaint because the spring may not be able to return the camshaft to the idle position after a long highway trip. ● **SEE FIGURE 7–21**.

VARIABLE DISPLACEMENT SYSTEMS

PURPOSE AND FUNCTION Some engines are designed to be operated on four of eight or three of six cylinders during low-load conditions to improve fuel economy. The powertrain computer monitors engine speed, coolant temperature, throttle position, and load. It also determines when to deactivate cylinders.

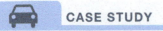
The Case of the Wrong Oil

A Dodge Durango was in the shop for routine service, including a tire rotation and an oil change.

Shortly after, the customer returned and stated that the "check engine" light was on. A scan tool was used to retrieve any diagnostic trouble codes. A P0521, "oil pressure not reaching specified value at 1,250 RPM," was set. A check of service information showed that this code could be set if the incorrect viscosity engine oil was used. The shop had used SAE 10W-30, but the 5.7 liter Hemi V-8 with multiple displacement system (MDS) required SAE 5W-20 oil. The correct oil was installed and the DTC cleared. A thorough test-drive confirmed that the fault had been corrected and the shop learned that the proper viscosity oil is important to use in all vehicles.

Summary:

- **Complaint**—The check engine light was on after an oil change.
- **Cause**—The incorrect viscosity oil was used.
- **Correction**—The oil was replaced with the specified viscosity and the DTC was cleared.

Systems that can deactivate cylinders are called:

- Cylinder cutoff system
- Variable displacement system
- Displacement on Demand (DOD) (now called Active Fuel Management) for General Motors
- Multiple Displacement System (MDS) for Chrysler

PARTS AND OPERATION The key to this process is the use of two-stage hydraulic valve lifters. In normal operation, the inner and outer lifter sleeves are held together by a pin and operate as an assembly. When the computer determines that the cylinder can be deactivated, oil pressure is delivered to a passage.

This depresses the pin and allows the outer portion of the lifter to follow the contour of the cam, while the inner portion remains stationary, keeping the valve closed. The electronic operation is achieved through the use of a lifter oil manifold containing solenoids to control the oil flow, which is used to activate or deactivate the cylinders. ● **SEE FIGURES 7-22 AND 7-23.**

ACTIVATION SEQUENCE OF EVENTS The following sequence of events occurs to trap an exhaust charge in a cylinder during deactivation:

STEP 1 After a normal combustion event has occurred, the exhaust valve is disabled.

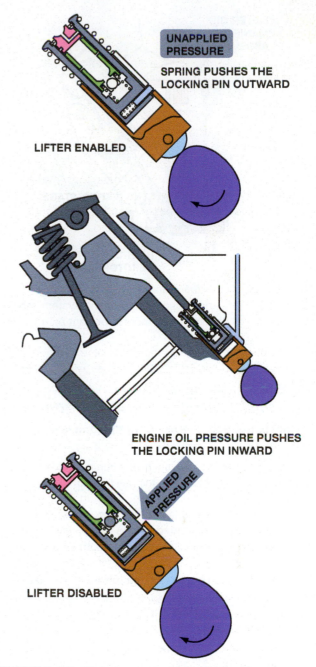

FIGURE 7-22 Oil pressure applied to the locking pin causes the inside of the lifter to freely move inside the outer shell of the lifter, thereby keeping the valve closed.

STEP 2 The intake valve is disabled and the fuel injection is stopped.

STEP 3 The sequence is repeated according to the firing order on the engine. The trapped charge creates an air spring, and the ignition for the disabled cylinders is disabled.

DEACTIVATION SEQUENCE OF EVENTS When the engine returns to firing on all cylinders after a cylinder deactivation event, the following sequence of events occurs:

STEP 1 The exhaust valve is opened, which releases the trapped charge out of the Exhaust.

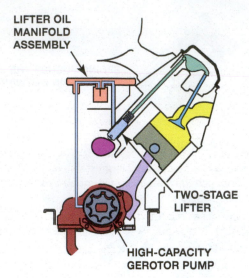

FIGURE 7-23 Active fuel management includes many different components and changes to the oiling system, which makes routine oil changes even more important on engines equipped with this system.

FIGURE 7-24 The driver information display on a Chevrolet Impala with a 5.3 liter V-8 equipped with active fuel management. The transition between four-cylinder mode and eight-cylinder mode is so smooth that most drivers are not aware that the switch is occurring.

 FREQUENTLY ASKED QUESTION

How Is the Engine Kept from Shaking When Cylinders Are Disabled?

If a cylinder is disabled, such as when a cylinder misfires due to a fault with the fuel injector of ignition, the engine does not operate smoothly. In an engine equipped with a variable displacement system that cuts off two or more cylinders, the following is often performed by the PCM to ensure smooth engine operation:

- The electronic throttle control (ETC) and the deactivation are synchronized to trap a burned charge in the combustion chamber.
- The ETC is used to open the throttle to compensate for the loss of power produced by the deactivated cylinders.
- When the cylinders are reactivated, the spark is retarded for a short time to reduce torque when the cylinders start to produce power. Using the ETC is not fast enough to react to the changes.

STEP 2 The fuel injector is reenergized allowing the fuel into the cylinder.

STEP 3 The intake valve is opened.

STEP 4 The ignition occurs, producing a normal combustion event.

STEP 5 The sequence of events is repeated, occurring to the firing order that results in the engine operating normally on all cylinders.

VARIABLE DISPLACEMENT SYSTEM DIAGNOSIS

DASH DISPLAY A cylinder deactivation system, also called cylinder cutoff system or variable displacement system, often displays when the system is active on the driver information display. ● **SEE FIGURE 7-24.**

DIAGNOSTIC PROCEDURE The diagnosis of the variable displacement system usually starts as a result of a check engine light (malfunction indicator lamp or MIL) turning on. The diagnostic procedure specified by the vehicle manufacturer usually includes the following steps:

STEP 1 Verify the customer concern. With a cylinder deactivation system, the customer concern could be lower than expected fuel economy.

STEP 2 Check for any stored diagnostic trouble codes (DTCs). A fault code set for an emission-related fault could cause the PCM to disable cylinder deactivation.

STEP 3 Perform a thorough visual inspection, including checking the oil level and condition.

STEP 4 Check scan tool data for related parameters to see if any of the sensors are out of the normal range.

STEP 5 Determine the root cause and perform the repair as specified in service information.

STEP 6 Test-drive the vehicle to verify proper operation.

SUMMARY

1. Cam timing specifications are stated in terms of the angle of the crankshaft in relation to top dead center (TDC) or bottom dead center (BDC) when the valves open and close.

2. The camshaft is driven by:
   - Timing gears
   - Timing chains
   - Timing belts

3. Variable valve timing is used to improve engine performance and reduce exhaust emissions.

4. Intake cam phasing is used to improve low-speed torque and high-speed power.

5. Exhaust cam phasing is used to reduce exhaust emissions and increase fuel economy by reducing pumping losses.

6. The use of variable valve timing on overhead valve engines is used to reduce NO_x emissions.

7. Variable valve timing faults are often the result of extended oil change intervals, which can clog the screen on the cam phaser. As a result of the clogged screen, oil cannot flow to and adjust the valve timing, thereby setting valve timing-related diagnostic trouble codes (DTCs).

8. Oil flow to the phasers is controlled by the powertrain control module (PCM). If a 50% duty cycle is shown on a scan tool, the phaser has reached the commanded position.

9. If the duty cycle is other than 50% while operating the vehicle under steady conditions, there is a fault in the system because the cam phaser is not able to reach the commanded position.

10. Variable valve timing and lift electronic control (VTEC) is used on most Honda/Acura vehicles to improve performance.

11. Control of the variable valve timing (VVT) solenoid can be either ground side switching or power side switching.

12. Common variable valve timing diagnostic trouble codes include P0011, P0021, P0012, and P0022.

13. Cylinder deactivation systems improve fuel economy by disabling half of the cylinders during certain driving conditions, such as steady speed cruising.

REVIEW QUESTIONS

1. What is the advantage of varying the intake camshaft timing?
2. What is the advantage of varying the exhaust camshaft timing?
3. Why must the engine oil be changed regularly on an engine equipped with variable valve timing?
4. What sensors does the PCM monitor to determine the best camshaft timing?
5. What diagnostic trouble codes are associated with the variable valve timing (VVT) system?

CHAPTER QUIZ

1. The operation of the valvetrain determines _____.
   a. the distance the valves open
   b. the timing of when the valves are opened and closed
   c. the duration of the opening and closing of the valves
   d. All of the above

2. To reduce oxides of nitrogen (NO_x) exhaust emissions, which camshaft is varied?
   a. Exhaust camshaft only
   b. Intake camshaft only
   c. Both the intake and exhaust camshaft
   d. The exhaust camshaft is advanced and the intake camshaft is advanced.

3. What is different about the Atkinson cycle valve timing?
   a. Improves engine efficiency
   b. Increases low speed torque output of the engine
   c. Uses a shorter exhaust valve timing
   d. The engine with an Atkinson cycle uses a lower compression ratio

4. All of the following could cause noise in the valvetrain EXCEPT _____.
   a. oil level too low
   b. oil level too high
   c. an original equipment oil filter
   d. worn cam lobe

5. What sensors are used by the PCM to determine the best position of the camshafts for maximum power and lowest possible exhaust emissions?
   a. Engine speed (RPM)
   b. Crankshaft position (CKP) sensor
   c. Camshaft position (CMP) sensor
   d. All of the above

6. How is the camshaft actuator controlled?
   a. On only when conditions are right
   b. Pulse-width-modulated (PWM) signal
   c. Spring-loaded to the correct position based on engine speed
   d. Vacuum-controlled valve

7. If the engine oil is not changed regularly, what is the most likely fault that can occur to an engine equipped with variable valve timing (VVT)?
   a. Low oil pressure diagnostic trouble code (DTC)
   b. A no-start condition because the camshaft cannot rotate
   c. The filter screens on the actuator control valve become clogged
   d. Any of the above

8. How quickly can the rocker arms be switched from the low-speed camshaft profile to the high-speed camshaft profile on a Honda equipped with a VTEC system?
   a. 50 milliseconds
   b. 100 milliseconds
   c. 250 milliseconds
   d. 500 milliseconds

9. What sequence of events occurs to trap some exhaust in the cylinder during a cylinder deactivation event?
   a. After a normal combustion event has occurred, the exhaust valve is disabled
   b. The intake valve is disabled and the fuel injection is stopped.
   c. The sequence is repeated according to the firing order on the engine.
   d. All of the above.

10. If the incorrect grade of engine oil is used in an engine equipped with a variable displacement engine, what diagnostic trouble code (DTC) could be set?
   a. P0521
   b. P0300
   c. P0420
   d. P0011

chapter 8
ENGINE AND MISFIRE DIAGNOSIS

LEARNING OBJECTIVES

After studying this chapter, the reader should be able to:

1. List typical engine mechanical-related complaints.
2. Discuss how to diagnose engine operation problems using visual checks, engine noise, engine smoke, and oil pressure testing.
3. List the possible causes of an engine misfire.
4. Describe how to perform a cylinder power balance, cylinder contribution test, and cylinder pressure testing.
5. Describe how to perform dry, wet, and running compression tests.
6. Explain how to perform a cylinder leakage test.
7. Discuss vacuum testing to determine engine condition.
8. Describe how to test for excessive exhaust system back pressure.
9. Explain how to diagnose head gasket failure.

KEY TERMS

Back pressure 131
Cranking compression test 125
Cylinder contribution test 123
Cylinder leakage test 128
Dynamic compression test 127

Misfire 121
Power balance test 123
Running compression test 127
Wet compression test 126

EXHAUST SMOKE COLOR	POSSIBLE CAUSES
Blue	Blue exhaust indicates that the engine is burning oil. Oil is getting into the combustion chamber either past the piston rings or past the valve guides/stem seals. Blue smoke only after start-up is usually due to defective valve stem seals.
Black	Black exhaust smoke is due to excessive fuel being burned in the combustion chamber. Typical causes include a defective or misadjusted throttle body, leaking fuel injector, or excessive fuel system pressure.
White (steam)	White smoke or steam from the exhaust is normal during cold weather and represents condensed steam. Every engine creates about 1 gallon of water for each gallon of gasoline burned. If the steam from the exhaust is excessive, then water (coolant) is getting into the combustion chamber. Typical causes include a defective cylinder head gasket, a cracked cylinder head, or in severe cases, a cracked block. ● SEE FIGURE 8–1.

CHART 8–1

Exhaust smoke colors and possible causes.

ENGINE-RELATED COMPLAINTS

If there is an engine operation problem, the cause could be any one of many items, including the engine itself. The condition of the engine should be tested when the operation of the engine is not satisfactory. Many drivability problems are *not* caused by engine mechanical problems. A thorough inspection and testing of the ignition and fuel systems should be performed before testing for mechanical engine problems. Typical engine mechanical-related complaints include the following:

- Excessive oil consumption
- Engine misfiring
- Loss of power
- Smoke from the engine or exhaust
- Engine noise

FIGURE 8–1 White steam is usually an indication of a blown (defective) cylinder head gasket that allows engine coolant to flow into the combustion chamber where it is turned to steam.

ENGINE SMOKE DIAGNOSIS

The color of engine exhaust smoke can indicate what type of engine problem might exist. ● SEE CHART 8–1.

VISUAL CHECKS

OIL LEVEL AND CONDITION   The first step for visual inspection is checking oil level and condition.

1. Oil should be to the proper level.
2. Oil condition (check for abnormal color or odor).

COOLANT LEVEL AND CONDITION   Most mechanical engine problems are caused by overheating. The proper operation of the cooling system is critical to the life of any engine.

WARNING

Check the coolant level in the radiator only when the radiator is cool. If the radiator is hot and the radiator cap is removed, the drop in pressure above the coolant will cause the coolant to boil immediately and as the coolant explosively expands upward and outward from the radiator opening, it can cause severe burns and personal injury.

1. The coolant level in the coolant recovery container should be within the limits indicated on the overflow bottle. If this level is too low or the coolant recovery container is empty, then check the level of coolant in the radiator (only when cool) and also check the operation of the pressure cap.
2. The coolant should be checked with a hydrometer or refractometer for boiling and freezing temperatures. This

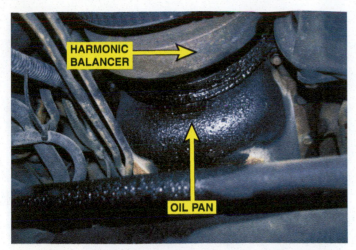

FIGURE 8–2 What looks like an oil pan gasket leak can be a valve or cam cover gasket leak. Always look for the highest most forward place that looks wet as oil always tends to move downward due to gravity and rearward due to vehicle movement.

test indicates if the concentration of the antifreeze is sufficient for proper protection.

3. Pressure-test the cooling system and look for leakage. Coolant leakage can often be seen around hoses or cooling system components because it will often cause the following:
   a. Grayish white stain
   b. Rusty stain
   c. Dye stains from antifreeze (red, orange, green, or yellow depending on the type of coolant)
4. Check for cool areas of the radiator indicating clogged sections.
5. Check operation and condition of the fan clutch, electric fan, and coolant pump drive belt.

OIL LEAKS Oil leaks can lead to severe engine damage if the resulting low oil level is not corrected. Besides causing an oily mess where the vehicle is parked, the oil leak can cause blue smoke to occur under the hood as leaking oil drips on the exhaust system. Finding the source location of the oil leak can often be difficult. ● SEE FIGURE 8–2.

ENGINE NOISE DIAGNOSIS

An engine knocking noise is often difficult to diagnose. Use a mechanical or electronic stethoscope to listen for engine related noises, or a short length of rubber hose or a long screwdriver. Items that may cause engine noise include the following:

- **Valves clicking.** This can happen because of lack of oil to the lifters. The noise is most noticeable at idle when the oil pressure is the lowest. It can also be due to a fault in the valve train. ● SEE FIGURE 8–3.

FIGURE 8–3 The weird sounding engine noise was finally found to be a damaged roller lifter and camshaft.

FIGURE 8–4 An accessory belt tensioner. Most tensioners have a mark that indicates normal operating location. If the belt has stretched, this indicator mark will be outside of the normal range. Anything wrong with the belt or tensioner can cause noise.

- **Torque converter.** The attaching bolts or nuts may be loose on the flex plate and cause a deep knocking noise that is often thought to be main or rod bearing-related. This noise is most noticeable at idle or when there is no load on the engine.
- **Cracked flex plate.** The noise of a cracked flex plate is often mistaken for a rod or main bearing noise.
- **Loose or defective drive belts or tensioners.** If an accessory drive belt is loose or defective, the flopping noise often sounds similar to a bearing knock. ● SEE FIGURE 8–4.

TYPICAL NOISE	POSSIBLE CAUSE
Clicking noise, like the clicking of a ballpoint pen	1. Loose spark plug 2. Loose accessory mount (air-conditioning compressor, alternator, power steering pump) 3. Loose/worn rocker arm 4. Worn camshaft 5. Exhaust leak ● **SEE FIGURE 8–5.** 6. Spark plug wire arcing
Clacking noise, like tapping on metal	1. Worn piston pin 2. Broken piston 3. Excessive valve clearance 4. Timing chain hitting cover 5. Valve lifter
Knock, like knocking on a door	1. Rod bearing(s) 2. Main bearing(s) 3. Thrust bearing(s) 4. Loose torque converter 5. Cracked flex plate (drive plate)
Rattle, like a baby rattle	1. Broken harmonic balancer 2. Loose accessory mounts 3. Loose accessory drive belt or tensioner
Clatter, like rolling marbles	1. Rod bearings 2. Piston pin 3. Loose timing chain
Whine, like an electric motor running	1. Alternator bearing 2. Power steering (low fluid level or bad pump) 3. Belt noise (accessory drive or timing belt)
Clunk, like a door closing	1. Engine mount 2. Driveaxle shaft U-joint or constant velocity (CV) joint

CHART 8–2

Typical engine-related noises and possible causes.

■ **Piston pin knock.** This knocking noise is usually not affected by load on the cylinder. If the clearance is too great, a double knock noise is heard when the engine idles. If disabling cylinders one at a time does not change the sound, then a defective piston pin could be the cause.

■ **Piston slap.** A piston slap is usually caused by an undersized or improperly shaped piston or oversized cylinder bore. A piston slap is most noticeable when the engine is cold and tends to decrease or stop making noise as the piston expands during engine operation.

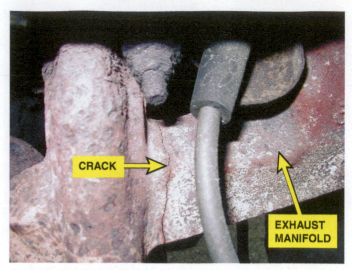

FIGURE 8–5 A cracked exhaust manifold can make a clicking sound that is often difficult to find.

■ **Timing chain noise.** An excessively loose timing chain can cause a severe knocking noise when the chain hits the timing chain cover. This noise can often sound like a rod bearing knock.

■ **Rod bearing noise.** The noise from a defective rod bearing is usually load sensitive and changes in intensity as the load on the engine increases and decreases. A rod bearing failure can often be detected by grounding out the spark plugs one cylinder at a time. If the knocking noise decreases or is eliminated when a particular cylinder is grounded (disabled), then the grounded cylinder is the one from which the noise is originating.

■ **Main bearing knock.** A main bearing knock often cannot be isolated to a particular cylinder. The sound can vary in intensity and may disappear at times depending on engine load. Regardless of the type of loud knocking noise, after the external causes of the knocking noise have been eliminated, the engine should be disassembled and carefully inspected to determine the exact cause. ● **SEE CHART 8–2** for examples of noises and possible causes.

OIL PRESSURE TESTING

TEST PROCEDURE Proper oil pressure is very important for the operation of any engine. Low oil pressure can cause engine wear, and engine wear can cause low oil pressure. If the main, thrust, cam, or rod bearings are worn, oil pressure is reduced because of oil leakage around the bearings. Oil pressure testing is usually performed using the following steps.

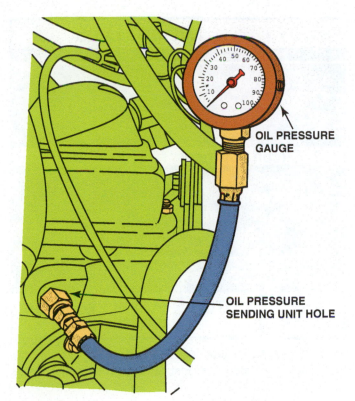

FIGURE 8–6 To measure engine oil pressure, remove the oil pressure sending (sender) unit usually located near the oil filter. Screw the pressure gauge into the oil pressure sending unit hole.

STEP 1 Operate the engine until normal operating temperature is achieved.

STEP 2 With the engine off, remove the oil pressure sending unit or sender, usually located near the oil filter. Thread an oil pressure gauge into the threaded hole. ● **SEE FIGURE 8–6.**

STEP 3 Start the engine and observe the gauge. Record the oil pressure at idle speed and at 2500 RPM. Most vehicle manufacturers recommend a minimum oil pressure of 10 PSI per 1000 RPM. Therefore, at 2500 RPM, the oil pressure should be at least 25 PSI. Always compare the test results with the manufacturer's recommended oil pressure. Besides engine bearing wear, other possible causes for low oil pressure include:

- Low oil level
- Diluted oil
- Worn oil pump or stuck oil pressure relief valve
- Restricted oil pump pickup screen

OIL PRESSURE WARNING LAMP The red oil pressure warning lamp in the dash usually lights when the oil pressure is less than 4 to 7 PSI, depending on vehicle and engine. The oil light should not be on during driving. If the oil warning lamp

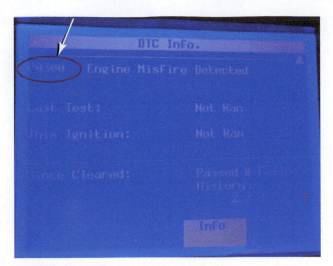

FIGURE 8–7 A General Motor's Tech 2 scan tool display showing a random misfire DTC has been detected.

🔧 **TECH TIP**

Do Not Clear Codes

When diagnosing an engine misfire, do not clear codes. When the codes are cleared, all of the Mode $06 data are also erased. Mode $06 is very helpful to identify which cylinder is causing the misfire and to what degree. Mode $06 can also be used to verify that the repair has been successful in solving the misfire fault. See Chapter 11 for details on Mode $06.

is on, stop the engine immediately. Always confirm oil pressure with a reliable mechanical gauge before performing engine repairs. The sending unit or circuit may be defective.

MISFIRE DIAGNOSIS

DEFINITION OF A MISFIRE An engine **misfire** is when a cylinder does not fire or fire well enough to contribute to the operation of the engine. When the engine is running properly, each cylinder contributes equally and the engine speed is consistent. If a cylinder is misfiring, the engine speed drops slightly instead of increasing slightly when each cylinder is operating correctly. It is this change in engine speed that is detected by the crankshaft position (CKP) sensor, which indicates to the PCM that a misfire has occurred. When a misfire is detected, the powertrain control module (PCM) usually sets a P0300 (random misfire detected) diagnostic trouble code (DTC) and turns on the malfunction indicator lamp (MIL). ● **SEE FIGURE 8–7.**

FIGURE 8–8 A broken accessory drive belt tensioner can cause the engine speed to vary as the belt loosens and then tightens causing what is measured by the CKP as uneven engine speed and a possible P0300 random misfire diagnostic trouble code.

Misfire Data		
IC Circuit Cylinder	1	OK
IC Circuit Cylinder	2	OK
IC Circuit Cylinder	3	OK
IC Circuit Cylinder	4	OK
IC Circuit Cylinder	5	Fault
IC Circuit Cylinder	6	OK
IC Circuit Cylinder	7	OK
IC Circuit Cylinder	8	OK
TCC Enable Sol.		Disabled
		39 / 46 - ▼
IC Circuit Cylinder	5	
Select Items	DTC	Quick Snapshot	More

FIGURE 8–9 A scan tool, such as a Tech 2, can often identify ignition system related faults that can be the cause of a misfire.

TECH TIP

Take Off the Accessory Drive Belt

Sometimes, a misfire condition can be caused by a fault with the A/C compressor or another accessory such as the alternator or even the power steering pump. Just to make sure that none of the accessories are the source of the misfire, remove the drive belt and start the engine and recheck the scan tool data for misfires. ● **SEE FIGURE 8–8.**

CAUSES OF MISFIRES An engine misfire can be caused by any one of more of the following systems:

1. **Engine Mechanical Fault** Any fault with the cylinder head or engine block assembly that affects the engine compression can be the source of a misfire. Typical causes can include the following:

   - Burned valves that would cause a lower-than-normal compression and less than normal combustion.
   - Blown head gasket that can affect one or more cylinders depending on the location and type of fault.
   - Valve timing issues, such as worn timing chain or skipped timing belt, can affect all cylinders and create multiple misfires if it affects cylinder compression.
   - A fault with the variable valve (cam) timing system can cause a misfire condition.
   - Piston or cylinder wear that causes a lower-than-normal compression will cause a misfire to occur.
   - A defective harmonic balancer or cracked flexplate can be the cause of a misfire.

2. **Ignition System Fault** Any fault in the ignition system can cause an engine to misfire. Typical causes can include the following:

   - An ignition coil fault can cause a lack of spark or proper spark to ignite the air–fuel mixture under all engine operating conditions.
   - A spark plug fault, such as being excessively worn or cracked porcelain, can cause a misfire.
   - Any faults in the secondary ignition circuit wiring, such as spark plug wires, can cause a misfire. ● **SEE FIGURE 8–9.**
   - Ignition timing faults caused by a defective crankshaft position (CKP) sensor or an engine mechanical fault can cause a misfire.

3. **Fuel System Fault** Any fault in the fuel system can cause an engine to misfire. Typical causes can include the following:

   - A defective or clogged fuel injector(s) can cause a leaner-than-normal air–fuel mixture, which can cause an engine misfire.
   - Low fuel pressure caused by a weak fuel pump, clogged fuel filter, or some other fault can cause a leaner-than-normal air–fuel mixture, which can cause an engine misfire.
   - A fault emission control system, such as a fault with the PCV or EVAP system that can cause a leaner-than-normal or a richer-than-normal air–fuel mixture, can cause an engine misfire.

For additional information on how fuel system faults can be detected, see Chapter 21 on fuel trim diagnosis.

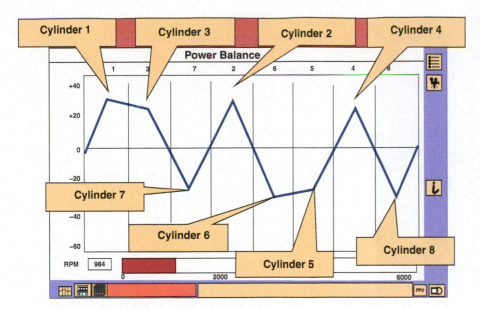

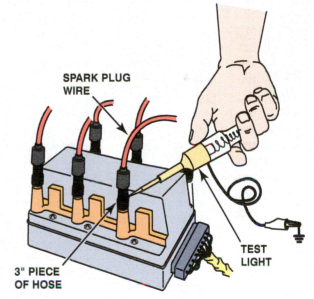

FIGURE 8–10 The Ford IDS scan tool has a graph function that allows the technician to view the data on the cylinder contribution test visually, making diagnosis easier. In this example, the cylinders on bank 2 on a Ford V-8 (cylinders 7, 6, 5, and 8) were weak and were caused by a stuck variable cam solenoid on bank 2.

ENGINE-RELATED MISFIRE DIAGNOSIS

CYLINDER CONTRIBUTION TEST One of the fastest ways to check to see if all cylinders are mechanically able to contribute to the operation of the engine is to perform a cylinder contribution test using a scan tool. A **cylinder contribution test**, also called an *injector power balance test*, is an automated test that a scan tool performs by turning the fuel injectors off one cylinder at the time and monitors the drop, or increase in engine speed. This change in engine speed should be the same for all cylinders if all cylinders are working correctly. For example, a Ford IDS scan tool can be used by selecting this function and following the on-screen instructions. ● **SEE FIGURE 8–10.**

CYLINDER BALANCE TEST Most large engine analyzers and scan tools have a cylinder power balance feature. The purpose of a cylinder **power balance test** is to determine if all cylinders are contributing power equally. This is determined by shorting out (disabling) one cylinder at a time. If the engine speed (RPM) does not drop as much for one cylinder as for other cylinders of the same engine, then the shorted cylinder must be weaker than the other cylinders. ● **SEE FIGURE 8–11.**

For example:

Cylinder number drop when ignition is shorted (disabled) (RPM)

Cylinder #1-75
Cylinder #2-70
Cylinder #3-15
Cylinder #4-65

FIGURE 8–11 Using a vacuum hose and a test light to ground one cylinder at a time on a waste spark ignition system. Use a standard 12-volt test light. Do not use an LED test light because the high voltage will damage the electronics in the test light. To avoid possible damage to the catalytic converter, do not short out a cylinder for longer than five seconds.

Cylinder #5-75
Cylinder #6-70
Cylinder #3 is the weak cylinder.

The cylinder with the least RPM drop is the cylinder not producing its share of power.

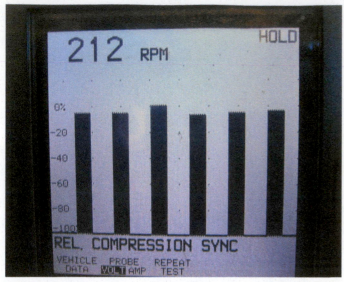

(a)

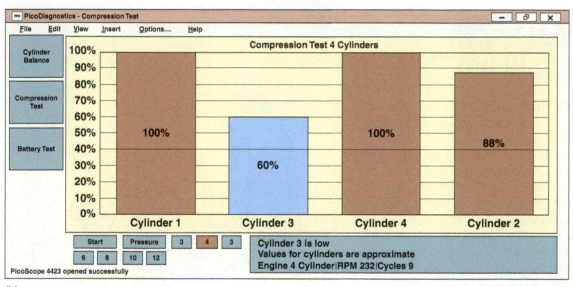

(b)

FIGURE 8–12 (a) A relative compression test shown on a Fluke scope. (b) A relative compression test as shown on a Pico scope.

RELATIVE COMPRESSION TEST
A digital storage oscilloscope (DSO) and a current clamp can be used to measure the change in current that occurs when an engine is cranking to determine the relative compression. This relative compression test uses the starter motor current to determine the compression values of all cylinders. The advantage of a relative compression test is that no pressure sensors are needed to check each individual cylinder and all cylinders can be tested at the same time. Most DSOs have this function built into the unit and can be performed by following the on-screen instructions. The scope records the relative current flow needed to crank the engine and uses these data to display relative compression.

- If a cylinder has high compression, the starter motor will draw more current.
- If a cylinder has lower compression, the starter motor will draw less current.

- The scope software then compares the highest current draw cylinder and flags that as having a relative compression of 100%.
- The other cylinders are then displayed as a percentage of the best cylinder. ● **SEE FIGURE 8–12.**

CYLINDER PRESSURE TRANSDUCER TESTING
Using a pressure transducer connected to a DSO is an excellent method to obtain dynamic cylinder pressure information. An in-cylinder pressure transducer test can provide information to help detect the following faults:

- Help determine if camshaft timing is correct
- Help determine if the cylinder pressure (compression) is normal
- Help determine if the exhaust valves are too tight, or too loose.
- Verify if there is a problem with the valves sealing properly ● **SEE FIGURE 8–13.**

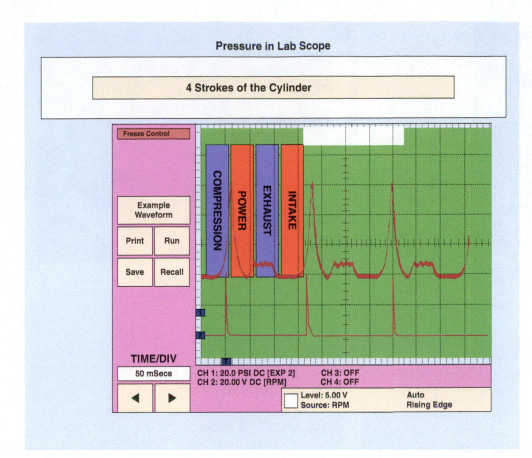

Pressure in Lab Scope

4 Strokes of the Cylinder

Freeze Control

Example Waveform

Print | Run

Save | Recall

COMPRESSION | POWER | EXHAUST | INTAKE

TIME/DIV

50 mSecs

CH 1: 20.0 PSI DC [EXP 2]   CH 3: OFF
CH 2: 20.00 V DC [RPM]   CH 4: OFF

Level: 5.00 V   Auto
Source: RPM   Rising Edge

FIGURE 8–13 A pressure waveform display showing the pressures inside the cylinder during engine cranking through all four strokes (720° of crankshaft rotation). The peaks shown on the waveform represent the pressure in the cylinder when the engine is on the compression stroke.

To conduct an electronic cylinder pressure test, perform the following steps:

STEP 1 Remove the spark plug from the cylinder to be tested and connect an electronic pressure transducer into the spark plug hole and disconnect the electrical connector to the coil (COP-type ignition) or ground spark plug wire (waste-spark system). ● SEE FIGURE 8–14.

STEP 2 Connect the pressure transducer to a digital storage oscilloscope and set to capture a pressure waveform when the engine is started. ● SEE FIGURE 8–15.

STEP 3 Start the engine and run at idle speed, then capture a cylinder pressure waveform.

See pressure transducer waveform sequence images at the end of the chapter for detailed analysis of how the pressure transducer test can help pinpoint engine mechanical faults.

COMPRESSION TEST

CRANKING COMPRESSION TEST An engine **cranking compression test** is one of the fundamental engine diagnostic tests that can be performed. For smooth engine operation, all

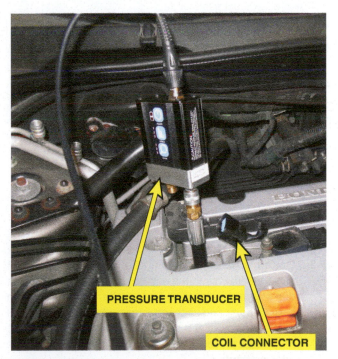

PRESSURE TRANSDUCER

COIL CONNECTOR

FIGURE 8–14 The coil-on-plug ignition coil and spark plug were removed and the pressure transducer was threaded into the spark plug hole.

PRESSURE TRANSDUCER

SCOPE CONNECTED TO PRESSURE TRANSDUCER AND LAPTOP COMPUTER

FIGURE 8–15 A Pico scope connected to a laptop computer is being used to capture the cylinder pressure waveform.

FIGURE 8–16 It often requires an assistant to perform a compression test: one person watches the first puff reading on the gauge and the other person cranks the engine.

TECH TIP

Quick and Easy Math

To make the math quick and easy, think of 10% of 150, which is 15 (move the decimal point to the left by one place). Now double it: $15 \times 2 = 30$. This represents 20%.

cylinders must have equal compression. An engine can lose compression when air leaks through one or more of the following three routes:

- Intake or exhaust valve or seat
- Piston rings (or piston, if there is a hole)
- Cylinder head gasket

For best results, the engine should be warmed to normal operating temperature before testing. An accurate compression test should be performed as follows:

STEP 1 Carefully remove all spark plugs. This allows the engine to be cranked to an even speed. Be sure to label all spark plug wires.

CAUTION: Disable the ignition system by disconnecting the primary leads from the ignition coil(s). Also disable the fuel-injection system to prevent the squirting of fuel into the cylinder.

STEP 2 Open the throttle to permit the maximum amount of air to be drawn into the engine. This step also ensures consistent compression test results. If working on an engine equipped with an electronic throttle control (ETC) system, check service information for the exact procedure to follow to safely open the throttle without causing harm.

STEP 3 Thread a compression gauge into one spark plug hole and crank the engine. Continue cranking the engine through *four* compression strokes. Each compression stroke makes a puffing sound and causes the gauge

needle to pulse. Note the reading on the compression gauge after the first puff. This reading should be at least one-half the final reading. For example, if the final, highest reading is 150 PSI, then the reading after the first puff should be at least one-half of the final reading or higher than 75 PSI in this example. A low first-puff reading indicates possible weak piston rings or a leaking valve or valve seat. Release the pressure on the gauge and repeat for the other cylinders. ● **SEE FIGURE 8–16**.

STEP 4 Record the test results for all cylinders and compare the results. Most vehicle manufacturers specify the minimum compression reading and the maximum allowable variation among cylinders. Most manufacturers specify a maximum difference of 20% between the highest and lowest readings. For example:

If the highest reading is 150 PSI

Subtract 20% (–30 PSI)

Lowest allowable compression is 120 PSI

WET COMPRESSION TEST If the compression test reading indicates low compression on one or more cylinders, add three squirts of oil to the cylinder and retest. This is called a **wet compression test**, because oil is used to help seal around the piston rings.

FIGURE 8–17 A leaking valve will cause a lower-than-normal compression reading.

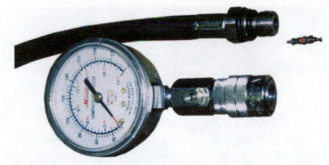

FIGURE 8–18 A two-piece compression gauge showing the Schrader valve removed from the end that is screwed into the spark plug hole.

CAUTION: Do not use more than three squirts oil from a hand-operated oil squirt can. Too much oil can cause a hydrostatic lock, which can damage or break pistons or connecting rods or even crack a cylinder head.

Perform the compression test again and observe the results. If the first-puff readings greatly improve and the readings are much higher than without the oil, the cause of the low compression is worn or defective piston rings. If the compression readings increase only slightly (or not at all), then the cause of the low compression is usually defective valves. ● SEE FIGURE 8–17.

NOTE: During both the dry and wet compression tests, be sure that the battery and starting system are capable of cranking the engine at normal cranking speed.

RUNNING (DYNAMIC) COMPRESSION TEST A compression test is commonly used to help determine engine condition and is usually performed with the engine cranking. What is the RPM of a cranking engine? An engine idles at about 600 to 900 RPM, and the starter motor obviously cannot crank the engine as fast as the engine idles. Most manufacturing specifications require the engine to crank at 80 to 250 cranking RPM. Therefore, a check of the engine's compression at cranking speed determines the condition of an engine that does not run at such low speeds. A **running compression test**, also called a **dynamic compression test**, is used to test the engine for valve train–related faults that do not show up during a cranking compression test. A running compression test is performed with the engine running rather than during engine cranking as is done in a regular compression test.

But what should be the compression of a running engine? Some would think that the compression would be substantially higher, because the valve overlap of the cam is more effective at higher engine speeds that would tend to increase the compression. Actually, the compression pressure of a running engine is much *lower* than cranking compression pressure. This results from the volumetric efficiency. The engine is revolving faster, so there is less *time* for air to enter the combustion chamber. With less air to compress, the compression pressure is lower. Typically, the higher the engine RPM is, the lower the running compression. For most engines, the value ranges are as follows:

■ Compression during cranking: 125 to 160 PSI
■ Compression at idle: 60 to 90 PSI
■ Compression at 2000 RPM: 30 to 60 PSI

As with cranking compression, the running compression of all cylinders should be equal. Therefore, a problem is not likely to be detected by single compression values, but by *variations* in running compression values among the cylinders. Engine faults that are often detected by performing a running compression test include:

■ Broken valve springs
■ Worn valve guides
■ Bent pushrods
■ Worn cam lobes

To perform a running compression test, perform the following steps:

STEP 1 Remove the Schrader valve from the end of the compression tester. ● SEE FIGURE 8–18.

STEP 2 Remove just one spark plug at a time.

STEP 3 With one spark plug removed from the engine, use a jumper wire to *ground* the spark plug wire to a good engine ground or disconnect the primary wire connecter at the coil (COP system). This prevents possible ignition coil damage.

STEP 4 Start the engine, push the pressure release on the gauge, and read the compression. Increase the engine speed to about 2000 RPM and push the pressure release on the gauge again. Read the gauge and record the reading.

FIGURE 8–19 A typical handheld cylinder leakage tester.

STEP 5 Stop the engine, install the spark plug, reattach the spark plug wire, and repeat the test for each of the remaining cylinders.

Results: Just like the cranking compression test, the running compression test can inform a technician of the *relative* compression of all the cylinders.

CYLINDER LEAKAGE TEST

TEST PROCEDURE One of the best tests that can be used to determine engine condition is the **cylinder leakage test**. This test involves injecting air under pressure into the cylinders one at a time. The amount and location of any escaping air helps the technician determine the condition of the engine. The air is injected into the cylinder through a cylinder leakage gauge installed in the spark plug hole. ● **SEE FIGURE 8–19**.

STEP 1 For best results, the engine should be at normal operating temperature (upper radiator hose hot and pressurized).

STEP 2 The cylinder being tested must be at top dead center (TDC) of the compression stroke. ● **SEE FIGURE 8–20.**

NOTE: The greatest amount of wear occurs at the top of the cylinder because of the heat generated near the top of the cylinders. The piston ring flex also adds to the wear at the top of the cylinder.

STEP 3 Connect the tester to shop air not over 100 PSI (700 kPa).

FIGURE 8–20 A whistle stop used to find top dead center. Remove the spark plug and install the whistle stop, then rotate the engine by hand. When the whistle stops making a sound, this means that the piston is at the top.

STEP 4 Calibrate the cylinder leakage unit as per manufacturer's instructions.

STEP 5 Inject air into the cylinders one at a time, rotating the engine as necessitated by firing order to test each cylinder at TDC on the compression stroke.

STEP 6 Evaluate the results:

Less than 10% leakage: good

Less than 20% leakage: acceptable

Less than 30% leakage: poor

More than 30% leakage: definite problem

NOTE: If leakage seems unacceptably high, repeat the test, being certain that it is being performed correctly and that the cylinder being tested is at TDC on the compression stroke.

STEP 7 Check the source of air leakage.

a. If air is heard escaping from the oil filler cap, the *piston rings* are worn or broken.

b. If air is observed bubbling out of the radiator, there is a possible blown head gasket or cracked cylinder head.

c. If air is heard coming from the throttle body, there is a defective intake valve(s).

d. If air is heard coming from the tailpipe, there is a defective exhaust valve(s).

VACUUM TESTS

PURPOSE Engine vacuum is pressure below atmospheric pressure and is measured in **inches (or millimeters) of mercury (Hg)**. An engine in good mechanical condition will run with high manifold vacuum. Manifold vacuum is developed by the pistons as they move down during the intake stroke to draw the fuel and air charge from the throttle body and intake manifold. The air needed to refill the manifold flows past the throttle plate into the manifold. Vacuum will increase anytime the engine turns faster or has better cylinder sealing while the throttle plate remains in a fixed position. Manifold vacuum will decrease when the engine turns more slowly or when the cylinders no longer do an efficient job of pumping.

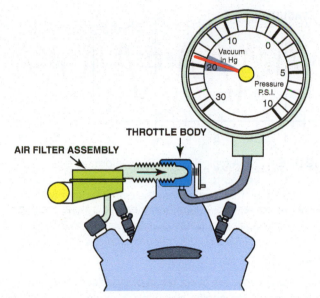

FIGURE 8-21 An engine in good mechanical condition should produce 17 to 21 in. Hg of vacuum at idle at sea level.

IDLE VACUUM TEST

An engine in proper condition should idle with a steady vacuum between 17 in. Hg and 21 in. Hg. ● **SEE FIGURE 8-21.**

NOTE: Engine vacuum readings vary with altitude. A reduction of 1 in. Hg per 1,000 ft (300 m) of altitude should be subtracted from the expected values if testing a vehicle above 1,000 ft (300 m). For example, a vehicle in good operating condition would have an idle vacuum of 12 to 16 in. Hg in Denver, Colorado (elevation 5,100 ft). The same vehicle would read 17 to 21 in. Hg at sea level.

LOW AND STEADY VACUUM

If the vacuum is lower than normal, yet the gauge reading is steady, the most common causes include:

- Retarded cam/ignition timing (Check the timing chain for excessive slack or the timing belt for proper installation.)
- Vacuum leaks. ● **SEE FIGURE 8-22.**

FLUCTUATING VACUUM

If the needle drops, then returns to a normal reading, then drops again, and again returns, this indicates a sticking valve. A common cause of sticking valves is lack of lubrication of the valve stems. ● **SEE FIGURES 8-23 THROUGH 8-28.**

If the vacuum gauge fluctuates above and below a center point, burned valves or weak valve springs may be indicated. If the fluctuation is slow and steady, unequal fuel mixture could be the cause.

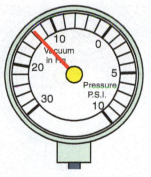

FIGURE 8-22 A steady but low reading could indicate retarded valve or ignition timing.

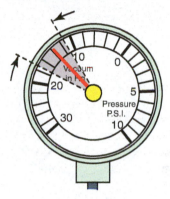

FIGURE 8-23 A gauge reading with the needle fluctuating 3 to 9 in. Hg below normal often indicates a vacuum leak in the intake system.

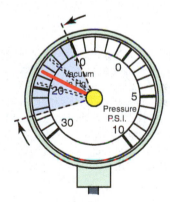

FIGURE 8-24 A leaking head gasket can cause the needle to vibrate as it moves through a range from below to above normal.

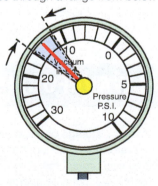

FIGURE 8-25 An oscillating needle 1 or 2 in. Hg below normal could indicate an incorrect air-fuel mixture (either too rich or too lean).

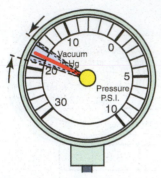

FIGURE 8–26 A rapidly vibrating needle at idle that becomes steady as engine speed is increased indicates worn valve guides.

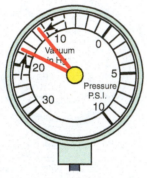

FIGURE 8–27 If the needle drops 1 or 2 in. Hg from the normal reading, one of the engine valves is burned or is not seating properly.

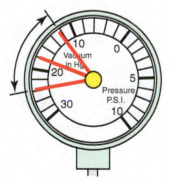

FIGURE 8–28 Weak valve springs will produce a normal reading at idle, but as engine speed increases, the needle will fluctuate rapidly between 12 and 24 in. Hg.

VACUUM WAVEFORMS

PRINCIPLES A digital storage oscilloscope can be used to create a vacuum waveform if a vacuum transducer is attached to an intake manifold vacuum source. A transducer is a device that converts pressure, vacuum, temperature, or other input signals into an electrical signal that will vary with changes in input levels. Transducers allow meters and scopes to accurately measure other things besides electricity. Vacuum created

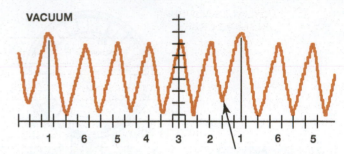

VACUUM

FIGURE 8–29 A typical vacuum waveform as displayed on a scope connected to a vacuum transducer and connected to the intake manifold. Notice that the cylinder number 2 vacuum waveform does not go down as low as the others. This indicates that the cylinder is not sealing.

during cranking is the direct result of cylinder sealing and therefore indicates the engine condition. Vacuum waveform is not affected by any of the following:

- Ignition timing or faults in the ignition system
- Fuel injector faults
- Fuel delivery faults

INTERPRETING A VACUUM WAVEFORM A vacuum waveform will display the pressure (vacuum) in the intake manifold.

The lower the waveform is, the higher is the vacuum. ● **SEE FIGURE 8–29**.

Determining which cylinder relates to which waveform using a vacuum waveform can be a challenge. Most scopes or testers that are equipped to display vacuum waveforms also trigger off of cylinder number 1. Vacuum waveform testing is an excellent way to determine engine condition. A diagram that indicates where the highest vacuum (lowest part of the waveform) will be for each cylinder is shown in ● **FIGURE 8–30**.

Always follow the oscilloscope manufacturer's recommended procedures as found in the instruction manual.

EXHAUST BACKPRESSURE TESTING

PURPOSE OF THE TESTS If the exhaust system is restricted, the engine will be low on power yet will operate smoothly. Common causes of **restricted exhaust** include the following:

- **Clogged catalytic converter.** Always check the ignition and fuel-injection systems for faults that could cause excessive amounts of unburned fuel to be exhausted. Excessive unburned fuel can overheat the catalytic converter and cause the beads or structure of the converter to fuse together, creating the restriction.

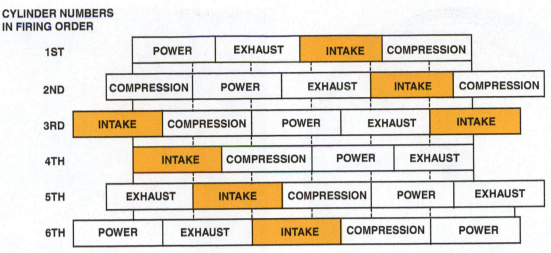

1ST	POWER	EXHAUST	INTAKE	COMPRESSION
2ND	COMPRESSION	POWER	EXHAUST	INTAKE	COMPRESSION
3RD	INTAKE	COMPRESSION	POWER	EXHAUST	INTAKE
4TH	INTAKE	COMPRESSION	POWER	EXHAUST
5TH	EXHAUST	INTAKE	COMPRESSION	POWER	EXHAUST
6TH	POWER	EXHAUST	INTAKE	COMPRESSION	POWER

FIGURE 8–30 The relationship among cylinders showing where the intake stroke occurs in relation to other cylinders.

- **Clogged or restricted muffler.** This can cause low power. Often a defective catalytic converter will shed particles that can clog a muffler. Broken internal baffles can also restrict exhaust flow.

USING A VACUUM GAUGE

A vacuum gauge can be used to measure manifold vacuum at a high idle (2000–2500 RPM). If the exhaust system is restricted, pressure increases in the exhaust system. This pressure is called **back pressure**. Manifold vacuum will drop gradually if the engine is kept at a constant speed if the exhaust is restricted.

- If the exhaust system is not restricted, the vacuum reading will be the same or higher than the vacuum reading when the engine was at idle speed. For example, if the vacuum reading at idle speed is 20 in. Hg, then a good reading would be 21 inches or higher with the engine speed at 2500 RPM.

- If the vacuum reading is lower at 2500 RPM than when it was at idle speed, then an exhaust restriction is indicated. For example, if the vacuum reading at idle speed is 20 in. Hg, then a bad reading would be 20 inches or lower.

The reason the vacuum will drop is that all exhaust leaving the engine at the higher engine speed cannot get through the restriction. After a short time (within one minute), the exhaust tends to "pile up" above the restriction and eventually remains in the cylinder of the engine at the end of the exhaust stroke. Therefore, at the beginning of the intake stroke, when the piston traveling downward should be lowering the pressure (raising the vacuum) in the intake manifold, the extra exhaust in the cylinder *lowers* the normal vacuum. If the exhaust restriction is severe enough, the vehicle can become undrivable because cylinder filling cannot occur except at idle.

USING A PRESSURE GAUGE

Exhaust system back pressure can be measured directly by installing a pressure gauge into an exhaust opening. This can be accomplished in one of the following methods.

FIGURE 8–31 A technician-made adapter used to test exhaust system back pressure.

- **With an oxygen sensor** Use a back pressure gauge and adapter or remove the inside of a discarded oxygen sensor and thread in an adapter to convert to a vacuum or pressure gauge.

  NOTE: An adapter can be easily made by inserting a metal tube or pipe. A short section of brake line works well, too. The pipe can be brazed to the oxygen sensor housing or it can be glued in with epoxy. An 18 mm compression gauge adapter can also be adapted to fit into the oxygen sensor opening. ● SEE FIGURES 8–31 AND 8–32.

- **With the exhaust gas recirculation (EGR) valve** Remove the EGR valve and fabricate a plate to connect to a pressure gauge.

- **With the air-injection reaction (AIR) check valve** Remove the check valve from the exhaust tubes leading down to the exhaust manifold. Use a rubber cone with a tube inside to seal against the exhaust tube. Connect the tube to a pressure gauge. At idle, the maximum back pressure should be less than 1.5 PSI (10 kPa), and it should be less than 2.5 PSI (15 kPa) at 2500 RPM.

FIGURE 8–32 A technician marked pressure gauge showing a green line for acceptable backpressure readings and the red line indicating excessive backpressure readings.

FIGURE 8–33 A tester that uses a blue liquid to check for exhaust gases in the exhaust, which would indicate a head gasket leak problem.

DIAGNOSING HEAD GASKET FAILURE

TESTS AND INDICATIONS The following items can be used to help diagnose a head gasket failure:

- **Exhaust gas analyzer.** With the radiator cap removed, place the probe from the exhaust analyzer above the radiator filler neck. If the hydrocarbon (HC) reading increases, the exhaust (unburned fuel) is getting into the coolant from the combustion chamber.

- **Chemical test.** A chemical tester using blue liquid is also available. The liquid turns yellow if combustion gases are present in the coolant. ● SEE FIGURE 8–33.

- **Bubbles in the coolant.** Remove the coolant pump belt to prevent pump operation. Remove the radiator cap and start the engine. If bubbles appear in the coolant before it begins to boil, a defective head gasket or cracked cylinder head is indicated.

- **Excessive exhaust steam.** If excessive water or steam is observed coming from the tailpipe, this means that coolant is getting into the combustion chamber from a defective head gasket or a cracked head. If there is leakage between cylinders, the engine usually misfires and a power balance test and/or compression test can be used to confirm the problem.

- **Install a pressure gauge to the radiator.** If a head gasket failure is suspected, then an increase in cooling system pressure will often be detected before the coolant temperature becomes hot enough to boil.

If any of the preceding indicators of head gasket failure occur, remove the cylinder head(s) and check all of the following:

1. Head gasket, for signs of leakage
2. Sealing surfaces, for warpage
3. Castings, for cracks

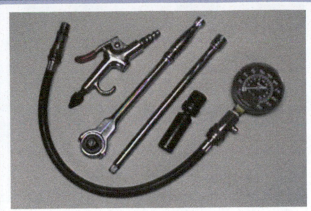

1 The tools and equipment needed to perform a compression test include a compression gauge, an air nozzle, and the socket ratchets and extensions that may be necessary to remove the spark plugs from the engine.

2 To prevent ignition and fuel-injection operation while the engine is being cranked, remove both the fuel-injection fuse and the ignition fuse. If the fuses cannot be removed, disconnect the wiring connectors for the injectors and the ignition system.

3 Block open the throttle. Here a screwdriver is being used to wedge the throttle linkage open. Keeping the throttle open ensures that enough air will be drawn into the engine so that the compression test results will be accurate.

4 Before removing the spark plugs, use an air nozzle to blow away any dirt that may be around the spark plug. This step helps prevent debris from getting into the engine when the spark plugs are removed.

5 Remove all of the spark plugs. Be sure to mark the spark plug wires so that they can be reinstalled onto the correct spark plugs after the compression test has been performed.

6 Select the proper adapter for the compression gauge. The threads on the adapter should match those on the spark plug.

CONTINUED ▶

7 If necessary, connect a battery charger to the battery before starting the compression test. It is important that consistent cranking speed be available for each cylinder being tested.

8 Make a note of the reading on the gauge after the first "puff," which indicates the first compression stroke that occurred on that cylinder as the engine was being rotated. If the first puff reading is low and the reading gradually increases with each puff, weak or worn piston rings may be indicated.

9 After the engine has been cranked for four "puffs," stop cranking the engine and observe the compression gauge.

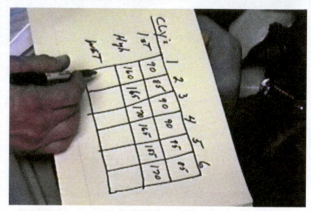

10 Record the first puff and this final reading for each cylinder. The final readings should all be within 20% of each other.

11 If a cylinder(s) is lower than most of the others, use an oil can and squirt two squirts of engine oil into the cylinder and repeat the compression test. This is called performing a wet compression test.

12 If the gauge reading is now much higher than the first test results, then the cause of the low compression is due to worn or defective piston rings. The oil in the cylinder temporarily seals the rings which causes the higher reading.

CYLINDER PRESSURE TRANSDUCER WAVEFORM SEQUENCE

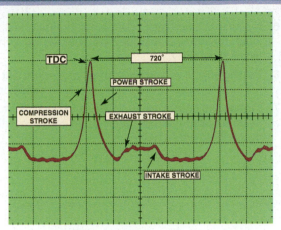

1 The crankshaft rotates 720° between the two peaks, which show the pressure at top dead center (TDC) of the cylinder.

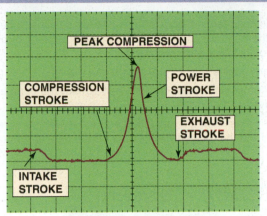

2 At the beginning of the intake stroke, the pressure inside the cylinder is at atmospheric pressure and then drops as the piston travels downward on the intake stroke.

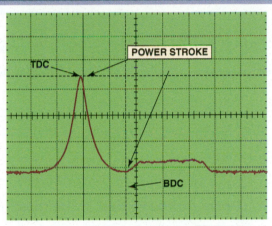

3 The scope is being triggered by the ignition as it fires number one cylinder and the power stroke ends when the piston is near bottom dead center (BDC).

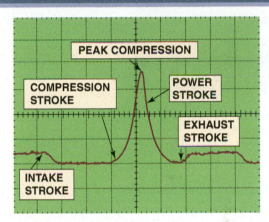

4 Waveform showing when the intake and exhaust valves open and close.

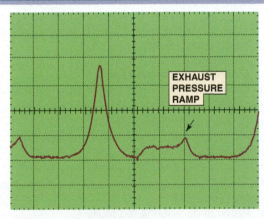

5 A waveform pattern showing a cylinder with excessive exhaust valve clearance.

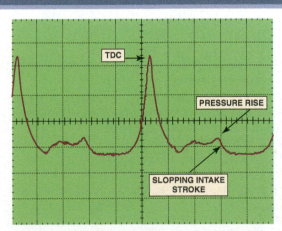

6 A waveform showing a pattern on an engine with a worn intake cam lobe.

SUMMARY

1. The first step in diagnosing engine condition is to perform a thorough visual inspection, including a check of oil and coolant levels and their condition.

2. Many engine-related problems make a characteristic noise.

3. A compression test can be used to test the condition of valves and piston rings.

4. A cylinder leakage test fills the cylinder with compressed air, and the gauge indicates the percentage of leakage.

5. Cylinder balance test, relative compression test, and cylinder contribution test indicate whether all cylinders are working normally.

6. Testing engine vacuum is another procedure that can help the service technician determine engine condition.

7. Testing the engine using a DSO and pressure transducer helps pinpoint the root cause of an engine condition or a misfire problem.

REVIEW QUESTIONS

1. What are four visual checks that should be performed on an engine if a mechanical malfunction is suspected?

2. What engine faults can be determined using a compression test?

3. How is a cylinder leakage test performed?

4. What is a cylinder contribution test and how is it performed?

5. What part of a cylinder pressure waveform indicates a valve issue?

CHAPTER QUIZ

1. Which of the following is *not* likely to be an engine mechanical fault?
   a. Poor fuel economy
   b. Exhaust smoke
   c. Engine noise
   d. Excessive oil consumption

2. A misfire is detected by what sensor(s)?
   a. Camshaft position (CMP)
   b. Crankshaft position (CKP)
   c. Knock sensor (KS)
   d. MAF and/or MAP

3. How could a technician pinpoint a noise made by a defective rod bearing?
   a. By disabling cylinders
   b. By coasting in neutral
   c. By looking at the spark plug gaps
   d. By removing the valve cover and listening while the engine is running

4. Engine oil pressure is being measured. A good engine should be able to produce how much oil pressure?
   a. 10 PSI or more per 1000 RPM
   b. 20 PSI or less
   c. 3-7 PSI at 2500 RPM
   d. More than 100 PSI

5. A good reading for a cylinder leakage test would be _____.
   a. within 20% between cylinders
   b. all cylinders below 20% leakage
   c. all cylinders above 20% leakage
   d. all cylinders above 70% leakage and within 7% of each other

6. An engine in good condition should have about _____ in. Hg at idle.
   a. 10 to 12
   b. 17 to 21
   c. no more than 15
   d. at least 29

7. A cylinder contribution test is performed using a _____.
   a. scan tool
   b. digital storage oscilloscope (DSO)
   c. compression gauge
   d. cylinder leakage tester

8. A relative compression test uses a DSO to monitor _____ to determine the relative compression of each cylinder in the engine while it is being cranked.
   a. injector pulse-width
   b. fuel pressure drop
   c. secondary ignition voltage
   d. battery draw by the starter motor

9. When should a wet compression test be performed?
   a. Before a dry compression test
   b. After a cylinder fails a dry compression test
   c. When the engine is cold
   d. When a defective head gasket is suspected

10. A running compression test is used to locate what type of engine problems?
   a. Piston or connecting rod faults
   b. Valve train–related faults
   c. Leaking intake manifold gasket faults
   d. Excessive exhaust system back pressure

chapter 9

CAN AND NETWORK COMMUNICATIONS

LEARNING OBJECTIVES

After studying this chapter, the reader should be able to:

1. Explain the advantages of connecting modules together in a network.
2. Describe the types of networks and serial communications used on vehicles.
3. Discuss how the networks connect to the data link connector and to other modules in various types of protocols.
4. Explain how to diagnose module communication faults.

This chapter will help you prepare for the ASE Electrical/Electronic Systems (A6) certification test content area "A" (General Electrical/Electronic System Diagnosis).

KEY TERMS

Breakout box (BOB) 148
BUS 139
CAN 141
Class 2 142
E & C 142
GMLAN 143
Keyword 142
Multiplexing 139
Network 139
Node 138
Programmable controller interface (PCI) 146
Serial communications interface (SCI) 146
Serial data 139
Splice pack 139
Standard corporate protocol (SCP) 144
State of health (SOH) 151
SWCAN 143
Terminating resistors 151
Twisted pair 139
UART 142
UART-based protocol (UBP) 144

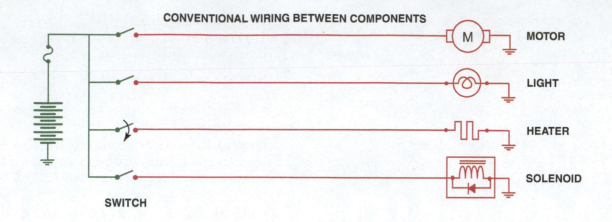

CONVENTIONAL WIRING BETWEEN COMPONENTS

MOTOR

LIGHT

HEATER

SOLENOID

SWITCH

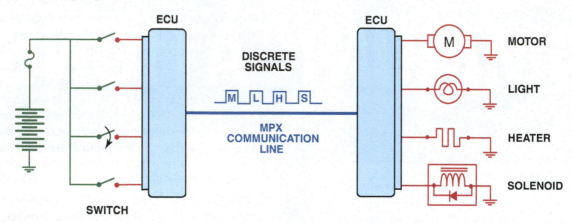

ECU

ECU

DISCRETE
SIGNALS

M L H S

MPX
COMMUNICATION
LINE

MOTOR

LIGHT

HEATER

SOLENOID

SWITCH

FIGURE 9–1 Module communications makes controlling multiple electrical devices and accessories easier by utilizing simple low-current switches to signal another module, which does the actual switching of the current to the device.

MODULE COMMUNICATIONS AND NETWORKS

NEED FOR NETWORK Since the 1990s, vehicles have used modules to control the operation of most electrical components. A typical vehicle will have 10 or more modules and they communicate with each other over data lines or hard wiring, depending on the application.

ADVANTAGES Most modules are connected together in a network because of the following advantages.

- A decreased number of wires are needed, thereby saving weight and cost, as well as helping with installation at the factory and decreased complexity, making servicing easier.

- Common sensor data can be shared with those modules that may need the information, such as vehicle speed, outside air temperature, and engine coolant temperature.
- **SEE FIGURE 9–1.**

NETWORK FUNDAMENTALS

MODULES AND NODES Each module, also called a **node**, must communicate to other modules. For example, if the driver depresses the window-down switch, the power window switch sends a window-down message to the body control module. The body control module then sends the request to the driver's side window module. This module is responsible for actually performing the task by supplying power and ground to the window lift motor in the current polarity to cause the window to go down. The module also contains a circuit that monitors the current flow through the motor and will stop and/or reverse the window motor if an obstruction causes the window motor to draw more than the normal amount of current.

TYPES OF COMMUNICATION The types of communications include the following:

- **Differential.** In the differential form of BUS communication, a difference in voltage is applied to two wires, which

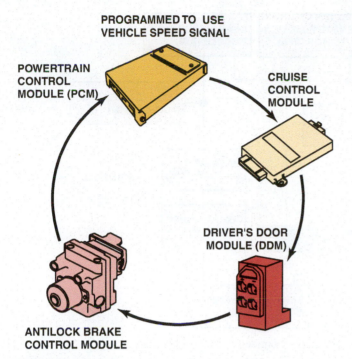

FIGURE 9–2 A network allows all modules to communicate with other modules.

are twisted to help reduce electromagnetic interference (EMI). These transfer wires are called a **twisted pair**.

- **Parallel.** In the parallel type of BUS communication, the send and receive signals are on different wires.

- **Serial data.** The **serial data** is data transmitted by a series of rapidly changing voltage signals pulsed from low to high or from high to low.

- **Multiplexing.** The process of **multiplexing** involves the sending of multiple signals of information at the same time over a signal wire and then separating the signals at the receiving end.

This system of intercommunication of computers or processors is referred to as a **network**. ● SEE FIGURE 9–2.

By connecting the computers together on a communications network, they can easily share information back and forth. This multiplexing has the following advantages.

- Elimination of redundant sensors and dedicated wiring for these multiple sensors

- Reduction of the number of wires, connectors, and circuits

- Addition of more features and option content to new vehicles

- Weight reduction due to fewer components, wires, and connectors, thereby increasing fuel economy

- Changeable features with software upgrades versus component replacement

MODULE COMMUNICATIONS CONFIGURATION

The three most common types of networks used on vehicles include the following:

1. **Ring link networks.** In a ring-type network, all modules are connected to each other by a serial data line (in a line) until all are connected in a ring. ● SEE FIGURE 9–3.

2. **Star link networks.** In a star link network, a serial data line attaches to each module and then each is connected to a central point. This central point is called a **splice pack**, abbreviated SP, such as in "SP 306." The splice pack uses a bar to splice all of the serial lines together. Some GM vehicles use two or more splice packs to tie the modules together. When more than one splice pack is used, a serial data line connects one splice pack to the others. In most applications, the BUS bar used in each splice pack can be removed. When the BUS bar is removed, a special tool (J 42236) can be installed in place of the removed BUS bar. Using this tool, the serial data line for each module can be isolated and tested for a possible problem. Using the special tool at the splice pack makes diagnosing this type of network easier than many others. ● SEE FIGURE 9–4.

3. **Ring/star hybrid.** In a ring/star network, the modules are connected using both types of network configurations. Check service information (SI) for details on how this network is connected on the vehicle being diagnosed and always follow the recommended diagnostic steps.

NETWORK COMMUNICATIONS CLASSIFICATIONS

The Society of Automotive Engineers (SAE) standards include the following three categories of in-vehicle network communications.

 FREQUENTLY ASKED QUESTION

What Is a BUS?

A **BUS** is a term used to describe a communications network. Therefore, there are *connections to the BUS* and *BUS communications*, both of which refer to digital messages being transmitted among electronic modules or computers.

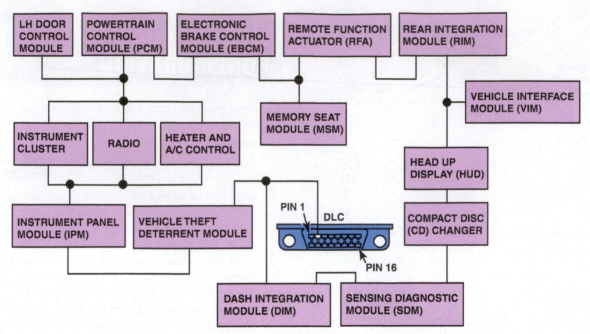

FIGURE 9-3 A ring link network reduces the number of wires it takes to interconnect all of the modules.

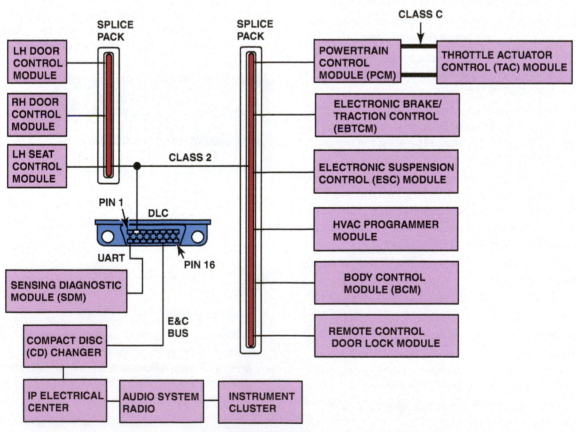

FIGURE 9-4 In a star link network, all of the modules are connected using splice packs.

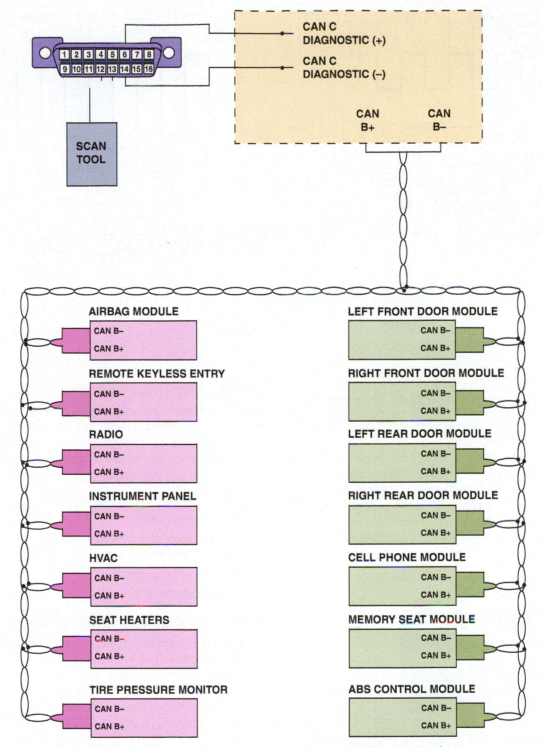

FIGURE 9–5 A typical BUS system showing module CAN communications and twisted pairs of wire.

CLASS A Low-speed networks, meaning less than 10,000 bits per second (bps, or 10 Kbs), are generally used for trip computers, entertainment, and other convenience features.

CLASS B Medium-speed networks, meaning 10,000 to 125,000 bps (10 to 125 Kbs), are generally used for information transfer among modules, such as instrument clusters, temperature sensor data, and other general uses.

CLASS C High-speed networks, meaning 125,000 to 1,000,000 bps, are generally used for real-time powertrain and vehicle dynamic control. High-speed BUS communication systems now use a **controller area network (CAN)**. ● SEE FIGURE 9–5.

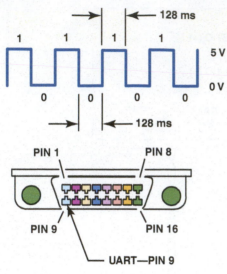

FIGURE 9–6 UART serial data master control module is connected to the data link connector (DLC) at pin 9.

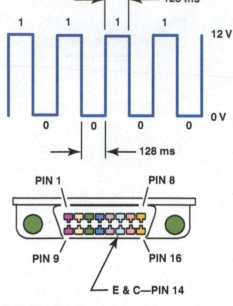

FIGURE 9–7 The E & C serial data is connected to the data link connector at pin 14.

GENERAL MOTORS COMMUNICATIONS PROTOCOLS

UART General Motors and others use UART communications for some electronic modules or systems. **UART** is a serial data communications protocol that stands for **universal asynchronous receive and transmit**. UART uses a master control module connected to one or more remote modules. The master control module is used to control message traffic on the data line by poling all of the other UART modules. The remote modules send a response message back to the master module.

UART uses a fixed pulse-width switching between 0 and 5 volts. The UART data BUS operates at a baud rate of 8,192 bps. ● **SEE FIGURE 9–6**.

ENTERTAINMENT AND COMFORT COMMUNICATION

The GM **entertainment and comfort (E & C)** serial data is similar to UART, but uses a 0 to 12 volts toggle. Like UART, the E & C serial data uses a master control module connected to other remote modules, which could include the following:

- Compact disc (CD) player
- Instrument panel (IP) electrical center
- Audio system (radio)
- Heating, ventilation, and air-conditioning (HVAC) programmer and control head
- Steering wheel controls
  - ● **SEE FIGURE 9–7**.

CLASS 2 COMMUNICATIONS **Class 2** is a serial communications system that operates by toggling between 0 and 7 volts at a transfer rate of 10.4 Kbs. Class 2 is used for most high-speed communications between the powertrain control module and other control modules, plus to the scan tool. Class 2 is the primary high-speed serial communications system used by GMCAN (CAN). ● **SEE FIGURE 9–8**.

KEYWORD COMMUNICATION **Keyword** 81, 82, and 2000 serial data are also used for some module-to-module communication on GM vehicles. Keyword data BUS signals are toggled from 0 to 12 volts when communicating. The voltage or the datastream is 0 volt when not communicating. Keyword serial communication is used by the seat heater module and others, but is not connected to the data link connector (DLC). ● **SEE FIGURE 9–9**.

GMLAN General Motors, like all vehicle manufacturers, must use high-speed serial data to communicate with scan tools on

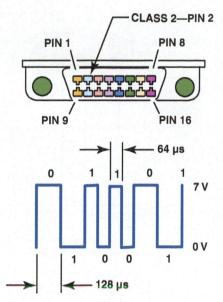

FIGURE 9–8 Class 2 serial data communication is accessible at the data link connector at pin 2.

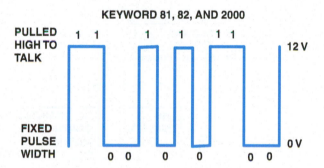

FIGURE 9–9 Keyword 82 operates at a rate of 8,192 bps, similar to UART, and keyword 2000 operates at a baud rate of 10,400 bps (the same as a Class 2 communicator).

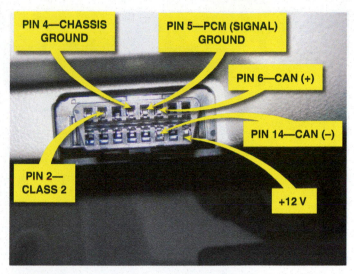

FIGURE 9–10 GMLAN uses pins at terminals 6 and 14. Pin 1 is used for low-speed GMLAN on 2006 and newer GM vehicles.

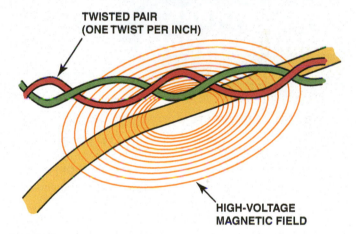

FIGURE 9–11 A twisted pair is used by several different network communications protocols to reduce interference that can be induced in the wiring from nearby electromagnetic sources.

all vehicles effective with the 2008 model year. As mentioned, the standard is called controller area network (CAN), which General Motors calls **GMLAN**, which stands for **GM local area network**.

General Motors uses two versions of GMLAN.

- **Low-speed GMLAN.** The low-speed version is used for driver-controlled functions, such as power windows and door locks. The baud rate for low-speed GMLAN is 33,300 bps. The GMLAN low-speed serial data is not connected directly to the data link connector and uses one wire. The voltage toggles between 0 and 5 volts after an initial 12 volts spike, which indicates to the modules to turn on or wake up and listen for data on the line. Low-speed GMLAN is also known as **single-wire CAN**, or **SWCAN**, and is located at pin 1 of the DLC.

- **High-speed GMLAN.** The baud rate is almost real time at 500 Kbs. This serial data method uses a two-twisted-wire circuit, which is connected to the data link connector on pins 6 and 14. ● SEE FIGURE 9–10.

 FREQUENTLY ASKED QUESTION

Why Is a Twisted Pair Used?

A twisted pair is where two wires are twisted to prevent electromagnetic radiation from affecting the signals passing through the wires. By twisting the two wires about once every inch (9 to 16 times per foot), the interference is canceled by the adjacent wire. ● SEE FIGURE 9–11.

A CANDi (CAN diagnostic interface) module is required to be used with the Tech 2 to be able to connect a GM vehicle equipped with GMLAN. ● SEE FIGURE 9–12.

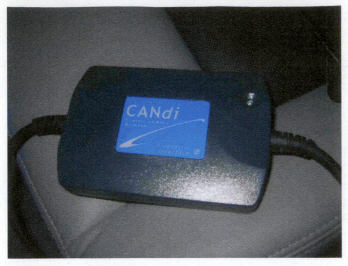

FIGURE 9-12 A CANDi module will flash the green LED rapidly if communication is detected.

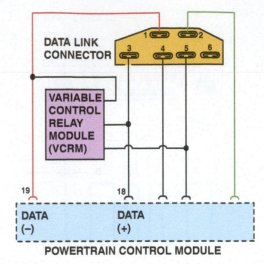

FIGURE 9-13 A Ford OBD-I diagnostic link connector showing that SCP communication uses terminals in cavities 1 (upper left) and 3 (lower left).

FORD NETWORK COMMUNICATIONS PROTOCOLS

STANDARD CORPORATE PROTOCOL Only a few Fords had scan tool data accessible through the OBD-I data link connector. To identify an OBD-I (1988–1995) on a Ford vehicle that is equipped with **standard corporate protocol (SCP)** and be able to communicate through a scan tool, look for terminals in cavities 1 and 3 of the DLC. ● **SEE FIGURE 9-13**.

SCP uses the J-1850 protocol and is active with the key on. The SCP signal is from 4 volts negative to 4.3 volts positive, and a scan tool does not have to be connected for the signal to be detected on the terminals. OBD-II (EECV) Ford vehicles use terminals 2 (positive) and 10 (negative) of the 16 pin data link connector for network communication, using the SCP module communications.

UART-BASED PROTOCOL Newer Fords use the CAN for scan tool diagnosis, but still retain SCP and **UART-based protocol (UBP)** for some modules. ● **SEE FIGURES 9-14 AND 9-15**.

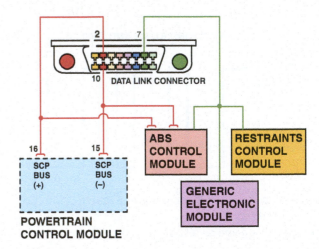

FIGURE 9-14 A scan tool can be used to check communications with the SCP BUS through terminals 2 and 10 and to the other modules connected to terminal 7 of the data link connector.

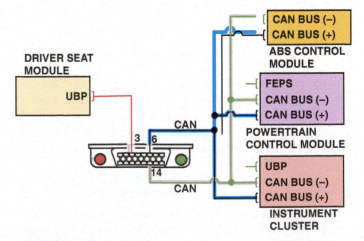

FIGURE 9-15 Many Fords use UBP module communications along with CAN.

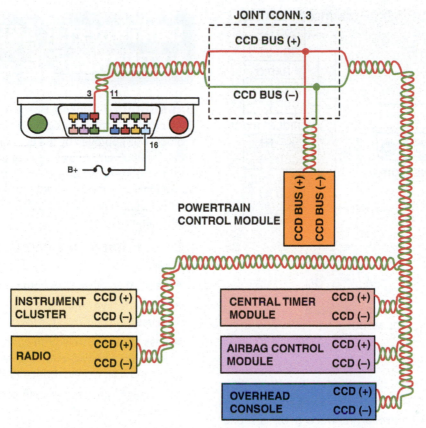

FIGURE 9–16 CCD signals are labeled plus (+) and minus (−) and use a twisted pair of wires. Notice that terminals 3 and 11 of the data link connector are used to access the CCD BUS from a scan tool. Pin 16 is used to supply 12 volts to the scan tool.

CHRYSLER COMMUNICATIONS PROTOCOLS

CCD Since the late 1980s, the Chrysler Collision Detection (CCD) multiplex network is used for scan tool and module communications. It is a differential-type communication and uses a twisted pair of wires. The modules connected to the network apply a bias voltage on each wire. CCD signals are divided into plus and minus (CCD+ and CCD−) and the voltage difference does not exceed 0.02 volt. The baud rate is 7,812.5 bps.

NOTE: The "collision" in the Chrysler Collision Detection BUS communications refers to the program that avoids conflicts of information exchange within the BUS, and does not refer to airbags or other accident-related circuits of the vehicle.

The circuit is active without a scan tool command. ● SEE FIGURE 9–16.

The modules on the CCD BUS apply a bias voltage on each wire by using termination resistors. ● SEE FIGURE 9–17.

The difference in voltage between CCD+ and CCD− is less than 20 millivolts. For example, using a digital meter with

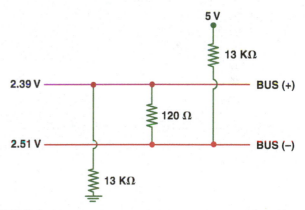

FIGURE 9–17 The differential voltage for the CCD BUS is created by using resistors in a module.

the black meter lead attached to ground and the red meter lead attached at the data link connector, a normal reading could include:

- Terminal 3 = 2.45 volts
- Terminal 11 = 2.47 volts

This is an acceptable reading because the readings are 20 millivolts (0.020 V) of each other. If both had been exactly 2.5 volts, then this could indicate that the two data lines are shorted together. The module providing the bias voltage is usually the body control module on passenger cars and the front control module on Jeeps and trucks.

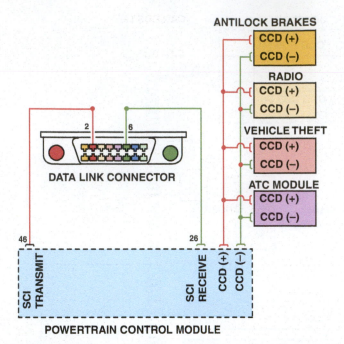

FIGURE 9–18 Many Chrysler vehicles use both SCI and CCD for module communication.

PROGRAMMABLE CONTROLLER INTERFACE

The Chrysler **programmable controller interface (PCI)** is a one-wire communication protocol that connects at the OBD-II DLC at terminal 2. The PCI BUS is connected to all modules on the BUS in a star configuration and operates at a baud rate of 10,200 bps. The voltage signal toggles between 7.5 and 0 volt. If this voltage is checked at terminal 2 of the OBD-II DLC, a voltage of about 1 volt indicates the average voltage and means that the BUS is functioning and is not shorted-to-ground. PCI and CCD are often used in the same vehicle. ● **SEE FIGURE 9–18.**

SERIAL COMMUNICATIONS INTERFACE

Chrysler used **serial communications interface (SCI)** for most scan tool and flash reprogramming functions until it was replaced with CAN. SCI is connected at the OBD-II data link connector (DLC) at terminals 6 (SCI receive) and 2 (SCI transmit). A scan tool must be connected to test the circuit.

CONTROLLER AREA NETWORK

BACKGROUND Robert Bosch Corporation developed the CAN protocol, which was called CAN 1.2, in 1993. The CAN protocol was approved by the Environmental Protection Agency (EPA) for 2003 and newer vehicle diagnostics, and became a legal requirement for all vehicles by 2008. The CAN diagnostic systems use pins 6 and 14 in the standard 16 pin OBD-II (J-1962) connector. Before CAN, the scan tool protocol had been manufacturer specific.

CAN FEATURES The CAN protocol offers the following features.

- Faster than other BUS communication protocols
- Cost-effective because it is an easier system than others to use
- Less affected by electromagnetic interference (Data is transferred on two wires that are twisted together, called twisted pair, to help reduce EMI interference.)
- Message based rather than address based, which makes it easier to expand
- No wake-up needed because it is a two-wire system
- Supports up to 15 modules plus a scan tool
- Uses a 120 ohm resistor at the ends of each pair to reduce electrical noise
- Applies 2.5 volts on both wires:

  H (high) goes to 3.5 volts when active
  L (low) goes to 1.5 volts when active
  ● **SEE FIGURE 9–19.**

CAN CLASS A, B, AND C There are three classes of CAN and they operate at different speeds. The CAN A, B, and C networks can all be linked using a gateway within the same vehicle. The gateway is usually one of the many modules in the vehicle.

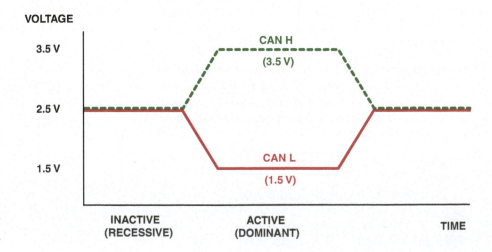

FIGURE 9–19 CAN uses a differential type of module communication where the voltage on one wire is the equal, but opposite voltage on the other wire. When no communication is occurring, both wires have 2.5 volts applied. When communication is occurring, CAN H goes up 1 to 3.5 volts and CAN L goes down 1 to 1.5 volts.

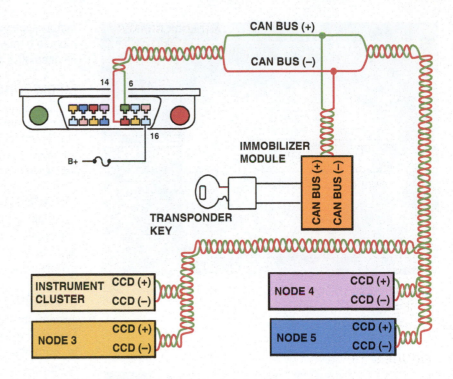

FIGURE 9–20 A typical (generic) system showing how the CAN BUS is connected to various electrical accessories and systems in the vehicle.

■ **CAN A.** This class operates on only one wire at slow speeds and is therefore less expensive to build. CAN A operates a data transfer rate of 33.33 Kbs in normal mode and up to 83.33 Kbs during reprogramming mode. CAN A uses the vehicle ground as the signal return circuit.

■ **CAN B.** This class operates on a two-wire network and does not use the vehicle ground as the signal return circuit. CAN B uses a data transfer rate of 95.2 Kbs. Instead, CAN B (and CAN C) uses two network wires for differential signaling. This means that the two data signal voltages are opposite to each other and used for error detection by constantly being compared. In this case, when the signal voltage at one of the CAN data wires goes high (CAN H), the other one goes low (CAN L), hence the name *differential signaling*. Differential signaling is also used for redundancy, in case one of the signal wires shorts out.

■ **CAN C.** This class is the highest speed CAN protocol with speeds up to 500 Kbs. Beginning with 2008 models, all vehicles sold in the United States must use CAN BUS for scan tool communications. Most vehicle manufacturers started using CAN in older models, and it is easy to determine if a vehicle is equipped with CAN. The CAN BUS communicates to the scan tool through terminals 6 and 14 of the DLC indicating that the vehicle is equipped with CAN. ● **SEE FIGURE 9–20.**

The total voltage remains constant at all times and the electromagnetic field effects of the two data BUS lines cancel each other out. The data BUS line is protected against received radiation and is virtually neutral in sending radiation.

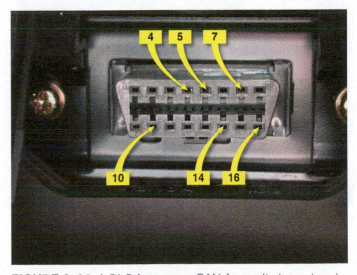

FIGURE 9–21 A DLC from a pre-CAN Acura. It shows terminals in cavities 4, 5 (grounds), 7, 10, 14, and 16 (B+).

HONDA/TOYOTA COMMUNICATIONS

The primary BUS communication on pre-CAN-equipped vehicles is ISO 9141-2 using terminals 7 and 15 at the OBD-II DLC. ● **SEE FIGURE 9–21.**

A factory scan tool or an aftermarket scan tool equipped with enhanced original equipment (OE) software is needed to access many of the BUS messages. ● **SEE FIGURE 9–22.**

FIGURE 9–22 A Chrysler scan display showing a B and two U codes, all indicating a BUS-related problem(s).

FIGURE 9–23 A typical 38-cavity diagnostic connector as found on many BMW and Mercedes vehicles under the hood. The use of a breakout box (BOB) connected to this connector can help gain access to module BUS information.

EUROPEAN BUS COMMUNICATIONS

UNIQUE DIAGNOSTIC CONNECTOR Many different types of module communications protocols are used on European vehicles, such as Mercedes and BMW.

Most of these communication BUS messages cannot be accessed through the data link connector. To check the operation of the individual modules, a scan tool equipped with factory-type software will be needed to communicate with the module through the gateway module. ● **SEE FIGURE 9–23** for an alternative access method to the modules.

MEDIA-ORIENTED SYSTEM TRANSPORT BUS The media-oriented system transport (MOST) BUS uses fiber optics for module-to-module communications in a ring or star configuration. This BUS system is currently being used for entertainment equipment data communications for videos, CDs, and other media systems in the vehicle.

MOTOROLA INTERCONNECT BUS Motorola interconnect (MI) is a single-wire serial communications protocol, using one master control module and many slave modules. Typical application of the MI BUS protocol is with power and memory mirrors, seats, windows, and headlight levelers.

DISTRIBUTED SYSTEM INTERFACE BUS Distributed system interface (DSI) BUS protocol was developed by Motorola and uses a two-wire serial BUS. This BUS protocol is currently being used for safety-related sensors and components.

BOSCH-SIEMENS-TEMIC BUS The Bosch-Siemens-Temic (BST) BUS is another system that is used for safety-related components and sensors in a vehicle, such as airbags. The BST BUS is a two-wire system and operates up to 250,000 bps.

BYTEFLIGHT BUS The byteflight BUS is used in safety critical systems, such as airbags, and uses the time division multiple access (TDMA) protocol, which operates at 10 million bps using a plastic optical fiber (POF).

? FREQUENTLY ASKED QUESTION

How Do You Know What System Is Used?

Use service information to determine which network communication protocol is used. However, due to the various systems on some vehicles, it may be easier to look at the data link connection to determine the system. All OBD-II vehicles have terminals in the following cavities.

Terminal 4: chassis ground
Terminal 5: computer (signal) ground
Terminal 16: 12 volts positive

The terminals in cavities 6 and 14 mean that this vehicle is equipped with CAN as the only module communication protocol available at the DLC. To perform a test of the BUS, use a **breakout box (BOB)** to gain access to the terminals while connecting to the vehicle, using a scan tool. ● **SEE FIGURE 9–24** or a typical OBD-II connector breakout box.

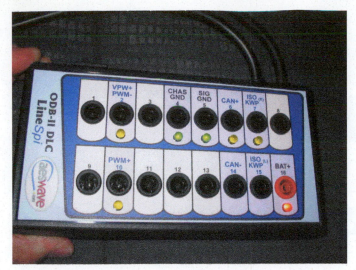

FIGURE 9–24 A breakout box (BOB) used to access the BUS terminals while using a scan tool to activate the modules. This breakout box is equipped with LEDs that light when circuits are active.

PIN	DESCRIPTION	PIN	DESCRIPTION
1	Vendor Option	9	Vendor Option
2	J1850 Bus+	10	J1850 Bus−
3	Vendor Option	11	Vendor Option
4	Chassis Ground	12	Vendor Option
5	Signal Ground	13	Vendor Option
6	CAN (J-2234) High	14	CAN (J-2234) Low
7	ISO 9141-2 K-Line	15	ISO 9141-2 L-Line
8	Vendor Option	16	Battery Power

FIGURE 9–25 A 16 pin OBD-II DLC with terminals identified. Scan tools use the power pin (16) and ground pin (4) for power so that a separate cigarette lighter plug is not necessary on OBD-II vehicles.

FLEXRAY BUS FlexRay BUS is a version of byteflight and is a high-speed serial communication system for in-vehicle networks. FlexRay is commonly used for steer-by-wire and brake-by-wire systems.

DOMESTIC DIGITAL BUS The domestic digital BUS, commonly designated D2B, is an optical BUS system connecting audio, video, computer, and telephone components in a single-ring structure with a speed of up to 5,600,000 bps.

LOCAL INTERCONNECT NETWORK BUS Local interconnect network (LIN) is a BUS protocol used between intelligent sensors and actuators and has a BUS speed of 19,200 bps.

OBD-II DATA LINK CONNECTOR

All OBD-II vehicles use a 16 pin connector that includes:

Pin 4 = chassis ground

Pin 5 = signal ground

Pin 16 = battery power (4 A max)

● **SEE FIGURE 9–25.**

GENERAL MOTORS VEHICLES

■ SAE J-1850 (VPW, Class 2, 10.4 Kbs) standard, which uses pins 2, 4, 5, and 16, but not 10

■ GM Domestic OBD-II

Pins 1 and 9: CCM (comprehensive component monitor) slow baud rate, 8,192 UART (prior to 2006)

Pin 1 (2006+): low-speed GMLAN

Pins 2 and 10: OEM enhanced, fast rate, 40,500 baud rate

Pins 7 and 15: generic OBD-II, ISO 9141, 10,400 baud rate

Pins 6 and 14: GMLAN

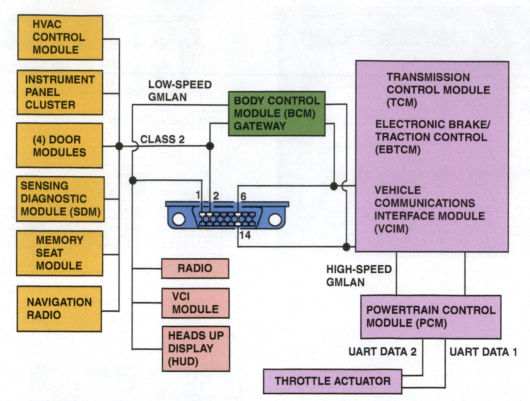

FIGURE 9–26 This schematic of a Chevrolet Equinox shows that the vehicle uses a GMLAN BUS (DLC pins 6 and 14), plus a Class 2 (pin 2) and UART. Pin 1 connects to the low-speed GMLAN network.

ASIAN, CHRYSLER, AND EUROPEAN VEHICLES

- ISO 9141-2 standard, which uses pins 4, 5, 7, 15, and 16
- Chrysler Domestic Group OBD-II

  Pins 2 and 10: CCM
  Pins 3 and 14: OEM enhanced, 60,500 baud rate
  Pins 7 and 15: generic OBD-II, ISO 9141, 10,400 baud rate

FORD VEHICLES

- SAE J-1850 (PWM, 41.6 Kbs) standard, which uses pins 2, 4, 5, 10, and 16
- Ford Domestic OBD-II

  Pins 2 and 10: CCM
  Pins 6 and 14: OEM enhanced, Class C, 40,500 baud rate
  Pins 7 and 15: generic OBD-II, ISO 9141, 10,400 baud rate

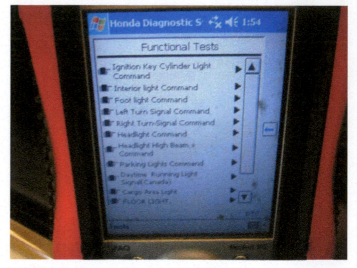

FIGURE 9–27 This Honda scan tool allows the technician to turn on individual lights and operate individual power windows and other accessories that are connected to the BUS system.

NETWORK COMMUNICATIONS DIAGNOSIS

STEPS TO FINDING A FAULT When a network communications fault is suspected, perform the following steps.

STEP 1 **Check everything that does and does not work.** Often accessories that do not seem to be connected can help identify which module or BUS circuit is at fault.

STEP 2 **Perform module status test.** Use a factory level scan tool or an aftermarket scan tool equipped with enhanced software that allows OE-like functions. Check if the components or systems can be operated through the scan tool. ● **SEE FIGURE 9–27.**

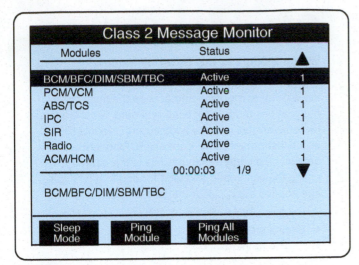

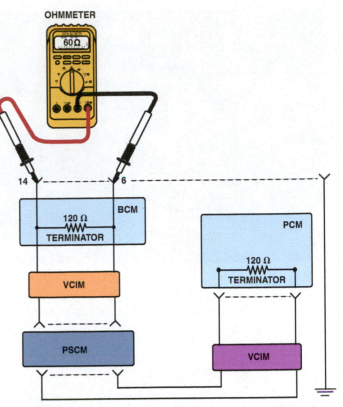

FIGURE 9–28 Modules used in a General Motors vehicle can be "pinged" using a Tech 2 scan tool.

- **Ping modules.** Start the Class 2 diagnosis by using a scan tool and select *diagnostic circuit check.* If no diagnostic trouble codes (DTCs) are shown, there could be a communication problem. Select *message monitor,* which will display the status of all of the modules on the Class 2 BUS circuit. The modules that are awake will be shown as active and the scan tool can be used to ping individual modules or command all modules. The ping command should change the status from "active" to "inactive." ● **SEE FIGURE 9–28.**

NOTE: If an excessive parasitic draw is being diagnosed, use a scan tool to ping the modules in one way to determine if one of the modules is not going to sleep and cause excessive battery drain.

- **Check state of health.** All modules on the Class 2 BUS circuit have at least one other module responsible for reporting **state of health (SOH)**. If a module fails to send a state of health message within five seconds, the companion module will set a diagnostic trouble code for the module that did not respond. The defective module is not capable of sending this message.

STEP 3 **Check the resistance of the terminating resistors.** Most high-speed BUS systems use resistors at each end, called **terminating resistors**. These resistors are used to help reduce interference into other systems in the vehicle. Usually two 120 ohm resistors are installed at each end and are therefore connected electrically in parallel. Two 120 ohm resistors connected in parallel would measure 60 ohms if tested using an ohmmeter. ● **SEE FIGURE 9–29.**

STEP 4 **Check data BUS for voltages.** Use a digital multimeter set to DC volts to monitor communications and

FIGURE 9–29 Checking the terminating resistors using an ohmmeter at the DLC.

🚗 **CASE STUDY**

The Radio Caused No-Start Story

A GMC pickup truck did not start. A technician checked with a subscription-based helpline service and discovered that a fault with the Class 2 data circuit could prevent the engine from starting. The advisor suggested that a module should be disconnected one at a time to see if one of them was taking the data line to ground. The first one the technician disconnected was the radio. The engine started and ran. Apparently the Class 2 serial data line was shorted-to-ground inside the radio, which took the entire BUS down. When BUS communication is lost, the PCM is not able to energize the fuel pump, ignition, or fuel injectors, so the engine would not start. The radio was replaced to solve the no-start condition.

Summary:

- **Complaint**—The engine did not start.
- **Cause**—A hot line service helped the technician narrow the cause to a fault in the radio that took the Class 2 data line to ground.
- **Correction**—The radio was replaced which restored proper operation of the Class 2 data bus.

FIGURE 9–30 Use front-probe terminals to access the data link connector. Always follow the specified back-probe and front-probe procedures as found in service information.

check the BUS for proper operation. Some BUS conditions and possible causes include:

- **Signal is zero volt all of the time.** Check for short-to-ground by unplugging modules one at a time to check if one module is causing the problem.

- **Signal is high or 12 volts all of the time.** The BUS circuit could be shorted to 12 volts. Check with the customer to see if any service or body repair work was done recently. Try unplugging each module one at a time to pin down which module is causing the communications problem.

- **A variable voltage usually indicates that messages are being sent and received.** CAN and Class 2 can be identified by looking at the data link connector for a terminal in cavity number 2. Class 2 is active all of the time the ignition is "on," and therefore voltage variation between 0 and 7 volts can be measured using a DMM set to read DC volts. ● SEE FIGURE 9–30.

STEP 5 **Use a digital storage oscilloscope to monitor the waveforms of the BUS circuit.** Using a scope on the data line terminals can show if communication is being transmitted. Typical faults and their causes include the following:

- **Normal operation.** Normal operation shows variable voltage signals on the data lines. It is impossible to know what information is being transmitted, but if there is activity with short sections of inactivity, this indicates normal data line transmission activity. ● SEE FIGURE 9–31.

- **High voltage.** If there is a constant high-voltage signal without any change, this indicates that the data line is shorted-to-voltage.

- **Zero or low voltage.** If the data line voltage is zero or almost zero and not showing any higher voltage signals, then the data line is short-to-ground.

STEP 6 **Follow factory service information instructions to isolate the cause of the fault.** This step often involves disconnecting one module at a time to see if it is the cause of a short-to-ground or an open in the BUS circuit.

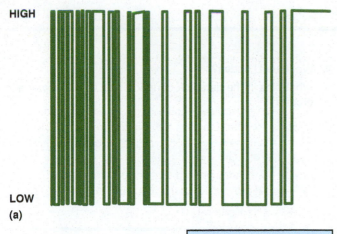

(a)

CAN BUS LOOKS GOOD

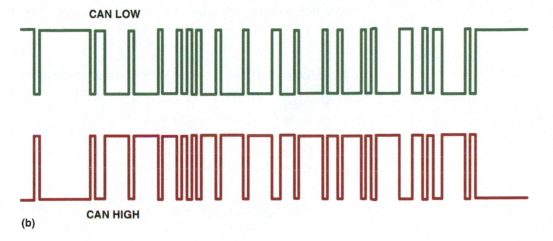

FIGURE 9–31 (a) Data is sent in packets, so it is normal to see activity and then a flat line between messages. (b) A CAN BUS should show voltages that are opposite when there is normal communications. CAN H circuit should go from 2.5 volts at rest to 3.5 volts when active. The CAN L circuit goes from 2.5 volts at rest to 1.5 volts when active.

SUMMARY

1. The use of a network for module communications reduces the number of wires and connections needed.

2. Module communication configurations include ring link, star link, and ring/star hybrid systems.

3. The SAE communication classifications for vehicle communications systems include Class A (low speed), Class B (medium speed), and Class C (high speed).

4. Various module communications used on General Motors vehicles include UART, E & C, Class 2, keyword communications, and GMLAN (CAN).

5. Types of module communications used on Ford vehicles include SCP, UBP, and CAN.

6. Chrysler brand vehicles use SCI, CCD, PCI, and CAN communications protocols.

7. Many European vehicles use an underhood electrical connector that can be used to access electrical components and modules using a breakout box (BOB) or special tester.

8. Diagnosis of network communications includes checking the terminating resistor value and checking for changing voltage signals at the DLC.

1. Why is a communication network used?

2. Why are the two wires twisted if used for network communications?

3. Why is a gateway module used?

4. What are U codes?

5. What pins in the data link connector (DLC) are power and ground?

CHAPTER QUIZ

1. Technician A says that module communications networks are used to reduce the number of wires in a vehicle. Technician B says that a communications network is used to share data from sensors, which can be used by many different modules. Which technician is correct?
   a. Technician A only
   b. Technician B only
   c. Both Technicians A and B
   d. Neither Technician A nor B

2. A module is also known as a _____.
   a. BUS
   b. node
   c. terminator
   d. resistor pack

3. A high-speed CAN BUS communicates with a scan tool through which terminal(s)?
   a. 6 and 14
   b. 2
   c. 7 and 15
   d. 4 and 16

4. Network diagnosis is being discussed. Technician A says that a test light can be used at the DLC to determine if the CAN bus has activity. Technician B says that a break-out box can be used to determine if there is activity on the CAN bus. Which technician is correct?
   a. Technician A only
   b. Technician B only
   c. Both technicians are correct
   d. Neither technician is correct

5. GM Class 2 communication toggles between _____.
   a. 5 and 7 volts
   b. 0 and 12 volts
   c. 7 and 12 volts
   d. 0 and 7 volts

6. Which terminal of the data link connector does General Motors use for Class 2 communication?
   a. 1
   b. 2
   c. 3
   d. 4

7. GMLAN is the General Motors term for which type of module communication?
   a. UART
   b. Class 2
   c. High-speed CAN
   d. Keyword 2000

8. How do CAN H and CAN L operate?
   a. CAN H is at 2.5 volts when not transmitting.
   b. CAN L is at 2.5 volts when not transmitting.
   c. CAN H goes to 3.5 volts when transmitting.
   d. All of the above

9. Which terminal of the OBD-II data link connector is the signal ground for all vehicles?
   a. 1
   b. 3
   c. 4
   d. 5

10. Terminal 16 of the OBD-II data link connector is used for what?
    a. Chassis ground
    b. 12 V positive
    c. Module (signal ground)
    d. Manufacturer's discretion

ON-BOARD DIAGNOSIS

LEARNING OBJECTIVES

After studying this chapter, the reader should be able to:

1. Understand the purpose and function of on-board diagnostics generation-II (OBD-II) systems.
2. Discuss the numbering designation of OBD-II diagnostic trouble codes.
3. List the types of information obtained from a freeze-frame.
4. Understand the information obtained from an on-board diagnostics monitor and the criteria to enable an OBD monitor.
5. List the continuous and noncontinuous monitors.

KEY TERMS

California Air Resources Board (CARB) 156
Catalyst monitor 163
Comprehensive component monitor (CCM) 161
Continuous monitors 160
Diagnostic executive 158
Enable criteria 159
Evaporative emissions monitor 163
Exhaust Gas Recirculation (EGR) Monitor 164
Exponentially weighted moving average (EWMA) monitor 160
Federal Test Procedure (FTP) 156

Freeze-frame 157
Fuel trim monitor 162
Functionality 161
Malfunction indicator lamp (MIL) 156
Misfire monitor 161
Monitor 160
On-board diagnosis (OBD) 156
Oxygen sensor monitor 162
Oxygen Sensor Heater Monitor 163
Pending codes 157
Rationality 161
Society of Automotive Engineers (SAE) 156
Task manager 158

ON-BOARD DIAGNOSTICS GENERATION–II (OBD-II) SYSTEMS

PURPOSE AND FUNCTION OF OBD-II During the 1980s, most manufacturers began equipping their vehicles with full-function control systems capable of alerting the driver of a malfunction and of allowing the technician to retrieve codes that identify circuit faults. These early diagnostic systems were meant to reduce emissions and speed up vehicle repair.

The automotive industry calls these systems **On-Board Diagnostics (OBDs)**. The **California Air Resources Board (CARB)** developed the first regulation requiring manufacturers selling vehicles in that state to install OBD. OBD Generation I (OBD I) applies to all vehicles sold in California beginning with the 1988 model year. It specifies the following requirements:

1. An instrument panel warning lamp able to alert the driver of certain control system failures, now called a **malfunction indicator lamp (MIL)**. ● **SEE FIGURE 10–1.**

2. The system's ability to record and transmit diagnostic trouble codes (DTCs) for emission-related failures.

3. Electronic system monitoring of the HO2S, EGR valve, and evaporative purge solenoid. Although not U.S. EPA required, during this time most manufacturers also equipped vehicles sold outside of California with OBD-I.

By failing to monitor the catalytic converter, the evaporative system for leaks, and the presence of engine misfire, OBD-I did not do enough to lower automotive emissions. This led the CARB and the EPA to develop OBD Generation II (OBD-II).

OBD-II OBJECTIVES Generally, the CARB defines an OBD-II-equipped vehicle by its ability to do the following:

1. Detect component degradation or a faulty emission related system that prevents compliance with federal emission standards.

2. Alert the driver of needed emission-related repair or maintenance.

3. Use standardized DTCs and accept a generic scan tool.

These requirements apply to all 1996 and later model light-duty vehicles. The Clean Air Act of 1990 directed the EPA to develop new regulations for OBD. The primary purpose of OBD-II is emission related, whereas the primary purpose of OBD-I (1988) was to detect faults in sensors or sensor circuits. OBD-II regulations require that not only sensors but also all exhaust emission control devices be tested,, and that they are verified for proper operation.

All new vehicles must pass the **Federal Test Procedure (FTP)** for exhaust emissions while being tested for 1874 seconds on dynamometer rollers that simulate the urban drive cycle around downtown Los Angeles.

FIGURE 10–1 A typical malfunction indicator lamp (MIL) often labeled "check engine" or "service engine soon" (SES).

NOTE: IM 240 is simply a shorter 240-second version of the 1874-second federal test procedure.

The regulations for OBD-II vehicles state that the vehicle computer must be capable of testing for, and determining, if the exhaust emissions are within 1.5 times the FTP limits. To achieve this goal, the computer must do the following:

- Test all exhaust emission system components for correct operation.

- Actively operate the system and measure the results.

- Continuously monitor all aspects of the engine operation to be certain that the exhaust emissions do not exceed 1.5 times the FTP limit.

- Check engine operation for a misfire.

- Turn on the MIL (check engine) if the computer senses a fault in a circuit or system.

- Record a freeze-frame, which is a snapshot of all key engine data at the time the DTC was set.

- Flash the MIL if an engine misfire occurs that could damage the catalytic converter.

OBD-II DTC NUMBERING DESIGNATION

A scan tool is required to retrieve DTCs from an OBD-II vehicle. Every OBD-II scan tool will be able to read all generic **Society of Automotive Engineers (SAE)** DTCs from any vehicle. ● **SEE FIGURE 10–2** for definitions and explanations of OBD alphanumeric DTCs.

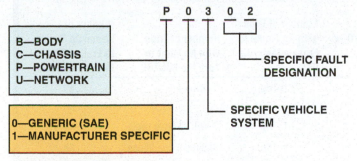

EXAMPLE: P0302 = CYLINDER 2 MISFIRE DETECTED

P 0 3 0 2

B—BODY
C—CHASSIS
P—POWERTRAIN
U—NETWORK

0—GENERIC (SAE)
1—MANUFACTURER SPECIFIC

SPECIFIC FAULT DESIGNATION

SPECIFIC VEHICLE SYSTEM

FIGURE 10–2 OBD-II DTC identification format.

The diagnostic trouble codes (DTCs) are grouped into major categories, depending on the location of the fault on the system involved:

- **Pxxx codes**—powertrain DTCs (engine, transmission-related faults)
- **Bxxx codes**—body DTCs (accessories, interior-related faults)
- **Cxxx codes**—chassis DTCs (suspension and steering-related faults)
- **Uxxx codes**—network DTCs (module communication-related faults)

DTC NUMBERING EXPLANATION The number in the hundredth position indicates the specific vehicle system or subgroup that failed. This position should be consistent for P0xxx and P1xxx-type codes. The following numbers and systems were established by SAE:

- **P0100**—Air metering and fuel system fault
- **P0200**—Fuel system (fuel injector only) fault
- **P0300**—Ignition system or misfire fault
- **P0400**—Emission control system fault
- **P0500**—Idle speed control, vehicle speed (VS) sensor fault
- **P0600**—Computer output circuit (relay, solenoid, etc.) fault
- **P0700**—Transaxle, transmission faults

NOTE: The tens and ones numbers indicate the part of the system at fault.

TYPES OF DTCS Not all OBD-II DTCs are of the same importance for exhaust emissions. Each type of DTC has different requirements for it to set, and the computer will turn on the MIL only for emissions-related DTCs.

Type A Codes: A type A DTC is emission related and will cause the MIL to be turned on in the first trip if the computer has detected a problem. Engine misfire or a very rich or lean air–fuel ratio, for example, would cause a type A DTC. These codes alert the driver to an emission problem that may cause damage to the catalytic converter.

? FREQUENTLY ASKED QUESTION

What Are Pending Codes?

Pending codes are set when operating conditions are met and the component or circuit is not within the normal range, yet the conditions have not been met to set a DTC. For example, a sensor may require two consecutive faults before a DTC is set. If a scan tool displays a pending code or a failure, a driveability concern could also be present. The pending code can help the technician to determine the root cause before the customer complains of a check engine light illumination.

Type B Codes: A type B code will be stored, and the MIL will be turned on during the second consecutive trip, alerting the driver to the fact that a diagnostic test was performed and failed.

NOTE: Type A and B codes are emission-related codes that will cause the lighting of the malfunction indicator lamp (MIL), usually labeled "check engine" or "service engine soon."

Type C and D Codes: Type C and D codes are for use with non–emission related diagnostic tests. They will cause the lighting of a "service" lamp (if the vehicle is so equipped). Type C codes are also called type C1 codes, and D codes are also called type C0 codes.

DIAGNOSTIC TROUBLE CODE PRIORITY CARB has also mandated that all diagnostic trouble codes (DTCs) be stored according to individual priority. DTCs with a higher priority overwrite those with a lower priority. The OBD-II System DTC Priority is listed here:

Priority 0—Non–emission related codes
Priority 1—One-trip failure of two-trip fault for nonfuel, non-misfire codes
Priority 2—One-trip failure of two-trip fault for fuel or misfire codes
Priority 3—Two-trip failure or matured fault of nonfuel, non-misfire codes
Priority 4—Two-trip failure or matured fault for fuel or misfire codes

OBD-II FREEZE-FRAME

To assist the service technician, OBD-II requires the computer to take a "snapshot" or **freeze-frame** of all data at the instant an emission-related DTC is set. A scan tool is required to retrieve this data.

Monitor Name	Monitor Type (How Often It Completes)	Number of Faults on Separate Trips to Set a Pending DTC	Number of Separate Consecutive Trips to Light MIL, Store a DTC	Number of Trips with No Faults to Erase a Maturing DTC	Number of Trips with No Fault to Turn the MIL Off	Number of Warm-Up Cycles to Erase DTC after MIL Is Turned Off
CCM	Continuous (when trip conditions allow it)	1	2	1–Trip	3–Trips	40
Catalyst	Once per drive cycle	1	3	1–Trip	3–OBD-II drive cycle	40
Misfire Type A	Continuous		1	1–Trip	3–Similar conditions	80
Misfire Type B	Continuous	1	2	1–Trip	3–Similar conditions	80
Fuel System	Continuous	1	2	1–Trip	3–Similar conditions	80
Oxygen Sensor	Once per trip	1	2	1–Trip	3–Trips	40
EGR	Once per trip	1	2	1–Trip	3–Trips	40
EVAP	Once per trip	1	1	1–Trip	3–Trips	40
AIR	Once per trip	1	2	1–Trip	3–Trips	40

CHART 10–1

PCM determination of faults chart.

NOTE: Although OBD-II requires that just one freeze-frame of data be stored, the instant an emission-related DTC is set, vehicle manufacturers usually provide expanded data about the DTC beyond that required, such as General Motor's *failure recorders*. However, retrieving this enhanced data usually requires the use of the vehicle-specific scan tool.

Freeze-frame items include the following:

- Calculated load value
- Engine speed (RPM)
- Short-term and long-term fuel trim percent
- Fuel system pressure (on some vehicles)
- Vehicle speed (mph)
- Engine coolant temperature
- Intake manifold pressure
- Closed-open-loop status
- Fault code that triggered the freeze-frame
- If a misfire code is set, identify which cylinder is misfiring

A DTC should not be cleared from the vehicle computer memory unless the fault has been corrected, and the technician is so directed by the diagnostic procedure. If the problem that caused the DTC to be set has been corrected, the computer will automatically clear the DTC after 40 consecutive warm-up cycles with no further faults detected. (Misfire and excessively rich or lean condition codes require 80 warm-up cycles.) The codes can also be erased by using a scan tool. ● **SEE CHART 10–1.**

NOTE: Disconnecting the battery may not erase OBD-II DTCs or freeze-frame data. Most vehicle manufacturers recommend using a scan tool to erase DTCs rather than disconnecting the battery because the memory for the radio, seats, and learned engine operating parameters is lost if the battery is disconnected.

DIAGNOSTIC EXECUTIVE OR TASK MANAGER

PURPOSE On OBD-II systems, the powertrain control module (PCM) incorporates a special segment of software to perform the task needed. On Ford and GM systems, this software is called the diagnostic executive. On Chrysler systems, it is called the **task manager**. This software program is designed to manage the operation of all OBD-II monitors by controlling the sequence of steps necessary to execute the diagnostic tests and monitors.

ENABLING CRITERIA With so many different tests (monitors) to run, the PCM needs an internal director to keep track of when each monitor should run. As mentioned, different manufacturers have different names for this director, such as the diagnostic executive or the task manager. Each monitor has enabling criteria. These criteria are a set of conditions that must be met before the task manager will give the go-ahead for each monitor to run. Most enabling criteria follow simple logic, such as the following:

- The task manager will not authorize the start of the O2S monitor until the engine has reached operating temperature and the system has entered closed loop.
- The task manager will not authorize the start of the EGR monitor when the engine is at idle because the EGR is always closed at this time.

Because each monitor is responsible for testing a different part of the system, the enabling criteria can differ greatly from one monitor to the next. The task manager must decide when each monitor should run, and in what order, to avoid confusion.

There may be a conflict if two monitors were to run at the same time. The results of one monitor might also be tainted if a second monitor were to run simultaneously. In such cases, the task manager decides which monitor has a higher priority. Some monitors also depend on the results of other monitors before they can run.

A monitor may be classified as pending if a failed sensor or other system fault is keeping it from running on schedule. The task manager may suspend a monitor if the conditions are not correct to continue. For example, if the catalyst monitor is running during a road test and the PCM detects a misfire, the catalyst monitor will be suspended for the duration of the misfire.

GLOBAL DISABLE   Monitors can be *globally disabled* for certain defined parameters (as defined by the EPA and CARB) because of the potential for false failures during the test. Not all global disablers apply to every monitor. Conditions that could disable a monitor include:

- New catalyst Bank 2
- New catalyst Bank 1
- Very low battery voltage
- High ethanol content
- Power Take Off (PTO) Engage
- Low fuel level
- High fuel level
- High altitude
- Low battery voltage
- High battery voltage
- Low ambient temperature
- Very low ambient temperature

PENDING   Under some situations the PCM will not run a monitor if the MIL is illuminated and a fault is stored from another monitor. In these situations, the PCM postpones monitors, pending a resolution of the original fault. The PCM does not run the test until the problem is remedied.

For example, when the MIL is illuminated for an oxygen sensor fault, the PCM does not run the catalyst monitor until the oxygen sensor fault is remedied. Since the catalyst monitor is based on signals from the oxygen sensor, running the test would produce inaccurate results.

CONFLICT   There are also situations when the PCM does not run a monitor if another monitor is in progress. In these situations, the effects of another monitor running could result in an erroneous failure. If this conflict is present, the monitor is not run until the conflicting condition passes. Most likely, the monitor will run later after the conflicting monitor has passed.

For example, if the fuel system monitor is in progress, the PCM does not run the EGR monitor. Since both tests monitor changes in air–fuel ratio and adaptive fuel compensation, the monitors conflict with each other.

SUSPEND   Occasionally, the PCM may not allow a two-trip fault to mature. The PCM will suspend the maturing fault if a condition exists that may induce erroneous failure. This prevents illuminating the MIL for the wrong fault and allows more precise diagnosis.

For example, if the PCM is storing a one-trip fault for the oxygen sensor and the EGR monitor, the PCM may still run the EGR monitor, but will suspend the results until the oxygen sensor monitor either passes or fails. At that point, the PCM can determine if the EGR system is actually failing or if an oxygen sensor is failing.

TRIP   A trip is defined as a key-on condition that contains the necessary conditions for a particular test to be performed followed by a key-off. These conditions are called the **enable criteria**. For example, for the EGR test to be performed, the engine must be at normal operating temperature and decelerating for a minimum amount of time. Some tests are performed when the engine is cold, whereas others require that the vehicle be cruising at a steady highway speed.

WARM-UP CYCLE   Once a MIL is deactivated, the original code will remain in memory until 40 warm-up cycles are completed without the fault reappearing. A warm-up cycle is defined as a trip with an engine temperature increase of at least 40°F, and where engine temperature reaches at least 160°F (71°C).

MIL CONDITION: OFF   This condition indicates that the PCM has not detected any faults in an emissions-related component or system or that the MIL circuit is not working.

MIL CONDITION: ON STEADY   This condition indicates a fault in an emissions-related component or system that could affect the vehicle emission levels.

MIL CONDITION: FLASHING   This condition indicates a misfire or fuel control system fault that could damage the catalytic converter.

NOTE: In a misfire condition with the MIL on steady, if the driver reaches a vehicle speed and load condition with the engine misfiring at a level that could cause

catalyst damage, the MIL would start flashing. It would continue to flash until engine speed and load conditions caused the level of misfire to subside. Then, the MIL would go back to the on-steady condition. This situation might result in a customer complaint of a MIL with an intermittent flashing condition.

MIL OFF The PCM will turn off the MIL if any of the following actions or conditions occurs:

- The codes are cleared with a scan tool.
- Power to the PCM is removed at the battery or with the PCM power fuse for an extended period of time (may be up to several hours or longer).
- A vehicle is driven on three consecutive trips with a warm-up cycle and meets all code set conditions without the PCM detecting any faults.

The PCM will set a code if a fault is detected that could cause tailpipe emissions to exceed 1.5 times the FTP standard. However, the PCM will not deactivate the MIL until the vehicle has been driven on three consecutive trips with vehicle conditions similar to actual conditions present when the fault was detected. This is not merely three vehicle start-ups and trips. It means three trips during which certain engine operating conditions are met so that the OBD-II monitor that found the fault can run again and pass the diagnostic test.

EXPONENTIALLY WEIGHTED MOVING AVERAGE (EWMA) MONITORS

The **exponentially weighted moving average (EWMA) monitor** is a mathematical method used to determine performance. This method smooths out any variables in the readings over time and results in a running average. Some manufacturers use this strategy to test a system multiple times during a single drive cycle to get more reliable test results. This method is used by some vehicle manufacturers for two monitors.

1. Catalyst monitor.
2. EGR monitor.

MONITORS

DEFINITION A **monitor** is an organized method of testing a specific part of the system. Monitors are simply tests that the computer performs to evaluate components and systems. If a component or system failure is detected while a monitor is running, a DTC will be stored and the MIL illuminated during the second trip. The two types of monitors are continuous and noncontinuous (once-per-trip).

CONTINUOUS MONITORS **Continuous monitors** are run after the required enabling conditions are met. These continuous monitors will run for the remainder of the vehicle drive cycle.

? FREQUENTLY ASKED QUESTION

What Is a Drive Cycle?

A **drive cycle** is a vehicle being driven under specified speed and times that will allow all monitors to run. In other words, the powertrain control module (PCM) is looking at a series of data points representing speed and time, and determines from these data points when the conditions are right to perform a monitor or a test of a component. These data points, and therefore the drive cycle, are vehicle specific and are not the same for each vehicle. Some common conditions for a drive cycle to successfully run all of the monitors include:

1. Cold start intake air temperature (IAT) and engine coolant temperature (ECT) close to each other, indicating that the engine has cooled to the temperature of the surrounding air temperature.
2. Fuel level within a certain range usually between 15% and 85%.
3. Vehicle speed within a certain speed range for a certain amount of time, usually 4 to 12 minutes.
4. Stop and idle for a certain time. Each monitor requires its own set of parameters needed to run the test, and sometimes these conditions cannot be met. For example, some evaporate emissions control (EVAP) systems require a temperature that may not be possible in winter months in a cold climatic area.

A typical universal drive cycle that works for many vehicles includes the following steps.

- MIL must be off.
- No DTCs present.
- Fuel fill between 15% and 85%.
- Cold start—Preferred = 8-hour soak at 68°F to 86°F.
- Alternative = ECT below 86°F.

STEP 1 With the ignition off, connect a scan tool.

STEP 2 Start engine and drive between 20 and 30 mph for 22 minutes, allowing speed to vary.

STEP 3 Stop and idle for 40 seconds, gradually accelerate to 55 mph.

STEP 4 Maintain 55 mph for 4 minutes using a steady throttle input.

STEP 5 Stop and idle for 30 seconds, then accelerate to 30 mph.

STEP 6 Maintain 30 mph for 12 minutes.

STEP 7 Repeat steps 4 and 5 four times.

Using scan tool, check readiness. Always check service information for the exact drive cycle conditions for the vehicle being serviced for best results.

COMPREHENSIVE COMPONENT MONITOR (CCM)

The **Comprehensive Component Monitor (CCM)** watches the sensors and actuators in the OBD-II system. Sensor values are constantly compared with known-good values stored in the PCM's memory. The CCM is an internal program in the PCM designed to monitor a failure in any electronic component or circuit (including emission-related and non–emission related circuits) that provides input or output signals to the PCM. The PCM considers that an input or output signal is inoperative when a failure exists because of an open circuit or out-of-range value or if an onboard rationality check fails. If an emission-related fault is detected, the PCM will set a code and activate the MIL (requires two consecutive trips).

Many PCM sensors and output devices are tested at key-on or immediately after engine start-up. However, some devices are tested by the CCM only after the engine meets certain engine conditions. The number of times the CCM must detect a fault before it will activate the MIL depends upon the manufacturer, but most require two consecutive trips to activate the MIL. The components tested by the CCM include the following:

- Four-wheel-drive low switch
- Brake switch
- Camshaft (CMP) and crankshaft (CKP) sensors
- Clutch switch (manual transmissions/transaxles only)
- Cruise servo switch
- Engine coolant temperature (ECT) sensor
- EVAP purge sensor or switch
- Fuel composition sensor
- Intake air temperature (IAT) sensor
- Knock sensor (KS)
- Manifold absolute pressure (MAP) sensor
- Mass airflow (MAF) sensor
- Throttle-position (TP) sensor
- Transmission temperature sensor
- Transmission turbine speed sensor
- Vacuum sensor
- Vehicle speed (VS) sensor
- EVAP canister purge and EVAP purge vent solenoid
- Idle air control (IAC)
- Ignition control system
- Transmission torque converter clutch solenoid
- Transmission shift solenoids

ELECTRICAL TEST The electrical test refers to the PCM check of both input and outputs for the following:

- Open circuits
- Shorts to voltage
- Shorts to ground

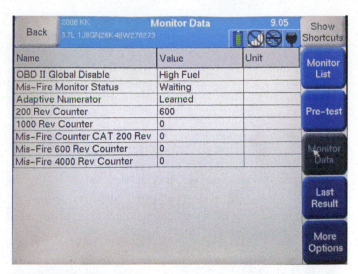

FIGURE 10–3 A screen capture of a misfire on a scan tool.

Example:

ECT Shorted high (input to PCM) above capable voltage; that is, a 5-volt sensor with 12-volt input to PCM would indicate a short to voltage.

RATIONALITY TEST A **rationality test** is applied by the PCM and constantly being monitored for rationality. This means that the input signal is compared against other inputs and information to see if it makes sense under the current conditions.

FUNCTIONALITY TEST A **functionality test** refers to PCM inputs checking the operation of the outputs to see that they are functioning as designed:

Example:

- PCM commands IAC to increase engine speed
- PCM monitors engine RPM
- Functionality test fails if engine speed does not increase

MISFIRE MONITOR The **misfire monitor** looks at engine misfire. The PCM uses the information received from the crankshaft position sensor (CKP) to calculate the time between the edges of the reluctor, as well as the rotational speed and acceleration. By comparing the acceleration of each firing event, the PCM can determine if a cylinder is not firing correctly. ● **SEE FIGURE 10–3.**

Misfire Type A. Upon detection of a misfire type A (200 revolutions), which would cause catalyst damage, the MIL will blink once per second during the actual misfire, and a DTC will be stored.

Misfire Type B. Upon detection of a misfire type B (1000 revolutions), which will exceed 1.5 times the EPA federal test procedure (FTP) standard or cause a vehicle to fail an inspection and maintenance tailpipe emissions test, the MIL will illuminate and a DTC will be stored.

Misfire codes can be set for a variety of failures. The systems that can cause a misfire code to set include the ignition, fuel,

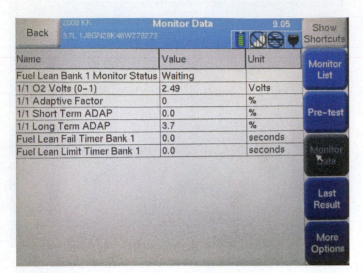

FIGURE 10–4 A Chrysler fuel trim monitor.

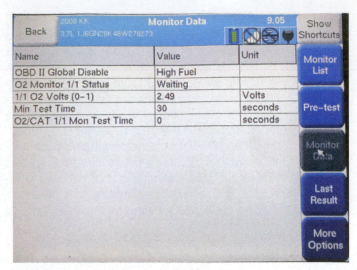

FIGURE 10–5 An example of an upstream oxygen sensor monitor as displayed on a scan tool.

the air induction, and engine mechanical. Once the repairs have been completed, it is helpful to complete a misfire monitor good trip to ensure the problem has been resolved. Most misfire monitors require that a "pass" occur under the same conditions that the failure occurred. In order to find the "similar conditions" window, it is helpful to review the freeze-frame data to see what conditions were present when the failure occurred.

The DTC associated with multiple cylinder misfire for a type A or type B misfire is DTC P0300. The DTCs associated with an individual cylinder misfire for a type A or type B misfire are DTCs P0301, P0302, P0303, P0304, P0305, P0306, P0307, P0308, P0309, and P0310.

FUEL TRIM MONITOR The PCM uses the **fuel trim monitor** to continuously monitor short- and long-term fuel trim. Constantly updated adaptive fuel tables are stored in long-term memory (KAM) and used by the PCM for compensation due to wear and aging of the fuel system components. The MIL will illuminate when the PCM determines the total fuel trim values have reached and stayed at their limits for too long a period of time. The percentage of fuel addition or subtraction that the monitor fails is not necessarily the same as the PCM's total ability to add or subtract fuel. In many cases, the PCM will continue to add or subtract fuel beyond the monitor failure point in an effort to keep the vehicle operating. ● **SEE FIGURE 10–4**.

Generally, fuel trim monitors fail because of fuel delivery or air induction concerns. After the failure is corrected, it is helpful to pass a fuel trim monitor to ensure the problem has been corrected. Fuel trim monitors typically have to pass under the same conditions in which they failed. To determine the similar conditions window it is helpful to review the freeze-frame data.

The codes associated with a fuel trim monitor include:

- **P0171**—Fuel Trim Lean Bank 1
- **P0174**—Fuel Trim Lean Bank 2
- **P0172**—Fuel Trim Rich Bank 1
- **P0175**—Fuel Trim Rich Bank 2

NONCONTINUOUS (ONCE-PER-TRIP) MONITORS

The following data generally applies to all noncontinuous or once-per-trip monitors:

- Monitor runs once per trip, pass or fail
- Two-trip DTCs
- MIL, DTC, freeze-frame after two consecutive faults
- Freeze-frame is priority 1 on first trip
- Freeze-frame is priority 3 on maturing trip
- Three consecutive good trips are used to extinguish the MIL
- Forty warm-up cycles are used to erase DTC and freeze-frame

OXYGEN SENSOR MONITOR The **oxygen sensor monitor** is a once-per-trip monitor that tests the performance of both the upstream and downstream oxygen sensors. The monitor tests the ability of the sensors to switch fast enough and that the voltage can change far enough.

To enable the monitor to run, the powertrain control module will ensure the engine, the exhaust system, and the oxygen sensor have reached a minimum temperature. Generally, this involves driving the vehicle at a minimum speed with a minimum throttle angle with the engine closed for a specific amount of time. ● **SEE FIGURE 10–5**.

Once the monitor is ready to run under specific operating conditions, the powertrain control module will monitor the signal being generated by the oxygen sensor. The signal will be monitored to see how many switches or half-cycles occurred in a specific amount of time, and how high and low the voltage reached during each switch. The criteria for an upstream oxygen sensor are different from the downstream oxygen sensor because of the presence of the catalytic converter.

Generally, a failed oxygen sensor performance monitor is a result of an older oxygen sensor that has deteriorated over time. It is important to make sure the exhaust system is in good condition and not leaking before condemning the sensor. A leaking exhaust system will allow unmonitored oxygen into the exhaust stream and may cause a false failure.

Pass or fail, once the monitor has been completed, the oxygen sensor performance is no longer monitored for the balance of the drive cycle. The circuit continuity of the sensor, however, is still continuously monitored throughout the drive cycle by the comprehensive component monitor. An oxygen sensor monitor that fails two consecutive monitors will set a hard code and illuminate the MIL.

After the failure has been corrected the vehicle should be driven in a manner that will allow the oxygen sensor to run to completion. If the system passes the monitor, it is likely the vehicle has been correctly repaired. If the system fails the monitor, it is likely other problems are still present.

The codes associated with a failed oxygen sensor monitor are:

- P1131 HO2S lack of switching
- P0132 HO2S over voltage
- P0133 HO2S slow response

OXYGEN SENSOR HEATER MONITOR
The **Oxygen Sensor Heater Monitor** tests the oxygen sensor heater separately from the sensor output of the oxygen sensor. It is a once-per-trip monitor and is typically tested on a cold start. All oxygen sensor heaters are tested at the same time. Generally, the current flow through the circuit is monitored by the PCM to determine if the heater is functional. On many vehicles this is the first monitor to run during the drive cycle.

The PCM can control the ground side or the power side of the circuit, depending on how the system is designed. The heater can be provided switched battery power and the PCM can pulse-width modulate the ground side of the circuit using a low-side driver. The PCM can also control the voltage to a heater using a high-side driver on a sensor that is always grounded.

Typically, the only enabling criteria for this monitor are that the engine is cold and the battery voltage is above a minimum level.

A failed oxygen sensor heater monitor is most generally associated with a failed heater. An easy way to test the circuit is to unplug the sensor and connect a test light across the heater circuit in the connector. Start the vehicle and if the test light illuminates the PCM and the circuits are both good, this leaves the heater to be the only possible bad component.

The codes associated with a failed oxygen sensor heater are:

- **P0135**—Upstream O₂ Sensor Heater Malfunction
- **P0141**—Downstream O₂ Sensor Heater Malfunction

CATALYST MONITOR
The **catalyst monitor** is a once-per-trip monitor that monitors the efficiency of the catalytic converter. The catalytic converter is designed to reduce the levels of hydrocarbons

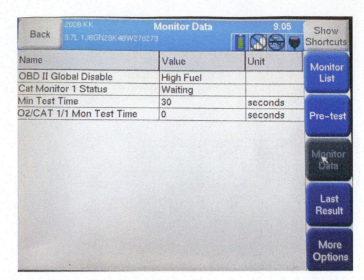

FIGURE 10–6 An EWMA catalyst monitor on a scan tool.

(HC), carbon monoxide (CO), and oxides of nitrogen (NO_x) to the certified level of the vehicle's particular emissions package.

The efficiency of the catalytic converter is monitored using an upstream and a downstream oxygen sensor. Under specific operating conditions, the switch rate of the two sensors are monitored and compared. During normal operating conditions, the upstream oxygen sensor will be switching between a low voltage (0.2 V) and a high voltage (0.8 V) as it keeps the vehicle in normal fuel control. If the catalyst is good, the downstream oxygen sensor will show very little activity. As the catalyst begins to fail, the switch rate of the downstream oxygen sensor will begin to approach the switch rate of the upstream oxygen sensor. When a specific switch rate percentage is surpassed, the monitor will fail, indicating the emissions have increased to 1.5 times the Federal Test Procedure (FTP) standards.

To enable a monitor to operate, specific criteria must be met. Although it varies by vehicle, the criteria focus on operating temperature, vehicle speed, and throttle angle. Generally, the fuel level must be above 15% and the engine must be in closed loop fuel control. The engine must be at normal operating temperature and the vehicle speed and throttle angle must indicate the engine is under enough load to get the exhaust system hot enough to test. ● **SEE FIGURE 10–6**.

Before condemning a catalyst, it is recommended that the fuel trims be checked and the integrity of the exhaust system be inspected. A fuel system that is adding or subtracting more than 10% of the fuel, or an exhaust system that leaks, may create a false failure and set an erroneous code.

The codes associated with a catalyst monitor failure include:

- **P0420**—Catalyst Efficiency below Threshold (Bank 1)
- **P0430**—Catalyst Efficiency below Threshold (Bank 2)

EVAPORATIVE EMISSIONS MONITOR
The purpose of the **evaporative emissions monitor** is to ensure the evaporative emissions system flows properly and does not leak unburned hydrocarbons (HCS) to the atmosphere. Evaporative emissions systems are generally divided into two categories:

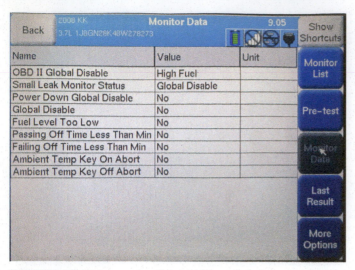

FIGURE 10–7 An evaporative emissions monitor on a pressure type (LDP) system on a Chrysler.

pressure based and vacuum based. Because of these differences, the monitors are not the same.

Regardless of the style of the evaporative system, the enabling criteria to get the monitor ready to run are very similar. The engine must cold soak and the ambient temperature must be between 40 and 90 degrees. The fuel level must be between 15% and 85% and the intake air temperature and coolant temperature must be within 10 degrees of each other.

A vacuum-style evaporative system monitor runs on a cold start. The vent solenoid is energized closing the valve. The purge solenoid is energized allowing the system to flow. This operation will pull the evaporative system into a vacuum. The pressure level is monitored for a specific amount of time to determine if the system is leaking and flowing properly. A system that fails to hold the vacuum for the specified amount of time will fail.

A pressure-style system also runs on a cold start using a leak detection pump. The purge valve is de-energized, sealing the system, and the pump is energized to pressurize the system. The system pressure is monitored for a specific amount of time. A system that fails to hold for the specific amount of time will fail for a leak. ● **SEE FIGURE 10–7.**

System failures for leaks are the most common. Failures of components, such as vent solenoids, deterioration of lines, and loose gas caps, are the common causes of the failure. The use of scan data and smoke machines can help to identify these

failures. This monitor is very difficult to operate after a repair has been completed because of the cold soak requirement. Many manufacturers provide a service bay or other test that will simulate the monitor to help with the repair verification process. Codes associated with an evaporative emission failure are:

- **P0456**—Evaporative Emission System Small Leak Detected
- **P0457**—Evaporative Emission System Large Leak Detected

EXHAUST GAS RECIRCULATION (EGR) MONITOR The **Exhaust Gas Recirculation (EGR) Monitor** is a once-per-trip monitor that measures the flow of exhaust gases back into the engine. The EGR system is designed to displace oxygen in the combustion chamber with exhaust gases to lower combustion temperatures and the level of oxides of nitrogen (NO_x). The monitor ensures that the flow is not too low or too high.

The many different designs of an EGR system affect the operation of the EGR monitor. Some systems will monitor intake manifold pressure during change while others will monitor exhaust oxygen level change. The enabling criteria for different systems are very similar. The engine must be at operating condition with the fuel system in closed loop. The engine load, vehicle speed, and throttle angle must be in a specific range. During the operation of the monitor, the EGR valve is either turned on or off and the specific pressure or exhaust oxygen level change is measured. If the level of change is in the expected range, the monitor will pass. If the level change is too low or too high, the system will fail.

Failures for insufficient flow and excessive flow are common. EGR valve failures are common, but it is important to inspect the system for the presence of carbon. Carbon build-up is a common source of ERG system failures. It may restrict system flow and cause a failure for insufficient flow, or it may not allow a valve to close creating an excessive flow failure. Carbon can be cleaned from the system using dispersants, such as Simple Green.

Once the repairs have been completed, the drive cycle for the EGR monitor should be completed to ensure the system is operating normally. Failures associated with EGR monitor failures include:

- **P0401**—EGR Insufficient Flow Detected
- **P0402**—EGR Excessive Flow Detected

SUMMARY

1. If the MIL is on, retrieve the DTC and follow the manufacturer's recommended procedure to find the root cause of the problem.

2. All monitors must have the enable criteria achieved before a test is performed.

3. OBD-II vehicles use common generic DTCs.

4. OBD-II includes generic (SAE) as well as vehicle manufacturer-specific DTCs and data display.

5. All OBD-II monitors can be divided into two categories: continuous and noncontinuous (once-per-trip).

1. What does the PCM do during a trip to test emission-related components?
2. What is the difference between a type A and type B OBD-II DTC?
3. What is the difference between a trip and a warm-up cycle?
4. What could cause the MIL to flash?
5. What does it mean for an OBD-II monitor to be globally disabled?

CHAPTER QUIZ

1. A freeze-frame is generated on an OBD-II vehicle _____.
   a. when a type C or D diagnostic trouble code is set
   b. when a type A or B diagnostic trouble code is set
   c. every other trip
   d. when the PCM detects a problem with the O2S

2. An ignition misfire or fuel mixture problem is an example of what type of DTC?
   a. Type A
   b. Type B
   c. Type C
   d. Type D

3. The comprehensive component monitor checks computer-controlled devices for _____.
   a. opens
   b. rationality
   c. shorts-to-ground
   d. All of the above

4. OBD-II has been on all passenger vehicles in the United States since _____.
   a. 1986
   b. 1991
   c. 1996
   d. 2000

5. Which is a continuous monitor?
   a. Fuel trim monitor
   b. EGR monitor
   c. Oxygen sensor monitor
   d. Catalyst monitor

6. The OBD-II task manager software is responsible for _____.
   a. calculating spark timing
   b. calculating fuel injector timing
   c. controlling the timing of diagnostic tests
   d. measuring the coolant temperature

7. DTC P0302 is a _____.
   a. generic DTC
   b. vehicle manufacturer–specific DTC
   c. idle speed–related DTC
   d. transmission/transaxle-related DTC

8. Freeze-frame data includes all of the following EXCEPT _____.
   a. RPM
   b. date of the failure
   c. coolant temperature
   d. vehicle speed

9. The computer will automatically clear a DTC if there are no additional detected faults after _____.
   a. forty consecutive warm-up cycles
   b. eighty warm-up cycles
   c. two consecutive trips
   d. four key-on/key-off cycles

10. A vehicle has a flashing MIL when warmed up and driving. What does this mean?
    a. OBD-II self-test complete
    b. Possible catalytic converter damage
    c. Low tailpipe flow
    d. Fuel pressure too low

chapter 11

GLOBAL OBD II AND MODE $06

After studying this chapter, the reader should be able to:

1. Explain Global OBD-II and its modes of operation.
2. List the steps for diagnosing problems using mode $06.
3. Access global OBD II on a scan tool.
4. Describe how mode $06 can be used to identify a problem.
5. Explain how to convert raw numbers to usable data for various types of mode $06 tests.
6. Describe permanent fault codes and how to clear them.
7. State where mode $06 information can be obtained.

KEY TERMS

CID 167
Generic OBD II 167
Global OBD II 167
MID 167
Mode $06 168
PID 167
TID 167

WHAT IS GLOBAL OBD II?

Global OBD II, also called **generic OBD II**, is the standardized format of on-board diagnostics, following SAE standard J1962. Global OBD II was designed for engineers to check the operation of noncontinuously monitored systems. When OBD II was first introduced, it was not intended to be used by service technicians.

PURPOSES AND FUNCTIONS The purposes and functions of global OBD II include:

1. It can check the powertrain control module (PCM) to determine what it has detected about a failure.

2. It can be used by service technicians to verify a repair.

3. It can check the test results performed by the PCM to see if the results are close to a failure level. This information will show what is at fault even though no diagnostic trouble codes are set.

4. Since the data displayed is very technical, it often need to be converted to give the service technician usable information.

5. An estimated 80% of the PCM DTCs can be diagnosed using the global OBD II function of the scan tool.

6. All global OBD-II functions are standardized, which is not the case when looking at original equipment manufacturer (OEM) data.

7. Some DTCs may be displayed using the global OBD-II function of the scan tool that is not displayed on an OEM, or by using the enhanced mode OBD-II function of the scan tool.

GLOBAL OBD II MODES

All OBD-II vehicles must be able to display data on a global (generic) scan tool under ten different modes of operation. These modes include:

Mode One	Current powertrain data (parameter identification display or **PID**)
Mode Two	Freeze-frame data
Mode Three	Diagnostic trouble codes
Mode Four	Clear and reset diagnostic trouble codes (DTCs), freeze-frame data, and readiness status monitors for noncontinuous monitors only
Mode Five	Oxygen sensor monitor test results
Mode Six	Onboard monitoring of test results for noncontinuous monitored systems
Mode Seven	Onboard monitoring of test results for continuously monitored systems
Mode Eight	Bidirectional control of onboard systems

FREQUENTLY ASKED QUESTION

How Can You Tell Global from Factory?

When using a scan tool on an OBD-II equipped vehicle, if the display asks for make, model, and year of manufacture, then the factory or enhanced part of the PCM is being accessed. This is true for most scan tools except the Chrysler DRB III and Star Scans being used on a Chrysler vehicle. These scan tools can determine vehicle information from the PCM and do not need to be entered by the service technician. If the global or generic part of the PCM is being scanned, then there is no need to know the vehicle details.

Mode Nine	Module identification
Mode Ten ($0A)	Permanent diagnostic trouble codes (DTCs)

HEXADECIMAL NUMBERS Generic (global) data is used by most state emission programs. Generic OBD-II displays often use hexadecimal numbers, which use 16 numbers instead of 10. The numbers 0 to 9 (zero counts as a number) make up the first 10 and then capital letters A to F complete the 16 numbers. To help identify the number as being in a hexadecimal format, a dollar sign ($) is used in front of the number or letter. See the following conversion chart:

Decimal Number	Hexadecimal Code
0	$0
1	$1
2	$2
3	$3
4	$4
5	$5
6	$6
7	$7
8	$8
9	$9
10	$A
11	$B
12	$C
13	$D
14	$E
15	$F

Hexadecimal coding is also used to identify tests (**Test Identification [TID]** and **Component Identification [CID]**). CAN-equipped vehicles use **monitor identification (MID)** and TID.

FIGURE 11–1 Global OBD II can be accessed from the main menu on all aftermarket and some original equipment scan tools.

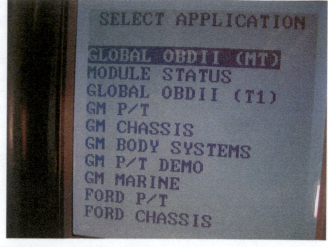

FIGURE 11–2 A photo of a Master Tech display, showing where to select global OBD II from the menu.

DIAGNOSING PROBLEMS USING MODE $06

Mode $06 information can be used to diagnose faults by following three steps:

STEP 1 Check the monitor status before starting repairs. This step will show how the system failed.

STEP 2 Look at the component or parameter that triggered the fault. This step will help pin down the root cause of the failure.

STEP 3 Look to the monitor enable criteria, which will show what it takes to fail or pass the monitor.

ACCESSING GLOBAL OBD II

Global (generic) OBD II is used by inspectors where emission testing is performed. Aftermarket scan tools are designed to retrieve global OBD II; however, some original equipment scan tools, such as the Tech 2 used on General Motors vehicles, are not able to retrieve the information without special software. Global OBD II is accessible using ISO-9141-2, KWP 2000, J1850 PWM, J1850 VPW, and CAN. ● SEE FIGURE 11–1.

SNAP-ON 2500 An older Snap-on scan tool, often called "the brick" that was used in the aftermarket for many year.

SNAP-ON SOLUS From the main menu select "Generic OBD II/EOBD" and then follow the on-screen instructions to select the desired test.

SNAP-ON MODIS Select the scanner using the down arrow key and then select "Global OBD II." Follow on-screen instructions to get to "start communication" and then to the list of options to view.

OTC GENISYS From the main menu select "Global OBD II" and then follow the on-screen instructions. Select "special tests" to get access to mode $06 information and parameters.

MASTER TECH From the main menu, select "Global OBD II." At the next screen, select "OBD II functions," then "system tests," and then "other results" to obtain mode $06 data. ● SEE FIGURE 11–2.

MODE $06

Mode $06 is used by service technicians to monitor the PCM test results of various systems. While other modes are used for monitoring other functions, mode $06 is used to maintain all noncontinuous monitors and pending DTCs. The continuous monitors include fuel system monitors, misfire monitors, and comprehensive component monitors (CCM). The noncontinuous monitors include catalyst efficiency, EGR, EVAP, oxygen sensor monitors, oxygen sensor heater, secondary air injection (SAI), and thermostats.

USING MODE $06

Mode $06 is used to monitor all of the tests of the system and components. Mode $06 allows the service technician to view what the computer is doing and see the results of all of the tests that are being performed. Mode $06 can be used for the following:

- **See test results that are close to failing.** This means that a diagnostic trouble code may be set in the future because results of the test are close to the set limit, which would cause a DTC to set. Therefore, by looking at mode $06 data, the technician can be forewarned of a problem; in that case the customer can be told that a "check engine" light may come on and why.

- **Verify a repair.** By looking at mode $06 test results, the service technician can determine whether or not the repair that caused the check engine light to come on was in fact repaired correctly. If the test results are close to the upper or lower limit allowed, the repair was not completed successfully. If, however, the test results are far from the upper or lower limit, the repair was successful and the vehicle can be returned to the owner with the satisfaction of knowing that the check engine light will not come on again due to the same concern.

READING MODE $06 DATA

Some scan tools translate the raw hexadecimal data into English, such as Auto Enginuity scan tool software, which is used with a PC. However, the data is difficult to read. In addition, data from Ford vehicles needs to be multiplied by a conversion factor to achieve a usable value.

SELECT MONITOR

The first step is to select the monitor (fuel trim, misfire, catalyst, etc.). There could be three results:

- **Incomplete.** This means that the computer has not yet completed the test for the selected monitor.

- **Pass.** This means that the monitor was tested to completion and that the test passed. This pass could have been close to failing; looking at the test results will indicate how close it came to failing.

- **Fail.** The monitor test failed. Checking the test results will help the service technician determine why it failed and by how much, which will help in diagnosing the root cause.

DATA DISPLAY

The test data displayed often includes upper limit and/or lower limit (often not both), test results, and units.

The "unit" may be just a number. However, by looking at the upper and lower limits, the technician can judge how close the test results were to failing the test. Many scan tools display component and test information in plain English while others just display the hexadecimal number. If just the hexadecimal number is shown, it has to be translated into English to show which component or test is being displayed. Check service information for the exact translation or refer to the following charts for a typical example.

Chart 1

$03	Fuel System 1
$03	Fuel System 2
$04	Calculated Load Percentage
$05	Engine Coolant Temp Sensor (Celsius)
$06	Short-Term Fuel Trim Bank 1 (%)
$07	Long-Term Fuel Trim Bank 1 (%)
$08	Short-Term Fuel Trim Bank 2 (%)
$09	Long-Term Fuel Trim Bank 2 (%)
$0A	Fuel Pressure Gauge (KPA)
$0B	Intake MAP (KPA)
$0C	Engine Speed (1/min)
$0D	Vehicle Speed (km/h)
$0E	Ignition Timing Advance (degrees)
$0F	Intake Air Temperature (Celsius)
$10	Air Flow Rate (g/s)
$11	Absolute Throttle Position (%)
$12	Commanded Secondary AIR Status
$13	O2S Bank 1-Sensor 1
$13	O2S Bank 1-Sensor 2
$13	O2S Bank 1-Sensor 3
$13	O2S Bank 1-Sensor 4
$13	O2S Bank 2-Sensor 1
$13	O2S Bank 2-Sensor 2
$13	O2S Bank 2-Sensor 3
$13	O2S Bank 2-Sensor 4
$14	O2S Voltage Bank 1-Sensor 1 (V)
$14	Short-Term Fuel Trim Bank 1-Sensor 1 (%)
$15	O2S Voltage Bank 1-Sensor 2 (V)
$15	Short-Term Fuel Trim Bank 1-Sensor 2 (%)
$16	O2S Voltage Bank 1-Sensor 3 (V)
$16	Short-Term Fuel Trim Bank 1-Sensor 3 (%)
$17	O2S Voltage Bank 1-Sensor 4 (V)
$17	Short-Term Fuel Trim Bank 1-Sensor 4 (%)
$18	O2S Voltage Bank 2-Sensor 1 (V)
$18	O2S Voltage Bank 3-Sensor 1 (V)
$18	Short-Term Fuel Trim Bank 2-Sensor 1 (%)
$18	Short-Term Fuel Trim Bank 3-Sensor 1 (%)
$19	O2S Voltage Bank 2-Sensor 2 (V)
$19	O2S Voltage Bank 3-Sensor 2 (V)
$19	Short-Term Fuel Trim Bank 2-Sensor 2 (%)
$19	Short-Term Fuel Trim Bank 3-Sensor 2 (%)
$1A	O2S Voltage Bank 2-Sensor 3 (V)
$1A	O2S Voltage Bank 4-Sensor 1 (V)
$1A	Short-Term Fuel Trim Bank 2-Sensor 3 (%)
$1A	Short-Term Fuel Trim Bank 4-Sensor 1 (%)
$1B	O2S Voltage Bank 2-Sensor 4 (V)

$1B	O2S Voltage Bank 4-Sensor 2 (V)	$3B	O2S Current Bank 2-Sensor 4 (ma)
$1B	Short-Term Fuel Trim Bank 2-Sensor 4 (%)	$3B	O2S Current Bank 3-Sensor 4 (ma)
$1B	Short-Term Fuel Trim Bank 4-Sensor 2 (%)	$3C	Catalyst Temperature Bank 1-Sensor 1°C
$1C	OBD Requirements	$3D	Catalyst Temperature Bank 2-Sensor 1°C
$1D	O2S Bank 1-Sensor 1	$3E	Catalyst Temperature Bank 1-Sensor 2°C
$1D	O2S Bank 1-Sensor 2	$3F	Catalyst Temperature Bank 2-Sensor 2°C
$1D	O2S Bank 2-Sensor 1	$42	Control Module Voltage
$1D	O2S Bank 2-Sensor 2	$43	Absolute Load Value (%)
$1D	O2S Bank 3-Sensor 1	$44	Commanded Equivalence Ratio
$1D	O2S Bank 3-Sensor 2	$45	Relative Throttle Position (%)
$1D	O2S Bank 4-Sensor 1	$46	Ambient Air Temperature °C
$1D	O2S Bank 4-Sensor 2	$47	Absolute Throttle Position B (%)
$1E	Power Take Off Status	$48	Absolute Throttle Position C (%)
$1F	Time since Engine Start(s)	$49	Accelerator Pedal Position D (%)
$21	Distance While MIL Active (km/miles)	$4A	Accelerator Pedal Position E (%)
$22	Relative Fuel Pressure (kPa)	$4B	Accelerator Pedal Position F (%)
$23	Fuel Pressure Gauge (kPa)	$4C	Commanded Throttle ACT. Control (%)
$24	Equivalence Ratio Bank 1-Sensor 1 (:1)	$4D	Engine Run Time with MIL Active (min.)
$25	Equivalence Ratio Bank 1-Sensor 2 (:1)	$4E	Time since DTCs Cleared (min.)
$26	Equivalence Ratio Bank 1-Sensor 3 (:1)		
$27	Equivalence Ratio Bank 1-Sensor 4 (:1)		
$28	Equivalence Ratio Bank 2-Sensor 1 (:1)		
$28	Equivalence Ratio Bank 3-Sensor 1 (:1)		
$29	Equivalence Ratio Bank 2-Sensor 2 (:1)		
$29	Equivalence Ratio Bank 3-Sensor 2 (:1)		
$2A	Equivalence Ratio Bank 2-Sensor 3 (:1)		
$2A	Equivalence Ratio Bank 3-Sensor 3 (:1)		
$2B	Equivalence Ratio Bank 2-Sensor 4 (:1)		
$2B	Equivalence Ratio Bank 3-Sensor 4 (:1)		
$2C	Commanded EGR (%)		
$2D	EGR Error (%)		
$2E	Commanded Evaporative Purge (%)		
$2F	Fuel Level Input (%)		
$30	Number of Warm-Ups since DTCs Cleared		
$31	Distance since DTCs Cleared		
$32	EVAP System Vapor Pressure (Pa)		
$33	Barometric Pressure (kPa)		
$34	O2S Current Bank 1-Sensor 1 (ma)		
$35	O2S Current Bank 1-Sensor 2 (ma)		
$36	O2S Current Bank 1-Sensor 3 (ma)		
$37	O2S Current Bank 1-Sensor 4 (ma)		
$38	O2S Current Bank 2-Sensor 1 (ma)		
$38	O2S Current Bank 3-Sensor 1 (ma)		
$39	O2S Current Bank 2-Sensor 2 (ma)		
$39	O2S Current Bank 3-Sensor 2 (ma)		
$3A	O2S Current Bank 2-Sensor 3 (ma)		
$3A	O2S Current Bank 3-Sensor 3 (ma)		

Chart 2

Test ID	Numbers (oxygen sensor)
$01	Rich to Lean Sensor Threshold
$02	Lean to Rich Sensor Threshold
$03	Low Sensor Voltage for Switch Time Calculation
$04	High Sensor Voltage for Switch Time Calculation
$05	Rich to Lean Sensor Switch Time
$06	Lean to Rich Sensor Switch Time
$07	Minimum Sensor Voltage for Test Cycle
$08	Maximum Sensor Voltage for Test Cycle
$09	Time between Sensor Transitions
$0A	Sensor Period

OXYGEN SENSOR HEATER MODE $06 TEST (GENERAL MOTORS)

This fault can set a P0141 DTC for bank 1, sensor 1 (B1S1). Checking service information indicates the following enable criteria for the code to set:

1. Cold engine start

2. Engine at idle speed

3. Engine operating temperature below 150°F (66°C)

The following monitors are suspended:

1. EVAP
2. Oxygen sensor performance
3. Catalyst

Mode $06 data for B1S1 heater circuit in TID-06, CID-41:

1. The maximum limit = 186
2. Measure value = 33
3. Minimum limit = -----
4. Result = passed

Note that the technician cannot determine what is being measured nor what the number 186 indicates. Also note that there is no minimum limit and the measured value of 33 is far below the maximum limit of 186. This means that the oxygen sensor heater test easily passed.

ENGINE MISFIRE TESTS (FORD)

A misfire fault can set a random misfire DTC of P0300 or one or more individual misfire DTCs P0301 through P0310 for cylinders one through 10. The enable criteria for these codes to set include:

1. Time since engine start 5 seconds
2. Engine coolant temperature 20°F (–7°C) to 250°F (121°C)
3. RPM range from idle to redline or fuel cutoff
4. Fuel level 15% minimum

Test ID is used to identify several related tests, including:

$50—Total engine misfire (updated every 1,000 revolutions)

$53—Cylinder-specific misfire

For example, a Ford being checked using mode $06 for TID-50 had the following results:

Maximum limit = 1,180

Measured value = 0

Minimum value = -----

Result = passed

What is the percentage of misfire allowed? The value shown for maximum has to be converted to get the actual percentage.

According to service information, to get the actual percentage of misfire the value has to be multiplied by 0.000015. Therefore, the raw value for maximum misfire was 1,180 × 0.000015, which equals 1.7%. In other words, the maximum allowable misfire before a DTC is set is 1.7%. By looking at mode $06 data, the technician can determine how close the engine is to failing the misfire monitor.

For individual cylinder misfires, check test ID $53. For example, if a value of 17,482 is displayed, the test failed. Multiplying the test results (17,482) by the conversion factor (0.000015) shows a misfire of 26%.

Type A misfire codes are those that can cause damage to the catalytic converter. The misfire usually ranges from 40% at idle to about 4% at high engine speeds.

Type B misfire codes are set if the misfire exceeds 2% to 4%, depending on the engine, make, model, and year.

FORD OXYGEN SENSOR MODE $06 TEST

Ford and other companies have many tests performed on the oxygen sensor, including voltage amplitude. For example, Ford TID $01, CID $21 for HO2S1 shows:

Minimum value = 512

Maximum value = N/A

Current value = 794

According to Ford service information, the numbers have to be converted into volts by multiplying the value by 0.00098. Therefore, the current value is 0.778 volts, which is above the minimum allowable voltage of 0.50 (512 × 0.0098 = 0.50).

GENERAL MOTORS CAN OXYGEN SENSOR MODE $06 TEST

One of the oxygen sensor tests performed on a General Motors vehicle equipped with CAN (GMCAN) is the rich-to-lean sensor switch time. Typical test results show:

Monitor ID (MID) $01

Test ID $05

Maximum limit = 0.155 sec.

Measured value = 0.030 sec.

Minimum value = 0.000 sec.

Result = passed

This mode $06 test clearly shows that the oxygen sensor is able to reset very quickly to a change in air–fuel mixture from rich to lean by reacting in 30 ms (0.030 sec.). Normally this information can only be determined by a service technician using a scope of the waveform who forces the system lean and watches the reaction time on the scope display. Using mode $06 and a scan tool, especially on vehicles equipped with CAN, is a fast and easy way to determine oxygen sensor health without having to do time-consuming tests.

FORD EGR TESTS

Ford checks many functions of the exhaust gas recirculation (EGR) system, including flow testing and tests of the sensor used to check the flow of exhaust gases. The duty cycle of the EGR solenoid can be checked using mode $06 by looking at the following:

TID $4B

CID $30

Maximum limit = 26,214

Measured value = 14,358

Minimum value = -----

Test results = passed

These results at the limits, like many other Ford mode $06 data, must be converted to give usable values. Multiply the measured set limit value by 0.0000305 to get the duty cycle as a percentage (%).

Maximum limit = 26,214 × 0.0000305 = 80%

Measured value = 14.358 × 0.0000305 = 43%

FORD DELTA PRESSURE FOR EGR FLOW TEST

In this test, the following occurred on a test vehicle:

TID $4A

CID $30

Maximum limit =

Measured value = 2,226

Minimum limit = 768

Result = passed

The values shown need to be compared and corrected as follows:

- If the value is greater than 32,767, the value is negative.
- If the value is less than 32,767, the value is positive.
- Multiply the value by 0.0078 to get inches of water.

The value was 2,226 × 0.0078 = 17.7 inches of water (in. H_2O) of vacuum (negative pressure).

GENERAL MOTORS CATALYST EFFICIENCY TEST

The scan tool displays data that do not need to be converted, although the units are often unknown. The service technician can, however, see how close the test results come to either the maximum or the minimum limits. For example, a General

Motors idle catalyst efficiency test could have the results following:

TID $0C

CID $60

Maximum limit = 33,234

Measured value = 17,708

Minimum limit = -----

Result = passed

What do the numbers represent? The numbers are created as a result of the test and cannot be determined by the technician. However, it is clear by the reading and the maximum limit that the catalyst efficiency test easily passed. This is an excellent test to check if the efficiency of the catalytic converter needs to be determined.

GENERAL MOTORS EVAP TEST (CAN)

One of the evaporative (EVAP) system tests that can be monitored using a scan tool and mode $06 data is the engine off, natural vacuum test. An example of a typical result includes:

MID EVAP = 0.020

TID 201

Minimum value = 0.000

Maximum value = 0.601

Current value = 0.023

The values do not need to be converted, although the units are unknown. However, it is clear from the test results that the current value is not even close to the maximum limit, which means that the EVAP system being tested by the natural vacuum method is free from faults.

PERMANENT CODES

DEFINITION Starting in 2010 all vehicles support "permanent fault codes," which are stored in nonvolatile RAM and cannot be cleared when the battery is disconnected and only go away when the problem is fixed.

There are three different types of OBDII codes defined under the SAE J1979 standard:

1. Mode $03 "confirmed" trouble codes
2. Mode $07 "pending" trouble codes
3. Mode $0A "permanent" trouble codes

Permanent trouble codes cannot be simply "cleared" by any tool, even factory scan tools. These codes can only be cleared by the PCM once it has determined that the malfunction is no longer present. This usually requires that the vehicle be driven enough so it can pass the self tests.

NEED TO CLEAR Many shops and dealers require that their technicians make sure that the permanent codes are cleared by the PCM before the vehicle is released back to the customer.

This helps insure that the vehicle has been properly repaired and can pass an emission test.

WHERE TO GET MODE $06 INFORMATION

Many scan tools display all of the parameters and information needed so that additional mode $06 data is not needed. Many vehicle manufacturers post mode $06 information on the service information websites. This information is often free, unlike other service information. Refer to the National Automotive Service Task Force (NASTF) website for the website address of all vehicle manufacturers' service information sites (www. NASTF.org)

Two examples include:

http://service.gm.com (free access to mode $06 information)

www.motorcraftservice.com (search for mode $06 free access)

SUMMARY

1. Global OBD II can be used by a service technician to do the following:
   a. Check the PCM regarding what it has detected as a fault
   b. Verify a repair
   c. Check if the test results are close to failure, which could trigger the MIL
2. Global OBD II has 10 modes, each covering a certain aspect of the diagnostic system.

3. Mode $06 is the most commonly used mode of global OBD II because it includes data on the noncontinuous monitored system.
4. Most aftermarket scan tools and some original equipment scan tools can access global OBD II data.
5. Many Ford mode $06 data requires that the displayed number be converted to show usable values.

REVIEW QUESTIONS

1. What are the 10 modes of global (generic) OBD II?
2. How do hexadecimal numbers differ from base 10 numbers?
3. Why does some mode $06 data need to be translated into plain English?

4. Where can mode $06 data information be obtained?
5. Why do some shops require their technicians to make sure that any permanent codes are cleared before the vehicle is released back to the customer?

1. What is global (generic) OBD II?
   a. A standardized format that meets SAE standard J1962
   b. A format originally designed for engineers
   c. The same for all numbers and models of vehicles
   d. All of the above

2. Mode $06 can be used to verify a repair by checking _____.
   a. the component system test passed
   b. DTCs
   c. sensor values
   d. a captured freeze-frame

3. Mode $06 is the mode that checks which systems?
   a. Oxygen sensors
   b. Continuously monitored systems
   c. Noncontinuously monitored systems
   d. Current powertrain data (PIDs)

4. When using mode $06 to diagnose a problem, when should the technician access the mode $06 data?
   a. Before starting the repair
   b. During a test drive
   c. During the repair
   d. During a snap-throttle

5. Technician A says that by looking at the mode $06 data, the technician can determine how close a component or system came to passing the onboard test. Technician B says that the data shown may have to be converted to obtain values that are meaningful to the technician. Which technician is correct?
   a. Technician A only
   b. Technician B only
   c. Both Technicians A and B
   d. Neither Technician A nor B

6. Which of the following scan tools would NOT be used to access global OBD-II information?
   a. Master Tech
   b. Snap-On Modis
   c. GM Tech 2
   d. OTC Genisys

7. An oxygen sensor switch time from rich to lean is identified as test identification (TID) _____.
   a. $05   c. $02
   b. $0A   d. $09

8. How can permanent DTCs be cleared from the PCM?
   a. Disconnect the battery
   b. Only with a generic scan tool
   c. Push the DTC reset button
   d. Drive the vehicle after the repair

9. A General Motors vehicle is being checked using mode $06 for the proper operation of the oxygen sensor. The rich-to-lean sensor switch time is 0.030 seconds. Technician A says that this indicates a slow reacting oxygen sensor. Technician B says that the oxygen sensor is reacting correctly and is okay. Which technician is correct?
   a. Technician A only
   b. Technician B only
   c. Both Technicians A and B
   d. Neither Technician A nor B

10. Mode $06 information can be accessed at _____.
   a. http://service.gm.com
   b. www.motorcraftservice.com
   c. www.nastf.org
   d. All of the above

chapter 12
IMMOBILIZER SYSTEMS

LEARNING OBJECTIVES

After studying this chapter, the reader should be able to:

1. Describe the purpose and function of a security system.

2. Explain how an immobilizer system works and the major components involved.

3. Describe the types of immobilizer systems used by various manufacturers.

4. Explain how to diagnosis a fault with an immobilizer system.

KEY TERMS

Key fob 177
Locksmith ID 180
Passlock III 182
Radio frequency identification (RFID) 177

Remote keyless entry (RKE) 177
Transceiver 178
Transponder 177

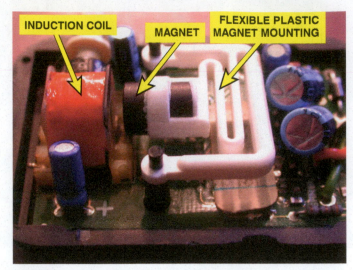

FIGURE 12–1 A shock sensor used in alarm and antitheft systems. If the vehicle is moved, the magnet will move relative to the coil, inducing a small voltage that will trigger the alarm.

FIGURE 12–2 The security system symbol used on a Ford. The symbol varies by make model and year so check service information to determine what symbol is used on the vehicle being diagnosed.

VEHICLE SECURITY SYSTEMS

PURPOSE AND FUNCTION The purpose and function of a security system on a vehicle is to prevent the unauthorized use (theft) of the vehicle. This function is accomplished by installing the following locks:

1. A lock on the doors to help prevent unauthorized entry to the interior of the vehicle.

2. A lock for the ignition so a key is needed to crank and start the engine and unlock the steering wheel, starting in 1970.

 FREQUENTLY ASKED QUESTION

What Is Content Theft Protection?

Content theft protection is a security system that includes sensors that detect glass breakage or entry into the vehicle and sounds an alarm when these occur. The purpose of the content theft system is to prevent the theft of objects inside the vehicle and sound an alarm when someone enters the vehicle without using the proper remote or key. Most systems use a motion detector for content theft protection system as well as switches in the doorjambs, trunk, and hood provide an input signal to the control module. Some antitheft systems are more complex and also have electronic sensors that trigger the alarm if glass is broken or a change in battery current draw. These sensors also provide an input signal to the control module, which may be a separate antitheft unit or may be incorporated into the PCM or BCM. ● **SEE FIGURE 12–1.**

Early vehicle theft security systems only monitored the doors for a valid unlock signal. If the vehicle did not receive this signal, an alarm would go off when the door was opened. In many cases, the vehicle would still start even though the alarm was going off. While these locks have worked, vehicles can still be easily stolen if access to the interior and the ignition switch is accessible. It is the purpose and function of an immobilizer system to prevent the vehicle from being started if the correct ignition key is not used even if an intruder gets access to the interior of the vehicle and tries to use a key that fits the lock cylinder.

IMMOBILIZER SYSTEMS

NORMAL OPERATION A vehicle equipped with an immobilizer system operates normally as follows:

■ When a valid key is used, and is rotated to the start position, the engine cranks and starts and the immobilizer symbol on the dash will flash on and off for about two seconds, and then go off. ● **SEE FIGURE 12–2.**

■ If there is a fault with an invalid key, the dash symbol will flash continuously and the engine will not start or if it does crank and start, the engine will not continue to run.

POSSIBLE IMMOBILIZER CAUSED FAULTS Faults with the immobilizer system can be the cause of one of the following conditions depending on the exact make and model of a vehicle:

■ No crank condition (the starter motor does not operate)

■ The engine cranks but does not start (fuel disabled in most vehicles)

■ The engine starts but then almost immediately stalls.

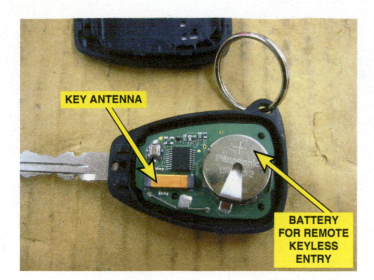

FIGURE 12–3 A typical key with the cover removed showing the battery used to power the door lock and the antenna used for the immobilizer system.

KEY ANTENNA

BATTERY FOR REMOTE KEYLESS ENTRY

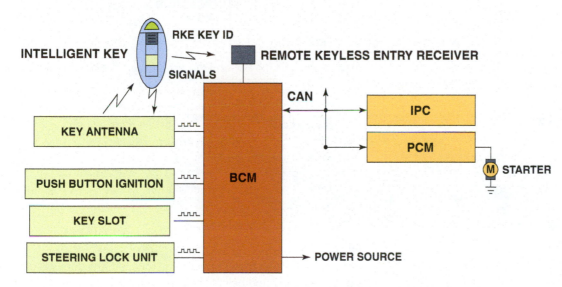

INTELLIGENT KEY

RKE KEY ID

REMOTE KEYLESS ENTRY RECEIVER

SIGNALS

KEY ANTENNA

PUSH BUTTON IGNITION

KEY SLOT

STEERING LOCK UNIT

BCM

CAN

IPC

PCM

M STARTER

POWER SOURCE

FIGURE 12–4 The remote keyless entry is used to unlock the doors as well as create the signals to the powertrain control module (PCM) used to control the starter motor and/or the fuel system and the warning lamp on the instrument panel cluster (IPC).

Therefore, if a customer concern involves any of these situations, a fault in the immobilizer system is a possible cause rather than a fault with the ignition or fuel system.

IMMOBILIZER SYSTEM PARTS Most security systems today use a **Radio Frequency Identification (RFID)** security system, which has two main components:

1. A **key fob** is the object that is a decoration on a key ring and usually contains a transmitter used to unlock a vehicle. While the **remote keyless entry (RKE)** part of the key fob has a battery to power the transmitter, the RFID chip part of the key fob does not require a battery to function. The **transponder** is mounted in the key or the body of the key fob. A transponder has an antenna, which consists of a coil of wire as well as a circuit board containing the processing electronics and data memory. ● SEE FIGURE 12–3.

2. The transponder key has the transponder electronics integrated in its plastic body. It consists of the following components:

■ A microchip contains the unique internal identification (ID) number. To prevent an unauthorized scanning of the ID number, the code changes with each transfer and uses several million different coding possibilities. ● SEE FIGURE 12–4.

■ The coil antenna in the key consists of a copper coil wound up in a ring case and an integrated circuit to create a high-frequency alternating voltage for the inductive coupling. Through inductive (electromagnetic) coupling, the data from the key is transferred to the immobilizer module.

■ Another coil is installed around the lock cylinder and connected to the control module of the immobilizer system. This coil transfers and receives all data signals to and from the immobilizer control module using the coil antenna/transceiver. It does not need to be reprogrammed to the immobilizer system in case of replacement.

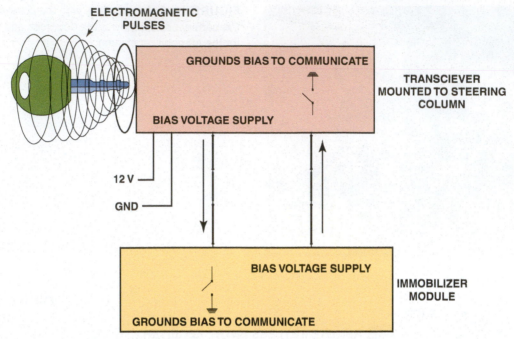

FIGURE 12–5 A typical immobilizer circuit showing the communication between the key and the transceiver. The transceiver then communicates with the immobilizer module over data lines.

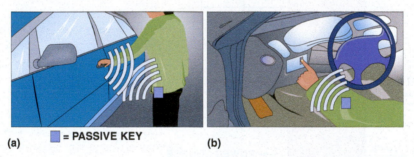

= PASSIVE KEY

(a)   (b)

FIGURE 12–6 (a) If the passive key is within about 15 feet (5 m) of the vehicle when the door handle is touched, the door will unlock allowing access to the interior. (b) The engine will start if the smart key is detected being inside the vehicle.

■ A **transceiver** is inside the vehicle and receives the signal transmitted by the transponder in the key.
A "transceiver" functions as both a reviewer and a transmitter. The transceiver is usually mounted on the steering column assembly. The antenna for the transceiver is a coil of wire mounted within the plastic ring that mounts around the lock cylinder. ● **SEE FIGURE 12–5**.

PASSIVE KEYLESS ENTRY SYSTEM   A **passive keyless entry** system uses the key fob as a transmitter, which communicates with the vehicle as it comes into a specific range. ● **SEE FIGURE 12–6**.

The key is identified using one of several antennas around the body of the vehicle and a radio pulse generator in the key housing. Depending on the system, the vehicle is automatically unlocked when a button or sensor on the door handle or trunk release is depressed. ● **SEE FIGURE 12–7**.

Vehicles with a passive (smart) key system can also have a mechanical backup, usually in the form of a key blade built into the fob. Vehicles with a smart key system are generally started by pressing a start button. In the event of a system failure, the vehicle can be started by one of two ways. In some models the driver must insert the key blade in a mechanical switch. The location of the mechanical switch varies and sometimes requires the driver to take the cover off the button to gain access. On other models, the fob must be placed in a specific location where the vehicle can recognize the fob even when the battery is dead. ● **SEE FIGURE 12–8**.

When leaving a vehicle equipped with a smart key system, the vehicle is locked, depending on make, model, and year of manufacture by:

■ Pressing a button on one of the door handles

■ Touching a capacitive area on the door handle

■ Simply walking away from the vehicle and the doors will lock when the key fob goes out of communication range

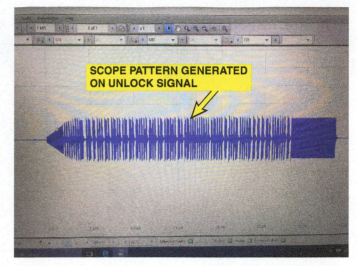

SCOPE PATTERN GENERATED
ON UNLOCK SIGNAL

FIGURE 12–7 (a) The keyless entry signal detector is used on the driver's door handle to verify its functionality. (b) The scope pattern that was generated by the vehicle on the unlock command verified the functionality of the circuit.

SLOT IN
CENTER
CONSOLE

KEY FOB

FIGURE 12–8 The placement of the passive key fob in the slot in the center console is an example of how an immobilizer system is able to recognize the fob even when the key is dead and allow the vehicle to start.

IMMOBILIZER SYSTEM OPERATION When the ignition key in inserted, the transceiver sends out an electromagnetic energy pulse. This energy pulse is received by the coil inside the key transponder, which creates a voltage. The information or data in the magnetic pulses is in the form of a frequency modulated signal.

A typical immobilizer system consists of transponder key, coil antenna, key reminder switch, separate immobilizer module, PCM, and security light. Most immobilizer systems work as follows:

- The key identification (ID) numbers are stored in a non-volatile memory of the immobilizer module. At each start the module compares the ID number of the transponder key used with those stored in the memory.

- If the verification has been successful, the immobilizer module sends a request signal to the PCM to compare the key ID number with the numbers registered in the PCM.

- Each immobilizer module has its unique code word that is stored in the PCM. After the verification of the ID number, the immobilizer module requests the code word from the PCM.

- The immobilizer module controls the starter circuit and the security light and signals the PCM to activate fuel injection and ignition when the ID number and code word verification have been successful.

- The signals between immobilizer module and PCM are transmitted via a serial data line.

SECURITY LIGHT OPERATION Normal operation of the security light includes a self-test and flashes a few times then goes out. However, if a fault is detected, the security light will

(a) (b) (c)

FIGURE 12–9 (a) Avoid using a key where the key ring is over the top of the key, which can interfere with the operation of the immobilizer system. (b) Do not angle another key upward from the key being used to help prevent interference with the magnetic field used to energize the key. (c) Do not have the keys from another vehicle near the key being used.

🔧 **TECH TIP**

Do Not Have Other Keys Near

Whenever diagnosing an immobilizer system, keep other key fobs away from the area. If another key fob were close, it could be transmitting a signal that is not recognized by the vehicle and the security system could prevent proper vehicle operation. Even having other metal objects near the key can affect the strength of the electromagnetic pulses and could interfere with the immobilizer system and prevent it from working as designed. ● **SEE FIGURE 12–9**.

continue to flash and the engine may not start. If a fault occurs with the immobilizer system when the engine is running, then the security light will come on but the engine will not be shut off as this condition is not a theft attempt.

PRECAUTIONS To avoid damage to the key, do not allow the key to:

- Be dropped onto a hard surface
- Get wet
- Exposed to any kind of magnetic field
- Exposed to high temperatures on places such as the top of the dash under direct sunlight.

A system malfunction may occur if any of the following items touches the key or is near the key head:

- A metal object
- Spare keys or keys for other vehicles equipped with an immobilizer system
- An electronic device, such as cards with magnetic strips

TESTING KEY FOB OR PASSIVE KEY BATTERIES Over time, the batteries in a key fob or a passive key system may become weak or fail. Before opening the fob or passive key to replace the battery, test it to make sure it is the problem. Using a stand-alone fob signal detection tool or a TPMS tool equipped with the key fob signal detection option, press each button and observe the signal strength. This will not only check battery strength, it will also check the functionality of each button. ● **SEE FIGURE 12–10**.

TYPICAL IMMOBILIZER CIRCUITS The diagnostic process involved with positively identifying the defective security system component can be quick and accurate. At the transceiver check for power, ground, and proper communication on data transmission lines. ● **SEE FIGURE 12–11**.

CAUTION: Do not leave the key in the ignition as this will often keep the immobilizer system alive and will drain the vehicle battery. If leaving the vehicle, take the key out of the ignition and best to place it 15 feet (5 m) away to help avoid possible issues.

VEHICLE SECURITY PROFESSIONAL—LOCKSMITH ID When a key fob or passive key is replaced, it must be programmed into the vehicles immobilizer system. Most manufacturers require the security codes, or key-specific information must be re-entered during the process. In order to obtain this information, the shop or service technician must be a registered vehicle security professional and have a **locksmith ID** number.

CHRYSLER IMMOBILIZER SYSTEM

Beginning in 1998, Chrysler started a security system known as the **Sentry Key Immobilizer System (SKIS)**. When an attempt to start a vehicle arises, the onboard computer sends out a radio-frequency (RF) signal that is read by the electronic transponder chip embedded in the key. The transponder then returns a unique signal back to the SKIM, giving it the okay for the vehicle to start and continue to run. This all happens in under a second, and is completely transparent to the vehicle driver. For additional security, two preprogrammed keys are needed in order to register additional keys into the system. In the event of the loss of all keys, special programming equipment is needed to register new keys into the system.

CHRYSLER SELF-PROGRAMMING ADDITIONAL SENTRY KEYS (REQUIRES TWO ORIGINAL KEYS) Quick steps:

STEP 1 Purchase a blank key and have it cut to fit the lock cylinder.

STEP 2 Insert the original key #1 into the ignition and turn to ON.

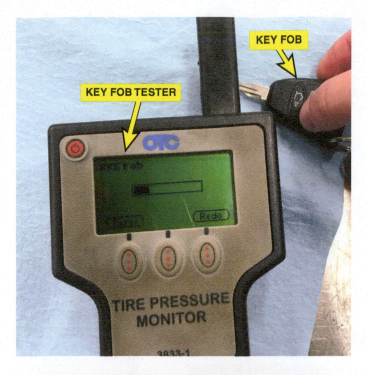

FIGURE 12–10 The RKE test equipment indicates a signal from the key fob when the unlock button was pushed indicating that portion of the fob is functional and the battery strength was sufficient.

STEP 3 Wait 5 seconds and turn the key to OFF.

STEP 4 Immediately insert the original key #2 into the ignition and turn to ON.

STEP 5 Wait 10 seconds for the SKIS indicator in the dash to start to flash.

STEP 6 Turn the ignition off, insert the new blank key, and turn the ignition back on.

STEP 7 Once the SKIS light stops flashing and turns off, the new key is programmed.

FORD PATS SYSTEM

Ford uses a responder key for their antitheft system, which is called the **Passive Antitheft System** (**PATS**).

FORD PROGRAMMING FOR ADDITIONAL (PATS) KEYS This procedure will work only if two or more programmed ignition keys are available. The steps include:

STEP 1 Insert the first programmed ignition key into the ignition lock cylinder. Turn the ignition switch from the LOCK to RUN position (ignition switch must stay in the run position for 1 second). Turn the ignition switch to the LOCK position and remove the ignition key from the ignition lock cylinder.

STEP 2 Within 5 seconds of turning the ignition switch to the LOCK position, insert the second programmed ignition key into the ignition lock cylinder. Turn the ignition switch from the LOCK to RUN position (ignition switch must stay in the RUN position for 1 second). Turn the ignition switch to the LOCK position and remove the second ignition key from the ignition lock cylinder.

STEP 3 Within 5 seconds of turning the ignition switch to the LOCK position, insert a new un-programmed ignition key into the ignition lock cylinder. Turn the ignition switch from the LOCK to RUN position (the ignition switch must stay in the RUN position for 1 second). Turn the ignition switch to the LOCK position and remove the ignition key from the ignition lock cylinder. The new ignition key should now be programmed. To program additional key(s), repeat the key programming procedure from Step 1.

GENERAL MOTORS ANTITHEFT SYSTEM

The type of antitheft system used on General Motors vehicles has included many different systems starting with an antitheft system that used a resistor pellet in the ignition

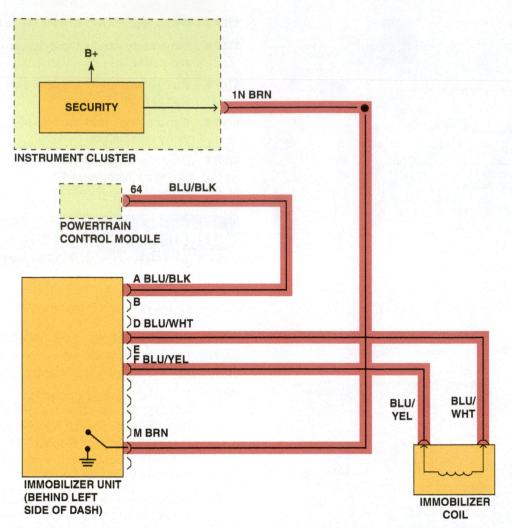

FIGURE 12–11 Check service information for the exact wiring diagram (schematic) for the vehicle being tested. Highlighting the wires and noting their color will help when following the specified testing procedures.

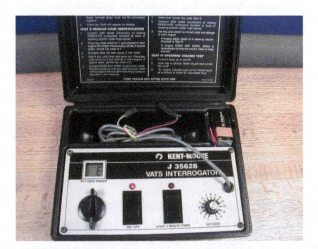

FIGURE 12–12 A special tool is needed to diagnose a General Motors VATS security system and special keys that contain a resistor pellet.

key. If the key fit the lock cylinder and the resistance was the correct value, the engine would crank and start. This system was called the **Vehicle Antitheft System** or **(VATS)**. A special tester was required to test this system. ● **SEE FIGURE 12–12**.

Newer systems include the **Passkey I** and **Passkey II**, which also use a resistor pellet in the ignition key. **Passlock I, Passlock II,** and **Passlock III** systems use a Hall-effect sensor and magnets in the lock cylinder with a conventional key. ● **SEE FIGURE 12–13**.

Passkey III systems use a transponder embedded into the head of the key, which is stamped "SK3." Most of the systems disable the starter and the fuel injectors, but Passlock I disables fuel after the engine starts and the security light will then flash. Due to the various systems, service information must be used and followed to diagnose and repair a fault in these systems.

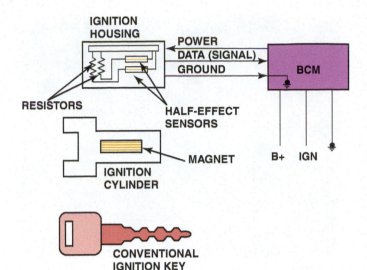

FIGURE 12–13 The Passlock series of General Motors security systems uses a conventional key. The magnet is located in the ignition lock cylinder and triggers the Hall-effect sensors.

FIGURE 12–14 Scan tools, such as this factory tool being used on a Chrysler, are capable of many diagnostic functions that can help the technician zero in on the root cause of a problem.

TESTING IMMOBILIZER SYSTEMS

DIAGNOSTIC STEPS Most vehicle manufacturers recommend a series of steps that a technician should follow when diagnosing a fault with the immobilizer system.

STEP 1 **Verify the Customer Concern**—A fault with the immobilizer system will often cause the engine to not start or start then stall. Faults can also be intermittent because many systems will "time out" after 20 minutes if an error occurs and then works normally after the wait period. A "no-start" condition can also occur that is not associated with the immobilizer system and should be handled using normal diagnostic procedures as specified by the vehicle manufacturer for a no-start condition.

STEP 2 **Visual Inspection**—Most vehicle manufacturers specify that the first step after the customer concern has been verified is that a visual inspection be performed. A visual inspection includes checking the security light status. A typical security light status includes:

- **Normal**—The security dash lamp comes on for 2 to 5 seconds for a bulb check when the ignition is turned on, then goes out.

- **Tamper mode**—The security lamp flashes about once per second if the system detects a bad key, lock cylinder, or security-related wiring problem. The engine will not start or if it does start, will not continue to run.

- **Fail enable mode**—If a fault with the security system occurs when the vehicle is running, the security light will remain on but the immobilizer system

will be disabled because it is apparently, not a theft attempt. Therefore, the engine will start and run as normal except that the security warning light on the dash will be on all the time.

Check for the presence of aftermarket accessories such as an add-on remote starter system. These systems require the use of a spare key that is held near the lock cylinder, thereby allowing the engine to start using a remote control. A fault with the aftermarket system could have an effect on the proper operation of the immobilizer system.

STEP 3 **Check for Diagnostic Trouble Codes**—Use a factory or enhanced factory level aftermarket scan tool and retrieve diagnostic trouble codes. Check service information for

DTC	DESCRIPTION OF FAULT
P0513	Incorrect Immobilizer Key
P1570	Fault in antenna detected
P1517	Reference code not compatible with ECM
P1572	Communications failure with ECM
B2957	Security System Data Circuit Low
B2960	Security System Data Wrong But Valid
U2017	Loss of communication with Body Control System

CHART 12–1

Sample diagnostic trouble codes for an immobilizer system. These codes vary by make, model, and year of manufacture, so check service information for the exact vehicle being diagnosed.

the exact codes for the vehicle being checked. ● **SEE CHART 12–1** for some sample DTCs and their meaning.

STEP 4 **Check for Technical Service Bulletins**—Technical service bulletins (TSBs) are issued by vehicle and aftermarket manufacturers to inform technicians of a situation or technical problem and give the corrective steps and a list of parts needed to solve the problem. Any diagnostic trouble codes should be retrieved before looking at the technical service bulletins because many bulletins include what DTCs may or may not be present. ● **SEE FIGURE 12–15.**

While some of these TSBs concern minor problems covering few vehicles, many contain very helpful solutions to hard-to-find problems that cover many vehicles. TSBs can also be purchased through aftermarket companies that are licensed and available on a website. Visit the National Automotive Service Task Force (NASTF) website (www.NASTF.org) for a list of the Web addresses for all vehicle manufacturers' sites where the full text of TSBs can be purchased directly. Factory TSBs can often save the technician many hours of troubleshooting.

STEP 5 **Perform Pinpoint Tests**—Following the specified diagnostic steps found in service information, check for the system for proper voltage at each of the components.

STEP 6 **Determine the Root Cause**—By following the specified diagnostic routine, the root cause can often be determined. If a module is replaced, it will usually have to be programmed to accept the ignition key and this can be a huge problem if a used module is chosen instead of a new one. Always check service information for the exact procedure to follow.

STEP 7 **Verify the Repair**—After the repairs or service procedures have been performed, verify that the system is working as designed. If needed, operate the vehicle under the same conditions that it was when the customer concern was corrected to verify the repair. Document the work order and return the vehicle to the customer in clean condition.

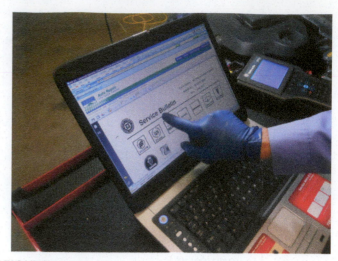

FIGURE 12–15 After checking for stored diagnostic trouble codes (DTCs), the wise technician checks service information for any technical service bulletins (TSBs) that may relate to the vehicle being serviced.

LIGHT EMITTING DIODE (LED)

FIGURE 12–16 Immobilizer coil detectors can be found online by searching for immobilizer transponder coil detector.

TECH TIP

Use an Antenna Coil Tester to Save Time

The procedure for testing the antenna coil using an antenna tester includes:

- Insert the ignition key into the ignition lock cylinder. On some vehicles, inserting the key will cause the transceiver to activate. On some vehicles, the key must be rotated to the ON position.

- Use a handheld tester to check that the transceiver is able to transmit a signal. A coil detector is used to check the immobilizer coil that surrounds the lock cylinder. The coil is working normally if the LED lights up as the key is inserted into the lock cylinder. If the coil is defective, this can save the technician a lot of time troubleshooting the system. The coil can be replaced without the need to reprogram the keys. ● **SEE FIGURE 12–16.**

SUMMARY

1. Faults with the immobilizer system can cause one of the following conditions:
   - No crank condition (the starter motor does not operate)
   - The engine cranks but does not start
   - The engine starts but then almost immediately stalls.

2. Most security systems today use a Radio Frequency Identification (RFID) security system.

3. The transponder key has the transponder electronic integrated in its plastic handle where it is encapsulated in a glass or plastic body.

4. The transceiver is usually mounted to the steering column assembly. The antenna for the transceiver is a coil of wire mounted within the plastic ring that mounts around the lock cylinder.

5. A typical immobilizer system consists of transponder key, coil antenna, key reminder switch, separate immobilizer module, PCM, and security light.

6. Normal operation of the security light includes a self-test and flashes a few times then goes out. However, if a fault is detected, the security light will continue to flash and the engine may not start.

7. To diagnose an immobilizer system, use a factory or enhanced factory level aftermarket scan tool and retrieve diagnostic trouble codes, then follow the specified diagnostic procedures.

REVIEW QUESTIONS

1. What faults will an immobilizer system cause?

2. How is the security information transferred from the key to the vehicle?

3. A typical immobilizer system consists of what parts?

4. To avoid damage to the key, what precautions are needed to be performed?

5. What is a passive keyless entry system?

CHAPTER QUIZ

1. What is the purpose and function of an immobilizer system?
   a. To prevent entry inside the vehicle
   b. Only allows the use of the ignition key that is properly matched to the lock cylinder
   c. Prevents the vehicle from starting or running if the correct key is not used
   d. Requires that the driver enter a password to start the vehicle

2. The battery in the key fob is used to power _____.
   a. the shock sensor
   b. the remote keyless entry (RKE)
   c. the immobilizer circuit
   d. Both the remote keyless entry and the immobilizer circuit

3. What can occur if the immobilizer system is not working as designed?
   a. No crank condition (the starter motor does not operate)
   b. The engine cranks but does not start
   c. The engine starts but then almost immediately stalls
   d. Any of the above

4. An immobilizer fault may occur if the _____.
   a. the key is dropped onto a hard surface
   b. the key gets wet
   c. the key is exposed to any kind of magnetic field
   d. Any of the above

5. How is data transmitted between the key and the steering column (lock cylinder)?
   a. By inductive coupling
   b. By electrical contacts inside the lock cylinder
   c. Transmitted from the key to the vehicle using the battery inside the key
   d. Transferred from the key to the BCM using a small transmitter in the key

6. A typical Ford immobilizer system is called _____.
   a. VATS
   b. PATS
   c. Passlock
   d. SKIS

7. A typical Chrysler immobilizer system is called _____.
   a. VATS
   b. PATS
   c. Passlock
   d. SKIS

8. The security dash lamp comes on for 2 to 5 seconds and then goes out. This indicates what condition _____?
   a. a fault has been detected in the key transponder
   b. a fault has been detected in the wiring near the ignition lock cylinder
   c. normal security light operation
   d. the system has entered tamper mode

9. Immobilizer diagnostic trouble codes are often found under what area?
   a. Engine-related "P" codes
   b. Body-related "B" codes
   c. Chassis-related "C" codes
   d. Any of the above

10. If an immobilizer-related module is replaced, what needs to be performed?
   a. The module will need to be programmed with the security information to be able to function with the existing key
   b. All the immobilizer-related modules need to be replaced at the same time so they all work together
   c. The key(s) will need to be replaced to match the new module
   d. Any of the above depending on the make, model, and year of manufacture vehicle

chapter 13

STARTING AND CHARGING SYSTEM DIAGNOSIS

LEARNING OBJECTIVES

After studying this chapter, the reader should be able to:

1. Describe the purpose, function, and types of batteries.
2. Discuss methods for checking the condition of a battery.
3. Describe how to perform a battery drain test and isolate a problem.
4. Explain battery charging and coding.
5. Describe the components and operation of cranking systems.
6. Describe the purpose and operation of stop/start systems.
7. List the steps necessary to perform a voltage-drop test.
8. Explain how to test the charging circuit.

KEY TERMS

Absorbed glass mat (AGM) 188
AC ripple voltage 196
Ampere-hour 188
Battery 188
Battery electrical drain test 190
CA 188
CCA 188
Charging circuit 188
Conductance tester 189
Cranking circuit 188
DE 195
Enhanced flooded battery (EFB) 188
Flooded lead acid (FLA) 188
Generator (alternator) 188
IOD 190
MCA 188
Neutral safety switch 192
Parasitic load 190
Reserve capacity 188
Ripple current 197
State of charge 190
Voltage-drop 193

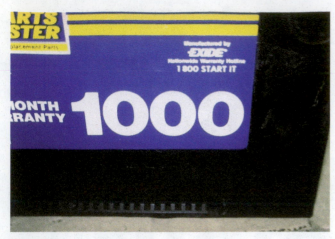

FIGURE 13–1 This battery has a cranking amperes (CA) rating of 1,000. This means that this battery is capable of cranking an engine for 30 seconds at a temperature of 32°F (0°C) at a minimum of 1.2 volts per cell (7.2 volts for a 12-volt battery).

- **Cranking Amperes** The **cranking amperes (CA)** are not the same as CCA but are often advertised and labeled on batteries. The designation CA refers to the number of amperes that can be supplied by the battery at 32°F (0°C). This rating results in a higher number than the more stringent rating of CCA.
- **Marine Cranking Amperes** The **marine cranking amperes (MCA)** rating is similar to the cranking amperes (CA) rating and is tested at 32°F (0°C).
- **Ampere-Hour Rating** The **Ampere-Hour (Ah)** is how many amperes can be discharged from the battery before dropping to 10.5 volts over a 20-hour period. A battery that is able to supply 3.75 amperes for 20 hours has a rating of 75 ampere hours ($3.75 \times 20 = 75$).
- **Reserve Capacity** The **reserve capacity** rating for batteries is *the number of minutes* for which the battery can produce 25 amperes and still have a battery voltage of 1.75 volts per cell (10.5 volts for a 12-volt battery). This rating is actually a measurement of the time for which a vehicle can be driven in the event of a charging system failure.

BATTERIES

PURPOSE AND FUNCTION
The primary purpose of an automotive **battery** is to provide a source of electrical power for starting and for electrical demands that exceed alternator output. The battery also acts as a voltage stabilizer for the entire electrical system. The battery is a voltage stabilizer because it acts as a reservoir where large amounts of current (amperes) can be removed quickly during starting, and replaced gradually by the **alternator** during charging. The battery *must* be in good (serviceable) condition before the charging system and the cranking system can be tested. For example, if a battery is discharged, the **cranking circuit** (starter motor) could test as being defective because the battery voltage might drop below specifications.

The **charging circuit** could also test as being defective because of a weak or discharged battery. Therefore, the vehicle battery should be tested and confirmed serviceable before testing the cranking or charging system.

BATTERY RATINGS
- **Cold-Cranking Amperes** Every automotive battery must be able to supply electrical power to crank the engine in cold weather and still provide voltage high enough to operate the ignition system for starting. The cold-cranking power of a battery is the number of amperes that can be supplied at 0°F (−18°C) for 30 seconds while the battery still maintains a voltage of 1.2 volts per cell or higher. This means that the battery voltage would be 7.2 volts for a 12-volt battery and 3.6 volts for a 6-volt battery. The cold-cranking performance rating is called **cold-cranking amperes (CCA)**. Try to purchase a battery that offers the highest CCA for the money. ● **SEE FIGURE 13–1.**

BATTERY CONSTRUCTION TYPES

FLOODED BATTERIES Conventional batteries use a liquid electrolyte and are called **flooded lead acid (FLA)** batteries. In this design, vents are used to allow the gases (hydrogen and oxygen) to escape. It is this loss of the hydrogen and oxygen that results in a battery using water during normal use.

ENHANCED FLOODED BATTERIES An **enhanced flooded battery (EFB)** is a flooded battery (NOT an absorbed glass mat battery) that is optimized to work with stop/start vehicle systems. Using wet cells, the design allows for improved charge acceptance and greater durability when being operated in a vehicle that uses a stop/start system.

ABSORBED GLASS MAT The acid used in an **absorbed glass mat (AGM)** battery is totally absorbed into the separator, making the battery leak-proof and spill-proof. The battery is assembled by compressing the cell about 20%, then inserting it into the container. The compressed cell helps reduce damage caused by vibration and helps keep the acid tightly against the plates. The sealed maintenance-free design uses a pressure release valve in each cell. Unlike conventional batteries that use a liquid electrolyte, called flooded cell batteries, most of the hydrogen and oxygen given off during charging remains inside the battery. The separator or mat is only 90%–95% saturated with electrolyte, thereby allowing a portion of the mat to be filled with gas. The gas spaces provide channels to allow the

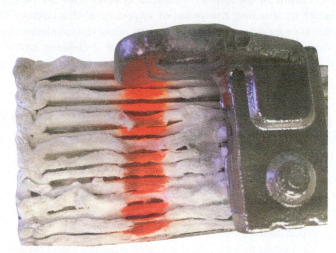

FIGURE 13–2 A close-up of an AGM cell showing the mat totally encasing the plates.

FIGURE 13–3 An AGM battery under the floor next to the spare tire on a Lexus NX300h hybrid electric vehicle.

FIGURE 13–4 Corrosion on a battery cable could be an indication that the battery itself is either being overcharged or is sulfated, creating a lot of gassing of the electrolyte.

FIGURE 13–5 A visual inspection on this battery shows the electrolyte level is below the plates in all cells.

hydrogen and oxygen gases to recombine rapidly and safely. Because the acid is totally absorbed into the glass mat separator, an AGM battery can be mounted in any direction. AGM batteries also have a longer service life, often lasting 7 to 10 years. Absorbed glass mat batteries are used as standard equipment in some vehicles, such as the Chevrolet Corvette and in most Toyota/Lexus hybrid electric vehicles. ● SEE FIGURES 13–2 AND 13–3.

BATTERY TESTING

VISUAL INSPECTION The battery and battery cables should be included in the list of items checked during a thorough visual inspection. Check the battery cables for corrosion and tightness. ● SEE FIGURE 13–4.

NOTE: On side-post batteries, grasp the battery cable near the battery and attempt to move the cable in a clockwise direction in an attempt to tighten the battery connection.

If possible, remove the covers and observe the level of the electrolyte. ● SEE FIGURE 13–5.

BATTERY CONDUCTANCE TESTING General Motors Corporation, Chrysler Corporation, Ford, and other vehicle manufacturers specify that a **conductance tester** be used to test batteries in vehicles still under factory warranty. The tester uses its internal electronic circuitry to determine the state of charge and capacity of the battery by measuring the voltage and conductance of the plates. ● SEE FIGURE 13–6.

Connect the tester to the positive and negative terminals of the battery, and after entering the CCA rating (if known), push the arrow keys. The tester determines one of the following:

- **Good battery.** The battery can return to service.
- **Charge and retest.** Fully recharge the battery and return it to service.

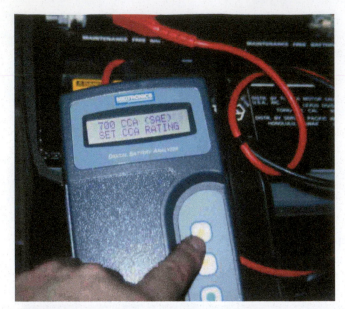

FIGURE 13–6 A conductance tester is very easy to use and has proved to accurately determine battery condition if the connections are properly made. Follow the instructions on the display exactly for best results.

- ■ **Replace the battery.** The battery is not serviceable and should be replaced.
- ■ **Bad cell—replace.** The battery is not serviceable and should be replaced.

If the message states that the battery should be charged and retested, this means that the battery may or may not require replacement. Always follow the tester's recommended steps and procedures.

BATTERY DRAIN TEST

PURPOSE The **battery electrical drain test** determines if some component or circuit in a vehicle or truck is causing a drain on the battery when everything is off. This test is also called the **ignition off-draw (IOD)** or **parasitic load** test. This test should be performed whenever one of the following conditions exists:

1. Whenever a battery is being charged or replaced (a battery drain could have been the cause for charging or replacing the battery)
2. Whenever the battery is suspected of being drained, normal battery drain on a vehicle equipped with electronic radio, climate control, computerized fuel injection, and so forth, is usually about 20 to 30 milliamperes (0.02 to 0.03 A). Most vehicle manufacturers recommend repairing the cause of any drain that exceeds 50 mA (0.05 A).

NOTE: Some manufacturers relate maximum allowable parasitic load to the size of the battery. The higher the battery capacity, the greater the allowable load. The maximum allowable drain on a battery can be calculated by dividing the reserve capacity of the battery in minutes by 4 to get the maximum allowable drain in milliamps. For example, if a battery had a reserve capacity of 100 minutes, it would have a maximum allowable parasitic load of 25 mA (100/4 = 25 mA).

BATTERY ELECTRICAL DRAIN TESTING USING AN AMMETER There are two ways to measure battery electrical drain (parasitic draw).

METHOD 1 Use an inductive clamp-on ammeter (preferred method).

METHOD 2 Connect a digital meter set to read amperes in series between the battery terminal and the disconnected battery clamp or install a parasitic load tester adapter. Normal battery drain is 0.020 to 0.030 A and any drain greater than 0.050 A should be found and corrected. If after disconnecting these components the battery drain can draw more than 50 mA (0.05 A), disconnect one fuse at a time from the fuse box until the test light goes out or the ammeter reading drops. If the drain drops to normal after one fuse is disconnected, the source of the drain is located in that particular circuit, as labeled on the fuse box. As fuses are pulled, they should not be reinstalled until the end of the test. Reinstalling a fuse can reset a module and foul up the test. Start at the fuses farthest from the battery and work toward the battery until the faulty circuit is found. Note that many vehicles have multiple fuse boxes. Then, disconnect the *power-side* wire connectors from each component included in that particular circuit until the ammeter reads a normal amount of draw. The source of the battery drain can then be traced to an individual component or part of one circuit. If none of the fuses causes the drain to stop, disconnect the alternator output lead. A shorted diode in the alternator could be the cause.

BATTERY CHARGING

RATE OF CHARGING If the **state-of-charge** of a battery is low, it must be recharged. It is best to slow-charge any battery to prevent possible overheating damage to the battery. It may require 8 hours or more to charge a fully discharged battery. The initial charge rate should be about 35 amperes for 30 minutes to help start the charging process. Fast-charging a battery increases the temperature of the battery and can cause warping of the plates inside the battery. Fast-charging also increases the amount of gassing (release of hydrogen and oxygen), which can create a health and fire hazard. The battery temperature should not exceed 125°F (hot to the touch). Most batteries should be charged at a rate equal to 1% of the battery's CCA rating. ● **SEE FIGURE 13–7.**

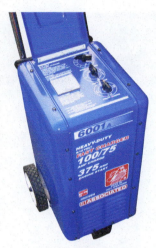

FIGURE 13–7 A typical industrial battery charger. Be sure that the ignition switch is in the off position before connecting any battery charger. Connect the cables of the charger to the battery before plugging the charger into the outlet. This helps prevent a voltage spike and spark that could occur if the charger happened to be accidentally left on. Always follow the battery charger manufacturer's instructions.

- Fast charge: 15 amperes maximum
- Slow charge: 5 amperes maximum

● **SEE CHART 13–1** for battery charging times at various battery voltages and charging rates.

CAUTION: Always use the "AGM" setting on the charger when charging absorbed glass mat batteries. AGM batteries should never be charged at a voltage higher than 15 volts.

BATTERY REGISTRATION

PURPOSE Some vehicle manufacturers require that a new battery be registered when installed in the vehicle. Some vehicle manufacturers, usually European brands, design the charging system with an algorithm that varies the rate of charge by the age and type of the battery installed.

PROCEDURE Registering a new battery resets the algorithm back to optimal charging voltage for the specified battery. Check service information for the vehicle being serviced to determine if a new replacement battery needs to be coded after being installed. Failure to complete this procedure may result in an undercharge or overcharge condition of the new battery. Check service information for the vehicle being serviced to determine if a new replacement battery needs to be coded after being installed.

CRANKING SYSTEMS

PARTS INVOLVED The cranking circuit includes those mechanical and electrical components required to crank the engine for starting. The cranking circuits include the following:

1. **Starter motor.** The starter is normally a 0.5–2.6 horsepower (0.4–2.0 kW) electric motor that can develop nearly 8 horsepower (6 kW) for a very short time when first cranking a cold engine.
2. **Battery.** The battery must be of the correct capacity and be at least 75% charged to provide the necessary current and voltage for correct operation of the starter.
3. **Starter solenoid or relay.** The high current required by the starter must be able to be turned on and off. A large switch would be required if the current were controlled by the driver directly. Instead, a small current switch (ignition switch) operates a solenoid or relay that controls the high starter current.
4. **Ignition Switch/Button.** The ignition switch and safety control switches control the starter motor operation. The ignition switch will not operate the starter unless the

OPEN CIRCUIT VOLTAGE	BATTERY SPECIFIC GRAVITY*	STATE OF CHARGE	CHARGING TIME TO FULL CHARGE AT 80°F**					
			at 60 amps	at 50 amps	at 40 amps	at 30 amps	at 20 amps	at 10 amps
12.6	1.265	100%	FULL CHARGE					
12.4	1.225	75%	15 min.	20 min.	27 min.	35 min.	48 min.	90 min.
12.2	1.190	50%	35 min.	45 min.	55 min.	75 min.	95 min.	180 min.
12.0	1.155	25%	50 min.	65 min.	85 min.	115 min.	145 min.	260 min.
11.8	1.120	0%	65 min.	85 min.	110 min.	150 min.	195 min.	370 min.

CHART 13–1

Battery charging guideline showing the charging times that vary according to state of charge, temperature, and charging rate. It may take eight hours or more to charge a fully discharged battery.
*Correct for temperature.
**If colder, it'll take longer.

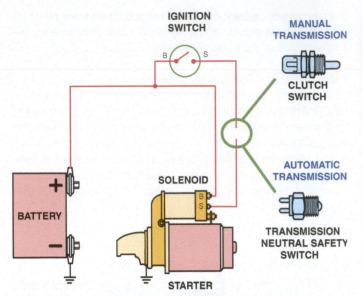

FIGURE 13–8 To prevent the engine from cranking, an electrical switch is usually installed to open the circuit between the ignition switch and the starter solenoid. The control circuit includes the small wiring and components needed to control the solenoid. The starter solenoid controls the electrical current flow through the large battery cables of the power circuit which operates the starter motor.

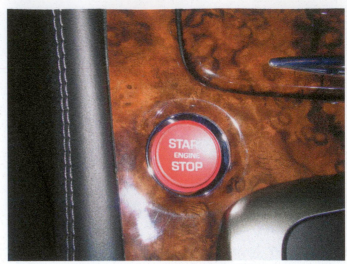

FIGURE 13–9 Instead of using an ignition key to start the engine, some vehicles are using a start button which is also used to stop the engine, as shown on this Jaguar.

automatic transmission is in neutral or park. This is to prevent an accident that might result from the vehicle moving forward or backward when the engine is started. Many automobile manufacturers use a **neutral safety switch** that opens the circuit between the ignition switch and the starter to prevent starter motor operation unless the gear

selector is in neutral or park. The safety switch can either be attached to the steering column inside the vehicle near the floor or on the side of the transmission/transaxle. ● **SEE FIGURES 13–8 AND 13–9.**

CRANKING CIRCUIT OPERATION
The engine is cranked by an electric motor that is controlled by a key-operated ignition switch or the PCM on vehicles equipped with electronic starting. According to vehicle manufacturing engineers, starters can be expected to start an engine 25,000 times during normal life of the vehicle. ● **SEE FIGURE 13–10.**

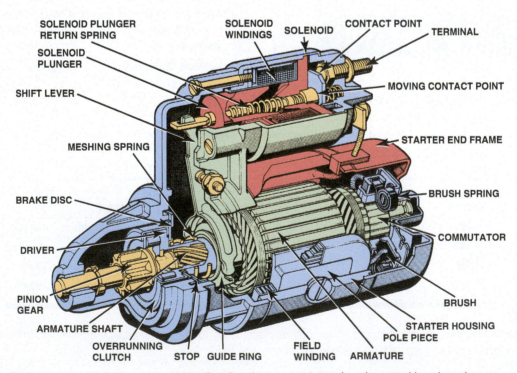

FIGURE 13–10 A cutaway of a typical starter motor showing the commutator, brushes, and brush spring.

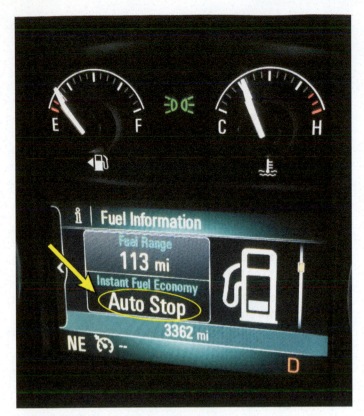

FIGURE 13–11 A Buick Auto Stop system lets the driver know when the engine is stopped.

STOP/START SYSTEMS

PURPOSE AND FUNCTION Stop/start systems are designed to increase fuel economy and reduce exhaust emissions. Fuel economy and the reduction of CO_2 emissions are estimated to be 5%–10%, depending on the vehicle and how it is being operated. With stop-start mechanism, the engine is stopped to reduce the fuel consumption when the vehicle is stopped at traffic signals or in stop and go traffic conditions.

Various vehicle manufacturers refer to stop-start systems using different terms, including:

- Auto Stop—● **SEE FIGURE 13–11.**
- Stop-Start
- Idle-Stop (Honda)
- Smart Stop (Toyota)
- Intelligent Stop and Go (Kia)
- Auto Start/Stop (BMW)
- Engine Stop-Start (ESS)—Chrysler

CONDITIONS FOR STOP/START TO OCCUR Before the PCM will engage the stop/start function, the following parameters must be achieved:

- Engine speed is within idling range.
- Accelerator pedal is not depressed.

- Vehicle speed is low or zero, depending on the type of starter used.
- Battery state-of-charge (SOC) is above threshold.
- Hood is closed.

START/STOP SYSTEM COMPONENTS It is estimated that a stop/start system will start the engine about 500,000 times in the life of the vehicle compared to about 25,000 times for a conventional starting system. A typical stop/start system includes the following components:

1. An absorbed glass-mat (AGM) or enhanced lead-acid (ELA) battery
2. Battery sensor used by the PCM to determine the current entering and leaving the battery in order to estimate the battery state-of-charge.
3. Hood switch used by the PCM to disengage stop/start if the hood is open.
4. HVAC control unit used to start the engine if cooling or heat is required in the passenger compartment.

STOP/START STARTER MOTOR DESIGNS Because the engine needs to be restarted many times a day if driving in heavy congested traffic, the starter used must be robust and capable of starting the engine over 500,000 times during the life of the system. There are three designs of starters used in stop/start system, including:

1. **Advanced Engagement (AE) Starter** An advanced engagement starter works like a typical starter. When energized, the pinion shifts forward by the starter solenoid and engages with the engine's ring gear/flywheel, and immediately spins.
2. **Tandem Solenoid (TS) Starter** Using a starter that has two solenoids allows the starter to engage the flywheel of the engine when it is still moving, such as when the vehicle is coasting to a stop. A tandem solenoid starter design is also able to start the engine within 0.5 and 1.5 seconds compared to about 3 seconds for a conventional starter.
3. **Permanently Engaged (PE) Starter** A permanently engaged starter delivers the quickest and quietest restart times of all starter motor–based systems. In this system, the starter and flywheel gears are permanently connected, so there are no concerns with gear engagement and disengagement.

CRANKING CIRCUIT VOLTAGE-DROP TESTING

PURPOSE **Voltage-drop** is the drop in voltage that occurs when current is flowing through a resistance. For example, a voltage drop is the difference between voltage at the source and voltage at the electrical device to which it is flowing. The higher the voltage drop, the greater the resistance in the circuit. Even though voltage-drop testing can be performed on any electrical

FIGURE 13–12 The stop-start system on this Ford F-150 pickup truck can be turned off using a switch on the dash.

 FREQUENTLY ASKED QUESTION

Can a Stop-Start System Be Turned Off?

Sometimes. Some vehicles equipped with a stop-start system can be turned off using a button on the dash or center stack. ● SEE FIGURE 13–12.

circuit, the most common areas of testing include the cranking circuit, and the charging circuit wiring and connections.

A high-voltage drop (high resistance) in the cranking circuit wiring can cause slow engine cranking with less-than-normal starter amperage drain as a result of the excessive circuit resistance. If the voltage drop is high enough, such as could be caused by dirty battery terminals, the starter may not operate. A typical symptom of low battery voltage or high resistance in the cranking circuit is a "clicking" of the starter solenoid.

PERFORMING A VOLTAGE DROP TEST Voltage-drop testing of the wire involves connecting any voltmeter (on the low scale) to the suspected high-resistance cable ends and cranking the engine. ● SEE FIGURES 13–13 THROUGH 13–15.

NOTE: Before a difference in voltage (voltage drop) can be measured between the ends of a battery cable, current must be flowing through the cable. *Resistance is not effective unless current is flowing.* If the engine is not being cranked, current is not flowing through the battery cables and the voltage drop cannot be measured.

Crank the engine with a voltmeter connected to the battery and record the reading. Crank the engine with the voltmeter connected across the starter and record the reading. If the difference in the two readings exceeds 0.5 volt, perform the following steps to determine the exact location of the voltage drop.

STEP 1 Connect the positive voltmeter test lead to the most positive end of the cable being tested. The most positive end of a cable is the end closest to the positive terminal of the battery.

STEP 2 Connect the negative voltmeter test lead to the other end of the cable being tested. With no current flowing through the cable, the voltmeter should read zero because there is the same voltage at both ends of the cable.

STEP 3 Crank the engine. The voltmeter should read less than 0.2 volt.

STEP 4 Evaluate the results. If the voltmeter reads zero, the cable being tested has no resistance and is good. If the voltmeter reads higher than 0.2 volt, the cable

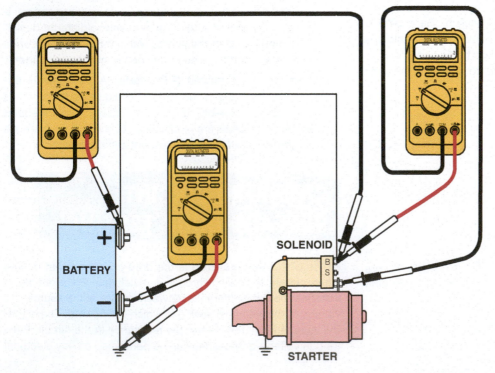

FIGURE 13–13 Voltmeter hookups for voltage drop testing of a solenoid-type cranking circuit.

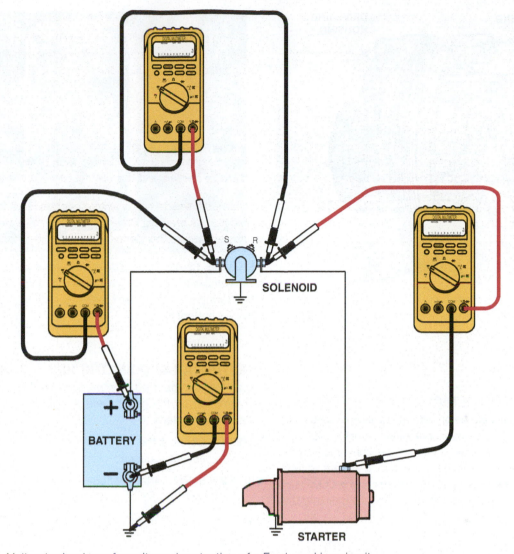

FIGURE 13–14 Voltmeter hookups for voltage drop testing of a Ford cranking circuit.

FIGURE 13–15 To test the voltage drop of the battery cable connection, place one voltmeter lead on the battery terminal and the other voltmeter lead on the cable end and crank the engine. The voltmeter will read the difference in voltage between the two leads, which should not exceed 0.20 volt (200 mV).

has excessive resistance and should be replaced. However, before replacing the cable, make certain that the connections at both ends of the cable being tested are clean and tight.

CHARGING CIRCUIT

PARTS AND OPERATION An alternator is constructed of a two-piece cast-aluminum housing. Aluminum is used because of its lightweight, nonmagnetic properties and heat transfer properties, which are needed to help keep the alternator cool. A front ball bearing is pressed into the front housing (called the **drive-end [DE]** housing) to provide the support and friction reduction necessary for the belt-driven rotor assembly. The rear housing (called the **slip ring end [SRE]**) usually contains a roller-bearing support for the rotor and mounting for the brushes, diodes, and internal voltage regulator (if the alternator is so equipped). ● **SEE FIGURE 13–16.**

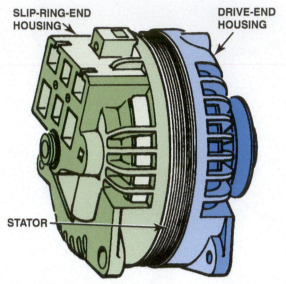

FIGURE 13–16 The end frame toward the drive belt is called the drive-end housing and the rear section is called the slip-ring-end housing.

FIGURE 13–17 The digital multimeter should be set to read DC volts, with the red lead connected to the positive (+) battery terminal and the black meter lead connected to the negative (−) battery terminal.

CHARGING SYSTEM VOLTAGE TEST

The charge indicator light on the dash should be on with the ignition on, engine off (KOEO), but should be off when the engine is running (KOER). If the charge light remains on with the engine running, check the charging system voltage. To measure charging system voltage, connect the test leads of a digital multimeter to the positive (+) and negative (−) terminals of the battery. Set the multimeter to read DC volts.

CHARGING SYSTEM VOLTAGE SPECIFICATIONS

Most alternators are designed to supply between 13.5 and 15.0 volts at 2000 engine RPM. Be sure to check the vehicle manufacturer's specifications. For example, most General Motors Corporation vehicles specify a charging voltage of 14.7 volts - 14.7 volts plus or minus 0.5 (or between 14.2 and 15.2 volts) at 2000 RPM and no load.

CHARGING SYSTEM VOLTAGE TEST PROCEDURE

Charging system voltage tests should be performed on a vehicle with a battery at least 75% charged. If the battery is discharged (or defective), the charging voltage may be below specifications.

To measure charging system voltage, perform the following steps:

STEP 1 Connect the voltmeter. ● **SEE FIGURE 13–17.**

STEP 2 Set the meter to read DC volts.

STEP 3 Start the engine and raise to a fast idle (about 2000 RPM).

STEP 4 Read the voltmeter and compare with specifications.

If lower than specifications, charge the battery and test for excessive charging circuit voltage drop and for a possible open in the sensing wire before replacing the alternator.

TESTING AN ALTERNATOR USING A SCAN TOOL

A scan tool can be used on most vehicles that have data stream information on the battery and the charging system. Perform the following steps:

STEP 1 Connect the scan tool according to the manufacturer's instructions.

STEP 2 Select battery voltage and engine RPM on the scan tool.

STEP 3 Start the engine and operate at 2000 RPM.

STEP 4 Observe the battery voltage. This voltage should be between 13.5 and 15.0 volts (or within manufacturer's specifications).

NOTE: The scan tool voltage should be within 0.5 volt of the charging voltage as tested at the battery. In some PCM-controlled charging systems, such as the General Motor's electrical power management (EPM) system, the charging voltage can vary from 12 to 15 volts and be normal. Always check service information for the exact specification for the vehicle being tested to help avoid unnecessary repairs.

AC RIPPLE VOLTAGE

A good alternator should produce only a small amount of AC voltage. It is the purpose of the diodes in the alternator to rectify AC voltage into DC voltage. **AC ripple voltage** is the AC part of the DC charging voltage produced by the alternator. If the AC ripple voltage is higher than 0.5 volt, this can cause engine performance problems because the AC voltage can interfere with sensor signals. The procedure to check for AC voltage includes the following steps:

1. Set the digital meter to read AC volts.

2. Start the engine and operate it at 2000 RPM (fast idle).

MEASURING THE AC RIPPLE FROM THE ALTERNATOR TELLS A LOT ABOUT ITS CONDITION. IF THE AC RIPPLE IS ABOVE 500 MILLIVOLTS, OR 0.5 VOLT, LOOK FOR A PROBLEM IN THE DIODES OR STATOR. IF THE RIPPLE IS BELOW 500 MILLIVOLTS, CHECK THE ALTERNATOR OUTPUT TO DETERMINE ITS CONDITION.

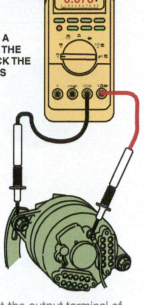

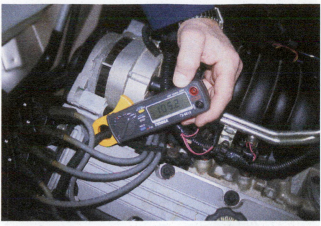

FIGURE 13–19 A mini clamp-on meter can be used to measure alternator output as shown here (105.2 A). Then the meter can be used to check AC current ripple by selecting AC amps on the rotary dial. AC ripple current should be less than 10% of the DC current output.

FIGURE 13–18 Testing AC ripple at the output terminal of the alternator is more accurate than testing at the battery due to the resistance of the wiring between the alternator and the battery. The reading shown on the meter, set to AC volts, is only 78 millivolts (0.078 V), far below what the reading would be if a diode were defective.

3. Connect the voltmeter leads to the positive and negative battery terminals.

4. Turn on the headlights to provide an electrical load on the alternator.

NOTE: A higher, more accurate reading can be obtained by touching the meter lead to the output terminal of the alternator. ● **SEE FIGURE 13–18.**

The results should be interpreted as follows: If the diodes are good, the voltmeter should read *less* than 0.4 volt AC. If the reading is *over* 0.5 volt AC, the rectifier diodes or stator are defective, indicating that the alternator should be replaced.

AC RIPPLE CURRENT The amount of AC current (also called **ripple current**) in amperes flowing from the alternator to the battery can be measured using a clamp-on digital multimeter set to read AC amperes. Attach the clamp of the meter around the alternator output wire or all of the positive or negative battery cables if the output wire is not accessible. Start the engine and turn on all lights and accessories to load the alternator and read the meter display. The maximum allowable AC current (amperes) from the alternator is less than 10% of the rated output of the alternator.

Because most newer alternators produce about 100 amperes DC, the maximum allowable AC amperes would be 10 amperes. If the reading is above 10 A (or 10%), this indicates that the rectifier diodes or a fault with the stator windings is present. ● **SEE FIGURE 13–19.**

 CASE STUDY

The Speedometer Works as If It Is a Tachometer

The owner of a Ford F-150 pickup truck complained that all of a sudden, the speedometer needle went up and down with engine speed, rather than vehicle speed. In fact, the speedometer needle went up and down with engine speed, even though the gear selector was in "park" and the vehicle was not moving. After hours of troubleshooting, the service technician went back and started checking the basics and discovered that the alternator had a bad diode. The technician measured over 1 volt AC and over 10 amperes AC ripple current using a clamp-on AC/DC ammeter. Replacing the alternator restored the proper operation of the speedometer.

Summary:

- **Complaint**—Customer stated that the speedometer would move in relation to engine speed and not vehicle speed.
- **Cause**—Tests confirmed that the alternator was producing excessive AC voltage due to a bad diode.
- **Correction**—Replacing the alternator restored proper operation of the speedometer.

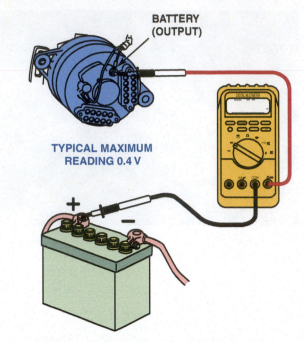

BATTERY
(OUTPUT)

TYPICAL MAXIMUM
READING 0.4 V

VOLTAGE DROP—INSULATED CHARGING CIRCUIT

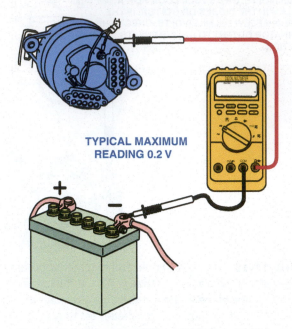

ENGINE AT 2000 RPM.
CHARGING SYSTEM
LOADED TO 20 A

TYPICAL MAXIMUM
READING 0.2 V

VOLTAGE DROP—CHARGING GROUND CIRCUIT

FIGURE 13–20 Voltmeter hookup to test the voltage drop of the charging circuit.

CHARGING SYSTEM VOLTAGE DROP TESTING For the proper operation of any charging system, there must be good electrical connections between the battery positive terminal and the alternator output terminal. The alternator must also be properly grounded to the engine block. Many vehicle manufacturers run the lead from the output terminal of the alternator to other connectors or junction blocks that are electrically connected to the positive terminal of the battery. If there is high resistance (a high-voltage drop) in these connections or in the wiring itself, the battery will not be properly charged. When there is a suspected charging system problem (with or without a charge indicator light on), simply follow these steps to measure the voltage drop of the insulated (power-side) charging circuit:

1. Start the engine and run it at a fast idle (about 2000 engine RPM).

2. Turn on the headlights to ensure an electrical load on the charging system.

3. Using any voltmeter, connect the positive test lead (usually red) to the output terminal of the alternator. Attach the negative test lead (usually black) to the positive post of the battery.

The results should be interpreted as follows:

1. If there is less than a 0.4-volt reading, all wiring and connections are satisfactory.

2. If the voltmeter reads higher than 0.4 volt, there is excessive resistance (voltage drop) between the alternator output terminal and the positive terminal of the battery.

3. If the voltmeter reads battery voltage (or close to battery voltage), there is an open circuit between the battery and the alternator output terminal (look for a positive open maxi fuse or fusible link).

To determine whether the alternator is correctly grounded, maintain the engine speed at 2000 RPM with the headlights on. Connect the positive voltmeter lead to the case of the alternator and the negative voltmeter lead to the negative terminal of the battery. The voltmeter should read less than 0.2 volt if the alternator is properly grounded. If the reading is over 0.2 volt, connect one end of an auxiliary ground wire to the case of the alternator and the other end to a good engine ground. ● SEE FIGURE 13–20.

ALTERNATOR SCOPE TESTING Defective diodes and open or shorted stators can be detected on an ignition scope. Connect the scope leads as usual, *except* for the coil negative connection, which attaches to the alternator output ("BAT") terminal. With the pattern selection set to "raster" (stacked), start the engine and run to approximately 1000 RPM (slightly higher-than-normal idle speed). The scope should show an even ripple pattern reflecting the slight alternating up-and-down level of the alternator output voltage.

If the alternator is controlled by an electronic voltage regulator, the rapid on-and-off cycling of the field current can create vertical spikes evenly throughout the pattern. These spikes are normal. If the ripple pattern is jagged or uneven, a defective diode (open or shorted) or a defective stator is indicated. ● **SEE FIGURES 13–21 THROUGH 13–23**. If the alternator scope pattern does not show even ripples, the alternator should be replaced.

FIGURE 13–21 Normal alternator scope pattern. This AC ripple is on top of a DC voltage line. The ripple should be less than 0.50 volt high.

FIGURE 13–22 Alternator pattern indicating a shorted diode.

FIGURE 13–23 Alternator pattern indicating an open diode.

SUMMARY

1. Batteries can be tested with a voltmeter to determine the state of charge. A battery load test loads the battery to one-half of its CCA rating. A good battery should be able to maintain above 9.6 volts for the entire 15-second test period.

2. A battery drain test should be performed if the battery runs down.

3. Proper operation of the starter motor depends on the battery being at least 75% charged and the battery cables being of the correct size (gauge) and having no more than a 0.2-volt drop.

4. Voltage-drop testing includes cranking the engine, measuring the drop in voltage from the battery to the starter, and measuring the drop in voltage from the negative terminal of the battery to the engine block.

5. The cranking circuit should be tested for proper amperage draw.

6. An open in the control circuit can prevent starter motor operation.

7. Charging system testing requires that the battery be at least 75% charged to be assured of accurate test results. The charge indicator light should be on with the ignition switch on, but should go out whenever the engine is running. Normal charging voltage (at 2000 engine RPM) is 13.5–15.0 volts.

8. To check for excessive resistance in the wiring between the alternator and the battery, perform a voltage-drop test.

REVIEW QUESTIONS

1. How can a conductance tester be used to determine the battery state-of-charge?

2. What is the purpose and function of a stop-start system?

3. What are the steps needed to be performed for a voltage-drop test of the cranking circuit?

4. How is the voltage drop of the charging circuit determined?

5. What does testing the voltage or current AC ripple tell the technician about the condition of the alternator?

1. A battery conductance test is being performed and the test results show that the battery is discharged. Technician A says that the battery may or may not need to be replaced. Technician B says that the battery should be charged and retested. Which technician is correct?
   a. Technician A only
   b. Technician B only
   c. Both Technicians A and B
   d. Neither Technician A nor B

2. Normal battery drain (parasitic drain) with a vehicle with many computer and electronic circuits is ——————.
   a. 20 to 30 milliamperes
   b. 2 to 3 amperes
   c. 150 to 300 milliamperes
   d. None of the above

3. Electrical resistance of the cranking and charging circuits is best determined by what type of test?
   a. Resistance testing using an ohmmeter
   b. Voltage drop testing
   c. Ammeter testing of the system to determine the current flow
   d. Checking the wiring and cables with an ohmmeter

4. Battery testers usually use what battery rating?
   a. CCA
   b. CA
   c. Reserve capacity
   d. Amp-hour

5. Which type of meter can be used to measure battery drain, starter amperage draw, and alternator output without having to disconnect wiring connections?
   a. Ohmmeter
   b. Clamp-on ammeter
   c. Voltmeter
   d. Any of the above

6. The purpose and function of a stop/start system is to ——————.
   a. reduce noise, vibration, and harshness
   b. improve fuel economy and reduce exhaust emissions
   c. reduce noise and vibration at idle
   d. replace the starter motor saving weight

7. Registering a new battery is sometimes needed because ——————.
   a. it resets the algorithm back to optional charging voltage
   b. allows a different battery size to be used in the vehicle
   c. the battery warranty may have expired
   d. the number of cells of the replacement battery must be inputted into the PCM memory

8. An acceptable charging circuit voltage on a 12-volt system is ——————.
   a. 13.5 to 15.0 volts
   b. 12.6 to 15.6 volts
   c. 12.0 to 14.0 volts
   d. 14.9 to 16.1 volts

9. Technician A says that a voltage-drop test of the charging circuit should only be performed when current is flowing through the circuit. Technician B says to connect the leads of a voltmeter to the positive and negative terminals of the battery to measure the voltage drop of the charging system. Which technician is correct?
   a. Technician A only
   b. Technician B only
   c. Both Technicians A and B
   d. Neither Technician A nor B

10. An AGM battery should never be charged with more than —————— volts.
    a. 12
    b. 14
    c. 15
    d. All of these are too high

chapter 14

IGNITION SYSTEM OPERATION AND DIAGNOSIS

LEARNING OBJECTIVES

After studying this chapter, the reader should be able to:

1. Describe the purpose and function of the ignition system.
2. Discuss ignition switching and triggering.
3. Explain the purpose and function of distributor ignition systems.
4. Discuss waste-spark ignition systems and coil-on-plug ignition systems.
5. Discuss the purpose and function of knock sensors.
6. Explain ignition system diagnosis.
7. List the steps to perform a current ramp test of the ignition coils.
8. Explain spark plug construction, service, and how to conduct a spark plug wire inspection.
9. Explain ignition timing and scope testing and discuss the symptoms of a faulty ignition system.

KEY TERMS

Coil-on-plug (COP) system 202
Companion cylinders 207
Detonation 211
Distributor ignition (DI) 202
Electronic ignition (EI) 202
EMI 202
Firing order 206
Hall effect 204
ICM 203
Ignition coil 202
Ignition timing 221
Ion-sensing ignition 210
Iridium spark plugs 219
Knock sensors 211
Magnetic pulse alternator 204
Pickup coil 204
Ping 211
Platinum spark plugs 219
Primary ignition circuit 203
Primary winding 202
Schmitt trigger 205
Secondary ignition circuit 203
Secondary winding 202
Spark knock 211
Spark plugs 218
Spark tester 213
Switching 204
Track 217
Transistor 204
Trigger 204
Turns ratio 202
Waste-spark system 202

PURPOSE AND FUNCTION The ignition system includes components and wiring necessary to create and distribute a high voltage (up to 40,000 volts or more) and send to the spark plug. A high-voltage arc occurs across the gap of a spark plug inside the combustion chamber. The spark raises the temperature of the air–fuel mixture and starts the combustion process inside the cylinder.

BACKGROUND All ignition systems apply battery voltage (close to 12 volts) to the positive side of the ignition coil(s) and pulse the negative side to ground.

- **Electronic ignition.** Since the mid-1970s, ignition systems have used sensors, such as a pickup coil and reluctor (trigger wheel), to trigger or signal an electronic module that switches the primary ground circuit of the ignition coil. **Distributor ignition (DI)** is the term specified by the Society of Automotive Engineers (SAE) for an ignition system that uses a distributor. **Electronic ignition (EI)** is the term specified by the SAE for an ignition system that does not use a distributor. Electronic ignition system types include:

1. **Waste-spark system.** This type of system uses one ignition coil to fire the spark plugs for two cylinders at the same time.

2. **Coil-on-plug (COP) system.** This type of system uses a single ignition coil for each cylinder with the coil placed above or near the spark plug.

IGNITION COIL CONSTRUCTION The heart of any ignition system is the **ignition coil**. When the coil negative lead is grounded, the primary (low-voltage) circuit of the coil is complete and a magnetic field is created around the coil windings. When the circuit is opened, the magnetic field collapses and induces a high voltage in the secondary winding of the ignition coil.

The coil creates a high-voltage spark by electromagnetic induction. Many ignition coils contain two separate but electrically connected windings of copper wire. Other coils are true transformers in which the primary and secondary windings are not electrically connected. ● SEE FIGURE 14–1.

The center of an ignition coil contains a core of laminated soft iron (thin strips of soft iron). This core increases the magnetic strength of the coil.

- **Secondary coil winding.** Surrounding the laminated core are approximately 20,000 turns of fine wire (approximately 42 gauge). The winding is called the **secondary winding**.
- **Primary coil winding.** Surrounding the secondary windings are approximately 150 turns of heavy wire (approximately 21 gauge). The winding is called the **primary winding**. The secondary winding has about 100 times the number of turns of the primary winding, referred to as the **turns ratio** (approximately 100:1).

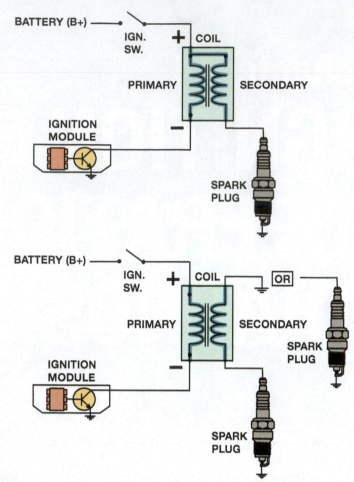

FIGURE 14–1 Some ignition coils are electrically connected, called married (top figure), whereas others use separate primary and secondary windings, called divorced (lower figure). The polarity (positive or negative) of a coil is determined by the direction in which the coil is wound.

In older coils, these windings are surrounded with a thin metal shield and insulating paper and placed into a metal container filled with transformer oil to help cool the coil windings. Other coil designs use an air-cooled, epoxy-sealed E coil. The *E coil* is so named because the laminated, soft iron core is E shaped, with the coil wire turns wrapped around the center "finger" of the E and the primary winding wrapped inside the secondary winding. ● SEE FIGURES 14–2 AND 14–3.

IGNITION COIL OPERATION All ignition systems use electromagnetic induction to produce a high-voltage spark from the ignition coil. **Electromagnetic induction (EMI)** means that a current can be created in a conductor (coil winding) by a moving magnetic field. The magnetic field in an ignition coil is produced by current flowing through the primary winding of the coil. An ignition coil is able to increase battery voltage to 40,000 volts or more in the following way.

FIGURE 14–2 The steel lamination used in an E coil helps increase the magnetic field strength, which helps the coil produce higher energy output for a more complete combustion in the cylinders.

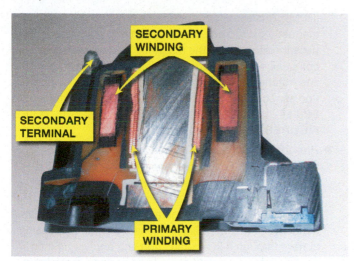

FIGURE 14–3 The primary windings are inside the secondary windings on this General Motors coil.

- Battery voltage is applied to the primary winding.
- A ground is provided to the primary winding by the **ignition control module (ICM)**, igniter, or PCM.
- Current (approximately 2 to 6 amperes) flows in the primary coil creating a magnetic field.
- When the ground is opened by the ICM, the built-up magnetic field collapses.
- The movement of the collapsing magnetic field induces a voltage of 250 to 400 volts in the primary winding and 20,000 to 40,000 volts or more in the secondary winding with a current of 0.020 to 0.080 ampere.
- The high voltage created in the secondary winding is high enough to jump the air gap at the spark plug.
- The electrical arc at the spark plug ignites the air–fuel mixture in the combustion chamber of the engine.
- For each spark that occurs, the coil must be charged with a magnetic field and then discharged.

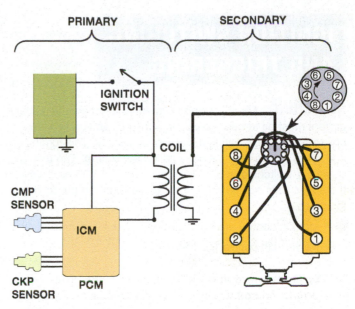

FIGURE 14–4 The primary ignition system is used to trigger and therefore create the secondary (high-voltage) spark from the ignition coil.

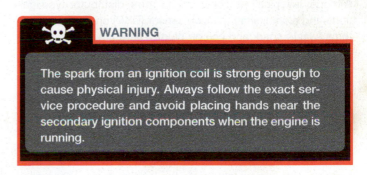

WARNING

The spark from an ignition coil is strong enough to cause physical injury. Always follow the exact service procedure and avoid placing hands near the secondary ignition components when the engine is running.

The ignition components that regulate the current in the coil primary winding by turning it on and off are known collectively as the **primary ignition circuit**. When the primary circuit is carrying current, the secondary circuit is off. When the primary circuit is turned off, the secondary circuit has high voltage. The components necessary to create and distribute the high voltage produced in the secondary windings of the coil are called the **secondary ignition circuit**. ● **SEE FIGURE 14–4.**

These circuits include the following components.
- Primary ignition circuit
  1. Battery
  2. Ignition switch
  3. Primary windings of coil
  4. Pickup coil (crankshaft position sensor)
  5. Ignition module (igniter)
- Secondary ignition circuit
  1. Secondary windings of coil
  2. Distributor cap and rotor (if the vehicle is so equipped)
  3. Spark plug wires
  4. Spark plugs

IGNITION SWITCHING AND TRIGGERING

SWITCHING For any ignition system to function, the primary current must be turned on to charge the coil and off to allow the coil to discharge, creating a high-voltage spark. This turning on and off of the primary circuit is called **switching**. The unit that does the switching is an electronic switch, such as a power transistor. This power transistor can be found in the following locations.

- Ignition control module (ICM) or igniter
- Powertrain control module (PCM)

NOTE: On some coil-on-plug systems, the ICM is part of the ignition coil itself and is serviced as an assembly.

TRIGGERING The device that signals the switching of the coil on and off or just on in most instances is called the **trigger**. A trigger is typically a pickup coil in some distributor-type ignitions and a crankshaft position sensor (CKP) on electronic systems (waste spark and coil on plug). There are two commonly used types of devices used for triggering.

1. Magnetic sensor
2. Hall-effect switch

PRIMARY CIRCUIT OPERATION To get a spark out of an ignition coil, the primary coil circuit must be turned on and off. The primary circuit current switching is controlled by a **transistor** (electronic switch) inside the ignition module (or igniter) and is controlled by one of several devices, including:

- **Magnetic sensor.** A simple and common ignition electronic switching device is the magnetic pulse alternator system. This is a type of magnetic sensor, often called a **magnetic pulse alternator** or **pickup coil**, and is installed in the distributor housing. The pulse alternator consists of a trigger wheel (reluctor) and a pickup coil. The pickup coil consists of an iron core wrapped with fine wire, in a coil at one end and attached to a permanent magnet at the other end. The center of the coil is called the pole piece. The pickup coil signal triggers the transistor inside the module and is also used by the PCM for piston position information and engine speed (RPM). The reluctor is shaped so that the magnetic strength changes enough to create a usable varying signal for use by the module to trigger the coil.

  Magnetic crankshaft position sensors use the changing strength of the magnetic field surrounding a coil of wire to signal the module and computer. This signal is used by the electronics in the module and computer to determine piston position and engine speed

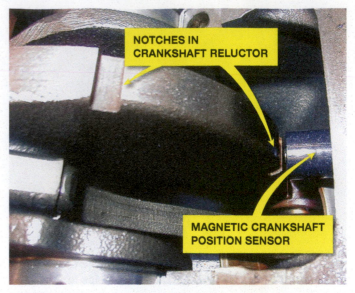

FIGURE 14–5 A typical magnetic crankshaft position sensor.

(RPM). This sensor operates similarly to the distributor magnetic pickup coil. The crankshaft position sensor uses the strength of the magnetic field surrounding a coil of wire to signal the ICM. The rotating crankshaft has notches cut into it that trigger the magnetic position sensor, which change the strength of the magnetic field as the notches pass by the position sensor. ● **SEE FIGURES 14–5 AND 14–6.**

- **Hall-effect switch.** This switch also uses a stationary sensor and rotating trigger wheel (shutter). Unlike the magnetic pulse the Hall-effect switch requires a small input voltage to generate an output or signal voltage. **Hall effect** has the ability to generate a voltage signal in semiconductor material (gallium arsenate crystal) by passing current through it in one direction and applying a magnetic field to it at a right angle to its surface. If the input current is held steady and the magnetic field fluctuates, an output voltage is produced that changes in proportion to field strength. Most Hall-effect switches in distributors have the following:

1. Hall element or device
2. Permanent magnet
3. Rotating ring of metal blades (shutters) similar to a trigger wheel (Another method uses a stationary sensor with a rotating magnet.) ● **SEE FIGURE 14–7.**

    Some blades are designed to hang down, typically found in Bosch and Chrysler systems, while others may be on a separate ring on the distributor shaft, typically found in General Motors and Ford Hall-effect distributors.

- When the shutter blade enters the gap between the magnet and the Hall element, it creates a magnetic shunt that changes the field strength through the Hall element.

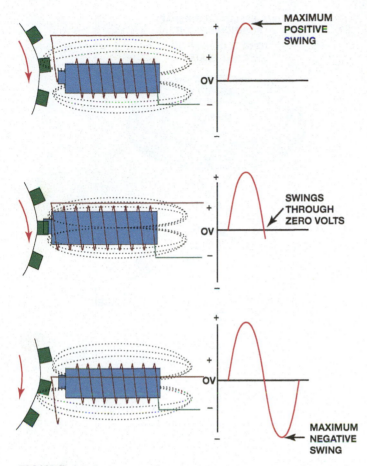

MAXIMUM POSITIVE SWING

OV

SWINGS THROUGH ZERO VOLTS

OV

OV

MAXIMUM NEGATIVE SWING

FIGURE 14–6 A magnetic sensor uses a permanent magnet surrounded by a coil of wire. The notches of the crankshaft (or camshaft) create a variable magnetic field strength around the coil. When a metallic section is close to the sensor, the magnetic field is stronger because metal is a better conductor of magnetic lines of force than air.

■ This analog signal is sent to a **Schmitt trigger** inside the sensor itself, which converts the analog signal into a digital signal. A digital (on or off) voltage signal is created at a varying frequency to the ignition module or onboard computer. ● **SEE FIGURE 14–8.**

FIGURE 14–7 A Hall-effect sensor produces an on-off voltage signal whether it is used with a blade or a notched wheel.

 **TECH TIP**

The Tachometer Trick

When diagnosing a no-start or intermediate missing condition, check the operation of the tachometer. If the tachometer does not indicate engine speed (no-start condition) or drops toward zero (engine missing), then the problem is due to a defect in the *primary* ignition circuit. The tachometer gets its signal from the pulsing of the primary winding of the ignition coil. The following components in the primary circuit could cause the tachometer to not work when the engine is cranking.

- Pickup coil
- Crankshaft position sensor
- Ignition module (igniter)
- Coil primary wiring

    If the vehicle is not equipped with a tachometer, use a scan tool to look at engine rpm. The results are as follows:

- No or an unstable engine RPM reading means the problem is in the primary ignition circuit.
- A steady engine RPM reading means the problem is in the secondary ignition circuit or is a fuel-related problem.

DISTRIBUTOR IGNITION (DI)

PURPOSE AND FUNCTION   The purpose of a distributor is to distribute the high-voltage spark from the output terminal of the ignition coil to the spark plugs for each cylinder. A gear or shaft drives the distributor that is connected to the camshaft and is driven at camshaft speed. Most distributor ignition systems also use a sensor to trigger the ignition control module. These triggering devices used in distributor ignition systems include:

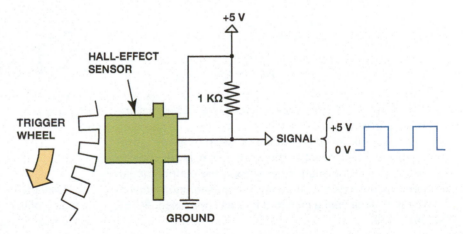

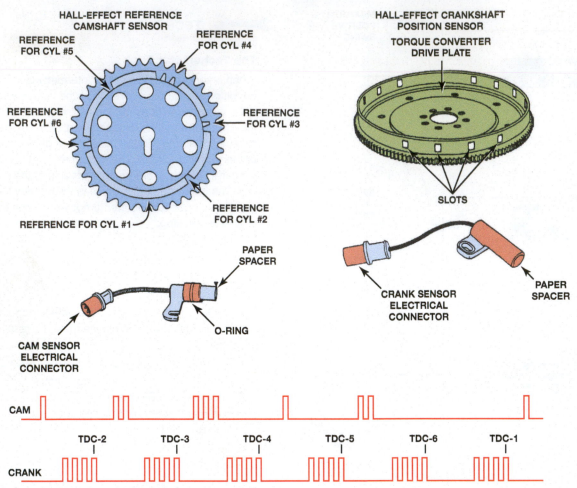

FIGURE 14–8 Some Hall-effect sensors look like magnetic sensors. This Hall-effect camshaft reference sensor and crankshaft position sensor have an electronic circuit built in that creates a 0 to 5 volt signal as shown at the bottom. These Hall-effect sensors have three wires: a power supply from the computer (controller), a signal (0 to 5 volts), and a signal ground.

- Magnetic pulse generator, also called pickup coils
- Hall-effect sensors located in the distributor
- Optical sensors located in the distributor

OPERATION OF DISTRIBUTOR IGNITION The distributor is used twice in most ignition systems that use a distributor.

- First, to trigger the ignition control module by the use of the rotating distributor shaft
- Second, by rotating the rotor to distribute the high-voltage spark to the individual spark plugs

FIRING ORDER **Firing order** means the order that the spark is distributed to the correct spark plug at the right time. The firing order of an engine is determined by crankshaft and camshaft design. The firing order is determined by the location of the spark plug wires in the distributor cap of an engine equipped with a distributor. The firing order is often cast into the intake manifold for easy reference. ● **SEE FIGURE 14–9.**

FIGURE 14–9 The firing order is cast or stamped on the intake manifold on most engines that have a distributor ignition.

Service information also shows the firing order and the direction of the distributor rotor rotation, as well as the location of the spark plug wires on the distributor cap.

CAUTION: Ford V-8s use two different firing orders depending on whether the engine is high output (HO) or standard. Using the incorrect firing order can cause the engine to backfire and could cause engine damage or personal injury. General Motors V-6 engines use different firing orders and different locations for cylinder 1 between the 60-degree V-6 and the 90-degree V-6. Using the incorrect firing order or cylinder number location chart could result in poor engine operation or a no start. Firing order is also important for waste-spark-type ignition systems. The spark plug wire can often be installed on the wrong coil pack, which can create a no-start condition or poor engine operation.

WASTE-SPARK IGNITION SYSTEMS

PARTS INVOLVED Waste-spark ignition is another name for distributorless ignition system (DIS) or electronic ignition (EI). Waste-spark ignition was introduced in the mid-1980s and uses the ignition control module (ICM) and/or the powertrain control module (PCM) to fire the ignition coils. A four-cylinder engine uses two ignition coils and a six-cylinder engine uses three ignition coils. Each coil is a true transformer because the primary winding and secondary winding are not electrically connected. Each end of the secondary winding is connected to a cylinder exactly opposite the other in the firing order, which is called a **companion (paired) cylinder.** ● **SEE FIGURE 14–10.**

WASTE-SPARK SYSTEM OPERATION *Both* spark plugs fire at the same time (within nanoseconds of each other).

- When one cylinder (for example, cylinder number 6) is on the compression stroke, the other cylinder (number 3) is on the exhaust stroke.

- The spark that occurs on the exhaust stroke is called the *waste spark,* because it does no useful work and is only used as a ground path for the secondary winding of the ignition coil. The voltage required to jump the spark plug gap on cylinder 3 (the exhaust stroke) is only 2 to 3 kV.

- The cylinder on the compression stroke uses the remaining coil energy.

- One spark plug of each pair always fires straight polarity and the other cylinder always fires reverse polarity. Spark plug life is not greatly affected by the reverse polarity. If there is only one defective spark plug wire or spark plug, two cylinders may be affected.

The coil polarity is determined by the direction the coil is wound (left-hand rule for conventional current flow) and cannot be changed.

Each spark plug for a particular cylinder always will be fired either with straight or reversed polarity, depending on its location in the engine and how the coils are wired. However, the compression and waste-spark condition flip-flops. When

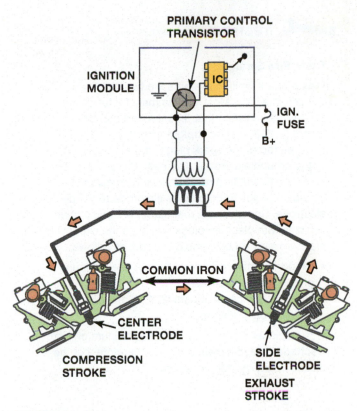

FIGURE 14–10 A waste-spark system fires one cylinder while its piston is on the compression stroke and into paired or companion cylinders while it is on the exhaust stroke. In a typical engine, it requires only about 2 to 3 kV to fire the cylinder on the exhaust stroke. The remaining coil energy is available to fire the spark plug under compression (typically about 8 to 12 kV).

? **FREQUENTLY ASKED QUESTION**

How Can You Determine the Companion Cylinder?

Companion cylinders are two cylinders in the same engine that both reach top dead center (tdc) at the same time.

- One cylinder is on the compression stroke.
- The other cylinder is on the exhaust stroke.

To determine which two cylinders are companion cylinders in the engine, follow these steps.

STEP 1 Determine the firing order (such as 165432 for a typical V-6 engine).

STEP 2 Write the firing order and then place the second half under the first half.

$$\frac{165}{432}$$

STEP 3 The cylinder numbers above and below each other are companion or paired cylinders.

In this case 1 and 4, 6 and 3, and 5 and 2 are companion cylinders.

Odds Fire Straight

Waste-spark ignition systems fire two spark plugs at the same time. Most vehicle manufacturers use a waste-spark system that fires the odd number cylinders (1, 3, and 5) by straight polarity (current flow from the top of the spark plug through the gap and to the ground electrode). The even number cylinders (2, 4, and 6) are fired reverse polarity, meaning that the spark jumps from the side electrode to the center electrode. Some vehicle manufacturers equip their vehicles with platinum plugs that have the expensive platinum alloy on only one electrode, as follows:

• On odd number cylinders (1, 3, 5), the platinum is on the center electrode.
• On even number cylinders (2, 4, 6), the platinum is on the ground electrode.

Replacement spark plugs use platinum on both electrodes (double platinum) and, therefore, can be placed in any cylinder location.

Cylinder 1	Always fires straight polarity (from the center electrode to the ground electrode), one time requiring 10 to 12 kV and one time requiring 3 to 4 kV.
Cylinder 4	Always fires reverse polarity (from the ground electrode to the center electrode), one time requiring 10 to 12 kV and one time requiring 3 to 4 kV.

Waste-spark ignitions require a sensor (usually a crankshaft sensor) to trigger the coils at the correct time. ● SEE FIGURE 14–11.

The crankshaft sensor cannot be moved to adjust ignition timing, because ignition timing is not adjustable. The slight adjustment of the crankshaft sensor is designed to position the sensor exactly in the middle of the rotating metal disc for maximum clearance.

COMPRESSION-SENSING WASTE-SPARK IGNITION

Some waste-spark ignition systems, such as those used on Saturns and others, use the slight difference (about 5 microseconds) between the actual firing of the two spark plugs that are triggered by the ignition control module (ICM). It requires a higher voltage to fire a spark plug under compression than it does when the spark plug is being fired on the exhaust stroke. The electronics in the coil and the PCM can detect which of the two companion (paired) cylinders that are triggered at the same time requires the higher voltage, and therefore indicates the cylinder that is on the compression stroke. For example, a typical 4-cylinder engine equipped with a waste-spark ignition

one cylinder is on compression, such as cylinder 1, then the paired cylinder (number 4) is on the exhaust stroke. During the next rotation of the crankshaft, cylinder 4 is on the compression stroke and cylinder 1 is on the exhaust stroke.

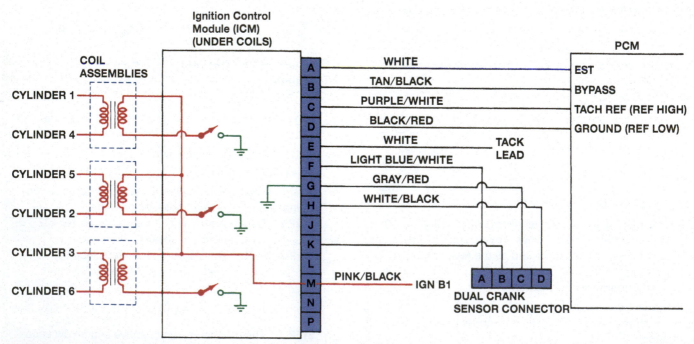

FIGURE 14–11 Typical wiring diagram of a V-6 waste-spark ignition system. The PCM uses input data from all of the engine sensors and determines the optimum ignition timing, then triggers the primary ignition circuit to fire the spark plug or sends the trigger signal to the ICM, if equipped.

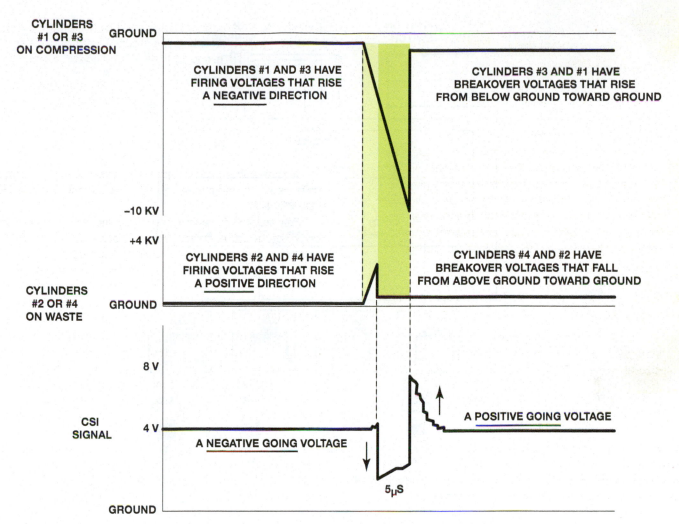

FIGURE 14–12 The slight (5 microseconds) difference in the firing of the companion cylinders is enough time to allow the PCM to determine which cylinder is firing on the compression stroke.

system will fire both cylinders 1 and 4. If cylinder 4 requires a higher voltage to fire, as determined by the electronics connected to the coil, then the PCM assumes that cylinder 4 is on the compression stroke. Engines equipped with compression-sensing ignition systems do not require the use of a camshaft position sensor to determine specific cylinder numbers. ● **SEE FIGURE 14–12**.

COIL-ON-PLUG IGNITION

TERMINOLOGY Coil-on-plug (COP) ignition uses one ignition coil for each spark plug. This system is also called *coil-by-plug, coil-near-plug,* or *coil-over-plug ignition.* ● **SEE FIGURES 14–13 AND 14–14**.

ADVANTAGES The coil-on-plug system eliminates the spark plug wires that are often the source of electromagnetic interference (EMI) that can cause problems to some computer

signals. The vehicle computer controls the timing of the spark. Ignition timing also can be changed (retarded or advanced) on a cylinder-by-cylinder basis for maximum performance and to respond to knock sensor signals.

TYPES OF COP SYSTEMS There are two basic types of coil-on-plug ignition systems.

- **Two primary wires.** This design uses the vehicle computer to control the firing of the ignition coil. The two wires include the ignition voltage feed and the pulse ground wire, which is controlled by the computer. The ignition control module is located in the PCM, which handles all ignition timing and coil on-time control.

- **Three primary wires.** This design includes an ignition module at each coil. The three wires include:

  - Ignition voltage
  - Ground
  - Pulse from the computer to the built-in ignition module

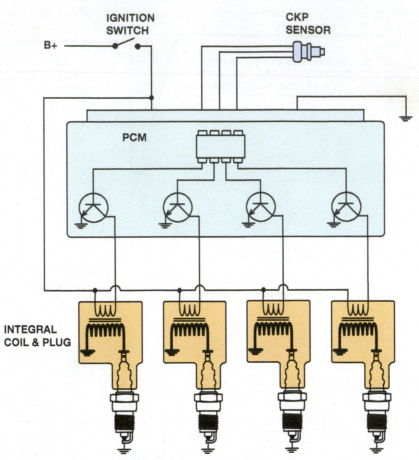

FIGURE 14–13 A typical coil-on-plug ignition system showing the triggering and the switching being performed by the pcm from input from the crankshaft position sensor.

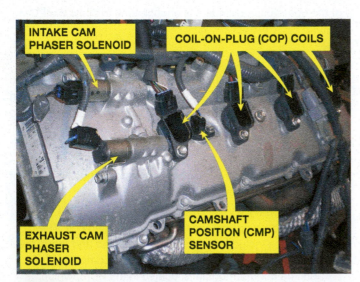

FIGURE 14–14 An overhead camshaft engine equipped with variable valve timing on both the intake and exhaust camshafts and coil-on-plug ignition.

Vehicles use a variety of coil-on-plug-type ignition systems, including:

- Many General Motors V-8 engines use a coil-near-plug system with individual coils and modules for each

individual cylinder that are placed on the valve covers. Short secondary ignition spark plug wires are used to connect the output terminal of the ignition coil to the spark plug, and therefore this system is called a *coil-near-plug* system.

- In a combination of coil-on-plug and waste-spark systems, the systems fire a spark plug attached to the coil plus use a spark plug wire attached to the other secondary terminal of the coil to fire another spark plug of the companion cylinder. This type of system is used in some Chrysler Hemi V-8 and Toyota V-6 engines. ● **SEE FIGURE 14–15**.

Most new engines use coil-over-plug-type ignition systems. Each coil is controlled by the PCM, which can vary the ignition timing separately for each cylinder based on signals the PCM receives from the knock sensor(s). For example, if the knock sensor detects that a spark knock has occurred after firing cylinder 3, then the PCM will continue to monitor cylinder 3 and retard timing on just this one cylinder if necessary to prevent engine-damaging detonation.

ION-SENSING IGNITION In an **ion-sensing ignition** system, the spark plug itself becomes a sensor. An ion-sensing ignition uses a coil-on-plug design where the ignition control

FIGURE 14–15 A Chrysler Hemi V-8 that has two spark plugs per cylinder. The coil on top of one spark fires that plug plus, through a spark plug wire, fires a plug in the companion cylinder.

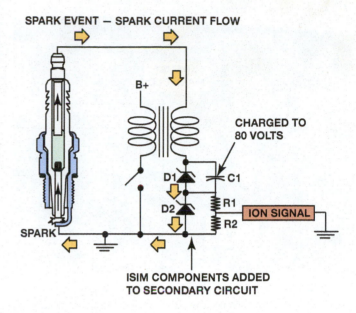

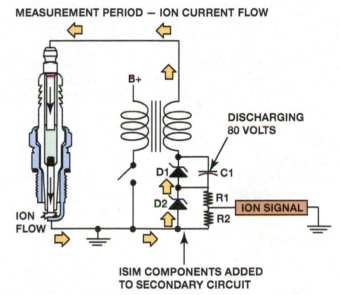

FIGURE 14–16 A DC voltage is applied across the spark plug gap after the plug fires and the circuit can determine if the correct air–fuel ratio was present in the cylinder and if knock occurred. The applied voltage for ion-sensing does not jump the spark plug gap, but determines the conductivity of the ionized gases left over from the combustion process.

module (ICM) applies a DC voltage across the spark plug gap *after* the ignition event to sense the ionized gases (called plasma) inside the cylinder. Ion-sensing ignition is used in the Saab four- and six-cylinder engines and on many Harley-Davidson motor-cycles. ● **SEE FIGURE 14–16.**

The secondary coil discharge voltage (10 to 15 kV) is electrically isolated from the ion-sensing circuit. The combustion flame is ionized and will conduct some electricity, which can be accurately measured at the spark plug gap. The purpose of this circuit includes:

- Misfire detection (required by OBD-II regulations)
- Knock detection (eliminates the need for a knock sensor)
- Ignition timing control (to achieve the best spark timing for maximum power with lowest exhaust emissions)
- Exhaust gas recirculation (EGR) control
- Air–fuel ratio control on an individual cylinder basis

Ion-sensing ignition systems still function the same as conventional coil-on-plug designs, but the engine does not need to be equipped with a camshaft position sensor for misfire

detection, or a knock sensor, because both of these faults are achieved using the electronics inside the ignition control circuits.

KNOCK SENSORS

PURPOSE AND FUNCTION **Knock sensors** are used to detect abnormal combustion, often called **ping**, **spark knock**, or **detonation**. Whenever abnormal combustion occurs, a rapid pressure increase occurs in the cylinder, creating a vibration in the engine block. It is this vibration that is detected by the

SAFETY TIP

Never Disconnect a Spark Plug Wire When the Engine Is Running!

Ignition systems produce a high-voltage pulse necessary to ignite a lean air–fuel mixture. If you disconnect a spark plug wire when the engine is running, this high-voltage spark could cause personal injury or damage to the ignition coil and/or ignition module.

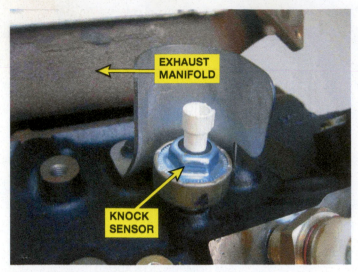

FIGURE 14–17 A typical knock sensor on the side of the block. Some are located in the "V" of a V-type engine and are not noticeable until the intake manifold has been removed.

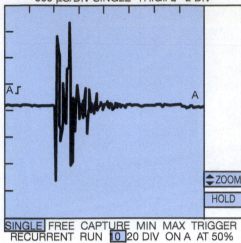

FIGURE 14–18 A typical waveform from a knock sensor during a spark knock event. This signal is sent to the computer which in turn retards the ignition timing. This timing retard is accomplished by an output command from the computer to either a spark advance control unit or directly to the ignition module.

knock sensor. The signal from the knock sensor is used by the PCM to retard the ignition timing until the knock is eliminated, thereby reducing the damaging effects of the abnormal combustion on pistons and other engine parts.

Inside the knock sensor is a piezoelectric element that is a type of crystal that produces a voltage when pressure or a vibration is applied to the unit. The knock sensor is tuned to the engine knock frequency, which is a range from 5 to 10 kHz, depending on the engine design. The voltage signal from the knock sensor is sent to the PCM. The PCM retards the ignition timing until the knocking stops. ● **SEE FIGURE 14–17**.

DIAGNOSING THE KNOCK SENSOR If a knock sensor diagnostic trouble code (DTC) is present, follow the specified testing procedure in the service information. A scan tool can be used to check the operation of the knock sensor, using the following procedure.

STEP 1 Start the engine and connect a scan tool to monitor ignition timing and/or knock sensor activity.

STEP 2 Create a simulated engine knocking sound by tapping on the engine block or cylinder head with a soft-faced mallet.

STEP 3 Observe the scan tool display. The vibration from the tapping should have been interpreted by the knock sensor as a knock, resulting in a knock sensor signal and a reduction in the spark advance.

A knock sensor also can be tested using a digital storage oscilloscope. ● **SEE FIGURE 14–18**.

NOTE: Some engine computers are programmed to ignore knock sensor signals when the engine is at idle speed to avoid having the noise from a loose accessory drive belt, or other accessory, interpreted as engine knock. Always follow the vehicle manufacturer's recommended testing procedure.

🚗 **Case Study**

The Low-Power Toyota

A technician talked about the driver of a Toyota who complained about poor performance and low fuel economy. The technician checked everything, and even replaced all secondary ignition components. Then the technician connected a scan tool and noticed that the knock sensor was commanding the timing to be retarded. Careful visual inspection revealed a "chunk" missing from the serpentine belt which caused a "noise" similar to a spark knock. Apparently the knock sensor was "hearing" the accessory drive belt noise and kept retarding the ignition timing. After replacing the accessory drive belt, a test drive confirmed that normal engine power was restored.

Summary:

Complaint—Driver complained of low performance and reduced fuel economy.

Cause—The accessory drive belt had a fault that caused the knock sensor to signal the PCM to retard ignition timing.

Correction—Replacing the accessory drive belt restored proper engine operation.

REPLACING A KNOCK SENSOR If replacing a knock sensor, be sure to purchase the exact replacement needed, because they often look the same, but the frequency range can vary according to engine design and location on the engine. Always tighten the knock sensor using a torque wrench and tighten to the specified torque to avoid causing damage to the piezoelectric element inside the sensor.

IGNITION SYSTEM DIAGNOSIS

CHECKING FOR SPARK
In the event of a no-start condition, the first step should be to check for secondary voltage out of the ignition coil or to the spark plugs. If the engine is equipped with a separate ignition coil, remove the coil wire from the center of the distributor cap, install a **spark tester**, and crank the engine. See the Tech Tip, "Always Use a Spark Tester." A good coil and ignition system should produce a blue spark at the spark tester. ● **SEE FIGURES 14–19 AND 14–20**.

If the ignition system being tested does not have a separate ignition coil, disconnect any spark plug wire from a spark plug and, while cranking the engine, test for spark available at the spark plug wire, again using a spark tester.

NOTE: An intermittent spark should be considered a no-spark condition.

Typical causes of a no-spark (intermittent spark) condition include the following:

1. Weak ignition coil
2. Low or no voltage to the primary (positive) side of the coil
3. High resistances, open coil wire, or spark plug wire
4. Negative side of the coil not being pulsed by the ignition module
5. Defective pickup coil or crankshaft position sensor
6. Defective ignition control module (ICM)
7. Defective main relay (can be labeled Main, EFI, ASD on Chrysler products; EEC on Ford vehicle relays)

The triggering sensor has to work to create a spark from the ignition coil(s). If there is a no-spark condition, check for triggering by using a scan tool and check for engine RPM while cranking the engine.

- If the engine speed (RPM) shows zero or almost zero while cranking, the most likely cause is a defective triggering sensor or sensor circuit fault.
- If the engine speed (RPM) is shown on the scan tool while cranking the engine, then the triggering sensor is working (in most cases).

Check service information for the exact procedure to follow for testing triggering sensors.

FIGURE 14–19 A spark tester looks like a regular spark plug with an alligator clip attached to the shell. This tester has a specified gap that requires at least 25,000 volts (25 kV) to fire.

FIGURE 14–20 A close-up showing the recessed center electrode on a spark tester. It is recessed 3/8 inch into the shell and the spark must then jump another 3/8 inch to the shell for a total gap of 3/4 inch.

IGNITION COIL TESTING USING AN OHMMETER
If an ignition coil is suspected of being defective, a simple ohmmeter check can be performed to test the resistance of the primary and secondary windings inside the coil. For accurate resistance measurements, the wiring to the coil should be removed before testing. To test the primary coil winding resistance, take the following steps. ● **SEE FIGURE 14–21**.

STEP 1 Set the meter to read low ohms.

STEP 2 Measure the resistance between the positive terminal and the negative terminal of the ignition coil. Most coils will give a reading between less than 1 and 3 ohms.

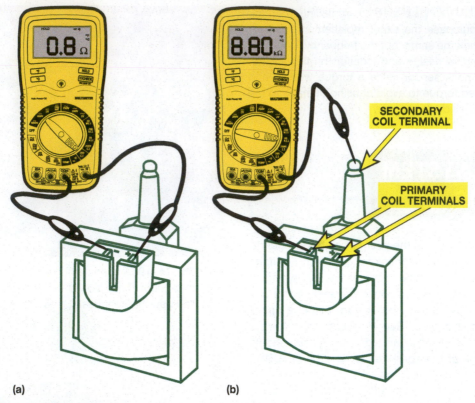

(a)　　　　　　　　　　**(b)**

FIGURE 14–21 (a) Set the digital meter to read Ohms and measure between the two the primary terminal of the coil. Most coils are less than one Ohm. (b) To measure the secondary winding. Connect one meter lead to one of the primary terminals and the other to the secondary terminal.

Check the manufacturer's specifications for the exact resistance values.

To test the secondary coil winding resistance, follow these steps.

STEP 1　Set the meter to read kilohms (kO).

STEP 2　Measure the resistance between either the primary terminal and the secondary coil tower or between the secondary towers. The normal resistance of most coils ranges between 6,000 and 30,000 ohms. Check the manufacturer's specifications for the exact resistance values.

 **TECH TIP**

Always use a Spark Tester

A spark tester looks like a spark plug except it has a recessed center electrode and no side electrode. The tester commonly has an alligator clip attached to the shell so that it can be clamped on a good ground connection on the engine. A good ignition system should be able to cause a spark to jump this wide gap at atmospheric pressure. Without a spark tester, a technician might assume that the ignition system is okay, because it can spark across a normal, grounded spark plug. The voltage required to fire a standard spark plug when it is out of the engine and not under pressure is about 3,000 volts or less. An electronic ignition spark tester requires a minimum of 25,000 volts to jump the 3/4 inch gap. Therefore, never assume that the ignition system is okay because it fires a spark plug – always use a spark tester. *Remember that an intermittent spark across a spark tester should be interpreted as a no-spark condition.*

CURRENT RAMPING IGNITION COILS

PURPOSE Testing an ignition coil for resistance does not always find a coil problem that occurs under actual heat and loads. However, by using a digital storage oscilloscope and a low-current probe, the ignition system can be checked for module current limits and the charging rise time.

Ignition coil operation begins with the ignition control module (ICM) completing the primary circuit through the ignition coil winding. The module allows primary current to ramp upward (primary charging time) to a preset limit. Once ramped to the preset limit, the coil remains on for a set period of time (primary saturation), known as the *dwell period*. Coil current is then turned off (open circuit) allowing the magnetic field built up through the dwell cycle to collapse inward, cutting across many turns of secondary coil windings, inducing a higher output voltage to fire the coil. The ignition systems used today must provide voltages of at least 25,000 volts and maintain spark duration of over 2 ms to assure good ignition over extended service intervals.

Using the digital storage oscilloscope and a current probe, a quick check can be made of the overall primary condition of the two most important parameters of the ignition circuit, the module current limits and the charging rise time of the circuit.

Actual circuit operation of the primary current control is a precise element in total ignition function and output. ● SEE FIGURE 14–22.

CURRENT RAMP TEST PROCEDURE
To perform a current ramp test of the ignition coil(s), take the following steps.

STEP 1 Every ignition system has a power feed circuit to the ignition coil(s). To perform current probe testing on the system, first locate the feed wire and make it current probe accessible. ● SEE FIGURE 14–23.

This will serve as a common point on all ignition systems and include both the DI and EI units.

STEP 2 Set up the scope to read approximately 100 mV per division and 2 ms per division. This may be adjusted to suit the waveform, but will give an initial referencepoint. A good current ramp waveform is shown in ● FIGURE 14–24.

Examples of some faults that a current waveform can detect are shown in **FIGURE 14–25**.

MAGNETIC SENSOR TESTING
The pickup coil, located under the distributor cap on many electronic ignition engines, can cause a no-spark condition if defective. The pickup coil must generate an AC voltage pulse to the ignition module so that the module can pulse the ignition coil.

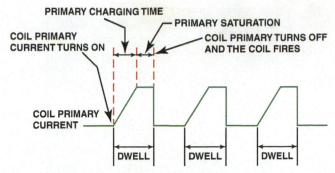

FIGURE 14–22 A waveform showing the primary current flow through the primary windings of an ignition coil.

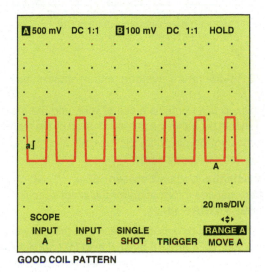

GOOD COIL PATTERN

FIGURE 14–24 An example of a good coil current flow waveform pattern. Note the regular shape of the rise time and slope. Duration of the waveform may change as the module adjusts the dwell. The dwell is usually increased as the engine speed is increased.

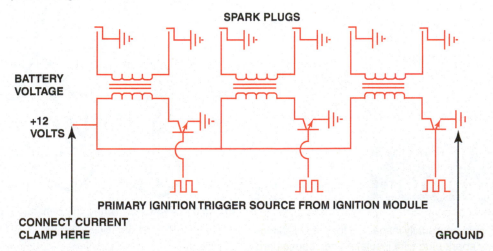

FIGURE 14–23 Schematic of a typical waste-spark ignition system showing the location for the power feed and grounds.

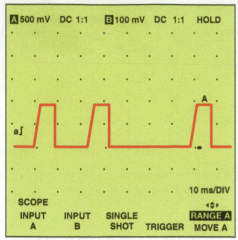

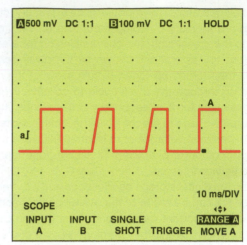

AN OPEN COIL PRIMARY WINDING WILL BE IDENTIFIED BY A MISSING PULSE IN THE CURRENT PATTERN.

(a)

A SHORTENED COIL WILL HAVE A SQUARE SHAPED CURRENT RAMP (DUE TO REDUCED PRIMARY COIL RESISTANCE).

(b)

FIGURE 14–25 (a) A waveform pattern showing an open in the coil primary. (b) A shorted coil pattern waveform.

A pickup coil contains a coil of wire, and the resistance of this coil should be within the range specified by the manufacturer.

Some common tests for pickup coils and magnetic crankshaft position sensors include:

- **Resistance.** Usually between 150 and 1,500 ohms, but check service information for the exact specifications. ● **SEE FIGURE 14–26.**

- **Coil shorted to ground.** Check that the coil windings are insulated from ground by checking for continuity using an ohmmeter. With one ohmmeter lead attached to ground, touch the other lead of the ohmmeter to the pickup coil terminal. The ohmmeter should read OL (over limit) with the ohmmeter set on the high scale. If the pickup coil resistance is not within the specified range or if it has continuity to ground, replace the pickup coil assembly.

- **AC voltage output.** The pickup coil also can be tested for proper voltage output. During cranking, most pickup coils should produce a minimum of 0.25 volt AC.

TESTING HALL-EFFECT SENSORS As with any other sensor, the output of the Hall-effect sensor should be tested first. Using a digital voltmeter, check for:

- Power and ground to the sensor
- Changing voltage (pulsed on and off or digital DC voltage) when the engine is being cranked
- Waveform, using an oscilloscope ● **SEE FIGURE 14–27.**

SPARK PLUG WIRE INSPECTION

Spark plug wires should be visually inspected for cuts or defective insulation. Faulty spark plug wire insulation can cause hard starting or no starting in rainy or damp weather conditions.

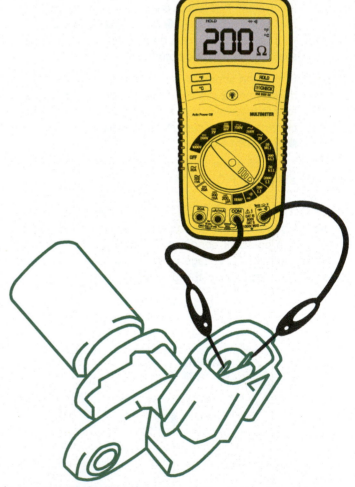

FIGURE 14–26 Measuring the resistance of an magnetic crankshaft position (CKP) sensor using an ohmmeter.

Crankshaft Position Sensor (CPK) and
Camshaft Position Sensor (CMP)

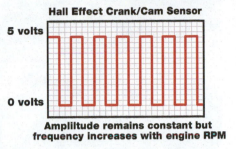

Hall Effect Crank/Cam Sensor

5 volts

0 volts

Amplitude remains constant but frequency increases with engine RPM

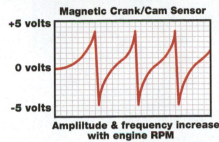

Magnetic Crank/Cam Sensor

+5 volts

0 volts

-5 volts

Amplitude & frequency increase with engine RPM

FIGURE 14–27 A Hall Effect sensor produces an square waveform whereas a magnetic sensor produces an analog waveform when viewed on scope

When removing a spark plug wire, be sure to rotate the boot of the wire at the plug before pulling it off the spark plug. This will help prevent damaging the wire as many wires are stuck to the spark plug and are often difficult to remove.

TECH TIP

Bad Wire? Replace the Coil!

When performing engine testing (such as a compression test), always ground the coil wire. Never allow the coil to discharge without a path to ground for the spark. High-energy ignition systems can produce 40,000 volts or more of electrical pressure. If the spark cannot spark to ground, the coil energy can (and usually does) arc inside the coil itself, creating a low-resistance path to the primary windings or the steel laminations of the coil. ● **SEE FIGURE 14–28.**

This low-resistance path is called a **track**, and could cause an engine misfire under load even though all of the remaining component parts of the ignition system are functioning correctly. Often these tracks do not show up on any coil test, including most scopes. Because the track is a lower resistance path to ground than normal, it requires that the ignition system be put under a load for it to be detected, and even then, the problem (engine missing) may be intermittent. If a misfire was the result of an open circuit in the secondary circuit, always replace the ignition coil.

When disabling an ignition system, perform one of the following procedures to prevent possible ignition coil damage.

1. Remove the power source wire from the ignition system to prevent any ignition operation.
2. On distributor-equipped engines, remove the secondary coil wire from the center of the distributor cap and connect a jumper wire between the disconnected coil wire and a good engine ground. This ensures that the secondary coil energy will be safely grounded and prevents high-voltage coil damage.

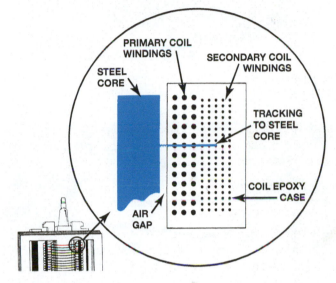

FIGURE 14–28 A track inside an ignition coil is not a short, but a low-resistance path or hole that has been burned through from the secondary wiring to the steel core.

VISUAL INSPECTION A thorough visual inspection should include a look at the following items.

- Check all spark plug wires for proper routing. All plug wires should be in the factory wiring separators and be clear of any metallic object that could damage the insulation and cause a short-to-ground fault.

- Check that all spark plug wires are securely attached to the spark plugs and to the distributor cap or ignition coil(s).

- Check that all spark plug wires are clean and free from excessive dirt or oil. Check that all protective covers normally covering the coil and/or distributor cap are in place and not damaged.

- Carefully check the cap and distributor rotor for faults or coil secondary terminal on waste spark coils. ● **SEE FIGURE 14–29.**

Visually check the wires and boots for damage. ● **SEE FIGURE 14–30.**

Check all spark plug wires with an ohmmeter for proper resistance. Good spark plug wires should measure less than 10,000 ohms per foot of length. ● **SEE FIGURE 14–31.**

FIGURE 14–29 Corroded terminals on a waste-spark coil can cause misfire diagnostic trouble codes to be set.

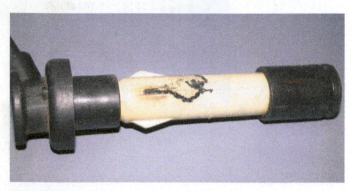

FIGURE 14–30 This spark plug boot on an overhead camshaft engine has been arcing to the valve cover causing a misfire to occur.

FIGURE 14–31 Measuring the resistance of a spark plug wire with a multimeter set to the ohms position. The reading of 16.03 kΩ (16,030 ohms) is okay because the wire is about 2 ft long. Maximum allowable resistance for a spark plug wire this long would be 20 kΩ (20,000 ohms).

FIGURE 14–32 This spark plug wire boot pliers is a handy addition to any tool box.

SPARK PLUGS

SPARK PLUG CONSTRUCTION **Spark plugs** are manufactured from ceramic insulators inside a steel shell. The threads of the shell are rolled and a seat is formed to create a gas-tight seal with the cylinder head. ● SEE FIGURE 14–34.

FIGURE 14–33 Always take the time to install spark plug wires back into the original holding brackets (wiring combs).

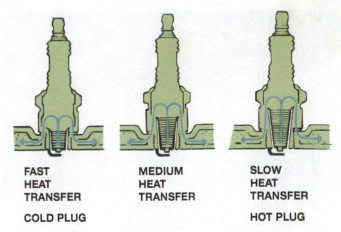

| FAST HEAT TRANSFER | MEDIUM HEAT TRANSFER | SLOW HEAT TRANSFER |
| COLD PLUG | | HOT PLUG |

FIGURE 14–35 The heat range of a spark plug is determined by distance the heat flows from the tip to the cylinder head.

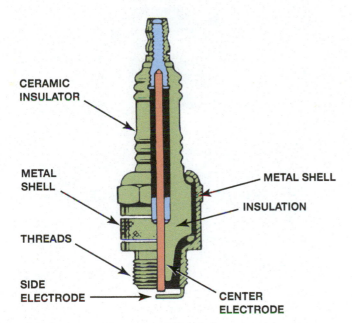

CERAMIC INSULATOR

METAL SHELL

METAL SHELL

INSULATION

THREADS

SIDE ELECTRODE

CENTER ELECTRODE

FIGURE 14–34 Parts of a spark plug.

The physical differences in spark plugs include:

- **Reach.** This is the length of the threaded part of the plug.
- **Heat range.** This refers to how rapidly the heat created at the tip is transferred to the cylinder head. A spark plug with a long ceramic insulator path will run hotter at the tip than one that has a shorter path, because the heat must travel farther. ● **SEE FIGURE 14–35**.
- **Type of seat.** Some spark plugs use a gasket and others rely on a tapered seat to seal.

RESISTOR SPARK PLUGS Most spark plugs include a resistor in the center electrode, which helps to reduce electromagnetic noise or radiation from the ignition system. The closer the resistor is to the actual spark or arc, the more effective it becomes. The value of the resistor is usually between 2,500 and 7,500 ohms.

PLATINUM SPARK PLUGS **Platinum spark plugs** have a small amount of the precious metal platinum included on the end of the center electrode, as well as on the ground or side electrode. Platinum is a gray-white metal that does not react with oxygen and, therefore, will not erode away as can occur with conventional nickel alloy spark plug electrodes. Platinum is also used as a catalyst in catalytic converters where it is able to start a chemical reaction without itself being consumed.

IRIDIUM SPARK PLUGS Iridium is a white precious metal and is the most corrosion-resistant metal known. Most **iridium spark plugs** use a small amount of iridium welded onto the tip of a small center electrode, 0.0015 to 0.002 inch (0.4 to 0.6 mm) in diameter. The small diameter reduces the voltage required to jump the gap between the center and the side electrode, thereby reducing possible misfires. The ground or side electrode is usually tipped with platinum to help reduce electrode gap wear.

Spark plugs should be inspected when an engine performance problem occurs and should be replaced at specified intervals to ensure proper ignition system performance.

- Nonplatinum spark plugs have a service life of over 20,000 miles (32,000 km).
- Platinum-tipped original equipment spark plugs have a typical service life of 60,000 to 100,000 miles (100,000 to 160,000 km) or longer.

SPARK PLUG INSPECTION Used spark plugs should *not* be cleaned and reused unless absolutely necessary. The labor required to remove and replace (R & R) spark plugs is the same whether the spark plugs are replaced or cleaned. Although cleaning spark plugs often restores proper engine operation, the service life of cleaned spark plugs is definitely shorter than that of new spark plugs. *Platinum-tipped spark plugs should not be regapped!* Using a gapping tool can break the platinum after it has been used in an engine. Check service information regarding the recommended type of spark plugs and the specified service procedures.

FIGURE 14–36 When removing spark plugs, it is wise to arrange them so that they can be compared and any problem can be identified with a particular cylinder.

SPARK PLUG SERVICE

When replacing spark plugs, perform the following steps.

STEP 1 Check service information. Check for the exact spark plug to use and the specified instructions and/or technical service bulletins that affect the number of plug to be used or a revised replacement procedure.

STEP 2 Allow the engine to cool before removing spark plugs. This is true especially on engines with aluminum cylinder heads.

STEP 3 Use compressed air or a brush to remove dirt from around the spark plug before removal. This step helps prevent dirt from getting into the cylinder of an engine while removing a spark.

STEP 4 Check the spark plug gap and correct as needed. Be careful not to damage the tip on the center electrode if adjusting a platinum or iridium type of spark plug.

STEP 5 Install the spark plugs by hand. After tightening by hand, use a torque wrench and tighten the spark plugs to factory specifications. ● **SEE FIGURES 14–36 AND 14–37.**

Spark plugs are the windows to the inside of the combustion chamber. A thorough visual inspection of the spark plugs often can lead to the root cause of an engine performance problem. Two indications on spark plugs and their possible root causes in engine performance include the following:

1. **Carbon fouling.** If the spark plug(s) has *dry black carbon* (soot), the usual causes include:
   - Excessive idling
   - Overly rich air–fuel mixture due to a fuel system fault
   - Weak ignition system output

2. **Oil fouling.** If the spark plug has *wet, oily* deposits with little electrode wear, oil may be getting into the combustion chamber from the following:
   - Worn or broken piston rings
   - Worn valve guides
   - Defective or missing valve stem seals

When removing spark plugs, place them in order so that they can be inspected to check for engine problems that might

FIGURE 14–37 A spark plug thread chaser is a low-cost tool that hopefully will not be used often, but is necessary to use to clean the threads before new spark plugs are installed.

FIGURE 14–38 A normally worn spark plug that uses a tapered platinum-tipped center electrode.

affect one or more cylinders. All spark plugs should be in the same condition, and the color of the center insulator should be light tan or gray. If all the spark plugs are black or dark, the engine should be checked for conditions that could cause an overly rich air–fuel mixture or possible oil burning. If only one or a few spark plugs are black, check those cylinders for proper firing (possible defective spark plug wire) or an engine condition affecting only those particular cylinders. ● **SEE FIGURES 14–38 THROUGH 14–41.**

If all spark plugs are white, check for possible overadvanced ignition timing or a vacuum leak causing a lean air–fuel mixture. If only one or a few spark plugs are white, check for a vacuum leak or injector fault affecting the air–fuel mixture only to those particular cylinders.

NOTE: The engine computer "senses" rich or lean air-fuel ratios by means of input from the oxygen sensor(s). If one cylinder is lean, the PCM may make all other cylinders richer to compensate.

FIGURE 14–39 A spark plug from an engine that had a blown head gasket. The white deposits could be from the additives in the coolant.

FIGURE 14–40 A worn spark plug showing fuel and/or oil deposits.

TECH TIP

Two-Finger Trick

To help prevent overtightening a spark plug when a torque wrench is not available, simply use two fingers on the ratchet handle. Even the strongest service technician cannot overtighten a spark plug by using two fingers.

FIGURE 14–41 A platinum tipped spark plug that is fuel soaked indicating a fault with the fuel system or the ignition system causing the spark plug to not fire.

Inspect all spark plugs for wear by first checking the condition of the center electrode. As a spark plug wears, the center electrode becomes rounded. If the center electrode is rounded, higher ignition system voltage is required to fire the spark plug.

When installing spark plugs, always use the correct tightening torque to ensure proper heat transfer from the spark plug shell to the cylinder head. ● **SEE CHART 14–1**.

NOTE: General Motors does not recommend the use of antiseize compound on the threads of spark plugs being installed in an aluminum cylinder head, because the spark plug will be overtightened. This excessive tightening torque places the threaded portion of the spark plug too far into the combustion chamber where carbon can accumulate and result in the spark plugs being difficult to remove. If antiseize compound is used on spark plug threads, reduce the tightening torque by 40%. Always follow the vehicle manufacturer's recommendations.

IGNITION TIMING

PURPOSE Ignition timing refers to when the spark plug fires in relation to piston position. The time when the spark occurs depends on engine speed and, therefore, must be advanced (spark plugs fire sooner) as the engine rotates faster. The ignition in the cylinder takes a certain amount of time, usually 30 milliseconds (30/1,000 of a second) and remains constant regardless of engine speed. Therefore, to maintain the most efficient combustion, the ignition sequence has to occur sooner as the engine speed increases. For maximum efficiency from the expanding gases inside the combustion chamber, the burning of the air–fuel mixture should end by about 10 degrees after top dead

SPARK PLUG TYPE	TORQUE WITH TORQUE WRENCH (LB-FT)		TORQUE WITHOUT TORQUE WRENCH (TURNS AFTER SEATED)	
	CAST-IRON HEAD	ALUMINUM HEAD	CAST-IRON HEAD	ALUMINUM HEAD
Gasket	26-30	18-22	1/4	1/4
14 mm	32-38	28-34	1/4	1/4
18 mm				
Tapered seat	7-15	7-15	1/16 (snug)	1/16 (snug)
14 mm	15-20	15-20	1/16 (snug)	1/16 (snug)
18 mm				

CHART 14–1

Typical spark plug installation torque.

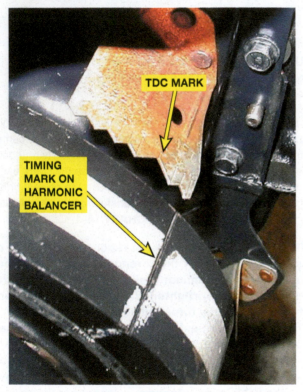

FIGURE 14–42 Ignition timing marks are found on the harmonic balancers on engines equipped with distributors that can be adjusted for timing.

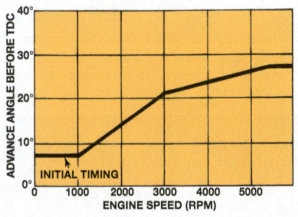

FIGURE 14–43 The initial (base) timing is where the spark plug fires at idle speed. The PCM then advances the timing based primarily on engine speed.

If the engine is equipped with a distributor, it may be possible to adjust the base or the initial timing. The initial timing is usually set to fire the spark plug between zero degrees (TDC) or slightly before TDC (BTDC). Ignition timing changes as mechanical wear occurs to the following:

- Timing chain
- Distributor gear
- Camshaft drive gear

center (ATDC). If the burning of the mixture is still occurring after that point, the expanding gases do not exert much force on the piston because the gases are "chasing" the piston as it moves downward.

Therefore, to achieve the goal of having the air–fuel mixture be completely burned by the time the piston reaches 10 degrees after top dead center, the spark must be advanced (occur sooner) as the engine speed increases. This timing advance is determined and controlled by the PCM on most vehicles. ● **SEE FIGURES 14–42 AND 18–43.**

IGNITION SCOPE TESTING

TERMINOLOGY All ignition systems must charge and discharge an ignition coil. With the engine off, ignition scopes will display a horizontal line. With the engine running, this horizontal (zero) line is changed to a pattern that will have sections both above and below the zero line. Sections of this pattern that are above the zero line indicate that the ignition coil is discharging. Sections of the scope pattern below the zero line indicate charging of the

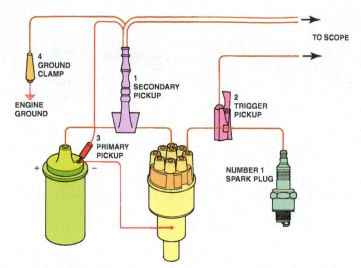

FIGURE 14–44 Typical engine analyzer hookup that includes a scope display. (1) Coil wire on top of the distributor cap if integral type of coil; (2) number 1 spark plug connection; (3) negative side of the ignition coil; (4) ground (negative) connection of the battery.

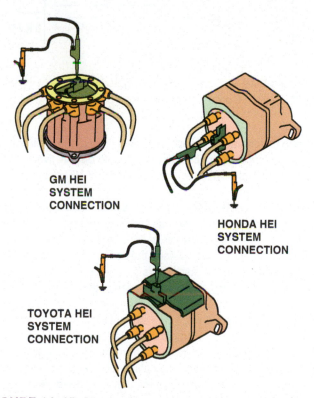

GM HEI SYSTEM CONNECTION

HONDA HEI SYSTEM CONNECTION

TOYOTA HEI SYSTEM CONNECTION

FIGURE 14–45 Clip-on adapters are used with an ignition system that uses an integral ignition coil.

ignition coil. The height of the scope pattern indicates voltage. The length (from left to right) of the scope pattern indicates time.
● **SEE FIGURES 14–44 AND 14–45** for typical scope hookups.

FIRING LINE The leftmost vertical (upward) line is called the **firing line**. The height of the firing line should be between 5,000 and 15,000 volts (5 and 15 kV) with not more than a 3 kV difference between the highest and the lowest cylinder's firing line.
● **SEE FIGURES 14–46 AND 14–47.**

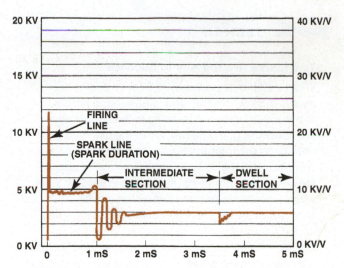

FIGURE 14–46 Typical secondary ignition oscilloscope pattern.

SECONDARY CONVENTIONAL (SINGLE)

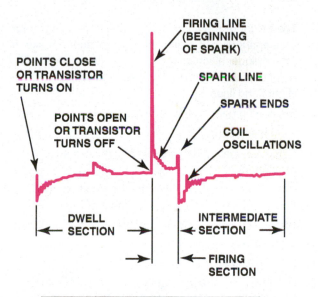

SECONDARY CONVENTIONAL (PARADE)

FIRING LINES SHOULD BE EQUAL. A SHORT LINE INDICATES LOW RESISTANCE IN THE WIRE. A HIGH LINE INDICATES HIGH RESISTANCE IN THE WIRE.

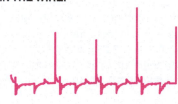

AVAILABLE VOLTAGE SHOULD BE ABOUT 10 KV ON A CONVENTIONAL IGNITION SYSTEM AND EVEN GREATER WITH AN ELECTRONIC SYSTEM

SPARK LINES CAN BE VIEWED SIDE-BY-SIDE FOR EASE OF COMPARISON

CYLINDERS ARE DISPLAYED IN FIRING ORDER

FIGURE 14–47 A single cylinder is shown at the top and a 4-cylinder engine at the bottom.

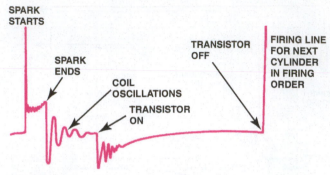

FIGURE 14–48 Drawing shows what is occurring electrically at each part of the scope pattern.

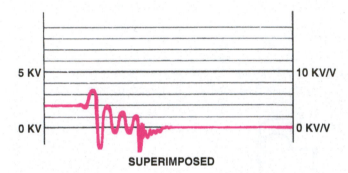

FIGURE 14–49 Typical secondary ignition pattern. Note the lack of firing lines on the superimposed pattern.

The height of the firing line indicates the *voltage* required to fire the spark plug. It requires a high voltage to make the air inside the cylinder electrically conductive (to ionize the air). One or more of the following conditions may cause higher-than-normal height firing lines.

1. Spark plug gapped too wide
2. Lean fuel mixture
3. Defective spark plug wire (excessive resistance or electrically open)

If the firing lines are higher than normal for *all* cylinders, then possible causes include one or more of the following:

1. Worn distributor cap and/or rotor (if the vehicle is so equipped)
2. Excessive wearing of all spark plugs
3. Defective coil wire (the high voltage could still jump across the open section of the wire to fire the spark plugs)

SPARK LINE The **spark line** is a short horizontal line connected to the firing line. The height of the spark line represents the voltage required to maintain the spark across the spark plug after the spark has started. The height of the spark line should be one-fourth of the height of the firing line (between 1.5 and 2.5 kV). The length (from left to right) of the line represents the length of time for which the spark lasts (duration). The spark duration should be between 0.8 and 2.2 milliseconds (usually between 1.0 and 2.0 ms). The spark stops at the end (right side) of the spark line, as shown in ●**FIGURE 14–48.**

INTERMEDIATE OSCILLATIONS After the spark has stopped, some energy remains in the coil. This remaining energy dissipates in the coil windings and the entire secondary circuit. The oscillations are also called the "ringing" of the coil as it is pulsed.

The secondary pattern amplifies any voltage variation occurring in the primary circuit because of the turns ratio

between the primary and secondary windings of the ignition coil. A correctly operating ignition system should display five or more "bumps" (oscillations) (three or more for a GM HEI system).

TRANSISTOR-ON POINT After the intermediate oscillations, the coil is empty (not charged), as indicated by the scope pattern being on the zero line for a short period. When the transistor turns on in an electronic ignition system, the coil is being charged. Note that the charging of the coil occurs slowly (coil-charging oscillations) because of the inductive reactance of the coil.

DWELL SECTION Dwell is the amount of time that the current is charging the coil from the transistor-on point to the transistor-off point. The end of the dwell section marks the beginning of the next firing line. This point is called "transistor off," and indicates that the primary current of the coil is stopped, resulting in a high-voltage spark out of the coil.

PATTERN SELECTION The entire pattern is not seen on a scope. Ignition oscilloscopes use three positions to view certain sections of the basic pattern more closely. These three positions are as follows:

1. **Superimposed.** This superimposed position is used to look at differences in patterns between cylinders in all areas except the firing line. There are no firing lines illustrated in superimposed positions. ● **SEE FIGURE 14–49**
2. **Raster (stacked).** Cylinder 1 appears at the bottom of the screen and all other cylinder patterns are displayed upward

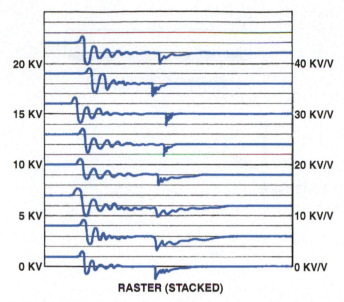

FIGURE 14–50 Raster is the best scope position to view the spark lines of all the cylinders to check for differences. Most scopes display cylinder 1 at the bottom. The other cylinders are positioned by firing order above cylinder 1.

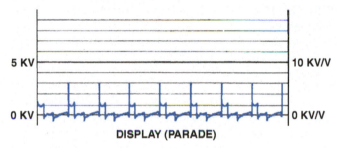

FIGURE 14–51 Display is the only position to view the firing lines of all cylinders. Cylinder 1 is displayed on the left (except for its firing line, which is shown on the right). The cylinders are displayed from left to right by firing order.

in the engine's firing order. Use the raster (stacked) position to look at the spark line length and transistor-on point. The raster pattern shows all areas of the scope pattern except the firing lines. ● SEE FIGURE 14–50

3. **Display (parade).** Display (parade) is the only position in which firing lines are visible and the cylinders are displayed on the screen from left to right in the engine's firing order. This selection is used to compare the height of firing lines among all cylinders. ● SEE FIGURE 14–51

READING THE SCOPE ON DISPLAY (PARADE)
Start the engine and operate at approximately 1000 RPM to ensure a smooth and accurate scope pattern. Firing lines are visible only on the display (parade) position. The firing lines should all be 5 to 15 kV in height and be within 3 kV of each other. If one or more cylinders have high firing lines, this could indicate a defective (open) spark plug wire, a spark plug gapped too far, or a lean fuel mixture affecting only those cylinders.

A lean mixture (not enough fuel) requires a higher voltage to ignite because there are fewer droplets of fuel in the cylinder for the spark to use as "stepping stones" for the voltage to jump across. Therefore, a lean mixture is less conductive than a rich mixture.

READING THE SPARK LINES
Spark lines can easily be seen on either superimposed or raster (stacked) position. On the raster position, each individual spark line can be viewed.

The spark lines should be level and one-fourth as high as the firing lines (1.5 to 2.5 kV, but usually less than 2 kV). The spark line voltage is called the **burn kV**. The *length* of the spark line is the critical factor for determining proper operation of the engine because it represents the spark duration time. There is only a limited amount of energy in an ignition coil. If most of the energy is used to ionize the air gaps of the rotor and the spark plug, there may not be enough energy remaining to create a spark duration long enough to completely burn the air–fuel mixture. Many scopes are equipped with a **millisecond (ms) sweep**. This means that the scope will sweep only that portion of the pattern that can be shown during a 5 ms or 25 ms setting.

Following are guidelines for spark line length.

- 0.8 ms: too short
- 1.5 ms: average
- 2.2 ms: too long

If the spark line is too short, possible causes include the following:

1. Spark plug(s) gapped too widely
2. Rotor tip to distributor cap insert distance gapped too widely (worn cap or rotor)
3. High-resistance spark plug wire
4. Air–fuel mixture too lean (vacuum leak, broken valve spring, etc.)

If the spark line is too long, possible causes include the following:

1. Fouled spark plug(s)
2. Spark plug(s) gapped too closely
3. Shorted spark plug or spark plug wire

Many scopes do not have a millisecond scale. Some scopes are labeled in degrees and/or percentage (%) of dwell. ● **CHART 14-2** can be used to determine acceptable spark line length.

SPARK LINE SLOPE
Downward-sloping spark lines indicate that the voltage required to maintain the spark duration is decreasing during the firing of the spark plug. Although it is normal for the spark line to angle downward slightly, a steep slope indicates that the spark energy is finding ground through spark plug deposits (the plug is fouled) or other ignition problems. ● SEE FIGURE 14–52.

An upward-sloping spark line usually indicates a mechanical engine problem. A defective piston ring or valve would tend to seal better in the increasing pressures of combustion. As the spark plug fires, the effective increase in pressures increases the

NORMAL SPARK LINE LENGTH (AT 700 TO 1200 RPM)			
NUMBER OF CYLINDERS	MILLISECONDS	PERCENTAGE (%) OF DWELL SCALE	DEGREES
4	1–2	3–6	3–5
6	1–2	4–9	2–5
8	1–2	6–13	3–6

CHART 14-2

Converting between units is sometimes needed depending on the type of scope used.

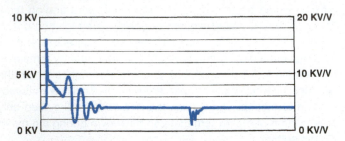

FIGURE 14–52 A downward-sloping spark line usually indicates high secondary ignition system resistance or an excessively rich air–fuel mixture.

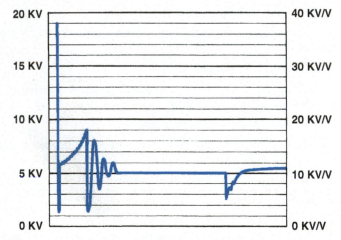

FIGURE 14–53 An upward-sloping spark line usually indicates a mechanical engine problem or a lean air–fuel mixture.

voltage required to maintain the spark, and the height of the spark line rises during the duration of the spark. ● **SEE FIGURE 14–53.**

An upward-sloping spark line can also indicate a lean air–fuel mixture. Typical causes include:

1. Clogged injector(s)
2. Vacuum leak
3. Sticking intake valve

● **SEE FIGURE 14–54** for an example showing the relationship between the firing line and the spark line.

READING THE INTERMEDIATE SECTION
The intermediate section should have three or more oscillations (bumps) for a correctly operating ignition system. Because approximately

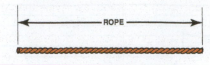

LENGTH OF ROPE REPRESENTS AMOUNT OF ENERGY STORED IN IGNITION COIL

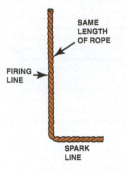

SAME LENGTH OF ROPE
FIRING LINE
SPARK LINE

SAME LENGTH OF ROPE (ENERGY). IF HIGH VOLTAGE IS REQUIRED TO IONIZE SPARK PLUG CAP, LESS ENERGY IS AVAILABLE FOR SPARK DURATION. (A LEAN CYLINDER IS AN EXAMPLE OF WHERE HIGHER VOLTAGE IS REQUIRED TO FIRE WITH A SHORTER-THAN-NORMAL DURATION.)

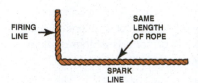

FIRING LINE
SAME LENGTH OF ROPE
SPARK LINE

IF LOW VOLTAGE IS REQUIRED TO FIRE THE SPARK PLUG (LOW FIRING LINE), MORE OF THE COIL'S ENERGY IS AVAILABLE TO PROVIDE A LONG-DURATION SPARK LINE. (A FOULED SPARK PLUG IS AN EXAMPLE OF LOW VOLTAGE TO FIRE, WITH A LONGER-THEN-NORMAL DURATION.)

FIGURE 14–54 The relationship between the height of the firing line and length of the spark line can be illustrated using a rope. Because energy cannot be destroyed, the stored energy in an ignition coil must dissipate totally, regardless of engine operating conditions.

250 volts are in the primary ignition circuit when the spark stops flowing across the spark plugs, this voltage is reduced by about 75 volts per oscillation. Additional resistances in the primary circuit would decrease the number of oscillations. If there are fewer than three oscillations, possible problems include the following:

1. Shorted ignition coil
2. Loose or high-resistance primary connections on the ignition coil or primary ignition wiring

DWELL AND CURRENT-LIMITING HUMP
Ignition systems use a dwell period to charge the coil. Dwell is the time that current is charging the coil, and changes with increasing RPM in many electronic ignition systems. This change in dwell with RPM should be considered normal.

Many EI systems also produce a "hump" in the dwell section, which reflects a current-limiting circuit in the control module. These current-limiting humps may have slightly different shapes depending on the exact module used. For example, the humps produced by various GM HEI modules differ slightly.

DWELL VARIATION (DISTRIBUTOR IGNITION)
A worn distributor gear, worn camshaft gear, or other distributor problem may cause engine performance problems, because the signal created in the distributor will be affected by the inaccurate distributor operation. However, many electronic ignitions vary the length of the dwell period electronically in the module

to maintain acceptable current flow levels through the ignition coil and ignition control module (ICM).

Different EI systems use one of three different designs. The dwell length characteristic and the types of EI systems that use each design are as follows:

1. Dwell time remains *constant* as the engine speed is increased.

2. Dwell time *decreases* as the engine speed is increased.

3. Dwell time *increases* as the engine speed is increased.

NOTE: Waste-spark and coil-on-plug ignition systems also vary dwell time electronically within the PCM or ignition module.

ACCELERATION CHECK   With the scope selector set on the display (parade) position, rapidly accelerate the engine (gear selector in park or neutral with the parking brake on). The results should be interpreted as follows:

1. All firing lines should rise evenly (not to exceed 75% of maximum coil output) for properly operating spark plugs.

2. If the firing lines on one or more cylinders fail to rise, this indicates fouled spark plugs.

ROTOR GAP VOLTAGE (DI SYSTEMS)   The rotor gap voltage test measures the voltage required to jump the gap (0.03 to 0.05 inches, or 0.8 to 1.3 mm) between the rotor and the inserts (segments) of the distributor cap. Select the display (parade) scope pattern and remove a spark plug wire (at the spark plug end), then using a jumper connected to a good ground, insert the jumper into the spark plug boot making sure it contacts the plug wire terminal. Start the engine and observe the height of the firing line for the cylinder being tested. Because the spark plug wire is connected directly to ground, the firing line height on the scope will indicate the voltage required to jump the air gap between the rotor and the distributor cap insert. The normal rotor gap voltage is 3 to 7 kV, and the voltage should not exceed 8 kV. If the rotor gap voltage indicated is near or above 8 kV, inspect and replace the distributor cap and/or rotor as required.

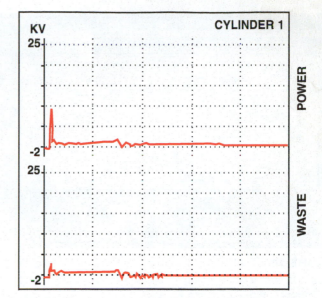

FIGURE 14–55   A dual trace scope pattern showing both the power and the waste spark from the same coil (cylinders 1 and 6). Note that the firing line is higher on the cylinder that is under compression (power); otherwise, both patterns are almost identical.

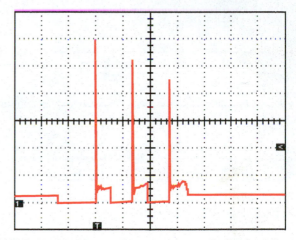

FIGURE 14–56   A secondary waveform of a Ford 4.6 liter V-8, showing three sparks occurring at idle speed.

SCOPE-TESTING A WASTE-SPARK SYSTEM

A handheld digital storage oscilloscope can be used to check the pattern of individual cylinders. Some larger scopes can be connected to all spark plug wires and therefore are able to display both power and waste-spark waveforms. ● **SEE FIGURE 14–55.**

Because the waste spark does not require as high a voltage level as the cylinder on the power stroke, the waste-spark firing line will be normally lower. The high and low firing lines will alternately change from high to low as the "paired" cylinders change from the compression to the exhaust strokes.

SCOPE-TESTING A COP SYSTEM

On a coil-on-plug (COP) type of ignition system, the individual coils can be shown on a scope and using the proper cables and adapters, the waveform for all of the cylinders can be viewed at the same time. Always follow the scope equipment manufacturer's instructions. Many Ford COP systems use a triple-strike secondary spark event. The spark plugs are fired three times when the engine is at idle speed to improve idle quality and to reduce exhaust emissions. Above certain engine speeds, the ignition system switches to a single-fire event. ● **SEE FIGURE 14–56.**

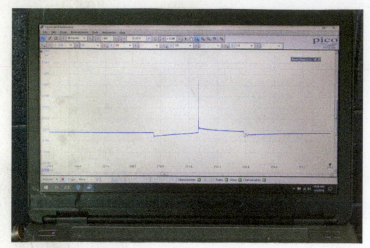

FIGURE 14–57 An inductive paddle being used on engine equipped with a coil-on-plug ignition to get a scope pattern on the laptop computer using a Pico scope.

FIGURE 14–58 The inductive paddle used with a Pico scope created the pattern showing normal ignition and engine operation.

ADVANCED IGNITION DIAGNOSIS As the use of coil-on-plug ignition systems has increased, so has the need for newer and more innovative technology to effectively diagnose misfire conditions. The inductive paddle and the oscilloscope is one of the newest and most efficient methods of diagnosing secondary ignition problems.● **SEE FIGURE 14–57**.

The inductive paddle is placed on the portion of the coil that gives the best pattern. The pattern typically will show when the coil is turned on, the inductive kick as well as the extra energy after the spark event.● **SEE FIGURE 14–58**.

IGNITION SYSTEM SYMPTOM GUIDE

Problem	Possible Causes and/or Solutions
No spark out of the coil	• Theft deterrent fault or theft deterrent system fault • Defective ignition control module • Defective triggering device (magnetic sensor, Hall-effect or optical sensor)
Engine misfire	• Defective (open) spark plug wire • Worn or fouled spark plugs • Defective ignition control module (ICM) • Defective ignition coil • Coil boot to plug shorted to cylinder head

SUMMARY

1. All inductive ignition systems supply battery voltage to the positive side of the ignition coil and pulse the negative side of the coil on and off to ground to create a high-voltage spark.

2. If an ignition system uses a distributor, it is a distributor ignition (DI) system.

3. If an ignition system does not use a distributor, it is an electronic ignition (EI) system.

4. A waste-spark ignition system fires two spark plugs at the same time.

5. A coil-on-plug ignition system uses an ignition coil for each spark plug.

6. A thorough visual inspection should be performed on all ignition components when diagnosing an engine performance problem.

7. Platinum spark plugs should not be regapped after use in an engine.

REVIEW QUESTIONS

1. How can 12 volts from a battery be changed to 40,000 volts for ignition?

2. How does a magnetic sensor work?

3. What harm can occur if the engine is cranked or run with an open (defective) spark plug wire?

4. Why should a spark tester be used to check for spark rather than a standard spark plug?

5. What are the sections of a secondary ignition scope pattern?

CHAPTER QUIZ

1. The primary (low-voltage) ignition system must be working correctly before any spark occurs from a coil. Which component is *not* in the primary ignition circuit?
   a. Spark plug wiring
   b. Ignition module (igniter)
   c. Pickup coil (pulse alternator)
   d. Ignition switch

2. The device that signals the switching of the coil on and off or just on in most instances is called the _____.
   a. trigger
   b. ignition switch
   c. module
   d. PCM

3. A spark tester should be used to check for spark because _____.
   a. a spark tester requires at least 25,000 volts to fire
   b. it is connected to the CKP sensor to check its output
   c. it can detect a cracked spark plug
   d. it can detect the gap of the spark plugs

4. Ignition coil primary resistance is usually _____ohms.
   a. 6,000 to 30,000
   b. 150 to 1,500
   c. Less than 1 to 3
   d. Zero

5. Spark plugs have a _____ in the center electrode to reduce electromagnetic noise.
   a. capacitor
   b. coil
   c. resistor
   d. calibrated gap

6. On a vehicle with a distributor, what is used to trigger the ignition control module (ICM) or the PCM?
   a. PCM
   b. Pick-up coil
   c. Ignition control module (ICM)
   d. Ignition coil

7. A coil is being tested using current ramping. The waveform should _____.
   a. slope downward
   b. slope upward
   c. remain flat
   d. start off flat then slope upward

8. Two technicians are discussing coil-on-plug ignition systems. Technician A says that they can be called coil-near-plug or coil-by-plug ignition systems. Technician B says that some can use ion sensing. Which technician is correct?
   a. Technician A only
   b. Technician B only
   c. Both Technicians A and B
   d. Neither Technician A nor B

9. An ignition scope pattern of the ignition secondary shows the firing line at 28 kV. This indicates _____.
   a. a normal voltage reading
   b. high resistance in the secondary ignition circuit
   c. a too wide spark plug gap
   d. Either b or c

10. What action will be taken if the knock sensor detects spark knock?
    a. PCM will lean out the fuel mixture
    b. PCM will retard ignition timing
    c. PCM will reduce EGR flow
    d. The sensor will rotate until the knock stops

chapter 15

TEMPERATURE SENSORS

LEARNING OBJECTIVES

After studying this chapter, the reader should be able to:

1. Discuss the function of engine coolant temperature sensors and the procedure to test them.
2. Explain the function of the intake air temperature sensors and the procedure to test them.
3. Explain transmission fluid, cylinder head, fuel, exhaust gas recirculation and engine oil temperature sensors.
4. Describe diagnostic trouble codes for temperature sensors.

KEY TERMS

Engine coolant temperature (ECT) 231

Negative temperature coefficient (NTC) 231

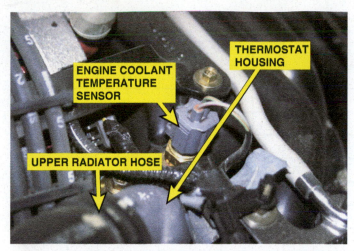

FIGURE 15–1 A typical engine coolant temperature (ECT) sensor. ECT sensors are located near the thermostat housing on many engines.

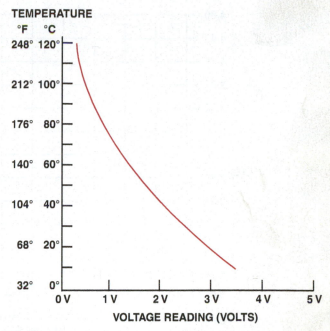

FIGURE 15–2 A typical ECT sensor temperature versus voltage curve.

ENGINE COOLANT TEMPERATURE SENSORS

PURPOSE AND FUNCTION Computer-equipped vehicles use an **engine coolant temperature (ECT)** sensor. When the engine is cold, the fuel mixture must be richer to prevent stalling and engine stumble. When the engine is warm, the fuel mixture can be leaner to provide maximum fuel economy with the lowest possible exhaust emissions. Because the powertrain control module (PCM) controls spark timing and fuel mixture, it will need to know the engine temperature. An engine coolant temperature (ECT) sensor screwed into the engine coolant passage will provide the PCM with this information. ● **SEE FIGURE 15–1.** This will be the most important (high-authority) sensor while the engine is cold. The ignition timing can also be tailored to engine (coolant) temperature. A hot engine cannot have the spark timing as far advanced as can a cold engine. The ECT sensor is also used as an important input for the following:

- Idle air control (IAC) position
- Oxygen sensor closed-loop status
- Canister purge on/off times
- Idle speed

ECT SENSOR CONSTRUCTION Engine coolant temperature sensors are constructed of a semiconductor material that decreases in resistance as the temperature of the sensor increases. Coolant sensors have very high resistance when the coolant is cold and low resistance when the coolant is hot. This is referred to as having a **negative temperature coefficient (NTC)**, which is opposite to the situation with most other electrical components. ● **SEE FIGURE 15–2.**

Therefore, if the coolant sensor has a poor connection (high resistance) at the wiring connector, the PCM will supply a richer-than-normal fuel mixture based on the resistance of the coolant sensor. Poor fuel economy and a possible-rich code

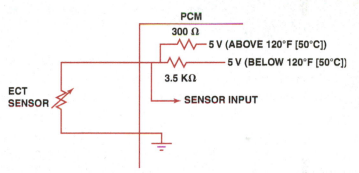

FIGURE 15–3 A two-step ECT circuit showing that when the coolant temperature is low, the PCM applies a 5-volt reference voltage differently to the ECT sensor than compared to when the temperature is higher.

can be caused by a defective sensor or high resistance in the sensor wiring. If the sensor was shorted or defective and had too low a resistance, a leaner-than-normal fuel mixture would be supplied to the engine. A too-lean fuel mixture can cause driveability problems and a possible-lean PCM code.

STEPPED ECT CIRCUITS Some vehicle manufacturers use a step-up resistor to effectively broaden the range of the ECT sensor. Chrysler and General Motors vehicles use the same sensor as a non-stepped ECT circuit but instead apply the sensor voltage through two different resistors:

- When the temperature is cold, usually below 120°F (50°C), the ECT sensor voltage is applied through a high-value resistor inside the PCM.
- When the temperature is warm, usually above 120°F (50°C), the ECT sensor voltage is applied through a much lower resistance value inside the PCM. ● **SEE FIGURE 15–3.**

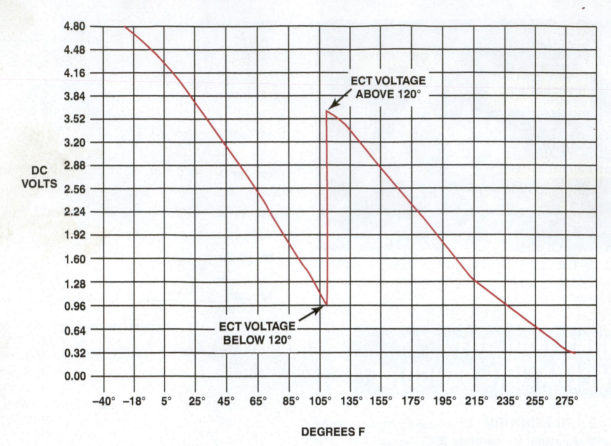

FIGURE 15–4 The transition between steps usually occurs at a temperature that would not interfere with cold engine starts or the cooling fan operation. In this example, the switch point between the two resistors occurs when the sensor voltage is about 1 volt and rises to about 3.6 volts.

The purpose of this extra circuit is to give the PCM a more accurate reading of the engine coolant temperature compared to the same sensor with only one circuit. ● SEE FIGURE 15–4.

TESTING THE ECT SENSOR

TESTING THE ECT SENSOR BY VISUAL INSPECTION
The correct functioning of the engine coolant temperature (ECT) sensor depends on the following items that should be checked or inspected:

- **Properly filled cooling system.** Check that the radiator reservoir bottle is full and that the radiator itself is filled to the top.

CAUTION: Be sure that the radiator is cool before removing the radiator cap to avoid being scalded by hot coolant.

The ECT sensor must be submerged in coolant to be able to indicate the proper coolant temperature.

- **Proper pressure maintained by the radiator cap.** If the radiator cap is defective and cannot allow the cooling system to become pressurized, air pockets could develop. These air pockets could cause the engine to

operate at a hotter-than-normal temperature and prevent proper temperature measurement, especially if the air pockets occur around the sensor.

- **Proper antifreeze–water mixture.** Most vehicle manufacturers recommend a 50/50 mixture of antifreeze and water as the best compromise between freezing protection and heat transfer ability.

- **Proper operation of the cooling fan.** If the cooling fan does not operate correctly, the engine may overheat.

TESTING THE ECT USING A MULTIMETER
Both the resistance (in ohms) and the voltage drop across the sensor can be measured and compared with specifications. ● SEE FIGURE 15–5. See the following charts showing examples of typical engine coolant temperature sensor specifications. Some vehicles use the PCM to attach another resistor in the ECT circuit to provide a more accurate measure of the engine temperature. ● SEE FIGURE 15–6. If resistance values match the approximate coolant temperature and there is still a coolant sensor trouble code, the problem is generally in the wiring between the sensor and the PCM. Always consult the manufacturer's recommended procedures for checking this wiring. If the resistance values do not match, the sensor may need to be replaced.

Normal operating temperature varies with vehicle make and model. Some vehicles are equipped with a thermostat with an opening temperature of 180°F (82°C), whereas other vehicles use

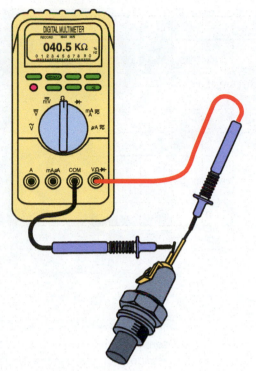

FIGURE 15–5 Measuring the resistance of the ECT sensor. The resistance measurement can then be compared with specifications .Most ECT sensors will measure about 3,000 ohms at 70 degrees F (20 degrees C).

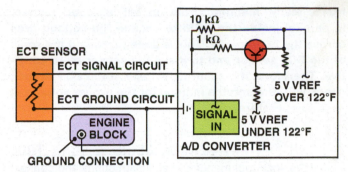

FIGURE 15–6 When the voltage drop reaches approximately 1.2 volts, the PCM turns on a transistor. The transistor connects a 1 − kΩ resistor in parallel with the 10 − kΩ resistor. Total circuit resistance now drops to around 909 ohms. This function allows the PCM to have full control at cold temperatures up to approximately 122°F and a second full control at temperatures greater than 122°F.

a thermostat that is 195°F (90°C) or higher. Before replacing the ECT sensor, be sure that the engine is operating at the temperature specified by the manufacturer. Most manufacturers recommend checking the ECT sensor after the cooling fan has cycled twice, indicating a fully warmed engine. To test for voltage at the ECT sensor, select DC volts on a digital meter and carefully back probe the sensor wire and read the voltage. ● SEE FIGURE 15–7.

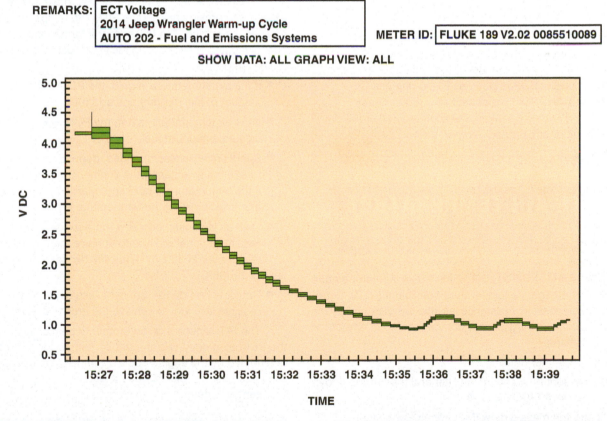

FIGURE 15–7 An ECT sensor being tested using a digital meter set to DC volts and in record mode. A chart showing the voltage decrease of the ECT sensor as the temperature increases from a cold start. The bumps at the bottom of the waveform represent temperature decreases when the thermostat opens and is controlling coolant temperature.

NOTE: Many manufacturers install another resistor in parallel inside the PCM to change the voltage drop across the ECT sensor. This is done to expand the scale of the ECT sensor and to make the sensor more sensitive. Therefore, if measuring *voltage* at the ECT sensor, check with the service manual for the proper voltage at each temperature.

TESTING THE ECT SENSOR USING A SCAN TOOL

Follow the scan tool manufacturer's instructions and connect a scan tool to the data link connector (DLC) of the vehicle. Comparing the temperature of the engine coolant as displayed on a scan tool with the actual temperature of the engine is an excellent method to test an engine coolant temperature sensor:

1. Record the scan tool temperature of the coolant (ECT).
2. Measure the actual temperature of the coolant using an infrared pyrometer or contact-type temperature probe.

The maximum difference between the two readings should be 10°F (5°C). If the actual temperature varies by more than 10°F from the temperature indicated on the scan tool, check the ECT sensor wiring and connector for damage or corrosion. If the connector and wiring are okay, check the sensor with a DVOM for resistance and compare to the actual engine temperature chart. If that checks out okay, check the PCM.

TECH TIP

The Unplug it Test

Using a scan tool, look at the ECT temperature and then unplug the connector. In most cases, the scan tool will show -40 degrees F (-40 degrees C). Sometimes the PCM will substitute a temperature when the circuit is open and the scan tool will show the default or substituted temperature.

INTAKE AIR TEMPERATURE SENSOR

PURPOSE AND FUNCTION The intake air temperature (IAT) sensor is a negative temperature coefficient (NTC) thermistor that decreases in resistance as the temperature of the sensor increases. The IAT sensor can be located in one of the following locations:

- In the air cleaner housing
- In the air duct between the air filter and the throttle body, as shown in ● **FIGURE 15–8**
- Built into the mass airflow (MAF) or airflow sensor
- Screwed into the intake manifold, where it senses the temperature of the air entering the cylinders

FIGURE 15–8 The IAT sensor on this General Motors 3800 V-6 engine is in the air passage duct between the air cleaner housing and the throttle body.

NOTE: An IAT installed in the intake manifold is the most likely to suffer damage because of an engine backfire, which can often destroy the sensor.

The purpose and function of the intake air temperature sensor is to provide the engine PCM the temperature of the air entering the engine. The IAT sensor information is used for fuel control (adding or subtracting fuel) and spark timing, depending on the temperature of incoming air:

- If the air temperature is cold, the PCM will modify the amount of fuel delivery and add fuel.
- If the air temperature is hot, the PCM will subtract the calculated amount of fuel.
- Spark timing is also changed, depending on the temperature of the air entering the engine. The timing is advanced if the temperature is cold and retarded from the base programmed timing if the temperature is hot.
- Cold air is denser, contains more oxygen, and therefore requires a richer mixture to achieve the proper air–fuel mixture. Air at 32°F (0°C) is 14% denser than air at 100°F (38°C).
- Hot air is less dense, contains less oxygen, and therefore requires less fuel to achieve the proper air–fuel mixture.

The IAT sensor is a low-authority sensor and is used by the PCM to modify the amount of fuel and ignition timing as determined by the engine coolant temperature sensor. The IAT sensor is used by the PCM as a backup in the event that the ECT sensor is determined to be inoperative.

NOTE: Some engines use a throttle-body temperature (TBT) sensor to sense the temperature of the air entering the engine, instead of an intake air temperature sensor.

Poor Fuel Economy? Black Exhaust Smoke? Look at the IAT

If the intake air temperature sensor is defective, it may be signaling the PCM that the intake air temperature is extremely cold when in fact it is warm. In such a case the PCM will supply a mixture that is much richer than normal. If a sensor is physically damaged or electrically open, the PCM will often set a diagnostic trouble code (DTC). This DTC is based on the fact that the sensor temperature did not change for a certain amount of time, usually about eight minutes. If, however, the wiring or the sensor itself has excessive resistance, a DTC will not be set and the result will be lower-than-normal fuel economy and, in serious cases, black exhaust smoke from the tailpipe during acceleration.

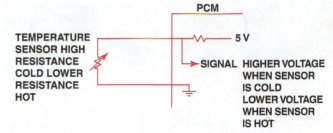

FIGURE 15–9 A transmission temperature sensor from an AXOD transmission.

Engine temperature is most accurately determined by looking at the engine coolant temperature (ECT) sensor. In certain conditions, the IAT has an effect on performance and drivability. One such condition is a warm engine being stopped in very cold weather. In this case, when the engine is restarted, the ECT may be near normal operating temperature such as 200°F (93°C), yet the air temperature could be −20°F (−30°C). In this case, the engine requires a richer mixture because of the cold air than the ECT would seem to indicate.

TESTING THE INTAKE AIR TEMPERATURE SENSOR

POSSIBLE TYPES OF FAILURES If the intake air temperature sensor circuit is damaged or faulty, a diagnostic trouble code (DTC) is set and the malfunction indicator lamp (MIL) may or may not turn on, depending on the condition and the type and model of the vehicle.

DIAGNOSTIC PROCEDURE To diagnose the IAT sensor, perform the following steps:

STEP 1 After the vehicle has been allowed to cool for several hours, use a scan tool, observe the IAT, and compare it to the engine coolant temperature (ECT). The two temperatures should be within 5°F of each other.

STEP 2 Perform a thorough visual inspection of the sensor and the wiring. If the IAT is screwed into the intake manifold, remove the sensor and check for damage.

STEP 3 Check the voltage and compare to the following chart.

TRANSMISSION FLUID TEMPERATURE SENSOR

PURPOSE AND FUNCTION The transmission fluid temperature (TFT), also called *transmission oil temperature (TOT)*, sensor is an important sensor for the proper operation of the automatic transmission. A TFT sensor is a negative temperature coefficient (NTC) thermistor that decreases in resistance as the temperature of the sensor increases. ● **SEE FIGURE 15–9**.

The transmission fluid temperature signal is used by the powertrain control module (PCM) to perform certain strategies based on the temperature of the automatic transmission fluid.

For example:

- If the temperature of the automatic transmission fluid is low (typically below 32°F [0°C]), the shift points may be delayed and overdrive disabled. The torque converter clutch also may not be applied to assist in the heating of the fluid.

- If the temperature of the automatic transmission fluid is high (typically above 260°F [130°C]), the overdrive is disabled and the torque converter clutch is applied to help reduce the temperature of the fluid.

NOTE: Check service information for the exact shift strategy based on high and low transmission fluid temperatures for the vehicle being serviced.

CYLINDER HEAD TEMPERATURE SENSOR

Some vehicles are equipped with cylinder head temperature (CHT) sensors: ● **SEE FIGURE 15–10**.

Example: VW Golf

$$14°F (−10°C) = 11,600 \, \Omega$$
$$68°F (20°C) = 2,900 \, \Omega$$
$$176°F (80°C) = 390 \, \Omega$$

FIGURE 15–10 A cylinder head temperature sensor on a V6 engine.

FIGURE 15–11 An EGR temperature sensor on a Ford Power Stroke diesel engine.

ENGINE FUEL TEMPERATURE (EFT) SENSOR

Some vehicles, such as many Ford vehicles that are equipped with an electronic returnless type of fuel injection, use an engine fuel temperature (EFT) sensor to give the PCM information regarding the temperature and, therefore, the density of the fuel.

EXHAUST GAS RECIRCULATION (EGR) TEMPERATURE SENSOR

Some engines, such as some gasoline engines and most diesel engines are equipped with exhaust gas recirculation (EGR) temperature sensors. EGR is an established method for reduction of NOx emissions in internal combustion engines. The exhaust gas contains unburned hydrocarbons, which are recirculated in the combustion process. Recirculation is controlled by valves, which operate as a function of exhaust gas speed, load, and temperature. The gas reaches a temperature of about 850°F (450°C) for which a special heavy-duty glass-encapsulated NTC sensor is available. ● **SEE FIGURE 15–11.**

The PCM monitors the temperature in the exhaust passage between the EGR valve and the intake manifold. If the temperature increases when the EGR is commanded on, the PCM can determine that the valve or related components are functioning.

ENGINE OIL TEMPERATURE SENSOR

Engine oil temperature sensors are used on many General Motors vehicles and are used as an input to the oil life monitoring system. The computer program inside the PCM calculates engine oil life based on run time, engine RPM, and oil temperature.

TEMPERATURE SENSOR DIAGNOSTIC TROUBLE CODES

The OBD-II diagnostic trouble codes that relate to temperature sensors include both high- and low-voltage codes as well as intermittent codes. High-voltage codes are generally caused by open circuits and low-voltage codes are generally caused by short circuits. When one of these codes is set, a good diagnostic process is to attempt to set the opposite code. If successful, this will verify the circuit and controller, leaving only the sensor as the potential failed component.

SUMMARY

1. The ECT sensor is a high-authority sensor at engine start-up and is used for closed-loop control as well as idle speed.

2. All temperature sensors that decrease in resistance as the temperature increases are considered negative temperature coefficient (NTC) sensors.

3. Some manufacturers use a stepped ECT circuit inside the PCM to broaden the accuracy of the sensor.

4. The ECT and IAT sensors can be tested visually as well as by using a digital multimeter or a scan tool.

5. Other temperature sensors include transmission fluid temperature (TFT), engine fuel temperature (EFT), exhaust gas recirculation (EGR) temperature, and engine oil temperature.

REVIEW QUESTIONS

1. How does a typical NTC temperature sensor work?

2. What is the difference between a stepped and a non-stepped ECT circuit?

3. What temperature should be displayed on a scan tool if the ECT sensor is unplugged with the key on, engine off?

4. What are the three ways that temperature sensors can be tested?

5. If the transmission fluid temperature is low, what would the PCM do to the transmission shifting points?

CHAPTER QUIZ

1. The sensor that most determines fuel delivery when a fuel injected engine is first started is the _____.
   a. O2S
   b. ECT sensor
   c. engine MAP sensor
   d. IAT sensor

2. What happens to the voltage measured at the ECT sensor when the thermostat opens?
   a. Increases slightly
   b. Increases about 1 volt
   c. Decreases slightly
   d. Decreases about 1 volt

3. Two technicians are discussing a stepped ECT circuit. Technician A says that the sensor used for a stepped circuit is different than one used in a non-stepped circuit. Technician B says that a stepped ECT circuit uses different internal resistance inside the PCM. Which technician is correct?
   a. Technician A only
   b. Technician B only
   c. Both Technicians A and B
   d. Neither Technician A nor B

4. When testing an ECT sensor on a vehicle, a digital multimeter (DMM) can be used and the signal wire tested with the connector attached the ignition on (engine off). What DMM setting should the technician use to test the sensor?
   a. AC volts
   b. DC volts
   c. Ohms
   d. Hz (hertz)

5. When testing the ECT sensor with the connector disconnected, the technician should select what position on the DMM?
   a. AC volts
   b. DC volts
   c. Ohms
   d. Hz (hertz)

6. Why does the PCM monitor engine oil temperature on some vehicles?
   a. To limit RPM in case of hot oil
   b. It is an OBD-II requirement
   c. Used to calculate engine oil life
   d. All of the above

7. Two technicians are discussing the IAT sensor. Technician A says that the IAT sensor is more important to the operation of the engine (higher authority) than the ECT sensor. Technician B says that the PCM will add fuel if the IAT indicates that the incoming air temperature is cold. Which technician is correct?
   a. Technician A only
   b. Technician B only
   c. Both Technicians A and B
   d. Neither Technician A nor B

8. An ECT sensor ECT sensor reads about 3,000 ohms when tested using a DMM. This resistance represents a temperature of about _____.
   a. −40°F (−40°C)
   b. 70°F (20°C)
   c. 120°F (50°C)
   d. 284°F (140°C)

9. If the transmission fluid temperature (TFT) sensor indicates cold automatic transmission fluid temperature, what would the PCM do to the shifts?
   a. Normal shifts and normal operation of the torque converter clutch
   b. Disable torque converter clutch; normal shift points
   c. Delayed shift points and torque converter clutch disabled
   d. Normal shifts, but overdrive will be disabled

10. An exhaust gas recirculation (EGR) temperature sensor is used on_____.
   a. some gasoline engines
   b. most diesel engines
   c. All V-8 engines
   d. Both a and b

chapter 16

THROTTLE POSITION SENSORS

LEARNING OBJECTIVES

After studying this chapter, the reader should be able to:

1. Explain the operation of a potentiometer and a Hall-effect throttle position sensor.
2. Describe the interaction between the throttle position sensor and the PCM.
3. Discuss how to test a TP sensor using a digital multimeter, scope, and scan tool.

KEY TERMS

Hall-effect style throttle position sensor 240

Potentiometer 240

Throttle Position (TP) sensor 240

FIGURE 16–1 A typical TP sensor mounted on the throttle body of this port-injected engine.

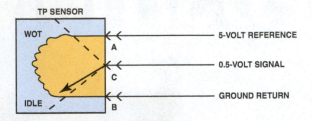

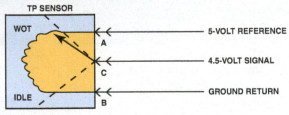

FIGURE 16–2 The signal voltage from a throttle position sensor increases as the throttle is opened because the moveable contact is closer to the 5-volt reference. At idle, the resistance of the sensor winding effectively reduces the signal voltage output to the PCM.

THROTTLE POSITION SENSOR

PURPOSE AND FUNCTION Most engines use a **throttle position (TP) sensor** to signal to the powertrain control module (PCM) the position of the throttle. ● SEE FIGURE 16–1. The TP sensor consists of a **potentiometer**, a type of variable resistor.

POTENTIOMETERS A potentiometer is a variable-resistance sensor with three terminals. One end of the resistor receives reference voltage, while the other end is grounded. The third terminal is attached to a movable contact that slides across the resistor to vary its resistance. Depending on whether the contact is near the supply end or the ground end of the resistor, return voltage is high or low. ● SEE FIGURE 16–2.

Throttle position sensors are among the most common potentiometer-type sensors. The PCM uses their input to determine the amount of throttle opening and the rate of change.

A typical sensor has three wires:
- A 5-volt reference feed wire from the PCM
- Signal return wire (a ground wire back to the PCM)
- A voltage signal wire back to the PCM (as the throttle is opened, the voltage to the PCM changes)

Normal throttle position voltage on most vehicles is about 0.5 volt at idle (closed throttle) and 4.5 volts at wide-open throttle (WOT).

NOTE: The TP sensor voltage at idle is usually about 10% of the TP sensor voltage when the throttle is wide open, but can vary from as low as 0.3 to 1.2 volts, depending on the make and model of vehicle.

HALL-EFFECT STYLE TP SENSORS Some manufacturers use a **Hall-effect style throttle position sensor**. This style of sensor is solid-state and noncontact, which provides for longer durability and a smoother signal than a conventional potentiometer style of sensor. As the throttle blade angle changes, a digital signal is generated. The signal is processed internally in the sensor and an analog signal is outputted to the powertrain control module for use in fuel injection and other calculations. ● SEE FIGURE 16–3.

TP SENSOR PCM INPUT FUNCTIONS

- The PCM senses any change in throttle position and changes the fuel mixture and ignition timing. The actual change in fuel mixture and ignition timing is also partly determined by the other sensors, such as the manifold pressure (engine vacuum), engine RPM, the coolant temperature, and oxygen sensor(s). Some throttle position sensors are adjustable and should be set according to the exact engine manufacturer's specifications.

- The throttle position (TP) sensor used on fuel-injected vehicles acts as an "electronic accelerator pump." This means that the PCM will pulse additional fuel from the injectors when the throttle is depressed. Because the air can quickly flow into the engine when the throttle is opened, additional fuel must be supplied to prevent the air–fuel mixture from going lean, causing the engine to hesitate when the throttle is depressed. If the TP sensor is unplugged or defective, the engine may still operate satisfactorily, but may hesitate upon acceleration.

- The PCM supplies the TP sensor with a regulated voltage that ranges from 4.8 to 5.1 volts. This reference voltage is usually referred to as a 5-volt reference or "Vref." The TP output signal is an input to the PCM, and the TP sensor ground also flows through the PCM.

See the Ford throttle position (TP) sensor chart for an example of how sensor voltage changes with throttle angle.

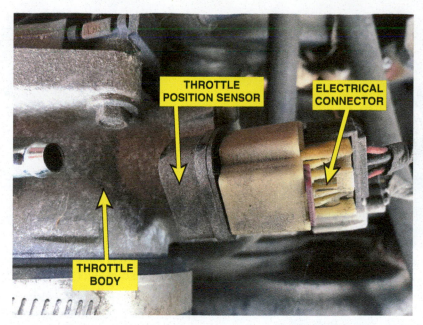

FIGURE 16–3 An example of a Hall-effect style of throttle position sensor on a Chrysler 3.7 liter engine.

Ford Throttle Position (TP) Sensor Chart	
Throttle Angle (Degrees)	**Voltage (V)**
0	0.5
10	0.97
20	1.44
30	1.9
40	2.37
50	2.84
60	3.31
70	3.78
80	4.24

NOTE: Generally, any reading higher than 80% represents wide-open throttle.

PCM USES FOR THE TP SENSOR

The TP sensor is used by the powertrain control module (PCM) for the following reasons.

- **Clear Flood Mode** If the throttle is depressed to the floor during engine cranking, the PCM will either greatly reduce or entirely eliminate any fuel-injector pulses to aid in cleaning a flooded engine. If the throttle is depressed to the floor and the engine is not flooded with excessive fuel, the engine may not start.

- **Torque Converter Clutch Engagement and Release** The torque converter clutch will be released if the PCM detects rapid acceleration to help the transmission deliver maximum torque to the drive wheels. The torque converter clutch is applied when the vehicle is lightly accelerating, and during cruise conditions to improve fuel economy.

- **Rationality Testing for MAP and MAF Sensors** As part of the rationality tests for the MAP and/or MAF sensor, the TP sensor signal is compared to the reading from other sensors to determine if they match. For example, if the throttle position sensor is showing wide-open throttle (WOT), the MAP and/or MAF reading should also indicate that this engine is under a heavy load. If not, a diagnostic trouble code could be set for the TP, as well as the MAP and/or MAF sensors.

- **Automatic Transmission Shift Points** The shift points are delayed if the throttle is opened wide to allow the engine speed to increase, thereby producing more power and aiding in the acceleration of the vehicle. If the throttle is barely open, the shift point occurs at the minimum speed designed for the vehicle.

- **Target Idle Speed (Idle Control Strategy)** When the TP sensor voltage is at idle, the PCM controls idle speed using the idle air control (IAC) and/or spark timing variation to maintain the commanded idle speed. If the TP sensor indicates that the throttle has moved off idle, fuel delivery and spark timing are programmed for acceleration. Therefore, if the throttle linkage is stuck or binding, the idle speed may not be correct.

- **Air-Conditioning Compressor Operation** The TP sensor is also used as an input sensor for air-conditioning compressor operation. If the PCM detects that the throttle is at or close to wide open, the air-conditioning compressor is disengaged.

- **Fail-Safe for Other Sensors** The TP sensor is used as part of a fail-safe or limp-in strategy to the MAP sensor and/or MAF in the event the PCM detects that one or both are not functioning correctly. The PCM then calculates fuel needs and spark timing based on the engine speed (RPM) and throttle position.

FIGURE 16–4 A meter lead connected to a T-pin that was gently pushed along the signal wire of the TP sensor until the point touched the metal terminal inside the plastic connector.

TESTING THE THROTTLE POSITION SENSOR

TYPES OF TEST EQUIPMENT
A TP sensor can be tested using one or more of the following tools:

- A digital voltmeter with three test leads connected in series between the sensor and the wiring harness connector, or back probing using T-pins or other recommended tool that will not cause harm to the connector or wiring.

- A scan tool or a specific tool recommended by the vehicle manufacturer.

- A breakout box that is connected in series between the computer and the wiring harness connector(s). A typical breakout box includes test points at which TP voltages can be measured with a digital voltmeter.

- An oscilloscope.

TEST PROCEDURE USING A DMM
Use jumper wires and T-pins to back-probe the wires or a breakout box to gain electrical access to the wiring to the TP sensor. ● **SEE FIGURE 16–4**.

NOTE: The procedure that follows is the method used by many manufacturers. Always refer to service information for the exact recommended procedure and specifications for the vehicle being tested.

The procedure for testing the sensor using a digital multimeter is as follows:

1. Turn the ignition switch on (engine off).
2. Set the digital meter to read to DC volts and measure the voltage between the signal wire and ground (reference low) wire. The voltage should be about 0.5 volt.

NOTE: Check service information for exact wire colors or locations.

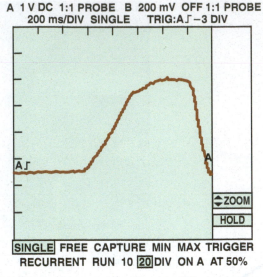

FIGURE 16–5 A typical waveform of a TP sensor signal as recorded on a DSO when the accelerator pedal was depressed with the ignition on (engine off). Clean transitions and the lack of any glitches in this waveform indicate a good sensor.

3. With the engine still not running (but with the ignition still on), slowly increase the throttle opening. The voltage signal from the TP sensor should also increase. Look for any "dead spots" or open circuit readings as the throttle is increased to the wide-open position. ● **SEE FIGURE 16–5** for an example of how a good TP sensor would look when tested with a digital storage oscilloscope (DSO).

NOTE: Use the accelerator pedal to depress the throttle because this applies the same forces on the TP sensor as the driver does during normal driving. Moving the throttle by hand under the hood may not accurately test the TP sensor.

4. With the voltmeter still connected, slowly return the throttle down to the idle position.

The voltage from the TP sensor should also decrease evenly on the return to idle. The TP sensor voltage at idle should be within the acceptable range as specified by the manufacturer. Some TP sensors can be adjusted by loosening their retaining screws and moving the sensor in relation to the throttle opening. This movement changes the output voltage of the sensor. All TP sensors should also provide a smooth transition voltage reading from idle to WOT, and back to idle. Replace the TP sensor if erratic voltage readings are obtained or if the correct setting at idle cannot be obtained.

TESTING USING THE MIN/MAX FUNCTION
Many digital multimeters are capable of recording voltage readings over time and then displaying the minimum, maximum, and average readings. To perform a MIN/MAX test of the TP sensor, manually set the meter to read higher than 4 volts:

STEP 1 Connect the red meter lead to the signal wire and the black meter lead to a good ground or the ground return wire at the TP sensor.

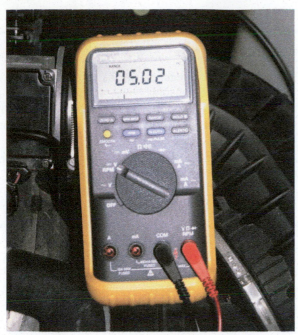

FIGURE 16–6 Checking the 5-volt reference from the computer being applied to the TP sensor with the ignition on (engine off). The reading for this vehicle (5.02 volts DC) is within the normal range for the reference voltage of 4.9 to 5.1 volts.

STEP 2 With the ignition on, engine off, slowly depress and release the accelerator pedal from inside the vehicle.

STEP 3 Check the minimum and maximum voltage reading on the meter display. Any 0-volt or 5-volt reading would indicate a fault or short in the TP sensor.

TESTING USING A SCAN TOOL A scan tool can be used to check for proper operation of the throttle position sensor, using the following steps:

STEP 1 With the key on, engine off, the TP sensor voltage display should be about 0.5 volt, but can vary from as low as 0.3 volt to as high as 1.2 volts.

FIGURE 16–7 Checking the voltage drop between the TP sensor ground and a good engine ground with the ignition on (engine off). A reading of greater than 0.2 volt (200 mV) represents a bad computer ground.

STEP 2 Check the scan tool display for the percentage of throttle opening. The reading should be zero and gradually increase in percentage as the throttle is depressed.

STEP 3 The idle air control (IAC) counts should increase as the throttle is opened and decrease as the throttle is closed. Start the engine and observe the IAC counts as the throttle is depressed.

STEP 4 Start the engine and observe the TP sensor reading. Use a wedge at the throttle stop to increase the throttle opening slightly. The throttle percentage reading should increase. Shut off and restart the engine. If the percentage of throttle opening returns to 0%, the PCM determines that the increased throttle opening is now the new minimum, and resets the idle position of the TP sensor. Remove the wedge and cycle the ignition key. The throttle position sensor should again read 0%.

NOTE: Some engine computers are not capable of resetting the throttle position sensor.

TP SENSOR DIAGNOSTIC TROUBLE CODES

The diagnostic trouble codes (DTCs) associated with the throttle position sensor include the following:

- P0122 TP sensor low voltage
- P0123 TP sensor high voltage
- P0121 TP sensor voltage does not agree with MAP
- P0124 TP sensor signal intermittent

SUMMARY

1. A throttle position (TP) sensor is a three-wire variable resistor called a potentiometer.

2. The three wires on the TP sensor include a 5-volt reference voltage from the PCM, plus the signal wire to the PCM, and a ground, which also goes to the PCM.

3. The TP sensor is used by the PCM for clear flood mode, torque converter engagement and release, and automotive transmission shift points, as well as rationality testing for the MAP and MAF sensors.

4. The TP sensor signal voltage should be about 0.5 volt at idle and increase to about 4.5 volts at wide-open throttle (WOT).

5. A TP sensor can be tested using a digital multimeter, a digital storage oscilloscope (DSO), or a scan tool.

REVIEW QUESTIONS

1. What is the purpose of each of the three wires on a typical TP sensor?

2. What all does the PCM do with the TP sensor signal voltage?

3. What is the procedure to follow when checking the 5-volt reference and TP sensor ground?

4. How can a TP sensor be diagnosed using a scan tool?

5. What makes a Hall-effect style of TP sensor different from a potentiometer style of sensor?

CHAPTER QUIZ

1. Which sensor is generally considered to be the electronic accelerator pump of a fuel-injected engine?
   a. O2S
   b. ECT sensor
   c. Engine MAP sensor
   d. TP sensor

2. Typical TP sensor voltage at idle is about _____.
   a. 2.5 to 2.8 volts
   b. 0.5 volt or 10% of WOT TP sensor voltage
   c. 1.5 to 2.8 volts
   d. 13.5 to 15 volts

3. A TP sensor is what type of sensor?
   a. Rheostat
   b. Voltage generating
   c. Potentiometer
   d. Piezoelectric

4. Most TP sensors have how many wires?
   a. One   c. Three
   b. Two   d. Four

5. Which sensor does the TP sensor back up if the PCM determines that a failure has occurred?
   a. Oxygen sensor   c. MAP sensor
   b. MAF sensor   d. Either b or c

6. Which wire on a TP sensor should be back-probed to check the voltage signal to the PCM?
   a. 5-volt reference (Vref)
   b. Signal
   c. Ground
   d. Meter should be connected between the 5-volt reference and the ground

7. After a TP sensor has been tested using the MIN/MAX function on a DMM, a reading of 0 volts is displayed. What does this reading indicate?
   a. The TP sensor is open at one point during the test.
   b. The TP sensor is shorted.
   c. The TP sensor signal is shorted to 5-volt reference.
   d. Both b and c are possible.

8. After a TP sensor has been tested using the MIN/MAX function on a DMM, a reading of 5 volts is displayed. What does this reading indicate?
   a. The TP sensor is open at one point during the test.
   b. The TP sensor is shorted.
   c. The TP sensor signal is shorted to 5-volt reference.
   d. Both b and c are possible.

9. A technician attaches one lead of a digital voltmeter to the ground terminal of the TP sensor, and the other meter lead to the negative terminal of the battery. The ignition is switched to on, engine off, and the meter displays 37.3 mV. Technician A says that this is the signal voltage and is a little low. Technician B says that the TP sensor ground circuit has excessive resistance. Which technician is correct?
   a. Technician A only
   b. Technician B only
   c. Both Technicians A and B
   d. Neither Technician A nor B

10. A P0122 DTC is retrieved using a scan tool. This DTC means _____.
   a. the TP sensor voltage is low
   b. the TP sensor could be shorted-to-ground
   c. the TP sensor signal circuit could be shorted-to-ground
   d. Any of the above

chapter 17

MANIFOLD ABSOLUTE PRESSURE AND MASS AIRFLOW SENSORS

MANIFOLD ABSOLUTE PRESSURE/BAROMETRIC PRESSURE SENSORS

PURPOSE AND FUNCTION A **manifold absolute pressure (MAP)** sensor is used on many engines for the PCM to determine the load on the engine. A **barometric pressure (BARO)** sensor is used to measure atmospheric pressure. The relationship among barometer pressure, engine vacuum, and MAP sensor voltage includes the following:

- Absolute pressure is equal to barometric pressure minus intake manifold vacuum.
- A decrease in manifold vacuum means an increase in manifold pressure.
- The MAP sensor compares manifold vacuum to a perfect vacuum.
- The barometric pressure minus the MAP sensor reading equals intake manifold vacuum. Normal engine vacuum is 17 to 21 in. Hg.
- Supercharged and turbocharged engines require a MAP sensor that is calibrated for pressures above atmospheric, as well as for vacuum.

AIR PRESSURE—HIGH AND LOW

Think of an internal combustion engine as a big air pump. As the pistons move up and down in the cylinders, they pump in air and fuel for combustion and pump out exhaust gases. They do this by creating a difference in air pressure. The air outside an engine has weight and exerts pressure, as does the air inside an engine.

As a piston moves down on an intake stroke with the intake valve open, it creates a larger area inside the cylinder for the air to fill. This lowers the air pressure within the engine. Because the pressure inside the engine is lower than the pressure outside, air flows into the engine to fill the low-pressure area and equalize the pressure.

The low pressure within the engine is called vacuum. Vacuum causes the higher-pressure air on the outside to flow into the low-pressure area inside the cylinder. The difference in pressure between the two areas is called a *pressure differential*. ● **SEE FIGURE 17–1.**

PRINCIPLES OF PRESSURE SENSORS

Intake manifold pressure changes with changing throttle positions. At wide-open throttle, manifold pressure is almost the same as atmospheric pressure. On deceleration or at idle, manifold pressure is below atmospheric pressure, thus creating a vacuum. In cases where turbo- or supercharging is used, under part- or full-load condition, intake manifold pressure rises above atmospheric pressure. Also, oxygen content and barometric pressure change with differences in altitude, and the PCM must be able to compensate by making changes in the flow of fuel entering the engine. To provide the PCM with changing airflow information, a fuel-injection system may use the following:

- MAP sensor
- MAP sensor plus BARO sensor
- Barometric and manifold absolute pressure (BMAP) sensors combined

The MAP sensor may be a ceramic capacitor diaphragm, an aneroid bellows, or a piezoresistive crystal. It has a sealed vacuum reference input on one side; the other side is connected (vented) to the intake manifold. This sensor housing also contains signal conditioning circuitry. Pressure changes in the manifold cause the sensor to deflect, varying its analog or digital return signal to the PCM. As the air pressure increases, the MAP sensor generates a higher voltage or frequency return signal to the PCM. ● **SEE FIGURE 17–2.**

CONSTRUCTION OF MAP SENSORS

The MAP sensor is used by the PCM to sense engine load. The typical MAP sensor consists of a ceramic or silicon wafer sealed on one side with a perfect vacuum, and exposed to intake manifold vacuum on the other side. As the engine vacuum changes, the pressure difference on the wafer changes the output voltage or frequency of the MAP sensor.

SILICON-DIAPHRAGM STRAIN GAUGE MAP SENSOR This is the most commonly used design for a MAP sensor, and the output is a DC analog (variable) voltage. One side of a silicon wafer is exposed to engine vacuum, and the other side is exposed to a perfect vacuum.

There are four resistors attached to the silicon wafer, which changes in resistance when strain is applied to the wafer. This change in resistance due to strain is called **piezoresistivity**. The resistors are electrically connected to a Wheatstone bridge circuit and then to a differential amplifier, which creates a voltage in proportion to the vacuum applied.

A typical General Motors MAP sensor voltage varies from 0.88 to 1.62 at engine idle:

- 17 in. Hg is equal to about 1.62 volts.
- 21 in. Hg is equal to about 0.88 volts.

Therefore, a good reading should be about 1 volt from the MAP sensor on a sound engine at idle speed. See the following chart that shows engine load, engine vacuum, and MAP.

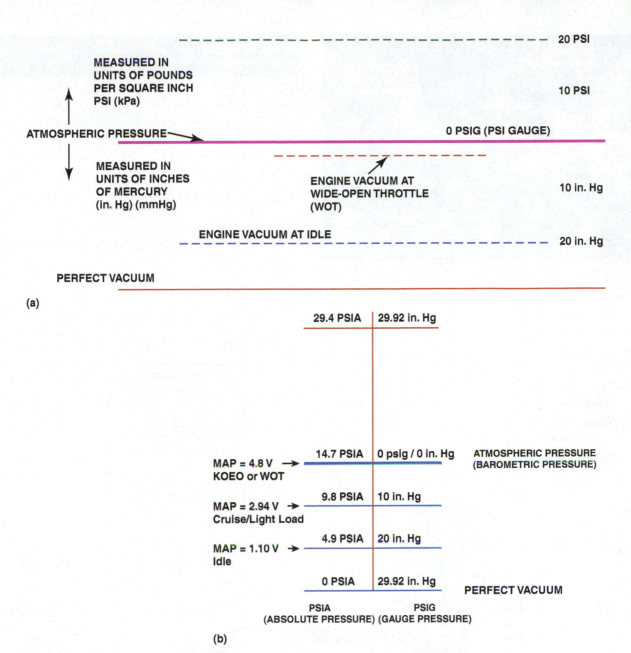

(a)

20 PSI

10 PSI

MEASURED IN
UNITS OF POUNDS
PER SQUARE INCH
PSI (kPa)

ATMOSPHERIC PRESSURE → 0 PSIG (PSI GAUGE)

MEASURED IN
UNITS OF INCHES
OF MERCURY
(in. Hg) (mmHg)

ENGINE VACUUM AT
WIDE-OPEN THROTTLE
(WOT)

10 in. Hg

ENGINE VACUUM AT IDLE

20 in. Hg

PERFECT VACUUM

(b)

29.4 PSIA | 29.92 in. Hg

MAP = 4.8 V → 14.7 PSIA | 0 psig / 0 in. Hg | ATMOSPHERIC PRESSURE
KOEO or WOT | | | (BAROMETRIC PRESSURE)

MAP = 2.94 V → 9.8 PSIA | 10 in. Hg
Cruise/Light Load

MAP = 1.10 V → 4.9 PSIA | 20 in. Hg
Idle

0 PSIA | 29.92 in. Hg | PERFECT VACUUM

PSIA | PSIG
(ABSOLUTE PRESSURE) (GAUGE PRESSURE)

FIGURE 17–1 (a) As an engine is accelerated under a load, the engine vacuum drops. This drop in vacuum is actually an increase in absolute pressure in the intake manifold. A MAP sensor senses all pressures greater than that of a perfect vacuum. (b) The relationship between absolute pressure, vacuum, and gauge pressure.

CAPACITOR-CAPSULE MAP SENSOR
A capacitor-capsule is a type of MAP sensor used by Ford which uses two ceramic (alumina) plates with an insulating washer spacer in the center to create a capacitor. Changes in engine vacuum cause the plates to deflect, which changes the capacitance. The electronics in the sensor then generate a varying digital frequency output signal, which is proportional to the engine vacuum. ● **SEE FIGURE 17–3**. ● **SEE FIGURE 17–4** for a scope waveform of a digital MAP sensor. Also see the Ford MAP sensor chart.

CERAMIC DISC MAP SENSOR
The ceramic disc MAP sensor is used by Chrysler. It converts manifold pressure into a capacitance discharge. The discharge controls the amount of voltage delivered by the sensor to the PCM. The output is the same as the previously used strain gauge/Wheatstone bridge design and is interchangeable. ● **SEE FIGURE 17–5**. See the Chrysler MAP sensor chart.

Ford MAP Sensor Chart		
MAP Sensor Output	Engine Operating Conditions	Intake Manifold Vacuum
156–159 Hz	Key on, engine off	0 in. Hg
102–109 Hz	Engine at idle (sea level)	17–21 in. Hg
156–159 Hz	Engine at wide-open throttle	Near 0 in. Hg

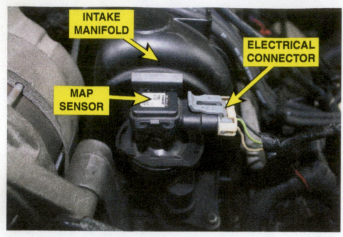

Chrysler MAP Sensor Chart	
Vacuum (in. Hg)	MAP Sensor Signal Voltage (V)
0.5	4.8
1	4.6
3	4.1
5	3.8
7	3.5
10	2.9
15	2.1
20	1.2
25	0.5

FIGURE 17–2 A MAP sensor on a GM 3.8 liter engine is used to measure intake manifold pressure changes.

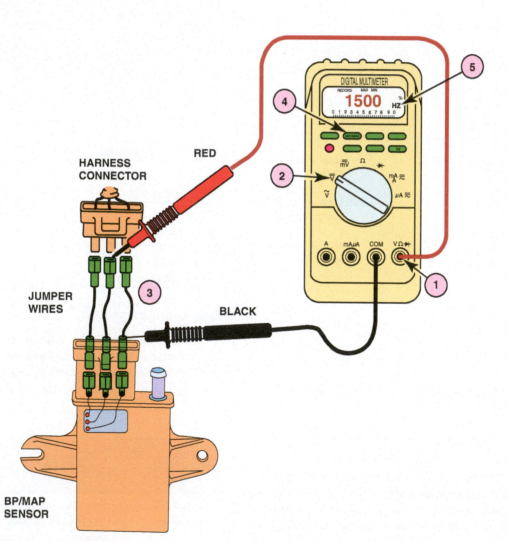

FIGURE 17–3 A digital multimeter is being used to test a three-wire MAP sensor. 1. The red lead is connected to the signal wire. 2. The meter has been set to DC volts. 3. The black lead is connected to the ground wire. 4. The meter has been set to measure hertz (Hz). The display will show the change in voltage (frequency) as the vacuum applied to the sensor changes.

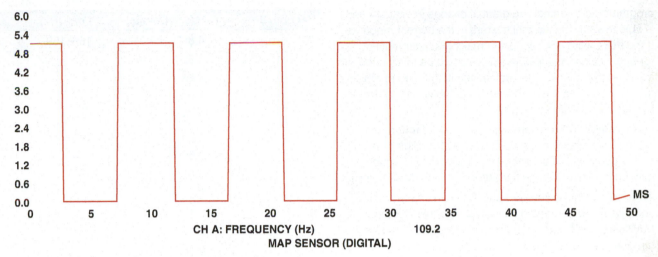

FIGURE 17–4 A waveform of a typical digital MAP sensor.

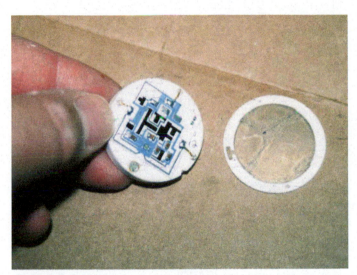

FIGURE 17–5 Shown is the electronic circuit inside a ceramic disc MAP sensor. The black areas are carbon resistors that are applied to the ceramic disc and used to measure pressure change.

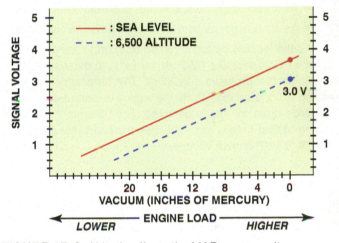

FIGURE 17–6 Altitude affects the MAP sensor voltage.

PCM USES OF THE MAP SENSOR

The PCM uses the MAP sensor to determine the following:

- **Load on the engine.** The MAP sensor is used on a speed density-type fuel-injection system to determine engine load, and therefore, the amount of fuel needed. On engines equipped with a mass airflow (MAF) sensor, the MAP is used as a backup to the MAF, for diagnosis of other sensors, and systems, such as the EGR system.

- **Altitude, fuel, and spark control calculations.** At key on, the MAP sensor determines the altitude (acts as a BARO sensor) and adjusts the fuel delivery and spark timing accordingly:

- If the altitude is high, generally over 5,000 feet (1,500 m), the PCM will reduce fuel delivery and advance the ignition timing.

- The altitude is also reset when the engine is accelerated to wide-open throttle and the MAP sensor is used to reset the altitude reading. ● **SEE FIGURE 17–6.**

- **EGR system operation.** As part of the OBD-II standards, the exhaust gas recirculation (EGR) system must be checked for proper operation. One method used by many vehicle manufacturers is to command the EGR valve on and watch the MAP sensor signal. The opening of the EGR pintle should decrease engine vacuum. If the MAP sensor does not react with the specified drop in manifold vacuum (increase in manifold pressure), an EGR flow rate problem diagnostic trouble code is set.

- **Detect deceleration (vacuum increases).** The engine vacuum rises when the accelerator is released, which changes the MAP sensor voltage. When deceleration is detected by the PCM, fuel is either stopped or greatly reduced to improve exhaust emissions.

- **Monitor engine condition.** As an engine wears, the intake manifold vacuum usually decreases. The PCM is programmed to detect the gradual change in vacuum and is able to keep the air–fuel mixture in the correct range. If the PCM were not capable of making adjustments for engine wear, the lower vacuum could be interpreted as increased load on the engine, resulting in too much fuel being injected, thereby reducing fuel economy and increasing exhaust emissions.

- **Load detection for returnless-type fuel injection.** On fuel delivery systems that do not use a return line back to the fuel tank, the engine load calculation for the fuel needed is determined by the signals from the MAP sensor.

- **Altitude and MAP sensor values.** On an engine equipped with a speed density-type fuel injection, the MAP sensor is the most important sensor needed to determine injection pulse width. Changes in altitude change the air density, as well as weather conditions. Barometric pressure and altitude are inversely related:

  - As altitude increases, barometric pressure decreases.
  - As altitude decreases, barometric pressure increases.

As the ignition switch is turned from off to the start position, the PCM reads the MAP sensor value to determine atmospheric and air pressure conditions. This barometric pressure reading is updated every time the engine is started and whenever wide-open throttle is detected. The barometric pressure reading at that time is updated. See the chart that compares altitude to MAP sensor voltage.

Vacuum (in. Hg)	GM (DC volts)	Ford (Hz)
0	4.8	156–159
1	4.52	
2	4.46	
3	4.26	
4	4.06	
5	3.88	141–143
6	3.66	
7	3.5	
8	3.3	
9	3.1	
10	2.94	127–130
11	2.76	
12	2.54	
13	2.36	
14	2.2	
15	2	114–117
16	1.8	
17	1.62	
18	1.42	
19	1.2	
20	1.1	102–104

TECH TIP

Use the MAP Sensor as a Vacuum Gauge

A MAP sensor measures the pressure inside the intake manifold compared with absolute zero (perfect vacuum). For example, an idling engine that has 20 in. Hg of vacuum has a lower pressure inside the intake manifold than when the engine is under a load and the vacuum is at 10 in. Hg. A decrease in engine vacuum results in an increase in manifold pressure. A normal engine should produce between 17 and 21 in. Hg at idle. Comparing the vacuum reading with the voltage reading output of the MAP sensor indicates that the reading should be between 1.62 and 0.88 volt or 109 to 102 Hz or lower on Ford MAP sensors. Therefore, a digital multimeter (DMM), scan tool, or scope can be used to measure the MAP sensor voltage and be used instead of a vacuum gauge.

NOTE: This chart was developed by testing a MAP sensor at a location about 600 feet above sea level. For best results, a chart based on your altitude should be made by applying a known vacuum, and reading the voltage of a known good MAP sensor. Vacuum usually drops about 1 inch per 1,000 feet of altitude.

BAROMETRIC PRESSURE SENSOR

A barometric pressure (BARO) sensor is similar in design to a MAP sensor, but senses more subtle changes in barometric absolute pressure (atmospheric air pressure). It is vented directly to the atmosphere. The **barometric manifold absolute pressure (BMAP) sensor** is actually a combination of a BARO and MAP sensor in the same housing. The BMAP sensor has individual circuits to measure barometric and manifold pressure. This input not only allows the PCM to adjust for changes in atmospheric pressure due to weather, but also is the primary sensor used to determine altitude.

NOTE: A MAP sensor and a BARO sensor are usually the same sensor, but the MAP sensor is connected to the manifold and a BARO sensor is open to the atmosphere. The MAP sensor is capable of reading barometric pressure just as the ignition switch is turned to the on position before the engine starts. Therefore, altitude and weather changes are available to the PCM. During mountainous driving, it may be an advantage to stop and then restart the engine so that the PCM can take another barometric pressure reading and recalibrate fuel delivery based on the new altitude. See the Ford/BARO altitude

The Old Chevrolet Story

The owner of an old Chevrolet stated to a service technician that the "check engine" (MIL) was on. The technician found a diagnostic trouble code (DTC) for a MAP sensor. The technician removed the hose at the MAP sensor and discovered that gasoline had accumulated in the sensor and dripped out of the hose as it was being removed. The technician replaced the MAP sensor and test-drove the vehicle to confirm the repair. Almost at once the check engine light came on with the same MAP sensor code. After several hours of troubleshooting without success in determining the cause, the technician decided to start over again. Almost at once, the technician discovered that no vacuum was getting to the MAP sensor where a vacuum gauge was connected with a T-fitting in the vacuum line to the MAP sensor. The vacuum port in the base of the throttle body was clogged with carbon. After a thorough cleaning and clearing the DTC, the Cavalier again performed properly, and the check engine light did not come on again. The technician had assumed that if gasoline was able to reach the sensor through the vacuum hose, surely vacuum could reach the sensor. The technician learned to stop assuming when diagnosing a vehicle and concentrate more on testing the simple things first.

Summary:

- **Complaint**—MIL lamp illuminated.
- **Cause**—Vacuum port on the throttle body was blocked with carbon.
- **Correction**—Remove the carbon blocking the passage, which restored the vacuum signal to the MAP sensor.

chart for an example of how altitude affects intake manifold pressure. The PCM on some vehicles will monitor the throttle position sensor and use the MAP sensor reading at wide-open throttle (WOT) to update the BARO sensor if it has changed during driving.

TESTING THE MAP SENSOR

Most pressure sensors operate on 5 volts from the PCM and return a signal (voltage or frequency) based on the pressure (vacuum) applied to the sensor. If a MAP sensor is being tested, make certain that the vacuum hose and hose fittings are sound and making a good, tight connection to a manifold vacuum source on the engine.

Four different types of test instruments can be used to test a pressure sensor:

1. A digital voltmeter with three test leads connected in series between the sensor and the wiring harness connector or back-probe the terminals
2. A scope connected to the sensor output, power, and ground
3. A scan tool or a specific tool recommended by the vehicle manufacturer
4. A breakout box connected in series between the PCM and the wiring harness connection(s) (A typical breakout box includes test points at which pressure sensor values can be measured with a digital voltmeter set on DC volts—or frequency counter, if a frequency-type MAP sensor is being tested.)

NOTE: Always check service information for the exact testing procedures and specifications for the vehicle being tested.

TESTING THE MAP SENSOR USING A DMM OR SCOPE   Use jumper wires, T-pins to back-probe the connector, or a breakout box to gain electrical access to the wiring to the pressure sensor. Most pressure sensors use three wires:

1. A 5-volt wire from the PCM
2. A variable-signal wire back to the PCM
3. A ground or reference low wire

   The procedure for testing the sensor is as follows:

1. Turn the ignition on (engine off).
2. Measure the voltage (or frequency) of the sensor output.
3. Using a hand-operated vacuum pump (or other variable vacuum source), apply vacuum to the sensor.

A good pressure sensor should change voltage (or frequency) in relation to the applied vacuum. If the signal does not change or the values are out of range according to the manufacturer's specifications, the sensor must be replaced.

TESTING THE MAP SENSOR USING A SCAN TOOL   A scan tool can be used to test a MAP sensor by monitoring the injector pulse width (in milliseconds) when vacuum is being applied to the MAP sensor using a hand-operated vacuum pump. ● **SEE FIGURE 17–7.**

STEP 1   Apply about 20 in. Hg of vacuum to the MAP sensor and start the engine.

STEP 2   Observe the injector pulse width. On a warm engine, the injector pulse width will normally be 1.5 to 3.5 ms.

STEP 3   Slowly reduce the vacuum to the MAP sensor and observe the pulse width. A lower vacuum to the MAP sensor indicates a heavier load on the engine, and the injector pulse width should increase.

FIGURE 17–7 A typical hand-operated vacuum pump.

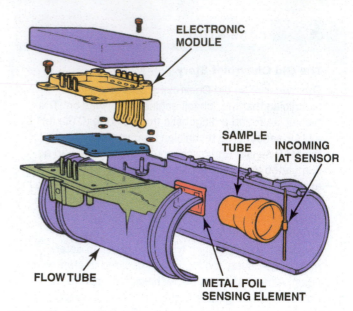

FIGURE 17–8 This five-wire mass airflow sensor consists of a metal foil sensing unit, an intake air temperature (IAT) sensor, and the electronic module.

NOTE: If 23 in. Hg or more vacuum is applied to the MAP sensor with the engine running, this high vacuum will often stall the engine. The engine stalls because the high vacuum is interpreted by the PCM to indicate that the engine is being decelerated, which shuts off the fuel. During engine deceleration, the PCM shuts off the fuel injectors to reduce exhaust emissions and increase fuel economy.

MAP/BARO DIAGNOSTIC CODES

The diagnostic trouble codes (DTCs) associated with the MAP and BARO sensors include the following:

- P0106 BARO sensor out-of-range at key on
- P0107 MAP sensor low voltage
- P0108 Map sensor high voltage

MASS AIRFLOW SENSORS

MASS AIRFLOW SENSOR TYPES Most new fuel injection systems use a mass airflow (MAF) sensor to calculate the amount of air volume delivered to the engine.

There are several types of mass airflow sensors.

HOT FILM SENSOR The hot film sensor uses a temperature-sensing resistor (thermistor) to measure the temperature of the incoming air. Through the electronics within the sensor, a conductive film is kept at a temperature 70°C above the temperature of the incoming air. ● SEE FIGURE 17–8.

Because both the amount and the density of the air tend to contribute to the cooling effect as the air passes through the sensor, this type of sensor can actually produce an output based on the mass of the airflow. Mass equals volume times density. For example, cold air is denser than warm air, so a small amount of cold air may have the same mass as a larger amount of warm air. Therefore, a mass airflow sensor is designed to measure the mass, not the volume, of the air entering the engine.

The output of this type of sensor is usually a frequency based on the amount of air entering the sensor. The more air that enters the sensor, the more the hot film is cooled. The electronics inside the sensor, therefore, increase the current flow through the hot film to maintain the 70°C temperature differential between the air temperature and the temperature of the hot film. This change in current flow is converted to a frequency output that the PCM can use as a measurement of airflow. Most of these types of sensors are referred to as mass airflow (MAF) sensors because, unlike the air vane sensor, the MAF sensor takes into account relative humidity, altitude, and temperature of the air. The denser the air, the greater the cooling effect on the hot film sensor, and the greater the amount of fuel required for proper combustion.

HOT WIRE SENSOR The hot wire sensor is similar to the hot-film type but uses a hot wire to sense the mass airflow instead of the hot film. Like the hot-film sensor, the hot-wire sensor uses a temperature-sensing resistor (thermistor) to measure the temperature of the air entering the sensor. ● SEE FIGURE 17–9. The electronic circuitry within the sensor keeps the temperature of the wire at 70°C above the temperature of the incoming air.

FIGURE 17–9 The sensing wire in a typical hot-wire mass airflow sensor.

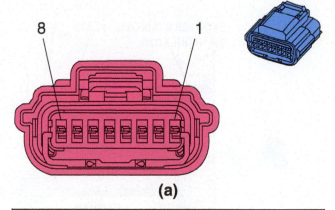

Both designs operate in essentially the same way. A resistor wire or screen installed in the path of intake airflow is heated to a constant temperature by electric current provided by the PCM. Air flowing past the screen or wire cools it. The degree of cooling varies with air velocity, temperature, density, and humidity. These factors combine to indicate the mass of air entering the engine. As the screen or wire cools, more current is required to maintain the specified temperature. As the screen or wire heats up, less current is required. The operating principle can be summarized as follows:

More intake air volume = a cooler sensor, more current

Less intake air volume = a warmer sensor, less current

The PCM constantly monitors the change in current and translates it into a voltage signal that is used to determine injector pulse width.

BURN-OFF CIRCUIT. Some hot wire-type MAF sensors use a burn-off circuit to keep the sensing wire clean of dust and dirt. A high current is passed through the sensing wire for a short time but long enough to cause the wire to glow because of the heat. The burn-off circuit is turned on when the ignition switch is switched off after the engine has been operating long enough to achieve normal operating temperature.

EIGHT-WIRE MASS AIRFLOW SENSOR

Recently manufacturers have begun to use an eight-wire type of mass airflow sensor. It has been sometimes referred to as a multifunction mass airflow sensor or a mini weather station. The sensor measures the following elements:

- Airflow
- Intake air temperature
- Barometric pressure
- Humidity

Measuring airflow, temperature, and barometric pressure is not new. Temperature and barometric pressure have an effect

Pin	Wire	Circuit	Function
1	0.5 L-BU	6289	IAT Sensor Signal
2	0.5 GY/WH	3201	5 Volt Reference A
3	0.5 L-BU	2760	Low Reference
4	0.5 YE/WH	3200	Throttle Inlet Absolute Pressure Sensor Signal
5	0.5 PK/BK	5294	PWR/TRN Relay Power
6	0.5 YE	492	MAF Sensor Signal
7	0.5 BK/WH	451	Ground
8	0.5 L-BU	7564	Humidity Sensor Signal

(b)

FIGURE 17–10 The (a) connector and (b) pinout are typical of an eight-wire mass airflow sensor used on a General Motors vehicle.

on the air density. Measuring the effect of humidity on airflow is new. Humidity, or water vapor, takes up space in the airflow and lowers the volume of air. Without this feature, high humidity could create a rich condition. The barometric pressure reading is also used in this calculation because the density of the air affects the amount of water vapor it can hold. The net result of this change is a more precise measurement of the air entering the engine than previous types of sensors. ● SEE FIGURE 17–10.

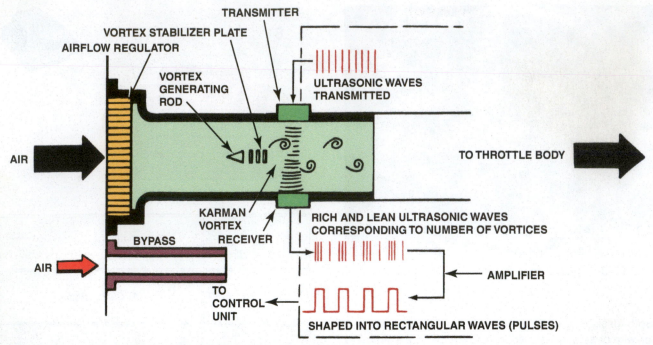

FIGURE 17–11 A Karman vortex sensor uses a triangle-shaped rod to create vortexes as the air flows through the sensor. The electronics in the sensor convert these vortexes to a digital square wave signal.

KARMAN VORTEX SENSORS

In 1912, a Hungarian scientist named Theodore Van Karman observed that vortexes were created when air passed over a pointed surface. This type of sensor sends a sound wave through the turbulence created by incoming air passing through the sensor. Air mass is calculated based on the time required for the sound waves to cross the turbulent air passage.

There are two basic designs of Karman vortex airflow sensors:

- **Ultrasonic.** This type of sensor uses ultrasonic waves to detect the vortexes that are produced and produces a digital (on-and-off) signal where frequency is proportional to the amount of air passing through the sensor. ● **SEE FIGURE 17–11.**

- **Pressure type.** Chrysler uses a pressure-type Karman vortex sensor that uses a pressure sensor to detect the vortexes. As the airflow through the sensor increases, so do the number of pressure variations. The electronics in the sensor convert these pressure variations to a square wave (digital DC voltage) signal, whose frequency is in proportion to the airflow through the sensor.

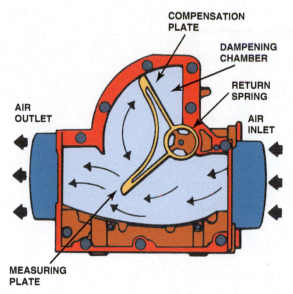

FIGURE 17–12 A vane airflow (VAF) sensor.

 CASE STUDY

The Dirty MAF Sensor Story

The owner of a Buick equipped with a 3800 V-6 engine complained that the engine would hesitate during acceleration, showed lack of power, and seemed to surge or miss at times. A visual inspection found everything to be like new, including a new air filter. There were no stored diagnostic trouble codes (DTCs). A look at the scan data showed airflow to be within the recommended 3 to 7 grams per second. A check of the frequency output showed the problem:

  Idle frequency = 2.177 kHz (2,177 Hz)

Normal frequency at idle speed should be 2.37 to 2.52 kHz. Cleaning the hot wire of the MAF sensor restored proper operation. The sensor wire was covered with what looked like fine fibers, possibly from the replacement air filter.

NOTE: Older GM MAF sensors operated at a lower frequency of 32 to 150 Hz, with 32 Hz being the average reading at idle and 150 Hz for wide-open throttle.

Summary:

- **Complaint**—Vehicle had a lack of power, hesitated on acceleration, and had a miss at times.
- **Cause**—MAF sensor was contaminated with fibers from the air filter.
- **Correction**—The MAF sensor was cleaned, which restored proper engine operation.

PCM USES FOR AIRFLOW SENSORS

The PCM uses the information from the airflow sensor for the following purposes:

- Airflow sensors are used mostly to determine the amount of fuel needed and base pulse-width numbers. The greater the mass of the incoming air, the longer the injectors are pulsed on.
- Airflow sensors back up the TP sensor in the event of a loss of signal or an inaccurate throttle position sensor signal. If the MAF sensor fails, then the PCM will calculate the fuel delivery needs of the engine based on throttle position and engine speed (RPM).

TESTING MASS AIRFLOW SENSORS

VISUAL INSPECTION Start the testing of a MAF sensor by performing a thorough visual inspection. Look at all the hoses that direct and send air, especially between the MAF sensor and the throttle body. Also check the electrical connector for the following:

- Corrosion
- Terminals that are bent or pushed out of the plastic connector
- Frayed wiring

MAF SENSOR OUTPUT TEST MAF sensors calculate air mass by weight in a given amount of time usually in grams per second (gm/sec). A digital multimeter, set to read DC volts on the signal wire circuit, can be used to check the MAF sensor. See the chart that shows the voltage output compared with the grams per second of airflow through the sensor. Normal airflow is 3 to 7 grams per second. ● **SEE FIGURE 17–13.**

TAP TEST With the engine running at idle speed, gently tap the MAF sensor with the fingers of an open hand. If the engine stumbles or stalls, the MAF sensor is defective. This test is commonly called the tap test.

DIGITAL METER TEST OF MAF SENSOR A digital multimeter can be used to measure the frequency (Hz) output of the sensor and compare the reading with specifications. The frequency output and engine speed in RPM can also be plotted on a graph to check to see if the frequency and RPM are proportional, resulting in a straight line on the graph.

Mass Airflow (gm/sec)	Sensor Voltage
0	0.20
2	0.70
4	1.00
8	1.50
15	2.00
30	2.50
50	3.00
80	3.50
110	4.00
150	4.50
175	4.80

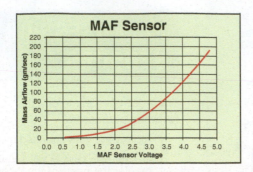

FIGURE 17–13 A typical analog MAF sensor.

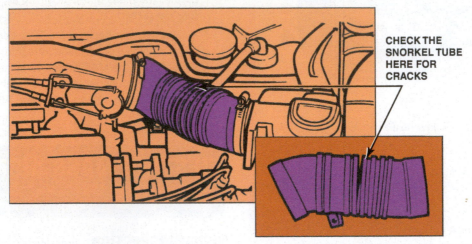

CHECK THE SNORKEL TUBE HERE FOR CRACKS

FIGURE 17–14 Carefully check the hose between the MAF sensor and the throttle body assembly for cracks or splits that could create extra (false) air into the engine that was not measured by the MAF sensor.

High-Authority Sensors	Low-Authority Sensors
ECT (Especially when the engine starts and is warming up)	IAT (Intake air temperature) sensors modify and back up the ECT)
O2S (after the engine reaches closed loop operation)	TFT (transmission fluid temperature)
MAP	PRNDL (shift position sensor)
MAF	KS (knock sensor)
TP (high authority during acceleration and deceleration)	EFT (engine fuel temperature)

 FREQUENTLY ASKED QUESTION

What Is Meant by a "High-Authority Sensor"?

A high-authority sensor is a sensor that has a major influence over the amount of fuel being delivered to the engine. For example, at engine start-up, the engine coolant temperature (ECT) sensor is a high-authority sensor, and the oxygen sensor (O2S) is a low-authority sensor. However, as the engine reaches operating temperature, the oxygen sensor becomes a high-authority sensor and can greatly affect the amount of fuel being supplied to the engine. See the following chart.

? FREQUENTLY ASKED QUESTION

What Is False Air?

Airflow sensors and mass airflow (MAF) sensors are designed to measure *all* the air entering the engine. If an air hose between the MAF sensor and the throttle body was loose or had a hole, extra air could enter the engine without being measured. This extra air is often called **false air**. ●SEE **FIGURE 17–14**. Because this extra air is unmeasured, the PCM does not provide enough fuel delivery, and the engine operates too lean, especially at idle. A small hole in the air inlet hose would represent a fairly large percentage of false air at idle, but would represent a very small percentage of extra air at highway speeds.

To begin diagnosis for false air, look at long-term fuel trim numbers at idle and at 3000 RPM.

NOTE: If the engine runs well in reverse, yet runs terrible in any forward gear, carefully look at the inlet hose for air leaks that would open when the engine torque moves the engine slightly on its mounts.

MAF SENSOR CONTAMINATION

Dirt, oil, silicon, or even spider webs can coat the sensing wire. Because it tends to insulate the sensing wire at low air-flow rates, a contaminated sensor often overestimates the amount of air entering the engine at idle, and therefore, causes the fuel system to go rich. At higher engine speeds near wide-open throttle (WOT), the contamination can cause the sensor to underestimate the amount of air entering the engine. As a result, the fuel system will go lean, causing spark knock and lack of power concerns. To check for contamination, check the fuel trim numbers.

If the fuel trim is negative (removing fuel) at idle, yet is positive (adding fuel) at higher engine speeds, a contaminated MAF sensor is a likely cause. Other tests for a contaminated MAF sensor include the following:

- At WOT, the grams per second, as read on a scan tool, should exceed 100 grams.

- At WOT, the voltage, as read on a digital voltmeter, should exceed 4 volts for an analog sensor.

- At WOT, the frequency, as read on a meter or scan tool, should exceed 7 kHz for a digital sensor.

If the readings do not exceed these values, then the MAF sensor is contaminated.

MAF-RELATED DAIGNOSTIC TROUBLE CODES

The DTCs associated with the mass airflow and air vane sensors include the following:

- P0100 Mass or volume airflow circuit problems

- P0101 Mass airflow circuit range problems

- P0102 Mass airflow circuit low output

- P0103 Mass airflow circuit high output

SUMMARY

1. Pressure below atmospheric pressure is called vacuum and is measured in inches of mercury.

2. A manifold absolute pressure sensor uses a perfect vacuum (zero absolute pressure) in the sensor to determine the pressure.

3. Three types of MAP sensors include the following:
   - Silicon-diaphragm strain gauge
   - Capacitor-capsule design
   - Ceramic disc design

4. A heavy engine load results in low intake manifold vacuum and a high MAP sensor signal voltage.

5. A light engine load results in high intake manifold vacuum and a low MAP sensor signal voltage.

6. A MAP sensor is used to detect changes in altitude, as well as check other sensors and engine systems.

7. A MAP sensor can be tested by visual inspection, testing the output using a digital meter or scan tool.

8. A mass airflow sensor actually measures the density and amount of air flowing into the engine, which results in accurate engine control.

9. An air vane sensor measures the volume of the air, and the intake air temperature sensor is used by the PCM to calculate the mass of the air entering the engine.

10. 10. A hot-wire MAF sensor uses the electronics in the sensor itself to heat a wire 70°C above the temperature of the air entering the engine.

1. What is the relationship among atmospheric pressure, vacuum, and boost pressure in PSI?

2. What are two types (construction) of MAP sensors?

3. How does a hot-film MAF sensor work?

4. What type of voltage signal is produced by a MAF?

5. How is a MAF sensor tested?

CHAPTER QUIZ

1. As the load on an engine increases, the manifold vacuum decreases and the manifold absolute pressure _____
   a. increases
   b. decreases
   c. changes with barometric pressure only (altitude or weather)
   d. remains constant (absolute)

2. A typical MAP sensor compares the vacuum in the intake manifold to _____.
   a. atmospheric pressure
   b. a perfect vacuum
   c. barometric pressure
   d. the value of the IAT sensor

3. The MAP sensor is used when the OBD-II does a test of the _____ system.
   a. timing
   b. cooling
   c. feedback
   d. EGR

4. Which design of MAP sensor produces a frequency (digital) output signal?
   a. Silicon-diaphragm strain gauge
   b. Piezoresistivity design
   c. Capacitor-capsule
   d. Ceramic disc

5. When measuring the output signal of a MAP sensor on a General Motors vehicle, the digital multimeter should be set to read _____.
   a. DC V
   b. AC V
   c. Hz
   d. DC A

6. As the altitude of the vehicle increases, barometric pressure _____.
   a. increases
   b. does not change
   c. decreases
   d. None of the above

7. Which of these tools could be used to test a MAP sensor?
   a. Digital voltmeter
   b. Scan tool
   c. Hand-operated vacuum pump
   d. Any of the above

8. If the MAF sensor fails, the PCM will use _____ to calculate fuel delivery needs.
   a. MAP and throttle position
   b. RPM and throttle position
   c. throttle position and transmission RPM
   d. RPM alone

9. A MAF sensor on a General Motors 3800 V-6 is being tested for contamination. Technician A says that the sensor should show over 100 grams per second on a scan tool display when the accelerator is depressed to WOT on a running engine. Technician B says that the output frequency should exceed 7,000 Hz when the accelerator pedal is depressed to WOT on a running engine. Which technician is correct?
   a. Technician A only
   b. Technician B only
   c. Both Technicians A and B
   d. Neither Technician A nor B

10. An eight-wire mass airflow sensor senses all of these EXCEPT _____.
    a. airflow
    b. RPM
    c. humidity
    d. intake air temperature

chapter 18
ELECTRONIC THROTTLE CONTROL SYSTEM

LEARNING OBJECTIVES

After studying this chapter, the reader should be able to:

1. Describe the advantages of an electronic throttle control (ETC) system.
2. Explain how an electronic throttle control system works.
3. Explain how an accelerator pedal position sensor works.
4. List the parts of a typical electronic throttle body assembly.
5. Describe the two types of throttle position sensors.
6. Describe how to diagnose faults in an electronic throttle control system.
7. Explain how to service an electronic throttle system.

This chapter will help you prepare for ASE content area "E" (Computerized Engine Controls Diagnosis and Repair).

KEY TERMS

Accelerator pedal position (APP) sensor 260
Coast-down stall 266
Default position 261
Drive-by-wire 260
Electronic throttle control (ETC) 260
Fail safe position 261
Neutral position 261
Servomotor 261
Throttle position (TP) sensor 260

259

ELECTRONIC THROTTLE CONTROL (ETC) SYSTEM

ADVANTAGES OF ETC The absence of any mechanical linkage between the throttle pedal and the throttle body requires the use of an electric actuator motor. The electronic throttle system has the following advantages over the conventional cable:

- Eliminates the mechanical throttle cable, thereby reducing the number of moving parts.
- Eliminates the need for cruise control actuators and controllers.
- Helps reduce engine power for traction control (TC) and electronic stability control (ESC) systems.
- Delays rapid applications of torque to the transmission/transaxle to help improve drivability and to smooth shifts.
- Helps reduce pumping losses by using the electronic throttle to open at highway speeds with greater fuel economy. The electronic throttle control (ETC) opens the throttle to maintain engine and vehicle speed as the Powertrain Control Module leans the air–fuel ratio, retards ignition timing, and introduces additional exhaust gas recirculation (EGR) to reduce pumping losses.
- Provides smooth engine operation, especially during rapid acceleration.
- Eliminates the need for an idle air control valve.

The electronic throttle can be called **drive-by-wire**, but most vehicle manufacturers use the term **electronic throttle control (ETC)** to describe the system that opens the throttle valve electrically.

PARTS INVOLVED The typical ETC system includes the following components:

1. **Accelerator pedal position (APP)** sensor, also called *accelerator pedal sensor (APS)*
2. The electronic throttle actuator (servomotor), which is part of the electronic throttle body
3. A **throttle position (TP) sensor**
4. An electronic control unit, which is usually the Powertrain Control Module
   - ● **SEE FIGURE 18–1.**

NORMAL OPERATION OF THE ETC SYSTEM

Driving a vehicle equipped with an electronic throttle control system is about the same as driving a vehicle with a conventional mechanical throttle cable and throttle valve. However,

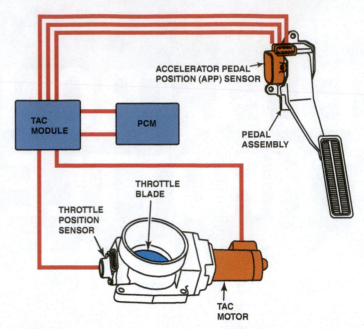

FIGURE 18–1 The throttle pedal is connected to the accelerator pedal position (APP) sensor. The electronic throttle body includes a throttle position sensor to provide throttle angle feedback to the vehicle PCM. Some systems use a Throttle Actuator Control (TAC) module to operate the throttle blade (plate).

the driver may notice some differences, which are to be considered normal. These normal conditions include:

- The engine may not increase above idle speed when depressing the accelerator pedal when the gear selector is in PARK.
- If the engine speed does increase when the accelerator is depressed with the transmission in PARK or NEUTRAL, the engine speed will likely be limited to less than 2000 RPM.
- While accelerating rapidly, there is often a slight delay before the engine responds. ● **SEE FIGURE 18–2.**
- While at cruise speed, the accelerator pedal may or may not cause the engine speed to increase if the accelerator pedal is moved slightly.

ACCELERATOR PEDAL POSITION SENSOR

CABLE-OPERATED SYSTEM Honda Accords until 2008 model year used a cable attached to the accelerator pedal to operate the APP sensor located under the hood. A similar arrangement was used in Dodge RAM trucks in 2003. In both of these applications, the throttle cable was simply moving the APP sensor and not moving the throttle plate. The throttle plate is controlled by the PCM and moved by the electronic throttle control motor.

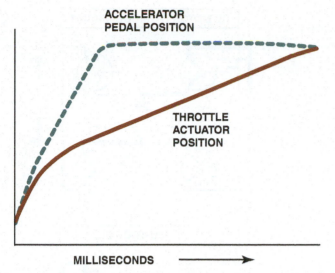

FIGURE 18–2 The opening of the throttle plate can be delayed as long as 30 milliseconds (0.030 sec) to allow time for the amount of fuel needed to catch up to the opening of the throttle plate.

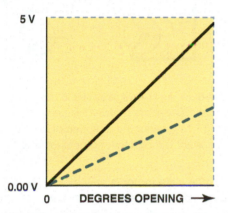

FIGURE 18–3 A typical accelerator pedal position (APP) sensor, showing two different output voltage signals that are used by the PCM to determine accelerator pedal position. Two (or three in some applications) are used as a double check because this is a safety-related sensor.

TWO SENSORS The accelerator pedal position sensor uses two and sometimes three separate sensors, which act together to give accurate accelerator pedal position information to the controller, but also are used to check that the sensor is working properly. They function just like a throttle position sensor, and two are needed for proper system function. One APP sensor output signal increases as the pedal is depressed and the other signal decreases. The controller compares the signals with a look-up table to determine the pedal position. Using two or three signals improves redundancy should one sensor fail, and allows the PCM to quickly detect a malfunction. When three sensors are used, the third signal can either decrease or increase with pedal position, but its voltage range will still be different from the other two. ● **SEE FIGURE 18–3**.

THROTTLE BODY ASSEMBLY

The throttle body assembly contains the following components:

- Throttle plate
- Electric actuator DC motor
- Dual throttle position (TP) sensors
- Gears used to multiply the torque of the DC motor
- Springs used to hold the throttle plate in the default location

THROTTLE PLATE AND SPRING The throttle plate is held slightly open by a concentric clock spring. The spring applies a force that will close the throttle plate if power is lost to the actuator motor. The spring is also used to open the throttle plate slightly from the fully closed position.

ELECTRONIC THROTTLE BODY MOTOR The actuator is a DC electric motor and is often called a **servomotor**. The throttle plate is held in a **default position** by a spring inside the throttle body assembly. This partially open position, also called the **neutral position** or the **fail safe position**, is about 16% to 20% open. This default position varies depending on the vehicle and usually results in an engine speed of 1200 to 1500 RPM.

- The throttle plate is driven closed to achieve speeds lower than the default position, such as idle speed.
- The throttle plate is driven open to achieve speeds higher than the default position, such as during acceleration.
  ● **SEE FIGURE 18–4**.

? **FREQUENTLY ASKED QUESTION**

What Is the "Spring Test"?
The spring test is a self-test performed by the PCM whenever the engine is started. The PCM operates the throttle to check if it can react to the command and return to the default (home) position. This self-test is used by the PCM to determine that the spring and motor are working correctly and may be noticed by some vehicle owners by the following factors:

- A slight delay in the operation of the starter motor. It is when the ignition is turned to the on position that the PCM performs the test. While it takes just a short time to perform the test, it can be sensed by the driver that there could be a fault in the ignition switch or starter motor circuits.
- A slight "clicking" sound may also be heard coming from under the hood when the ignition is turned on. This is normal and is related to the self-test on the throttle as it opens and closes.

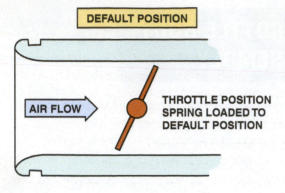

DEFAULT POSITION

AIR FLOW → THROTTLE POSITION SPRING LOADED TO DEFAULT POSITION

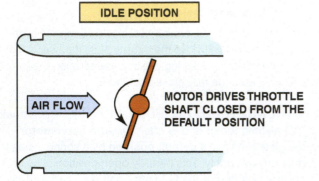

IDLE POSITION

AIR FLOW → MOTOR DRIVES THROTTLE SHAFT CLOSED FROM THE DEFAULT POSITION

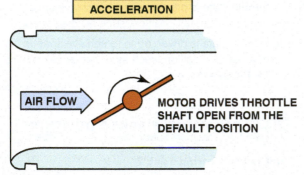

ACCELERATION

AIR FLOW → MOTOR DRIVES THROTTLE SHAFT OPEN FROM THE DEFAULT POSITION

FIGURE 18–4 The default position for the throttle plate is in slightly open position. The servomotor then is used to close it for idle and open it during acceleration.

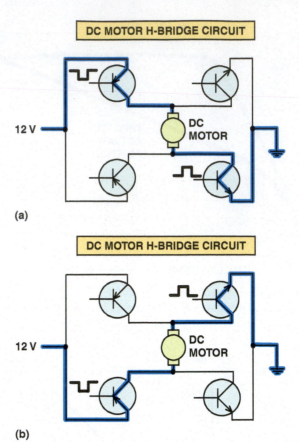

DC MOTOR H-BRIDGE CIRCUIT

12 V — DC MOTOR

(a)

DC MOTOR H-BRIDGE CIRCUIT

12 V — DC MOTOR

(b)

FIGURE 18–5 (a) An H-bridge circuit is used to control the direction of the DC electric motor of the electronic throttle control unit. (b) To reverse the direction of operation, the polarity of the current through the motor is reversed.

The throttle plate motor is driven by a bidirectional pulse-width modulated (PWM) signal from the PCM or electronic throttle control module using an H-bridge circuit. ● **SEE FIGURE 18–5**.

The H-bridge circuit is controlled by the Powertrain Control Module by:

■ Reversing the polarity of power and ground brushes to the DC motor
■ Pulse-width modulating (PWM) the current through the motor

The PCM monitors the position of the throttle from the two throttle position (TP) sensors. The PCM then commands the throttle plate to the desired position. ● **SEE FIGURE 18–6**.

THROTTLE POSITION (TP) SENSOR

Two throttle position sensors are used in the throttle body assembly to provide throttle position signals to the PCM. Two sensors are used as a fail-safe measure and for diagnosis. There are two types of TP sensors used in electronic throttle control systems: potentiometers and Hall-effect.

FREQUENTLY ASKED QUESTION

Why Not Use a Stepper Motor for ETC?

A stepper motor is a type of motor that has multiple windings and is pulsed by a PCM to rotate a certain number of degrees when pulsed. The disadvantage is that a stepper motor is too slow to react compared with a conventional DC electric motor and is the reason a stepper motor is not used in electronic throttle control systems.

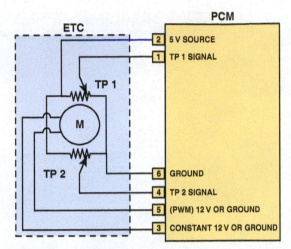

FIGURE 18–6 Schematic of a typical electronic throttle control (ETC) system. Note that terminal #5 is always pulse-width modulated and that terminal #3 is always constant, but both power and ground are switched to change the direction of the motor.

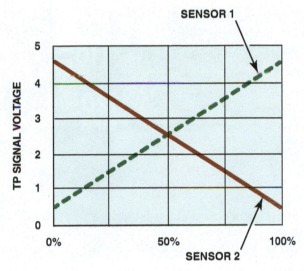

FIGURE 18–7 The two TP sensors used on the throttle body of an electronic throttle body assembly produce opposite voltage signals as the throttle is opened. The total voltage of both combined at any throttle plate position is 5 volts.

THREE-WIRE POTENTIOMETER SENSORS
These sensors use a 5 volt reference from the PCM and produce an analog (variable) voltage signal that is proportional to the throttle plate position. The two sensors produce opposite signals as the throttle plate opens:

- One sensor starts at low voltage (about 0.5 volt) and increases as the throttle plate is opened.
- The second sensor starts at a higher voltage (about 4.5 volt) and produces a lower voltage as the throttle plate is opened. ● SEE FIGURE 18–7.

HALL-EFFECT TP SENSORS
Some vehicle manufacturers such as Honda use a noncontact Hall-effect throttle position sensor. Because there is no physical contact, this type of sensor is less likely to fail due to wear.

DIAGNOSIS OF ELECTRONIC THROTTLE CONTROL SYSTEMS

FAULT MODE Electronic throttle control systems can have faults like any other automatic system. Due to the redundant sensors in accelerator pedal position sensors and throttle position sensors, many faults result in a "limp home" situation instead of a total failure. The limp home mode is also called the "fail-safe mode" and indicates the following actions performed by the Powertrain Control Module:

- Engine speed is limited to the default speed (about 1200 to 1600 RPM).
- There is slow or no response when the accelerator pedal is depressed.
- The cruise control system is disabled.
- A diagnostic trouble code (DTC) is set.
- An ETC warning lamp on the dash will light. The warning lamp may be labeled differently, depending on the vehicle manufacturer. For example:
  - **General Motors vehicle**—Reduced power lamp (● SEE FIGURE 18–8)
  - **Ford**—Wrench symbol (amber or green) (● SEE FIGURE 18–9)
  - **Chrysler**—Red lightning bolt symbol (● SEE FIGURE 18–10)
- The engine will run and can be driven slowly. This limp-in mode operation allows the vehicle to be driven off of the road and to a safe location.

(a)

(b)

FIGURE 18–8 (a) A "reduced power" warning light indicates a fault with the electronic throttle control system on some General Motors vehicles. (b) A symbol showing an engine with an arrow pointing down is used on some General Motors vehicles to indicate a fault with the electronic throttle control system.

The ETC may enter the limp-in mode if any of the following has occurred:

- Low battery voltage has been detected
- PCM failure
- One TP and the MAP sensor have failed
- Both TP sensors have failed
- The ETC actuator motor has failed
- The ETC throttle spring has failed

VACUUM LEAKS The electronic throttle control system is able to compensate for many vacuum leaks. A vacuum leak at the intake manifold, for example, will allow air into the engine

FIGURE 18–9 A wrench symbol warning lamp on a Ford vehicle. The symbol can also be green.

FIGURE 18–10 A symbol used on a Chrysler vehicle indicating a fault with the electronic throttle control.

that is not measured by the mass airflow sensor. The ETC system will simply move the throttle as needed to achieve the proper idle speed to compensate for the leak.

DIAGNOSTIC PROCEDURE If a fault occurs in the ETC system, check service information for the specified procedure to follow for the vehicle being checked. Most vehicle service information includes the following steps:

STEP 1 Verify the customer concern.

STEP 2 Use a factory scan tool or an aftermarket scan tool with original equipment capability and check for diagnostic trouble codes (DTCs).

STEP 3 If there are stored diagnostic trouble codes, follow service information instructions for diagnosing the system.

STEP 4 If there are no stored diagnostic trouble codes, check scan tool data for possible fault areas in the system.

CASE STUDY

The High Idle Toyota

The owner of a Toyota Camry complained that the engine would idle at over 1200 RPM compared with a normal 600 to 700 RPM. The vehicle would also not accelerate. Using a scan tool, a check for diagnostic trouble codes showed one code: P2101—"TAC motor circuit low."

Checking service information led to the inspection of the electronic throttle control throttle body assembly. With the ignition key out of the ignition and the inlet air duct off the throttle body, the technician used a screwdriver to see if the throttle plate worked.

Normal operation—The throttle plate should move and then spring back quickly to the default position.

Abnormal operation—If the throttle plate stays where it is moved or does not return to the default position, there is a fault with the throttle body assembly.
● **SEE FIGURE 18–11**.

The technician replaced the throttle body assembly with an updated version and proper engine operation was restored. The technician disassembled the old throttle body and found it was corroded inside due to moisture entering the unit through the vent hose. ● **SEE FIGURE 18–12**.

Summary:

• **Complaint**—Customer stated that the engine would idle at over 2000 RPM.

• **Cause**—A stored P2101 DTC was stored indicating a fault with the throttle body assembly.

• **Correction**—The throttle body was replaced with an improved version that placed the vent tube in a different position to help avoid water getting into the assembly.

FIGURE 18–11 The throttle plate stayed where it was moved, which indicates that there is a problem with the electronic throttle body control assembly.

FIGURE 18–12 A corroded electronic throttle control assembly shown with the cover removed.

■ **TP sensors 1 and 2.** The scan tool will display "agree" or "disagree." If the PCM or throttle actuator control (TAC) module receives a voltage signal from one of the TP sensors that is not in the proper relationship to the other TP sensor, the scan tool will display *disagree*.

ETC THROTTLE FOLLOWER TEST

On some vehicles, such as many Chrysler vehicles, the operation of the electronic throttle control can be tested using a factory or factory-level scan tool. To perform this test, use the "throttle follower test" procedure as shown on the scan tool. An assistant is needed to check that the throttle plate is moving as the accelerator pedal is depressed. This test cannot be done normally because the PCM does not normally allow the throttle plate to be moved unless the engine is running.

SCAN TOOL DATA Scan data related to the electronic throttle control system can be confusing. Typical data and the meaning include:

■ **APP indicated angle.** The scan tool will display a percentage ranging from 0% to 100%. When the throttle is released, the indicated angle should be 0%. When the throttle is depressed to wide open, the reading should indicate 100%.

■ **TP desired angle.** The scan tool will display a percentage ranging from 0% to 100%. This represents the desired throttle angle as commanded by the driver of the vehicle.

■ **TP indicated angle.** The TP indicated angle is the angle of the measured throttle opening and it should agree with the TP desired angle.

SERVICING ELECTRONIC THROTTLE SYSTEMS

ETC-RELATED PERFORMANCE ISSUES The only service that an electronic throttle control system may require is a cleaning of the throttle body. Throttle body cleaning is a routine service procedure on port fuel-injected engines and is still needed when the throttle is being opened by an electric motor rather than a throttle cable tied to a mechanical accelerator pedal. The throttle body may need cleaning if one or more of the following symptoms are present:

- Lower than normal idle speed
- Rough idle
- Engine stalls when coming to a stop (called a **coast-down stall**)

If any of the above conditions exists, a throttle body cleaning will often correct these faults.

CAUTION: Some vehicle manufacturers add a nonstick coating to the throttle assembly and warn that cleaning could remove this protective coating. Always follow the vehicle manufacturer's recommended procedures.

THROTTLE BODY CLEANING PROCEDURE Before attempting to clean a throttle body on an engine equipped with an electronic throttle control system, be sure that the ignition key is out of the vehicle and the ready light is off if working on a Toyota/Lexus hybrid electric vehicle to avoid the possibility of personal injury.

 WARNING

The electric motor that operates the throttle plate is strong enough to cut off a finger. ● SEE FIGURE 18–13.

To clean the throttle, perform the following steps:

STEP 1 With the ignition off and the key removed from the ignition, remove the air inlet hose from the throttle body.

STEP 2 Spray throttle body cleaner onto a shop cloth.

STEP 3 Open the throttle body and use the shop cloth to remove the varnish and carbon deposits from the throttle body housing and throttle plate.

STEP 4 Reinstall the inlet hose being sure that there are no air leaks between the hose and the throttle body assembly.

FIGURE 18–13 Notice the small motor gear on the left drives a larger plastic gear (black), which then drives the small gear in mesh with the section of a gear attached to the throttle plate. This results in a huge torque increase from the small motor and helps explain why it could be dangerous to insert a finger into the throttle body assembly.

CAUTION: Do not spray cleaner into the throttle body assembly. The liquid cleaner could flow into and damage the throttle position (TP) sensors.

STEP 5 Start the engine and allow the PCM to learn the correct idle. If the idle is not correct, check service information for the specified procedures to follow to perform a throttle relearn.

THROTTLE BODY RELEARN PROCEDURE When installing a new throttle body or Powertrain Control Module or sometimes after cleaning the throttle body, the throttle position has to be learned by the PCM. After the following conditions have been met, a typical throttle body relearn procedure for a General Motors vehicle includes:

- Accelerator pedal released
- Battery voltage higher than 8 volts
- Vehicle speed must be zero
- Engine coolant temperature (ECT) higher than 40°F (5°C) and lower than 212°F (100°C)
- Intake air temperature (IAT) higher than 40°F (5°C)
- No throttle diagnostic trouble codes set

If all of the above conditions are met, perform the following steps:

STEP 1 Turn the ignition on (engine off) for 30 seconds.

STEP 2 Turn the ignition off and wait 30 seconds.

Start the engine and the idle learn procedure should cause the engine to idle at the correct speed.

SUMMARY

1. Using an electronic throttle control (ETC) system on an engine has many advantages over a conventional method that uses a mechanical cable between the accelerator pedal and the throttle valve.

2. The major components of an electronic throttle control system include:
   - Accelerator pedal position (APP) sensor
   - Electronic throttle control actuator motor and spring
   - Throttle position (TP) sensor
   - Electronic control unit

3. The throttle position (TP) sensor is actually two sensors that share the 5 volt reference from the PCM and produce opposite signals as a redundant check.

4. Limp-in mode is commanded if there is a major fault in the system, which can allow the vehicle to be driven enough to be pulled off the road to safety.

5. The diagnostic procedure for the ETC system includes verifying the customer concern, using a scan tool to check for diagnostic trouble codes, and checking the value of the TP and APP sensors.

6. Servicing the ETC system includes cleaning the throttle body and throttle plate.

REVIEW QUESTIONS

1. What parts can be deleted if an engine uses an electronic throttle control (ETC) system instead of a conventional accelerator pedal and cable to operate the throttle valve?

2. How can the use of an ETC system improve fuel economy?

3. How is the operation of the throttle different on a system that uses an ETC system compared with a conventional mechanical system?

4. What component parts are included in an ETC system?

5. What is the default or limp-in position of the throttle plate?

CHAPTER QUIZ

1. The use of an ETC system allows the elimination of all *except* _____.
   a. accelerator pedal
   b. mechanical throttle cable (most systems)
   c. cruise control actuator
   d. idle air control

2. A vehicle with an electronic throttle is idling with the transmission in PARK. When the accelerator pedal is pressed down, the engine does not increase above idle speed. This means_____.
   a. there is a fault with the throttle system
   b. normal operation
   c. the air filter is restricted
   d. the throttle cable is mis-adjusted

3. What type of electric motor is the throttle plate actuator motor?
   a. Stepper motor
   b. DC motor
   c. AC motor
   d. Brushless motor

4. The actuator motor is controlled by the PCM through what type of circuit?
   a. Series
   b. Parallel
   c. H-bridge
   d. Series-parallel

5. When does the PCM perform a self-test of the ETC system?
   a. During cruise speed when the throttle is steady
   b. During deceleration
   c. During acceleration
   d. When the ignition switch is first rotated to the on position before the engine starts

6. What type is the throttle position sensor used in the throttle body assembly of an ETC system?
   a. A single potentiometer
   b. Two potentiometers that read in the opposite direction
   c. A Hall-effect sensor
   d. Either b or c

7. A green wrench symbol is displayed on the dash. What does this mean?
   a. A fault in the ETC in a Ford vehicle has been detected
   b. A fault in the ETC in a Honda vehicle has been detected
   c. A fault in the ETC in a Chrysler vehicle has been detected
   d. A fault in the ETC in a General Motors vehicle has been detected

8. The default position varies depending on the vehicle and usually results in an engine speed of _____.
   a. 1600 to 1800 RPM
   b. 1200 to 1500 RPM
   c. 500 to 600 RPM
   d. 100 to 300 RPM

9. The accelerator pedal position sensor contains _____ separate sensors.
   a. one
   b. two
   c. three
   d. b or c depending on the vehicle

10. The throttle body may be cleaned (if recommended by the vehicle manufacturer) if what conditions are occurring?
    a. Coast-down stall
    b. Rough idle
    c. Lower-than-normal idle speed
    d. Any of the above

chapter 19
OXYGEN SENSORS

LEARNING OBJECTIVES

After studying this chapter, the reader should be able to:

1. Discuss how oxygen sensors (O2S) work.
2. List the methods that can be used to test oxygen sensors.
3. Describe how a wide-band oxygen sensor works and how to test it.

KEY TERMS

Air–fuel ratio sensor 283
Ambient side electrode 270
Bias voltage 272
Closed loop 273
Cup design 270
Dual cell 281
Exhaust side electrode 270
False lean 276
False rich 275
Finger design 270
Fuel trim 273
HO2S 272
Light-off time (LOT) 280
Nernst cell 280

Open loop 273
Oxygen sensors (O2S) 270
Planar 280
Pump cell 281
Reference 281
Reference electrode 270
RTV 279
Signal electrode 270
Single cell 283
Thimble design 270
Titania 272
Wide-band O2S 279
Zirconia 270
ZrO2 270

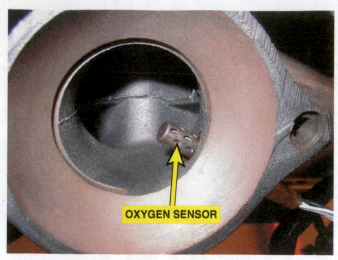

FIGURE 19–1 Many oxygen sensors are located in the exhaust manifold near its outlet so that the sensor can detect the air–fuel mixture in the exhaust stream for all cylinders that feed into the manifold.

OXYGEN SENSORS

PURPOSE AND FUNCTION Automotive computer systems use a sensor in the exhaust system to measure the oxygen content of the exhaust. These sensors are called **oxygen sensors (O2S)**. The oxygen sensor is installed in the exhaust manifold or located downstream from the manifold in the exhaust pipe. ● SEE FIGURE 19–1.

The oxygen sensor is directly in the path of the exhaust gas stream where it monitors oxygen levels in both the exhaust stream and the ambient air. A **zirconia** oxygen sensor is made of **zirconium dioxide (ZrO_2)**, an electrically conductive material capable of generating a small voltage in the presence of oxygen.

NARROW BAND A conventional zirconia oxygen sensor (O2S) is only able to detect if the exhaust is richer or leaner than 14.7:1. A conventional oxygen sensor is therefore referred to as the following:

- *Two-step sensor*, which is either rich or lean
- *Narrow-band sensor*, which informs the PCM whether the exhaust is rich or lean only

The voltage value where a zirconia oxygen sensor switches from rich to lean or from lean to rich is 0.45 V (450 mV).

- Above 0.45 V = rich
- Below 0.45 V = lean
  - ● SEE FIGURE 19–2.

CONSTRUCTION A typical zirconia oxygen sensor has the sensing element in the shape of a thimble; therefore, it is often referred to as one of the following:

- **Thimble design**
- **Cup design**
- Finger design
  - ● SEE FIGURE 19–3.

A typical zirconia oxygen sensor has a heater inside the thimble and does not touch the inside of the sensor. The sensor is similar to a battery that has two electrodes and an electrolyte. The electrolyte is solid and is the zirconia (zirconium dioxide). There are also two porous platinum electrodes, which have the following functions.

- **Exhaust side electrode** is exposed to the exhaust stream.
- **Ambient side electrode** is exposed to outside (ambient) air and is the **signal electrode**, also called the **reference electrode**.
  - ● SEE FIGURE 19–4.

The electrolyte (zirconia) is able to conduct electrons as follows:

- If the exhaust is rich, O_2 from the reference (inner) electrode wants to flow to the exhaust side electrode, which results in the generation of a voltage.
- If the exhaust is lean, O_2 flow is not needed. As a result, there is little if any electron movement and, therefore, no voltage is produced.

OPERATION Exhaust from the engine passes through the end of the sensor where the gases contact the outer side of the thimble. Atmospheric air enters through the other end of the sensor or through the wire of the sensor and contacts the inner side of the thimble. The inner and outer surfaces of the thimble are plated with platinum. The inner surface becomes a negative electrode and the outer surface is a positive electrode. The atmosphere contains a relatively constant 21% of oxygen. Exhaust gases created by burning a rich air–fuel mixture contain little oxygen. Exhaust gases from burning a lean air–fuel mixture contain more oxygen.

Negatively charged oxygen ions are drawn to the thimble where they collect on both the inner and outer surfaces.

Because the oxygen present in the atmosphere exceeds that in the exhaust gases, the air side of the thimble draws more negative oxygen ions than the exhaust side. The difference between the two sides creates an electrical potential, or voltage. When the concentration of oxygen on the exhaust side of the thimble is low, a high voltage (0.60 to 1.0 V) is generated between the electrodes. As the oxygen concentration on the exhaust side increases, the voltage generated drops low (0.0 to 0.3 V).

An O2S does not send a voltage signal until its tip reaches a temperature of about 572°F (300°C). Also, oxygen sensors provide their fastest response to mixture changes at about 1,472°F (800°C). When the engine starts and the O2S is cold, the PCM operates the engine in the open-loop mode, drawing on prerecorded data in the PROM for fuel control on a cold engine, or when O2S output is not within certain limits.

If the exhaust contains very little oxygen, the PCM assumes that the intake charge is rich (too much fuel) and

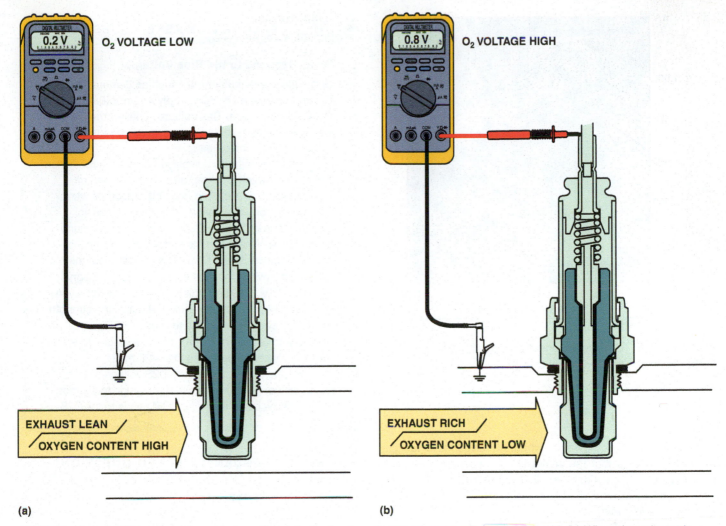

O₂ VOLTAGE LOW

0.2 V

EXHAUST LEAN
OXYGEN CONTENT HIGH

(a)

O₂ VOLTAGE HIGH

0.8 V

EXHAUST RICH
OXYGEN CONTENT LOW

(b)

FIGURE 19–2 (a) When the exhaust is lean, the output of a zirconia oxygen sensor is below 450 mV. (b) When the exhaust is rich, the output of a zirconia oxygen sensor is above 450 mV.

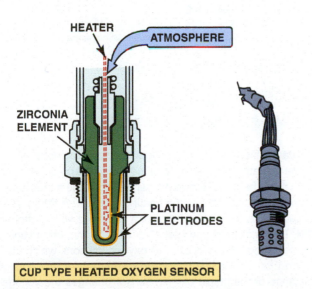

HEATER ATMOSPHERE

ZIRCONIA
ELEMENT

PLATINUM
ELECTRODES

CUP TYPE HEATED OXYGEN SENSOR

FIGURE 19–3 Most conventional zirconia oxygen sensors and some wide-band oxygen sensors use the cup (finger) type of design.

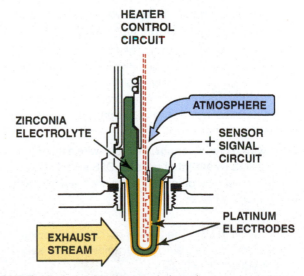

HEATER
CONTROL
CIRCUIT

ATMOSPHERE

ZIRCONIA
ELECTROLYTE

+ SENSOR
− SIGNAL
CIRCUIT

PLATINUM
ELECTRODES

EXHAUST
STREAM

FIGURE 19–4 A typical heated zirconia oxygen sensor, showing the sensor signal circuit that uses the outer (exhaust) electrode as the negative and the ambient air side electrode as the positive.

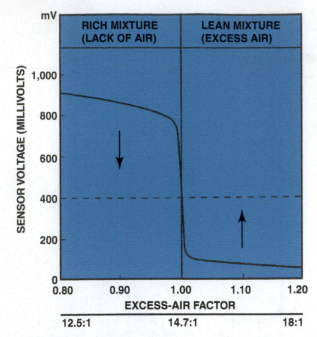

FIGURE 19–5 The oxygen sensor provides a quick response at the stoichiometric air–fuel ratio of 14.7:1.

reduces fuel delivery. However, when the oxygen level is high, the PCM assumes that the intake charge is lean (not enough fuel) and increases fuel delivery. ● **SEE FIGURE 19–5.**

There are several different designs of oxygen sensors, including the following:

- **One-wire oxygen sensor.** The single wire of the one-wire oxygen sensor is the O2S signal wire. The ground for the O2S is through the shell and threads of the sensor and through the exhaust manifold.

- **Two-wire oxygen sensor.** The two-wire sensor has a signal wire and a ground wire for the O2S.

- **Three-wire oxygen sensor.** The three-wire sensor design uses an electric resistance heater to help get the O2S up to temperature more quickly and to help keep the sensor at operating temperature even at idle speeds. The three wires include the O2S signal, the power, and ground for the heater.

- **Four-wire oxygen sensor.** The four-wire sensor is a **heated O2S (HO2S)** that uses an O2S signal wire and signal ground. The other two wires are the power and ground for the heater.

HEATER CIRCUITS The heater circuit on conventional oxygen sensors requires 0.8 to 2.0 amperes and keeps the sensor at about 600°F (315°C).

A wide-band oxygen sensor operates at a higher temperature than a conventional HO2S, from 1,200°F to 1,400°F (650°C to 760°C). The amount of electrical current needed for a wide-band oxygen sensor is about 8 to 10 amperes.

? FREQUENTLY ASKED QUESTION

What Happens to the Bias Voltage?

Some vehicle manufacturers such as General Motors Corporation have the PCM apply 450 mV (0.45 V) to the O2S signal wire. This voltage is called the **bias voltage** and represents the threshold voltage for the transition from rich to lean.

This bias voltage is displayed on a scan tool when the ignition switch is turned on with the engine off. When the engine is started, the O2S becomes warm enough to produce a usable voltage, and bias voltage "disappears" as the O2S responds to a rich and lean mixture. What happens to the bias voltage that the PCM applies to the O2S? The voltage from the O2S simply overcomes the very weak voltage signal from the PCM. This bias voltage is so weak that even a 20 megohm impedance DMM will affect the strength enough to cause the voltage to drop to 426 mV. Other meters with only 10 megohms of impedance will cause the bias voltage to read less than 400 mV.

Therefore, even though the O2S voltage is relatively low powered, it is more than strong enough to override the very weak bias voltage the PCM sends to the O2S.

? FREQUENTLY ASKED QUESTION

Where Is HO2S1?

Oxygen sensors are numbered according to their location in the engine. On a V-type engine, heated oxygen sensor number 1 (HO2S1) is located in the exhaust system upstream of the catalytic converter on the side of the engine where cylinder 1 is located. ● **SEE FIGURE 19–6.**

TITANIA OXYGEN SENSOR

The **titania** (titanium dioxide) oxygen sensor does not produce a voltage but rather changes resistance due to the presence of oxygen in the exhaust. All titania oxygen sensors use a four-terminal variable resistance unit with a heating element. A titania sensor samples exhaust air only and uses a reference voltage from the PCM. Titania oxide oxygen sensors use a 14 mm thread and are not interchangeable with zirconia oxygen sensors, which use an 18 mm thread. One volt is applied to the sensor; the changing resistance of the titania oxygen sensor changes the voltage of the sensor circuit. As with a zirconia oxygen sensor, the voltage signal is above 450 mV when the exhaust is rich and low (below 450 mV) when the exhaust is lean.

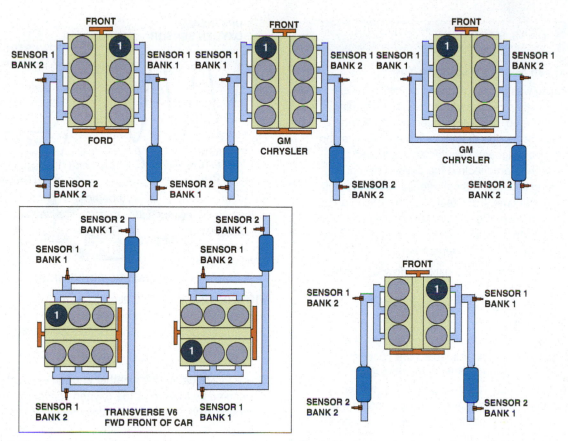

FIGURE 19–6 Number and label designations for oxygen sensors. Bank 1 is the bank where cylinder 1 is located.

PCM USES OF THE OXYGEN SENSOR

FUEL CONTROL The amount of fuel delivered to an engine is determined by the powertrain control module (PCM) based on inputs from the engine coolant temperature (ECT), throttle position (TP) sensor, and others until the oxygen sensor is capable of supplying a usable signal. When the PCM alone is determining the amount of fuel needed, it is called **open-loop** operation. As soon as the oxygen sensor (O2S) is capable of supplying rich and lean signals, PCM adjustments can be made to fine-tune the correct air–fuel mixture. This checking and adjusting of the PCM is called **closed-loop** operation.

The upstream oxygen sensors are among the high-authority senors used for fuel control while operating in closed loop. Before the oxygen sensors are hot enough to give accurate exhaust oxygen information to the PCM, fuel control is determined by other sensors and the anticipated injector pulse width determined by those sensors. After the control system achieves closed-loop status, the oxygen sensor provides feedback to actual exhaust gas oxygen content.

FUEL TRIM The **fuel trim** numbers are determined from the signals by the oxygen sensor(s). If the engine has been operating too lean, short-term and long-term fuel time programming inside the PCM can cause an increase in the commanded injector pulse

 CASE STUDY

The Chevrolet Pickup Truck Story

The owner of a Chevrolet pickup truck complained that the engine ran terribly. It would hesitate and surge, yet there were no diagnostic trouble codes (DTCs). After hours of troubleshooting, the technician discovered while talking to the owner that the problem started after the transmission had been repaired. However, the transmission shop said that the problem was an engine problem and not related to the transmission.

A thorough visual inspection revealed that the front and rear oxygen sensor connectors had been switched. The PCM was trying to compensate for an air–fuel mixture condition that did not exist. Reversing the O2S connectors restored proper operation of the truck.

Summary:
- **Complaint**—Vehicle owner complained that the pickup truck ran terribly.
- **Cause**—During a previous repair, the upstream and downstream oxygen sensor connectors were reversed.
- **Correction**—The connectors were moved to their correct locations which restored proper engine operation.

width to bring the air–fuel mixture back into the proper range. Fuel trim can be negative (subtracting fuel) or positive (adding fuel).

The Oxygen Sensor Is Lying to You

A technician was trying to solve a drivability problem with an older V-6 passenger car. The car idled roughly, hesitated, and accelerated poorly. A thorough visual inspection did not indicate problems and there were no diagnostic trouble codes stored.

The technician checked the oxygen sensor activity using a DMM. The voltage stayed above 600 mV most of the time. If the technician removed a large vacuum hose, the oxygen sensor voltage would temporarily drop to below 450 mV and then return to a reading of over 600 mV. Remember:

- High O2S readings = rich exhaust (low O_2 content in the exhaust)
- Low O2S readings = lean exhaust (high O_2 content in the exhaust)

As part of a thorough visual inspection, the technician removed and inspected the spark plugs. All the spark plugs were white, indicating a lean mixture, not the rich mixture that the oxygen sensor was indicating. The high O2S reading signaled the PCM to reduce the amount of fuel, resulting in an excessively lean operation.

After replacing the oxygen sensor, the engine ran great. But what killed the oxygen sensor? The technician finally learned from the owner that the head gasket had been replaced over a year ago. The silicate and phosphate additives in the antifreeze coolant had coated the oxygen sensor. Because the oxygen sensor was coated, the oxygen content of the exhaust could not be detected, resulting in a false rich signal from the oxygen sensor.

Summary:

- **Complaint**—Vehicle owner complained that the car equipped with a V-6 engine ran terribly.
- **Cause**—The oxygen sensor was contaminated by the additives in the coolant caused by a previously repaired head gasket failure.
- **Correction**—Replacing the oxygen sensors restored proper engine operation.

OXYGEN SENSOR DIAGNOSIS

PCM SYSTEM TESTS The oxygen sensors are used for diagnosis of other systems and components. For example, the exhaust gas recirculation (EGR) system is tested by the PCM, by commanding the EGR valve to open during the test.

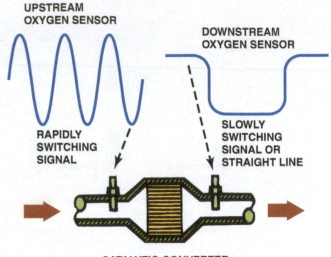

FIGURE 19–7 The OBD-II catalytic converter monitor compares the signals of the upstream and downstream oxygen sensor to determine converter efficiency.

Some PCMs determine whether enough exhaust gas flows into the engine by looking at the oxygen sensor response (fuel trim numbers). The upstream and downstream oxygen sensors are also used to determine the efficiency of the catalytic converter. Therefore, if a fault occurs with an oxygen sensor, the PCM may not be able to test other systems. ● **SEE FIGURE 19–7.**

VISUAL INSPECTION Whenever an oxygen sensor is replaced, the old sensor should be carefully inspected to help determine the cause of the failure. This is an important step because if the cause of the failure is not discovered, it could lead to another sensor failure.

Inspection may reveal the following:

1. Black sooty deposits usually indicate a rich air–fuel mixture.
2. White chalky deposits are characteristic of silica contamination. Usual causes for this type of sensor failure include silica deposits in the fuel or a technician having used the wrong type of silicone sealant during the servicing of the engine.
3. White sandy or gritty deposits are characteristic of antifreeze (ethylene glycol) contamination. A defective cylinder head or intake manifold gasket could be the cause, or a cracked cylinder head or engine block. Antifreeze may also cause the oxygen sensor to become green as a result of the dye used in antifreeze.
4. Dark brown deposits indicate excessive oil consumption. Possible causes include a defective positive crankcase ventilation (PCV) system or a mechanical engine problem such as defective valve stem seals or piston rings.

DIGITAL VOLTMETER TESTING The oxygen sensor can be checked for proper operation using a digital high-impedance voltmeter.

The Missing Ford

A Ford was being analyzed for poor engine operation. The engine ran perfectly during the following conditions:

1. Engine cold or operating in open loop

2. Engine at idle

3. Engine operating at or near wide-open throttle

After hours of troubleshooting, the technician determined the cause to be a poor ground connection for the oxygen sensor. The engine ran okay during times when the PCM ignored the oxygen sensor. Unfortunately, the service technician did not have a definite plan during the diagnostic process and as a result checked and replaced many unnecessary parts. An oxygen sensor test early in the diagnostic procedure would have indicated that the oxygen (O2S) signal was not correct. The poor ground caused the oxygen sensor voltage level to be too high, indicating to the PCM that the mixture was too rich. The PCM then subtracted fuel, which caused the engine to miss and run roughly as the result of the now too lean air–fuel mixture.

Summary:

- **Complaint**—Vehicle owner complained of poor engine operation except at idle and at wide open throttle conditions.
- **Cause**—A poor ground connection for the oxygen sensor causes the O2S to read incorrectly.
- **Correction**—The ground connection was cleaned and this restored proper engine operation under all operating conditions.

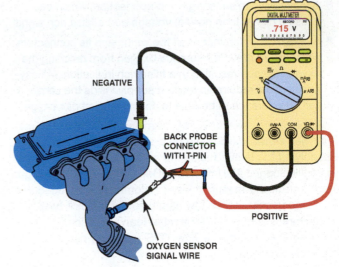

FIGURE 19–8 Testing an oxygen sensor using a DMM set on DC volts. With the engine operating in closed loop, the oxygen voltage should read over 800 mV and lower than 200 mV and be constantly fluctuating.

TECH TIP

Do Not Solder Oxygen Sensor Wires

Oxygen sensors must have outside oxygen to compare with the oxygen content in the exhaust. Most oxygen sensors breathe through the signal wire and, if soldered, would block the flow of outside air to the sensor. If a replacement oxygen sensor is used, always use the factory replacement, using the original connectors or a crimp-and-seal connector that will seal out any moisture and still allow air to flow through the connector.

1. With the engine off, connect the red lead of the meter to the oxygen sensor signal wire and the black meter lead to a good engine ground. ● **SEE FIGURE 19–8.**

2. Start the engine and allow it to reach closed-loop operation.

3. In closed-loop operation, the oxygen sensor voltage should be constantly changing as the fuel mixture is being controlled.

   The results should be interpreted as follows:

   - If the oxygen sensor fails to respond, and its voltage remains at about 450 mV, the sensor may be defective and require replacement. Before replacing the oxygen sensor, check the manufacturer's recommended procedures.
   - If the oxygen sensor reads high all the time (above 550 mV), the fuel system could be supplying too rich

a fuel mixture or the oxygen sensor may be contaminated. An oxygen sensor reading that is high could be due to other things besides a rich air–fuel mixture. When the O2S reads high as a result of other factors besides a rich mixture, it is often called a **false rich** indication.

False rich indications (high O2S readings) can be attributed to the following:

- Contaminated O2S due to additives in the engine coolant or due to silicon poisoning
- A stuck open EGR valve (especially at idle)
- A spark plug wire too close to the oxygen sensor signal wire, which can induce a higher than normal voltage in the signal wire, thereby indicating to the PCM a false rich condition

- A loose oxygen sensor ground connection, which can cause a higher than normal voltage and a false rich signal
- A break or contamination of the wiring and its connectors, which could prevent reference oxygen from reaching the oxygen sensor, resulting in a false rich indication. (All oxygen sensors require an oxygen supply inside the sensor itself for reference to be able to sense exhaust gas oxygen.)

If the oxygen sensor voltage remains low (below 350 mV), the oxygen sensor itself could be bad or the fuel system could be supplying too lean a fuel mixture. Check for a vacuum leak or partially clogged fuel injector(s). Before replacing the oxygen sensor, check the manufacturer's recommended procedures. If an oxygen sensor reads low as a result of a factor besides a lean mixture, it is often called a **false lean** indication.

False lean indications (low O2S readings) can be attributed to the following:

1. **Ignition misfires.** An ignition misfire due to a defective spark plug wire, fouled spark plug, and so forth, causes no burned air and fuel to be exhausted past the O2S. The O2S "sees" the oxygen (not the unburned gasoline) and the O2S voltage is low.

2. **Exhaust leak in front of the O2S.** An exhaust leak between the engine and the oxygen sensor causes outside oxygen to be drawn into the exhaust and past the O2S. This oxygen is "read" by the O2S and produces a lower than normal voltage. The PCM interprets the lower than normal voltage signal from the O2S as meaning that the air–fuel mixture is lean. The PCM will cause the fuel system to deliver a richer air–fuel mixture.

3. **Spark plug misfire.** The PCM does not know that the extra oxygen going past the oxygen sensor is not due to a lean air–fuel mixture. The PCM commands a richer mixture, which could cause the spark plugs to foul, increasing the rate of misfiring.

MIN/MAX TESTING   A digital meter set on DC volts can be used to record the minimum and maximum voltage with the engine running. A good oxygen sensor should be able to produce a value of less than 300 mV and a maximum voltage above 800 mV. ● **SEE FIGURE 19–9.**

Replace any oxygen sensor that fails to go above 700 mV or below 300 mV. ● **SEE CHART 19–1.**

SCAN TOOL TESTING   A good oxygen sensor should sense the oxygen content and change voltage outputs rapidly. How fast an oxygen sensor switches from high (above 450 mV) to low (below 350 mV) is measured as frequency, or the number of times the voltage switches per second.

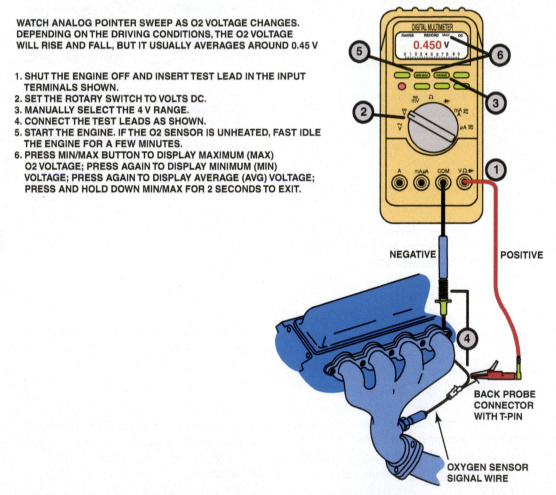

WATCH ANALOG POINTER SWEEP AS O2 VOLTAGE CHANGES. DEPENDING ON THE DRIVING CONDITIONS, THE O2 VOLTAGE WILL RISE AND FALL, BUT IT USUALLY AVERAGES AROUND 0.45 V

1. SHUT THE ENGINE OFF AND INSERT TEST LEAD IN THE INPUT TERMINALS SHOWN.
2. SET THE ROTARY SWITCH TO VOLTS DC.
3. MANUALLY SELECT THE 4 V RANGE.
4. CONNECT THE TEST LEADS AS SHOWN.
5. START THE ENGINE. IF THE O2 SENSOR IS UNHEATED, FAST IDLE THE ENGINE FOR A FEW MINUTES.
6. PRESS MIN/MAX BUTTON TO DISPLAY MAXIMUM (MAX) O2 VOLTAGE; PRESS AGAIN TO DISPLAY MINIMUM (MIN) VOLTAGE; PRESS AGAIN TO DISPLAY AVERAGE (AVG) VOLTAGE; PRESS AND HOLD DOWN MIN/MAX FOR 2 SECONDS TO EXIT.

NEGATIVE   POSITIVE

BACK PROBE CONNECTOR WITH T-PIN

OXYGEN SENSOR SIGNAL WIRE

FIGURE 19–9 Using a digital multimeter to test an oxygen sensor using the MIN/MAX record function of the meter.

MIN/MAX OXYGEN SENSOR TEST CHART

MINIMUM VOLTAGE	MAXIMUM VOLTAGE	AVERAGE VOLTAGE	TEST RESULTS
Below 200 mV	Above 800 mV	400–500 mV	Oxygen sensor is okay.
Above 200 mV	Any reading	400–500 mV	Oxygen sensor is defective.
Any reading	Below 800 mV	400–500 mV	Oxygen sensor is defective.
Below 200 mV	Above 800 mV	Below 400 mV	System is operating lean.[*]
Below 200 mV	Below 800 mV	Below 400 mV	System is operating lean. (Add propane to the intake air to see if the oxygen sensor reacts. If not, the sensor is defective.)
Below 200 mV	Above 800 mV	Above 500 mV	System is operating rich.
Above 200 mV	Above 800 mV	Above 500 mV	System is operating rich. (Remove a vacuum hose to see if the oxygen sensor reacts. If not, the sensor is defective.)

CHART 19–1

The test results of using a digital meter set to read minimum and maximum values while testing a narrow-band oxygen sensor.
[*] Check for an exhaust leak upstream from the O2S or ignition misfire that can cause a false lean indication before further diagnosis.

 FREQUENTLY ASKED QUESTION

Why Does the Oxygen Sensor Voltage Read 5 Volts on Many Chrysler Vehicles?

Many Chrysler vehicles apply a 5 v reference to the signal wire of the oxygen sensor. The purpose of this voltage is to allow the PCM to detect if the oxygen sensor signal circuit is open or grounded.

- If the voltage on the signal wire is 4.5 v or more, the PCM assumes that the sensor is open.
- If the voltage on the signal wire is zero, the PCM assumes that the sensor is shorted-to-ground.

    If either condition exists, the PCM can set a diagnostic trouble code (DTC).

NOTE: On a fuel-injected engine at 2000 engine RPM, 1 to 5 Hz (one to five switches per second) is normal.

Using a scan tool, observe the oxygen sensor voltages with the engine running at 2000 RPM. Look for numbers higher than 800 mV and lower than 200 mV.

If the frequency of switching is low, the oxygen sensor may be contaminated, or the fuel delivery system is delivering a constant rich or lean air–fuel mixture. If the frequency of switching is higher than 5 Hz, look for misfire conditions.

1. Connect the scan tool and start the engine.
2. Operate the engine at a fast idle (2500 RPM) for two minutes to allow time for the oxygen sensor to warm to operating temperature.
3. Observe the oxygen sensor activity on the scan tool to verify closed-loop operation. Select the "snapshot" mode, hold the engine speed steady, and start recording.
4. Play back snapshot and place a mark beside each range of oxygen sensor voltage for each frame of the snapshot.

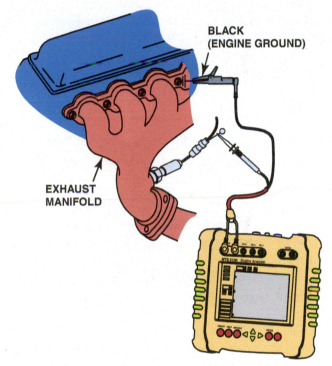

FIGURE 19–10 Connecting a handheld digital storage oscilloscope to an oxygen sensor signal wire. Check the instructions for the scope as some require a filter to be installed in the test lead to reduce electromagnetic interference, which can affect the oxygen sensor waveform.

A good oxygen sensor and PCM should result in the most snapshot values at both ends (0 to 300 mV and 600 to 1,000 mV). If most of the readings are in the middle, the oxygen sensor is not working correctly.

SCOPE TESTING A scope can also be used to test an oxygen sensor. Connect the scope to the signal wire and ground for the sensor (if it is so equipped). ● **SEE FIGURE 19–10.**

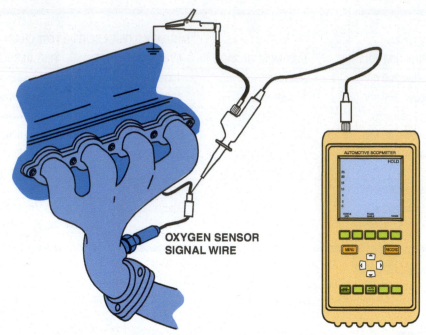

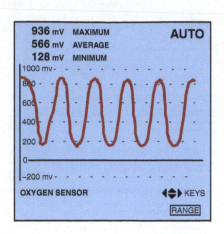

936 mV MAXIMUM
566 mV AVERAGE
128 mV MINIMUM

AUTO

1000 mv
800
600
400
200
0
−200 mv

OXYGEN SENSOR

KEYS

RANGE

OXYGEN SENSOR
SIGNAL WIRE

FIGURE 19–11 The waveform of a good oxygen sensor as displayed on a digital storage oscilloscope (DSO). Note that the maximum reading is above 800 mV and the minimum reading is less than 200 mV.

 TECH TIP

The Key On, Engine Off Oxygen Sensor Test

This test works on General Motors vehicles and may work on others if the PCM applies a bias voltage to the oxygen sensors. Zirconia oxygen sensors become more electrically conductive as they get hot. To perform this test, be sure that the vehicle has not run for several hours.

STEP 1 Connect a scan tool and get the display ready to show oxygen sensor data.

STEP 2 Key the engine on without starting the engine. The heater in the oxygen sensor will start heating the sensor.

STEP 3 Observe the voltage of the oxygen sensor. The applied bias voltage of 450 mV should slowly decrease for all oxygen sensors as they become more electrically conductive as the bias voltage is flowing to ground.

STEP 4 A good oxygen sensor should indicate a voltage of less than 100 mV after three minutes. Any sensor that displays a higher than usual voltage or seems to stay higher longer than the others could be defective or skewed high.

With the engine operating in closed loop, the voltage signal of the sensor should be constantly changing. ● **SEE FIGURE 19–11.**

Check for rapid switching from rich to lean and lean to rich and change between once every two seconds and five times per second (0.5 to 5.0 Hz).

NOTE: General Motors warns not to base the diagnosis of an oxygen sensor problem solely on its scope pattern. The varying voltage output of an oxygen sensor can easily be mistaken for a fault in the sensor itself, rather than a fault in the fuel delivery system.

POST-CATALYTIC CONVERTER OXYGEN SENSOR TESTING

The oxygen sensor located behind the catalytic converter is used on OBD-II vehicles to monitor converter efficiency. A changing air–fuel mixture is required for the most efficient operation of the converter. If the converter is working correctly, the oxygen content after the converter should be fairly constant. ● **SEE FIGURE 19–12.**

The post-catalytic converter oxygen sensor is also used to modify the amount of fuel delivered to the engine to allow the converter to work efficiently. If, for example, the rear oxygen

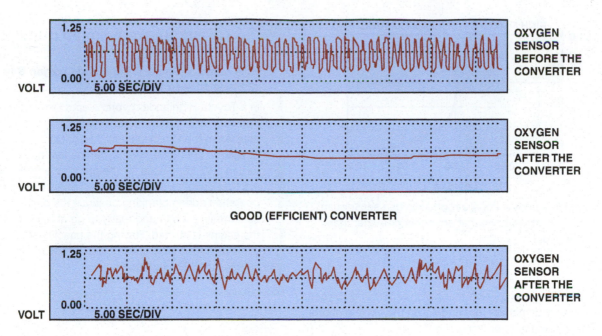

FIGURE 19–12 The post-catalytic converter oxygen sensor should display very little activity if the catalytic converter is efficient.

sensor voltage stayed high, the PCM will try to increase the amount of oxygen entering the converter by leaning the air–fuel mixture to the engine. This process is often called the target upstream fuel trim. Therefore, instead of the PCM commanding a target air–fuel mixture of 14.7:1, the new target may specify an air–fuel ratio of 14.9:1 or slightly leaner than normal to help provide a little extra oxygen for use by the catalytic converter. This target air–fuel ratio or fuel trim is displayed on scan tools.

WIDE-BAND OXYGEN SENSORS

TERMINOLOGY Honda was the first manufacturer to use **wide-band oxygen sensors** beginning in 1992. Today, they are used by most vehicle manufacturers to ensure that the exhaust

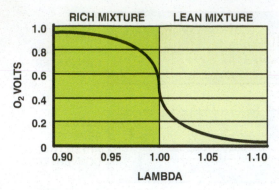

FIGURE 19–13 A conventional zirconia oxygen sensor can only reset to exhaust mixtures that are richer or leaner than 14.7:1 (lambda 1.00).

? FREQUENTLY ASKED QUESTION

How Quickly Can a Wide-Band Oxygen Sensor Achieve Closed Loop?

In a Toyota Highlander hybrid electric vehicle, the operation of the gasoline engine is delayed for a short time when the vehicle is first driven. During this time of electric operation, the oxygen sensor heaters are turned on in readiness for the gasoline engine starting. The gasoline engine often achieves closed-loop operation during cranking because the oxygen sensors are fully warm and ready to go at the same time the engine is started. Having the gasoline engine achieve closed loop quickly, allows it to meet the stringent SULEV standards.

emissions can meet the current standard. Wide-band oxygen sensors have various names, depending on the vehicle and/or oxygen sensor manufacturer, including:

- Wide-band oxygen sensor
- Broadband oxygen sensor
- Wide-range oxygen sensor
- Air–fuel ratio (AFR) sensor
- Wide-range air–fuel (WRAF) sensor
- Lean-air fuel (LAF) sensor
- Air–fuel (AF) sensor

Wide-band oxygen sensors are also manufactured in dual cell and single cell designs.

INTRODUCTION A conventional zirconia oxygen sensor reacts to an air–fuel mixture that is either richer or leaner than 14.7:1. This means that the sensor cannot be used to detect the exact air–fuel mixture. ● **SEE FIGURE 19–13.**

The need for more stringent exhaust emission standards, such as the national low-emission vehicle (NLEV), plus the ultra low-emission vehicle (ULEV) and the super-ultra low-emission vehicle (SULEV), requires more accurate fuel control than can be provided by a traditional oxygen sensor.

PURPOSE AND FUNCTION A wide-band oxygen sensor is capable of supplying air–fuel ratio information to the PCM over a much broader range. Compared with a conventional zirconia oxygen sensor, the wide-band oxygen sensor has the following features:

1. The ability to detect exhaust air–fuel ratio from as rich as 10:1 to as lean as 23:1 in some cases
2. Cold start activity within as little as 10 seconds

PLANAR DESIGN In 1998, Bosch introduced a wide-band oxygen sensor that is flat and thin (1.5 mm or 0.006 in.), known as a planar design and not in the shape of a thimble as previously constructed. Now several manufacturers produce a

similar **planar** design wide-band oxygen sensor. Its thin design makes it easier to heat than older styles of oxygen sensors and, as a result, it can achieve closed loop in less than 10 seconds. This fast heating, called **light-off time (LOT)**, helps improve fuel economy and reduces cold-start exhaust emissions. The type of construction is not noticed by the technician, nor does it affect the testing procedures.

A conventional oxygen sensor can also be constructed using a planar design instead of the thimble-type design. A planar design has the following features:

- The elements including the zirconia electrolyte and the two electrodes and heater are stacked together in a flat-type design.
- It allows faster warm-up because the heater is in direct contact with the other elements.
- Planar oxygen sensors are the most commonly used. Some planar designs are used as a conventional narrow-band oxygen sensor.

The sandwich-type designs of the planar style of oxygen sensor have the same elements and operate the same, but are stacked in the following way from the exhaust side to the ambient air side:

Exhaust stream

Outer electrode

Zirconia (Zr_2) (electrolyte)

Inner electrode (reference or signal)

Outside (ambient) air

Heater
● **SEE FIGURE 19–14.**

NOTE: Another name for a conventional oxygen sensor is a Nernst cell, named for Walther Nernst, 1864–1941, a German physicist known for his work in electrochemistry.

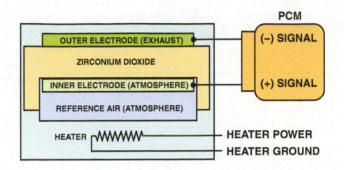

FIGURE 19–14 A planar design zirconia oxygen sensor places all of the elements together, which allows the sensor to reach operating temperature quickly.

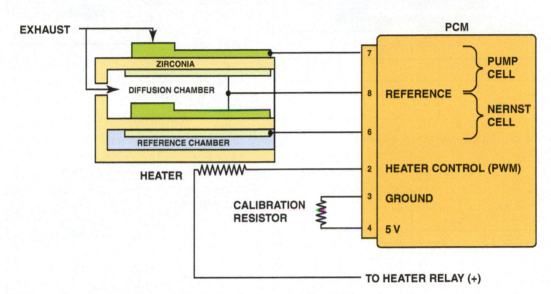

FIGURE 19–15 The reference electrodes are shared by the Nernst cell and the pump cell.

DUAL CELL PLANAR WIDE-BAND SENSOR OPERATION

CONSTRUCTION In a conventional zirconia oxygen sensor, a bias or reference voltage can be applied to the two platinum electrodes, and then oxygen ions can be forced (pumped) from the ambient reference air side to the exhaust side of the sensor. If the polarity is reversed, the oxygen ion can be forced to travel in the opposite direction.

A **dual cell** planar-type wide-band oxygen sensor is made like a conventional planar O2S, or Nernst cell. Above the Nernst cell is another zirconia layer with two electrodes, called the **pump cell**. The two cells share a common ground, called the **reference**. There are two internal chambers:

- The air reference chamber is exposed to ambient air.
- The diffusion chamber is exposed to the exhaust gases.

Platinum electrodes are on both sides of the zirconia electrolyte elements, which separate the air reference chamber and the exhaust exposed diffusion chamber.

OPERATION The basic principle of operation of a typical wide-band oxygen sensor is that it uses a positive or negative voltage signal to keep a balance between two sensors. Oxygen sensors do not measure the quantity of free oxygen in the exhaust. Instead, oxygen sensors produce a voltage that is based on the ion flow between the platinum electrodes of the sensor to maintain a stoichiometric balance.

For example:

- If there is a lean exhaust, there is oxygen in the exhaust and the ion flow from the ambient side to the exhaust side is low.
- If there is rich exhaust, the ion flow is increased to help maintain balance between the ambient air side and the exhaust side of the sensor.

The PCM can apply a small current to the pump cell electrodes, which causes oxygen ions through the zirconia into or out of the diffusion chamber. The PCM pumps O_2 ions in and out of the diffusion chamber to bring the voltage back to 0.45 V, using the pump cell.

The operation of a wide-band oxygen sensor is best described by looking at what occurs when the exhaust is stoichiometric, rich, and lean. ● **SEE FIGURE 19–15.**

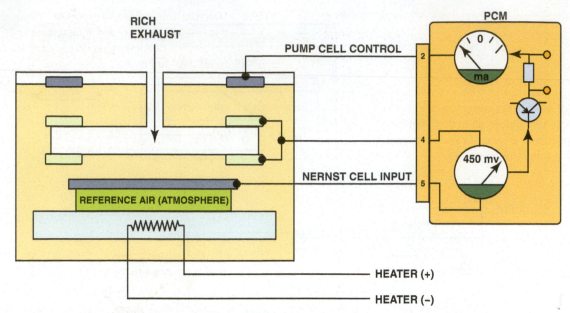

FIGURE 19–16 When the exhaust is rich, the PCM applies a negative current into the pump cell.

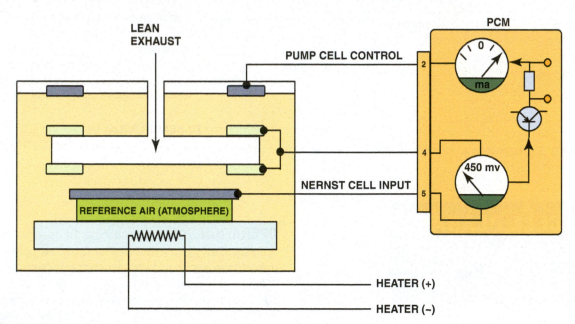

FIGURE 19–17 When the exhaust is lean, the PCM applies a positive current into the pump cell.

STOICHIOMETRIC

- When the exhaust is at stoichiometric (14.7:1 air–fuel ratio), the voltage of the Nernst cell is 450 mV (0.45 V).
- The voltage between the diffusion chamber and the air reference chamber changes from 0.45 V. This voltage will be:
  - Higher if the exhaust is rich
  - Lower if the exhaust is lean

The reference voltage remains constant, usually at 2.5 V, but can vary depending on the year of manufacture, make, and model of vehicle and the type of sensor. Typical reference voltages include:

- 2.2 V
- 2.5 V
- 2.7 V
- 3.3 V
- 3.6 V

RICH EXHAUST. When the exhaust is rich, the voltage between the common (reference) electrode and the Nernst cell electrode that is exposed to ambient air is higher than 0.45 V. The PCM applies a negative current in milliamperes to the pump cell electrode to bring the circuit back into balance. ● **SEE FIGURE 19–16.**

LEAN EXHAUST. When the exhaust is lean, the voltage between the common (reference) electrode and the Nernst cell electrode is lower than 0.45 V. The PCM applies a positive current in milliamperes to the pump cell to bring the circuit back into balance. ● **SEE FIGURE 19–17.**

FACTORY SCAN TOOL	OBD II SCAN TOOL	AIR–FUEL RATIO
2.50 V	0.50 V	12.5:1
3.00 V	0.60 V	14.0:1
3.30 V	0.66 V	14.7:1
3.50 V	0.70 V	15.5:1
4.00 V	0.80 V	18.5:1

CHART 19–2

A comparison showing what a factory scan tool and a generic OBD-II scan tool might display at various air–fuel ratios.

DUAL CELL DIAGNOSIS

SCAN TOOL DIAGNOSIS   Most service information specifies that a scan tool be used to check the wide-band oxygen sensor, because the PCM performs tests of the unit and can identify faults. However, even wide-band oxygen sensors can be fooled if there is an exhaust manifold leak or other fault, which could lead to false or inaccurate readings. If the oxygen sensor reading is false, the PCM will command an incorrect amount of fuel. The scan data shown on a generic (global) OBD-II scan tool will often be different than the reading on the factory scan tool. ● **SEE CHART 19–2** for an example of a Toyota wide-band oxygen sensor being tested using a factory scan tool and a generic OBD-II scan tool.

SCAN TOOL DATA (PID)   The following information will be displayed as a scan tool when looking at data for a wide-band oxygen sensor.

H02S1 = _____ mA ÷	If the current is positive, this means that the PCM is pumping current in the diffusion gap due to a rich exhaust. If the current is negative, the PCM is pumping current out of the diffusion gap due to a lean exhaust.
Air–fuel ratio = _____	Usually expressed in lambda. One means that the exhaust is at stoichiometric (14.7:1 air–fuel ratio) and numbers higher than one indicate a lean exhaust and numbers lower than one indicate a rich exhaust.

DIGITAL METER TESTING   When testing a wide-band oxygen sensor for proper operation, perform the following steps:

STEP 1   Check service information and determine the circuit and connector terminal identification.

STEP 2   Measure the calibration resistor. While the value of this resistor can vary widely, depending on the type of sensor, the calibrating resistor should still be checked for opens and shorts.

NOTE: The calibration resistor is usually located within the connector itself.

- If open, the ohmmeter will read OL (infinity ohms).
- If shorted, the ohmmeter will read zero or close to zero.

STEP 3   Measure the heater circuit for proper resistance or current flow.

STEP 4   Measure the reference voltage relative to ground. This can vary but is generally 2.4 to 2.6 V.

STEP 5   Using jumper wires, connect an ammeter and measure the current in the pump cell control wire.

RICH EXHAUST   When the exhaust is rich (lambda less than 1.00), the Nernst cell voltage will move higher than 0.45 V. The PCM will pump oxygen from the exhaust into the diffusion gap by applying a negative voltage to the pump cell.

LEAN EXHAUST   When the exhaust is lean (lambda higher than 1.00), the Nernst cell voltage will move lower than 0.45 V. The PCM will pump oxygen out of the diffusion gap by applying a positive voltage to the pump cell.

Pump cell is used to pump oxygen into the diffusion gap when the exhaust is rich. The pump cell applies a negative voltage to do this.

- Positive current = lean exhaust
- Negative current = rich exhaust
- ● **SEE FIGURE 19–18.**

SINGLE CELL WIDE-BAND OXYGEN SENSORS

CONSTRUCTION   A typical **single cell** wide-band oxygen sensor looks similar to a conventional four-wire zirconia oxygen sensor. The typical single cell wide-band oxygen sensor, usually called an **air–fuel ratio sensor**, has the following construction features:

- It can be made using the cup or planar design.
- Oxygen (O_2) is pumped into the diffusion layer similar to the operation of a dual cell wide-band oxygen sensor. ● **SEE FIGURE 19–19.**
- Current flow reverses positive and negative.
- There are two cell wires and two heater wires (power and ground).
- The heater usually requires 6 amperes and the ground side is pulse-width modulated.

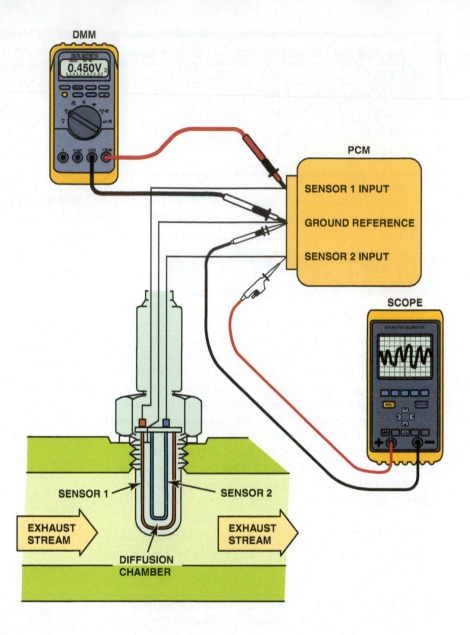

FIGURE 19–18 Testing a dual cell wide-band oxygen sensor can be done using a voltmeter or a scope. The meter reading is attached to the Nernst cell (sensor 1) and should read stoichiometric (450 mV) at all times. The scope is showing activity to the pump cell (sensor 2) with commands from the PCM to keep the Nernst cell at 14.7:1 air–fuel ratio.

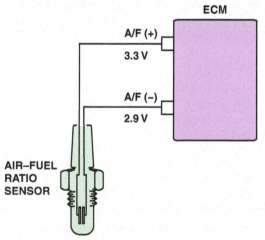

FIGURE 19–19 A single cell wide-band oxygen sensor has four wires with two for the heater and two for the sensor itself. The voltage applied to the sensor is 0.4 V (3.3 − 2.9 = 0.4) across the two leads of the sensor.

MILLIAMMETER TESTING

The PCM controls the single cell wide-band oxygen sensor by maintaining a voltage difference of 300 mV (0.3 V) between the two sensor leads. The PCM keeps the voltage difference constant under all operating conditions by increasing or decreasing current between the element of the cell.

- Zero (0 mA) represents lambda or stoichiometric air–fuel ratio of 14.7:1
- +10 mA indicates a lean condition
- −10 mA indicates a rich condition

SCAN TOOL TESTING

A scan tool will display a voltage reading, which can vary depending on the type and maker of the scan tool. ● **SEE FIGURE 19–20.**

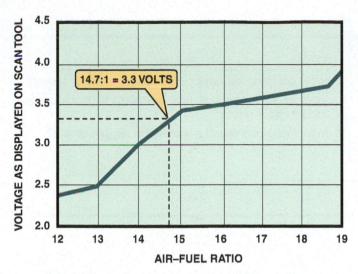

FIGURE 19–20 The scan can display various voltages but will often show 3.3 V because the PCM is controlling the sensor through applying a low current to the sensor to achieve balance.

WIDE-BAND OXYGEN PATTERN FAILURES

Wide-band oxygen sensors have a long life, but they can fail. Most of the failures will cause a diagnostic trouble code (DTC) to set, usually causing the malfunction indicator (check engine) lamp to light.

However, one type of failure may not set a DTC, such as when the following occur:

1. Voltage from the heater circuit bleeds into the Nernst cell.

2. This voltage will cause the engine to operate extremely lean and may or may not set a diagnostic trouble code.

3. When testing indicates an extremely lean condition, unplug the connector to the oxygen sensor. If the engine starts to operate correctly with the sensor unplugged, this is confirmation that the wide-band oxygen sensor has failed and requires replacement.

OXYGEN SENSOR-RELATED DIAGNOSTIC TROUBLE CODES

Diagnostic trouble codes (DTCs) associated with the oxygen sensor include the following:

Diagnostic Trouble Codes	Description	Possible Causes
P0131	Upstream HO2S grounded	• Exhaust leak upstream of HO2S (bank 1) • Extremely lean air–fuel mixture • HO2S defective or contaminated • HO2S signal wire shorted-to-ground
P0132	Upstream HO2S shorted	• Upstream HO2S (bank 1) shorted • Defective HO2S • Fuel-contaminated HO2S
P0133	Upstream HO2S slow response	• Open or short in heater circuit • Defective or fuel-contaminated HO2S • EGR or fuel system fault

SUMMARY

1. An oxygen sensor produces a voltage output signal based on the oxygen content of the exhaust stream.

2. If the exhaust has little oxygen, the voltage of the oxygen sensor will be close to 1 volt (1,000 mV) and close to zero if there is high oxygen content in the exhaust.

3. Oxygen sensors can have one, two, three, four, or more wires, depending on the style and design.

4. A wide-band oxygen sensor, also called a lean air–fuel (LAF) or linear air–fuel ratio sensor, can detect air–fuel ratios from as rich as 12:1 to as lean as 22:1.

5. The oxygen sensor signal determines fuel trim, which is used to tailor the air–fuel mixture for the catalytic converter.

6. Conditions can occur that cause the oxygen sensor to be fooled and give a false lean or false rich signal to the PCM.

7. Oxygen sensors can be tested using a digital meter, scope, or scan tool.

REVIEW QUESTIONS

1. How does an oxygen sensor detect oxygen levels in the exhaust?

2. What is the difference between open-loop and closed-loop engine operation?

3. What are the three ways oxygen sensors can be tested?

4. Why would an exhaust leak upstream from the oxygen sensor cause issues?

5. What is the purpose of a wide-band oxygen sensor?

CHAPTER QUIZ

1. The voltage output of a zirconia oxygen sensor when the exhaust stream is lean (excess oxygen) is _____.
   a. relatively high (close to 1 volt)
   b. about in the middle of the voltage range
   c. relatively low (close to 0 volt)
   d. either a or b, depending on atmospheric pressure

2. A high O2S voltage could be due to a _____.
   a. rich exhaust
   b. lean exhaust
   c. defective spark plug wire
   d. both a and c

3. A low O2S voltage could be due to a _____.
   a. rich exhaust
   b. lean exhaust
   c. defective spark plug wire
   d. both b and c

4. An oxygen sensor is being tested with a digital multimeter (DMM), using the MIN/MAX function. The readings are: minimum = 78 mV; maximum = 932 mV; average = 442 mV. Technician A says that the engine is operating correctly. Technician B says that the oxygen sensor is skewed too rich. Which technician is correct?
   a. Technician A only
   b. Technician B only
   c. Both Technicians A and B
   d. Neither Technician A nor B

5. An oxygen sensor is being tested using a digital storage oscilloscope (DSO). A good oxygen sensor should display how many transitions (switches) per second?
   a. 1 to 5
   b. 5 to 10
   c. 10 to 15
   d. 15 to 20

6. A wide-band oxygen sensor was first used on a Honda in what model year?
   a. 1992
   b. 1996
   c. 2000
   d. 2006

7. A wide-band oxygen sensor is capable of detecting the air–fuel mixture in the exhaust from _____ (rich) to _____ (lean).
   a. 12:1; 15:1
   b. 13:1; 16.7:1
   c. 10:1; 23:1
   d. 8:1; 18:1

8. A wide-band oxygen sensor needs to be heated to what operating temperature?
   a. 600°F (315°C)
   b. 800°F (427°C)
   c. 1,400°F (760°C)
   d. 2,000°F (1,093°C)

9. A wide-band oxygen sensor heater could draw how much current (amperes)?
   a. 0.8 to 2 A
   b. 2 to 4 A
   c. 6 to 8 A
   d. 8 to 10 A

10. A P0133 DTC is being discussed. Technician A says that a defective heater circuit could be the cause. Technician B says that a contaminated sensor could be the cause. Which technician is correct?
    a. Technician A only
    b. Technician B only
    c. Both Technicians A and B
    d. Neither Technician A nor B

chapter 20
FUEL TRIM DIAGNOSIS

LEARNING OBJECTIVES

After studying this chapter, the reader should be able to:

1. Explain the purpose and function of fuel trim.
2. Discuss the difference between speed density and mass air flow fuel control.
3. Explain how the PCM determines the base injector pulse width.
4. Compare short-term and long-term fuel trim.
5. Explain how fuel trim can aid in diagnosis.
6. List factors that can affect the accuracy of the mass air flow sensor.
7. Describe how knowing the volumetric efficiency of the engine can help diagnose engine performance concerns.

KEY TERMS

Alpha 293
Base pulse width 288
Equivalence ratio (ER) 288
Fuel trim 288
Fuel trim cells 292
Lambda 288
Long-term fuel trim (LTFT) 291
Short-term fuel trim (STFT) 290
Stoichiometric 288
Volumetric efficiency (VE) 295

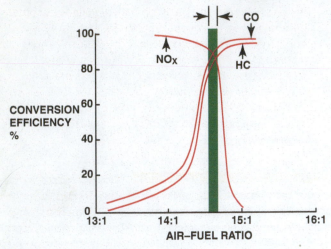

FIGURE 20–1 The catalytic converter is most efficient when the exhaust ratio is closest to 14.7:1.

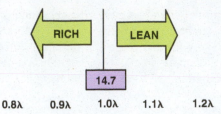

FIGURE 20–2 Shown is lambda. The equivalence ratio is opposite lambda.

Most new vehicles are designed to operate between 0.98 and 1.02 lambda or, stated another way, within 2% of stoichiometric.

EQUIVALENCE RATIO The equivalence ratio (ER) is the inverse of lambda, with 1.0 equal to 1.0 lambda; however, 0.9 ER is equal to 1.1 lambda. Equivalence ratio (ER) = $1/\lambda$ (lambda), which is the inverse of lambda. Therefore, a rich air–fuel mixture has an equivalence ratio of greater than 1 and a lean mixture less than 1. ● **SEE FIGURE 20–2.**

NOTE: Engineers and many technical articles of fuel trim use equivalence ratios instead of lambda.

BASE PULSE WIDTH

PURPOSE AND FUNCTION The base pulse width is the injector pulse width that is calculated by the PCM using information from sensors before the oxygen sensor(s) is operating and supplying air–fuel ratio information. The PCM uses information from the following sensors to determine the base pulse width for the fuel injectors.

- RPM (engine speed)
- Manifold absolute pressure (MAP) or mass air flow (MAF)
- BARO (altitude)
- Throttle position (TPS)
- Engine coolant temperature (ECT) (used mostly when the engine is cold)
- Intake air temperature (IAT)
- Battery voltage B+
- Amount of exhaust gas (EGR) or (VVT)
- Canister purge flow amount

A general formula for the calculation is:

$$((\textbf{RPM} \times \textbf{MAP or MAF}/\textbf{BARO}) \times (\textbf{ECT} \times \textbf{TPS}) \times$$
$$(\textbf{IAT} \times \textbf{B+})) \times \textbf{O2} \times (\textbf{STFT} \times \textbf{LTFT})$$

The cam and crank sensors are used to determine how fast the engine is turning (RPM). The barometer reading (BARO) and the manifold absolute pressure (MAP) sensor or the mass air flow (MAF) sensors are used to determine the amount and the density of air entering the engine. These

FUEL TRIM

PURPOSE AND FUNCTION The Powertrain Control Module (PCM) does not measure or check the air–fuel mixture entering the cylinders. Instead, the PCM measures the air mass, and then calculates the amount of fuel needed. Fuel trim provides a method that is capable of changing the amount of fuel delivered to the engine based on feedback from the oxygen sensors. The primary purpose of the fuel trim is to keep the air–fuel mixture as close to 14.7:1 as possible. When the air–fuel ratio is kept at 14.7:1, the efficiency of the catalytic converter is the highest, which results in the lowest possible exhaust emissions. ● **SEE FIGURE 20–1.**

LAMBDA Lambda is a Greek letter used to represent ratio, as in air–fuel ratio. If an engine is operating at exactly 14.7:1, the air–fuel ratio on gasoline, the ratio is called **stoichiometric** and is assigned a lambda of 1.0.

- Air–fuel ratios lower than 1.0 indicate a rich mixture.
- Air–fuel ratios higher than 1.0 indicate a lean mixture.

To determine the air–fuel ratio if lambda is given, multiply lambda times 14.7.

Example 1:

A lambda of 1.05 means that the engine is operating 5% lean and has an air–fuel mixture of 15.4:1 ($14.7 \times 1.05 = 15.4$).

Example 2:

A lambda of 0.97 means that the engine is operating 3% rich and has an air–fuel mixture of 14.3:1 ($0.97 \times 1.47 = 14.28$).

The usual lambda limits include:

- 0.9 lambda (13.2:1) is 10% rich and results in maximum power.
- 1.15 lambda (16.9:1) is 15% lean; in this case, a lean misfire is likely to occur.

values together generate a base load calculation. The engine coolant temperature (ECT) sensor and the throttle position sensor (TPS) are major modifiers to the base load calculation. The intake air temperature (IAT) and battery voltage (B+) are minor modifiers to the base load calculation. Other factors, such as purge flow and exhaust gasses, are considered. The fuel is injected into the cylinder. After the combustion process, the oxygen sensor (O2) is used to determine how much oxygen is left in the exhaust stream. The PCM uses the feedback from the O2 sensor to adjust short-term fuel trim (STFT) and long-term fuel trim (LTFT) values to achieve the stoichiometric ratio target.

SPEED DENSITY MODIFIER

Besides the MAP sensor, other sensors are used to fine-tune or modify the mathematical calculations needed to determine the injector pulse width. The input sensors that affect fuel trim in a speed density system include:

BARO. The BARO sensor or MAP sensor reading at key on determines the atmospheric pressure.

IAT. The intake air temperature (IAT) sensor measures the temperature of the air entering the engine. The PCM uses this information to calculate the density of the air.

RPM. All speed density calculations need the speed of the engine to calculate injector pulse width.

EGR. The PCM needs to determine the amount of exhaust gases being recirculated into the intake manifold to make an accurate measurement of air mass entering the cylinders. Various vehicle designs are used for this calculation and include one or more of the following:

- EGR valve pintle position
- EGR passage temperature sensor
- Pressure differential in the EGR passage
- ECT. The engine coolant temperature is used to add fuel when the engine is cold, but has little effect on fuel trim after the engine has been run for a while on newer vehicles.
- TP sensor. The PCM uses the position of the throttle in three places to determine basic calculations.

These three positions are:

- Idle
- Cruise
- Wide-open throttle (WOT)

The TP sensor is also monitored for rate of change. If the throttle is rapidly depressed, this indicates that a large gulp of air is going to be entering the engine and additional fuel will need to be provided up to about five times (500%) more than normal. If the throttle is rapidly released, the fuel needs to be removed (fuel cut off) from the cylinders to keep the engine from stalling.

- Battery voltage correction. The PCM attempts to keep the emissions low and protect the catalytic converter and

the engine from damage. If the battery voltage becomes lower than normal, the fuel injectors will be slower to open and, as a result, deliver less than the calculated amount of fuel. Therefore, the PCM uses a program called *battery voltage correction* that adds time to the injector pulse width if battery voltage is low. This correction will prevent a possible lean air–fuel condition, which could cause damage to the catalytic converter and/or the engine itself.

MASS AIR FLOW MODIFIERS

Using a mass air flow sensor provides the PCM with a direct reading of the volume of air entering the engine. As a result, a MAF-equipped engine is able to provide a more accurate air–fuel ratio under all conditions. A MAF system has the following advantages compared with a speed density system:

- The system measures the actual mass of the air entering the engine.
- Altitude and temperature corrections are not needed.
- The amount of exhaust gas recirculation does not need to be calculated.

However, some calculations need to be made to the air–fuel ratios if the throttle is rapidly depressed. Many General Motors systems use both a MAP sensor and a MAF sensor.

One of the purposes of the MAP sensor, besides helping to diagnose the proper operation of the EGR system, is to provide the PCM with intake manifold pressure changes that occur when the throttle is rapidly closed or opened.

Electronic throttle control (ETC) systems help the PCM maintain proper air–fuel mixtures because the computer can control the rate of change of throttle opening. Therefore, it can determine what is happening directly rather than indicating it through information provided by the MAP sensor.

MEASURING PULSE WIDTH

The PCM determines the base injector pulse width based on the reading from the sensors and the calculations from lookup tables stored in read-only memory. This base pulse width is the best guess as to the correct amount of fuel that the engine needs. Pulse width is measured in milliseconds (ms) and represents the amount of time the fuel injectors are commanded on. A typical engine at idle speed will have a pulse width of about 2 to 5 ms, depending on the size of the engine. If there is a fault in one of the sensors, the calculated base pulse width may be incorrect. Because the air–fuel ratio is very important for the proper operation of the catalytic converter, the PCM uses data from the oxygen sensor to modify, if needed, the commanded pulse width. This correction from the base pulse width using data from the oxygen sensor is called fuel trim.

Does the Air–Fuel Ratio Have to Vary from Rich to Lean?

No. The catalytic converter is most efficient when the air–fuel mixture is at 14.7:1 (stoichiometric). However, when carburetors were used for fuel control, they were not capable of providing exactly 14.7:1 and did fluctuate rich and lean within about 5% of stoichiometric. Older fuel-injection systems (multiport or gang-fired systems) were capable of providing an air–fuel mixture within about 2% of stoichiometric. Vehicles equipped with sequential port fuel injectors can be kept within 1% of 14.7:1, which greatly increases the efficiency of the catalytic converter.

 FREQUENTLY ASKED QUESTION

Is There Less Oxygen in the Air at High Altitude?

No. At altitudes above sea level, the atmospheric pressure and air density are lower, but the amount of oxygen (21%) remains the same at all altitudes. Three basic altitude-related factors are:

- Physical altitude. This is the altitude measured above sea level.
- Pressure altitude. This is the atmospheric pressure corrected to sea level according to the International Standard Atmosphere (ISA). Pressure altitude is primarily used for airplane performance calculations using 101 kPa as the standard for atmospheric pressure at sea level. See the following chart.

Pressure Altitude (ft)	Static Pressure (kPa)	In Hg	PSI
0	101.325	29.92	14.7
1,000	97.715	28.86	14.2
2,500	92.5	27.32	13.4
5,000	84.306	24.9	12.2
10,000	69.681	20.58	10.1
20,000	46.563	13.75	6.8
30,000	30.089	8.89	4.4
36,090	22.631	6.68	3.3

- Density altitude. This altitude factor is important for engine operation. Density altitude is the number of oxygen molecules that are entering the engine. The density is affected by temperature. Therefore, the use of the intake air temperature sensor data is important in determining air density.

 **TECH TIP**

One Millisecond per Liter

A rule-of-thumb that usually works to determine if the pulse width is within reason is to remember that the size of the engine does affect the amount of fuel needed. While injector flow rates are higher for larger engines, it is generally true that, at idle on a warm engine, the injector pulse width will be about 1 millisecond per liter of displacement.

2 liters = 2 milliseconds

3 liters = 3 milliseconds

4 liters = 4 milliseconds

5 liters = 5 milliseconds

6 liters = 6 milliseconds

Therefore, if the injector pulse width is far from being normal, determine if the engine has a vacuum leak (if numbers are too high) or if the purge valve is stuck open (if the numbers are too low).

FUEL TRIM OPERATION

THE NEED FOR FUEL TRIM The purpose of fuel trim is to provide the catalytic converter with a stoichiometric air–fuel mixture, which it needs to reduce NO_X exhaust emissions and to help oxidize *HC* and *CO* into harmless carbon dioxide (CO_2) and water (H_2O) vapor. If the exhaust is always rich, the catalytic converter cannot reduce CO and HC emissions. If the exhaust is always lean, the catalytic converter cannot reduce NO_X emissions; therefore, the air–fuel mixture must alternate between rich and lean. The computer is therefore designed to provide as close to a 14.7:1 mixture as possible by using the oxygen sensor, as well as the short-term and long-term fuel trim program, to accomplish this feat. ● SEE FIGURE 20–3.

NOTE: On some vehicles, while operating under full load, the oxygen sensor data is ignored and the PCM commands the richer-than-normal air–fuel mixture needed for maximum power based on inputs from the other sensors.

SHORT-TERM FUEL TRIM Short-term fuel trim (STFT) is a percentage measurement of the amount the computer is adding or subtracting from a calculated value. Electronic fuel-injector systems use the oxygen sensor (O2S) to determine whether the exhaust is rich or lean. Without the O2S,

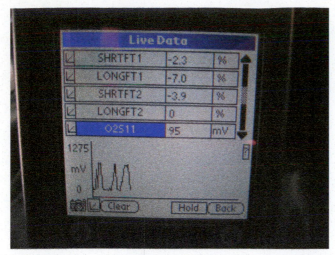

FIGURE 20–3 A scan tool display showing both long-term and short-term fuel trim. Both LTFT and STFT should be less than 10%.

fuel delivery is controlled by the computer alone using the programmed pulse width commands based on other sensor inputs, such as engine coolant temperature (ECT), throttle position (TP), and engine load (MAP). When the engine is operating in closed loop, the O2S signal can modify or change the preprogrammed fuel delivery. Fuel trim is expressed as a percentage (%), either positive (+) or negative (−), and represents the amount of fuel different from the anticipated amount. For example, if a small vacuum leak occurs, the O2S produces a lower voltage signal, which is interpreted by the computer as meaning the air–fuel mixture is too lean. As a result, the pulse width is increased slightly to compensate for this slight vacuum leak. The amount of this additional fuel is seen on a scan tool as a positive short-term fuel trim.

A short-term fuel trim of +20% indicates that 20% additional fuel had to be added to achieve the proper air–fuel mixture. A −20% short-term fuel trim indicates that fuel had to be removed by shortening the injector pulse width to achieve the proper air–fuel mixture.

Short-term fuel trim represents actions by the computer over a relatively short time. The purpose of the STFT is to provide a varying air–fuel mixture so that the catalytic converter can efficiently reduce HC, CO, and NO_X exhaust emissions. If, for example, a large vacuum leak were to occur, then the fuel delivery would have to be increased even more and for a longer time. Therefore, electronic fuel-injection system computers also incorporate a long-term fuel trim program.

LONG-TERM FUEL TRIM Long-term fuel trim (LTFT)
is designed to add or subtract fuel for a longer amount of time than short-term fuel trim. For this reason, LTFT should be looked at by the service technician as a guide to whether the computer has been adding or subtracting fuel in order to achieve the proper air–fuel mixture. For example, if a vacuum hose splits open, the engine will be leaner than normal. Short-term fuel trim will attempt to add fuel right away to

CASE STUDY

The Red Pickup Truck Story

A 4-cylinder 2.2-liter engine was replaced due to excessive oil consumption. The replacement engine never ran correctly, especially at idle and low speeds. The scan tool data showed a −25% long-term fuel trim, indicating that the oxygen sensor was measuring a very rich (low oxygen content) exhaust stream. Because the engine was operating so badly, the service technician believed the oxygen sensor was indicating a false rich condition. The service technician then checked the following:

- Poor oxygen sensor ground (this can cause a higher-than-normal oxygen sensor voltage)
- Oxygen sensor wiring shorted to voltage or near a spark plug wire
- A contaminated (coated) oxygen sensor that will read higher than normal

None of the false rich conditions was found. Remembering that the engine ran terribly even when cold and the problem started after the engine was replaced, the technician started to look for faults that could have occurred when parts were switched from the original engine to the replacement engine. The technician found an incorrect EGR gasket. This caused exhaust gases to flow into the cylinders all the time. The exhaust gases also displaced the oxygen that normally would be in the cylinder, thereby reducing the amount of oxygen measured by the oxygen sensor. Replacing the EGR gasket restored proper engine operation.

Summary:

- **Complaint**—A replacement engine never ran correctly after being installed into the pickup truck.
- **Cause**—The incorrect EGR base gasket had been installed allowing exhaust gasses to enter cylinders at all times.
- **Correction**—The correct EGR base gasket was installed which corrected the poor engine operation.

adjust. If the resulting air (vacuum) leak remains for longer than a few seconds to a minute, the computer will revise the long-term fuel trim to compensate for the leak over a larger period of time. When the LTFT makes an adjustment, the STFT can still make short and quick changes in the air–fuel mixture needed to provide the catalytic converter with an alternating rich, then lean, then rich exhaust. *The purpose of long-term fuel trim is to keep short-term fuel trim as close to zero as possible.*

USING FUEL TRIM AS A DIAGNOSTIC AID

Fuel trim values can only be observed with a scan tool. A scan tool will display both short-term and long-term fuel trim. For system diagnosis, refer to the long-term fuel trim because it represents a longer amount of time (history) and a greater amount of mixture correction.

NOTE: The object of STFT and LTFT is to be able to make corrections to the amount of fuel delivered to the engine to achieve the proper air–fuel mixture. For example, a reading of +30% LTFT will indicate the computer must deliver 30% more than the calibrated amount of fuel to achieve the proper air–fuel mixture. This also means that the engine is now operating with the correct air–fuel mixture. The LTFT number simply tells the technician what the computer had to do to achieve the proper mixture.

TECH TIP

Think of a Small Faucet and a Large Faucet

The purpose of fuel trim is to add or subtract fuel as needed to maintain the proper air–fuel mixture so the catalytic converter can operate properly. STFT is fast, but can add or subtract only a small amount of fuel. This can be visualized as being similar to a small water faucet adding water to a sink. For example, if a small vacuum hose becomes disconnected, the STFT will add a little extra fuel to compensate for the added amount of air being drawn into the engine. If a large hose becomes disconnected, the STFT cannot supply the needed fuel required; therefore, the LTFT is needed to supply additional fuel to overcome the large air leak. This can be visualized as being similar to a large water faucet adding a greater amount of water to a sink. Because the LTFT indicates a larger amount of fuel being added or subtracted than STFT, many service technicians simply ignore the STFT readings and use the LTFT numbers to see if they are within 10%. If LTFT is greater than 10%, either positive (+) or negative (−), then a fault should be corrected. The maximum value for STFT and LTFT depends on the exact make, model, and year of manufacture of vehicle but is usually limited to 25% to 30% for either.

The following are three examples of readings and possible explanations:

Example 1

$$STFT = +5\%, LTFT = 20\%$$

Explanation: The computer is responding to a lean condition. The LTFT indicates that the programmed amount of fuel had to be increased by 20% to achieve the proper air–fuel mixture to the level where the STFT could "toggle" the mixture rich and lean for the most catalytic converter efficiency. Look for a vacuum leak or low fuel pressure.

Example 2

$$STFT = +5\%, LIFT = 0\%$$

Explanation: These readings are perfect. It is normal for the STFT to add or subtract up to 10% to achieve the proper air–fuel mixture.

Example 3

$$STFT = -10\%, LIFT = -30\%$$

Explanation: The engine was rich because the LTFT had to remove 30% of the anticipated amount of fuel to achieve the proper air–fuel mixture. Look for a defective (stuck-open) injector, defective fuel pressure regulator, or a restriction in the intake air passage.

FUEL TRIM CELLS

Both STFTs and LTFTs react to oxygen sensor voltage to modify fuel delivery. Most vehicles set aside different fuel trim cells for each combination of engine speed (RPM) and load. The computer can then correct for slight differences in fuel mixture separately for each cell. For example, General Motors uses 16 cells plus 2 for deceleration and 2 for idle only. ● **SEE FIGURE 20–4**.

TECH TIP

Movie Mode Diagnosis

A scan tool will display fuel trim values, but only those in the cell where the engine is operating. For example, if an engine lacks power while towing a trailer up a hill, looking at the fuel trim values at idle in the shop will show the values in the cell or cells that the engine is operating. To observe the true fuel trim values, the vehicle will have to be operated under similar conditions and the data recorded on the scan tool. Use snap-shot or movie mode during the test drive, scroll through the recorded values, and look for the fuel trim cell and the LTFT and STFT values to help determine if there is a fuel delivery or other fuel trim-related problem.

Load			
12	13	14	15
8	9	10	11
4	5	6	7
0	1	2	3
RPM ──────────▶			

Deceleration Cells	Idle Cells
Greater than 1225 RPM = 17	A/C on = 18
Less than 1225 RPM = 16	A/C off = 19

FIGURE 20–4 An example of a fuel cell map.

Fuel Trim Diagnostic Chart		
Fuel Trim @ Idle	**Fuel Trim @ 3000 RPM**	**Possible Cause(s)**
Adding fuel	No correction	Vacuum leak
No correction	Adding fuel	Low fuel volume, weak fuel pump, or restricted fuel filter
Adding fuel	Adding fuel	Dirty (clogged) fuel injectors, low fuel pump pressure
Subtracting fuel	No correction	Gasoline in the engine oil (drawn into the engine through the PCV valve)
Subtracting fuel	Subtracting fuel	High fuel pressure, defective fuel pressure regulator, leaking or stuck-open injector(s)

FIGURE 20–5 A fuel trim diagnostic chart example.

FUEL TRIM CELL DIAGNOSIS

To use fuel trim as a diagnostic aid, the data should be observed during the same condition as the problem. For example, notice that there are two cells for idle—one with the air conditioning (A/C) on and one for the A/C off. If the problem or customer's concern only occurs when the A/C is on, then observe the fuel trim numbers on the scan tool with the engine operating at idle and with the A/C on. The same thing is true of a problem that may be occurring at 55 MPH (90 km/h). Looking at fuel trim in the service bay (stall) with the engine at idle will not help the technician at all. The vehicle must be driven under similar conditions to best duplicate the condition when the problem occurs. Only then will the correct fuel cell be displayed. Then the long-term fuel trim information should be valid. See the following fuel trim diagnostic chart. ● **SEE FIGURE 20–5.**

MASS AIR FLOW ACCURACY

In an engine equipped with a MAF sensor, the accuracy of the sensor is critical for the PCM to provide the current pulse

FIGURE 20–6 Any fault in the air cleaner assembly can disrupt the airflow through the MAF sensor.

  FREQUENTLY ASKED QUESTION

What Is the Alpha PID?

Alpha is the air–fuel ratio parameter displayed on Nissan/Infiniti vehicles.

$$100 = 14.7:1$$

Higher than 100 = PCM is adding fuel

Lower than 100 = PCM is subtracting fuel

Alpha is used as a single parameter that replaces both long-term fuel trim and short-term fuel trim.

width command to the fuel injectors. Factors that can affect the accuracy of the MAF sensor readings include:

- **Vacuum leaks.** A vacuum leak represents air entering the combustion chambers that was not measured by the MAF sensor, and affects the air–fuel mixture mostly at idle. Above idle, the effects of a vacuum leak are reduced.

- **False air.** False or unmeasured air is air that is entering the intake system after the MAF sensor. This false air can have a great effect on the air–fuel mixture at idle and, like a vacuum leak, tends to have less of an effect at higher engine speeds.

- **PCV airflow.** The airflow through the PCV system is not measured by the MAF sensor. Therefore, all openings to the crankcase must be sealed to prevent unmeasured air from entering.

- **Airflow disturbance (disruption).** If the incorrect air filter is installed or the air inlet system is modified, airflow through the MAF sensor may not be straight. If air turbulence passes through the MAF sensor, the accuracy of the amount of airflow will not be correct. ● **SEE FIGURE 20–6.**

CASE STUDY

Negative Fuel Trim Bank #1; Positive Fuel Trim Bank #2

The owner of a Chevrolet Camaro V-8 complained that the engine seemed to lack the power it used to have. The service technical found that, while there were no diagnostic trouble codes, the left bank (bank #1) had a negative total fuel trim, whereas the right bank had a positive total fuel trim. If one bank of a V-8 engine has a restricted exhaust on one bank, the fuel trim numbers will be negative on the bank that is restricted and positive on the bank that is not restricted. A restricted converter was found to be the root cause as the substrate had cracked and the broken sections restricted the flow of exhaust. ● **SEE FIGURES 20–7 THROUGH 20–10.**

Summary:

- **Complaint**—The customer complained of a lack of power.
- **Cause**—A restricted exhaust on the left bank due to a broken substrate inside the catalytic converter.
- **Correction**—The catalytic converter was replaced, which restored normal engine power delivery.

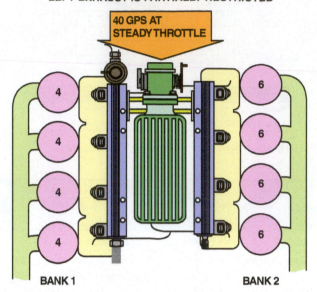

FIGURE 20–8 If the exhaust system on the left bank (bank #1) were to become restricted, the total airflow through the MAF sensor would also decrease. The cylinders on the right Bank (bank #2) would draw the same 6 GPS as before and the cylinders on bank #1, which have a restricted exhaust, would draw just 4 GPS.

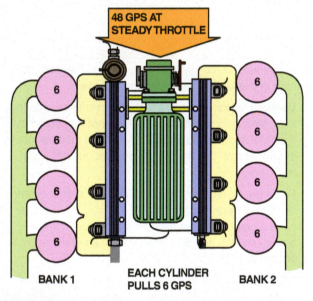

FIGURE 20–7 This properly operating engine is drawing in 48 grams per second of air for all eight cylinders. This indicates that each cylinder will be receiving 6 grams per second (GPS).

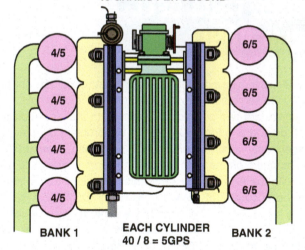

FIGURE 20–9 If all cylinders were equal and showed the 40 grams per second, then each cylinder will be drawing 5grams per second (5 × 8 cylinders = 40 GPS). Bank #1 is being supplied 4/5ths of the air needed, whereas bank #2 is being supplied 6/5ths of the air needed causing bank #1 to operate too rich and bank # 2 to operate too lean.

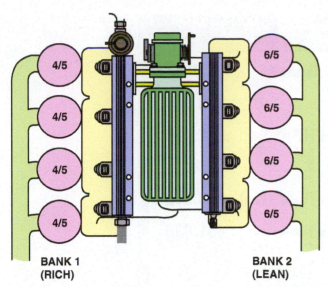

BANK 1 (RICH)   BANK 2 (LEAN)

FIGURE 20-10 As a result of the restricted exhaust on bank #1, the restricted bank will operate too rich and bank #2 will operate too lean. The long-term fuel trim will be negative for bank #1 and positive for bank #2.

VOLUMETRIC EFFICIENCY

DEFINITION OF VOLUMETRIC EFFICIENCY Volumetric efficiency (VE) is the percentage of air entering the engine compared to the theoretical airflow. Volumetric efficiency testing can help diagnose low engine power concerns if it is lower than normal. Typical normally aspirated engines will test having a VE of 75% to 90%. Older two-valve cylinder head engines will test lower than newer engines equipped with four valves per cylinder. Percentages above 100% are possible on supercharged or turbocharged engines.

A VE calculator can be downloaded from (free):

www.jameshalderman.com

Click on "ASE/NATEF"

Click on "Service Information" and then select "Volumetric Efficiency Calculator for Windows."

The calculation requires data to be captured using a scan tool while the vehicle is being driven at wide-open throttle. This test should be conducted in a safe location away from traffic and does not need to be performed at high vehicle speeds. The data needed includes:

- Engine size in cubic inches
- Engine speed (RPM)
- MAF (grams per second)
- Intake air temperature (IAT)

Example 1

A Chevrolet Trailblazer equipped with a 4.2-liter 6-cylinder engine is tested using the following information and results:

$$\text{Engine size} = 256 \text{ cu. in. } (4.2 \text{ liters})$$

$$\text{Engine RPM} = 6097$$

$$\text{MAF (gm/s)} = 225.4$$

$$\text{IAT (°F)} = 66$$

The calculated airflow through the engine is 395 cu. ft per sec. The theoretical airflow through the engine is 451 cu. ft per second. The VE is 87%. This result indicates that the MAF sensor is accurately measuring the airflow and the engine is in good mechanical condition. ● **SEE FIGURE 20-11**.

Example 2

A Cadillac Deville is equipped with a 4.6-liter V-8. The customer's concern is poor performance. Fuel trim numbers are within ±2% 2from idle to cruise. A check of the VE indicates the following:

$$\text{Engine size} = 281 \text{ cu. in. } (4.6 \text{ liters})$$

$$\text{Engine RPM} = 3400$$

$$\text{MAF (gm/s)} = 80$$

$$\text{IAT (°F)} = 95$$

The calculated volumetric efficiency is 53%. A clogged catalytic converter is discovered to be the cause. ● **SEE FIGURE 20-12**.

 TECH TIP

MAF Sensor or Airflow Problem?

If a MAF sensor reading is lower than normal, such as at wide-open throttle, it could be an engine breathing problem or a defective/contaminated MAF sensor. To determine which the case is, check the following:

- If the fuel trim numbers follow the airflow, there is an airflow measurement error (MAF sensor related problem).
- If the fuel trim numbers are okay, the MAF is okay.
- If the BARO reading is lower than normal, there is an engine breathing issue, such as a restricted intake or exhaust.

TECH TIP

Possible Restricted Exhaust? Check the IAT.

If the exhaust system is restricted, all of the exhaust will be unable to exit the engine, especially at wide-open throttle. Using a scan tool, look at the values displayed for the intake air temperature (IAT) sensor. The IAT temperature should decrease slightly at WOT normally due to the increased airflow. If the IAT temperature reading increases, this is an indication of a restricted exhaust.

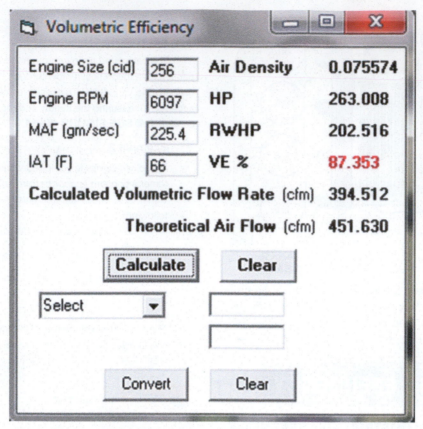

FIGURE 20–11 The data shows a normally operating engine.

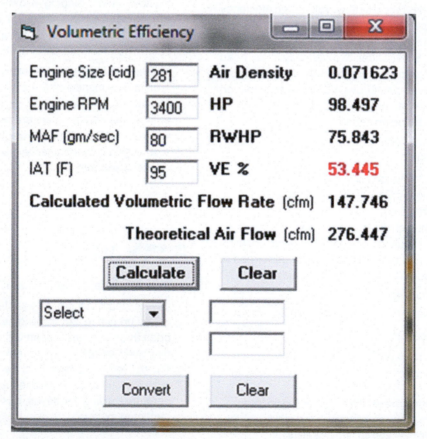

FIGURE 20–12 The data indicates a restriction.

1. Lambda is a Greek letter used to represent air–fuel ratio. Lambda of 1.0 is equal to an air–fuel rate of 14.7:1.

2. Equivalence ratio is the inverse of lambda.

3. Base pulse width is determined by the PCM based on input from many sensors.

4. Speed density fuel control uses calculations based on the input from various sensors, such as the TP and MAP sensor to determine the amount of fuel needed.

5. Mass air flow systems use a mass air flow sensor to measure the mass of the air entering the engine directly.

6. Fuel trim uses the oxygen sensor data to fine-tune the air–fuel mixture to ensure lowest emissions.

7. Short-term fuel trim (STFT) is capable of quickly adding or subtracting fuel, but only a limited amount.

8. Long-term fuel trim (LTFT) is capable of adding or subtracting more fuel than STFT, but is slower to react.

9. Volumetric efficiency is the percentage of air entering the engine compared to the theoretical airflow.

REVIEW QUESTIONS

1. What is the difference between lambda and equivalence ratio?

2. How is base pulse width determined?

3. Why is fuel trim needed?

4. What is the difference between short-term and long-term fuel trim?

5. How can volumetric efficiency be used to diagnose a low power condition?

CHAPTER QUIZ

1. If the air–fuel ratio is 14.7:1, what is lambda?
   - **a.** 1.0
   - **b.** 0.9
   - **c.** 1.1
   - **d.** 14.7

2. If lambda is 0.98, this means the _____.
   - **a.** mixture is lean.
   - **b.** air–fuel mixture is within 2% of stoichiometric
   - **c.** air–fuel mixture is slightly rich
   - **d.** Both b and c

3. Base pulse width is determined by _____.
   - **a.** oxygen sensor data
   - **b.** computer calculations
   - **c.** input from many sensors, except the oxygen sensor
   - **d.** Both b and c

4. The air at high altitude has _____.
   - **a.** 21% oxygen
   - **b.** less than 21% oxygen
   - **c.** a higher pressure
   - **d.** a higher density

5. The MAF sensor may give an inaccurate measurement if the _____ is modified.
   - **a.** cooling fan
   - **b.** radiator
   - **c.** air inlet system
   - **d.** AC system

6. The catalytic converter is most efficient when the air–fuel mixture is _____.
   - **a.** at 14.7:1 air/fuel ratio
   - **b.** at 1.0 lambda
   - **c.** varying from rich to lean (0.9 to 1.1 lambda)
   - **d.** Both a and b

7. Injector pulse width is measured in _____.
   - **a.** percentage (%)
   - **b.** milliseconds (ms)
   - **c.** duty cycle (%)
   - **d.** frequency (Hz)

8. What is *not* true about short-term fuel trim?
   - **a.** It is able to react quickly to add or subtract fuel.
   - **b.** It can add or subtract a large amount of fuel.
   - **c.** It uses the oxygen sensor.
   - **d.** It is expressed in percentages.

9. A Nissan is being checked, using a scan tool, and Alpha is 107. This means _____.
   - **a.** the PCM is adding fuel
   - **b.** the PCM is subtracting fuel
   - **c.** the PCM represents STFT only
   - **d.** the PCM represents LTFT only

10. A contaminated or defective MAF sensor is indicated if _____.
    - **a.** the fuel trim number follows the airflow
    - **b.** the VE is low
    - **c.** the fuel trim numbers are within 62%
    - **d.** the BARO reading is lower than normal

chapter 21

FUEL PUMPS, LINES, AND FILTERS

LEARNING OBJECTIVES

After studying this chapter, the reader should be able to:

1. Explain the role of fuel tanks in the fuel delivery system.
2. Describe the different methods of rollover leakage protection.
3. Discuss the different types of fuel lines.
4. Explain the different types of electric fuel pumps.
5. Describe the purpose and function of fuel filters.
6. Describe how to test and replace fuel pumps.

This chapter will help you prepare for Engine Repair (A8) ASE certification test content area "C" (Fuel, Air Induction, and Exhaust Systems Diagnosis and Repair).

KEY TERMS

Accumulator 307
Baffle 299
Gerotor 304
Hydrokinetic pump 304
Inertia switch 301
Onboard refueling vapor recovery (ORVR) 299
Peripheral pump 304
Residual or rest pressure 304

Roller cell 303
Rotary vane pump 304
Side-channel pump 304
Turbine pump 304
Vapor lock 301
Volatile organic compound (VOC) 302

FUEL DELIVERY SYSTEM

Creating and maintaining a correct air–fuel mixture requires a properly functioning fuel and air delivery system. Fuel delivery (and return) systems use many if not all of the following components to make certain that fuel is available under the right conditions to the fuel-injection system:

- Fuel storage tank, filler neck, and gas cap
- Fuel tank pressure sensor
- Fuel pump
- Fuel filter(s)
- Fuel delivery lines and fuel rail
- Fuel-pressure regulator
- Fuel return line (if equipped with a return-type fuel delivery system)

FUEL TANKS

A vehicle fuel tank is made of corrosion-resistant steel or polyethylene plastic. Some models, such as sport utility vehicles (SUVs) and light trucks, may have an auxiliary fuel tank.

Tank design and capacity are a compromise between available space, filler location, fuel expansion room, and fuel movement. Some later-model tanks deliberately limit tank capacity by extending the filler tube neck into the tank low enough to prevent complete filling, or by providing for expansion room. ● SEE FIGURE 21–1. A vertical **baffle** in this same tank limits fuel sloshing as the vehicle moves.

Regardless of size and shape, all fuel tanks incorporate most if not all of the following features:

- Inlet or filler tube through which fuel enters the tank
- Filler cap with pressure holding and relief features
- An outlet to the fuel line leading to the fuel pump or fuel injector
- Fuel pump mounted within the tank
- Tank vent system
- Fuel pickup tube and fuel level sending unit

TANK LOCATION AND MOUNTING Most vehicles use a horizontally suspended fuel tank, usually mounted below the rear of the floor pan, just ahead of or behind the rear axle. Fuel tanks are located there so that frame rails and body components protect the tank in the event of a crash. To prevent squeaks, some models have insulated strips cemented on the top or sides of the tank wherever it contacts the underbody.

Fuel inlet location depends on the tank design and filler tube placement. It is located behind a filler cap and is often a hinged door in the outer side of either rear fender panel.

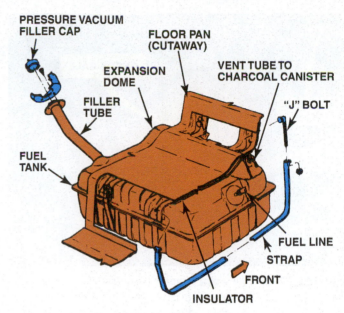

FIGURE 21–1 A typical fuel tank installation.

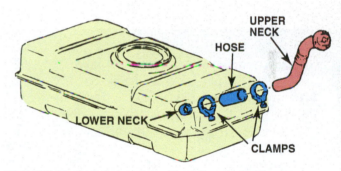

FIGURE 21–2 A three-piece filler tube assembly.

Generally, a pair of metal retaining straps holds a fuel tank in place. Underbody brackets or support panels hold the strap ends using bolts. The free ends are drawn underneath the tank to hold it in place, then bolted to other support brackets or to a frame member on the opposite side of the tank.

FILLER TUBES Fuel enters the tank through a large tube extending from the tank to an opening on the outside of the vehicle. ● SEE FIGURE 21–2.

Effective in 1993, federal regulations require manufacturers to install a device to prevent fuel from being siphoned through the filler neck. Federal authorities recognized methanol as a poison, and methanol used in gasoline is a definite health hazard. Additionally, gasoline is a suspected carcinogen (cancer-causing agent). To prevent siphoning, manufacturers welded a filler-neck check-ball tube in fuel tanks. To drain check ball–equipped fuel tanks, a technician must disconnect the check-ball tube at the tank and attach a siphon directly to the tank. ● SEE FIGURE 21–3.

Onboard refueling vapor recovery (ORVR) systems have been developed to reduce evaporative emissions during refueling. ● SEE FIGURE 21–4. These systems add components

FIGURE 21–3 A view of a typical filler tube with the fuel tank removed. Notice the ground strap used to help prevent the buildup of static electricity as the fuel flows into the plastic tank. The check ball looks exactly like a ping-pong ball.

FIGURE 21–4 Vehicles equipped with onboard refueling vapor recovery usually have a reduced-size fill tube.

to the filler neck and the tank. One ORVR system utilizes a tapered filler neck with a smaller diameter tube and a check valve. When fuel flows down the neck, it opens the normally closed check valve. The vapor passage to the charcoal canister is opened. The decreased size neck and the opened air passage allow fuel and vapor to flow rapidly into the tank and the canister, respectively. When the fuel has reached a predetermined level, the check valve closes, and the fuel tank pressure increases. This forces the nozzle to shut off, thereby preventing the tank from being overfilled.

PRESSURE-VACUUM FILLER CAP
Fuel and vapors are sealed in the tank by the safety filler cap. The safety cap must release excess pressure or excess vacuum. Either condition could cause fuel tank damage, fuel spills, and vapor escape. Typically, the cap will release if the pressure is over 1.5 to 2.0 PSI (10 to 14 kPa) or if the vacuum is 0.15 to 0.30 PSI (1 to 2 kPa).

FUEL PICKUP TUBE
The fuel pickup tube is usually a part of the fuel sender assembly or the electric fuel pump assembly.

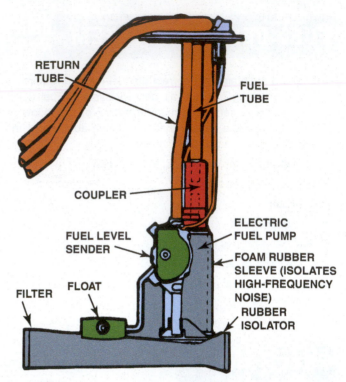

FIGURE 21–5 The fuel pickup tube is part of the fuel sender and pump assembly.

Since dirt and sediment eventually gather on the bottom of a fuel tank, the fuel pickup tube is fitted with a filter sock or strainer to prevent contamination from entering the fuel lines. The woven plastic strainer also acts as a water separator by preventing water from being drawn up with the fuel. The filter sock usually is designed to filter out particles that are larger than 70 to 100 microns, or 30 microns if a gerotor-type fuel pump is used. One micron is 0.000039 inch. ● SEE FIGURE 21–5.

NOTE: The human eye cannot see anything smaller than about 40 microns.

The filter is made from woven Saran resin (copolymer of vinylidene chloride and vinyl chloride). The filter blocks any water that may be in the fuel tank, unless it is completely submerged in water. In that case, it will allow water through the filter. This filter should be replaced whenever the fuel pump is replaced.

TANK VENTING REQUIREMENTS
Fuel tanks must be vented to prevent a vacuum lock as fuel is drawn from the tank. As fuel is used and its level drops in the tank, the space above the fuel increases. As the air in the tank expands to fill this greater space, its pressure drops. Without a vent, the air pressure inside the tank would drop below atmospheric pressure, developing a vacuum, which prevents the flow of fuel. Under extreme pressure variance, the tank could collapse. Venting the tank allows outside air to enter as the fuel level drops, preventing a vacuum from developing.

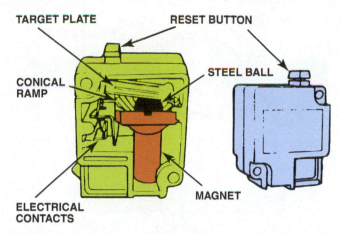

TARGET PLATE   RESET BUTTON

CONICAL RAMP   STEEL BALL

ELECTRICAL CONTACTS   MAGNET

FIGURE 21–6 Ford uses an inertia switch to turn off the electric fuel pump in case of an accident.

An EVAP system vents gasoline vapors from the fuel tank directly to a charcoal-filled vapor storage canister, and uses an unvented filler cap. Many filler caps contain valves that open to relieve pressure or vacuum above specified safety levels. Systems that use completely sealed caps have separate pressure and vacuum relief valves for venting.

Because fuel tanks are not vented directly to the atmosphere, the tank must allow for fuel expansion, contraction, and overflow that can result from changes in temperature or overfilling. One way is to use a dome in the top of the tank. Many General Motors vehicles use a design that includes a vertical slosh baffle which reserves up to 12% of the total tank capacity for fuel expansion.

ROLLOVER LEAKAGE PROTECTION

All vehicles have one or more devices to prevent fuel leaks in case of vehicle rollover or a collision in which fuel may spill.

Variations of the basic one-way check valve may be installed in any number of places between the fuel tank and the engine. The valve may be installed in the fuel return line, vapor vent line, or fuel tank filler cap.

In addition to the rollover protection devices, some vehicles use devices to ensure that the fuel pump shuts off when an accident occurs. Some pumps depend upon an oil pressure or an engine speed signal to continue operating; these pumps turn off whenever the engine dies.

Ford vehicles use an **inertia switch**. ● **SEE FIGURE 21–6**. The inertia switch is installed in the rear of the vehicle between the electric fuel pump and its power supply. With any sudden impact, such as a jolt from another vehicle in a parking lot, the inertia switch opens and shuts off power to the fuel pump. The switch must be reset manually by pushing a button to restore current to the pump.

FUEL LINES

Fuel and vapor lines made of steel, nylon tubing, or fuel-resistant rubber hoses connect the parts of the fuel system. Fuel lines supply fuel to the throttle body or fuel rail. They also return excess fuel and vapors to the tank. Depending on their function, fuel and vapor lines may be either rigid or flexible.

Fuel lines must remain as cool as possible. If any part of the line is located near too much heat, the gasoline passing through it vaporizes and **vapor lock** occurs. When this happens, the fuel pump supplies only vapor that passes into the injectors. Without liquid gasoline, the engine stalls and a hot restart problem develops.

The fuel delivery system supplies 10 to 15 PSI (69 to 103 kPa) or up to 35 PSI (241 kPa) to many throttle-body injection units and up to 50 PSI (345 kPa) for multiport fuel-injection systems. Fuel-injection systems retain residual or rest pressure in the lines for a half hour or longer when the engine is turned off to prevent hot engine restart problems. Higher-pressure systems such as these require special fuel lines.

RIGID LINES   All fuel lines fastened to the body, frame, or engine are made of seamless steel tubing. Steel springs may be wound around the tubing at certain points to protect against impact damage.

Only steel tubing, or that recommended by the manufacturer, should be used when replacing rigid fuel lines. *Never substitute copper or aluminum tubing for steel tubing.* These materials do not withstand normal vehicle vibration and could combine with the fuel to cause a chemical reaction.

FLEXIBLE LINES   Most fuel systems use synthetic rubber hose sections where flexibility is needed. Short hose sections often connect steel fuel lines to other system components. The fuel delivery hose inside diameter (ID) is generally larger (3/16 to 3/8 inches or 8 to 10 millimeters) than the fuel return hose ID (1/4 inches or 6 millimeters).

Fuel-injection systems require special-composition reinforced hoses specifically made for these higher-pressure systems. Similarly, vapor vent lines must be made of materials that resist fuel vapors. Replacement vent hoses are usually marked with the designation "EVAP" to indicate their intended use.

FUEL LINE MOUNTING   Fuel supply lines from the tank to a throttle body or fuel rail are routed to follow the frame along the underbody of the vehicle. Vapor and return lines may be routed with the fuel supply line. All rigid lines are fastened to the frame rail or underbody with screws and clamps, or clips. ● **SEE FIGURE 21–7**.

FUEL-INJECTION LINES   Hoses used for fuel-injection systems are made of materials with high resistance to oxidation and deterioration. Replacement hoses for injection systems should always be equivalent to original equipment manufacturer (OEM) hoses.

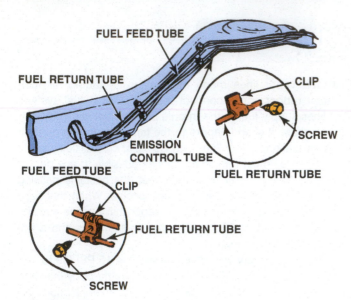

FIGURE 21–7 Fuel lines are routed along the frame or body and secured with clips.

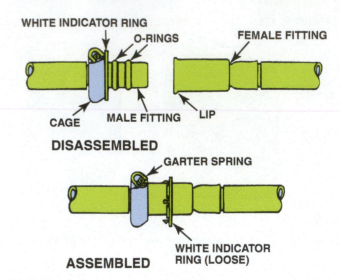

FIGURE 21–8 Some Ford metal line connections use spring-locks and O-rings.

CAUTION: *Do not use spring-type clamps on fuel-injected engines*—they cannot withstand the fuel pressures involved.

FUEL-INJECTION FITTINGS AND NYLON LINES

Because of their operating pressures, fuel-injection systems often use special kinds of fittings to ensure leakproof connections. Some high-pressure fittings on GM vehicles with port fuel-injection systems use O-ring seals instead of the traditional flare connections. When disconnecting such a fitting, inspect the O-ring for damage and replace it if necessary. *Always* tighten O-ring fittings to the specified torque value to prevent damage.

Other manufacturers also use O-ring seals on fuel line connections. In all cases, the O-rings are made of special materials that withstand contact with gasoline and oxygenated fuel blends. Some manufacturers specify that the O-rings be replaced every time the fuel system connection is opened. When replacing one of these O-rings, a new part specifically designed for fuel system service must be used.

Ford also uses spring-lock connectors to join male and female ends of steel tubing. ● **SEE FIGURE 21–8.** The coupling is held together by a garter spring inside a circular cage. The flared end of the female fitting slips behind the spring to lock the coupling together.

General Motors has used nylon fuel lines with quick-connect fittings at the fuel tank and fuel filter since the early 1990s. Like the GM threaded couplings used with steel lines, nylon line couplings use internal O-ring seals. Unlocking the metal connectors requires a special quick-connector separator tool; plastic connectors can be released without the tool. ● **SEE FIGURES 21–9 AND 21–10.**

FUEL LINE LAYOUT
Fuel pressures have tended to become higher to prevent vapor lock, and a major portion of the fuel

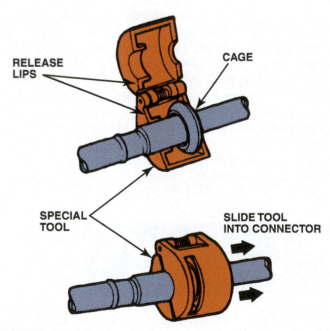

FIGURE 21–9 Ford spring-lock connectors require a special tool for disassembly.

routed to the fuel-injection system returns to the tank by way of a fuel return line or return-type systems. This allows better control, within limits, of heat absorbed by the gasoline as it is routed through the engine compartment. Throttle-body and multiport injection systems have typically used a pressure regulator to control fuel pressure in the throttle body or fuel rail, and also allow excess fuel not used by the injectors to return to the tank. However, the warmer fuel in the tank may create problems, such as an excessive rise in fuel vapor pressures in the tank.

With late-model vehicles, there has been some concern about too much heat being sent back to the fuel tank, causing rising in-tank temperatures and increases in fuel vaporization and **volatile organic compound (VOC)** (hydrocarbon)

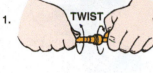

METAL COLLAR
QUICK-CONNECT FITTING

PLASTIC COLLAR
QUICK-CONNECT FITTING

FIGURE 21–10 Typical quick-connect steps.

REMOVAL

INSTALLATION

1. TWIST

1.

2. BLOW

2. →← ←

3. OR

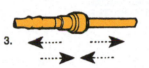

3. ←⋯⋯ ⋯⋯→
   ⋯⋯→ ←⋯⋯

4.

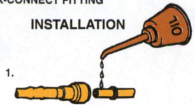

? FREQUENTLY ASKED QUESTION

Just How Much Fuel Is Recirculated?

Approximately 80% of the available fuel-pump volume is released to the fuel tank through the fuel-pressure regulator at idle speed. For example, a passenger vehicle cruising down the road at 60 mph gets 30 mpg. With a typical return-style fuel system pumping about 30 gallons per hour from the tank, it would therefore burn 2 gallons per hour, and return about 28 gallons per hour to the tank!

emissions. To combat this problem, manufacturers have placed the pressure regulator back by the tank instead of under the hood on mechanical returnless systems. In this way, returned fuel is not subjected to the heat generated by the engine and the underhood environment. To prevent vapor lock in these systems, pressures have been raised in the fuel rail, and injectors tend to have smaller openings to maintain control of the fuel spray under pressure.

? FREQUENTLY ASKED QUESTION

How Can an Electric Pump Work Inside a Gas Tank and Not Cause a Fire?

Even though fuel fills the entire pump, no burnable mixture exists inside the pump because there is no air and no danger of commutator brush arcing, igniting the fuel.

Not only must the fuel be filtered and supplied under adequate pressure, but there must also be a consistent *volume* of fuel to assure smooth engine performance even under the heaviest of loads.

ELECTRIC FUEL PUMPS

The electric fuel pump is a pusher unit. When the pump is mounted in the tank, the entire fuel supply line to the engine can be pressurized. Because the fuel, when pressurized, has a higher boiling point, it is unlikely that vapor will form to interfere with fuel flow.

Most vehicles use the impeller or turbine pumps. ● **SEE FIGURE 21–11.** All electrical pumps are driven by a small electric motor, but the turbine pump turns at higher speeds and is quieter than the others.

POSITIVE DISPLACEMENT PUMP A positive displacement pump is a design that forces everything that enters the pump to leave the pump.

In the **roller cell** or vane pump, the impeller draws fuel into the pump, and then pushes it out through the fuel line to the injection system. All designs of pumps use a variable-sized chamber to draw in fuel. When the maximum volume has been reached, the supply port closes and the discharge opens. Fuel is then forced out the discharge as this volume decreases. The chambers are formed by rollers or gears in a rotor plate. Since this type of pump uses no valves to move the fuel, the fuel flows steadily through the pump housing. Since fuel flows steadily through the entire pump, including the electrical portion, the

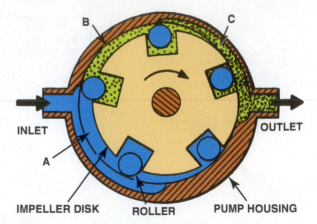

FIGURE 21–12 The pumping action of an impeller or rotary vane pump.

B C

INLET OUTLET

A

IMPELLER DISK ROLLER PUMP HOUSING

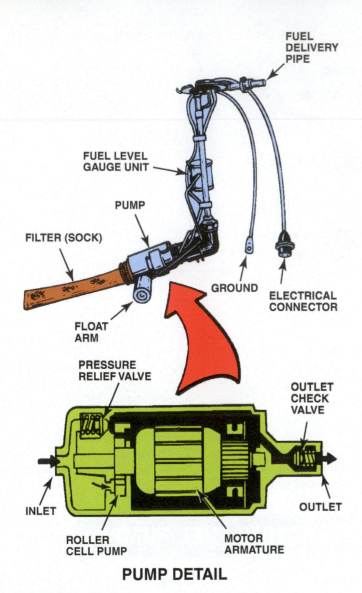

FUEL
DELIVERY
PIPE

FUEL LEVEL
GAUGE UNIT

PUMP

FILTER (SOCK)

GROUND

ELECTRICAL
CONNECTOR

FLOAT
ARM

PRESSURE
RELIEF VALVE

OUTLET
CHECK
VALVE

INLET

OUTLET

ROLLER
CELL PUMP

MOTOR
ARMATURE

PUMP DETAIL

FIGURE 21–11 A roller cell-type electric fuel pump.

pump stays cool. Usually, only when a vehicle runs out of fuel is there a risk of pump damage.

Most electric fuel pumps are equipped with a fuel outlet check valve that closes to maintain fuel pressure when the pump shuts off. **Residual or rest pressure** prevents vapor lock and hot-start problems on these systems.

● **FIGURE 21–12** shows the pumping action of a **rotary vane pump**. The pump consists of a central impeller disk, several rollers or vanes that ride in notches in the impeller, and a pump housing that is offset from the impeller center-line. The impeller is mounted on the end of the motor armature and spins whenever the motor is running. The rollers are free to slide in and out within the notches in the impeller to main-tain sealing contact. Unpressurized fuel enters the pump, fills the spaces between the rollers, and is trapped between the impeller, the housing, and two rollers. An internal gear pump, called a **gerotor**, is another type of positive displacement pump that is often used in engine oil pumps. It uses the mesh-ing of internal and external gear teeth to pressurize the fuel.

● **SEE FIGURE 21–13** for an example of a gerotor-type fuel pump that uses an impeller as the first stage and is used to move the fuel gerotor section where it is pressurized.

HYDROKINETIC FLOW PUMP DESIGN
The word *hydro* means liquid and the term *kinetic* refers to motion, so the term **hydrokinetic pump** means that this design of pump rapidly moves the fuel to create pressure. This design of pump is a nonpositive displacement pump design.

A **turbine pump** is the most common because it tends to be less noisy. Sometimes called turbine, **peripheral**, and **side-channel**, these units use an impeller that accelerates the fuel particles before actually discharging them into a tract where they generate pressure via pulse exchange. Actual pump volume is controlled by using a different number of impel-ler blades, and in some cases a higher number of impellers, or different shapes along the side discharge channels. These units are fitted more toward lower operating pressures of less than 60 PSI. ● **SEE FIGURE 21–14** for an example of a two-stage turbine pump. The turbine impeller has a staggered blade design to minimize pump harmonic noise and to separate vapor from the liquid fuel. The end cap assembly contains a pressure relief valve and a radio-frequency interference (RFI) suppression module. The check valve is usually located in the upper fuel pipe connector assembly.

After it passes through the strainer, fuel is drawn into the lower housing inlet port by the impellers. It is pressurized and delivered to the convoluted fuel tube for transfer through a check valve into the fuel feed pipe. A typical electric fuel pump used on a fuel-injection system delivers about 40 to 50 gallons per hour or 0.6 to 0.8 gallons per minute at a pressure of 70 to 90 PSI.

MODULAR FUEL SENDER ASSEMBLY
The modular fuel sender consists of a fuel level sensor, a turbine pump, and a jet pump. The reservoir housing is attached to the cover con-taining fuel pipes and the electrical connector. Fuel is trans-ferred from the pump to the fuel pipe through a convoluted (flexible) fuel pipe. The convoluted fuel pipe eliminates the need

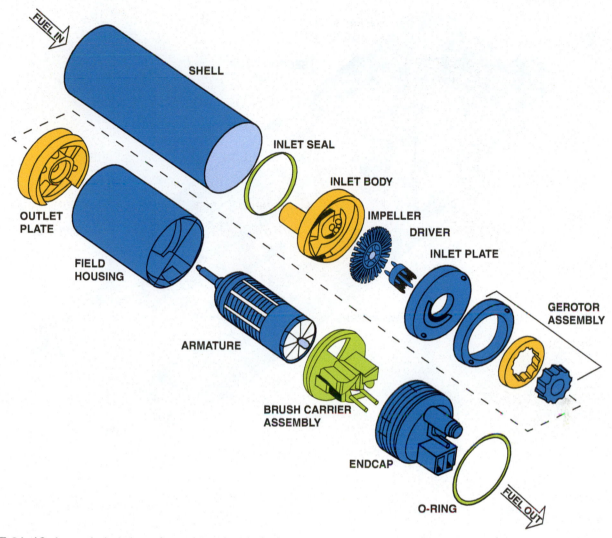

FUEL IN

SHELL

INLET SEAL

INLET BODY

IMPELLER

DRIVER

INLET PLATE

OUTLET PLATE

FIELD HOUSING

GEROTOR ASSEMBLY

ARMATURE

BRUSH CARRIER ASSEMBLY

ENDCAP

O-RING

FUEL OUT

FIGURE 21–13 An exploded view of a gerotor electric fuel pump.

for rubber hoses, nylon pipes, and clamps. The reservoir dampens fuel slosh to maintain a constant fuel level available to the roller vane pump; it also reduces noise.

Some of the flow, however, is returned to the jet pump for recirculation. Excess fuel is returned to the reservoir through one of the three hollow support pipes. The hot fuel quickly mixes with the cooler fuel in the reservoir; this minimizes the possibility of vapor lock. In these modules, the reservoir is filled by the jet pump. Some of the fuel from the pump is sent through the jet pump to lift fuel from the tank into the reservoir.

ELECTRIC PUMP CONTROL CIRCUITS
Fuel-pump circuits are controlled by the fuel-pump relay. Fuel-pump relays are activated initially by turning the ignition key to on, which allows the pump to pressurize the fuel system. As a safety precaution, the relay de-energizes after a few seconds until the key is moved to the crank position. On some systems, once an ignition coil signal, or "tach" signal, is received by the engine control computer, indicating the engine is rotating, the relay remains energized even with the key released to the run position.

CHRYSLER. On older Chrysler vehicles, the PCM must receive an engine speed (RPM) signal during cranking before it can energize a circuit driver inside the power module to activate an automatic shutdown (ASD) relay to power the fuel pump, ignition coil, and injectors. As a safety precaution, if the RPM signal to the logic module is interrupted, the logic module signals the power module to deactivate the ASD, turning off the pump, coil, and injectors. In some vehicles, the oil pressure switch circuit may be used as a safety circuit to activate the pump in the ignition switch run position.

GENERAL MOTORS. General Motors systems energize the pump with the ignition switch to initially pressurize the fuel lines, but then deactivate the pump if an RPM signal is not received within one or two seconds. The pump is reactivated as soon as engine cranking is detected. The oil pressure sending unit serves as a backup to the fuel-pump relay on some vehicles. In case of pump relay failure, the oil pressure switch will operate the fuel pump once oil pressure reaches about 4 PSI (28 kPa).

FORD. Older fuel-injected Fords used an inertia switch between the fuel pump relay and fuel pump.

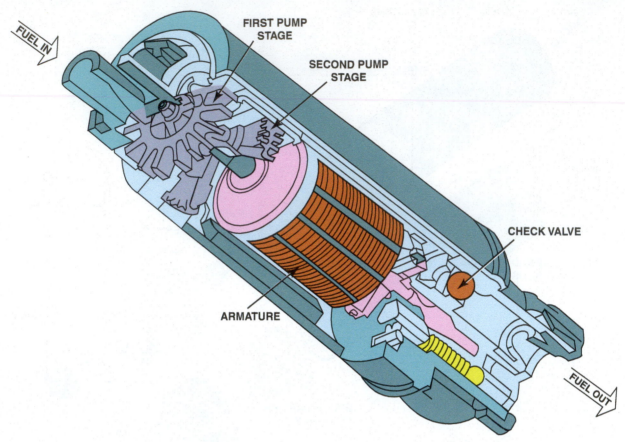

FIGURE 21–14 A cutaway view of a typical two-stage turbine electric fuel pump.

FUEL IN

FIRST PUMP
STAGE

SECOND PUMP
STAGE

CHECK VALVE

ARMATURE

FUEL OUT

 FREQUENTLY ASKED QUESTION

Why Are Many Fuel-Pump Modules Spring-Loaded?

Fuel modules that contain the fuel pickup sock, fuel pump, and fuel level sensor are often spring-loaded when fitted to a plastic fuel tank. The plastic material shrinks when cold and expands when hot, so having the fuel module spring-loaded ensures that the fuel pickup sock will always be the same distance from the bottom of the tank. ● **SEE FIGURE 21–15.**

The inertia switch opens under a specified impact, such as a collision. When the switch opens, current to the pump shuts off because the fuel-pump relay will not energize. The switch must be reset manually by opening the trunk and depressing the reset button before current flow to the pump can be restored. ● **SEE FIGURE 21–16** for a schematic of a typical fuel system that uses an inertia switch in the power feed circuit to the electric fuel pump.

Since about 2008, the inertial switch has been replaced with a signal input from the airbag module. If the airbag is deployed, the circuit to the fuel pump is opened and the fuel pump stops.

FIGURE 21–15 A typical fuel-pump module assembly, which includes the pickup strainer and fuel pump, as well as the fuel-pressure sensor and fuel level sensing unit.

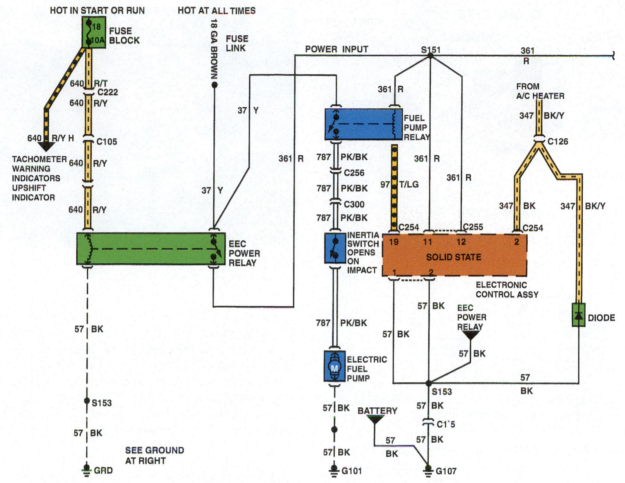

FIGURE 21–16 A schematic showing that an inertia switch is connected in series between the fuel-pump relay and the fuel pump.

PUMP PULSATION DAMPENING Some manufacturers use an **accumulator** in the system to reduce pressure pulses and noise. Others use a pulsator located at the outlet of the fuel pump to absorb pressure pulsations that are created by the pump. These pulsators are usually used on roller vane pumps and are a source of many internal fuel leaks. ● **SEE FIGURE 21–17.**

NOTE: Some experts suggest that the pulsator be removed and replaced with a standard section of fuel line to prevent the loss of fuel pressure that results when the connections on the pulsator loosen and leak fuel back into the tank.

VARIABLE SPEED PUMPS Another way to help reduce noise, current draw, and pump wear is to reduce the speed of the pump when less than maximum output is required. Pump speed and pressure can be regulated by controlling the voltage supplied to the pump with a resistor switched into the circuit, or by using a separate fuel pump driver module to supply a pulse-width modulated (PWM) voltage to the pump. With slower pump speed and pressure, less noise is produced.

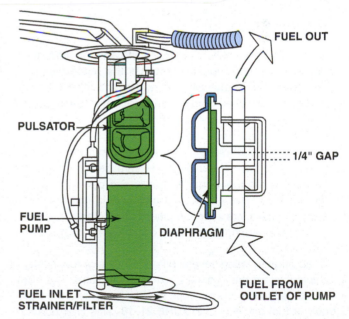

FIGURE 21–17 A typical fuel pulsator used mostly with roller vane-type pumps to help even out the pulsation in pressure that can cause noise.

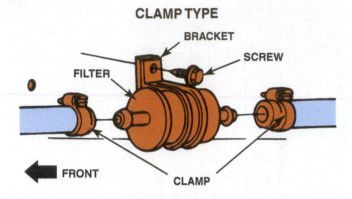

CLAMP TYPE

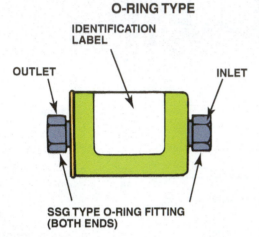

O-RING TYPE

FIGURE 21–18 Inline fuel filters are usually attached to the fuel line with screw clamps or threaded connections. The fuel filter must be installed in the proper direction or a restricted fuel flow can result.

FIGURE 21–19 A dim headlight indicates excessive resistance in fuel pump circuit.

Fuel filters may be mounted on a bracket on the fender panel, a shock tower, or another convenient place in the engine compartment. They may also be installed under the vehicle near the fuel tank. Fuel filters should be replaced according to the vehicle manufacturer's recommendations, which range from every 30,000 miles (48,000 km) to 100,000 miles (160,000 km) or longer. Fuel filters that are part of the fuel-pump module assemblies usually do not have any specified service interval.

 **TECH TIP**

Use a Headlight to Test for Power and Ground

When replacing a fuel pump, always check for proper power and ground. If the supply voltage is low due to resistance in the circuit or the ground connection is poor, the lower available voltage to the pump will result in lower pump output and could also reduce the life of the pump. While a voltage drop test can be preformed, a quick and easy test is to use a headlight connected to the circuit. If the headlight is bright, then both the power side and the ground side of the pump circuit are normal. If the headlight is dim, then more testing will be needed to find the source of the resistance in the circuit(s). ● **SEE FIGURE 21–19**.

FUEL FILTERS

Despite the care generally taken in refining, storing, and delivering gasoline, some impurities get into the automotive fuel system. Fuel filters remove dirt, rust, water, and other contamination from the gasoline before it can reach the fuel injectors. Most fuel filters are designed to filter particles that are 10 to 20 microns or larger in size.

The useful life of many filters is limited, but vehicles that use a returnless-type fuel-injection system usually use filters that are part of the fuel pump assembly and do not have any specified interval. This means that they should last the life of the vehicle. If fuel filters are not replaced according to the manufacturer's recommendations, they can become clogged and restrict fuel flow.

In addition to using several different types of fuel filters, a single fuel system may contain two or more filters. The inline filter is located in the line between the fuel pump and the throttle body or fuel rail. ● **SEE FIGURE 21–18**. This filter protects the system from contamination, but does not protect the fuel pump. The inline filter usually is a metal or plastic container with a pleated paper element sealed inside.

FUEL-PUMP TESTING

Fuel-pump testing includes many different tests and procedures. Even though a fuel pump can pass one test, it does not mean that there is not a fuel-pump problem. For example, if the pump motor is rotating slower than normal, it may be able to produce the specified pressure, but not enough volume to meet the needs of the engine while operating under a heavy load.

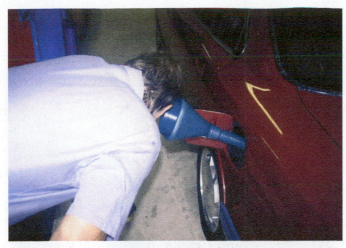

(a)

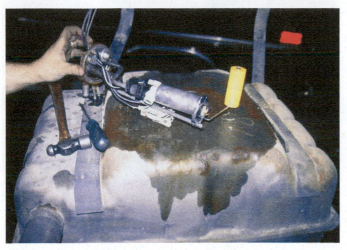

(b)

FIGURE 21–20 (a) A funnel helps in hearing if the electric fuel pump inside the gas tank is working. (b) If the pump is not running, check the wiring and current flow before going through the process of dropping the fuel tank to remove the .

TECH TIP

The Ear Test

No, this is not a test of your hearing, but rather using your ear to check that the electric fuel pump is operating. The electric fuel pump inside the fuel tank is often difficult to hear running, especially in a noisy shop environment. A commonly used trick to better hear the pump is to use a funnel in the fuel filter neck. ● **SEE FIGURE 21–20.**

TESTING FUEL-PUMP PRESSURE Fuel pump-regulated pressure has become more important than ever with a more exact fuel control. Although an increase in fuel pressure does increase fuel volume to the engine, this is *not* the preferred method to add additional fuel as some units will not open

FIGURE 21–21 The Schrader valve on this General Motors 3800 V-6 is located next to the fuel-pressure regulator.

correctly at the increased fuel pressure. On the other side of the discussion, many newer engines will not start when fuel pressure is just a few PSI low. Correct fuel pressure is very important for proper engine operation. Most fuel-injection systems operate at either a low pressure of about 10 PSI or a high pressure of between 35 and 45 PSI.

Normal Operating Pressure	(PSI)	Maximum Pump Pressure (PSI)
Low-pressure TBI units	9–13	18–20
High-pressure TBI units	25–35	50–70
Port fuel-injection systems	35–45	70–90
Central port fuel injection (GM)	55–64	90–110

In both types of systems, maximum fuel-pump pressure is about double the normal operating pressure to ensure that a continuous flow of cool fuel is being supplied to the injector(s) to help prevent vapor from forming in the fuel system. Although vapor or foaming in a fuel system can greatly affect engine operation, the cooling and lubricating flow of the fuel must be maintained to ensure the durability of injector nozzles.

To measure fuel-pump pressure, locate the Schrader valve and attach a fuel-pressure gauge. ● **SEE FIGURE 21–21.**

NOTE: Some vehicles, such as those with General Motors TBI fuel-injection systems, require a specific fuel-pressure gauge that connects to the fuel system. Always follow the manufacturers' recommendations and procedures.

REST PRESSURE TEST If the fuel pressure is acceptable, then check the system for leakdown. Observe the pressure gauge after five minutes. ● **SEE FIGURE 21–22.** The pressure should be the same as the initial reading. If not, then the pressure regulator, fuel-pump check valve, or the injectors are leaking.

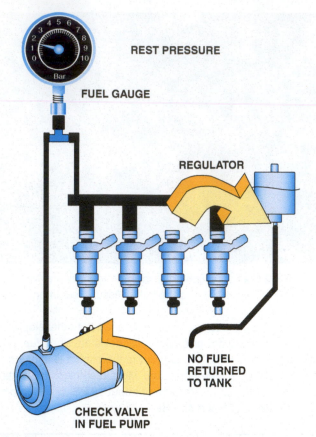

REST PRESSURE

FUEL GAUGE

REGULATOR

NO FUEL
RETURNED
TO TANK

CHECK VALVE
IN FUEL PUMP

FIGURE 21–22 The fuel system should hold pressure if the system is leak free.

FUEL PRESSURE
REGULATOR

FIGURE 21–23 If the vacuum hose is removed from the fuel-pressure regulator when the engine is running, the fuel pressure should increase. If it does not increase, then the fuel pump is not capable of supplying adequate pressure or the fuel-pressure regulator is defective. If gasoline is visible in the vacuum hose, the regulator is leaking and should be replaced.

🔧 TECH TIP

The Rubber Mallet Trick

Often a no-start condition is due to an inoperative electric fuel pump. A common trick is to tap on the bottom of the fuel tank with a rubber mallet in an attempt to jar the pump motor enough to work. Instead of pushing a vehicle into the shop, simply tap on the fuel tank and attempt to start the engine. This is not a repair, but rather a confirmation that the fuel pump does indeed require replacement.

🔧 TECH TIP

The Fuel-Pressure Stethoscope Test

When the fuel pump is energized and the engine is not running, fuel should be heard flowing back to the fuel tank at the outlet of the fuel-pressure regulator. ● SEE FIGURE 21–24. If fuel is heard flowing through the return line, the fuel-pump pressure is higher than the regulator pressure. If no sound of fuel is heard, either the fuel pump or the fuel-pressure regulator is at fault.

DYNAMIC PRESSURE TEST To test the pressure dynamically, start the engine. If the pressure is vacuum referenced, then the pressure should change when the throttle is cycled. If it does not, then check the vacuum supply circuit. Remove the vacuum line from the regulator and inspect for any presence of fuel. ● SEE FIGURE 21–23. There should never be any fuel present on the vacuum side of the regulator diaphragm. When the engine speed is increased, the pressure reading should remain within the specifications.

Some engines do not use a vacuum-referenced regulator. The running pressure remains constant, which is typical for a mechanical returnless-type fuel system. On these systems, the

pressure is higher than on return-type systems to help reduce the formation of fuel vapors in the system.

TESTING FUEL-PUMP VOLUME Fuel pressure alone is not enough for proper engine operation. ● SEE FIGURE 21–25. Sufficient fuel capacity (flow) should be at least 2 pints (1 liter) every 30 seconds or 1 pint in 15 seconds. Fuel flow

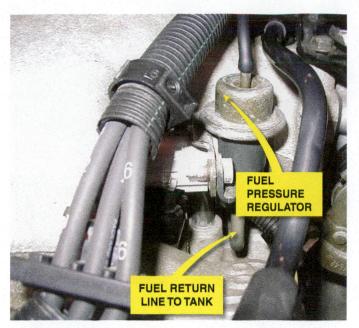

FIGURE 21-24 Fuel should be heard returning to the fuel tank at the fuel return line if the fuel pump and fuel-pressure regulator are functioning correctly.

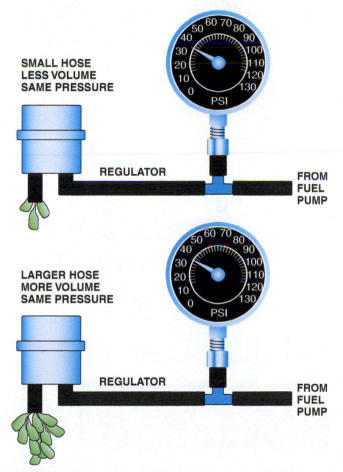

FIGURE 21-25 A fuel-pressure reading does not confirm that there is enough fuel volume for the engine to operate correctly.

FIGURE 21-26 A fuel system tester connected in series in the fuel system so all of the fuel used flows through the meter, which displays the rate of flow and the fuel pressure.

specifications are usually expressed in gallons per minute. A typical specification would be 0.5 gallons per minute or more. Volume testing is shown in ● **FIGURE 21-26**.

All fuel must be filtered to prevent dirt and impurities from damaging the fuel system components and/or engine. The first filter is inside the gas tank and is usually not replaceable separately but is attached to the fuel pump (if the pump is electric) and/or fuel gauge sending unit. The replaceable fuel filter is usually located between the fuel tank and the fuel rail or inlet to the fuel-injection system. Most vehicle manufacturers state in service information when to replace the fuel filter. Most newer vehicles, that use returnless-type fuel-injection systems, do not have replaceable filters as they are built into the fuel pump module assembly. (Check the vehicle manufacturers' recommendations for exact time and mileage intervals.)

If the fuel filter becomes partially clogged, the following are likely to occur:

1. There will be low power at higher engine speeds. The vehicle usually will not go faster than a certain speed (engine acts as if it has a built-in speed governor).

2. The engine will cut out or miss on acceleration, especially when climbing hills or during heavy-load acceleration.

A weak or defective fuel pump can also be the cause of the symptoms just listed. If an electric fuel pump for a fuel-injected engine becomes weak, additional problems include the following:

1. The engine may be hard to start.

2. There may be a rough idle and stalling.

3. There may be erratic shifting of the automatic transmission as a result of engine missing due to lack of fuel-pump pressure and/or volume.

CAUTION: Be certain to consult the vehicle manufacturers' recommended service and testing procedures before attempting to test or replace any component of a high-pressure electronic fuel-injection system.

Quick and Easy Fuel Volume Test

Testing for pump volume involves using a specialized tester or a fuel-pressure gauge equipped with a hose to allow the fuel to be drawn from the system into a container with volume markings to allow for a volume measurement. This test can be hazardous because of expanding gasoline. An alternative test involves connecting a fuel-pressure gauge to the system with the following steps:

STEP 1 Start the engine and observe the fuelpressure gauge. The reading should be within factory specifications (typically between 35 and 45 PSI).

STEP 2 Remove the hose from the fuel-pressure regulator. The pressure should increase if the system uses a demand-type regulator.

STEP 3 Rapidly accelerate the engine while watching the fuel-pressure gauge. If the fuel volume is okay, the fuel pressure should not drop more than 2 PSI. If the fuel pressure drops more than 2 PSI, replace the fuel filter and retest.

STEP 4 After replacing the fuel filter, accelerate the engine and observe the pressure gauge. If the pressure drops more than 2 PSI, replace the fuel pump.

NOTE: The fuel pump could still be delivering less than the specified volume of fuel, but as long as the volume needed by the engine is met, the pressure will not drop. If, however, the vehicle is pulling a heavy load, the demand for fuel volume may exceed the capacity of the pump.

Remove the Bed to Save Time?

The electric fuel pump is easier to replace on many General Motors pickup trucks if the bed is removed. Access to the top of the fuel tank, where the access hole is located, for the removal of the fuel tank sender unit and pump is restricted by the bottom of the pickup truck bed. It would take several people (usually other technicians in the shop) to lift the truck bed from the frame after removing only a few fasteners.
● **SEE FIGURE 21–27.**

CAUTION: Be sure to clean around the fuel pump opening so that dirt or debris does not enter the tank when the fuel pump is removed.

FIGURE 21–27 Removing the bed from a pickup truck makes gaining access to the fuel pump a lot easier.

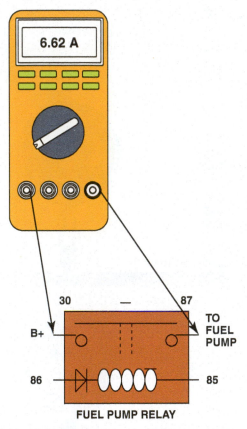

FIGURE 21–28 Hookup for testing fuel-pump current draw on any vehicle equipped with a fuel-pump relay.

FUEL-PUMP CURRENT DRAW TEST

Another test that can and should be performed on a fuel pump is to measure the current draw in amperes. This test is most often performed by connecting a digital multimeter set to read DC amperes and test the current draw. ● **SEE FIGURE 21–28.**

Fuel-Pump Current Draw Table			
AMPERAGE READING	EXPECTED VALUE	AMPERAGE TOO HIGH	AMPERAGE TOO LOW
Throttle-Body Fuel-Injection Engines	2–5 A	• Check the fuel filter. • Check for restrictions in other fuel line areas. • Replace the fuel pump.	• Check for a high-resistance connection. • Check for a high-resistance ground fault. • Replace the fuel pump.
Port Fuel-Injection Engines	4–8 A	• Check the fuel filter. • Check for restrictions in other fuel line areas. • Replace the fuel pump.	• Check for a high-resistance connection. • Check for a high-resistance ground fault. • Replace the fuel pump.
Turbo Engines	6–10 A	• Check the fuel filter. • Check for restrictions in other fuel line areas. • Replace the fuel pump.	• Check for a high-resistance connection. • Check for a high-resistance ground fault. • Replace the fuel pump.
GM CPI Truck Engines	8–12 A	• Check the fuel filter. • Check for restrictions in other fuel line areas. • Replace the fuel pump.	• Check for a high-resistance connection. • Check for a high-resistance ground fault. • Replace the fuel pump.

CHART 21–1

Fuel-pump draw and possible faults that could cause either too high or too low an amperage reading.

for the hookup for vehicles equipped with a fuel-pump relay. Compare the reading to factory specifications. ● **SEE CHART 21–1** for an example of typical fuel-pump current draw readings.

NOTE: Testing the current draw of an electric fuel pump may not indicate whether the pump is good. A pump that is not rotating may draw normal current.

FUEL-PUMP REPLACEMENT

The following recommendations should be followed whenever replacing an electric fuel pump:

- The fuel-pump strainer (sock) should be replaced with the new pump.
- If the original pump had a deflector shield, it should always be used to prevent fuel return bubbles from blocking the inlet to the pump.
- Always check the interior of the fuel tank for evidence of contamination or dirt.
- Double-check that the replacement pump is correct for the application.
- Check that the wiring and electrical connectors are clean and tight.

 CASE STUDY

The Case of the Stalling Chevrolet Suburban

The owner of a Chevrolet Suburban with 187,000 miles complained that it has died several times when driving on the highway. Before it died, the driver felt as if the vehicle was rumbling and had a jerky feeling. Then the truck lost power and stalls. After the truck was allowed to sit on the shoulder of the road for a few minutes, it started and ran normally.

The service technician checked the fuel pump for proper current draw and while it was within specification, the technician thought that the symptoms were perfect for a fuel pump failure because it was intermittent. Using a digital storage oscilloscope (DSO) connected to the pump power wire at the fuel pump relay, showed a pattern that indicated worn brushes. The fuel pump was replaced and the owner reported back that the intermittent stalling had not occurred since the repair.

Summary:

- **Complaint**—The owner complained that the truck would intermittently stall when driving on the highway.
- **Cause**—A worn fuel pump was the root cause of the intermittent stalling.
- **Correction**—The fuel pump was replaced, which solved the stalling problem.

Fuel Supply–Related Symptom Guide	
PROBLEM	**POSSIBLE CAUSES**
Pressure too high after engine start-up.	1. Defective fuel-pressure regulator 2. Restricted fuel return line 3. Excessive system voltage 4. Restricted return line 5. Wrong fuel pump
Pressure too low after engine start-up.	1. Stuck-open pressure regulator 2. Low voltage 3. Poor ground 4. Plugged fuel filter 5. Faulty inline fuel pump 6. Faulty in-tank fuel pump 7. Partially clogged filter sock 8. Faulty hose coupling 9. Leaking fuel line 10. Wrong fuel pump 11. Leaking pulsator 12. Restricted accumulator 13. Faulty pump check valves 14. Faulty pump installation
Pressure drops off with key on/ engine off. **With key off, the pressure does not hold.**	1. Leaky pulsator 2. Leaking fuel-pump coupling hose 3. Faulty fuel pump (check valves) 4. Faulty pressure regulator 5. Leaking fuel injector 6. Leaking cold-start fuel injector 7. Faulty installation 8. Lines leaking

SUMMARY

1. The fuel delivery system includes the following items:
   - Fuel tank
   - Fuel pump
   - Fuel filter(s)
   - Fuel lines

2. A fuel tank is either constructed of steel with a tin plating for corrosion resistance or polyethylene plastic.

3. Fuel tank filler tubes contain an anti-siphoning device.

4. Accident and rollover protection devices include check valves and inertia switches.

5. Most fuel lines are made of nylon plastic.

6. Electric fuel-pump types include roller cell, gerotor, and turbine.

7. Fuel filters remove particles that are 10 to 20 microns or larger in size and should be replaced regularly.

8. Fuel pumps can be tested by checking:
   - Pressure
   - Volume
   - Specified current draw

REVIEW QUESTIONS

1. What are the three most commonly used pump designs?

2. What is the proper way to disconnect and connect plastic fuel line connections?

3. Where are the fuel filters located in the fuel system?

4. What accident and rollover devices are installed in a fuel delivery system?

5. What three methods can be used to test a fuel pump?

1. The first fuel filter in the sock inside the fuel tank normally filters particles larger than _____.
   a. 0.001 to 0.003 inch
   b. 0.010 to 0.030 inch
   c. 10 to 20 microns
   d. 70 to 100 microns

2. If it is tripped, which type of safety device will keep the electric fuel pump from operating?
   a. Rollover valve
   b. Inertia switch
   c. Anti-siphoning valve
   d. Check valve

3. Fuel lines are constructed from _____.
   a. seamless steel tubing
   b. nylon plastic
   c. copper and/or aluminum tubing
   d. both a and b

4. What prevents the fuel pump inside the fuel tank from catching the gasoline on fire?
   a. Electricity is not used to power the pump
   b. No air is around the motor brushes
   c. Gasoline is hard to ignite in a closed space
   d. All of the above

5. A good fuel pump should be able to supply how much fuel per minute?
   a. 1/4 pint
   b. 1/2 pint
   c. 1 pint
   d. 0.6 to 0.8 gallons

6. Technician A says that fuel pump modules are spring-loaded so that they can be compressed to fit into the opening. Technician B says that they are spring-loaded to allow for expansion and contraction of plastic fuel tanks. Which technician is correct?
   a. Technician A only
   b. Technician B only
   c. Both Technicians A and B
   d. Neither Technician A nor B

7. Most fuel filters are designed to remove particles larger than _____.
   a. 10 microns
   b. 20 microns
   c. 70 microns
   d. 100 microns

8. The amperage draw of an electric fuel pump is higher than specified. What could be the cause?
   a. Clogged fuel filter
   b. Restriction in the fuel line
   c. Defective fuel pump
   d. Any of the above

9. A fuel pump is being replaced for the third time. Technician A says that the gasoline could be contaminated. Technician B says that wiring to the pump could be corroded. Which technician is correct?
   a. Technician A only
   b. Technician B only
   c. Both Technicians A and B
   d. Neither Technician A nor B

10. The amperage draw of an electric fuel pump is lower than specified. What is the most likely cause?
    a. Corroded electrical connections at the pump motor
    b. Clogged fuel filter
    c. Restriction in the fuel line
    d. Stuck fuel pump impeller blades

chapter 22

FUEL-INJECTION COMPONENTS AND OPERATION

LEARNING OBJECTIVES

After studying this chapter, the reader should be able to:

1. List the types of fuel-injection systems and explain their modes of operation.
2. Describe how throttle-body injection and port fuel-injection systems work.
3. Discuss the function of the fuel-pressure regulator and describe a vacuum-biased fuel-pressure regulator.
4. Describe the different types of returnless fuel systems and how they function.
5. Describe the purpose and function of a demand delivery system.
6. Discuss fuel injectors and fuel-injection modes of operation.
7. Explain the operation of the idle control system.

This chapter will help you prepare for Engine Repair (A8) ASE certification test content area "C" (Fuel, Air Induction, and Exhaust Systems Diagnosis and Repair).

KEY TERMS

Demand delivery system (DDS) 323
Electronic air control (EAC) 327
Electronic returnless fuel system (ERFS) 323
Flare 328
Fuel rail 325
Gang fired 320
Idle speed control (ISC) motor 328

Mechanical returnless fuel system (MRFS) 323
Port fuel-injection 318
Pressure control valve (PCV) 323
Pressure vent valve (PVV) 323
Sequential fuel injection (SFI) 321
Throttle-body-injection (TBI) 318

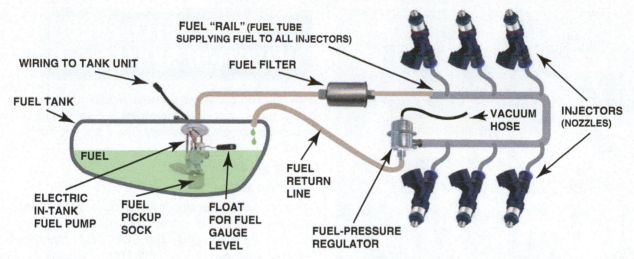

FIGURE 22–1 Typical port fuel-injection system, indicating the location of various components. Notice that the fuel-pressure regulator is located on the fuel return side of the system. The computer does not control fuel pressure, but does control the operation of the electric fuel pump (on most systems) and the pulsing on and off of the injectors.

ELECTRONIC FUEL-INJECTION OPERATION

Electronic fuel-injection systems use the computer (PCM) to control the following operation of fuel injectors and other functions based on information sent to the PCM from the various sensors. Most electronic fuel-injection systems share the following:

1. Electric fuel pump (usually located inside the fuel tank)
2. Fuel-pump relay (usually controlled by the PCM)
3. Fuel-pressure regulator (mechanically operated spring-loaded rubber diaphragm maintains proper fuel pressure)
4. Fuel-injector nozzle or nozzles

● **SEE FIGURE 22–1.** Most electronic fuel-injection systems uses 12 volts from the ignition and the PCM to control the following aspects of their operation:

1. **Pulsing the fuel injectors on and off.** The longer the injectors are held open, the greater the amount of fuel injected into the intake manifold near the intake valve.
2. **Operating the fuel-pump relay circuit.** The PCM usually controls the operation of the electric fuel pump located inside (or near) the fuel tank. The PCM uses signals from the ignition switch and RPM signals from the ignition module or system to energize the fuel-pump relay circuit.

NOTE: This is a safety feature, because if the engine stalls and the tachometer (engine speed) signal is lost, the PCM will shut off (de-energize) the fuel-pump relay and stop the fuel pump.

Computer-controlled fuel-injection systems are normally reliable systems if the proper service procedures are followed. Fuel-injection systems use the gasoline flowing through the injectors to lubricate and cool the injector electrical windings and pintle valves.

NOTE: The fuel does not actually make contact with the electrical windings because the injectors have O-rings at the top and bottom of the winding spool to keep fuel out.

TECH TIP

"Two Must-Do's"

For long service life of the fuel system, always do the following:

1. Avoid operating the vehicle on a near-empty tank of fuel. The water or alcohol becomes more concentrated when the fuel level is low. Dirt that settles near the bottom of the fuel tank can be drawn through the fuel system and cause damage to the pump and injector nozzles.
2. Replace the fuel filter at regular service intervals, if applicable.

FIGURE 22–2 A dual-nozzle TBI unit on a Chevrolet 5.0 L V-8 engine. The fuel is squirted above the throttle plate where the fuel mixes with air before entering the intake manifold.

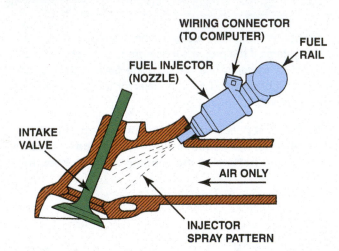

FIGURE 22–3 A typical port fuel-injection system squirts fuel into the low pressure (vacuum) of the intake manifold, about 3 inch (70 to 100 mm) from the intake valve.

There are two types of electronic fuel-injection systems:

- **Throttle-body-injection (TBI)** type. A TBI system delivers fuel from a nozzle(s) into the air above the throttle plate. ● **SEE FIGURE 22–2**.
- **Port fuel-injection** type. A port fuel-injection design uses a nozzle for each cylinder and the fuel is squirted into the intake manifold about 2 to 3 inches (70 to 100 mm) from the intake valve. ● **SEE FIGURE 22–3**.

SPEED-DENSITY FUEL-INJECTION SYSTEMS

Fuel-injection computer systems require a method for measuring the amount of air the engine is breathing in, in order to match the correct fuel delivery. There are two basic methods used:

1. Speed density
2. Mass airflow

The speed-density method does not require an air quantity sensor, but rather calculates the amount of fuel required by the engine. The PCM uses information from sensors such as the MAP and TP to calculate the needed amount of fuel.

- **MAP sensor.** The value of the intake (inlet) manifold pressure (vacuum) is a direct indication of engine load.

- **TP sensor.** The position of the throttle plate and its rate of change are used as part of the equation to calculate the proper amount of fuel to inject.

- **Temperature sensors.** Both engine coolant temperature (ECT) and intake air temperature (IAT) are used to calculate the density of the air and the need of the engine for fuel. A cold engine (low-coolant temperature) requires a richer air–fuel mixture than a warm engine.

On speed-density systems, the PCM calculates the amount of air in each cylinder by using manifold pressure and engine rpm. The amount of air in each cylinder is the major factor in determining the amount of fuel needed. Other sensors provide information to modify the fuel requirements. The formula used to determine the injector pulse width (PW) in milliseconds (ms) is:

Injector pulse width = MAP/BARO × RPM/maximum RPM

The formula is modified by values from other sensors, including:

- Throttle position (TP)
- Engine coolant temperature (ECT)
- Intake air temperature (IAT)
- Oxygen sensor voltage (O2S)
- Adaptive memory

A fuel injector delivers atomized fuel into the airstream where it is instantly vaporized. All throttle-body (TB) fuel-injection systems and many multipoint (port) injection systems use the speed-density method of fuel calculation.

MASS AIRFLOW FUEL-INJECTION SYSTEMS

The formula used by fuel-injection systems that use a mass airflow (MAF) sensor to calculate the injection base pulse width is:

Injector pulse width = airflow/RPM

The formula is modified by other sensor values such as:

- Throttle position
- Engine coolant temperature
- Barometric pressure
- Adaptive memory

NOTE: Many four-cylinder engines do not use a MAF sensor because, due to the time interval between intake events, some reverse airflow can occur in the intake manifold. The MAF sensor would "read" this flow of air as being additional air entering the engine, giving the PCM incorrect airflow information. Therefore, most four-cylinder engines use the speed-density method of fuel control.

THROTTLE-BODY INJECTION

The PCM controls injector pulses in one of two ways:

- Synchronized
- Nonsynchronized

If the system uses a synchronized mode, the injector pulses once for each distributor reference pulse. In some vehicles, when dual injectors are used in a synchronized system, the injectors pulse alternately. In a nonsynchronized system, the injectors are pulsed once during a given period (which varies according to calibration) completely independent of distributor reference pulses.

The injector always opens the same distance, and the fuel pressure is maintained at a controlled value by the pressure regulator. The regulators used on throttle-body injection systems are not connected to a vacuum like many port fuel-injection systems. The strength of the spring inside the regulator determines at what pressure the valve is unseated, sending the fuel back to the tank and lowering the pressure. ●SEE FIGURE 22–4. The amount of fuel delivered by the injector depends on the amount of time (on-time) that the nozzle is open. This is the injector pulse width—the on-time in milliseconds that the nozzle is open.

The PCM commands a variety of pulse widths to supply the amount of fuel that an engine needs at any specific moment.

- A long pulse width delivers more fuel.
- A short pulse width delivers less fuel.

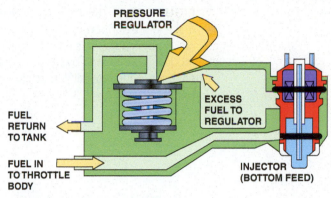

FIGURE 22–4 The tension of the spring in the fuel-pressure regulator determines the operating pressure on a throttle-body fuel-injection unit.

? FREQUENTLY ASKED QUESTION

How Do the Sensors Affect the Pulse Width?

The base pulse width of a fuel-injection system is primarily determined by the value of the MAF or MAP sensor and engine speed (RPM). However, the PCM relies on the input from many other sensors, such as the following, to modify the base pulse width as needed:

- **TP Sensor.** This sensor causes the PCM to command up to 500% (five times) the base pulse width if the accelerator pedal is depressed rapidly to the floor. It can also reduce the pulse width by about 70% if the throttle is rapidly closed.
- **ECT.** The value of this sensor determines the temperature of the engine coolant, helps determine the base pulse width, and can account for up to 60% of the determining factors.
- **BARO.** The BARO sensor compensates for altitude and adds up to about 10% under high-pressure conditions and subtracts as much as 50% from the base pulse width at high altitudes.
- **IAT.** The intake air temperature is used to modify the base pulse width based on the temperature of the air entering the engine. It is usually capable of adding as much as 20% if very cold air is entering the engine or reducing the pulse width by up to 20% if very hot air is entering the engine.
- **O2S.** This is one of the main modifiers to the base pulse width and can add or subtract up to about 20% to 25% or more, depending on the oxygen sensor activity.

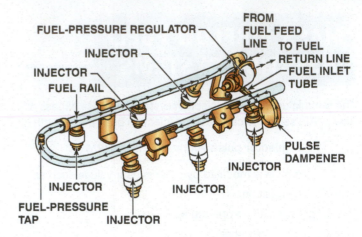

FIGURE 22–5 The injectors receive fuel and are supported by the fuel rail. A pulse damper is used to help reduce noise caused by the pressure changes in the fuel rail during injector pulsing operation.

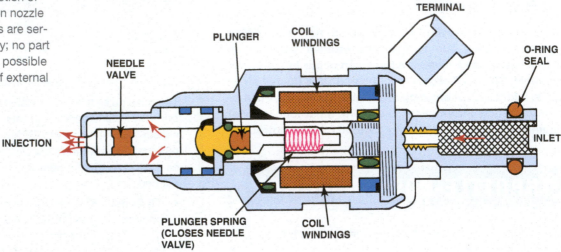

FIGURE 22–6 Cross section of a typical port fuel-injection nozzle assembly. These injectors are serviced as an assembly only; no part replacement or service is possible except for replacement of external O-ring seals.

PORT-FUEL INJECTION

The advantages of port fuel-injection design also are related to characteristics of intake manifolds:

- Fuel distribution is equal to all cylinders because each cylinder has its own injector. ● **SEE FIGURE 22–5**.

- The fuel is injected almost directly into the combustion chamber, so there is no chance for it to condense on the walls of a cold intake manifold.

- Because the manifold does not have to carry fuel to properly position a TBI unit, it can be shaped and sized to tune the intake airflow to achieve specific engine performance characteristics.

An EFI injector is simply a specialized solenoid. ● **SEE FIGURE 22–6**. It has an armature winding to create a magnetic field, and a needle (pintle), a disc, or a ball valve. A spring holds the needle, disc, or ball closed against the valve seat, and when energized, the armature winding pulls open the valve when it receives a current pulse from the Powertrain Control Module (PCM). When the solenoid is energized, it unseats the valve to inject fuel.

Electronic fuel-injection systems use a solenoid-operated injector to spray atomized fuel in timed pulses into the manifold or near the intake valve. ● **SEE FIGURE 22–7**. Injectors may be sequenced and fired in one of several ways, but their pulse width is determined and controlled by the PCM.

Port systems have an injector for each cylinder, but they do not all fire the injectors in the same way. Domestic systems use one of three ways to trigger the injectors:

- Grouped double-fire
- Simultaneous double-fire
- Sequential

GROUPED DOUBLE-FIRE This system divides the injectors into two equalized groups. The groups fire alternately; each group fires once each crankshaft revolution, or twice per four-stroke cycle. The fuel injected remains near the intake valve and enters the engine when the valve opens. This method of pulsing injectors in groups is sometimes called **gang fired**.

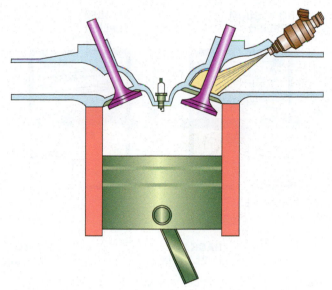

FIGURE 22–7 Port fuel injectors spray atomized fuel into the intake manifold about 3 inches (75 mm) from the intake valve.

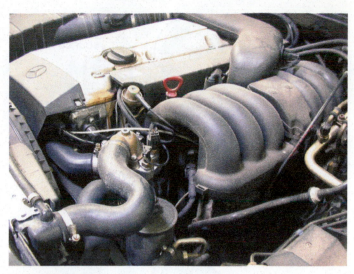

FIGURE 22–8 A port fuel-injected engine that is equipped with long, tuned intake-manifold runners.

SIMULTANEOUS DOUBLE-FIRE This design fires all of the injectors at the same time once every engine revolution: two pulses per four-stroke cycle. Many port fuel-injection systems on four-cylinder engines use this pattern of injector firing. It is easier for engineers to program this system and it can make relatively quick adjustments in the air–fuel ratio, but it still requires the intake charge to wait in the manifold for varying lengths of time.

SEQUENTIAL Sequential firing of the injectors according to engine firing order is the most accurate and desirable method of regulating port fuel injection. However, it is also the most complex and expensive to design and manufacture. In this system, the injectors are timed and pulsed individually, much like the spark plugs are sequentially operated in firing order of the engine. This system is often called **sequential fuel injection** or **SFI**. Each cylinder receives one charge every two crankshaft revolutions, just before the intake valve opens. This means that the mixture is never static in the intake manifold and mixture adjustments can be made almost instantaneously between the firing of one injector and the next. A camshaft position sensor (CMP) signal or a special distributor reference pulse informs the PCM when the No. 1 cylinder is on its compression stroke. If the sensor fails or the reference pulse is interrupted, some injection systems shut down, while others revert to pulsing the injectors simultaneously.

The major advantage of using port injection instead of the simpler throttle-body injection is that the intake manifolds on port fuel-injected engines only contain air, not a mixture of air and fuel. This allows the engine design engineer the opportunity to design long, "tuned" intake-manifold runners that help the engine produce increased torque at low engine speeds. ● **SEE FIGURE 22–8.**

NOTE: Some port fuel-injection systems used on engines with four or more valves per cylinder may use two injectors per cylinder. One injector is used all the time, and the second injector is operated by the PCM when high-engine speed and high-load conditions are detected by the PCM. Typically, the second injector injects fuel into the high-speed intake ports of the manifold. This system permits good low-speed power and throttle responses as well as superior high-speed power.

FUEL-PRESSURE REGULATOR

PURPOSE AND FUNCTION The pressure regulator and fuel pump work together to maintain the required pressure drop at the injector tips. The fuel-pressure regulator typically consists of a spring-loaded, diaphragm-operated valve in a metal housing.

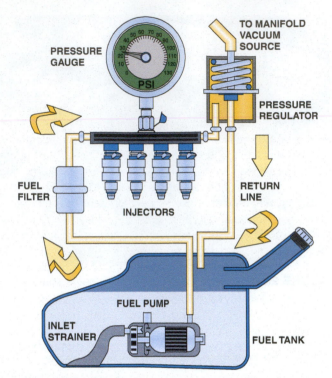

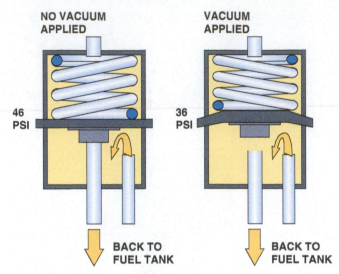

FIGURE 22–10 A typical fuel-pressure regulator that has a spring that exerts 46 pounds of force against the fuel. If 20 inches of vacuum are applied above the spring, the vacuum reduces the force exerted by the spring on the fuel, allowing the fuel to return to the tank at a lower pressure.

FIGURE 22–9 A typical port fuel-injected system showing a vacuum-controlled fuel-pressure regulator.

Fuel-pressure regulators on fuel-return-type fuel-injection systems are installed on the return (downstream) side of the injectors at the end of the fuel rail, or are built into or mounted upon the throttle-body housing. Downstream regulation minimizes fuel-pressure pulsations caused by pressure drop across the injectors as the nozzles open. It also ensures positive fuel pressure at the injectors at all times and holds residual pressure in the lines when the engine is off. On mechanical returnless systems, the regulator is located back at the tank with the fuel filter.

OPERATION In order for excess fuel (about 80% to 90% of the fuel delivered) to return to the tank, fuel pressure must overcome spring pressure on the spring-loaded diaphragm to uncover the return line to the tank. This happens when system pressure exceeds operating requirements. With TBI, the regulator is close to the injector tip, so the regulator senses essentially the same air pressure as the injector.

The pressure regulator used in a port fuel-injection system has an intake-manifold vacuum line connection on the regulator vacuum chamber. This allows fuel pressure to be modulated by a combination of spring pressure and manifold vacuum acting on the diaphragm. ● SEE FIGURES 22–9 AND 22–10.

In both TBI and port fuel-injection systems, the regulator shuts off the return line when the fuel pump is not running. This maintains pressure at the injectors for easy restarting after hot soak as well as reducing vapor lock.

FIGURE 22–11 A lack of fuel flow could be due to a restricted fuel-pressure regulator. Notice the fine screen filter. If this filter were to become clogged, higher than normal fuel pressure would occur.

TECH TIP

Don't Forget the Regulator
Some fuel-pressure regulators contain a 10 micron filter. If this filter becomes clogged, a lack of fuel flow would result. ● SEE FIGURE 22–11.

Port fuel-injection systems generally operate with pressures at the injector of about 30 to 55 PSI (207 to 379 kPa).

VACUUM-BIASED FUEL-PRESSURE REGULATOR

The primary reason why many port fuel-injected systems use a vacuum-controlled fuel-pressure regulator is to ensure that there is a constant pressure drop across the injectors. In a throttle-body fuel-injection system, the injector squirts into the atmospheric pressure regardless of the load on the engine. In a port fuel-injected engine, however, the pressure inside the intake manifold changes as the load on the engine increases.

ENGINE OPERATING CONDITION	INTAKE-MANIFOLD VACUUM	FUEL PRESSURE
Idle or cruise	High	Lower
Heavy load	Low	Higher

The PCM can best calculate injector pulse width based on all sensors if the pressure drop across the injector is the same under all operating conditions. A vacuum-controlled fuel-pressure regulator allows the equal pressure drop by reducing the force exerted by the regulator spring at high vacuum (low-load condition), yet allowing the full force of the regulator spring to be exerted when the vacuum is low (high-engine-load condition).

ELECTRONIC RETURNLESS FUEL SYSTEM

This system is unique because it does not use a mechanical valve to regulate rail pressure. Fuel pressure at the rail is sensed by a pressure transducer, which sends a low-level signal to a controller. The controller contains logic to calculate a signal to the pump power driver. The power driver contains a high-current transistor that controls the pump speed using pulse width modulation (PWM). This system is called the **electronic returnless fuel system (ERFS)**. ● SEE FIGURE 22–12. This transducer can be differentially referenced to manifold pressure for closed-loop feedback, correcting and maintaining the output of the pump to a desired rail setting. This system is capable of continuously varying rail pressure as a result of engine vacuum, engine fuel demand, and fuel temperature (as sensed by an external temperature transducer, if necessary). A **pressure vent valve (PVV)** is employed at the tank to relieve overpressure due to thermal expansion of fuel. In addition, a supply-side bleed, by means of an in-tank reservoir using a supply-side jet pump, is necessary for proper pump operation.

MECHANICAL RETURNLESS FUEL SYSTEM

The first production returnless systems employed the **mechanical returnless fuel system (MRFS)** approach. This system has a bypass regulator to control rail pressure that is located in close proximity to the fuel tank. Fuel is sent by the in-tank pump to a chassis-mounted inline filter with excess fuel returning to the tank through a short return line. ● SEE FIGURE 22–13. The inline filter may be mounted directly to the tank, thereby eliminating the shortened return line. Supply pressure is regulated on the downstream side of the inline filter to accommodate changing restrictions throughout the filter's service life. This system is limited to constant rail pressure (*CRP) system calibrations, whereas with ERFS, the pressure transducer can be referenced to atmospheric pressure for CRP systems or differentially referenced to intake-manifold pressure for constant differential injector pressure (**CIP) systems.

NOTE: *CRP is referenced to atmospheric pressure, has lower operating pressure, and is desirable for calibrations using speed/air density sensing. **CIP is referenced to manifold pressure, varies rail pressure, and is desirable in engines that use mass airflow sensing.

DEMAND DELIVERY SYSTEM (DDS)

Given the experience with both ERFS and MRFS, a need was recognized to develop new returnless technologies that could combine the speed control and constant injector pressure attributes of ERFS together with the cost savings, simplicity, and reliability of MRFS. This new technology also needed to address pulsation dampening/hammering and fuel transient response. Therefore, the **demand delivery system (DDS)** technology was developed. A different form of demand pressure regulator has been applied to the fuel rail. It mounts at the head or port entry and regulates the pressure downstream at the injectors by admitting the precise quantity of fuel into the rail as consumed by the engine. Having demand regulation at the rail improves pressure response to flow transients and provides rail pulsation dampening. A fuel pump and a low-cost, high-performance bypass regulator are used within the appropriate fuel sender. ● SEE FIGURE 22–14. They supply a pressure somewhat higher than the required rail set pressure to accommodate dynamic line and filter pressure losses. Electronic pump speed control is accomplished using a smart regulator as an integral flow sensor. A **pressure control valve (PCV)** may also be used and can readily reconfigure an existing design fuel sender into a returnless sender.

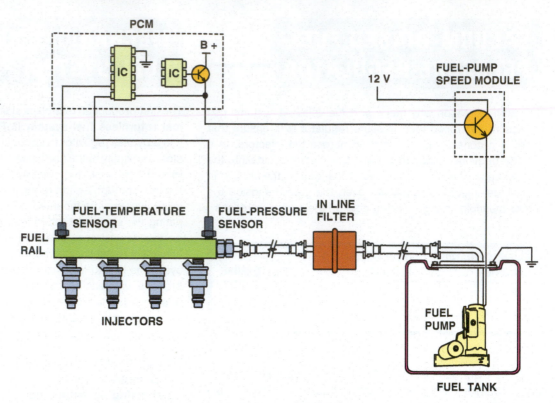

FIGURE 22–12 The fuel-pressure sensor and fuel-temperature sensor are often constructed together in one assembly to help give the PCM the needed data to control the fuel-pump speed.

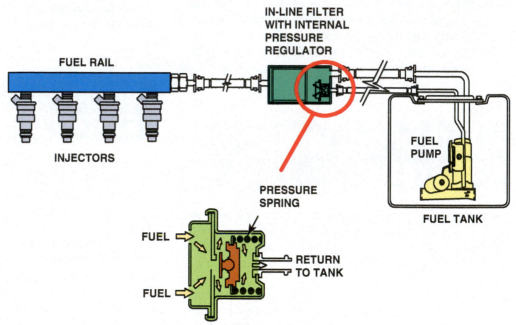

FIGURE 22–13 A mechanical returnless fuel system. The by-pass regulator in the fuel tank controls fuel line pressure.

FUEL INJECTORS

EFI systems use solenoid-operated injectors. ● **SEE FIGURE 22–16**. This electromagnetic device contains an armature and a spring-loaded needle valve or ball valve assembly. When the PCM energizes the solenoid, voltage is applied to the solenoid coil until the current reaches a specified level. This permits a quick pull-in of the armature during turn-on. The armature is pulled off of its seat against spring force, allowing fuel to flow through the inlet filter screen to the spray nozzle, where it is sprayed in a pattern that varies with application. ● **SEE FIGURE 22–17**. The injector opens the same amount each time it is energized, so the amount of fuel injected depends on the length of time the injector remains open. By angling the director hole plates, the injector sprays fuel more directly at the intake valves, which further atomizes and vaporizes the fuel before it enters the combustion chamber. PFI injectors typically are a top-feed design in which fuel enters the top of the injector and passes through its entire length to keep it cool before being injected.

Ford introduced two basic designs of deposit-resistant injectors on some engines. The design, manufactured by

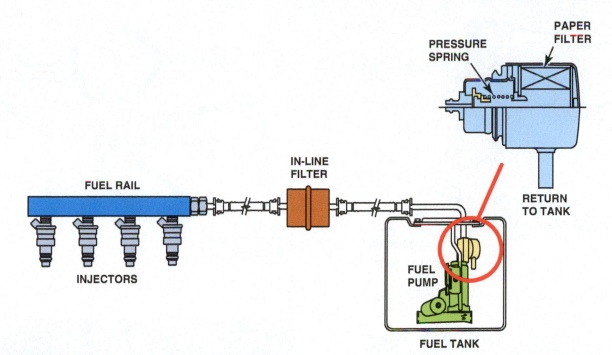

FIGURE 22–14 A demand delivery system uses a fuel-pressure regulator attached to the fuel pump assembly inside the fuel tank.

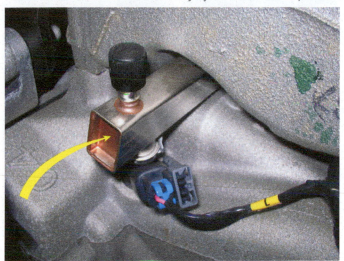

FIGURE 22–15 A rectangular-shaped fuel rail is used to help dampen fuel system pulsations and noise caused by the injectors opening and closing.

 FREQUENTLY ASKED QUESTION

Why Are Some Fuel Rails Rectangular Shaped?

A port fuel-injection system uses a pipe or tubes to deliver fuel from the fuel line to the intended fuel injectors. This pipe or tube is called the **fuel rail**. Some vehicle manufacturers construct the fuel rail in a rectangular cross section. ● **SEE FIGURE 22–15.** The sides of the fuel rail are able to move in and out slightly, thereby acting as a fuel pulsator evening out the pressure pulses created by the opening and closing of the injectors to reduce underhood noise. A round cross-sectional fuel rail is not able to deform and, as a result, some manufacturers have had to use a separate dampener.

? **FREQUENTLY ASKED QUESTION**

How Can the Proper Injector Size Be Determined?

Most people want to increase the output of fuel to increase engine performance. Injector sizing can sometimes be a challenge, especially if the size of injector is not known. In most cases, manufacturers publish the rating of injectors, in pounds of fuel per hour (lb/hr). The rate is figured with the injector held open at 3 bars (43.5 PSI). An important consideration is that larger flow injectors have a higher minimum flow rating. Here is a formula to calculate injector sizing when changing the mechanical characteristics of an engine.

Flow rate = hp × BSFC/number of cylinders × maximum duty cycle (of on − time of the injectors)

- **hp** is the projected horsepower. Be realistic!
- **BSFC** is brake-specific fuel consumption in pounds per horsepower-hour. Calculated values are used for this, 0.4 to 0.8 lb. In most cases, start on the low side for naturally aspirated engines and the high side for engines with forced induction.
- **Number of cylinders** is actually the number of injectors being used.
- **Maximum duty cycle** is considered at 0.8 (80%). Above this, the injector may overheat, lose consistency, or not work at all.

  For example:
  5.7 liter V − 8 = 240 hp × 0.65/8 cylinders × 8
  = 24.37 lb/hr injectors required

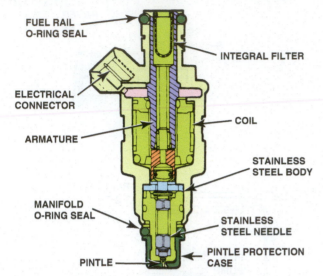

FIGURE 22–16 A multiport fuel injector. Notice that the fuel flows straight through and does not come in contact with the coil windings.

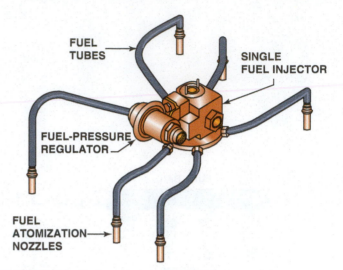

FIGURE 22–18 A central port fuel-injection system.

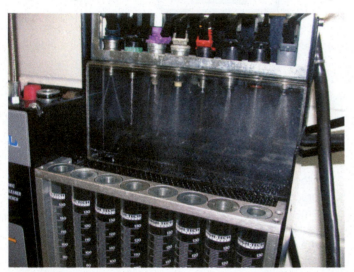

FIGURE 22–17 Each of the eight injectors shown are producing a correct spray pattern for the applications. While all throttle-body injectors spray a conical pattern, most port fuel injections do not.

Bosch, uses a four-hole director/metering plate similar to that used by the Rochester Multec injectors. The design manufactured by Nippondenso uses an internal upstream orifice in the adjusting tube. It also has a redesigned pintle/seat containing a wider tip opening that tolerates deposit buildup without affecting injector performance.

CENTRAL PORT INJECTION

A cross between port fuel injection and throttle-body injection, CPI was introduced in the early 1990s by General Motors. The CPI assembly consists of a single fuel injector, a pressure regulator, and six poppet nozzle assemblies with nozzle tubes. ● SEE FIGURE 22–18. The central sequential fuel injection (CSFI) system has six injectors in place of just one used on the CPI unit.

When the injector is energized, its armature lifts off of the six fuel tube seats and pressurized fuel flows through the nozzle

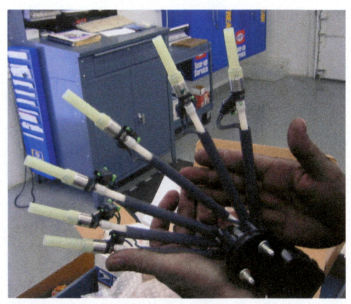

FIGURE 22–19 A factory replacement unit for a CSFI unit that has individual injectors at the ends that go into the intake manifold instead of poppet valves.

tubes to each poppet nozzle. The increased pressure causes each poppet nozzle ball to also lift from its seat, allowing fuel to flow from the nozzle. This hybrid injection system combines the single injector of a TBI system with the equalized fuel distribution of a PFI system. It eliminates the individual fuel rail while allowing more efficient manifold tuning than is otherwise possible with a TBI system. Newer versions use six individual solenoids to fire one for each cylinder. ● SEE FIGURE 22–19.

FUEL-INJECTION MODES OF OPERATION

All fuel-injection systems are designed to supply the correct amount of fuel under a wide range of engine operating conditions. These modes of operation include:

- Starting (cranking)
- Clear flood
- Idle (run)
- Acceleration enrichment
- Deceleration enleanment
- Fuel shutoff

STARTING MODE When the ignition is turned to the start (on) position, the engine cranks and the PCM energizes the fuel-pump relay. The PCM also pulses the injectors on, basing the pulse width on engine speed and engine coolant temperature. The colder the engine is, the greater the pulse width. Cranking mode air–fuel ratio varies from about 1.5:1 at −40°F (−40°C) to 14.7:1 at 200°F (93°C).

CLEAR FLOOD MODE If the engine becomes flooded with too much fuel, the driver can depress the accelerator pedal to greater than 80% to enter the clear flood mode. When the PCM detects that the engine speed is low (usually below 600 RPM) and the throttle-position (TP) sensor voltage is high (WOT), the injector pulse width is greatly reduced or even shut off entirely, depending on the vehicle.

OPEN-LOOP MODE Open-loop operation occurs during warm-up before the oxygen sensor can supply accurate information to the PCM. The PCM determines injector pulse width based on values from the MAF, MAP, TP, ECT, and IAT sensors.

CLOSED-LOOP MODE Closed-loop operation is used to modify the base injector pulse width as determined by feedback from the oxygen sensor to achieve proper fuel control.

ACCELERATION ENRICHMENT MODE During acceleration, the throttle-position (TP) voltage increases, indicating that a richer air–fuel mixture is required. The PCM then supplies a longer injector pulse width and may even supply extra pulses to supply the needed fuel for acceleration.

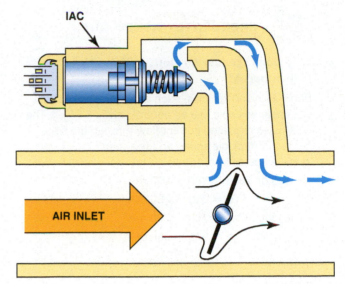

FIGURE 22–20 The small arrows indicate the air bypassing the throttle plate in the closed throttle position. This air is called minimum air. The air flowing through the IAC is the airflow that determines the idle speed.

DECELERATION ENLEANMENT MODE When the engine decelerates, a leaner air–fuel mixture is required to help reduce emissions and to prevent deceleration backfire. If the deceleration is rapid, the injector may be shut off entirely for a short time and then pulsed on enough to keep the engine running.

FUEL SHUTOFF MODE Besides shutting off fuel entirely during periods of rapid deceleration, PCM also shuts off the injector when the ignition is turned off to prevent the engine from continuing to run.

IDLE CONTROL

PURPOSE AND FUNCTION Before electronic throttle control (ETC) systems, the idle speed was controlled by using an air bypass control unit. ● SEE FIGURE 22–20. This air bypass or regulator provides needed additional airflow, and thus more fuel. The engine needs more power when cold to maintain its normal idle speed to overcome the increased friction from cold lubricating oil. It does this by opening an intake air passage to let more air into the engine just as depressing the accelerator pedal would open the throttle valve, allowing more air into the engine. The system is calibrated to maintain engine idle speed at a specified value regardless of engine temperature.

Most PFI systems use an idle air control (IAC) motor to regulate idle bypass air. The IAC is computer-controlled, and is either a solenoid-operated valve or a stepper motor that regulates the airflow around the throttle. The idle air control valve is also called an **electronic air control (EAC)** valve.

FREQUENTLY ASKED QUESTION

What Is Battery Voltage Correction?

Battery voltage correction is a program built into the PCM that causes the injector pulse width to increase if there is a drop in electrical system voltage. Lower battery voltage would cause the fuel injectors to open slower than normal and the fuel pump to run slower. Both of these conditions can cause the engine to run leaner than normal if the battery voltage is low. Because a lean air–fuel mixture can cause the engine to overheat, the PCM compensates for the lower voltage by adding a percentage to the injector pulse width. This richer condition will help prevent serious engine damage. The idle speed is also increased to turn the generator (alternator) faster if low battery voltage is detected.

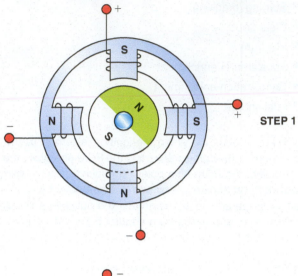

? **FREQUENTLY ASKED QUESTION**

Why Does the Idle Air Control Valve Use Milliamperes?

Some Chrysler vehicles, such as the Dodge minivan, use linear solenoid idle air control valves (LSIAC). The PCM uses regulated current flow through the solenoid to control idle speed and the scan tool display is in milliamperes (mA).

Closed position = 180 − 200 mA

Idle = 300 − 450 mA

Light cruise = 500 − 700 mA

Fully open = 900 − 950 mA

When the engine stops, most IAC units will retract outward to get ready for the next engine start. When the engine starts, the engine speed is high to provide for proper operation when the engine is cold. Then, as the engine gets warmer, the PCM reduces engine idle speed gradually by reducing the number of counts or steps commanded by the IAC.

When the engine is warm and restarted, the idle speed should momentarily increase, then decrease to normal idle speed. This increase and then decrease in engine speed is often called an engine **flare**. If the engine speed does not flare, then the IAC may not be working (it may be stuck in one position).

STEPPER MOTOR OPERATION A digital output is used to control stepper motors. Stepper motors are direct-current motors that move in fixed steps or increments from de-energized (no voltage) to fully energized (full voltage). A stepper motor often has as many as 120 steps of motion.

A common use for stepper motors is as an idle air control (IAC) valve, which controls engine idle speeds and prevents stalls due to changes in engine load. When used as an IAC, the stepper motor is usually a reversible DC motor that moves in increments, or steps. The motor moves a shaft back and forth to operate a conical valve. When the conical valve is moved back, more air bypasses the throttle plates and enters the engine, increasing idle speed. As the conical valve moves inward, the idle speed decreases.

When using a stepper motor that is controlled by the PCM, it is very easy for the PCM to keep track of the position of the stepper motor. By counting the number of steps that have been sent to the stepper motor, the PCM can determine the relative position of the stepper motor. While the PCM does not actually receive a

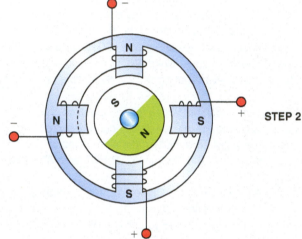

FIGURE 22–21 Most stepper motors use four wires, which are pulsed by the PCM to rotate the armature in steps.

feedback signal from the stepper motor, it does know how many steps forward or backward the motor should have moved.

A typical stepper motor uses a permanent magnet and two electromagnets. Each of the two electromagnetic windings is controlled by the PCM. The PCM pulses the windings and changes the polarity of the windings to cause the armature of the stepper motor to rotate 90 degrees at a time. Each 90-degree pulse is recorded by the PCM as a "count" or "step"; therefore, the name given to this type of motor. ● **SEE FIGURE 22–21.**

Idle airflow in a TBI system travels through a passage around the throttle and is controlled by a stepper motor. In some applications, an externally mounted permanent magnet motor called the **idle speed control (ISC) motor** mechanically advances the throttle linkage to advance the throttle opening.

SUMMARY

1. A fuel-injection system includes the electric fuel pump and fuel-pump relay, fuel-pressure regulator, and fuel injectors (nozzles).

2. The two types of fuel-injection systems are the throttle-body design and the port fuel-injection design.

3. The two methods of fuel-injection control are the speed-density system, which uses the MAP to measure the load on the engine, and the mass airflow, which uses the MAF sensor to directly measure the amount of air entering the engine.

4. The amount of fuel supplied by fuel injectors is determined by how long they are kept open. This opening time is called the pulse width and is measured in milliseconds.

5. The fuel-pressure regulator is usually located on the fuel return on return-type fuel-injection systems.

6. TBI-type fuel-injection systems do not use a vacuum-controlled fuel-pressure regulator, whereas many port fuel-injection systems use a vacuum-controlled regulator to monitor equal pressure drop across the injectors.

7. Other fuel designs include the electronic returnless, the mechanical returnless, and the demand delivery systems.

REVIEW QUESTIONS

1. What are the two basic methods used for measuring the amount of air the engine is breathing in, in order to match the correct fuel delivery?

2. What is the purpose of the vacuum-controlled (biased) fuel-pressure regulator?

3. How many sensors are used to determine the base pulse width on a speed-density system?

4. How many sensors are used to determine the base pulse width on a mass airflow system?

5. What are the three types of returnless fuel-injection systems?

CHAPTER QUIZ

1. Technician A says that the fuel-pump relay is usually controlled by the PCM. Technician B says that a TBI injector squirts fuel above the throttle plate. Which technician is correct?
   a. Technician A only
   b. Technician B only
   c. Both Technicians A and B
   d. Neither Technician A nor B

2. Why are some fuel rails rectangular in shape?
   a. Increases fuel pressure
   b. Helps keep air out of the injectors
   c. Reduces noise
   d. Increases the speed of the fuel through the fuel rail

3. Which fuel-injection system uses the MAP sensor as the primary sensor to determine the base pulse width?
   a. Speed density
   b. Mass airflow
   c. Demand delivery
   d. Mechanical returnless

4. Why is a vacuum line attached to a fuel-pressure regulator on many port fuel-injected engines?
   a. To draw fuel back into the intake manifold through the vacuum hose
   b. To create an equal pressure drop across the injectors
   c. To raise the fuel pressure at idle
   d. To lower the fuel pressure under heavy engine load conditions to help improve fuel economy

5. Which sensor has the greatest influence on injector pulse width besides the MAF sensor?
   a. IAT
   b. BARO
   c. ECT
   d. TP

6. Technician A says that the port fuel-injection injectors operate using 5 volts from the computer. Technician B says that sequential fuel injectors all use a different wire color on the injectors. Which technician is correct?
   a. Technician A only
   b. Technician B only
   c. Both Technicians A and B
   d. Neither Technician A nor B

7. Which type of port fuel-injection system uses a fuel-temperature and/or fuel-pressure sensor?
   a. All port fuel-injected engines
   b. TBI units only
   c. Electronic returnless systems
   d. Demand delivery systems

8. The injectors on an EFI equipped engine are opened using _____ to lift the spray needle.
   a. a solenoid
   b. oil pressure
   c. engine vacuum
   d. a cam

9. Where is the fuel-pressure regulator located on a vacuum-biased port fuel-injection system?
   a. In the tank
   b. At the inlet of the fuel rail
   c. At the outlet of the fuel rail
   d. Near or on the fuel filter

10. What type of device is used in a typical idle air control?
   a. DC motor
   b. Stepper motor
   c. Pulsator-type actuator
   d. Solenoid

chapter 23
GASOLINE DIRECT-INJECTION SYSTEMS

LEARNING OBJECTIVES

After studying this chapter, the reader should be able to:

1. Explain how a gasoline direct-injection system works.
2. Describe the differences between port fuel-injection and gasoline direct-injection systems.
3. List the various modes of operation of a gasoline direct-injection system.
4. Discuss how to troubleshoot a gasoline direct-injection system.

This chapter will help you prepare for Engine Repair (A8) ASE certification test content area "C" (Fuel, Air Induction, and Exhaust Systems Diagnosis and Repair).

KEY TERMS

Gasoline direct injection (GDI) 331

Homogeneous mode 335

Spark ignition direct injection (SIDI) 331

Stratified mode 335

DIRECT FUEL INJECTION

PORT INJECTION VS. DIRECT INJECTION

In a port fuel injection system, the fuel is squirted into the intake manifold or in the intake port upstream from the intake valve. The atomized fuel then mixes with the air entering the cylinder in its way to the combustion chamber.

In a **gasoline direct injection (GDI)** system, the fuel is squired directly into the combustion chamber. ● **SEE FIGURE 23–1.**

Unlike a port fuel-injection system, a gasoline direct injection system varies the fuel pressure to achieve greater fuel delivery using a very short pulse time, which is usually less than 1 millisecond.

- Port Fuel Injection—constant fuel pressure but variable injector pulse-width.
- GDI—almost constant injector pulse-width with varying fuel pressure.

General Motors refers to as a **spark ignition direct injection (SIDI)** system.

PARTS AND OPERATION

A direct-injection system sprays high-pressure fuel, up to 2,900 PSI, into the combustion chamber as the piston approaches the top of the compression stroke. With the combination of high-pressure swirl injectors and modified combustion chamber, almost instantaneous vaporization occurs. This combined with a higher compression ratio allows a direct-injected engine to operate using a leaner-than-normal air–fuel ratio, which results in improved fuel economy with higher power output and reduced exhaust emissions. ● **SEE FIGURE 23–2.**

ADVANTAGES OF GASOLINE DIRECT INJECTION

The use of direct injection compared with port fuel injection has many advantages, including:

- Improved fuel economy due to reduced pumping losses and heat loss
- Allows a higher compression ratio for higher engine efficiency
- Allows the use of lower-octane gasoline
- The volumetric efficiency is higher
- Less need for extra fuel for acceleration
- Improved cold starting and throttle response
- Allows the use of greater percentage of EGR to reduce exhaust emissions
- Up to 25% improvement in fuel economy
- 12% to 15% reduction in exhaust emissions

DISADVANTAGES OF GASOLINE DIRECT INJECTION

- Higher cost due to high-pressure pump and injectors
- More components compared with port fuel injection
- Due to the high compression, a NO_x storage catalyst is sometimes required to meet emission standards, especially in Europe. (● **SEE FIGURE 23–3.**)
- Uses up to six operating modes depending on engine load and speed, which requires more calculations to be performed by the Powertrain Control Module (PCM).

DIRECT-INJECTION FUEL DELIVERY SYSTEM

LOW-PRESSURE SUPPLY PUMP

The fuel pump in the fuel tank supplies fuel to the high-pressure fuel pump at a pressure of approximately 60 PSI. The fuel filter is located in the fuel tank and is part of the fuel pump assembly. It is not usually serviceable as a separate component; the engine control module (ECM) controls the output of the high-pressure pump, which has a range between 500 PSI (3,440 kPa) and 2,900 PSI (15,200 kPa) during engine operation. ● **SEE FIGURES 23–3 AND 23–4.**

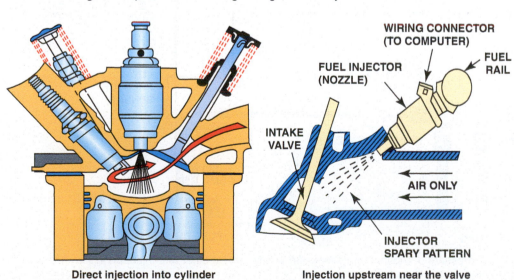

FIGURE 23–1 A comparison of a port fuel injection system (right) to a gasoline direct injection system on the left.

WIRING CONNECTOR (TO COMPUTER)

FUEL INJECTOR (NOZZLE)

FUEL RAIL

INTAKE VALVE

AIR ONLY

INJECTOR SPARY PATTERN

Direct injection into cylinder

Injection upstream near the valve

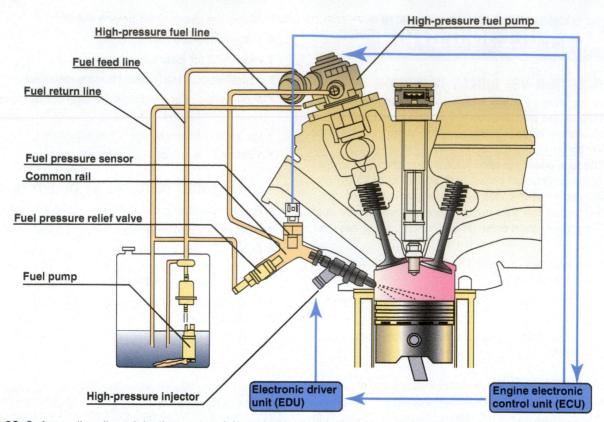

FIGURE 23–2 A gasoline direct-injection system injects fuel under high pressure directly into the combustion chamber.

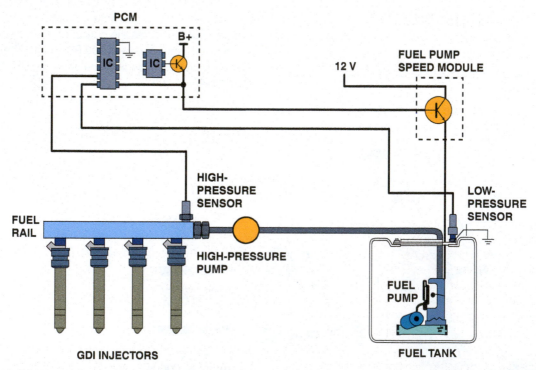

FIGURE 23–3 A GDI system uses a low-pressure pump in the gas tank similar to other types of fuel-injection systems. The PCM controls the pressure of the high-pressure pump using sensor inputs.

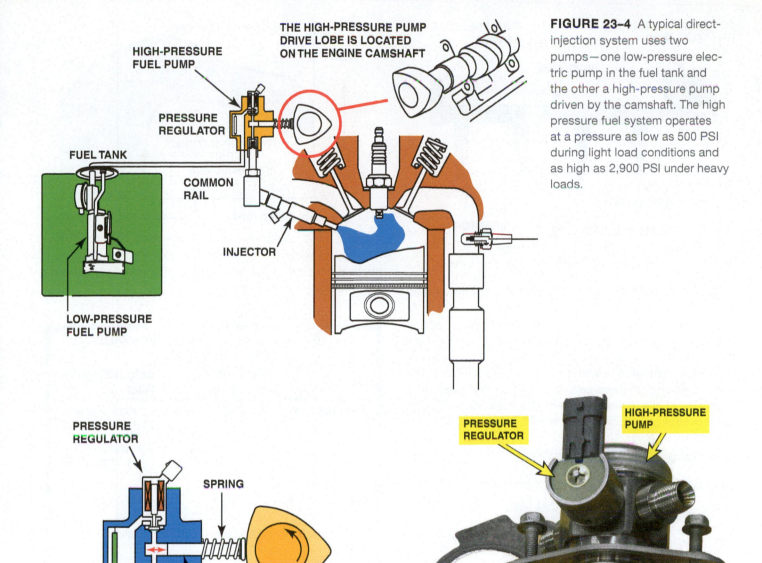

HIGH-PRESSURE FUEL PUMP

PRESSURE REGULATOR

THE HIGH-PRESSURE PUMP DRIVE LOBE IS LOCATED ON THE ENGINE CAMSHAFT

FUEL TANK

COMMON RAIL

INJECTOR

LOW-PRESSURE FUEL PUMP

FIGURE 23–4 A typical direct-injection system uses two pumps—one low-pressure electric pump in the fuel tank and the other a high-pressure pump driven by the camshaft. The high pressure fuel system operates at a pressure as low as 500 PSI during light load conditions and as high as 2,900 PSI under heavy loads.

PRESSURE REGULATOR

SPRING

PISTON

CHECK BALL

CAMSHAFT

PRESSURE REGULATOR

HIGH-PRESSURE PUMP

FIGURE 23–5a A typical camshaft-driven high-pressure pump used to increase fuel pressure to 2,000 PSI or higher.

FIGURE 23–5b The high-pressure pump assembly removed from the engine. Many GDI engines use a roller where the high-pressure pump rides against the cam lobes to help reduce friction and wear.

HIGH-PRESSURE PUMP In a General Motors system, the ECM controls the output of the high-pressure pump, which has a range between 500 PSI (3,440 kPa) and 2,900 PSI (15,200 kPa) during engine operation. The high-pressure fuel pump connects to the pump in the fuel tank through the low-pressure fuel line. The pump consists of a single-barrel piston pump, which is driven by the engine camshaft. The pump plunger rides on a three-lobed cam on the camshaft. The high-pressure pump is cooled and lubricated by the fuel itself. ● **SEE FIGURE 23–5.**

FUEL RAIL The fuel rail stores the fuel from the high-pressure pump and stores high-pressure fuel for use to each injector. All injectors get the same pressure fuel from the fuel rail.

FUEL PRESSURE REGULATOR An electric pressure-control valve is installed between the pump inlet and outlet valves. The fuel rail pressure sensor connects to the PCM with three wires:

- 5 volt reference
- ground
- signal

The sensor signal provides an analog signal to the PCM that varies in voltage as fuel rail pressure changes. Low pressure results in a low-voltage signal and high pressure results in a high-voltage signal.

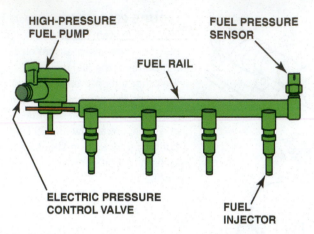

FIGURE 23–6 A gasoline direct-injection (GDI) fuel rail and pump assembly with the electric pressure control valve.

The PCM uses internal drivers to control the power feed and ground for the pressure control valve. When both PCM drivers are deactivated, the inlet valve is held open by spring pressure. This causes the high pressure fuel pump to default to low-pressure mode. The fuel from the high-pressure fuel pump flows through a line to the fuel rail and injectors. The actual operating pressure can vary from as low as 500 PSI (3,440 kPa) at idle to over 2,000 PSI (13,800 kPa) during high speed or heavy load conditions. ● SEE FIGURE 23–6.

GASOLINE DIRECT-INJECTION FUEL INJECTORS

Each high-pressure fuel injector assembly is an electrically magnetic injector mounted in the cylinder head. In the GDI system, the PCM controls each fuel injector with 50 to 90 volts (usually 60 to 70 volts), depending on the system, which is created by a boost capacitor in the PCM. During the high-voltage boost phase, the capacitor is discharged through an injector, allowing for initial injector opening. The injector is then held open with 12 volts. The high-pressure fuel injector has a small slit or six precision-machined holes that generate the desired spray pattern. The injector also has an extended tip to allow for cooling from a water jacket in the cylinder head.
● SEE CHART 23–1 for an overview of the differences between a port fuel-injection system and a gasoline direct-injection system.

PORT- AND DIRECT-INJECTION SYSTEMS

OVERVIEW Many vehicles use gasoline direct injection and in some engines they also use a conventional port fuel-injection system. The system combines direct-injection injectors located

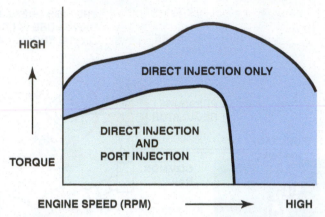

FIGURE 23–7 Notice that there are conditions when the port fuel-injector, located in the intake manifold, and the gasoline direct injector, located in the cylinder, both operate to provide the proper air–fuel mixture.

PORT FUEL-INJECTION SYSTEM COMPARED WITH GDI SYSTEM		
	PORT FUEL INJECTION	GASOLINE DIRECT INJECTION
Fuel pressure	35–60 PSI	Lift pump—50 to 60 PSI High-pressure pump—500 to 2,900 PSI
Injection pulse width at idle	1.5–3.5 ms	About 0.4 ms (400 μs)
Injector resistance	12–16 ohms	1–3 ohms
Injector voltage	6 V for low-resistance injectors, 12 V for most injectors	50–90 V
Number of injections per event	One	1–3
Engine compression ratio	8:1–11:1	11:1–13:1

CHART 23–1

A comparison chart showing the major differences between a port fuel-injection system and a gasoline direct-injection system.

in the combustion chamber with port fuel-injectors in the intake manifold near the intake valve. The two injection systems work together to supply the fuel needed by the engine. ● SEE FIGURE 23–7 for how the two systems are used throughout the various stages of engine operation.

COLD-START WARM-UP To help reduce exhaust emissions after a cold start, the fuel system uses a stratified change mode. This results in a richer air–fuel mixture near the spark plug and allows for the spark to be retarded to increase the temperature of the exhaust. As a result of the increased exhaust temperature, the catalytic converter rapidly reaches operating temperature, which reduces exhaust emissions.

MODES OF OPERATION

The two basic modes of operation include:

1. **Stratified mode.** In this mode of operation, the air–fuel mixture is richer around the spark plug than it is in the rest of the cylinder.

2. **Homogeneous mode.** In this mode of operation, the air–fuel mixture is the same throughout the cylinder.

There are variations of these modes that can be used to fine-tune the air–fuel mixture inside the cylinder. For example, Bosch, a supplier to many vehicle manufacturers, uses the following six modes of operation:

- **Homogeneous mode.** In this mode, the injector is pulsed one time to create an even air–fuel mixture in the cylinder. The injection occurs during the intake stroke. This mode is used during high-speed and/or high-torque conditions.

- **Homogeneous lean mode.** Similar to the homogeneous mode except that the overall air–fuel mixture is slightly lean for better fuel economy. The injection occurs during the intake stroke. This mode is used under steady, light-load conditions.

- **Stratified mode.** In this mode of operation, the injection occurs just before the spark occurs resulting in lean combustion, reducing fuel consumption.

- **Homogeneous stratified mode.** In this mode, there are two injections of fuel:
  - The first injection is during the intake stroke.
  - The second injection is during the compression stroke.

    As a result of these double injections, the rich air–fuel mixture around the spark plug is ignited first. Then, the rich mixture ignites the leaner mixture. The advantages of this mode include lower exhaust emissions than the stratified mode and less fuel consumption than the homogeneous lean mode.

- **Homogeneous knock protection mode.** The purpose of this mode is to reduce the possibility of spark knock from occurring under heavy loads at low engine speeds. There are two injections of fuel:
  - The first injection occurs on the intake stroke.
  - The second injection occurs during the compression stroke with the overall mixture being stoichiometric.

    As a result of this mode, the PCM does not need to retard ignition timing as much to operate knock-free.

- **Stratified catalyst heating mode.** In this mode, there are two injections:
  - The first injection is on the compression stroke just before combustion.

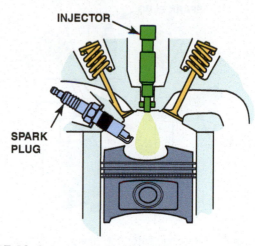

INJECTOR

SPARK PLUG

FIGURE 23–8 In this design, the fuel injector is at the top of the cylinder and sprays fuel into the cavity of the piston.

- The second injection is after combustion occurs to heat the exhaust. This mode is used to quickly warm the catalytic converter and to burn the sulfur from the NO_x catalyst.

PISTON TOP DESIGNS

Gasoline direct-injection (GDI) systems use a variety of shapes of piston and injector locations depending on make and model of engine. Three of the most commonly used designs include:

- **Spray-guided combustion.** In this design, the injector is placed in the center of the combustion chamber and injects fuel into the dished-out portion of the piston. The shape of the piston helps guide and direct the mist of fuel in the combustion chamber. ● **SEE FIGURE 23–8.**

- **Swirl combustion.** This design uses the shape of the piston and the position of the injector at the side of the combustion chamber to create turbulence and swirl of the air–fuel mixture. ● **SEE FIGURE 23–9.**

- **Tumble combustion.** Depending on when the fuel is injected into the combustion chamber helps determine how the air–fuel mixture is moved or tumbled. ● **SEE FIGURE 23–10.**

ENGINE START SYSTEM

An engine equipped with gasoline direct injection could use the system to start the engine. This is most useful during idle stop mode when the engine is stopped while the vehicle is at a traffic light to save fuel. The steps used in the Mazda start-stop system, called the *smart idle stop system (SISS)*, allow the

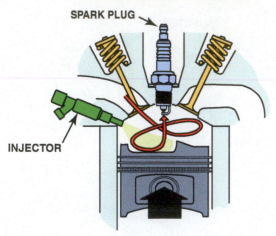

WALL-GUIDED (SWIRL) COMBUSTION

SPARK PLUG

INJECTOR

FIGURE 23–9 The side injector combines with the shape of the piston to create a swirl as the piston moves up on the compression stroke.

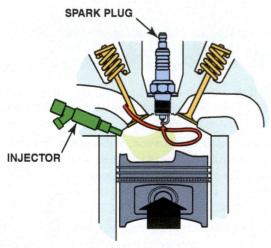

WALL-GUIDED (TUMBLE) COMBUSTION

SPARK PLUG

INJECTOR

FIGURE 23–10 The piston creates a tumbling force as it moves upward.

engine to be started without a starter motor and include the following steps:

STEP 1 The engine is stopped. The normal stopping position of an engine when it stops is 70 degrees before top dead center, plus or minus 20 degrees. This is because the engine stops with one cylinder on the compression stroke and the PCM can determine the cylinder position, using the crankshaft and camshaft position sensors.

STEP 2 When a command is made to start the engine by the PCM, fuel is injected into the cylinder that is on the compression stroke and ignited by the spark plug.

STEP 3 The piston on the compression stroke is forced downward forcing the crankshaft to rotate counterclockwise or in the opposite direction to normal operation.

STEP 4 The rotation of the crankshaft then forces the companion cylinder toward the top of the cylinder.

STEP 5 Fuel is injected and the spark plug is fired, forcing the piston down, causing the crankshaft to rotate in the normal (clockwise) direction. Normal combustion events continue allowing the engine to keep running.

GASOLINE DIRECT-INJECTION ISSUES

NOISE ISSUES Gasoline direct-injection systems operate at high pressure and the injectors can often be heard with the engine running and the hood open. This noise can be a customer concern because the clicking sound is similar to noisy valves. If a noise issue is the customer concern, check the following:

- Check a similar vehicle to determine if the sound is louder or more noticeable than normal.

- Check that nothing under the hood is touching the fuel rail. If another line or hose is in contact with the fuel rail, the sound of the injectors clicking can be transmitted throughout the engine, making the sound more noticeable.

- Check for any technical service bulletins (TSBs) that may include new clips or sound insulators to help reduce the noise.

CARBON ISSUES Carbon is often an issue in engines equipped with gasoline direct-injection systems. Carbon can affect engine operation by accumulating in two places:

- **On the injector itself.** Because the injector tip is in the combustion chamber, fuel residue can accumulate on the injector, reducing its ability to provide the proper spray pattern and amount of fuel. Some injector designs are more likely to be affected by carbon than others. For example, if the injector uses small holes, these tend to become clogged more than an injector that uses a single slit opening where the fuel being sprayed out tends to blast away any carbon. ● **SEE FIGURE 23–11**.

- **The backside of the intake valve.** This is a common place for fuel residue and carbon to accumulate on engines equipped with gasoline direct injection. The accumulation of carbon on the intake valve can become so severe that the engine will start and idle, but lack power to accelerate the vehicle. The carbon deposits restrict the airflow into the cylinder enough to decrease engine power.

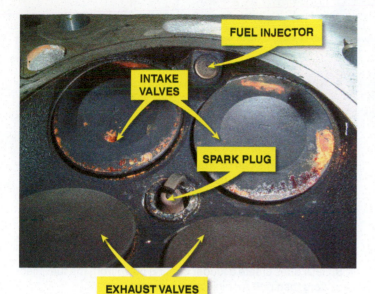

FIGURE 23–11 There may become a driveability issue because the gasoline direct-injection injector is exposed to combustion carbon and fuel residue.

NOTE: Engines that use both port and gasoline direct-injection injectors do not show intake valve deposits. It is thought that the fuel being sprayed onto the intake valve from the port injector helps keep the intake valve clean.

GDI SERVICE

CARBON PREVENTION Most experts recommend the use of Techron®, a fuel system dispersant, to help keep carbon from accumulating. The use of a dispersant every six months or every 6,000 miles has proven to help prevent injector and intake valve deposits.

If the lack of power is discovered and there are no stored diagnostic trouble codes, a conventional carbon cleaning procedure will likely restore power if the intake valves are coated.

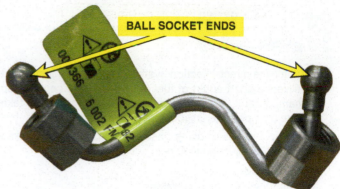

FIGURE 23–12 The high-pressure lines use a ball and socket connection. The ball end deforms when the line is tightened and must be replaced with a new part whenever it is removed.

SERVICING PRECAUTIONS Because of the high pressures involved, it is important to adhere to safety precautions when working on GDI system, which include:

- Don't reuse high-pressure lines. The ball-ends deform when tighten and will not seal if reused. ● **SEE FIGURE 23–12**.
- Always use a torque wrench when tightening fuel line fittings.
- Do not loosen any fuel fittings with the engine cranking or running.
- Always replace the Teflon seal whenever replacing or reinstalling a GDI injector. ● **SEE FIGURE 23–13**.

Always check service information for the exact procedures to follow when working on a GDI system.

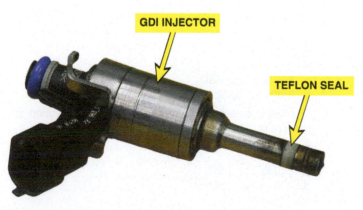

FIGURE 23–13 Whenever a GDI fuel injector is removed, a new Teflon seal must be installed to ensure a leak-free connection in the combustion chamber.

1. A gasoline direct-injection system uses a fuel injector that delivers a short squirt of fuel directly into the combustion chamber rather than in the intake manifold, near the intake valve on a port fuel-injection system.

2. The advantages of using gasoline direct injection instead of port fuel injection include:
   - Improved fuel economy
   - Reduced exhaust emissions
   - Greater engine power

3. Some of the disadvantages of gasoline direct-injection systems compared with a port fuel-injection system include:
   - Higher cost
   - The need for NO_x storage catalyst in some applications
   - More components

4. The operating pressure can vary from as low as 500 PSI during some low-demand conditions to as high as 2,900 PSI.

5. The fuel injectors are open for a very short period of time and are pulsed using a 50 to 90 volt pulse from a capacitor circuit.

6. GDI systems can operate in many modes, which are separated into the two basic modes:
   - Stratified mode
   - Homogeneous mode

7. GDI can be used to start an engine without the use of a starter motor for idle-stop functions.

8. GDI does create a louder clicking noise from the fuel injectors than port fuel-injection injectors.

9. Carbon deposits on the injector and the backside of the intake valve are a common problem with engines equipped with gasoline direct-injection systems.

REVIEW QUESTIONS

1. What are two advantages of gasoline direct injection compared with port fuel injection?

2. What are two disadvantages of gasoline direct injection compared with port fuel injection?

3. How is the fuel delivery system different from a port fuel-injection system?

4. What are the basic modes of operation of a GDI system?

5. What should be replaced anytime it is removed from the high-pressure GDI fuel system?

CHAPTER QUIZ

1. Where is the fuel injected in an engine equipped with gasoline direct injection?
   a. Into the intake manifold near the intake valve
   b. Directly into the combustion chamber
   c. Above the intake port
   d. In the exhaust port

2. The fuel pump inside the fuel tank on a vehicle equipped with gasoline direct injection produces about what fuel pressure?
   a. 5 to 10 PSI
   b. 10 to 20 PSI
   c. 20 to 40 PSI
   d. 50 to 60 PSI

3. The high-pressure fuel pumps used in gasoline direct-injection (GDI) systems are powered by _____.
   a. Electricity (DC motor)
   b. Electricity (AC motor)
   c. the camshaft
   d. the crankshaft

4. The high-pressure fuel pump pressure is regulated by using _____.
   a. an electric pressure-control valve
   b. a vacuum-biased regulator
   c. a mechanical regulator at the inlet to the fuel rail
   d. a non-vacuum biased regulator

5. The fuel injectors operate under a fuel pressure of about _____.
   a. 35 to 45 PSI
   b. 90 to 150 PSI
   c. 500 to 2,900 PSI
   d. 2,000 to 5,000 PSI

6. The fuel injectors used on a gasoline direct-injection system are pulsed on using what voltage?
   a. 12 to 14 volt
   b. 50 to 90 volt
   c. 100 to 110 volt
   d. 200 to 220 volt

7. Which mode of operation results in a richer air–fuel mixture near the spark plug?
   a. Stoichiometric
   b. Homogeneous
   c. Stratified
   d. Knock protection

8. All of the following are advantages of gasoline direct injection *except* _____.
   a. improved fuel economy
   b. higher engine efficiency
   c. able to use lower-octane gasoline
   d. decreased throttle response

9. All of the following are disadvantages of gasoline direct injection *except* _____.
   a. higher cost
   b. less need for extra fuel for acceleration
   c. NO_x storage catalyst may be needed
   d. more components compared to port fuel injection systems

10. A lack of power from an engine equipped with gasoline direct injection could be due to _____.
    a. noisy injectors
    b. carbon on the injectors
    c. carbon on the intake valves
    d. Both b and c

chapter 24

FUEL-INJECTION SYSTEM DIAGNOSIS AND SERVICE

LEARNING OBJECTIVES

After studying this chapter, the reader should be able to:

1. Explain how to check a fuel-pressure regulator.
2. Explain how to diagnose electronic fuel-injection problems.
3. Describe how to test fuel injectors.
4. Describe how to service the fuel-injection system.

This chapter will help you prepare for Engine Repair (A8) ASE certification test content area "C" (Fuel, Air Induction, and Exhaust Systems Diagnosis and Repair).

KEY TERMS

Graphing multimeter (GMM) 342
Idle air control (IAC) 350
Noid light 344
Peak-and-hold injector 348
Saturation 348

PORT FUEL-INJECTION PRESSURE REGULATOR DIAGNOSIS

Older port fuel-injected engines use a vacuum hose connected to the fuel-pressure regulator. At idle, the pressure inside the intake manifold is low (high vacuum). Manifold vacuum is applied above the diaphragm inside the fuel-pressure regulator. This reduces the pressure exerted on the diaphragm and results in a lower, about 10 PSI (69 kPa), fuel pressure applied to the injectors. To test a vacuum-controlled fuel-pressure regulator, follow these steps:

1. Connect a fuel-pressure gauge to monitor the fuel pressure. If the engine does not have a Schrader valve, check service information for the exact method and tools needed to perform a pressure test of the fuel injection system.

2. Locate the fuel-pressure regulator and disconnect the vacuum hose from the regulator.

   NOTE: If gasoline drips out of the vacuum hose when removed from the fuel-pressure regulator, the regulator is defective and will require replacement.

3. With the engine running at idle speed, reconnect the vacuum hose to the fuel-pressure regulator while watching the fuel-pressure gauge. The fuel pressure should drop (about 10 PSI or 69 kPa) when the hose is reattached to the regulator.

4. Using a hand-operated vacuum pump, apply vacuum (20 inches Hg) to the regulator. The regulator should hold vacuum. If the vacuum drops, replace the fuel-pressure regulator. ● **SEE FIGURE 24–1**.

Note: Some vehicles do not use a vacuum-regulated fuel-pressure regulator. Many of these vehicles use a regulator located inside the fuel tank that supplies a constant fuel pressure to the fuel injectors.

DIAGNOSING ELECTRONIC FUEL-INJECTION PROBLEMS USING VISUAL INSPECTION

All fuel-injection systems require the proper amount of clean fuel delivered to the system at the proper pressure and the

FUEL-PRESSURE REGULATOR

FIGURE 24–1 If the vacuum hose is removed from the fuel-pressure regulator when the engine is running, the fuel pressure should increase. If it does not increase, then the fuel pump is not capable of supplying adequate pressure or the fuel-pressure regulator is defective. If gasoline is visible in the vacuum hose, the regulator is leaking and should be replaced.

correct amount of filtered air. The following items should be carefully inspected before proceeding to more detailed tests:

- Check the air filter and replace as needed.
- Check the air induction system for obstructions.
- Check the conditions of all vacuum hoses. Replace any hose that is split, soft (mushy), or brittle.
- Check the positive crankcase ventilation (PCV) valve for proper operation or replacement as needed. ● **SEE FIGURE 24–3**.

NOTE: The use of an incorrect PCV valve can cause a rough idle or stalling.

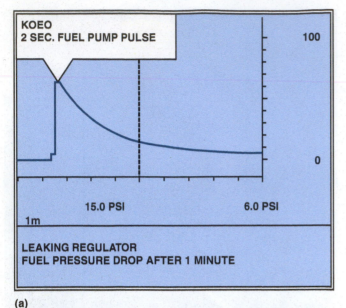

KOEO
2 SEC. FUEL PUMP PULSE

100

0

15.0 PSI   6.0 PSI

1m

LEAKING REGULATOR
FUEL PRESSURE DROP AFTER 1 MINUTE

(a)

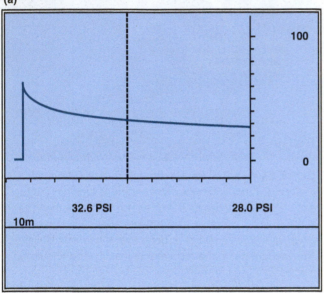

100

0

32.6 PSI   28.0 PSI

10m

(b)

FIGURE 24–2 (a) A fuel-pressure graph after key on, engine off (KOEO) on a TBI system. (b) Pressure drop after 10 minutes on a normal port fuel-injection system.

FIGURE 24–3 A clogged PCV system caused the engine oil fumes to be drawn into the air cleaner assembly. This is what the technician discovered during a visual inspection.

 **TECH TIP**

Pressure Transducer Fuel Pressure Test

Using a **pressure transducer** and a **graphing multimeter (GMM)** or digital storage oscilloscope (DSO) allows the service technician to view the fuel pressure over time. ● **SEE FIGURE 24–2(a)**. Note that the fuel pressure dropped from 15 PSI down to 6 PSI on a TBI-equipped vehicle after just one minute. A normal pressure holding capability is shown in ● **FIGURE 24–2(b)** when the pressure dropped only about 10% after 10 minutes on a port–fuel–injection system.

- Check all fuel-injection electrical connections for corrosion or damage.
- Check for gasoline at the vacuum port of the fuel-pressure regulator if the vehicle is so equipped. Gasoline in the vacuum hose at the fuel-pressure regulator indicates that the regulator is defective and requires replacement.

If a vacuum leak occurs on an engine equipped with a mass airflow-type fuel-injection system, the extra air causes the following to occur:

- The engine will operate leaner than normal because the extra air has not been measured by the MAF sensor.
- The idle speed will likely be lower due to the leaner- than-normal air–fuel mixture.

FIGURE 24–4 All fuel injectors should make the same sound with the engine running at idle speed. A lack of sound indicates a possible electrically open injector or a break in the wiring. A defective computer could also be the cause of a lack of clicking (pulsing) of the injectors.

FUEL-PRESSURE REGULATOR

FUEL RETURN LINE TO TANK

FIGURE 24–5 Fuel should be heard returning to the fuel tank at the fuel return line if the fuel-pump and fuel-pressure regulator are functioning correctly.

TECH TIP

Stethoscope Fuel-Injection Test

A commonly used test for injector operation is to listen to the injector using a stethoscope with the engine operating at idle speed. ● **SEE FIGURE 24–4**. All injectors should produce the same clicking sound. If any injector makes a clunking or rattling sound, it should be tested further or replaced. With the engine still running, place the end of the stethoscope probe to the return line from the fuel-pressure regulator. ● **SEE FIGURE 24–5**. Fuel should be heard flowing back to the fuel tank if the fuel-pump pressure is higher than the fuel-regulator pressure. If no sound of fuel is heard, then either the fuel pump or the fuel-pressure regulator is at fault.

TECH TIP

Quick and Easy Leaking Injector Test

Leaking injectors may be found by disabling the ignition, unhooking all injectors, and checking exhaust for hydrocarbons (HC) using a gas analyzer while cranking the engine (maximum HC should be 300 PPM).

TECH TIP

No Spark, No Squirt

Most electronic fuel-injection computer systems use the ignition primary (pickup coil or crank sensor) pulse as the trigger for when to inject (squirt) fuel from the injectors (nozzles). If this signal were not present, no fuel would be injected. Because this pulse is also necessary to trigger the module to create a spark from the coil, it can be said that "no spark" could also mean "no squirt." Therefore, if the cause of a no-start condition is observed to be a lack of fuel injection, do not start testing or replacing fuel-system components until the ignition system is checked for proper operation.

PORT FUEL-INJECTION SYSTEM DIAGNOSIS

To determine if a port fuel-injection system—including the fuel pump, injectors, and fuel-pressure regulator—is operating correctly, take the following steps:

1. Attach a fuel-pressure gauge to the Schrader valve on the fuel rail. ● **SEE FIGURE 24–7**.
2. Turn the ignition key on or start the engine to build up the fuel-pump pressure (to about 35 to 45 PSI).

FIGURE 24–6 Using a scan tool to check for IAC counts or percentage as part of a diagnostic routine.

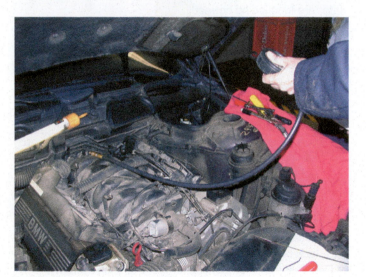

FIGURE 24–7 Checking the fuel pressure using a fuel-pressure gauge connected to the Schrader valve.

3. Wait 20 minutes and observe the fuel pressure retained in the fuel rail and note the PSI reading. The fuel pressure should not drop more than 20 PSI (140 kPa) in 20 minutes. If the drop is less than 20 PSI in 20 minutes, everything is okay; if the drop is *greater,* then there is a possible problem with:

- The check valve in the fuel pump
- Injectors, lines, or fittings
- A fuel-pressure regulator

To determine which unit is defective, perform the following:

- Reenergize the electric fuel pump.
- Clamp the fuel *supply* line, and wait 10 minutes (see CAUTION). If the pressure drop does not occur, replace the fuel pump. If the pressure drop still occurs, continue with the next step.

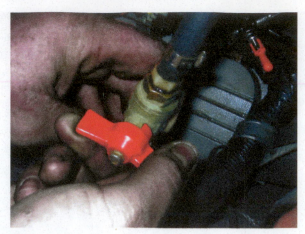

FIGURE 24–8 Shutoff valves must be used on vehicles equipped with plastic fuel lines to isolate the cause of a pressure drop in the fuel system.

- Repeat the pressure buildup of the electric pump and clamp the fuel return line. If the pressure drop time is now okay, replace the fuel-pressure regulator.
- If the pressure drop still occurs, one or more of the injectors is leaking. Remove the injectors with the fuel rail and hold over paper. Replace those injectors that drip one or more drops after 10 minutes with pressurized fuel.

CAUTION: Do not clamp plastic fuel lines. Connect shutoff valves to the fuel system to shut off supply and return lines. ● SEE FIGURE 24–8.

TESTING FOR AN INJECTOR PULSE

One of the first checks that should be performed when diagnosing a no-start condition is whether the fuel injectors are being pulsed by the computer. Checking for proper pulsing of the injector is also important in diagnosing a weak or dead cylinder.

A **noid light** is designed to electrically replace the injector in the circuit and to flash if the injector circuit is working correctly. ● SEE FIGURE 24–9. To use a noid light, disconnect the electrical connector at the fuel injector and plug the noid light into the injector harness connections. Crank or start the engine. The noid light should flash regularly.

NOTE: The term *noid* is simply an abbreviation of the word sole*noid.* Injectors use a movable iron core and are therefore solenoids. Therefore, a noid light is a replacement for the solenoid (injector).

Possible noid light problems and causes include the following:

1. **The light is off and does not flash.** The problem is an open in either the power side or ground side (or both) of the injector circuit.

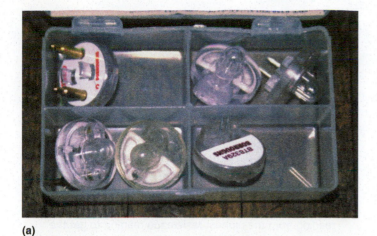

(a)

(b)

FIGURE 24–9 (a) Noid lights are usually purchased as an assortment so that one is available for any type or size of injector wiring connector. (b) The connector is unplugged from the injector and a noid light is plugged into the injector connector. The noid light should flash when the engine is being cranked if the power circuit and the pulsing to ground by the computer are functioning okay.

2. **The noid light flashes dimly.** A dim noid light indicates excessive resistance or low voltage available to the injector. Both the power and ground side must be checked.

3. **The noid light is on and does not flash.** If the noid light is on, then both a power and a ground are present. Because the light does not flash (blink) when the engine is being cranked or started, then a short-to-ground fault exists either in the computer itself or in the wiring between the injector and the computer.

CAUTION: A noid lamp must be used with caution. The computer may show a good noid light operation and have low supply voltage. ● SEE FIGURE 24–10.

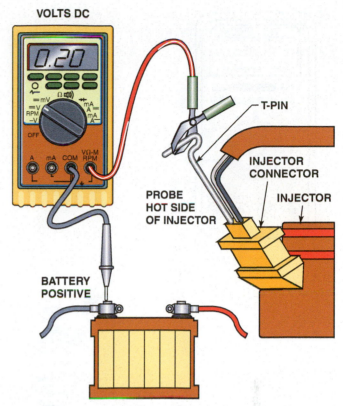

FIGURE 24–10 Use a DMM set to read DC volts to check the voltage drop of the positive circuit to the fuel injector. A reading of 0.5 volt or less is generally considered to be acceptable.

CHECKING FUEL-INJECTOR RESISTANCE

Each port fuel injector must deliver an equal amount of fuel or the engine will idle roughly or perform poorly.

The electrical balance test involves measuring the injector coil-winding resistance. For best engine operation, all injectors should have the same electrical resistance. To measure the resistance, carefully release the locking feature of the connector and remove the connector from the injector.

NOTE: Some engines require specific procedures to gain access to the injectors. Always follow the manufacturers' recommended procedures.

With an ohmmeter, measure the resistance across the injector terminals. Be sure to lower ohmmeter setting of the digital ohmmeter to read in tenths (0.1) of an ohm. ● **SEE FIGURES 24–11 AND 24–12.** Check service information for the resistance specification of the injectors. Measure the resistance of all of the injectors. Replace any injector that does not fall within the resistance range of the specification. The resistance

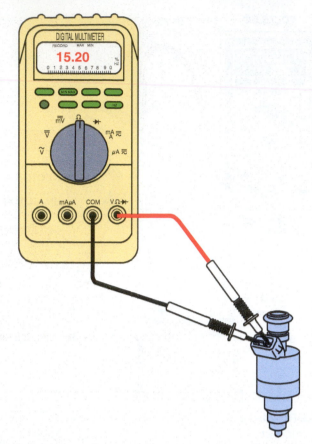

FIGURE 24–11 Connections and settings necessary to measure fuel-injector resistance.

FIGURE 24–12 To measure fuel-injector resistance, a technician constructed a short wiring harness with a double banana plug that fits into the V and COM terminals of the meter and an injector connector at the other end. This setup makes checking resistance of fuel injectors quick and easy.

of the injectors should be measured twice—once when the engine (and injectors) are cold and once after the engine has reached normal operating temperature. If any injector measures close to specification, make certain that the terminals of the injector are electrically sound, and perform other tests to confirm an injector problem before replacement.

TECH TIP

Equal Resistance Test

All fuel injectors should measure the specified resistance. However the specification often indicates the temperature of the injectors be at room temperature and of course will vary according to the temperature. Rather than waiting for all of the injectors to achieve room temperature, measure the resistance and check that they are all within 0.4 ohm of each other. To determine the difference, record the resistance of each injector and then subtract the lowest resistance reading from the highest resistance reading to get the difference. If more than 0.4 ohm then further testing will be needed to verify defective injector(s). ● SEE

FIGURES 24–13

TYPICAL RESISTANCE VALUES There are two basic types of injectors, which have an effect on their resistance including:

1. **Low-resistance injectors.** The features of a low-resistance injectors include:

   ■ Uses a "peak and hold" type firing where a high current, usually about 4 amperes, is used to open the injector, then it is held open by using a lower current, which is usually about 1 ampere.
   ■ All throttle body injection (TBI) injectors and some port fuel injectors are low-resistance injectors and are fired using a peak-and-hold circuit by the PCM.
   ■ The resistance value of a peak-and-hold-type injector is usually 1.5 to 4.0 ohms.

2. **Higher-resistance injectors.** The features of a higher-resistance injectors include:

   ■ Uses a constant low current, usually 1 ampere, to open the injector.
   ■ Is called a "saturated" type of injector because the current flows until the magnetic field is strong enough to open the injector.
   ■ Most port fuel injectors are of the saturated type.
   ■ The resistance value of a saturated injector is usually 12 to 16 ohms.

PRESSURE-DROP BALANCE TEST

The pressure balance test involves using an electrical timing device to pulse the fuel injectors on for a given amount of time, usually 500 milliseconds or 0.5 seconds, and observing the drop in pressure that accompanies the pulse. If the *fuel flow* through each injector is equal, the drop in pressure in the

FIGURE 24–13 If an injector has the specified resistance, this does not mean that it is okay. This injector had the specified resistance yet it did not deliver the correct amount of fuel because it was clogged.

FIGURE 24–14 Connect a fuel-pressure gauge to the fuel rail at the Schrader valve.

system will be equal. Most manufacturers recommend that the pressures be within about 1.5 PSI (10 kPa) of each other for satisfactory engine performance. This test method not only tests the electrical functioning of the injector (for definite time and current pulse), but also tests for mechanical defects that could affect fuel flow amounts.

The purpose of running this injector balance test is to determine which injector is restricted, inoperative, or delivering fuel differently than the other injectors. Replacing a complete set of injectors can be expensive. The basic tools needed are:

- Accurate pressure gauge with pressure relief
- Injector pulser with time control
- Necessary injector connection adapters
- Safe receptacle for catching and disposing of any fuel released

STEP 1 Attach the pressure gauge to the fuel delivery rail on the supply side. Make sure the connections are safe and leakproof.

STEP 2 Attach the injector pulser to the first injector to be tested.

STEP 3 Turn the ignition key to the on position to prime the fuel rail. Note the static fuel-pressure reading. ● **SEE FIGURE 24–14.**

STEP 4 Activate the pulser for the timed firing pulses.

STEP 5 Note and record the new static rail pressure after the injector has been pulsed.

STEP 6 Reenergize the fuel pump and repeat this procedure for all of the engine injectors.

STEP 7 Compare the two pressure readings and compute the pressure drop for each injector. Compare the pressure drops of the injectors to each other. Any variation

in pressure drops will indicate an uneven fuel delivery rate between the injectors.

For example:

Injector	1	2	3		4	5	6
Initial pressure	40	40	40		40	40	40
Second pressure	30	30	35		30	20	30
Pressure drop	10	10	5		10	20	10
Possible problem	OK	OK	Restriction		OK	Leak	OK

INJECTOR VOLTAGE-DROP TESTS

Another test of injectors involves pulsing the injector and measuring the voltage drop across the windings as current is flowing. A typical voltage-drop tester is shown in ● **FIGURE 24–15.** The tester, which is recommended for use by General Motors Corporation, pulses the injector while a digital multimeter is connected to the unit, which will display the voltage drop as the current flows through the winding.

CAUTION: Do not test an injector using a pulse-type tester more than once without starting the engine to help avoid a hydrostatic lock caused by the flow of fuel into the cylinder during the pulse test.

Record the highest voltage drop observed on the meter display during the test. Repeat the voltage-drop test for all of the injectors. The voltage drop across each injector should be within 0.1 volt of each other. If an injector has a higher-than-normal voltage drop, the injector windings have higher-than-normal resistance.

FIGURE 24-15 An injector tester being used to check the voltage drop through the injector while the tester is sending current through the injectors. This test is used to check the coil inside the injector. This same tester can be used to check for equal pressure drop of each injector by pulsing the injector on for 500 ms.

SCOPE-TESTING FUEL INJECTORS

A scope (analog or digital storage) can be connected into each injector circuit. There are three types of injector drive circuits and each type of circuit has its own characteristic pattern.
● **SEE FIGURE 24–16** for an example of how to connect a scope to read a fuel-injector waveform.

SATURATED SWITCH TYPE In a saturated switch-type injector-driven circuit, voltage (usually a full 12 volts) is applied to the injector. The ground for the injector is provided by the vehicle computer. When the ground connection is completed, current flows through the injector windings. Due to the resistance and inductive reactance of the coil itself, it requires a fraction of a second (about 3 milliseconds or 0.003 seconds) for the coil to reach **saturation** or maximum current flow. Most saturated switch-type fuel injectors have 12 to 16 ohms of resistance. This resistance, as well as the computer switching circuit, control and limit the current flow through the injector. A voltage spike occurs when the computer shuts off (opens the injector ground-side circuit) the injectors. ● **SEE FIGURE 24–17**.

PEAK-AND-HOLD TYPE A **peak-and-hold** type is typically used for TBI and some port low-resistance injectors. Full battery voltage is applied to the injector and the ground side is controlled through the computer. The computer provides a high initial current flow (about 4 amperes) to flow through the injector windings to open the injector core. Then the computer reduces the current to a lower level (about 1 ampere). The hold current is enough to keep the injector open, yet conserves energy

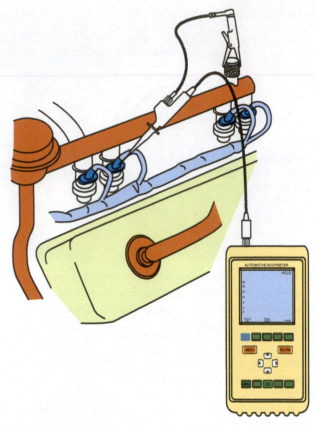

FIGURE 24-16 A digital storage oscilloscope can be easily connected to an injector by carefully back-probing the electrical connector.

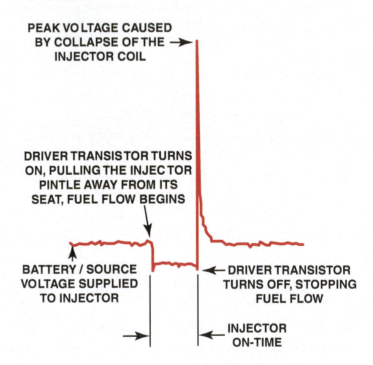

PEAK VOLTAGE CAUSED BY COLLAPSE OF THE INJECTOR COIL →

DRIVER TRANSISTOR TURNS ON, PULLING THE INJECTOR PINTLE AWAY FROM ITS SEAT, FUEL FLOW BEGINS

BATTERY / SOURCE VOLTAGE SUPPLIED TO INJECTOR

← DRIVER TRANSISTOR TURNS OFF, STOPPING FUEL FLOW

INJECTOR ON-TIME

FIGURE 24-17 The injector on-time is called the pulse width.

and reduces the heat buildup that would occur if the full current flow remains on as long as the injector is commanded on. Typical peak-and-hold-type injector resistance ranges from 2 to 4 ohms.

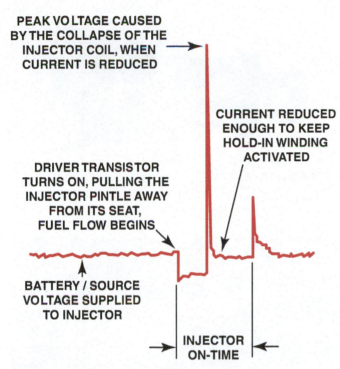

PEAK VOLTAGE CAUSED BY THE COLLAPSE OF THE INJECTOR COIL, WHEN CURRENT IS REDUCED

CURRENT REDUCED ENOUGH TO KEEP HOLD-IN WINDING ACTIVATED

DRIVER TRANSISTOR TURNS ON, PULLING THE INJECTOR PINTLE AWAY FROM ITS SEAT, FUEL FLOW BEGINS

BATTERY / SOURCE VOLTAGE SUPPLIED TO INJECTOR

INJECTOR ON-TIME

FIGURE 24–18 A typical peak-and-hold fuel-injector waveform. Most fuel injectors that measure less than 6 ohms will usually display a similar waveform.

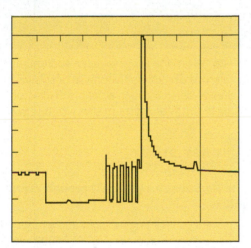

FIGURE 24–19 A waveform of a pulse-width-modulated fuel injector. At the end, when the voltage is removed, there is an inductive spike created similar to the spike created by other types of injectors.

The scope pattern of a typical peak-and-hold-type injector shows the initial closing of the ground circuit, then a voltage spike as the current flow is reduced. Another voltage spike occurs when the lower level current is turned off (opened) by the computer. ● **SEE FIGURE 24–18.**

PULSE-WIDTH MODULATED TYPE A pulse-width modulated type of injector drive circuit uses lower-resistance coil injectors. Battery voltage is available at the positive terminal of the injector and the computer provides a variable-duration connection to ground on the negative side of the injector.

FIGURE 24–20 A set of six reconditioned injectors. The sixth injector is barely visible at the far right.

The computer can vary the time intervals that the injector is grounded for very precise fuel control.

Each time the injector circuit is turned off (ground circuit opened), a small voltage spike occurs. It is normal to see multiple voltage spikes on a scope connected to a pulse-width modulated type of fuel injector. ● **SEE FIGURE 24–19.**

? FREQUENTLY ASKED QUESTION

If Three of Six Injectors Are Defective, Should I Also Replace the Other Three?

This is a good question. Many service technicians "recommend" that the three good injectors be replaced along with the other three that tested as being defective. The reasons given by these technicians include:

- All six injectors have been operating under the same fuel, engine, and weather conditions.
- The labor required to replace all six is just about the same as replacing only the three defective injectors.
- Replacing all six at the same time helps ensure that all of the injectors are flowing the same amount of fuel so that the engine is operating most efficiently.

With these ideas in mind, the customer should be informed and offered the choice. Complete sets of injectors such as those in ● **FIGURE 24–20** can be purchased at a reasonable cost.

IDLE AIR SPEED CONTROL DIAGNOSIS

On older engines equipped with fuel injection (TBI or port injection), the idle speed is controlled by increasing or decreasing the amount of air bypassing the throttle plate. Again, an

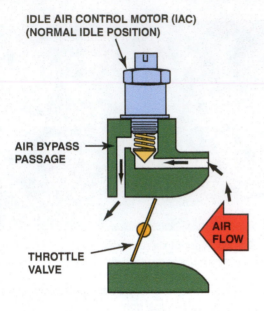

IDLE AIR CONTROL MOTOR (IAC)
(NORMAL IDLE POSITION)

AIR BYPASS
PASSAGE

THROTTLE
VALVE

AIR
FLOW

(FULLY EXTENDED POSITION)

AIR BYPASS
PASSAGE

FIGURE 24–21 An IAC controls idle speed by controlling the amount of air that passes around the throttle plate. More airflow results in a higher idle speed.

FIGURE 24–22 A typical IAC.

electronic stepper motor or pulse-width modulated solenoid is used to maintain the correct idle speed. This control is often called the **idle air control (IAC)**. ● **SEE FIGURES 24–21 THROUGH 24–22 24–23**.

When the engine stops, most IAC units will retract outward to get ready for the next engine start. When the engine starts, the engine speed is high to provide for proper operation when the engine is cold. Then, as the engine gets warmer, the computer reduces engine idle speed gradually by reducing the number of counts or steps commanded by the IAC.

FIGURE 24–23 Some IAC units are purchased with the housing as shown. Carbon buildup in these passages can cause a rough or unstable idling or stalling.

FIGURE 24–24 When the cover is removed from the top of the engine, a mouse or some other animal nest is visible. The animal had already eaten through a couple of injector wires. At least the cause of the intermittent misfire was discovered.

🚗 **CASE STUDY**

There Is No Substitute for a Thorough Visual Inspection

An intermittent "check engine" light and a random-misfire diagnostic trouble code (DTC) P0300 was being diagnosed. A scan tool did not provide any help because all systems seemed to be functioning normally. Finally, the technician removed the engine cover and discovered a mouse nest. ● **SEE FIGURE 24–24**.

Summary:

- **Complaint**—Customer stated that the "Check Engine" light was on.
- **Cause**—A stored P0300 DTC was stored indicating a random misfire had been detected caused by an animal that had partially eaten some fuel injector wires.
- **Correction**—The mouse nest was removed and the wiring was repaired.

When the engine is warm and restarted, the idle speed should momentarily increase, then decrease to normal idle speed. This increase and then decrease in engine speed is often called an engine-flare. If the engine speed does not flare, then the IAC may not be working (it may be stuck in one position).

FUEL-INJECTION SERVICE

NEED FOR SERVICE   All engines using fuel injection do require some type of fuel-system maintenance. Normal wear and tear with today's underhood temperatures and changes in gasoline quality contribute to the buildup of olefin wax, dirt, water, and many other additives. Unique to each engine is an air-control design that also may contribute different levels of carbon deposits, such as oil control.

FUEL INJECTION SERVICE   Fuel-injection system service should include the following operations:

1. **Check fuel-pump operating pressure and volume.** The missing link here is volume. Most working technicians assume that if the pressure is correct, the volume is also okay. Hook up a fuel-pressure tester to the fuel rail inlet to quickly test the fuel pressure with the engine running. At the same time, test the volume of the pump by sending fuel into the holding tank. (One ounce per second is the usual specification.) ● **SEE FIGURE 24–25**. A two-line system tester is the recommended procedure to use and is attached to the fuel inlet and the return on the fuel rail. The vehicle onboard system is looped and returns fuel to the tank.

2. **Test the fuel-pressure regulator for operation and leakage.** At this time, the fuel-pressure regulator would be tested for operational pressure and proper regulation, including leakage. (This works well as the operator has total control of rail pressure with a unit control valve.) Below are some points to consider:

   ■ Good pressure does not mean proper volume. For example, a clogged filter may test okay on pressure but the restriction may not allow proper volume under load. ● **SEE FIGURE 24–26**.
   ■ It is a good idea to use the vehicle's own gasoline to service the system versus a can of shop gasoline that has been sitting around for some time.
   ■ Pressure regulators do fail and a lot more do not properly shut off fuel, causing higher-than-normal pump wear and shorter service life.

3. **Flush the entire fuel rail and upper fuel-injector screens including the fuel-pressure regulator.** Raise the input pressure to a point above regulator setting to allow a constant flow of fuel through the inlet pressure side of the system, through the fuel rail, and out the open fuel-pressure regulator. In most cases the applied pressure is

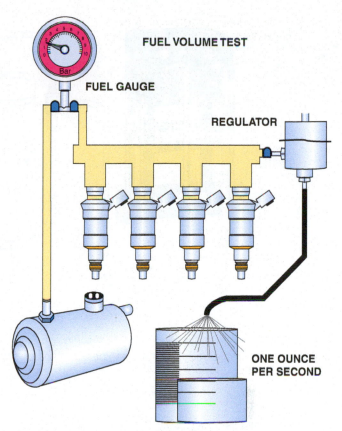

FIGURE 24–25 Checking fuel-pump volume using a hose from the outlet of the fuel-pressure regulator into a calibrated container.

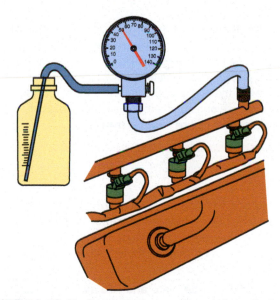

FIGURE 24–26 Testing fuel-pump volume using a fuel-pressure gauge with a bleed hose inserted into a suitable container. The engine is running during this test.

75 to 90 PSI (517 to 620 kPa), but will be maintained by the presence of a regulator. At this point, cleaning chemical is added to the fuel at a 5:1 mixture and allowed to flow through the system for 15 to 30 minutes. ● **SEE FIGURE 24–27**. Results are best on a hot engine with the fuel supply looped and the engine not running.

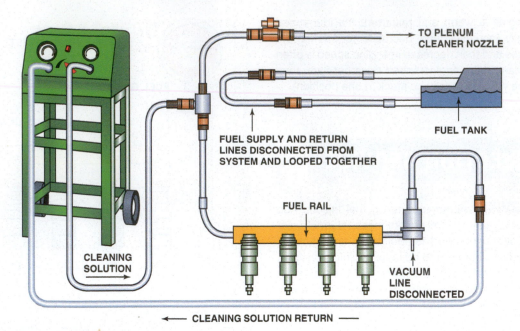

TO PLENUM
CLEANER NOZZLE

FUEL SUPPLY AND RETURN
LINES DISCONNECTED FROM
SYSTEM AND LOOPED TOGETHER

FUEL TANK

FUEL RAIL

VACUUM
LINE
DISCONNECTED

CLEANING
SOLUTION

← CLEANING SOLUTION RETURN →

FIGURE 24–27 A typical two-line cleaning machine hookup, showing an extension hose that can be used to squirt a cleaning solution into the throttle body while the engine is running on the cleaning solution and gasoline mixture.

🔧 **TECH TIP**

Check the Injectors at the "Bends and the Ends"

Injectors that are most likely to become restricted due to clogging of the filter basket screen are the injectors at the ends of the rail especially on returnless systems where dirt can accumulate. Also the injectors that are located at the bends of the fuel rail are also subject to possible clogging due to the dirt being deposited where the fuel makes a turn in the rail.

FIGURE 24–28 To thoroughly clean a throttle body, it is sometimes best to remove it from the vehicle. Dirty throttle plate(s) can cause a rough, unstable idle or stalling especially when the engine is warm.

4. **Decarbon the engine assembly.** On most vehicles, the injector spray will help the decarboning process. On others, you may need to enhance the operation with external addition of a mixture through the PCV hose, throttle plates, or idle air controls.

5. **Clean the throttle plate and idle air control passages.** Doing this service alone on most late-model engines will show a manifold vacuum increase of up to 2 inches Hg. ● SEE FIGURE 24–28. This works well as air is drawn into IAC passages on a running engine and will clean the passages without IAC removal.

6. **Relearn the onboard computer.** Some vehicles may have been running in such a poor state of operation that the onboard computer may need to be relearned. Consult service information for the suggested relearn procedures for each particular vehicle.

🔧 **TECH TIP**

Use an Injector Tester

The best way to check injectors is to remove them all from the engine and test them using an injector tester. A typical injector tester uses a special nonflammable test fluid that has the same viscosity as gasoline. The tester pulses the injectors, and the amount of fuel delivered as well as the spray pattern can be seen. Many testers are capable of varying the frequency of the pulse as well as the duration that helps find intermittent injector faults. ● SEE FIGURE 24–29.

All of the previously listed steps may be performed using a *two-line* fuel-injector service unit such as Carbon Clean, Auto Care, Injector Test, DeCarbon, or Motor-Vac.

FIGURE 24–29 The amount each injector is able to flow is displayed in glass cylinders are each injector for a quick visual check.

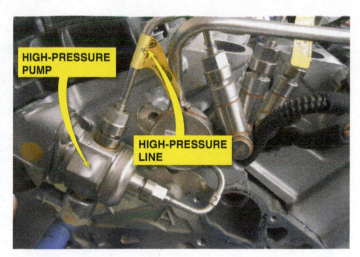

FIGURE 24–30 The line that has the yellow tag is a high-pressure line and this linßpart.

Fuel-Injection Symptom Chart

Symptom	Possible Causes
Hard cold starts	• Low fuel pressure
	• Leaking fuel injectors
	• Contaminated fuel
	• Low-volatility fuel
	• Dirty throttle plate
Garage stalls	• Low fuel pressure
	• Insufficient fuel volume
	• Restricted fuel injector
	• Contaminated fuel
	• Low-volatility fuel
Poor cold performance	• Low fuel pressure
	• Insufficient fuel volume
	• Contaminated fuel
	• Low-volatility fuel
Tip-in hesitation (hesitation just as the accelerator pedal is depressed)	• Low fuel pressure
	• Insufficient fuel volume
	• Intake valve deposits
	• Contaminated fuel
	• Low-volatility fuel

FUEL-SYSTEM SCAN TOOL DIAGNOSTICS

Diagnosing a faulty fuel system can be a difficult task. However, it can be made easier by utilizing the information available via the serial data stream. By observing the long-term fuel trim and the short-term fuel trim, to determine how the fuel system is performing. Short-term fuel trim and long-term fuel trim can help zero in on specific areas of trouble. Readings should be taken at idle and at 3000 RPM. ● **SEE CHART 24–1.**

> ☠ **WARNING**
>
> Before opening any part of the high-pressure section of a gasoline direct injection (GDI) system, the pressure must be bled off. The high pressures of this fuel system can cause injury or death. If any of the high-pressure lines are removed, even temporarily, they MUST be replaced because the ends use a ball-fitting that deforms to create the high-pressure seal. Once this seal has been opened, a new ball end must be used to insure a proper seal. ● SEE FIGURE 24–30.
>
> Always check service information for the exact procedures to follow for the vehicle being serviced.

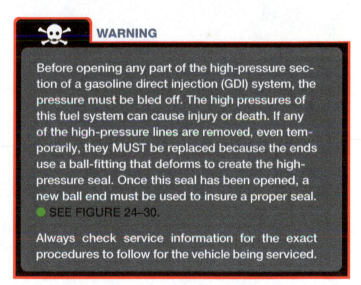

Condition	Long-Term Fuel Trim at Idle	Long-Term Fuel Trim at 3000 RPM
System normal	0% ± 10%	0% ± 10%
Vacuum leak	HIGH	OK
Fuel flow problem	OK	HIGH
Low fuel pressure	HIGH	HIGH
High fuel pressure	*OK or LOW	*OK or LOW

*High fuel pressure will affect trim at idle, at 3000 RPM, or both.

CHART 24–1

Fuel trim levels and possible causes if not within 10%.

FUEL-PUMP RELAY CIRCUIT DIAGNOSIS

1 The tools needed to diagnose a circuit containing a relay include a digital multimeter (DMM), a fused jumper wire, and an assortment of wiring terminals.

2 Start the diagnosis by locating the relay center. It is under the hood on this General Motors vehicle, so access is easy. Not all vehicles are this easy.

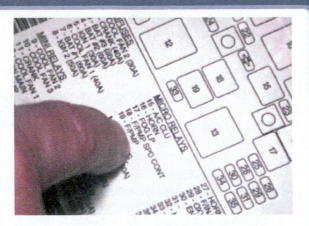

3 The chart under the cover for the relay center indicates the location of the relay that controls the electric fuel pump.

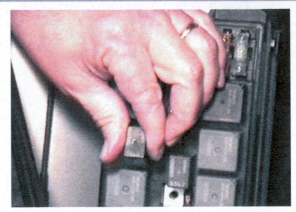

4 Locate the fuel-pump relay and remove by using a puller if necessary. Try to avoid rocking or twisting the relay to prevent causing damage to the relay terminals or the relay itself.

5 Terminals 85 and 86 represent the coil inside the relay. Terminal 30 is the power terminal, 87a is the normally closed contact, and 87 is the normally open contact.

6 The terminals are also labeled on most relays.

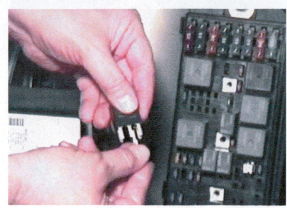

7 To help make good electrical contact with the terminals without doing any harm, select the proper-size terminal from the terminal assortment.

8 Insert the terminals into the relay socket in 30 and 87.

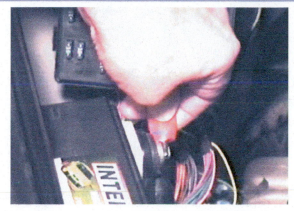

9 To check for voltage at terminal 30, use a test light or a voltmeter. Start by connecting the alligator clip of the test light to the positive (+) terminal of the battery.

10 Touch the test light to the negative (−) terminal of the battery or a good engine ground to check the test light.

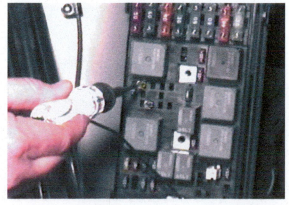

11 Use the test light to check for voltage at terminal 30 of the relay. The ignition may have to be in the on (run) position.

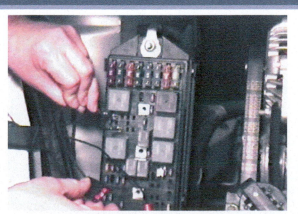

12 To check to see if the electric fuel pump can be operated from the relay contacts, use a fused jumper wire and touch the relay contacts that correspond to terminals 30 and 87 of the relay.

CONTINUED ▶

13 Connect the leads of the meter to contacts 30 and 87 of the relay socket. The reading of 4.7 amperes is okay because the specification is 4 to 8 amperes.

14 Set the meter to read ohms (V) and measure the resistance of the relay coil. The usual reading for most relays is between 60 and 100 ohms.

15 Measure between terminal 30 and 87a. Terminal 87a is the normally closed contact, and there should be little, if any, resistance between these two terminals, as shown.

16 To test the normally open contacts, connect one meter lead to terminal 30 and the other lead to terminal 87. The ohmmeter should show an open circuit by displaying OL.

17 Connect a fused jumper wire to supply 12 volts to terminal 86 and a ground to terminal 85 of the relay. If the relay clicks, then the relay coil is able to move the armature (movable arm) of the relay.

18 After testing, be sure to reinstall the relay and the relay cover.

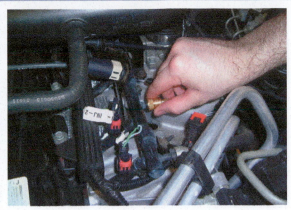

1 Start the fuel injector cleaning process by bringing the vehicle's engine up to operating temperature. Shut off the engine, remove the cap from the fuel rail test port, and install the appropriate adapter.

2 The vehicle's fuel pump is disabled by removing its relay or fuse. In some cases, it may be necessary to disconnect the fuel pump at the tank if the relay or fuse powers more than just the pump.

3 Turn the outlet valve of the canister to the OFF or CLOSED position.

4 Remove the fuel injector cleaning canister's top and regulator assembly. Note that there is an O-ring seal located here that must be in place for the canister's top to seal properly.

5 Pour the injection system cleaning fluid into the open canister. Rubber gloves are highly recommended for this step as the fluid is toxic.

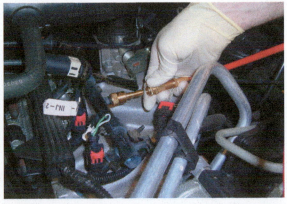

6 Replace the canister's top (making sure it is tight) and connect its hose to the fuel rail adapter. Be sure that the hose is routed away from exhaust manifolds and other hazards.

CONTINUED ▶

7 Hang the canister from the vehicle's hood and adjust the air pressure regulator to full OPEN position (CCW).

8 Connect shop air to the canister and adjust the air pressure regulator to the desired setting. Canister pressure can be read directly from the gauge.

9 Canister pressure should be adjusted to 5 PSI below system fuel pressure. An alternative for return-type systems is to block the fuel return line to the tank.

10 Open the outlet valve on the canister.

11 Start the vehicle's engine and let run at 1000–1500 RPM. The engine is now running on fuel injector cleaning fluid provided by the canister.

12 Continue the process until the canister is empty and the engine stalls. Remove the cleaning equipment, enable the vehicle's fuel pump, and run the engine to check for leaks.

1. A typical port fuel-injection system uses an individual fuel injector for each cylinder and squirts fuel directly into the intake manifold about 3 inches (80 mm) from the intake valve.

2. A typical fuel-injection system fuel pressure should not drop more than 20 PSI in 20 minutes.

3. A noid light can be used to check for the presence of an injector pulse.

4. Injectors can be tested for resistance and should be within 0.3 to 0.4 ohms of each other.

5. Different designs of injectors have a different scope waveform depending on how the computer pulses the injector on and off.

6. An idle air control unit controls idle speed and can be tested for proper operation using a scan tool or scope.

REVIEW QUESTIONS

1. List the ways fuel injectors can be tested.

2. List the steps necessary to test a fuel-pressure regulator.

3. What is wrong if a fuel injector measures 100 ohms of resistance?

4. Why should the throttle plate need cleaning?

5. What does an injector voltage drop test indicate?

CHAPTER QUIZ

1. Most port fuel-injected engines operate on how much fuel pressure?
   a. 3 to 5 PSI (21 to 35 kPa)
   b. 9 to 13 PSI (62 to 90 kPa)
   c. 35 to 45 PSI (240 to 310 kPa)
   d. 55 to 65 PSI (380 to 450 kPa)

2. Fuel injectors can be tested using _____.
   a. an ohmmeter
   b. a stethoscope
   c. a scope
   d. All of the above

3. Throttle-body fuel-injection systems use what type of injector driver?
   a. Peak and hold
   b. Saturated switch
   c. Pulse-width modu-
   lated
   d. Pulsed

4. Port fuel-injection systems generally use what type of injector driver?
   a. Peak and hold
   b. Saturated switch
   c. Pulse-width modulated
   d. Pulsed

5. The vacuum hose from the fuel-pressure regulator was removed from the regulator and gasoline dripped out of the hose. Technician A says that is normal and that everything is okay. Technician B says that one or more of the injectors may be defective, causing the fuel to get into the hose. Which technician is correct?
   a. Technician A only
   b. Technician B only
   c. Both Technicians A and B
   d. Neither Technician A nor B

6. The fuel pressure drops rapidly when the engine is turned off. Technician A says that one or more injectors could be leaking. Technician B says that a defective check valve in the fuel pump could be the cause. Which technician is correct?
   a. Technician A only
   b. Technician B only
   c. Both Technicians A and B
   d. Neither Technician A nor B

7. In a typical port fuel-injection system, which injectors are most subject to becoming restricted?
   a. Any of them equally
   b. The injectors at the end of the rail on a returnless system
   c. The injectors at the bends in the rail
   d. Either b or c

8. A visual inspection of the fuel injection system would include all of the following except _____.
   a. vacuum hose condition
   b. electrical connections
   c. air filter inspection
   d. injector resistance

9. Fuel-injection service is being discussed. Technician A says that the throttle plate(s) should be cleaned. Technician B says that the fuel rail should be cleaned. Which technician is correct?
   a. Technician A only
   b. Technician B only
   c. Both Technicians A and B
   d. Neither Technician A nor B

10. If the throttle plate needs to be cleaned, what symptoms will be present regarding the operation of the engine?
    a. Stalls
    b. Rough idle
    c. Hesitation on acceleration
    d. All of the above

chapter 25

ELECTRONIC TRANSMISSION CONTROLS

LEARNING OBJECTIVES

After studying this chapter, the reader should be able to:

1. Explain how the automatic transmissions/transaxles are controlled electronically.
2. Explain the function of sensors and switches for electronic control of transmission.
3. Identify the types of transmission solenoids.
4. Discuss adaptive strategies and controls for electronically controlled automatic transmissions/transaxles.
5. Explain the need for calibrating the transmission control module after it is replaced or reprogrammed.

KEY TERMS

Adaptive control 369
Adaptive learning 369
Brake on/off (BOO) 364
Clutch volume index (CVI) 369
Default (Limp in) 371
Electronic pressure control (EPC) 366
Input speed sensor (ISS) 363
Output speed sensor (OSS) 363
Pressure control solenoid (PCS) 366
Scan tool 369

Torque management 366
Transmission adapt pressure (TAP) 369
Transmission control module (TCM) 361
Transmission fluid temperature (TFT) 364
Transmission range (TR) switch 362
Turbine speed sensor (TSS) 363
Vehicle speed (VS) sensor 363

TRANSMISSION CONTROL MODULE

TCM All recent automatic transmissions are controlled by electronic components and circuits. Typical transmission control systems contain many components. An automatic transmission can be controlled by its own computer, called a **transmission control module (TCM)**, or a *transmission control unit (TCU)*. The transmission can also be controlled through either the body control module (BCM) or the powertrain control module (PCM). Each manufacturer has its own design criteria and terminology. The TCM is normally located outside the transmission in a protected, relatively cool and clean location. Some newer transmissions have the TCM mounted on the valve body inside the transmission. The primary advantage is the reduction of wiring and the elimination of electrical connectors, both sources of potential problems.

TERMINOLOGY When the TCM is located inside the transmission, this design is often called a *control solenoid valve assembly, mechatronic,* and *solenoid body* and reduces the number of wires entering the transmission because of the following:

- Input and output shaft speed sensors
- Transmission range sensor
- Fluid pressure sensors
- Fluid temperature sensor
- Shift and pressure control solenoids are connected directly to the TCM

The wire connections to the rest of the vehicle include:

- Hi and Lo CAN transmits data to and from the ECM, BCM, and PCM
- Ignition on
- Diagnostic connection
- Ground

The TCM in some transmissions is about the same size as a common credit card. A concern with an internal TCM is the possibility of overheating the electronic components. One design has a thermocouple temperature sensor(s) mounted in the TCM circuit board, and if the temperature rises above 288°F (142°C), it will go into failure mode/default. The TCM normally keeps relatively cool by contact with the transmission case, and a spring bracket is used to ensure tight contact. ● **SEE FIGURE 25–1**.

PURPOSE AND FUNCTION Many features of an electronic transmission, such as shift timing and quality, torque converter clutch apply timing, and quality, are software driven. A

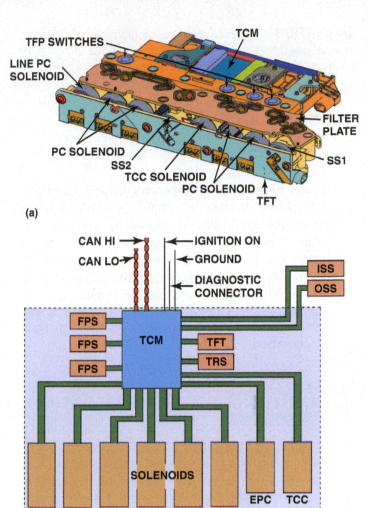

(a)

(b)

FIGURE 25–1 (a) This control solenoid assembly contains four transmission fluid pressure (TFP) switches, a line pressure control (PC) solenoid, four pressure control (PC) solenoids, two shift solenoids (SS), a torque converter clutch (TCC) solenoid, a transmission fluid temperature (TFT) sensor, and the transmission control module (TCM). It also has a vehicle harness connector and connectors to the shift position switch and the input and output speed sensors. (b) A simplified view is also shown.

vehicle manufacturer can use the same transmission and adjust the operating characteristics with software for variations of particular vehicles. Some transmission control modules allow calibration values to be reprogrammed by technicians in the field.

The TCM receives data from the sensors and other control modules, and when these signals match the program stored in the TCM's memory, the TCM sends a signal to one or more electrical actuators to control the shifting operation of the transmission.

OPERATION The TCM can be programmed to incorporate several different operating strategies that are stored in the memory. The types of memory include:

- **Random access memory (RAM).** This is temporary memory that is cleared every time the vehicle is turned off.

- **Read-only memory (ROM).** The TCM/processor can read from ROM, but cannot save any information to ROM.

- **Programmable read-only memory (PROM).** This is similar to a ROM, but is programmed for a specific vehicle.

- **Electronically erasable programmable read-only memory (EEPROM).** This is similar to PROM, but can be erased and reprogrammed. This is often called *reflashing*.

- **Keep alive memory (KAM).** ROM that is always connected to power so it retains memory. This can store information, such as transmission adaptive strategies, and the data will be lost if a battery becomes discharged or is disconnected.

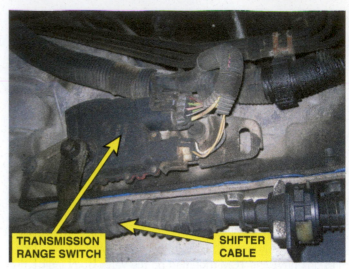

FIGURE 25–2 The transmission range switch is usually located on the case where the shifter cable attaches to the manual valve lever. The switch also includes the switch for the backup lights and the park/neutral switch, which is used to prevent the start being engaged unless the shifter is in park or neutral.

SENSORS
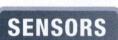

PURPOSE AND FUNCTION Sensors are the TCM inputs. They monitor the things that can affect transmission operation: vehicle speed, input shaft speed, transmission fluid temperature, the selected gear range, and engine coolant temperature, RPM, and load. A typical transmission sensor can be a switch that is made to open or close at certain pressures or temperatures, a transducer that senses pressure, a thermistor that senses temperature, or a speed sensor that measures vehicle speed or shaft RPM. The various sensor types (organized by the type of electrical signal) include the following:

- Frequency generators (creates an AC signal with a frequency relative to speed and the TCM monitors the signal frequency)

- Voltage generator (creates a voltage signal that is relative to speed and the TCM monitors the voltage)

- Potentiometer or variable resistor (alters resistance)

- Switches (an on–off signal)

- Thermistor (changes resistance relative to temperature)

- Transducer (changes resistance relative to pressure)

- Serial data (an on–off signal coming from another control module)

TRANSMISSION RANGE SWITCH The **transmission range (TR) switch**, also called the *manual lever position (MLP)* sensor, is used as an input to the PCM/TCM, which indicates the drive range requested by the driver. The transmission range switch is usually located on the outside of the case on

the transmission/transaxle housing and attached to the shifter. As the gear range selector is moved, the TR switch can make a variety of switch connections for each gear range. These inputs allow the TCM to determine which gear range has been selected. The TR switch is used by the TCM to:

- Keep the engine from starting in any gear position except park or neutral

- Allow a progressive 1–2–3–4 shift sequence in drive

- Limit upshifts in manual ranges

- Operate the backup lights in reverse. ● **SEE FIGURE 25–2.**

Some vehicles are equipped with a manual position where the driver can request one gear position by moving the shift lever to the manual position. ● **SEE FIGURE 25–3.**

SPEED SENSOR DESIGNS Speed sensors measure the speeds of the input and output shafts or sometimes of other shaft speeds in the automatic transmission or transaxle. The output shaft speed sensor is often used to provide vehicle speed information to the PCM and for adaptive learning. ● **SEE FIGURE 25–4.**

Speed sensor design includes:

- **Magnetic**—Most speed sensors use a coil of wire that is wrapped around a magnetic core. This sensor is mounted next to a toothed ring or wheel. As the toothed ring revolves, an alternating voltage is produced in the sensor. ● **SEE FIGURE 25–5.**

- **Hall-Effect**—Some speed sensors are Hall-effect and create an on–off square wave signal that is used directly by the PCM/TCM for speed detection.

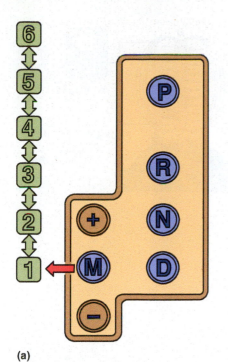

(a)

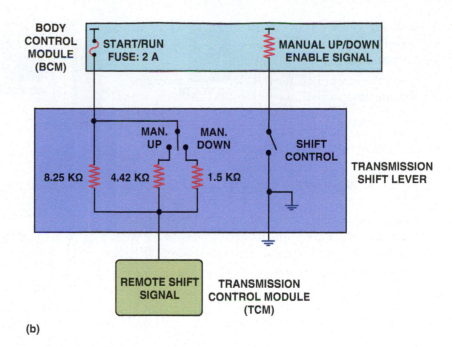

(b)

FIGURE 25–3 Moving the shift lever to the M (manual) position (a) activates the up/down, +/– switches that will cause an upshift or downshift. (b) The schematic of a typical circuit involving the transmission shift lever.

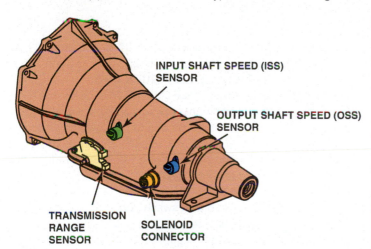

FIGURE 25–4 Speed sensors are used by the powertrain control module (PCM) or the transmission control module (TCM) to control shifts and detect faults such as slippage when the two speeds do not match the predetermined ratio for each gear commanded.

SPEED SENSOR LOCATIONS

- Speed sensors are used to detect the speeds of the input and output shafts on automatic transmissions/transaxles. **Input speed sensor (ISS)** measures the speed of the input shaft, which is the same or almost the same as the engine speed. This is also called **turbine speed sensor (TSS)** because it is used to determine the speed of the turbine shaft.
- The **output speed sensor (OSS)** is also called the **vehicle speed (VS) sensor** and is used by the PCM for speedometer and cruise control operation as well as for transmission/transaxle operation as well as shift-related fault detection.

PRESSURE SENSORS/SWITCHES Most pressure sensors use a transducer, which is a variable resistance that produces a signal that is relative to pressure. The *line pressure sensor (LPS)* is a transducer that converts line pressure to a variable resistance.

Many transmissions include *pressure switches* at the valve body. The signal from the pressure sensor tells the TCM that the circuit has pressure. The TCM uses these signals along with other information to determine TCC lockup and shift timing. ● **SEE FIGURE 25–6.**

? FREQUENTLY ASKED QUESTION

What Is Pressure Logic?

Pressure switches are used to monitor which clutch has pressure, but the PCM/TCM can use the information from the switches to verify which gear the transmission/transaxle is operating. Some pressure switches are normally open (N.O.) and others are normally closed (N.C.). The gear that the unit is operating in can be determined by the switch positions. An open circuit is represented by a binary code "1" and measures 12 volts while a grounded circuit binary code is "0" and measures 0 volts. Depending on the position of the manual valve, fluid is routed to the pressure switch manifold (PSM). The PCM/TCM uses information from the on/off positioning of the switches to adjust line pressure, torque converter clutch (TCM) apply, and to control shift solenoid operation. ● **SEE FIGURE 25–7.**

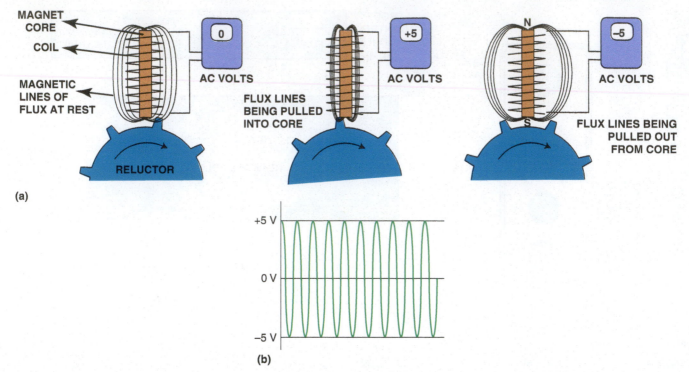

FIGURE 25–5 (a) The speed sensor switch will close as the magnet moves past it. (b) It will generate a sine wave signal, which is converted inside the PCM/TCM to a digital signal. The frequency of the signal is used to measure the speed.

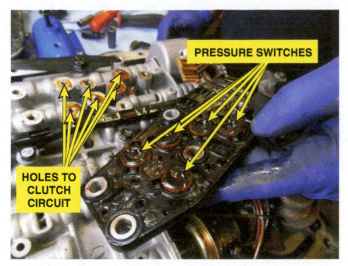

FIGURE 25–6 The pressure switch manifold (PSM) used in a GM 4L60-E consists of diaphragm switches with seals around each one that are bolted to the valve body over holes for each clutch circuit.

TEMPERATURE SENSORS The **transmission fluid temperature (TFT)** sensor can also be called a *transmission oil temperature (TOT) sensor*. Most temperature sensors are thermistors, a type of variable resistor that changes electrical resistance relative to temperature. These are called negative temperature coefficient (NTC) thermistors. The signal from a thermistor is the inverse of the temperature because it has high resistance at low temperatures and a low resistance at high temperatures. For example, a particular transmission fluid temperature sensor has a resistance of 37 to 100 ohms (Ω) at 32°F to 58°F (0°C to 20°C) and 1,500 to 2,700 ohms (Ω) at 195°F to 230°F (91°C to 110°C). ● **SEE FIGURE 25–8**.

This sensor is used by the PCM or TCM to detect the temperature of the automatic transmission fluid. This signal is used to determine the best shift points and to regulate line pressure. It will cause the PCM or the TCM to engage the torque converter clutch (TCC) sooner and disable overdrive, to help reduce the fluid temperature if it reaches higher than normal.

BRAKE SWITCH A brake switch mounted at the brake pedal provides a signal when the brake is depressed. It signals the TCM that the brake is applied, and the TCC should be released. The brake switch is also called a **brake on/off (BOO)** switch. ● **SEE FIGURE 25–9**.

INPUTS SHARED WITH THE PCM Many factors are used by the TCM to determine when to shift. Many sensors are used by the PCM for engine operation and are also used to help the engine and transmission/transaxle work together to provide smooth efficient operation. This produces the best performance with the lowest possible exhaust emission and the best possible fuel economy. The sensors that are used for both the engine and the transmission include the following:

- **Throttle position (TP) sensor.** This variable resistor (potentiometer) provides a voltage signal that is relative to throttle opening. It provides a throttle position signal to the TCM.

- **Engine coolant temperature (ECT).** This variable resistor (thermistor) monitors engine temperature. It signals the TCM that the engine is at operating temperature or approaching an overheat temperature.

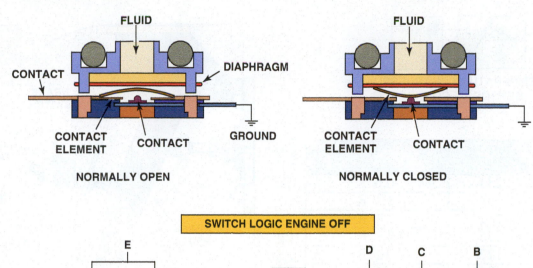

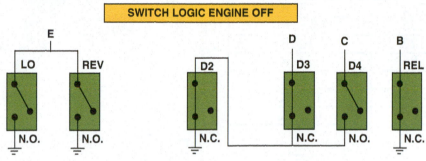

RANGE INDICATOR	FLUID					CIRCUIT		
	REV	D4	D3	D2	LO	E	D	C
PARK / NEUTRAL	0	0	0	0	0	0	1	0
REVERSE	1	0	0	0	0	1	1	0
OVERDRIVE	0	1	0	0	0	0	1	1
MANUAL THIRD	0	1	1	0	0	0	0	1
MANUAL SECOND	0	1	1	1	0	0	0	0
MANUAL FIRST	0	1	1	1	1	1	0	0

1 = PRESSURIZED   0 = EXHAUSTED

1 = GROUNDED (RESISTANCE < 50 OHMS, 0 OHMS)

0 = OPEN (RESISTANCE > 50 K OHMS, 12 VOLTS)

FIGURE 25–7 Some switches are electrically normally open (N.O.) and others are normally closed (N.C.) and are used to provide gear selection information to the PCM/TCM.

- **Manifold absolute pressure (MAP)** and *mass airflow sensor (MAF)*. These sensors provide engine load signal to the PCM.

TRANSMISSION SOLENOIDS

TYPES OF SOLENOIDS An electronic transmission controls the shift points by turning a solenoid(s) on and off. The solenoids in turn control the hydraulic pressure that moves the shift valves or operates the torque converter clutch. Solenoids used in electronically controlled automatic transmissions/transaxles are as follows:

- **On–off solenoids.** These can be normally open to fluid flow or normally closed to block fluid flow. Shift solenoids control the pressure force which in turn controls the position of the shift valve. They are commanded on or off by the PCM or TCM. The resistance of most on–off shift solenoids is 10 to 15 ohms. ● **SEE FIGURE 25–10.**

- **Linear solenoids.** This type of solenoid can be varied by changing the amount of on time to precisely control the fluid flow through the solenoid valve. The variable power or ground applied to the linear solenoids is pulse-width modulated (PWM) and allows the PCM precise control over the shifting and the fluid pressure. The resistance of most

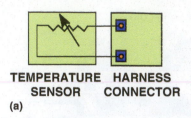

TEMPERATURE   HARNESS
SENSOR   CONNECTOR

(a)

Temperature		Resistance (Ohms)
°C	°F	
140	284	0.6 K
120	248	1.1 K
100	212	2.1 K
80	176	3.8 K
50	122	10 K
30	86	27 K
10	50	69 K
−10	14	193 K
−30	−22	600 K

(b)

FIGURE 25–8 (a) A transmission fluid temperature sensor can be checked by connecting an ohmmeter to the harness connector terminals. (b) The resistance should change as the temperature changes.

linear (PWM) shift solenoids is about half of the on–off type and ranges from 4 to 6 ohms. ● SEE FIGURE 25–11.

A PWM signal is a digital signal, usually 0 volts and 12 volts, which is cycling at a fixed frequency. Varying the length of time that the signal is on provides a signal that can vary the on and off time of an output. The ratio of on time relative to the period of the cycle is referred to as duty cycle. The torque converter clutch (TCC), pressure control solenoids (PCS), and some shift solenoids are pulse-width modulated-type solenoids. ● SEE FIGURE 25–12.

LOW-SIDE AND HIGH-SIDE DRIVERS Low-side drivers (LSD) are transistors that complete the ground path in the circuit. Ignition voltage is supplied to the solenoid and the computer output is connected to the ground side of the shift solenoid. The computer energizes the solenoid by completing the ground path. Low-side drivers can often perform a diagnostic circuit check by monitoring the voltage from the solenoid to check that the control circuit is complete. A low-side driver, however, cannot detect a short-to-ground.

High-side drivers (HSD) control the power side of the solenoid from the PCM/TCM. A ground is provided to the solenoid, so when the high-side driver switches, the solenoid will be energized. High-side drivers inside modules can detect electrical faults, such as a break in continuity when the circuit is not energized. ● SEE FIGURE 25–13.

ELECTRONIC PRESSURE CONTROL

- The transmission's hydraulic pump pressure regulator valve is controlled by the pressure regulator valve that is

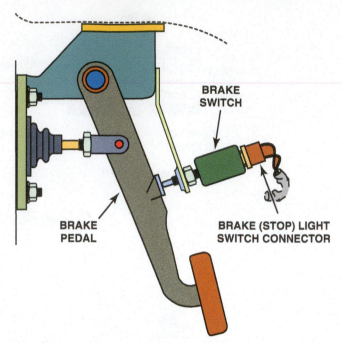

BRAKE
SWITCH

BRAKE
PEDAL

BRAKE (STOP) LIGHT
SWITCH CONNECTOR

FIGURE 25–9 The brake (stop light) switch is mounted at the brake pedal. It provides a brake-apply signal to the TCM.

controlled by a pulse-width-modulated solenoid called **Electronic pressure control (EPC)** or

- **Pressure control solenoid (PCS)** or
- **Variable force solenoid (VFS)** or
- **Force motor**

The EPC is normally closed, which results in high regulated pressure.

- Current (a maximum of about 1 ampere) allows the solenoid to open, which reduces the regulated pressure. The EPC PWM by the PCM/TCM operates at a fixed frequency, usually at 300 to 600 Hz depending on the unit.
- The higher the duty cycle, the more current and the lower the pressure.
- The lower the duty cycle, the less the current and the higher the pressure. ● SEE CHART 25–1.

? FREQUENTLY ASKED QUESTION

What Is Torque Control?

Accurate control of shift timing and quality provides a smoother driving experience. In addition to improving shift quality, altering the ignition timing during the shift decreases the load on the transmission and increases transmission life. This is called **torque management** or *torque reduction* and is controlled by the PCM/TCM. ● SEE FIGURE 25–14.

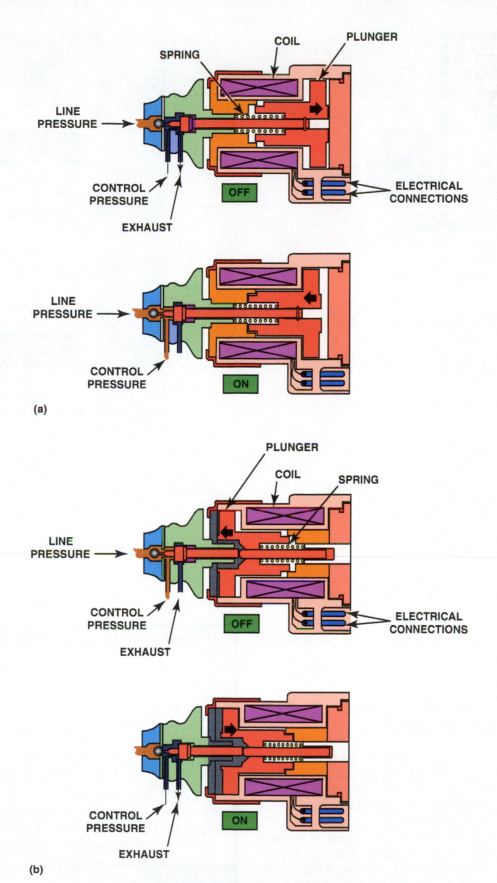

FIGURE 25–10 (a) The normally closed solenoid blocks fluid flow when it is off while opening the exhaust; and when it is on, it opens the valve. (b) The normally open solenoid allows fluid flow when it is off; and when it is on, it closes the valve while opening the exhaust.

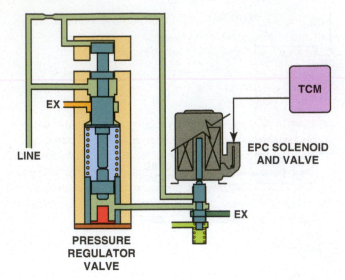

FIGURE 25–11 The signal from the TCM can cause the EPC solenoid to change the pressure regulator valve to adjust line pressure.

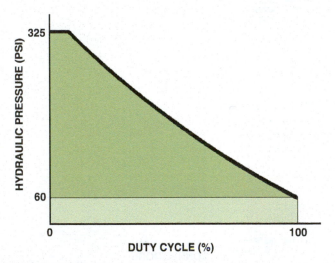

FIGURE 25–12 Line pressure increases as the duty cycle of the EPC solenoid decreases.

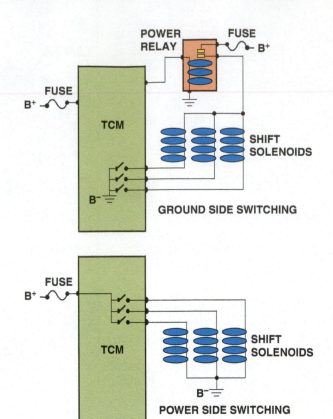

FIGURE 25–13 Top image shows that the TCM completes the ground side (B-) of the shift solenoids whereas the lower figure shows that the TCM completes the power side (B+) side of the shift solenoids.

HOW IT ALL WORKS

ELECTRONIC The transmission control module (TCM) uses information from the various engine and transmission/ transaxle sensors and then commands the shift solenoids to operate, which controls the timing of the shifts. ● SEE FIGURE 25–15.

HYDRAULIC A solenoid can be cycled (pulsed on and off) or line pressure can be increased or decreased by adjusting the electrical signal to the electronic pressure control (EPC) or shift solenoid. The solenoids in turn control the hydraulic pressure that moves the shift valves or operates the torque converter clutch. ● SEE FIGURE 25–16.

EPC AMPERES	PRESSURE PSI (KPA)
0.0	169–195 PSI (1,165–1,345 kPa)
0.1	167–194 PSI (1,151–1,338 kPa)
0.2	161–190 PSI (1,110–1,310 kPa)
0.3	155–186 PSI (1,069–1,282 kPa)
0.4	144–177 PSI (993–1,220 kPa)
0.5	133–167 PSI (917–1,151 kPa)
0.6	120–153 PSI (827–1,055 kPa)
0.7	102–138 PSI (703–952 kPa)
0.8	83–119 PSI (572–821 kPa)
0.9	62–97 PSI (427–669 kPa)
1.0	53–69 PSI (365–476 kPa)

CHART 25–1

Typical electronic pressure control (EPC) current and line pressure comparison.

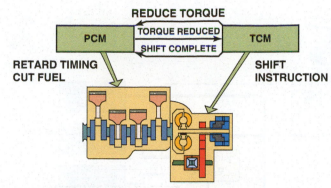

FIGURE 25–14 When the transmission control module (TCM) is ready to begin an upshift, it signals the powertrain control module (PCM) to reduce engine torque. This produces a smoother shift with less wear in the transmission.

TYPICAL ADAPTIVE CONTROLS Transmissions use input and output speed sensors, allowing the TCM to determine the gear ratio and how long it takes to make the shift.

- Chrysler refers to the adaptive control as the **clutch volume index (CVI)**, which is the length of time it takes to fill the clutches with fluid.

- General Motors call their adaptive control **Transmission Adapt Pressure (TAP)** system, which manages oil pressure to control clutch fill rates. The TAP values are sorted by cell, with each cell being a different throttle opening. The PCM/TCM can add pressure to compensate for clutch pack wear up to 30 PSI, which is displayed on a **scan tool**. ● SEE FIGURE 25–17.

ADAPTIVE STRATEGIES

DEFINITION Most late model electronically controlled automatic transmissions/transaxles use the PCM or TCM to monitor the time it takes to complete a shift. The PCM can determine this from the comparison between the engine speed and the output speed sensor data. When a shift is commanded, there should be a change in the speed of the output shaft. If the change in speed is more than normal, which could indicate normal wear in the clutch pack, the PCM can learn from this and start the shift sooner to allow time for the clutch to be fully engaged. The adjustment is called **adaptive control**, or **adaptive learning**, which keeps shift duration within a certain time period as determined by the driver's habits.

 FREQUENTLY ASKED QUESTION

What Is Fuzzy Logic?

A method used to improve shift timing is through a process called *fuzzy logic*. In most situations, shifts simply match vehicle speed and throttle position. Fuzzy logic adapts shifts to driving conditions such as mountains, upgrades and downgrades, and while turning corners. The shifts will be delayed and firmer because of increased load and multiple changes in throttle position. Fuzzy logic and advanced electronics allow improved shifts for many different situations. ● SEE FIGURE 25–18.

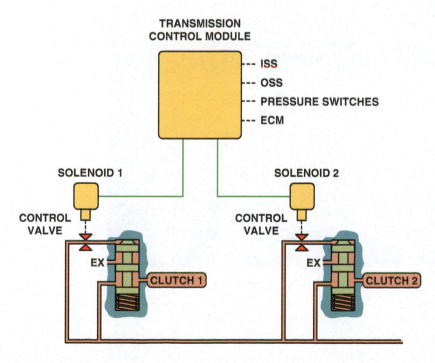

FIGURE 25–15 Using data from the various sensors, the TCM can apply or release the clutches. During an upshift, solenoid 1 can control how fast clutch 1 releases as solenoid 2 controls how fast clutch 2 applies to keep the shift time at the proper speed.

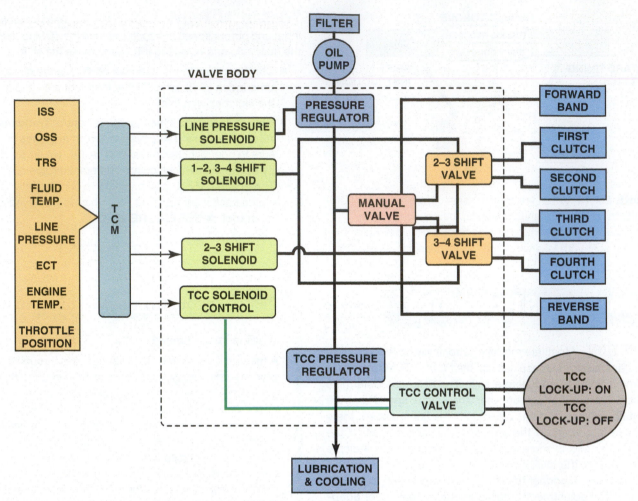

FIGURE 25–16 A diagram showing the relationship between the electronic and hydraulic controls.

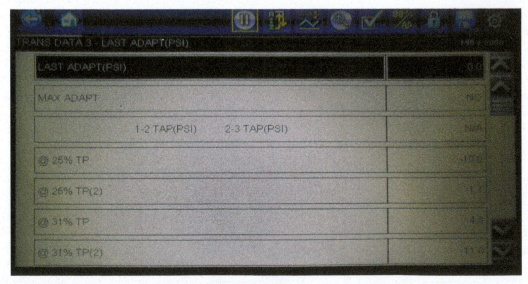

FIGURE 25–17 A scan tool display showing the adaptive (TAP) pressure changes at various throttle positions.

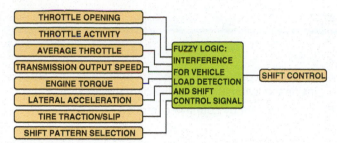

FIGURE 25–18 The fuzzy logic part of the TMC receives input signals, compares what the driver is doing with the throttle and what the vehicle is doing with normal operation, and adapts shift timing.

GENERAL MOTORS 4T60-E (FRONT-WHEEL-DRIVE TRANSAXLE)		
GEAR RANGE	**SOLENOID A**	**SOLENOID B**
First gear	ON	ON
Second gear	OFF	ON
Third gear	OFF	OFF
Fourth gear	ON	OFF

CHART 25–2

In this example, the vehicle would start out and remain in third gear if there was a fault with the computer or wiring.

- Honda calls it *clutch fill volume index*, which is shown on a scan tool as a number. The higher the number, the more fluid volume is required to fill a clutch and can be used to see if there are worn friction plates in a certain clutch pack.

Check service information for details for the proper clutch volumes on the unit being serviced.

Some vehicles have additional shift control modes, and these provide earlier or later and smoother or faster shifts.

- The driver can choose economy mode, which causes the transmission to shift early with a smooth shift feel.
- When switched to power mode, the transmission shifts later and more firmly.

GENERAL MOTORS 4L80-E (REAR-WHEEL-DRIVE TRANSMISSION)		
GEAR RANGE	**SOLENOID A**	**SOLENOID B**
First gear	ON	OFF
Second gear	OFF	OFF
Third gear	OFF	ON
Fourth gear	ON	ON

CHART 25–3

In this example, the vehicle would start out and remain in second gear if there was a fault with the computer or wiring.

TRANSMISSION CONTROL MODULE CALIBRATION

When a transmission control module is replaced or reprogrammed, certain parameters must be re-entered with a scan tool. The data that must be entered includes the tire size and the final drive ratio. This information is used by the transmission control module to control shift points. Failure to re-enter this information may result in incorrect shift points or an emission failure due to incorrect engine RPM. Any physical modifications to the transmission, such as changing gear ratios, may generate similar failures and result in the MIL being illuminated and a hard code being stored.

DEFAULT (LIMP-IN) A **default (or limp-in)** gear is the forward speed that is used if there is a failure in the electronic or computer system. If neither of two shift solenoids were engaged, then a default gear is actuated.

Depending on the exact make and model of the transmission or transaxle, the default gear can be second, third, or fourth gear. ● **SEE CHARTS 25–2 AND 25–3** for examples of two General Motors transmissions.

SUMMARY

1. Electronic controls are used for accurate automatic operation of the transmission/transaxle.
2. Electronic controls use sensors to monitor various operational inputs that will be used to control the operation of the transmission.
3. The hydraulic operation of the transmission is controlled by solenoids that are switched to redirect pressurized fluid to move shift valves or change the operational pressures.
4. The PCM/TCM receives the signals from the sensors and operates the solenoids to produce upshifts and downshifts at the proper speed.

REVIEW QUESTIONS

1. What are the four sensors that are used by the automatic transmission/transaxle controller to determine when to shift?

2. What are the types of computer memory used in the PCM/TCM?

3. What is the purpose and function of the input and output speed sensors?

4. What is the purpose and function of the pressure sensors inside the automatic transmission/transaxle?

5. What is meant by adaptive controls?

CHAPTER QUIZ

1. What electronic control module is used to control the shifting of an electronically controlled automatic transmission/transaxle?
   a. PCM
   b. TCM
   c. TCU
   d. Any of the above depending on application

2. A transmission control module (TCM) has just been replaced. Which parameters should be programmed into the TCM using a scan tool?
   a. odometer reading
   b. tire size
   c. vehicle emission control information
   d. vehicle weight

3. What type of sensor measures speed?
   a. Potentiometer
   b. Thermistor
   c. Transducer
   d. Frequency generator

4. The transmission range (TR) switch is used to _____.
   a. keep the engine from starting in any gear position except park or neutral
   b. limit upshifts in manual ranges
   c. operate the backup lights in reverse
   d. All of the above

5. The input speed sensor is also called a _____.
   a. Output speed sensor (OSS)
   b. Vehicle speed (VS) sensor
   c. Turbine speed sensor (TSS)
   d. Any of the above depending on make and model

6. The output speed sensor is also called a _____.
   a. Input speed sensor (ISS)
   b. Vehicle speed (VS) sensor
   c. Turbine speed sensor (TSS)
   d. Any of the above depending on make and model

7. What type of sensor is the transmission fluid temperature (TFT) sensor?
   a. Negative temperature coefficient (NTC) thermistor
   b. Potentiometer
   c. Rheostat
   d. Transducer

8. Linear solenoids are used for _____.
   a. TCC
   b. pressure control
   c. transducer
   d. All of the above depending on application

9. What does electronic pressure control (EPC) solenoid use to control mainline pressure?
   a. Resistance
   b. Current
   c. Torque
   d. Voltage

10. Adaptive control means _____.
    a. the time it takes to make a shift
    b. the delay between the command and when the shift occurs
    c. the change in the pressure or timing to keep the shift occurring at the same time to make up for wear
    d. the default position, which may be second, third, or fourth gear depending on application

chapter 26

VEHICLE EMISSIONS STANDARDS, AND TESTING

LEARNING OBJECTIVES

After studying this chapter, the reader should be able to:

1. Identify the reasons why excessive amounts of HC, CO, and NOx exhaust emissions are created.
2. Diagnose driveability and emissions problems resulting from malfunctions of interrelated systems.
3. Discuss emissions standards.
4. Describe how to test for various emissions products.

KEY TERMS

Carbon dioxide (CO_2) 374
Carbon monoxide (CO) 375
Federal Test Procedure (FTP) 381
Hydrocarbons (HC) 374
Lean indicator 376
Oxygen (O_2) 374
Oxides of nitrogen (NOx) 375
Ozone 379
Rich indicator 376
Smog 379
Stoichiometric ratio 374
Water (H_2O) 374

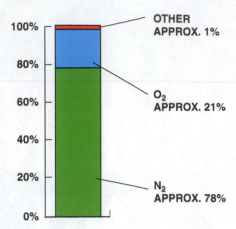

FIGURE 26–1 The air entering the engine consists of mostly nitrogen (78%) with about 21% oxygen and about 1% other gases.

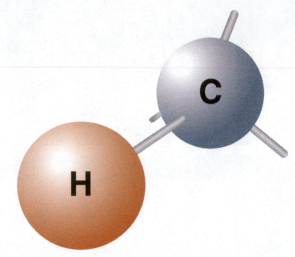

FIGURE 26–2 Hydrocarbons can include many combinations of hydrogen and carbon.

NORMAL ENGINE COMBUSTION

AIR AND GASOLINE Engines consume about 15 times more air than gasoline; this ratio of air to fuel is called the **stoichiometric ratio**. This ratio, which is 14.7:1 for gasoline, is the one where all of the fuel is consumed in the combustion process and uses all of the available oxygen.

- Entering the engine combustion chamber is fuel (HC) plus air (**nitrogen (N_2)** is 78% and **oxygen (O_2)** is 21% of the air). ● **SEE FIGURE 26–1**.

- During combustion, the HC combines with the air to form **water** (H_2O) and carbon dioxide (CO_2) in addition to nitrogen (N_2) and some other non-desirable gases.

- Engines consume about 15 times more air than gasoline (14.7:1 at stoichiometric ratio). The normal reaction results in water H_2O as a vapor and carbon dioxide (CO_2) as the result of the combustion process, but some of the other gases include:

  - Unburned **hydrocarbons (HC)** If perfect combustion occurred inside the engine, there should not be any leftover unburned fuel. If there are HC gases exiting the tailpipe, then something is wrong that prevented all of the fuel from being burned. ● **SEE FIGURE 26–2**.

  - **Carbon monoxide (CO)** During combustion, all of the carbon in the fuel should be converted to **carbon dioxide** (CO_2) if there was enough oxygen available. If there was not enough oxygen available in the combustion chamber, then incomplete combustion occurs, which creates CO instead of CO_2. ● **SEE FIGURE 26–3**.

  - **Oxides of Nitrogen** (**NOx**) Nitrogen is 78% of the air so having some left over is normal; however, if the combustion temperatures and pressures are high enough, some of the nitrogen (N_2) combines with

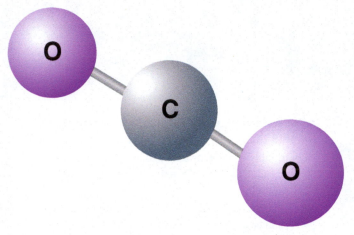

FIGURE 26–3 Carbon dioxide has two oxygen atoms attached to the one carbon atom and is a stable molecule.

the oxygen to form NO and NO_2. These are harmful exhaust gases and referred to as oxides of nitrogen, NOx, where the "x" represents any number of oxygen atoms. ● **SEE FIGURE 26–4**

? **FREQUENTLY ASKED QUESTION**

Why Is Steam Seen from the Tailpipe When Cold Outside, But Not Always?

Steam is water vapor and is invisible. However, when an engine is cold, the water vapor created by combustion partially condenses into small droplets of water that are visible as "steam" from the tailpipe of the vehicle. After the exhaust system has been heated, the water vapor no longer condenses in the exhaust system so it is not visible after the engine is warm. ● **SEE FIGURE 26–5**.

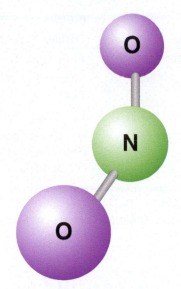

FIGURE 26–4 NO and NO_2 shown together are referred to as NOx.

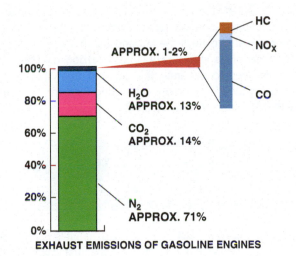

EXHAUST EMISSIONS OF GASOLINE ENGINES

FIGURE 26–5 A chart showing that about 13% of the exhaust emissions is water (H_2O) in the form of steam.

EXHAUST ANALYSIS AND COMBUSTION EFFICIENCY

The following section analyzes five gases and highlights their significance

HYDROCARBONS Hydrocarbons (HC) are unburned gasoline and are measured in parts per million (ppm). A correctly operating engine should burn (oxidize) almost all the gasoline; therefore, very little unburned gasoline should be present in the exhaust. Acceptable levels of HC are 50 PPM or less. High levels of HC could be due to excessive oil consumption caused by weak piston rings or worn valve guides. The most common

cause of excessive HC emissions is a fault in the ignition system. Items that should be checked include:

- Spark plugs
- Secondary ignition fault, such as coils, spark plug boots, or wiring

CARBON MONOXIDE Carbon monoxide (CO) is unstable and will easily combine with any oxygen to form stable carbon dioxide (CO_2). As CO combines with oxygen, it is considered as a poisonous gas (in the lungs, it combines with oxygen to form CO_2 and deprives the brain of oxygen). CO levels of a properly operating engine should be less than 0.5%. High levels of CO can be caused by clogged or restricted crankcase ventilation devices, such as the PCV valve, hose(s), and tubes. Other items that might cause excessive CO include:

- Incorrect idle speed
- Too-high fuel-pump pressure
- Any other items that can cause a rich condition

CARBON DIOXIDE (CO_2) Carbon dioxide (CO_2) is the result of oxygen in the engine combining with the carbon of the gasoline. An acceptable level of CO_2 is between 12% and 15%. A high reading indicates an efficiently operating engine. If the CO_2 level is low, the mixture may be either too rich or too lean.

OXYGEN There is about 21% oxygen in the atmosphere, and most of this oxygen should be "used up" during the combustion process to oxidize all the hydrogen and carbon (hydrocarbons) in the gasoline. Levels of O_2 should be very low (about 0.5%). High levels of O_2, especially at idle, could be due to an exhaust system leak.

NOTE: Adding 10% alcohol to gasoline provides additional oxygen to the fuel and will result in lower levels of CO and higher levels of O_2 in the exhaust.

OXIDES OF NITROGEN (NOₓ) An **oxide of nitrogen (NO)** is a colorless, tasteless, and odorless gas when it leaves the engine, but as soon as it reaches the atmosphere and mixes with more oxygen, nitrogen oxides (NO_2) are formed. NO_2 is reddish-brown and has an acid and pungent smell. NO and NO_2 are grouped together and referred to as NOx, where *x* represents any number of oxygen atoms. NOx, the symbol used to represent all oxides of nitrogen, is the fifth gas commonly tested using a five-gas analyzer. The exhaust gas recirculation (EGR) system is the major controlling device limiting the formation of NOx. ● SEE FIGURE 26–6.

SUMMARY OF EXHAUST GASES For a summary of the exhaust gases and what can cause them to form, ● SEE CHART 26–1.

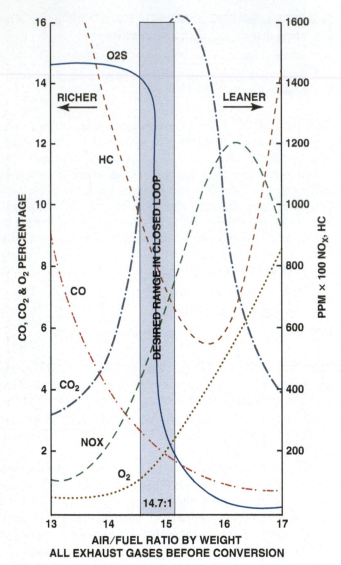

FIGURE 26–6 Exhaust emissions are very complex. When the air–fuel mixture becomes richer, some exhaust emissions are reduced, while others increase.

EXHAUST GAS	CAUSE
Hydrocarbons (HC)	Ignition misfire or incomplete combustion
Carbon monoxide (CO)	Exhaust too rich
Oxides of nitrogen (NO_x)	Engine operating too hot or too lean
Oxygen (O_2)	Exhaust is too lean
Carbon dioxide (CO_2)	Engine efficiency (the higher, the more efficient)

CHART 26–1

A summary of the measurable exhaust gases using a five-gas analyzer and the typical causes.

EXHAUST GAS	TYPICAL SPECIFICATIONS
Unburned hydrocarbons (HC)	30–50 ppm or less
Carbon monoxide (CO)	0.3%–0.5% or less
Oxygen (O_2)	0%–2%
Carbon dioxide (CO_2)	12%–15% or higher
Oxides of nitrogen (NO_x)	Less than 100 parts per million (PPM) at idle and less than 1,000 PPM at wide open throttle (WOT)

CHART 26–2

Typical specifications for gases on a vehicle equipped with a catalytic converter.

CATALYTIC CONVERTER

EFFECT ON EXHAUST GASES The catalytic converter is used to help reduce exhaust emissions by helping the oxygen in the exhaust to oxidize the HC and CO in the exhaust stream to form harmless water (H_2O) and carbon dioxide (CO_2). It also is used to separate the nitrogen from the oxygen in NOx to produce just nitrogen (N_2) and oxygen (O_2). ● **SEE FIGURE 26–7** and ● **CHART 26–2**.

EXHAUST ANALYSIS AS A DIAGNOSTIC TOOL

RICH OR LEAN EXHAUST If the exhaust is rich, CO emissions will be higher than normal. If the exhaust is lean, O_2 emissions will be higher than normal.

■ If CO is high, the exhaust is rich. This is why CO is called the "**rich indicator**."

■ If O_2 is high, the exhaust is lean. This is why O_2 is called the "**lean indicator**."

Therefore, if the CO reading is the same as the O_2 reading, the engine is operating correctly. For example, if both CO and O_2 are 0.5% and the engine develops a vacuum leak, the O_2 will rise. If a fuel-pressure regulator were to malfunction, the resulting richer air–fuel mixture would increase CO emissions. Therefore, if both the rich indicator (CO) and the lean indicator (O_2) are equal, the engine is operating correctly.

If the exhaust is rich (too much fuel or not enough air), then:

■ Both CO and HC will be high

■ O_2 will be low

■ CO_2 will be low

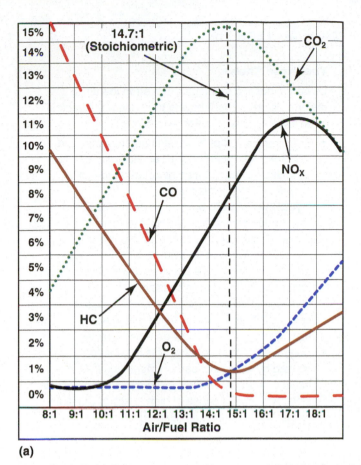

(a)

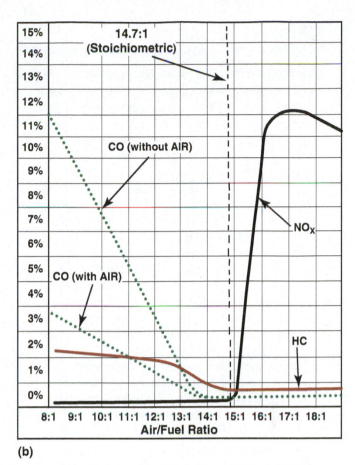

(b)

FIGURE 26–7 (a) Exhaust gases exiting an engine without a catalytic converter with rich exhaust being toward the left of the vertical line and lean exhaust to the right of the stoichiometric ratio line. (b) The exhaust after it has been treated by the catalytic converter.

**TECH TIP**

How to Find a Leak in the Exhaust System

A hole in the exhaust system can dilute the exhaust gases with additional oxygen (O_2). ● **SEE FIGURE 26–8.**

This additional O_2 in the exhaust can lead the service technician to believe that the air–fuel mixture is too lean. To help identify an exhaust leak, perform an exhaust analysis at idle and at 2,500 RPM (fast idle) and compare with the following:

- If O_2 is high at idle and at 2,500 RPM, the mixture is lean at both idle and at 2,500 RPM.
- If O_2 is low at idle and high at 2,500 RPM, this usually means that the vehicle is equipped with a working AIR pump.
- If O2 is high at idle, but okay at 2,500 RPM, a hole in the exhaust or a small vacuum leak that is "covered up" at higher speed is indicated.

If the exhaust is lean (not enough fuel or too much air), then:

■ O_2 will be high
■ CO_2 will be low

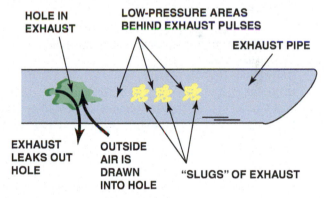

FIGURE 26–8 A hole in the exhaust system can cause outside air (containing oxygen) to be drawn into the exhaust system. This extra oxygen can be confusing to a service technician because the extra O2 in the exhaust stream could be misinterpreted as a too-lean air–fuel mixture.

ENGINE FAULT POSSIBILITIES

HC TOO HIGH High hydrocarbon exhaust emissions are usually caused by an engine misfire. What burns the fuel in an engine? The ignition system ignites a spark at the spark plug to

CASE STUDY

O2S Shows Rich, But Pulse Width Is Low

A service technician was attempting to solve a drive-ability problem. The PCM did not indicate any diagnostic trouble codes (DTCs). A check of the oxygen sensor voltage indicated a higher-than-normal reading almost all the time. The pulse width to the port injectors was lower than normal. The lower-than-normal pulse width indicates that the PCM is attempting to reduce fuel flow into the engine by decreasing the amount of on-time for all the injectors. What could cause a rich mixture if the injectors were being commanded to deliver a lean mixture?

Finally, the technician shut off the engine and took a careful look at the entire fuel-injection system. When the vacuum hose was removed from the fuel-pressure regulator, fuel was found dripping from the vacuum hose. The problem was a defective fuel-pressure regulator that allowed an uncontrolled amount of fuel to be drawn by the intake manifold vacuum into the cylinders. While the PCM tried to reduce fuel by reducing the pulse width signal to the injectors, the extra fuel being drawn directly from the fuel rail caused the engine to operate with too rich an air–fuel mixture.

Summary:

- **Complaint**–Customer stated that the engine did not perform correctly.
- **Cause**–No stored diagnostic trouble codes (DTCs) were found, but the oxygen sensor reading was higher than normal, indicating that the exhaust air–fuel mixture was too rich.
- **Correction**–The fuel pressure regulator was found to be leaking causing fuel to be drawn into the intake causing the richer-than-normal air–fuel mixture. Replacing the fuel pressure regulator solved the driveability complaint.

TECH TIP

Your Nose Knows

Using the nose, a technician can often identify a major problem without having to connect the vehicle to an exhaust analyzer. For example:

- The strong smell of exhaust is due to excessive unburned hydrocarbon (HC) emissions. Look for an ignition system fault that could prevent the proper burning of the fuel.
- If your eyes start to burn or water, suspect excessive oxides of nitrogen (NOx) emissions. The oxides of nitrogen combine with the moisture in the eyes to form a mild solution of nitric acid. The acid formation causes the eyes to burn and water. Excessive NOx exhaust emissions can be caused by a lack of proper amount of exhaust gas recirculation (EGR) or a variable valve timing issue (This is usually noticed above idle on most vehicles.)
- Dizzy feeling or headache. This is commonly caused by excessive carbon monoxide (CO) exhaust emissions. Get into fresh air as soon as possible. A probable cause of high levels of CO is an excessively rich air–fuel mixture.

CO TOO HIGH Excessive carbon monoxide is an indication of too rich an air–fuel mixture. CO is the rich indicator. The higher the CO reading, the richer the air–fuel mixture. High concentrations of CO indicate that not enough oxygen was available for the amount of fuel. Common causes of high CO include:

- Too-high fuel pressure
- Clogged air intake or PCV valve
- Defective injectors

O_2 AND CO_2 RELATIONSHIP Two gas exhaust analyzers (HC and CO) work well, but both HC and CO are consumed (converted) inside the catalytic converter. The amount of leftover oxygen coming out of the tailpipe is an indication of leanness. The higher the O_2 level, the leaner the exhaust. Oxygen, therefore, is the lean indicator. Acceptable levels of O_2 are 0% to 2%.

NOTE: A hole in the exhaust system can draw outside air (oxygen) into the exhaust system. Therefore, to be assured of an accurate reading, carefully check the exhaust system for leaks. Using a smoke machine is an easy method to locate leaks in the exhaust system.

Carbon dioxide (CO_2) is a measure of efficiency. The higher the level of CO_2 in the exhaust stream, the more efficiently the engine is operating. Levels of 12% to 17% are considered to be acceptable. Because CO_2 levels peak at an air–fuel mixture of 14.7:1, a lower level of CO_2 indicates either a too-rich or a too-lean condition. The CO_2 measurement by itself does not indicate which condition is present. For example:

---

ignite the proper mixture inside the combustion chamber. If a spark plug does not ignite the mixture, the resulting unburned fuel is pushed out of the cylinder on the exhaust stroke by the piston through the exhaust valves and into the exhaust system. Therefore, if any of the following ignition components or adjustments is not correct, excessive HC emission is likely:

1. Defective or worn spark plugs
2. Defective or loose spark plug boots or other faults in the primary or secondary ignition system

A lean air–fuel mixture can also cause a misfire. This condition is referred to as a *lean misfire*. A lean air–fuel mixture can be caused by low fuel pump pressure, a clogged fuel filter, or a restricted fuel injector.

The Case of the Retarded Exhaust Camshaft

A Toyota equipped with a double overhead camshaft (DOHC) six-cylinder engine failed the state-mandated enhanced exhaust emissions test for NOx. The engine ran perfectly without spark knocking (ping), which is usually a major reason for excessive NOx emissions. The technician checked the following:

- The cylinders, which were decarbonized using top engine cleaner
- The EGR valve, which was inspected and the EGR passages cleaned

After all the items were completed, the vehicle was returned to the inspection station where the vehicle again failed for excessive NOx emissions (better, but still over the maximum allowable limit).

After additional hours of troubleshooting, the technician decided to go back to basics and start over again. A check of the vehicle history with the owner indicated that the only previous work performed on the engine was a replacement timing belt over a year before. The technician discovered that the exhaust cam timing was retarded two teeth, resulting in late closing of the exhaust valve. The proper exhaust valve timing resulted in a slight amount of exhaust being retained in the cylinder. This extra exhaust helped reduce NOx emissions.

After repositioning the timing belt, the vehicle passed the emissions test well within the limits.

Summary:

- **Complaint**–Customer stated that the vehicle failed an emission test due to excessive NOx exhaust emissions.
- **Cause**–The exhaust cam was discovered to be retarded by two teeth as a result of the timing belt being incorrectly installed during a previous repair.
- **Correction**–The timing belt was properly aligned and the vehicle passed the emission test.

CO_2 is 8% (This means efficiency is low and the air–fuel mixture is not correct.)

Look at O_2 and CO levels. A high O_2 indicates lean and a high CO indicates rich.

SMOG AND NO$_X$ Oxides of nitrogen are formed by high temperature—over 2,500°F (1,370°C)—and/or pressures inside the combustion chamber. Oxides of nitrogen contribute to the formation of photochemical smog when sunlight reacts chemically with NOx and unburned hydrocarbons (HC). "**Smog**" is a term derived by combining the words *smoke* and *fog*. Ground-level ozone is a constituent of smog. **Ozone** is an enriched oxygen molecule with three atoms of oxygen (O_3) instead of the normal two atoms of oxygen (O_2). Ozone in the upper atmosphere is beneficial because it blocks out harmful ultraviolet rays that contribute to skin cancer. However, at ground level, this ozone (smog) is an irritant to the respiratory system. Because the formation of NOx occurs mostly under load, the most efficient method to test for NOx is to use a portable exhaust analyzer that can be carried in the vehicle while the vehicle is being driven under a variety of conditions.

From experience, a maximum reading of 1,000 parts per million (PPM) of NOx under loaded driving conditions will generally mean that the vehicle will pass an enhanced I/M roller test. A reading of over 100 PPM at idle should be considered excessive.

ABNORMAL GAS READINGS The exhaust gases each have their own cause for being higher than normal or lower than normal and they are interconnected. ● SEE CHART 26–3.

EMISSION STANDARDS

In the United States, emissions standards are managed by the Environmental Protection Agency (EPA), as well as some U.S. state governments. Some of the strictest standards in the world are formulated in California by the California Air Resources Board (CARB).

TIER 1 AND TIER 2 Federal emissions standards are set by the Clean Air Act Amendments (CAAA) of 1990 grouped by tier. All vehicles sold in the United States must meet Tier 1

CARBON MONOXIDE (CO)	CARBON DIOXIDE (CO_2)	HYDROCARBONS (HC)	OXYGEN (O_2)	POSSIBLE ISSUES
Low	High	Low	Low	Normal readings. No issues
High	Low	High	High	Rich exhaust and misfire
Low	Low	High	High	Lean exhaust and misfire
High	High	High	High	Catalytic converter not working as designed plus possible other air–fuel ratio issues
High	Low	High	High	Rich exhaust
High	Low	High	Low	Possible defective thermostat.

CHART 26–3

Possible issues based on the relative readings of the four exhaust gases.

standards that went into effect in 1994 and are the least stringent. Additional Tier 2 standards have been optional since 2001, and fully adopted by 2009. The current Tier 1 standards are different between automobiles and light trucks (SUVs, pickup trucks, and minivans), but Tier 2 standards will be the same for both types.

There are several ratings that can be given to vehicles, and a certain percentage of a manufacturer's vehicles must meet different levels in order for the company to sell its products in affected regions. Beyond Tier 1, and in order by stringency, are the following levels:

- **TLEV** (Transitional Low-Emission Vehicle). More stringent for HC than Tier 1.

- **LEV** (also known as LEV I) (Low-Emission Vehicle). An intermediate California standard about twice as stringent as Tier 1 for HC and NOx.

- **ULEV** (also known as ULEV I) (Ultra-Low-Emission Vehicle). A stronger California standard emphasizing very low HC emission.

- **ULEV II** (Ultra-Low-Emission Vehicle). A cleaner-than-average vehicle certified under the Phase II LEV standard.

Hydrocarbon and carbon monoxide emissions levels are nearly 50% lower than those of a LEV II-certified vehicle.

- **SULEV** (Super-Ultra-Low-Emission Vehicle). A California standard even tighter than ULEV, including much lower HC and NOx emissions; roughly equivalent to Tier 2 Bin 2 vehicles.

- **ZEV** (Zero-Emission Vehicle). A California standard prohibiting any tailpipe emissions. The ZEV category is largely restricted to electric vehicles and hydrogen-fueled vehicles.

In these cases, any emissions that are created are produced at another site, such as a power plant or hydrogen reforming center, unless such sites run on renewable energy.

NOTE: A battery-powered electric vehicle charged from the power grid will still be up to 10 times cleaner than even the cleanest gasoline vehicles over their respective lifetimes.

- **PZEV** (Partial Zero-Emission Vehicle). Compliant with the SULEV standard and has near-zero evaporative emissions and a 15-year/150,000-mile warranty on its emission control equipment. Tier 2 standards are even more stringent. Tier 2 variations are appended with "II," such as LEV II or SULEV II.

- **ILEV** (Inherently Low-Emission Vehicle). Used by some states that allow certain vehicles to use the HOV lanes regardless of the number of people in the vehicle. Check state and local laws and regulations for the list of vehicles included.

- **AT-PZEV** (Advanced Technology Partial Zero-Emission Vehicle). If a vehicle meets the PZEV standards and is using high-technology features, such as an electric motor or high-pressure gaseous fuel tanks for compressed natural gas, it qualifies as an AT-PZEV. Hybrid electric vehicles, such as the Toyota Prius, can qualify, as can

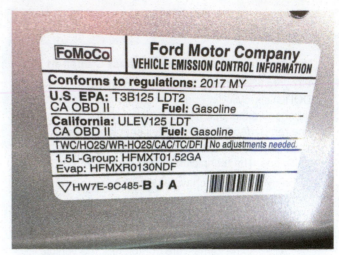

FIGURE 26–9 A vehicle emission control information (VECI) sticker for a vehicle showing that it meets Tier 3, Bin 1 (T2B3) EPA rating, and California ULEV125 standard.

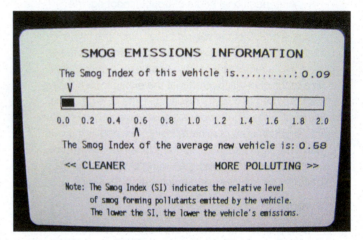

FIGURE 26–10 This label on a Toyota Camry hybrid shows the relative smog-producing emissions, but this does not include carbon dioxide (CO_2), which may increase global warming.

internal combustion engine vehicles that run on natural gas (CNG), such as the Honda Civic GX. These vehicles are classified as "partial" ZEV because they receive partial credit for the number of ZEV vehicles that automakers would otherwise be required to sell in California.

- **NLEV** (National Low-Emission Vehicle). All vehicles nationwide must meet this standard, which started in 2001.

FEDERAL EPA BIN NUMBER The higher the tier number, the newer the regulation; the lower the bin number, the cleaner the vehicle. The Toyota Prius is a very clean Bin 2, while dirtier vehicles are given a higher bin number. ● **SEE FIGURE 26–9.**

SMOG EMISSION INFORMATION New vehicles are equipped with a sticker that shows the relative level of smog-causing emissions created by the vehicle compared to others on the market. Smog-causing emissions include unburned hydrocarbons (HC) and oxides of nitrogen (NOx). ● **SEE FIGURE 26–10.**

EMISSION CATEGORY	NMOG + NOx GRAM PER MILE (G/MI)	CO GRAM PER MILE (G/MI)	PARTICULATE MATTER (PM) GRAM PER MILE (G/MI)
LEV 160	0.160	4.2	0.01
ULEV 125	0.125	2.1	0.01
ULEV 70	0.070	1.7	0.01
ULEV 50	0.050	1.7	0.01
SULEV 30	0.030	1.0	0.01
SULEV 20	0.020	1.0	0.01

CHART 26–4

Non-methane organic gases (NMOG) and oxides of nitrogen are combined under one limit meaning that the hydrocarbons and the NOx have to be both controlled to meet these standards. Particulate matter (PM) has in the past been associated with diesel engine emissions, but are now being tested on gasoline-powered vehicles.

CALIFORNIA STANDARDS The pre-2004 California Air Resources Board (CARB) standards as a whole were known as LEV I. Within that, there were four possible ratings: Tier 1, TLEV, LEV, and ULEV. The newest CARB rating system (since January 1, 2004) is known as LEV II. Within that rating system there are three primary ratings: LEV, ULEV, and SULEV. States other than California are given the option to use the federal EPA standards, or they can adopt California's standards.

LEV III The latest emission standards require that the vehicle manufacturer certify the vehicle for 150.000 miles.. The standards are more stringent than Tier 2 standards and include a number of other important changes:

- The required emission durability has been increased to 150,000 miles, up from 120,000 miles.
- Gasoline vehicles are tested—for exhaust and evaporative emissions—using gasoline containing 10% of ethanol (E10).
- Standards are for 2015–2025 vehicles sold in the United States.

● **SEE CHART 26–4**.

EUROPEAN STANDARDS

Exhaust emissions of nitrogen oxides (NOx), total hydrocarbon (THC), non-methane hydrocarbons (NMHC), carbon monoxide (CO), and particulate matter (PM) are regulated for most vehicle types, including cars and trucks in the European Union (EU). The EU also sets limits for CO_2 emission in units of grams per kilometer with the latest standard being 95 grams per km after 2020. Carbon dioxide is created by the combustion of fuel inside an internal combustion engine. Reducing the CO_2 emissions requires that less fuel be consumed, which is one way the EU is mandating fuel economy standards. The ratings include the following:

- **Euro 1** (1993)
- **Euro 2** (1996)
- **Euro 3** (2000)
- **Euro 4** (2005)
- **Euro 5** (2009)
- **Euro 6** (2014)

VEHICLE EMISSION TESTING

OBD-II TESTING In 1999, the EPA requested that states adopt OBD-II systems testing for 1996 and newer vehicles. The OBD-II system is designed to illuminate the MIL light and store trouble codes any time a malfunction exists that would cause the vehicle emissions to exceed 1 1/2 times the **Federal Test Procedure (FTP)** limits. If the OBD-II system is working correctly, the system should be able to detect a vehicle failure that would cause emissions to increase to an unacceptable level. The EPA has determined that the OBD-II system should detect emission failures of a vehicle even before that vehicle would fail an emissions test of the type that most states are employing.

The EPA has determined that, as the population of OBD-II-equipped vehicles increases and the population of older non-OBD-II-equipped vehicles decreases, tailpipe testing will no longer be necessary.

NOTE: If a state or local emission testing program still uses exhaust emission testing for older vehicles, check the information about the program and test procedures before having the vehicle tested.

The OBD-II testing program consists of a computer that can scan the vehicle OBD-II system using the DLC connector. The technician first performs a visual check of the vehicle MIL light to determine if it is working correctly. Next, the computer is connected to the vehicle's DLC connector. The computer will scan the vehicle OBD-II system and determine if there are any codes stored that are commanding the MIL light on. In addition, it will scan the status of the readiness monitors and determine if they have all run and passed. If the readiness monitors have all run and passed, it indicates that the OBD-II system has tested all the components of the emission control system. An OBD-II vehicle would fail this OBD-II test if:

- The MIL light does not come on with the key on, engine off
- The MIL is commanded on
- A number (varies by state) of the readiness monitors has not been run. If none of these conditions are present, the vehicle will pass the emissions test.

FIGURE 26–11 A partial stream sampling exhaust probe being used to measure exhaust gases in parts per million (PPM) or percent (%).

REMOTE SENSING The EPA requires that, in high enhanced areas, states perform on-the-road testing of vehicle emissions. The state must sample 0.5% of the vehicle population base in high-enhanced areas. This may be accomplished by using a remote sensing device. This type of sensing may be done through equipment that projects an infrared light through the exhaust stream of a passing vehicle. The reflected beam can then be analyzed to determine the pollutant levels coming from the vehicle. If a vehicle fails this type of test, the vehicle owner will receive notification in the mail that he or she must take the vehicle to a test facility to have the emissions tested.

RANDOM ROADSIDE TESTING Some states may implement random roadside testing that would usually involve visual checks of the emission control devices to detect tampering. Obviously, this method is not very popular as it can lead to traffic tie-ups and delays on the part of commuters. Exhaust analysis is an excellent tool to use for the diagnosis of engine performance concerns. In areas of the country that require exhaust testing to be able to get license plates, exhaust analysis must be able to:

- Establish a baseline for failure diagnosis and service.
- Identify areas of engine performance that are and are not functioning correctly.
- Determine that the service and repair of the vehicle have been accomplished and are complete.
- **SEE FIGURE 26–11**.

SUMMARY

1. Engines consume about 15 times more air than gasoline; this ratio of air to fuel is called the stoichiometric ratio. This ratio, which is 14.7:1 for gasoline, is the one where all of the fuel is consumed in the combustion process and uses all of the available oxygen.

2. Hydrocarbons (HC) are unburned gasoline and are measured in parts per million (ppm).

3. Carbon monoxide (CO) is unstable and will easily combine with any oxygen to form stable carbon dioxide (CO_2).

4. Carbon dioxide (CO_2) is the result of oxygen in the engine combining with the carbon of the gasoline. An acceptable level of CO_2 is between 12% and 15%.

5. An oxide of nitrogen (NO) is a colorless, tasteless, and odorless gas when it leaves the engine, but as soon as it reaches the atmosphere and mixes with more oxygen, nitrogen oxides (NO_2) are formed.

6. If the exhaust is rich, CO emissions will be higher than normal. If the exhaust is lean, O_2 emissions will be higher than normal.

7. *Smog* is a term derived by combining the words *smoke* and *fog*. Ground-level ozone is a constituent of smog. Ozone is an enriched oxygen molecule with three atoms of oxygen (O_3) instead of the normal two atoms of oxygen (O_2).

8. In the United States, emissions standards are managed by the Environmental Protection Agency (EPA) as well as some U.S. state governments. Some of the strictest standards in the world are formulated in California by the California Air Resources Board (CARB).

9. Particulate matter (PM) has in the past been associated with diesel engine emissions, but are now being tested on gasoline-powered vehicles.

10. A partial stream sampling exhaust probe is used to measure exhaust gases in parts per million (PPM) or percent (%).

REVIEW QUESTIONS

1. What are the five exhaust gases and their maximum allowable readings for a fuel-injected vehicle equipped with a catalytic converter?

2. How is water formed during the combustion process?

3. What is the stoichiometric ratio and what does it mean?

4. How are oxides of nitrogen (NO_x) formed?

5. What information is on the vehicle emission control information (VECI) sticker?

1. Technician A says that high HC emission levels are often caused by a fault in the ignition system. Technician B says that high CO_2 emissions are usually caused by a richer-than-normal air–fuel mixture. Which technician is correct?
   a. A only
   b. B only
   c. Both A and B
   d. Neither A nor B

2. HC and CO are high and CO_2 and O_2 are low. This could be caused by a_____.
   a. rich mixture
   b. lean mixture
   c. defective ignition component
   d. clogged EGR passage

3. Which gas is generally considered to be the rich indicator? (The higher the level of this gas, the richer the air–fuel mixture.)
   a. HC
   b. CO
   c. CO_2
   d. O_2

4. Which gas is generally considered to be the lean indicator? (The higher the level of this gas, the leaner the air–fuel mixture.)
   a. HC
   b. CO
   c. CO_2
   d. O_2

5. Which exhaust gas indicates efficiency? (The higher the level of this gas, the more efficient the engine operates.)
   a. HC
   b. CO
   c. CO_2
   d. O_2

6. All of the gases are measured in percentages except_____.
   a. HC
   b. CO
   c. CO_2
   d. O_2

7. After the following exhaust emissions were measured, how was the engine operating?
   HC 5,766 PPM; CO_2 5 8.2%; CO 5 4.6%; O_2 5 0.1%
   a. Too rich
   b. Too lean
   c. Operating at stoichiometric ratio
   d. Engine operating (coolant) temperature too high

8. Technician A says that carbon inside the engine can cause excessive NOx to form. Technician B says that excessive NOx could be caused by a cooling system fault causing the engine to operate too hot. Which technician is correct?
   a. A only
   b. B only
   c. Both A and B
   d. Neither A nor B

9. A clogged EGR passage could cause excessive exhaust emissions of which of these gases?
   a. HC
   b. CO
   c. NOx
   d. CO_2

10. An ignition fault could cause excessive exhaust emissions of which of these gases?
    a. HC
    b. CO
    c. NOx
    d. CO_2

chapter 27

EMISSION CONTROL DEVICES OPERATION AND DIAGNOSIS

LEARNING OBJECTIVES

After studying this chapter, the reader should be able to:

1. Explain exhaust gas recirculation systems.
2. Discuss OBD-II EGR monitoring strategies, diagnosing a defective EGR system, and EGR trouble codes.
3. Discuss crankcase ventilation, PCV system diagnosis, and PCV-related trouble codes.
4. Explain the secondary air-injection system and its diagnosis.
5. Explain the purpose and function of catalytic converters, their diagnosis, and guidelines to replace them.
6. Explain evaporative emission control system, and compare enhanced and nonenhanced evaporative control systems.
7. Discuss the leak detection pump system and onboard refueling vapor recovery.
8. Discuss the diagnosis of the EVAP system and state inspection EVAP tests.
9. Describe evaporative system monitors and typical EVAP monitors.

KEY TERMS

Most of the major advances in engines are a direct result of the need to improve fuel economy and reduce exhaust emissions. The engine changes needed to meet the latest emission standards include:

- More efficient combustion chambers
- Low friction engine components, such as low tension piston rings, roller camshaft followers (rockers), and roller lifters
- More precise ignition timing with coil-on-plug ignition systems, which have the ability to change ignition timing on individual cylinders as needed to achieve the highest possible efficiency
- Closer engine tolerances to reduce unburned fuel emissions and to improve power output
- Variable valve timing systems used to increase engine power and reduce exhaust emissions

It has been said that engine changes are due to the need to reduce three things.

1. Emissions
2. Emissions
3. Emissions

SMOG

DEFINITION AND TERMINOLOGY The common term used to describe air pollution is **smog**, a word that combines two words: *smoke* and *fog*. Smog is formed in the atmosphere when sunlight combines with unburned fuel (hydrocarbon, or HC) and oxides of nitrogen (NO_x) produced during the combustion process inside the cylinders of an engine. Carbon monoxide (CO) is a poisonous gas. Smog is ozone (O_3), a strong irritant to the lungs and eyes. Ozone is located in two places.

1. Upper-atmospheric ozone is desirable because it blocks out harmful ultraviolet rays from the sun.

2. Ground-level ozone is considered to be unhealthy smog.

   Emissions that are controlled include:

- **HC (unburned hydrocarbons).** Excessive HC emissions (unburned fuel) are controlled by the evaporative system (charcoal canister), the positive crankcase ventilation (PCV) system, the secondary air-injection (SAI) system, and the catalytic converter.
- **CO (carbon monoxide).** Excessive CO emissions are controlled by the positive crankcase ventilation (PCV) system, the secondary air-injection (SAI) system, and the catalytic converter.
- NO_x **(oxides of nitrogen).** Excessive NO_x emissions are controlled by the exhaust gas recirculation (EGR) system and the catalytic converter. An oxide of nitrogen (NO) is

FIGURE 27–1 Notice the red-brown haze which is often over many major cities. This haze is the result of oxides or nitrogen in the atmosphere.

a colorless, tasteless, and odorless gas when it leaves the engine, but as soon as it reaches the atmosphere and mixes with more oxygen, nitrogen oxides (NO_2) are formed, which appear as red-brown emissions. ● SEE FIGURE 27–1.

EXHAUST GAS RECIRCULATION SYSTEMS

INTRODUCTION **Exhaust gas recirculation (EGR)** is an emission control system that lowers the amount of **nitrogen oxides (NO_x)** formed during combustion. In the presence of sunlight, NO_x reacts with hydrocarbons in the atmosphere to form ozone (O_3) or photochemical smog, an air pollutant.

NO_x FORMATION Nitrogen (N_2) and oxygen (O_2) molecules are separated into individual atoms of nitrogen and oxygen during the combustion process. These molecules then bond to form NO_x (NO, NO_2). When combustion flame front temperatures exceed 2,500°F (1,370°C), NO_x is formed inside the cylinders, which is then discharged into the atmosphere from the tailpipe.

CONTROLLING NO_x To handle the NO_x generated above 2,500°F (1,370°C), the most efficient method to meet NO_x emissions, without significantly affecting engine performance, fuel economy, and other exhaust emissions, is to use exhaust gas recirculation (EGR). The EGR system routes small quantities, usually between 6% and 10%, of exhaust gas into the intake manifold.

Here, the exhaust gas mixes with and takes the place of some of the intake charge. This leaves less room for the intake charge to enter the combustion chamber. The recirculated exhaust gas is **inert** (chemically inactive) and does not

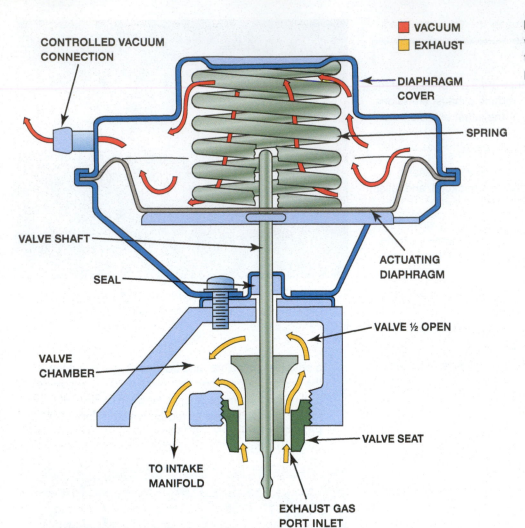

VACUUM

EXHAUST

CONTROLLED VACUUM CONNECTION

DIAPHRAGM COVER

SPRING

VALVE SHAFT

ACTUATING DIAPHRAGM

SEAL

VALVE ½ OPEN

VALVE CHAMBER

VALVE SEAT

TO INTAKE MANIFOLD

EXHAUST GAS PORT INLET

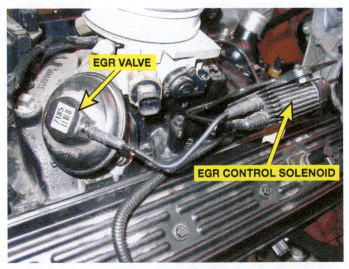

EGR VALVE

EGR CONTROL SOLENOID

FIGURE 27–3 A vacuum-operated EGR valve. The vacuum to the EGR valve is computer controlled by the EGR valve control solenoid.

enter into the combustion process. The result is a lower peak combustion temperature. When the combustion temperature is lowered, the production of oxides of nitrogen is reduced.

The EGR system has some means of interconnecting the exhaust and intake manifolds. ● **SEE FIGURES 27–2 AND 27–3.**

The EGR valve controls the flow of exhaust gases through the interconnecting passages.

- On V-type engines, the intake manifold crossover is used as a source of exhaust gas for the EGR system. A cast passage connects the exhaust crossover to the EGR valve. The exhaust gas is sent from the EGR valve to openings in the manifold.

- On inline-type engines, an external tube is generally used to carry exhaust gas to the EGR valve. This tube is often designed to be long so that the exhaust gas is cooled before it enters the EGR valve.

EGR SYSTEM OPERATION Since small amounts of exhaust are all that is needed to lower peak combustion temperatures, the orifice that the exhaust passes through is small.

EGR is usually *not* required during the following conditions because the combustion temperatures are low:

- Idle speed
- When the engine is cold
- At wide-open throttle (WOT) (Not allowing EGR allows the engine to provide extra power when demanded. While the NO_x formation is high during these times, the overall effect of not using EGR during wide-open throttle conditions is minor.)

The level of NO_x emission changes according to engine speed, temperature, and load. EGR is not used at wide-open throttle (WOT) because it would reduce engine performance and the engine does not operate under these conditions for a long period of time.

EGR BENEFITS
In addition to lowering NO_x levels, the EGR system also helps control detonation. Detonation, also called spark knock or ping, occurs when high pressure and heat cause the air–fuel mixture to ignite. This uncontrolled combustion can severely damage the engine.

Using the EGR system allows for greater ignition timing advance and for the advance to occur sooner without detonation problems, which increases power and efficiency.

POSITIVE AND NEGATIVE BACKPRESSURE EGR VALVES
Some vacuum-operated EGR valves used on older engines are designed with a small valve inside that bleeds off any applied vacuum and prevents the valve from opening.

- **Positive backpressure**. These types of EGR valves require a positive backpressure in the exhaust system. At low engine speeds and light engine loads, the EGR system is not needed, and the backpressure in it is also low. Without sufficient backpressure, the EGR valve does not open even though vacuum may be present at the EGR valve.

- **Negative backpressure**. On each exhaust stroke, the engine emits an exhaust "pulse." Each pulse represents a positive pressure. Behind each pulse is a small area of low pressure. Some EGR valves react to this low-pressure area by closing a small internal valve, which allows the EGR valve to be opened by vacuum.

The following conditions must occur before a backpressure-type vacuum-controlled EGR will operate.

1. Vacuum must be applied to the EGR valve itself. The vacuum source can be ported vacuum (above the throttle plate) or manifold vacuum (below the throttle plate) and by the computer through a solenoid valve.

2. Exhaust backpressure must be present to close an internal valve inside the EGR to allow the vacuum to move the diaphragm.

NOTE: Installing a high-performance exhaust system could prevent a backpressure vacuum-operated EGR valve from opening. If this occurs, excessive combustion chamber temperature leads to severe spark knock, piston damage, or a blown head gasket.

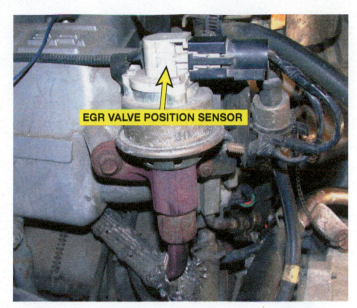

FIGURE 27–4 An EGR valve position sensor on top of an EGR valve.

COMPUTER-CONTROLLED EGR SYSTEMS
Many computer-controlled EGR systems have one or more solenoids controlling the EGR vacuum. The computer controls a solenoid to shut off vacuum to the EGR valve at cold engine temperatures, idle speed, and wide-open throttle operation. If two solenoids are used, one acts as an off-on control of supply vacuum, while the second solenoid vents vacuum when EGR flow is not desired or needs to be reduced. The second solenoid is used to control a vacuum air bleed, allowing atmospheric pressure in to modulate EGR flow according to vehicle operating conditions.

EGR VALVE POSITION SENSORS
Most computer-controlled EGR systems use a sensor to indicate EGR operation. Onboard diagnostics generation-II (OBD-II) EGR system monitors require an EGR sensor to verify that the valve opened. A linear potentiometer on the top of the EGR valve stem indicates valve position for the computer. This is called an **EGR valve position (EVP)** sensor. Some later-model Ford EGR systems, however, use a feedback signal provided by an EGR exhaust backpressure sensor that converts the exhaust backpressure to a voltage signal. This sensor is called a **pressure feedback EGR (PFE)** sensor.

On some EGR systems, the top of the valve contains a vacuum regulator and EGR pintle-position sensor in one assembly sealed inside a nonremovable plastic cover. The pintle-position sensor provides a voltage output to the PCM, which increases as the duty cycle increases, allowing the PCM to monitor valve operation. ● **SEE FIGURE 27–4.**

DIGITAL EGR VALVES
GM introduced a **digital EGR** valve design on some engines. Unlike vacuum-operated EGR valves, the digital EGR valve consists of three solenoids controlled by the powertrain control module (PCM). Each solenoid controls a different size orifice in the base—small, medium, and large. The PCM controls the ground circuit of each of the solenoids

FIGURE 27–5 Digital EGR valve.

FIGURE 27–6 A General Motors linear EGR valve.

 FREQUENTLY ASKED QUESTION

Where is the EGR valve?

Most newer vehicles that are equipped with variable valve timing (VVT) use the valve overlap to keep some exhaust gases in the combustion chamber. As a result, most newer engines do not use an EGR valve.

individually. It can produce any of seven different flow rates, using the solenoids to open the three valves in different combinations. The digital EGR valve offers precise control, and using a swivel pintle design helps prevent carbon deposit problems. ● **SEE FIGURE 27–5**.

LINEAR EGR Most General Motors and many other vehicles use a **linear EGR** that contains a pulse-width modulated solenoid to precisely regulate exhaust gas flow and a feedback potentiometer that signals the computer regarding the actual position of the valve. ● **SEE FIGURES 27–6 AND 27–7**.

OBD-II EGR MONITORING STRATEGIES

PURPOSE AND FUNCTION In 1996, the U.S. EPA began requiring OBD-II systems in all passenger cars and most light-duty trucks. These systems include emissions system monitors

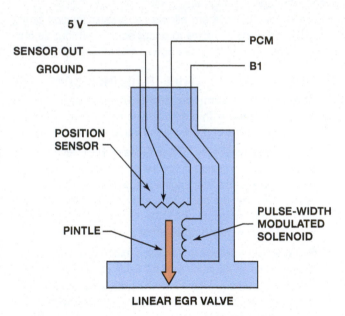

FIGURE 27–7 The EGR valve pintle is pulse-width modulated and a three-wire potentiometer provides pintle-position information back to the PCM.

that alert the driver and the technician if an emissions system is malfunctioning. The OBD-II system performs this test by opening and closing the EGR valve. The PCM monitors an EGR function sensor for a change in signal voltage. If the EGR system fails, a diagnostic trouble code (DTC) is set. If the system fails two consecutive times, the malfunction indicator light (MIL) is lit.

MONITORING STRATEGIES EGR monitoring strategies include the following:

- Some vehicle manufacturers, such as Chrysler, monitor the difference in the exhaust oxygen sensor voltage activity as the EGR valve opens and closes. Oxygen in

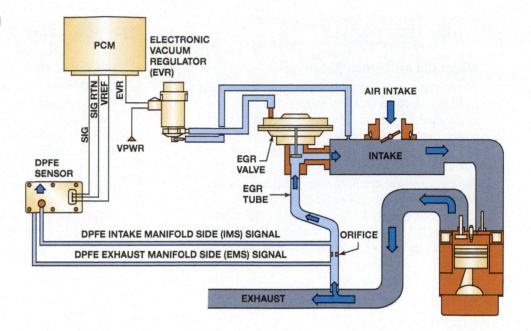

FIGURE 27–8 A DPFE sensor and related components.

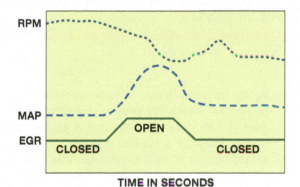

RPM

MAP

EGR   OPEN

CLOSED   CLOSED

TIME IN SECONDS

FIGURE 27–9 An OBD-II active test. The PCM opens the EGR valve and then monitors the MAP sensor and/or engine speed (RPM) to verify that it meets acceptable values.

the exhaust decreases when the EGR valve is open and increases when the EGR valve is closed. The PCM sets a DTC if the sensor signal does not change.

■ Most Fords use an EGR monitor test sensor called a **delta pressure feedback EGR (DPFE) sensor**. This sensor measures the pressure differential between two sides of a metered orifice positioned just below the EGR valve's exhaust side. Pressure between the orifice and the EGR valve decreases when the EGR opens because it becomes exposed to the lower pressure in the intake. The DPFE sensor recognizes this pressure drop, compares it to the relatively higher pressure on the exhaust side of the orifice, and signals the value of the pressure difference to the PCM. ● **SEE FIGURE 27–8**.

■ Many vehicle manufacturers use the manifold absolute pressure (MAP) sensor as the EGR monitor on some applications. After meeting the enable criteria (operating condition requirements), the EGR monitor is run. The PCM monitors the MAP sensor while it commands

the EGR valve to open. The MAP sensor signal should change in response to the sudden change in manifold pressure or the fuel trim changes created by a change in the oxygen sensor voltage. If the signal value falls outside the acceptable value in the look-up table, a DTC sets. If the EGR fails on two consecutive trips, the PCM lights the MIL. ● **SEE FIGURE 27–9**.

DIAGNOSING A DEFECTIVE EGR SYSTEM

SYMPTOMS   If the EGR valve is not opening or the flow of the exhaust gas is restricted, the following symptoms are likely.

■ Detonation (spark knock or ping) during acceleration or during cruise (steady-speed driving)

■ Excessive oxides of nitrogen (NO_x) exhaust emissions

If the EGR valve is stuck open or partially open, the following symptoms are likely.

■ Rough idle or frequent stalling

■ Poor performance/low power, especially at low engine speed

EGR TESTING PROCEDURES   The first step in almost any diagnosis is to perform a thorough visual inspection. To check for proper operation of a vacuum-operated EGR valve, follow these steps.

STEP 1   Check the vacuum diaphragm of the EGR valve to see if it can hold vacuum. Because many EGR valves require exhaust backpressure to function correctly, the engine should be running at a fast idle during this test. Always follow the specified testing procedures.

Watch Out for Carbon Balls!

Exhaust gas recirculation (EGR) valves can get stuck partially open by a chunk of carbon. The EGR valve or solenoid will test as defective. When the valve (or solenoid) is removed, small chunks or balls of carbon often fall into the exhaust manifold passage. When the replacement valve is installed, the carbon balls can be drawn into the new valve again, causing the engine to idle roughly or stall.

To help prevent this problem, start the engine with the EGR valve or solenoid removed. Any balls or chunks of carbon will be blown out of the passage by the exhaust. Stop the engine and install the replacement EGR valve or solenoid.

The Snake Trick

The EGR passages on many intake manifolds become clogged with carbon, which reduces the flow of exhaust and the amount of exhaust gases in the cylinders. This reduction can cause spark knock (detonation) and increased emissions of oxides of nitrogen (NO_x) (especially important in areas with enhanced exhaust emissions testing).

To quickly and easily remove carbon from exhaust passages, cut an approximately 1 foot (30 cm) length from stranded wire, such as garage door guide wire or an old speedometer cable. Flare the end and place the end of the wire into the passage. Set your drill on reverse, turn it on, and the wire will pull its way through the passage, cleaning the carbon as it goes, just like a snake in a drain pipe. Some vehicles, such as Hondas, require that plugs be drilled out to gain access to the EGR passages, as shown in ● FIGURE 27–10.

 CASE STUDY

The Blazer Story

The owner of a Chevrolet Blazer equipped with a 4.3 liter V-6 engine complained that the engine would stumble and hesitate at times. Everything seemed to be functioning correctly, except that the service technician discovered a weak vacuum going to the EGR valve at idle. This vehicle was equipped with an EGR valve-control solenoid, called an **electronic vacuum regulator valve (EVRV)** by General Motors Corporation. The computer pulses the solenoid to control the vacuum that regulates the operation of the EGR valve. The technician checked the service manual for details on how the system worked. The technician discovered that vacuum should be present at the EGR valve only when the gear selector indicates a drive gear (drive, low, reverse). Because the technician discovered the vacuum at the solenoid to be leaking, the solenoid was obviously defective and required replacement. After replacement of the solenoid (EVRV), the hesitation problem was solved.

Summary:

- **Complaint**—Vehicle owner complained that the engine would stumble and hesitate at times.
- **Cause**—The EGR vacuum solenoid was found to be leaking.
- **Correction**—The EGR solenoid was replaced which restored proper engine operation.

STEP 2 Apply vacuum from a hand-operated vacuum pump and check for proper operation. The valve itself should move when vacuum is applied, and the engine operation should be affected. The EGR valve should be able to hold the vacuum that was applied. If the vacuum drops off, then the valve is likely to be defective.

STEP 3 Monitor engine vacuum drop. Connect a vacuum gauge to an intake manifold vacuum source and monitor the engine vacuum at idle (should be 17 to 21 inch Hg at sea level). Raise the speed of the engine to 2500 RPM and note the vacuum reading (should be 17 to 21 inch Hg or higher).

Activate the EGR valve using a scan tool or vacuum pump, if vacuum controlled, and observe the vacuum gauge. The results are as follows:

- The vacuum should drop 6 to 8 inch Hg.
- If the vacuum drops less than 6 to 8 inch Hg, the valve or the EGR passages are clogged.

Results

- If the EGR valve is able to hold vacuum, but the engine is not affected when the valve is opened, the exhaust passage(s) must be checked for restriction.

See the Tech Tip, "The Snake Trick." If the EGR valve will not hold vacuum, the valve itself is likely to be defective and requires replacement.

FIGURE 27–10 Removing the EGR passage plugs from the intake manifold on a Honda.

FIGURE 27–11 A PCV valve in a cutaway valve cover, showing the baffles that prevent liquid oil from being drawn into the intake manifold.

EGR-RELATED OBD-II DIAGNOSTIC TROUBLE CODES

Diagnostic Trouble Code	Description	Possible Causes
P0400	Exhaust gas recirculation flow problems	▪ EGR valve ▪ EGR valve hose or electrical connection ▪ Defective PCM
P0401	Exhaust gas recirculation flow insufficient	▪ EGR valve ▪ Clogged EGR ports or passages
P0402	Exhaust gas recirculation flow excessive	▪ Stuck-open EGR valve ▪ Vacuum hose(s) misrouted ▪ Electrical wiring shorted

CRANKCASE VENTILATION

PURPOSE AND FUNCTION The problem of crankcase ventilation has existed since the beginning of the automobile, because no piston ring, new or old, can provide a perfect seal between the piston and the cylinder wall. When an engine is running, the pressure of combustion forces the piston downward. This same pressure also forces gases and unburned fuel from the combustion chamber, past the piston rings, and into the crankcase. **Blowby** is the term used to describe when combustion gases are forced past the piston rings and into the crankcase.

These combustion by-products, particularly unburned hydrocarbons (HC) caused by blowby, must be ventilated from the crankcase. However, the crankcase cannot be vented directly to the atmosphere, because the hydrocarbon vapors add to air pollution. **Positive crankcase ventilation (PCV)** systems were developed to ventilate the crankcase and recirculate the vapors to the engine's induction system so they can be burned in the cylinders. PCV systems help reduce HC and CO emissions.

All systems use the following:

1. PCV valve, calibrated orifice, or orifice and separator
2. PCV inlet air filter plus all connecting hoses ● **SEE FIGURE 27–11**.

An oil/vapor or oil/water separator is used in some systems instead of a valve or orifice, particularly with turbocharged and fuel-injected engines. The oil/vapor separator lets oil condense and drain back into the crankcase. The oil/water separator accumulates moisture and prevents it from freezing during cold engine starts.

The air for the PCV system is drawn after the air cleaner filter, which acts as a PCV filter.

NOTE: Some older designs drew from the dirty side of the air cleaner, where a separate crankcase ventilation filter was used.

PCV VALVES The PCV valve in most systems is a one-way valve containing a spring-operated plunger that controls valve flow rate. ● **SEE FIGURE 27–12**.

Flow rate is established for each engine and a valve for a different engine should not be substituted. The flow rate is determined by the size of the plunger and the holes inside the valve. PCV valves usually are located in the valve cover or intake manifold.

The PCV valve regulates airflow through the crankcase under all driving conditions and speeds. When manifold vacuum is high (at idle, cruising, and light-load operation), the PCV valve restricts the airflow to maintain a balanced air–fuel ratio. ● **SEE FIGURE 27–13**.

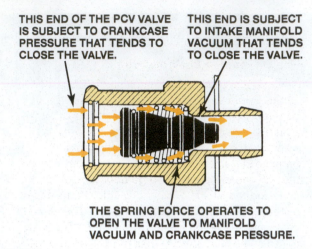

THIS END OF THE PCV VALVE IS SUBJECT TO CRANKCASE PRESSURE THAT TENDS TO CLOSE THE VALVE.

THIS END IS SUBJECT TO INTAKE MANIFOLD VACUUM THAT TENDS TO CLOSE THE VALVE.

THE SPRING FORCE OPERATES TO OPEN THE VALVE TO MANIFOLD VACUUM AND CRANKCASE PRESSURE.

FIGURE 27–12 Spring force, crankcase pressure, and intake manifold vacuum work together to regulate the flow rate through the PCV valve.

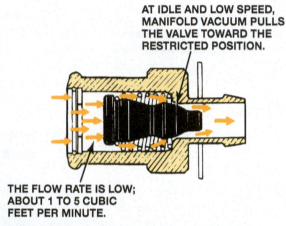

AT IDLE AND LOW SPEED, MANIFOLD VACUUM PULLS THE VALVE TOWARD THE RESTRICTED POSITION.

THE FLOW RATE IS LOW; ABOUT 1 TO 5 CUBIC FEET PER MINUTE.

FIGURE 27–13 Air flows through the PCV valve during idle, cruising, and light-load conditions.

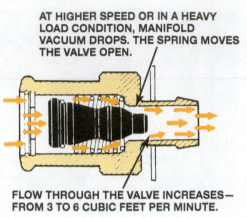

AT HIGHER SPEED OR IN A HEAVY LOAD CONDITION, MANIFOLD VACUUM DROPS. THE SPRING MOVES THE VALVE OPEN.

FLOW THROUGH THE VALVE INCREASES— FROM 3 TO 6 CUBIC FEET PER MINUTE.

FIGURE 27–14 Air flows through the PCV valve during acceleration and when the engine is under a heavy load.

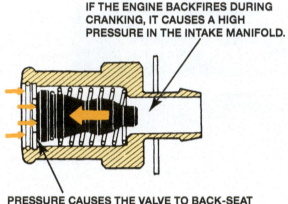

IF THE ENGINE BACKFIRES DURING CRANKING, IT CAUSES A HIGH PRESSURE IN THE INTAKE MANIFOLD.

PRESSURE CAUSES THE VALVE TO BACK-SEAT AND SEAL OFF THE INLET. THIS KEEPS THE BACKFIRE OUT OF THE CRANKCASE.

FIGURE 27–15 PCV valve operation in the event of a backfire.

It also prevents high intake manifold vacuum from pulling oil out of the crankcase and into the intake manifold. Under high speed or heavy loads, the valve opens and allows maximum airflow. ● **SEE FIGURE 27–14**.

If the engine backfires, the valve will close instantly to prevent a crankcase explosion. ● **SEE FIGURE 27–15**.

ORIFICE-CONTROLLED SYSTEMS The closed PCV system used on some 4-cylinder engines contains a calibrated orifice instead of a PCV valve. The orifice may be located in the valve cover or intake manifold, or in a hose connected between the valve cover, air cleaner, and intake manifold.

While most orifice flow control systems work the same as a PCV valve system, they may not use fresh air scavenging of the crankcase. Crankcase vapors are drawn into the intake manifold in calibrated amounts, depending on manifold pressure and the orifice size. If vapor availability is low, as during idle, air is drawn in with the vapors. During off-idle operation, excess vapors are sent to the air cleaner.

CASE STUDY

The Whistling Engine

An older vehicle was being diagnosed for a whistling sound whenever the engine was running, especially at idle. It was finally discovered that the breather in the valve cover was plugged and caused high vacuum in the crankcase. The engine was sucking air from what was likely the rear main seal lip, making the "whistle" noise. After replacing the breather and PCV, the noise stopped.

Summary:

- **Complaint**—Vehicle owner complained that the engine would make a whistling noise.
- **Cause**—The crankcase breather was clogged.
- **Correction**—The breather and the PCV valve were both replaced, which stopped the whistling noise when the engine was running.

At idle, PCV flow is controlled by a 0.05 inch (1.3 mm) orifice. As the engine moves off idle, ported vacuum pulls a spring-loaded valve off of its seat, allowing PCV flow to pass through a 0.09 inch (2.3 mm) orifice.

SEPARATOR SYSTEMS Turbocharged and many fuel-injected engines use an oil/vapor or oil/water separator and a calibrated orifice instead of a PCV valve. In the most common applications, the air intake throttle body acts as the source for crankcase ventilation vacuum and a calibrated orifice acts as the metering device.

PCV SYSTEM DIAGNOSIS

SYMPTOMS If the PCV valve or orifice is not clogged, intake air flows freely and the PCV system functions properly. Engine design includes the air and vapor flow as a calibrated part of the air–fuel mixture. In fact, some engines receive as much as 30% of the idle air through the PCV system. For this reason, a flow problem in the PCV system results in driveability problems.

A blocked or plugged PCV system can cause:

- Rough or unstable idle
- Excessive oil consumption
- Oil in the air filter housing
- Oil leaks due to excessive crankcase pressure

Before expensive engine repairs are attempted, check the condition of the PCV system.

PCV SYSTEM PERFORMANCE CHECK A properly operating positive crankcase ventilation system should be able to draw vapors from the crankcase and into the intake manifold. If the pipes, hoses, and PCV valve itself are not restricted,

vacuum is applied to the crankcase. A slight vacuum is created in the crankcase (usually less than 1 inch Hg if measured at the dipstick) and is also applied to other areas of the engine. Oil drainback holes provide a path for oil to drain back into the oil pan. These holes also allow crankcase vacuum to be applied under the rocker covers and in the valley area of most V-type engines. There are several methods that can be used to test a PCV system.

RATTLE TEST The rattle test is performed by simply removing the PCV valve and shaking it in your hand.

- If the PCV valve does *not* rattle, it is definitely defective and must be replaced.
- If the PCV valve *does* rattle, it does not necessarily mean that the PCV valve is good. All PCV valves contain springs that can become weaker with age and with heating and cooling cycles. Replace any PCV valve with the

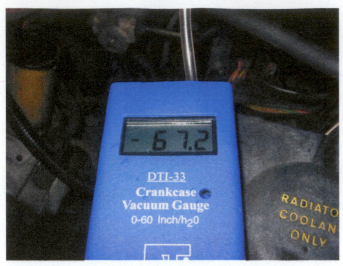

FIGURE 27–16 Using a gauge that measures vacuum in units of inches of water to test the vacuum at the dipstick tube, being sure that the PCV system is capable of drawing a vacuum on the crankcase. Note that 28 inches of water equals 1 PSI, or about 2 inches of mercury (inch Hg) of vacuum.

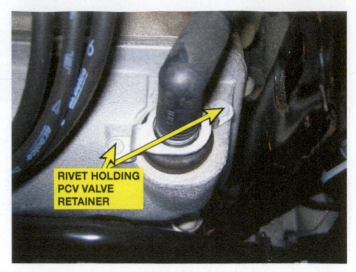

RIVET HOLDING PCV VALVE RETAINER

FIGURE 27–17 Most PCV valves used on newer vehicles are secured with fasteners, which makes it more difficult to disconnect, and therefore, less likely to increase emissions.

exact replacement according to the vehicle manufacturer's recommended intervals, usually every three years or 36,000 miles (60,000 km).

THE 3 × 5 CARD TEST

Remove the oil-fill cap (where oil is added to the engine) and start the engine.

NOTE: Use care on some overhead camshaft engines. With the engine running, oil may be sprayed from the open oil-fill opening.

Hold a 3 × 5 card over the opening (a dollar bill or any other piece of paper can be used for this test).

- If the PCV system, including the valve and hoses, is functioning correctly, the card should be held down on the oil-fill opening by the slight vacuum inside the crankcase.
- If the card will not stay, carefully inspect the PCV valve, hose(s), and manifold vacuum port for carbon buildup (restriction). Clean or replace as necessary.

NOTE: On some 4-cylinder engines, the 3 × 5 card may vibrate on the oil-fill opening when the engine is running at idle speed. This is normal because of the time intervals between intake strokes on a 4-cylinder engine.

SNAP-BACK TEST

The proper operation of the PCV valve can be checked by placing a finger over the inlet hole in the valve when the engine is running and removing the finger rapidly. Repeat several times. The valve should "snap back." If the valve does not snap back, replace the valve.

? FREQUENTLY ASKED QUESTION

Why Are There Wires at the PCV Valve?

Ford uses an electric heater to prevent ice from forming inside the PCV valve causing blockage. Water is a by-product of combustion and resulting moisture can freeze when the outside air temperature is low. General Motors and others clip a heater hose to the PCV hose to provide the heat needed to prevent an ice blockage.

CRANKCASE VACUUM TEST

Sometimes the PCV system can be checked by testing for a weak vacuum at the oil dipstick tube using an inches-of-water manometer or gauge, as follows:

STEP 1 Remove the oil-fill cap or vent PCV opening and cover the opening.

STEP 2 Remove the oil dipstick (oil level indicator).

STEP 3 Connect a water manometer or gauge to the dipstick tube.

STEP 4 Start the engine and observe the gauge at idle and at 2500 RPM.

● SEE FIGURE 27–16.

The gauge should show some vacuum, especially at 2500 RPM. If not, carefully inspect the PCV system for blockages or other faults.

PCV MONITOR

Starting with 2004 and newer vehicles, all vehicle PCMs monitor the PCV system for proper operation as part of the OBD-II system. The PCV monitor will fail if the PCM detects an opening between the crankcase and the PCV valve or between the PCV valve and the intake manifold. **● SEE FIGURE 27–17.**

Diagnostic Trouble Code	Description	Possible Causes
P0101	MAF or airflow circuit range problem	■ Defective PCV valve, hose/connections, or MAF circuit fault
P0505	Idle control system problem	■ Defective PCV valve or hose/connections

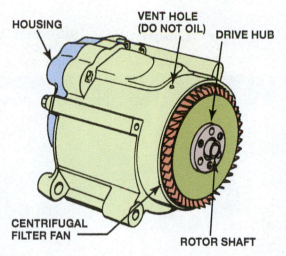

FIGURE 27–18 A typical belt-driven AIR pump. Air enters through the revolving fins behind the drive pulley. The fins act as an air filter because dirt is heavier than air, and therefore, the dirt is deflected off of the fins at the same time air is being drawn into the pump.

SECONDARY AIR-INJECTION SYSTEM

PURPOSE AND FUNCTION The **secondary air-injection (SAI)** system provides the air necessary for the oxidizing process either at the exhaust manifold or inside the catalytic converter.

NOTE: This system is commonly called AIR, meaning air-injection reaction. Therefore, an AIR pump does pump air.

PARTS AND OPERATION The SAI pump, also called an AIR pump, a **smog pump,** or a **thermactor pump,** is mounted at the front of the engine and can be driven by a belt from the crankshaft pulley. It pulls fresh air in through an external filter and pumps the air under slight pressure to each exhaust port through connecting hoses or a manifold. The typical SAI system includes the following components:

- A belt-driven pump with inlet air filter (older models) (●SEE FIGURE 27–18.)
- An electronic air pump (newer models)
- One or more air distribution manifolds and nozzles
- One or more exhaust check valves
- Connecting hoses for air distribution
- Air management valves and solenoids on all newer applications

With the introduction of NO_x reduction converters (also called dual-bed, **three-way converters,** or **TWC**), the output of the SAI pump is sent to the center of the converter where the extra air can help oxidize unburned hydrocarbons (HC), carbon monoxide (CO) into water vapor (H_2O), and carbon dioxide (CO_2).

The computer controls the airflow from the pump by switching on and off various solenoid valves.

AIR DISTRIBUTION MANIFOLDS AND NOZZLES The secondary air-injection system sends air from the pump to a nozzle installed near each exhaust port in the cylinder head. This provides equal air injection for the exhaust from each cylinder and makes it available at a point in the system where exhaust gases are the hottest.

Air is delivered to the exhaust system in one of two ways.

1. An external air manifold, or manifolds, distributes the air through injection tubes with stainless steel nozzles. The nozzles are threaded into the cylinder heads or exhaust manifolds close to each exhaust valve. This method is used primarily with smaller engines.

2. An internal air manifold distributes the air to the exhaust ports near each exhaust valve through passages cast in the cylinder head or the exhaust manifold. This method is used mainly with larger engines.

EXHAUST CHECK VALVES All air-injection systems use one or more one-way check valves to protect the air pump and other components from reverse exhaust flow. A **check valve** contains a spring-type metallic disc or reed that closes under exhaust backpressure. Check valves are located between the air manifold and the switching valve(s). If exhaust pressure exceeds injection pressure, or if the air pump fails, the check valve spring closes the valve to prevent reverse exhaust flow. ●SEE FIGURE 27–19.

NOTE: These check valves commonly fail, resulting in excessive exhaust emissions (CO especially). When the check valve fails, hot exhaust can travel up to and destroy the switching valve(s) and air pump itself.

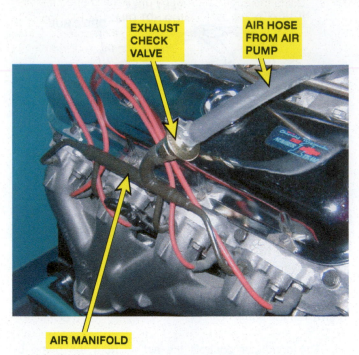

FIGURE 27–19 The external air manifold and exhaust check valve on a restored muscle car engine.

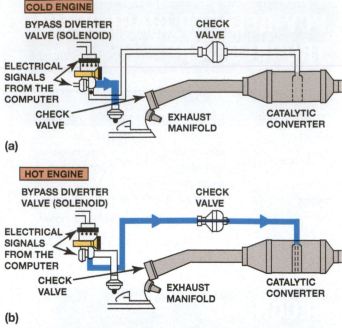

(a)

(b)

FIGURE 27–20 (a) When the engine is cold and before the oxygen sensor is hot enough to achieve closed loop, the air-flow from the air pump is directed to the exhaust manifold(s) through the one-way check valves which keep the exhaust gases from entering the switching solenoids and the pump itself. (b) When the engine achieves closed loop, the air is directed to the catalytic converter.

BELT-DRIVEN AIR PUMPS The belt-driven air pump uses a centrifugal filter just behind the drive pulley. As the pump rotates, underhood air is drawn into the pump and slightly compressed. The system uses either vacuum- or solenoid- controlled diverter valves to direct air to the following:

- Exhaust manifold when the engine is cold to help oxidize carbon monoxide (CO) and unburned hydrocarbons (HC) into carbon dioxide (CO_2) and water vapor (H_2O)
- Catalytic converter on many models to help provide the extra oxygen needed for the efficient conversion of CO and HC into CO_2 and H_2O
- Air cleaner during deceleration or wide-open throttle (WOT) engine operation ● SEE FIGURE 27–20.

ELECTRIC MOTOR-DRIVEN AIR PUMPS The electric motor-driven air pump is generally used only during cold engine operation and is computer controlled. The secondary air-injection (SAI) system helps reduce hydrocarbon (HC) and carbon monoxide (CO). It also helps to warm the three-way catalytic converters quickly on engine start-up so conversion of exhaust gases may occur sooner.

- The SAI pump solenoids are controlled by the PCM. The PCM turns on the SAI pump by providing the ground to complete the circuit which energizes the SAI pump solenoid relay. When air to the exhaust ports is desired, the PCM energizes the relay in order to turn on the solenoid and the SAI pump. ● SEE FIGURE 27–21.

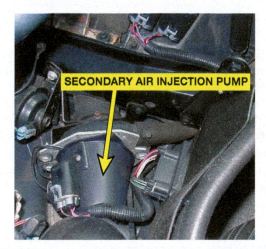

FIGURE 27–21 A typical electric motor-driven SAI pump. This unit is on a Chevrolet Corvette and only works when the engine is cold.

- The PCM turns on the SAI pump during start-up any time the engine coolant temperature is above 32°F (0°C). A typical electric SAI pump operates for a maximum of four minutes, or until the system enters closed-loop operation.

ENGINE OPERATION	NORMAL OPERATION OF A TYPICAL SAI SYSTEM
Cold engine (open-loop operation)	Air is diverted to the exhaust manifold(s) or cylinder head.
Warm engine (closed-loop operation)	Air is diverted to the catalytic converter.
Deceleration	Air is diverted to the air cleaner assembly.
Wide-open throttle	Air is diverted to the air cleaner assembly.

CHART 27–1

Typical SAI system operation showing the location of the airflow from the pump.

SECONDARY AIR-INJECTION SYSTEM DIAGNOSIS

SYMPTOMS The air pump system should be inspected if an exhaust emissions test failure occurs. In severe cases, the exhaust will enter the air cleaner assembly, resulting in a horribly running engine because the extra exhaust displaces the oxygen needed for proper combustion. With the engine running, check for normal operation. ● **SEE CHART 27–1**.

VISUAL INSPECTION Carefully inspect all secondary-air-injection (SAI) systems, including:

- Any hoses or pipes that have holes and leak air or exhaust, which require replacement
- Check valve(s), when a pump has become inoperative
- Exhaust gases that may have gotten past the check valve and damaged the pump (Look for signs of overheated areas upstream from the check valves. In severe cases, the exhaust can enter the air cleaner assembly and destroy the air filter and greatly reduce engine power.)
- Drive belt on an engine-driven pump, for wear and proper tension (If the belt is worn or damaged, check that the AIR pump rotates.)

FOUR-GAS EXHAUST ANALYSIS An SAI system can be easily tested using an exhaust gas analyzer and the following steps:

STEP 1 Start the engine and allow it to run until normal operating temperature is achieved.

STEP 2 Connect the analyzer probe to the tailpipe and observe the exhaust readings for hydrocarbons (HC) and carbon monoxide (CO).

STEP 3 Using the appropriate pinch-off pliers, shut off the airflow from the SAI system. Observe the HC and CO readings. If the SAI system is working correctly, the HC and CO should increase when the SAI system is shut off.

STEP 4 Record the O_2 reading with the SAI system still inoperative. Unclamp the pliers and watch the O_2 readings. If the system is functioning correctly, the O_2 level should increase by 1% to 4%.

SAI-RELATED DIAGNOSTIC TROUBLE CODE

Diagnostic Trouble Code	Description	Possible Causes
P0410	SAI solenoid circuit fault	■ Defective SAI solenoid ■ Loose or corroded electrical connections ■ Loose, missing, or defective rubber hose(s)

CATALYTIC CONVERTERS

PURPOSE AND FUNCTION A **catalytic converter** is an aftertreatment device used to reduce exhaust emissions outside of the engine. The catalytic converter uses a **catalyst**, which is a chemical that helps start a chemical reaction but does not enter into the chemical reaction.

- The catalyst materials on the surface of the material inside the converter help create a chemical reaction.
- The chemical reaction changes harmful exhaust emissions into nonharmful exhaust emissions.
- The converter, therefore, converts harmful exhaust gases into water vapor (H_2O) and carbon dioxide (CO_2).

This device is installed in the exhaust system between the exhaust manifold and the muffler, and usually is positioned beneath the passenger compartment. The location of the converter is important, since as much of the exhaust heat as possible must be retained for effective operation. The nearer it is to the engine, the better. ● **SEE FIGURE 27–22**.

CATALYTIC CONVERTER CONSTRUCTION Most catalytic converters are constructed of a ceramic material in a honeycomb shape with square openings for the exhaust gases.

- There are approximately 400 openings per square inch (62 openings per square centimeter) and the wall thickness is about 0.006 inch (1.5 mm).

FIGURE 27–22 Most catalytic converters are located as close to the exhaust manifold as possible, as seen in this display of a Chevrolet Corvette.

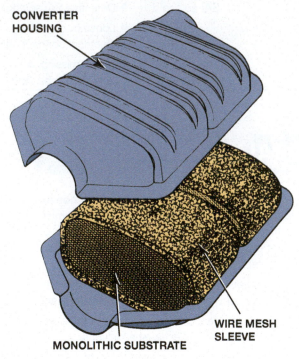

CONVERTER HOUSING

WIRE MESH SLEEVE

MONOLITHIC SUBSTRATE

FIGURE 27–23 A typical catalytic converter with a monolithic substrate.

- The substrate is then coated with a porous aluminum material called the **washcoat**, which makes the surface rough.
- The catalytic materials are then applied on top of the washcoat. The substrate is contained within a round or oval shell made by welding together two stamped pieces of stainless steel. ● **SEE FIGURE 27–23**.

The ceramic substrate in monolithic converters is not restrictive; however, the converter can be physically broken if exposed to shock or severe jolts. Monolithic converters can be serviced only as a unit.

An exhaust pipe is connected to the manifold or header to carry gases through a catalytic converter and then to the muffler or silencer. V-type engines can use dual converters or route the exhaust into one catalytic converter by using a Y-exhaust pipe.

CATALYTIC CONVERTER OPERATION The converter substrate contains small amounts of **rhodium**, **palladium**, and **platinum**. These elements act as catalysts, which, as mentioned, start a chemical reaction without becoming part of, or being consumed in, the process. In a three-way catalytic converter (TWC), all three exhaust emissions (NO_x, HC, and CO) are converted to carbon dioxide (CO_2) and water (H_2O). As the exhaust gas passes through the catalyst, oxides of nitrogen (NO_x) are chemically reduced (i.e., nitrogen and oxygen are separated) in the first section of the catalytic converter. In the second section of the catalytic converter, most of the hydrocarbons and carbon monoxide remaining in the exhaust gas are oxidized to form harmless carbon dioxide (CO_2) and water vapor (H_2O). ● **SEE FIGURE 27–24**.

Since the early 1990s, many converters also contain **cerium**, an element that can store oxygen. The purpose of the cerium is to provide oxygen to the oxidation bed of the converter when the exhaust is rich and lacks enough oxygen for proper oxidation. When the exhaust is lean, the cerium absorbs the extra oxygen. For the most efficient operation, the converter should have a 14.7:1 air–fuel ratio but can use a mixture that varies slightly.

- A rich exhaust is required for reduction—stripping the oxygen (O_2) from the nitrogen in NO_x.
- A lean exhaust is required to provide the oxygen necessary to oxidize HC and CO (combining oxygen with HC and CO to form H_2O and CO_2).

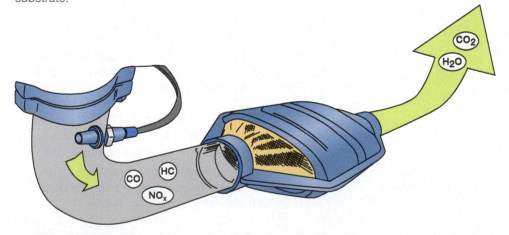

FIGURE 27–24 The three-way catalytic converter first separates the NO_x into nitrogen and oxygen and then converts the HC and CO into harmless water (H_2O) and carbon dioxide (CO_2).

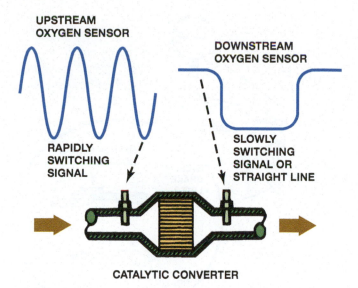

UPSTREAM OXYGEN SENSOR

RAPIDLY SWITCHING SIGNAL

DOWNSTREAM OXYGEN SENSOR

SLOWLY SWITCHING SIGNAL OR STRAIGHT LINE

CATALYTIC CONVERTER

FIGURE 27–25 The OBD-II catalytic converter monitor compares the signals of the upstream and downstream HO2S to determine converter efficiency.

If the catalytic converter is not functioning correctly, check that the air–fuel mixture being supplied to the engine is correct and that the ignition system is free of defects.

CONVERTER LIGHT-OFF TEMPERATURE The catalytic converter does not work when cold, and it must be heated to its **light-off temperature** of close to 500°F (260°C) before it starts working at 50% effectiveness. When fully effective, the converter reaches a temperature range of 900°F to 1,600°F (482°C to 871°C). In spite of the intense heat, however, catalytic reactions do not generate a flame associated with a simple burning reaction. Because of the extreme heat (almost as hot as combustion chamber temperatures), a converter remains hot long after the engine is shut off. Most vehicles use a series of heat shields to protect the passenger compartment and other parts of the chassis from excessive heat. Vehicles have been known to start fires because of the hot converter causing tall grass or dry leaves beneath the just-parked vehicle to ignite, especially if the engine is idling. This is most likely to occur if the heat shields have been removed from the converter.

CONVERTER USAGE A catalytic converter must be located as close as possible to the exhaust manifold to work effectively. The farther back the converter is positioned in the exhaust system, the more the exhaust gases cool before they reach the converter. Since positioning in the exhaust system affects the oxidation process, cars that use only an oxidation converter generally locate it underneath the front of the passenger compartment.

Some vehicles have used a small, quick heating oxidation converter called a **preconverter**, a **pup converter**, or a **mini converter** that connects directly to the exhaust manifold outlet. These have a small catalyst surface area close to the engine that heats up rapidly to start the oxidation process more quickly during cold engine warm-up. For this reason, they were

often called **light-off converters (LOCs)**. The larger main converter, under the passenger compartment, completes the oxidation reaction started in the LOC.

OBD-II CATALYTIC CONVERTER PERFORMANCE

With OBD-II equipped vehicles, catalytic converter performance is monitored by a **heated oxygen sensor (HO2S)**, both before and after the converter. The converters used on these vehicles have what is known as **oxygen storage capacity (OSC)**. This OSC is due mostly to the cerium coating in the catalyst rather than the precious metals used. When the three-way converter (TWC) is operating as it should, the postconverter HO2S is far less active than the preconverter sensor. The converter stores, then releases, the oxygen during normal reduction and oxidation of the exhaust gases, smoothing out the variations in O_2 being released.

Where a cycling sensor voltage output is expected before the converter, because of the converter action, the postconverter HO2S should read a steady signal without much fluctuation. ● **SEE FIGURE 27–25**.

CONVERTER-DAMAGING CONDITIONS Since converters have no moving parts, they require no periodic service. Under federal law, catalyst effectiveness is warranted for 80,000 miles or eight years.

The three main causes of premature converter failure are as follows:

- **Contamination.** Substances that can destroy the converter include exhaust that contains excess engine oil, antifreeze, sulfur (from poor fuel), and various other chemical substances.

- **Excessive temperatures.** Although a converter operates at high temperature, it can be destroyed by excessive temperatures. This most often occurs either when too much unburned fuel enters the converter, or with excessively lean mixtures. Excessive temperatures may be caused by long idling periods on some vehicles, since more heat develops at those times than when driving at normal highway speeds. Severe high temperatures can cause the converter to melt down, leading to the internal parts breaking apart and either clogging the converter or moving downstream to plug the muffler. In either case, the restricted exhaust flow severely reduces engine power.

- **Improper air-fuel mixtures.** Rich mixtures or raw fuel in the exhaust can be caused by engine misfiring, or an excessively rich air–fuel mixture resulting from a defective coolant temp sensor or defective fuel injectors. Lean mixtures are commonly caused by intake manifold leaks. When either of these circumstances occurs, the converter can become a catalytic furnace, causing the previously described damage.

To avoid excessive catalyst temperatures and the possibility of fuel vapors reaching the converter, follow these rules:

Can a Catalytic Converter Be Defective Without Being Clogged?

Yes. Catalytic converters can fail by being chemically damaged or poisoned without being mechanically clogged. Therefore, the catalytic converter should not only be tested for physical damage (clogging) by performing a backpressure or vacuum test and a rattle test, but also for temperature rise, usually with a pyrometer or propane test, to check the efficiency of the converter.

1. Do not use fuel additives or cleaners that are not converter safe.

2. Do not crank an engine for more than 40 seconds when it is flooded or misfiring.

3. Do not turn off the ignition switch when the vehicle is in motion.

4. Do not disconnect a spark plug wire for more than 30 seconds.

5. Repair engine problems such as dieseling, misfiring, or stumbling as soon as possible.

DIAGNOSING CATALYTIC CONVERTERS

THE TAP TEST The simple **tap test** involves tapping (not pounding) on the catalytic converter using a rubber mallet. If the substrate inside the converter is broken, the converter will rattle when hit. If the converter rattles, a replacement converter is required.

TESTING BACKPRESSURE WITH A PRESSURE GAUGE Exhaust system backpressure can be measured directly by installing a pressure gauge in an exhaust opening. This can be accomplished in one of the following ways:

1. To test backpressure, remove the inside of an old, discarded oxygen sensor and thread in an adapter to convert it to a vacuum or pressure gauge.

NOTE: An adapter can be easily made by inserting a metal tube or pipe into an old oxygen sensor housing. A short section of brake line works great. The pipe can be brazed to the oxygen sensor housing or it can be glued with epoxy. An 18 mm compression gauge adapter can also be adapted to fit into the oxygen sensor opening. ●**SEE FIGURE 27–26.**

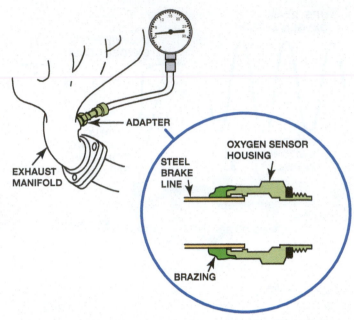

FIGURE 27–26 A back pressure tool can be made by using an oxygen sensor housing and epoxy or braze to hold the tube to the housing.

2. To test the exhaust backpressure at the exhaust gas recirculation (EGR) valve, remove the EGR valve and fabricate a plate equipped with a fitting for a pressure gauge.

3. To test at the secondary air-injection (SAI) check valve, remove the check valve from the exhaust tubes leading to the exhaust manifold. Use a rubber cone with a tube inside to seal against the exhaust tube. Connect the tube to a pressure gauge.

At idle, the maximum backpressure should be less than 1.5 PSI (10 kPa), and it should be less than 2.5 PSI (15 kPa) at 2500 RPM. Pressure readings higher than these indicate the exhaust system is restricted and further testing will be needed to determine the location of the restriction.

TESTING FOR BACKPRESSURE USING A VACUUM GAUGE An exhaust restriction can be tested indirectly by checking the intake manifold vacuum with the engine operating at a fast idle speed (about 2500 RPM). If the exhaust is restricted, some exhaust can pass and the effect may not be noticeable when the engine is at idle speed. However, when the engine is operating at a higher speed, the exhaust gases can build up behind the restriction and eventually will be unable to leave the combustion chamber. When some of the exhaust is left behind at the end of the exhaust stroke, the resulting pressure in the combustion chamber reduces engine vacuum. To test for an exhaust restriction using a vacuum gauge, perform the following steps:

STEP 1 Attach a vacuum gauge to an intake manifold vacuum source.

STEP 2 Start the engine. Record the engine manifold vacuum reading. The engine vacuum should read 17 to 21 inch Hg when the engine is at idle speed.

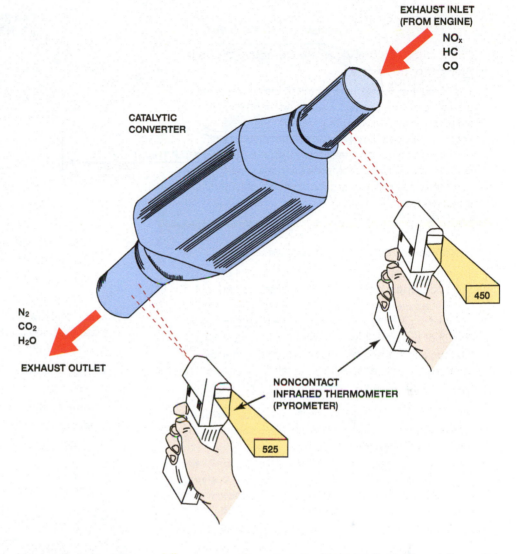

FIGURE 27–27 The temperature of the outlet should be at least 10% hotter than the temperature of the inlet. If a converter is not working, the inlet temperature will be hotter than the outlet temperature.

EXHAUST INLET
(FROM ENGINE)

NO_x
HC
CO

CATALYTIC
CONVERTER

N_2
CO_2
H_2O

EXHAUST OUTLET

NONCONTACT
INFRARED THERMOMETER
(PYROMETER)

450

525

STEP 3 Increase the engine speed to 2500 RPM and hold that speed for 60 seconds while looking at the vacuum gauge.

Results

- If the vacuum reading is equal to or higher than the vacuum reading when the engine was at idle speed, the exhaust system is *not* restricted.

- If the vacuum reading is lower than the vacuum reading when the engine was at idle speed, then the exhaust *is* restricted. Further testing will be needed to determine the location of the restriction.

TESTING A CATALYTIC CONVERTER FOR TEMPERATURE RISE A properly working catalytic converter should be able to reduce NO_x exhaust emissions into nitrogen (N) and oxygen (O_2) and oxidize unburned hydrocarbon (HC) and carbon monoxide (CO) into harmless carbon dioxide (CO_2) and water vapor (H_2O). During these chemical processes, the catalytic converter should increase in temperature at least 10% if the converter is working properly. To test the converter, operate the engine at 2,500 RPM for at least two minutes to

fully warm up the converter. Measure the inlet and the outlet temperatures using an **infrared thermometer (pyrometer)**, as shown in ● **FIGURE 27–27**.

NOTE: If the engine is extremely efficient, the converter may not have any excessive unburned hydrocarbons or carbon monoxide to convert! In this case, a spark plug wire could be grounded out using a vacuum hose and a test light to create some unburned hydrocarbon in the exhaust. Do not ground out a cylinder for longer than 10 seconds or the excessive amount of unburned hydrocarbon could overheat and damage the converter.

CATALYTIC CONVERTER EFFICIENCY TESTS The efficiency of a catalytic converter can be determined using an exhaust gas analyzer.

- **Oxygen level test.** With the engine warm and in closed loop, check the oxygen (O_2) and carbon monoxide (CO) levels. A good converter should be able to oxidize the extra hydrocarbons caused by the rapid acceleration.

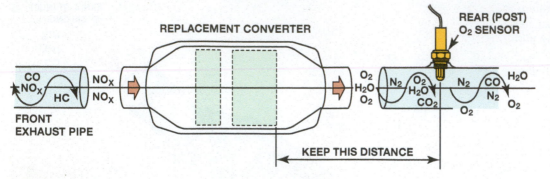

FRONT EXHAUST PIPE

REPLACEMENT CONVERTER

REAR (POST) O₂ SENSOR

KEEP THIS DISTANCE

FIGURE 27–28 Whenever replacing a catalytic converter with a universal unit, first measure the distance between the rear brick and the center of the rear oxygen sensor. Be sure that the replacement unit is installed to the same dimension.

TECH TIP

Aftermarket Catalytic Converters

Some replacement aftermarket (nonfactory) catalytic converters do not contain the same amount of cerium as the original part. Cerium is the element that is used in catalytic converters to store oxygen. As a result of the lack of cerium, the correlation between the oxygen storage and the conversion efficiency may be affected enough to set a false diagnostic trouble code (P0422).

NOTE: When an aftermarket converter is being installed, to be assured of proper operation, ensure that its distance from the rear of the catalyst block is the same as the distance between the rear oxygen sensor and the factory converter. Always follow the instructions that come with the replacement converter. ● SEE FIGURE 27–28.

- If O_2 is zero, go to the snap-throttle test.
- If O_2 is greater than zero, check the CO level.
- If CO is greater than zero, the converter is *not* functioning correctly.
- **Snap-throttle test.** With the engine warm and in closed loop, snap the throttle to wide open (WOT) in park or neutral and observe the oxygen reading.
  - The O_2 reading should not exceed 1.2%; if it does, the converter is *not* working.
  - If the O_2 rises to 1.2%, the converter may have low efficiency.
  - If the O_2 remains below 1.2%, then the converter is okay.

TECH TIP

Catalytic Converters Are Murdered

Catalytic converters start a chemical reaction but do not enter into the chemical reaction. Therefore, catalytic converters do not wear out and they do not die of old age. If a catalytic converter is found to be defective (nonfunctioning or clogged), look for the *root* cause. Remember this:

"Catalytic converters do not commit suicide—they're murdered."

Items that should be checked when a defective catalytic converter is discovered include all components of the ignition and fuel systems. Excessive unburned fuel can cause the catalytic converter to overheat and fail. The oxygen sensor must be working and fluctuating from 0.5 to 5 Hz (times per second) to provide the necessary air–fuel mixture variations for maximum catalytic converter efficiency.

CATALYTIC CONVERTER REPLACEMENT GUIDELINES

Because a catalytic converter is a major exhaust gas emission control device, the Environmental Protection Agency (EPA) has strict guidelines for its replacement, including:

- If a converter is replaced on a vehicle with less than 80,000 miles or eight years, depending on the year of the vehicle, an original equipment catalytic converter *must* be used as a replacement.
- The replacement converter must be of the same design as the original. If the original had an air pump fitting, so must the replacement.
- The old converter must be kept for possible inspection by the authorities for 60 days.
- A form must be completed and signed by both the vehicle owner and a representative from the service facility. This form must state the cause of the converter failure and must remain on file for two years.

CATALYTIC CONVERTER-RELATED DIAGNOSTIC TROUBLE CODE

Diagnostic Trouble Code	Description	Possible Causes
P0420	Catalytic converter efficiency failure	1. Engine mechanical fault 2. Exhaust leaks 3. Fuel contaminants, such as engine oil, coolant, or sulfur

FIGURE 27–29 A capless system from a Ford does not use a replaceable cap; instead, it has a spring-loaded closure.

EVAPORATIVE EMISSION CONTROL SYSTEM

PURPOSE AND FUNCTION The purpose of the evaporative (EVAP) emission control system is to trap and hold gasoline vapors, also called volatile organic compounds, or VOCs. The evaporative control system includes the charcoal canister, hoses, and valves. These vapors are routed into a charcoal canister, then into the intake airflow where they are burned in the engine instead of being released into the atmosphere.

COMMON COMPONENTS The fuel tank filler caps used on vehicles with modern EVAP systems are a special design. Most EVAP fuel tank filler caps have pressure-vacuum relief built into them. When pressure or vacuum exceeds a calibrated value, the valve opens. Once the pressure or vacuum has been relieved, the valve closes. If a sealed cap is used on an EVAP system that requires a pressure-vacuum relief design, a vacuum lock may develop in the fuel system, or the fuel tank may be damaged by fuel expansion or contraction. ● **SEE FIGURE 27–29**.

EVAPORATIVE CONTROL SYSTEM OPERATION The canister is located under the hood or underneath the vehicle, and is filled with activated charcoal granules that can hold up to one-third of their own weight in fuel vapors. ● **SEE FIGURE 27–30**.

NOTE: Some vehicles with large or dual fuel tanks may have dual canisters.

Activated charcoal is an effective vapor trap because of its great surface area. Each gram of activated charcoal has a surface area of 1,100 m^2 (more than a quarter acre). Typical canisters hold either 300 or 625 grams of charcoal *with a surface area equivalent to 80 or 165 football fields*. By a process called **adsorption**, the fuel vapor molecules adhere to the carbon

FREQUENTLY ASKED QUESTION

When Filling My Fuel Tank, Why Should I Stop When the Pump Clicks Off?

Every fuel tank has an upper volume chamber that allows for expansion of the fuel when hot. The volume of the chamber is between 10% and 20% of the volume of the tank. For example, if a fuel tank had a capacity of 20 gallons, the expansion chamber volume would be from 2 to 4 gallons. A hose is attached at the top of the chamber and vented to the charcoal canister. If extra fuel is forced into this expansion volume, liquid gasoline can be drawn into the charcoal canister. This liquid fuel can saturate the canister and create an overly rich air–fuel mixture when the canister purge valve is opened during normal vehicle operation. This extra-rich air–fuel mixture can cause the vehicle to fail an exhaust emissions test, reduce fuel economy, and possibly damage the catalytic converter. To avoid problems, simply add fuel to the next dime's worth after the nozzle clicks off. This will ensure that the tank is full, yet not overfilled.

surface. This attaching force is not strong, so the system purges the vapor molecules quite simply by sending a fresh airflow through the charcoal.

■ **Vapor purging.** During engine operation, stored vapors are drawn from the canister into the engine through a hose connected to the throttle body or the air cleaner. This "purging" process mixes HC vapors from the canister with the existing air–fuel charge. ● **SEE FIGURES 27–31** AND **27–32**.

FIGURE 27–30 A charcoal canister can be located under the hood or underneath the vehicle.

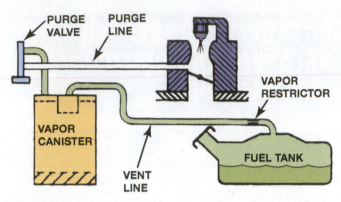

FIGURE 27–31 The evaporative emission control system includes all of the lines, hoses, and valves, plus the charcoal canister.

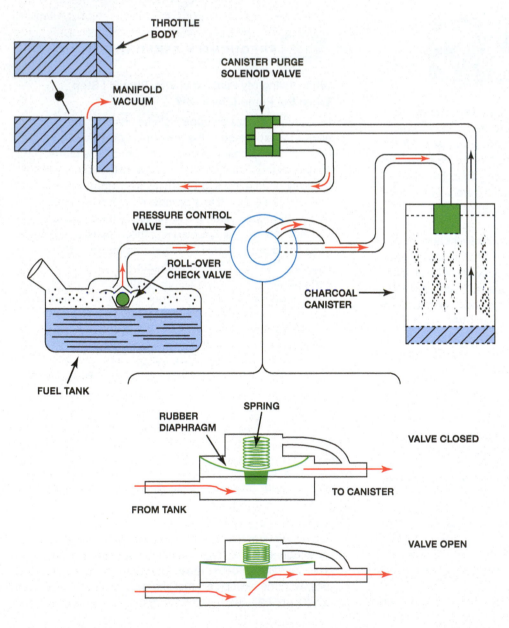

FIGURE 27–32 A typical evaporative emission control system. Note that when the computer turns on the canister purge solenoid valve, manifold vacuum draws any stored vapors from the canister into the engine. Manifold vacuum also is applied to the pressure control valve. When this valve opens, fumes from the fuel tank are drawn into the charcoal canister and eventually into the engine. When the solenoid valve is turned off (or the engine stops and there is no manifold vacuum), the pressure control valve is spring-loaded shut to keep vapors inside the fuel tank from escaping to the atmosphere.

- **Computer-controlled purge.** The PCM controls when the canister purges on most engines. This is done by an electric vacuum solenoid, and one or more purge valves. Under normal conditions, most engine control systems permit purging only during closed-loop operation at cruising speeds. During other engine operation conditions, such as open-loop mode, idle, deceleration, or wide-open throttle, the PCM prevents canister purging.

Pressures can build inside the fuel system and are usually measured in units of inches of water (inch H_2O) (28 inches of water equals 1 PSI). Some scan tools display other units of measure for the EVAP system that make understanding the system difficult. ● **SEE CHART 27–2** for the conversion among PSI, inch Hg, and inch H_2O.

Pressure buildup in the EVAP system can be caused by:

- Fuel evaporation rates (volatility)
- Gas tank size (fuel surface area and volume)
- Fuel level (liquid versus vapor)
- Fuel slosh (driving conditions)
- Hot temperatures (ambient, in-tank, close to the tank)
- Returned fuel from the rail

PRESSURE CONVERSIONS		
PSI	Inches Hg	Inches H_2O
14.7	29.93	407.19
1.0	2.036	27.7
0.9	1.8	24.93
0.8	1.63	22.16
0.7	1.43	19.39
0.6	1.22	16.62
0.5	1.018	13.85
0.4	0.814	11.08
0.3	0.611	8.31
0.2	0.407	5.54
0.1	0.204	2.77
0.09	0.183	2.49
0.08	0.163	2.22
0.07	0.143	1.94
0.06	0.122	1.66
0.05	0.102	1.385

CHART 27–2

The conversion between Pounds per square inch (PSI) and inches of Mercury (in. Hg.) and inches of water (inches of H_2O).

NOTE: Pressure conversions.

1 PSI = 28 inches H_2O

1/4 PSI = 7 inches H_2O

NONENHANCED EVAPORATIVE CONTROL SYSTEMS

Prior to 1996, evaporative systems were referred to as nonenhanced evaporative (EVAP) control systems. This term refers to evaporative systems that had limited diagnostic capabilities. While they are often PCM controlled, their diagnostic capability is usually limited to their ability to detect if purge has occurred. Many systems have a diagnostic switch that could sense if purge is occurring and set a code if no purge is detected. This system does not check for leaks. On some vehicles, the PCM also has the capability of monitoring the integrity of the purge solenoid and circuit. These systems' limitations are their ability to check the integrity of the evaporative system on the vehicle. They could not detect leaks or missing or loose gas caps that could lead to excessive evaporative emissions from the vehicle. Nonenhanced evaporative systems use either a canister purge solenoid or a vapor management valve to control purge vapor.

ENHANCED EVAPORATIVE CONTROL SYSTEM

BACKGROUND Beginning in 1996, with OBD-II vehicles, manufacturers were required to install systems that are able to detect both purge flow and evaporative system leakage.

- The systems on models produced between 1996 and 2000 must be able to detect a leak as small as 0.04 inch diameter.
- Beginning in the model year 2000, the enhanced systems started a phase-in of 0.020 inch diameter leak detection.
- All vehicles built after 1995 have enhanced evaporative systems that have the ability to detect purge flow and system leakage. If either of these two functions fails, the system is required to set a diagnostic trouble code (DTC) and turn on the MIL light to warn the driver of the failure.

CANISTER VENT VALVE The canister vent valve is a *normally open* valve and is only closed when commanded by the PCM during testing of the system. The vent valve is only closed during testing by the PCM as part of the mandated OBD-II standards. The vent solenoid is located under the vehicle in most cases and is exposed to the environment, making this valve subject to rust and corrosion.

CANISTER PURGE VALVE The purge valve, also called the **canister purge (CANP)** solenoid is *normally closed* and is pulsed open by the PCM during purging. The purge valve is connected to the intake manifold vacuum and this line is used to draw gasoline vapors from the charcoal canister into the

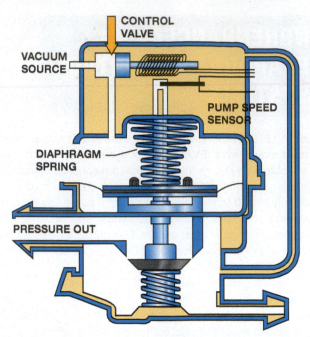

FIGURE 27–33 A leak detection pump (LDP) used on some Chrysler vehicles to pressurize (slightly) the fuel system to check for leaks.

Problems After Refueling? Check the Purge Valve

The purge valve is normally closed and open only when the PCM is commanding the system to purge. If the purge solenoid were to become stuck in the open position, gasoline fumes would be allowed to flow directly from the gas tank to the intake manifold. When refueling, this would result in a lot of fumes being forced into the intake manifold; and as a result, would cause a hard-to-start condition after refueling. This would also result in a rich exhaust (likely black) when first starting the engine after refueling. Although the purge solenoid is usually located under the hood of most vehicles and less subject to rust and corrosion, as with the vent valve, it can still fail.

engine when the purge valve is commanded open. Most purge valves are pulsed on and off to better control the amount of fumes being drawn into the intake manifold.

LEAK DETECTION PUMP SYSTEM

PURPOSE AND FUNCTION Many vehicles use a **leak detection pump (LDP)** as part of the evaporative control system diagnosis equipment. ● **SEE FIGURE 27–33.**

OPERATION The system works to test for leaks as follows:

- The purge solenoid is normally closed.
- The vent valve in the LDP is normally open. Filtered fresh air is drawn through the LDP to the canister.
- The LDP uses a spring attached to a diaphragm to apply pressure (7.5 inches H_2O) to the fuel tank.
- The PCM monitors the LDP switch that is triggered if the pressure drops in the fuel tank.
- The time between LDP solenoid off and LDP switch close is called the pump period. This time period is inversely proportional to the size of the leak. The shorter the pump period, the larger the leak. The longer the pump period, the smaller the leak.

  EVAP large leak (greater than 0.080 inches): less than 0.9 second

  EVAP medium leak (0.040 to 0.080 inches): 0.9 to 1.2 seconds

  EVAP small leak (0.020 to 0.040 inches): 1.2 to 6 seconds

ONBOARD REFUELING VAPOR RECOVERY

PURPOSE AND FUNCTION The onboard refueling vapor recovery (ORVR) system was first introduced on some 1998 vehicles. Previously designed EVAP systems allowed fuel vapor to escape to the atmosphere during refueling.

OPERATION The primary feature of most ORVR systems is the restricted tank filler tube, which is about 1 inch (25 mm) in diameter. This reduced size filler tube creates an aspiration effect, which tends to draw outside air into the filler tube. During refueling, the fuel tank is vented to the charcoal canister, which captures the gas fumes; and with air flowing into the filler tube, no vapors can escape to the atmosphere. ● **SEE FIGURE 27–34.**

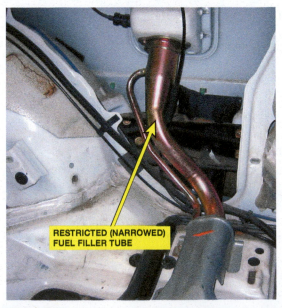

FIGURE 27–34 A restricted fuel fill pipe shown on a vehicle with the interior removed.

STATE INSPECTION EVAP TESTS

In some states, a periodic inspection and test of the fuel system are mandated along with a dynamometer test. The emissions inspection includes tests on the vehicle before and during the dynamometer test. Before the running test, the fuel tank and cap, fuel lines, canister, and other fuel system components must be inspected and tested to ensure that they are not leaking gasoline vapors into the atmosphere.

- First, the fuel tank cap is tested to ensure that it is sealing properly and holds pressure within specs.
- Next, the cap is installed on the vehicle, and using a special adapter, the EVAP system is pressurized to approximately 0.5 PSI and monitored for two minutes.
- Pressure in the tank and lines should not drop below approximately 0.3 PSI.

If the cap or system leaks, hydrocarbon emissions are likely being released, and the vehicle fails the test. If the system leaks, an ultrasonic leak detector may be used to find the leak.

Finally, with the engine warmed up and running at a moderate speed, the canister purge line is tested for adequate flow using a special flow meter inserted into the system. In one example, if the flow from the canister to the intake system when the system is activated is at least 1 liter per minute, the vehicle passes the canister purge test.

DIAGNOSING THE EVAP SYSTEM

SYMPTOMS Before vehicle emissions testing began in many parts of the country, little service work was done on the evaporative emission system. Common engine-performance problems that can be caused by a fault in this system include:

- **Poor fuel economy.** A leak in a vacuum-valve diaphragm can result in engine vacuum drawing in a constant flow of gasoline vapors from the fuel tank. This usually results in a drop in fuel economy of 2 to 4 miles per gallon (mpg). Use a hand-operated vacuum pump to check that the vacuum diaphragm can hold vacuum.
- **Poor performance.** A vacuum leak in the manifold or ported vacuum section of vacuum hose in the system can cause the engine to run rough. Age, heat, and time all contribute to the deterioration of rubber hoses.

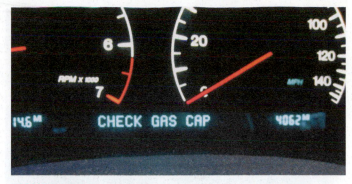

FIGURE 27–35 Some vehicles will display a message if an evaporative control system leak is detected that could be the result of a loose gas cap.

Enhanced exhaust emissions (I/M-240) testing tests the evaporative emission system. A leak in the system is tested by pressurizing the entire fuel system to a level below 1 pounds per sq. in. or 1 PSI (about 14 inches H_2O). The system is typically pressurized with nitrogen, a nonflammable gas that makes up 78% of our atmosphere. The pressure in the system is then shut off and monitored. If the pressure drops below a set standard, the vehicle fails the test. This test determines if there is a leak in the system.

NOTE: To help pass the evaporative section of an enhanced emissions test, arrive at the test site with less than one-half tank of fuel. This means that the rest of the volume of the fuel tank is filled with air. It takes longer for the pressure to drop from a small leak when the volume of the air is greater compared to when the tank is full and the volume of air remaining in the tank is small.

LOCATING LEAKS IN THE SYSTEM Leaks in the evaporative emission control system will cause the malfunction check gas cap indication lamp to light on some vehicles. ● **SEE FIGURE 27–35.**

A leak will also cause a gas smell, which would be most noticeable if the vehicle were parked in an enclosed garage. The first step is to determine if there is a leak in the system by setting the EVAP tester to rate the system, either a 0.040 inch or a 0.020 inch hole size leak. ● **SEE FIGURE 27–36.**

After it has been determined that a leak exists and that it is larger than specified, there are two methods that can be used to check for leaks in the evaporative system.

- **Smoke machine testing.** The most efficient method of leak detection is to introduce smoke under low pressure from a machine specifically designed for this purpose. ● **SEE FIGURE 27–37.**
- **Nitrogen gas pressurization.** This method uses nitrogen gas under a very low pressure (lower than 1 PSI) in the fuel system. The service technician then listens for the escaping air, using amplified headphones. ● **SEE FIGURE 27–38.**

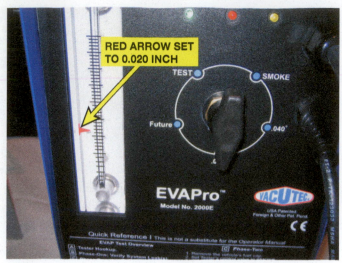

FIGURE 27–36 To test for a leak, this tester was set to the 0.020 inch hole and turned on. The ball rose in the scale on the left and the red arrow was moved to that location. When testing the system for leaks, if the ball rises higher than the arrow, the leak is larger than 0.020 inch. If the ball does not rise to the level of the arrow, the leak is smaller than 0.020 inch.

FIGURE 27–37 This unit is applying smoke to the fuel tank through an adapter and the leak was easily found to be the gas cap seal.

EVAPORATIVE SYSTEM MONITOR

OBD-II REQUIREMENTS OBD-II computer programs not only detect faults, but also *periodically test various systems* and alert the driver before emissions-related components are harmed by system faults.

- Serious faults cause a blinking malfunction indicator lamp (MIL) or even an engine shutdown.

FIGURE 27–38 An emission tester that uses nitrogen to pressurize the fuel system.

- Less serious faults may simply store a code, but not illuminate the MIL.

The OBD-II requirements did not affect fuel system design. However, one new component, a fuel evaporative canister purge line pressure sensor, was added for monitoring purge line pressure during tests. The OBD-II requirements state that vehicle fuel systems are to be routinely tested *while underway* by the PCM.

All OBD-II vehicles perform a canister purge system pressure test, as commanded by the PCM. While the vehicle is being driven, the vapor line between the canister and the purge valve is monitored for pressure changes.

- When the canister purge solenoid is open, the line should be under a vacuum since vapors must be drawn from the canister into the intake system. However, when the purge solenoid is closed, there should be no vacuum in the line. The pressure sensor detects if a vacuum is present, and the information is compared to the command given to the solenoid.

- If, during the canister purge cycle, no vacuum exists in the canister purge line, a code is set indicating a possible fault, which could be caused by an inoperative or clogged solenoid or a blocked or leaking canister purge fuel line. Likewise, if vacuum exists when no command for purge is given, a stuck solenoid is evident, and a code is set. The EVAP system monitor tests for purge volume and leaks.

A typical EVAP monitor first closes off the system to atmospheric pressure and opens the purge valve during cruise operation. A **fuel tank pressure (FTP)** sensor then monitors the rate with which vacuum increases in the system. The monitor uses this information to determine the purge volume flow rate. To test for leaks, the EVAP monitor closes the purge valve, creating a completely closed system. The fuel tank pressure sensor then monitors the leak-down rate. If the rate exceeds PCM-stored values, a leak greater than or equal to the OBD-II

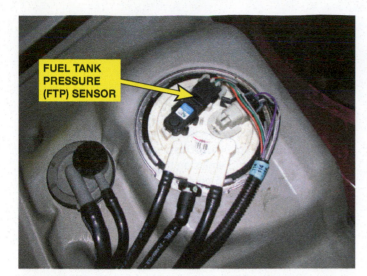

FIGURE 27–39 The fuel tank pressure sensor (black unit with three wires) looks like a MAP sensor and is usually located on top of the fuel pump module (white unit).

FIGURE 27–40 This Toyota cap has a warning. The check engine light will come on if not tightened until one click.

standard of 0.040 inch (1 mm) or 0.020 inch (0.5 mm) exists. After two consecutive failed trips testing either purge volume or the presence of a leak, the PCM lights the MIL and sets a DTC.

The fuel tank pressure sensor is similar to the MAP sensor, and instead of monitoring intake manifold absolute pressure, it is used to monitor fuel tank pressure. ● SEE FIGURE 27–39.

ENGINE-OFF NATURAL VACUUM System integrity (leakage) can also be checked after the engine is shut off. The premise is that a warm evaporative system will cool down after the engine is shut off and the vehicle is stable. A slight vacuum will be created in the gas tank during this cooling period. If a specific level of vacuum is reached and maintained, the system is said to have integrity (no leakage).

TYPICAL EVAP MONITOR

The PCM will run the EVAP monitor when the following enable criteria are met:

- Cold start
- Barometric pressure (BARO) greater than 70 kPa (20.7 inches Hg or 10.2 PSI)

TECH TIP

Always Tighten the Cap Correctly

Many diagnostic trouble codes (DTCs) are set because the gas cap has not been properly installed. To be sure that a screw-type gas cap is properly sealed, it may need to be tightened until it clicks three times. The clicking is a ratchet device and the clicking does not harm the cap. Therefore, if a P0440 or similar DTC is set, check the cap. ● SEE FIGURE 27–40.

TECH TIP

Keep the Fuel Tank Properly Filled

Most evaporative system monitors will not run unless the fuel level is between 15% and 85%. In other words, if a driver always runs with close to an empty tank or always tries to keep the tank full, the EVAP monitor may not run. ● SEE FIGURE 27–41.

- Intake air temperature (IAT) between 39°F and 86°F at engine start-up
- Engine coolant temperature (ECT) between 39°F and 86°F at engine start-up
- ECT and IAT within 39°F of each other at engine start-up
- Fuel level within 15% to 85%
- Throttle position (TP) sensor between 9% and 35%

RUNNING THE EVAP MONITOR There are three tests that are performed during a typical EVAP monitor. A DTC is assigned to each test.

1. **Weak vacuum test (P0440—large leak).** This test identifies gross leaks. During the monitor, the vent solenoid is closed and the purge solenoid is duty cycled. The fuel tank pressure (FTP) should indicate a vacuum of approximately 6 to 10 inches H_2O.

2. **Small leak test (P0442—small leak).** After the large leak test passes, the PCM checks for a small leak by keeping the vent solenoid closed and closing the purge solenoid. The system is now sealed. The PCM measures the change in FTP voltage over time.

3. **Excess vacuum test (P0446).** This test checks for vent path restrictions. With the vent solenoid open and purge commanded, the PCM should not see excessive vacuum in the EVAP system. Typical EVAP system vacuum with the vent solenoid open is about 5 to 6 inches H_2O.

FIGURE 27-41 The fuel level must be between 15% and 85% before the EVAP monitor will run on most vehicles.

EVAP SYSTEM-RELATED DIAGNOSTIC TROUBLE CODES

Diagnostic Trouble Code	Description	Possible Causes
P0440	Evaporative system fault	■ Loose gas cap ■ Defective EVAP vent ■ Cracked charcoal canister ■ EVAP vent or purge vapor line problems
P0442	Small leak detected	■ Loose gas cap ■ Defective EVAP vent or purge solenoid ■ EVAP vent or purge line problems
P0446	EVAP canister vent blocked	■ EVAP vent or purge solenoid electrical problems ■ Restricted EVAP canister vent line

TECH TIP

Check for Tampering

Tampering with, or deleting, vehicle emission control devices takes the vehicle out of compliance with emission standards and is against the law. Individuals who engage in these practices can be punished by state or federal agencies. Despite the law, changes are made to vehicle emission systems to improve performance or circumvent expensive repairs. When diagnosing a vehicle with a diagnostic trouble code (DTC) related to vehicle emissions, it is important to consider that a component may have been tampered with or removed, or the software in the control module may have been altered.

The under-hood emissions label will list all the emission components a vehicle is equipped with. A comparison of the vehicle to the list will help to identify if any components have been removed. When the vehicle control module software has been altered, the module ID number will no longer match the OEM numbers. A comparison of the module ID number in the controller with the OEM service calibrations may help identify this condition.

Changes to the vehicle emission hardware or software are likely to cause a failure at the vehicle emission test lane.

SUMMARY

1. Recirculating 6% to 10% inert exhaust gases back into the intake system by the EGR system reduces peak temperature inside the combustion chamber and reduces NO_x exhaust emissions.

2. EGR is usually not needed at idle, at wide-open throttle, or when the engine is cold.

3. Many EGR systems use a feedback potentiometer to signal the PCM the position of the EGR valve pintle.

4. OBD-II requires that the flow rate be tested and then is achieved by opening the EGR valve and observing the reaction of the MAP sensor.

5. Positive crankcase ventilation (PCV) systems use a valve or a fixed orifice to control and direct the fumes from the crankcase back into the intake system.

6. A PCV valve regulates the flow of fumes, depending on engine vacuum, and seals the crankcase vent in the event of a backfire.

7. As much as 30% of the air needed by the engine at idle speed flows through the PCV system.

8. The secondary air-injection (SAI) system forces air at low pressure into the exhaust to reduce CO and HC exhaust emissions.

9. A catalytic converter is an aftertreatment device that reduces exhaust emissions outside of the engine. A catalyst is an element that starts a chemical reaction, but is not consumed in the process.

10. The catalyst material used in a catalytic converter includes rhodium, palladium, and platinum.

11. The OBD-II system monitor compares the relative activity of a rear oxygen sensor to the precatalytic oxygen sensor to determine catalytic converter efficiency.

12. The purpose of the evaporative (EVAP) emission control system is to reduce the release of volatile organic compounds (VOCs) into the atmosphere.

13. A carbon (charcoal) canister is used to trap and hold gasoline vapors until they can be purged and run into the engine to be burned.

14. OBD-II regulation requires that the evaporative emission control system be checked for leakage and proper purge flow rates.

15. External leaks can best be located by pressurizing the fuel system with low-pressure smoke.

REVIEW QUESTIONS

1. How does the use of exhaust gas recirculation reduce NO_x exhaust emission?

2. How does the DPFE sensor work?

3. What exhaust emissions does the PCV valve and SAI system control?

4. How does a catalytic converter reduce NO_x to nitrogen and oxygen?

5. How does the computer monitor catalytic converter performance?

CHAPTER QUIZ

1. Two technicians are discussing clogged EGR passages. Technician A says clogged EGR passages can cause excessive NO_x exhaust emission. Technician B says that clogged EGR passages can cause the engine to ping (spark knock or detonation). Which technician is correct?
   a. Technician A only
   b. Technician B only
   c. Both Technicians A and B
   d. Neither Technician A nor B

2. The ORVR system is designed to capture _____ during re-fueling.
   a. excess liquid
   b. fuel vapors
   c. water vapor
   d. reserve fuel

3. How much air flows through the PCV system when the engine is at idle speed?
   a. 1% to 3%
   b. 5% to 10%
   c. 10% to 20%
   d. Up to 30%

4. Technician A says that if a PCV valve rattles, it is okay and does not need to be replaced. Technician B says that if a PCV valve does not rattle, it should be replaced. Which technician is correct?
   a. Technician A only
   b. Technician B only
   c. Both Technicians A and B
   d. Neither Technician A nor B

5. The switching valves on the AIR pump have failed several times. Technician A says that a defective exhaust check valve could be the cause. Technician B says that a leaking exhaust system at the muffler could be the cause. Which technician is correct?
   a. Technician A only
   b. Technician B only
   c. Both Technicians A and B
   d. Neither Technician A nor B

6. Two technicians are discussing testing a catalytic converter. Technician A says that a vacuum gauge can be used and observed to see if the vacuum drops with the engine at 2500 RPM for 60 seconds. Technician B says that a pressure gauge can be used to check for backpressure. Which technician is correct?
   a. Technician A only
   b. Technician B only
   c. Both Technicians A and B
   d. Neither Technician A nor B

7. At about what temperature does oxygen combine with the nitrogen in the air to form NO_x?
   a. 500°F (260°C)
   b. 750°F (400°C)
   c. 1,500°F (815°C)
   d. 2,500°F (1,370°C)

8. A state inspection of the EVAP system includes _____.
   a. Testing the gas cap for proper sealing
   b. Pressurizing the EVAP system
   c. checking the level of fuel in the tank
   d. Both a and b

9. Which EVAP valve(s) is(are) normally closed?
   a. Canister purge valve
   b. Canister vent valve
   c. Both canister purge and canister vent valves
   d. Neither canister purge nor canister vent valve

10. Before an evaporative emission monitor will run, the fuel level must be where?
    a. At least 75% full
    b. Over 25%
    c. Between 15% and 85%
    d. The level of the fuel in the tank is not needed to run the monitor test

chapter 28

MODULE REPROGRAMMING

LEARNING OBJECTIVES

After studying this chapter, the reader should be able to:

1. List the benefits of module reprogramming over previous methods of update.
2. Describe the regulatory requirements of J2534.
3. List the hardware and software used for programming.
4. Describe the methods of module reprogramming.
5. Explain the need for a battery maintainer during reprogramming.
6. Describe the concerns of programming in the shop.

KEY TERMS

Application Programming Interface (API) 415
Battery Maintainer 417
PROM 414
Electronically Erasable Programmable Read Only Memory (EEPROM) 414
Locksmith ID 416
NASTF 415
Pass-Through Device 415
SAE J2534 415
SAE J2534-1 415
SAE J2534-2 415
SAE J2534 version 5.00 415

FIGURE 28–1 The Toyota engine control module pictured in the figure is an example of a module that must be replaced to update the programming memory.

FIGURE 28–2A AND B The two General Motors engine control modules above are examples of two styles of removable PROMs used to update programmable memory.

MODULE SOFTWARE UPDATE

HISTORY OF MODULE PROGRAMMING Software programming has been used by the engine control module to meet air quality and emission standards since fuel injection replaced carburetors. The method of updating the software calibration has changed as technology has evolved. On early fuel-injected vehicles, it was necessary to change the computer when the calibration needed to be updated. ● SEE FIGURE 28–1.

In the early 1980s, the replacement **PROM** (programmable read only memory) was introduced. Instead of replacing the entire module, the technician would remove the PROM and install a replacement chip. Several versions of replaceable PROMs were used. ● SEE FIGURES 28–2A AND B.

In 1990, General Motors introduced flash reprogramming. This process allowed the technician to download the replacement software calibration from the manufacturer and to install it in the vehicles computer **EEPROM** (electronically erasable programmable read only memory). This eliminated the need to stock any parts which decreased the cost and the time needed for the repair.

In 1996 as part of the OBDII requirements, all modules that were responsible for emissions control were required to have EEPROM. The main purpose of this regulation was to make it more difficult for the technician to install a software calibration that would take the vehicle out of emission compliance. During this time period, module programming could typically only be performed by the dealer or by someone who had purchased manufacturer-specific tools. ● SEE FIGURE 28–3

FIGURE 28–3 The manufacturer scan tool is being used to reprogram the engine control module via the data link connector.

In 2004, it was mandated by CARB and the EPA that all vehicles manufactured after that point must be J2534 compliant, allowing for the reprogramming of emission-related modules. This mandate allowed for all individuals engaged in repair of emission-related failures the ability to update the software of these modules.

PURPOSE Designing a program that allows an engine to meet strict air quality and fuel economy standards while providing excellent performance is no small feat. However, this is only part of the challenge facing engineers assigned with the task of developing OBD-II software. The reason for this is the countless variables involved with running diagnostic monitors. Although programmers do their best to factor in any and all operating conditions when writing this complex code, periodic revisions are often required. Reprogramming consists of downloading new calibrations from the manufacturer into the PCM's electronically erasable programmable read only memory (EEPROM).

SAE STANDARDS

J2534- SAE created the standard **SAE J2534** for communications between a computer and a vehicle. The original standard was introduced in February of 2002, and was identified as version 02.02. The EPA and CARB regulations require all automakers to provide a J2534 service to everyone in the United States for re-flashing emission-related controllers. If the technician has a SAE J-2534 Pass-Through device, they can re-flash and, in some cases, diagnose vehicles with factory functionality. The EPA documentation requires OEMs to comply with SAE J2534 for pass-through reprogramming beginning with model year 2004. Reprogramming information also had to be made available within three months of vehicle introduction for new models. The original version of the standard was found to have some errors.

This original standard was updated in December of 2004. The new standard was identified as version 04.04 or more commonly as **SAE J2534-1**. The changes in the second version of the standard supported specific requirements of Ford and Chrysler that were not addressed in the first standard that related to J1850 class 2 communication protocols. It also defined specifics for the design of the vehicle communication interface device.

The standard was updated again and referred to as **SAE J2534-2**. These changes addressed issues related to single wire CAN Bus communication and issues related to the GM UART communication protocol. The new standard also provided a method for manufacturers to add optional features in a uniform way. An example of this is the ability to flash program modules that were not emission related.

The current standard is referred to as **SAE J2534 version 5.00**. The newest standard includes all the changes required in the previous updates and serves to improve the communication through the J1962 connector. It is important to have the most current equipment to ensure that that the flash reprogramming process will be completed without any malfunctions.

FIGURE 28–4 The GM MDI and Ford VCI are examples of manufacturer-specific pass-through devices.

PROGRAMMING HARDWARE

MANUFACTURER SPECIFIC Each manufacturer has developed their own J2534 **pass-through device** or **application programming interface (API)** that is specific to the brands the manufacturer sells. A pass-through device or API serves as a connection point that makes all the hardware look the same, and allows the computer with the reprogramming software to communicate with the vehicles control module through the data link connector (DLC). Generally, these tools are not designed with the functionality to support competitive brands. In many cases, these pass-through devices are designed to support the manufacturer scan tool in addition to providing reprogramming capabilities. The GM MDI and Ford VCI are both examples of this type of technology. ●**SEE FIGURE 28–4**.

GENERIC The generic J2534 pass-through device is designed to support multiple manufacturers. These tools typically do not have the same level of scan tool diagnostics as a manufacturer-specific tool. These tools are more often found outside of the dealership environment in the independent repair facilities. The Drew Technologies CarDAQ-Plus series of J2534 pass-through devices is an example of a generic tool. ●**SEE FIGURE 28–5**.

PROGRAMMING SOFTWARE

NASTF (NATIONAL AUTOMOTIVE SERVICE TASK FORCE) The **NASTF** is a cooperative effort of the automotive service industry, the tool industry, and the original equipment manufacturers to ensure that automotive professionals employed outside of the OEMs have all the information, training, and tools they need to diagnose and repair modern automobiles. The NASTF has created a portal for all automotive service professionals to access manufacturer-specific reprogramming

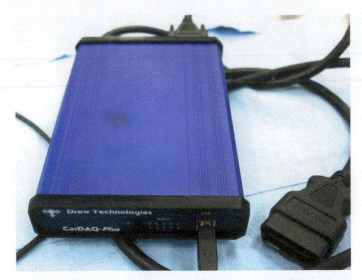

FIGURE 28–5 The CarDAQ Plus is a generic pass-through device.

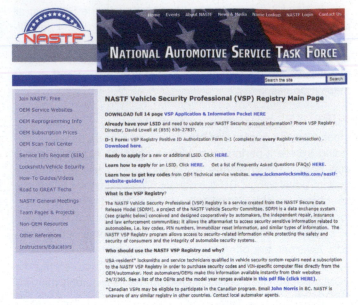

FIGURE 28–7 The screenshot from the NASTF website provides the resources for the technician to apply for a locksmith ID.

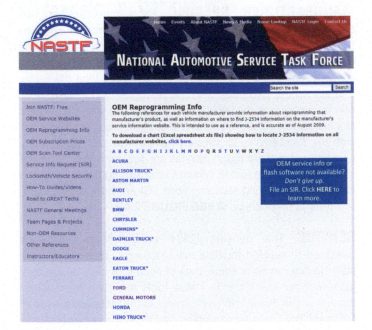

FIGURE 28–6 The screenshot of the NASTF website provides an access point for the aftermarket automotive professional to obtain the needed reprogramming information.

information. This includes where to access the information, the tools needed, and in many cases a short video on how to complete the task. ● **SEE FIGURE 28–6.**

VEHICLE SECURITY PROFESSIONAL – LOCKSMITH ID
Many times when a module must be reprogrammed or programmed upon replacement, the security codes or key specific information must be re-entered during the process. In order to obtain this information, the shop or service technician must be a registered vehicle security professional and have a **locksmith ID** number. The National Automotive Service Task Force (NASTF), in conjunction with automotive manufacturers,

insurance industry, independent repair, and law enforcement communities, has developed this system to allow the aftermarket repair industry to access to this sensitive data. The forms and instructions needed to apply for this identification number can be found on the NASTF website (*www.nasft.org*) under Locksmith/Vehicle Security. ● **SEE FIGURE 28–7.**

COMPUTERS AND CALIBRATIONS
The computers and their software used in the programming process need to be at the most current calibration. Before beginning the reprogramming of a module, it is important to make sure the needed software is at the correct level. It is not uncommon to find that two different manufacturers will have different software requirements for their reprogramming processes. In some cases, this will require that multiple computers are needed as software issues prevent their operating systems from being on the same unit. The incorrect software level on computer used in the reprogramming process may result in failed update of a control module.

NETWORK SECURITY
The equipment needed to reprogram vehicle modules has to be able to access the Internet for needed vehicle software files. As a result, repair shop network security has become a high priority as hackers increasingly try to gain electronic access to vehicles. A computer used in the reprogramming process in an open network can be accessed by hackers even when the computer is turned off. If unauthorized software is installed on the computer, the service technician may unknowingly install a virus in a vehicle during a reprogramming event. Computers used in the reprogramming process should only be used in a secure network that is password protected to minimize the chance of vehicle hacking.

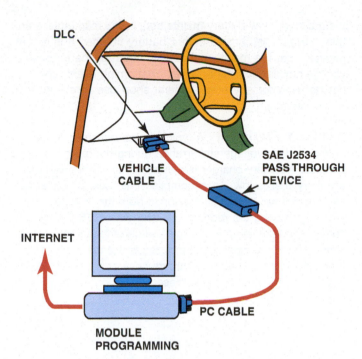

FIGURE 28–8 The J2534 device is being used to program the engine control module through the DLC.

FIGURE 28–9 The engine control module is being programmed at an off-board location.

REPROGRAMMING

ON-BOARD On-Board reprogramming of the controller is defined as having the module connected to the vehicle during the process. The module uses its normal connection points to provide the power, ground, communication links, and any other needed support. This is the type of programming that typically occurs in a service facility. ● SEE FIGURE 28–8.

OFF-BOARD Off-Board programming of the controller is defined as having the module programmed someplace other than in the vehicle. This could be anywhere that there is a computer and the needed power, ground and communication links. The purchase and programming of a module at a local parts store is an example of off-board programming. ● SEE FIGURE 28–9.

REMOTE Remote programming is a relatively new process. The servicing facility does not perform the reprogramming of the vehicle. Instead, the shop simply plugs in the equipment and follows the instructions of someone who is at a distant location. This process still requires an Internet connection and equipment. However, it relies on a third party who has the manufacturer subscription for the software. This option has become increasingly popular for shops that perform very few reprogramming events or lack the technical expertise to complete the task. ● SEE FIGURE 28–10.

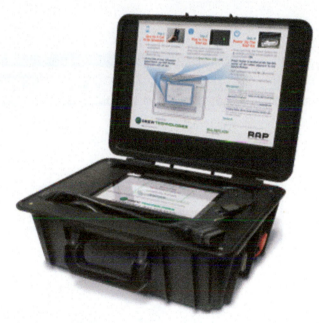

FIGURE 28–10 The Drew Technologies remote programming tool is an example of a tool that is connected to the vehicle and used remotely.

BATTERY VOLTAGE

BATTERY MAINTAINER In order to provide a stable vehicle voltage throughout the reprogramming process, it is recommended that a **battery maintainer** be connected to the vehicle during the repair. A battery maintainer is designed to hold the vehicle at a specific voltage throughout the duration of the repair. A unique feature of the battery maintainer is that it accomplishes this task without wide fluctuations in voltage or amperage. ● SEE FIGURES 28–11 AND 28–12. Currently

FIGURE 28–11 The Midtronics PSC-550 is an example of battery maintainer that meets the voltage and current requirements for reprogramming.

there are very few battery maintainers in the marketplace and they are more expensive than a battery charger. It is recommended that the maintainer be only used for the purpose of voltage stabilization during a reprogramming event, and they not be used for any other general shop use to ensure their proper operation.

BATTERY CHARGER A typical battery charger is not recommended for voltage stabilization during the reprogramming process. A battery charger is designed to raise the voltage of a battery that is low. To accomplish this task, a typical battery charger will have a fluctuation in both the voltage and the amperage during the recharge. ● **SEE FIGURES 28–13 AND 28–14**. The fluctuation in voltage and current can cause problems with the reprogramming process and is therefore not recommended. Some battery chargers have a reprogram feature that is designed to minimize these fluctuations, making them suitable for both tasks.

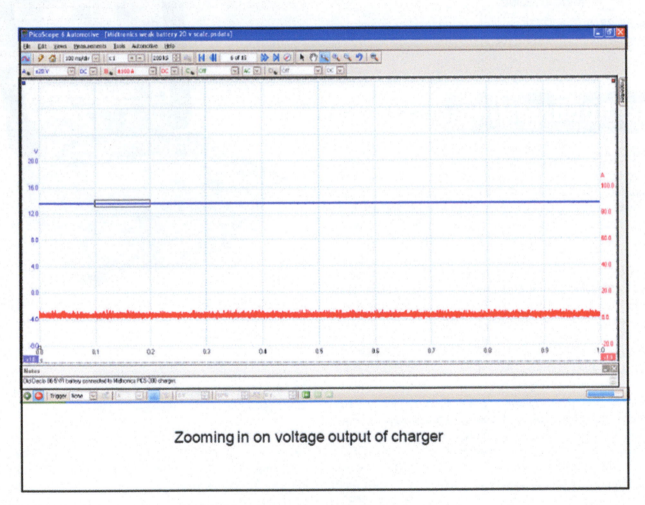

FIGURE 28–12 The scope patterns show stable voltage and current traces.

- Are not plug-and-play technology.
- PC-based scan tools may host J2534 operations, but are not J2534 hardware.
- IT skills (owner or technician) will need to improve.
- Different OEMs use different interfaces and some tools can be difficult to use with some models.
- Software, Java, browser settings, and PC requirements are critical to proper operation.

AFTERMARKET REPROGRAMMING

COMPLIANCE CONCERNS There are many aftermarket programmers or "tuners" available in the marketplace today. The primary purpose of the programs is to increase torque and horsepower or to defeat emission control devices. These programs take the vehicle out of emission compliance because they do not meet the EPA/CARB requirements and are therefore illegal for on- or off-road use. It is likely that the change in torque and horsepower will lead to physical failures of the powertrain due to the increased numbers. The changes in software may also lead to a failure at the emission test lane due to monitor failures or omissions. ● **SEE FIGURE 28–15**.

FIGURE 28–13 The Schumacher battery charger is an example of a device that does not meet the voltage and current requirements of a reprogramming event.

PROGRAMMING PROBLEMS AND CONCERNS

PROBLEMS AND CONCERNS IN THE FIELD The reprogramming of computers is relatively new to the automotive industry, and, as a result, there are many concerns related to the failure of the process and the damaging of the vehicle's module. The items listed below are some of the reasons some shops are hesitant to perform this type of repair.

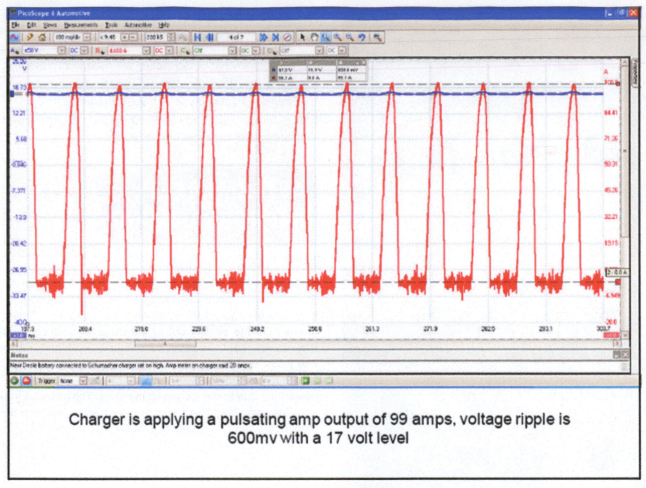

Charger is applying a pulsating amp output of 99 amps, voltage ripple is 600mv with a 17 volt level

FIGURE 28–14 The scope trace shows unstable voltage and fluctuating current.

FIGURE 28–15 The SCT aftermarket tuner is an example of device that takes the vehicle out of compliance when reprogramming the module.

1 Begin by plugging the J2534 device into the data link connector.

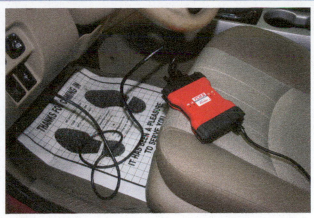

2 Ensure that the J2534 device is communicating with the vehicle and the computer.

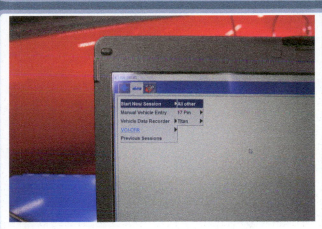

3 Start the program (in this case the Ford IDS).

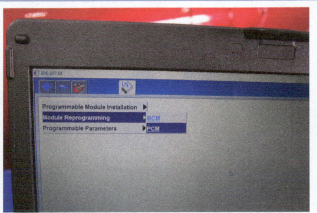

4 Start a new session.

5 Select module reprogramming.

6 Select the powertrain control module.

CONTINUED ▶

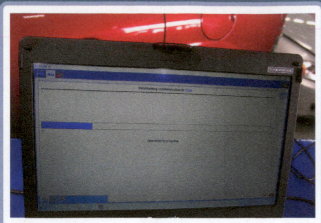

7 The program will establish communications with the PCM and identify the module.

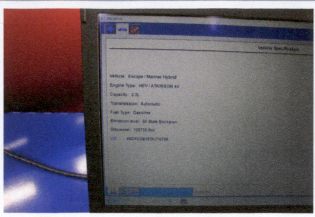

8 The program will confirm the vehicle and the module identification.

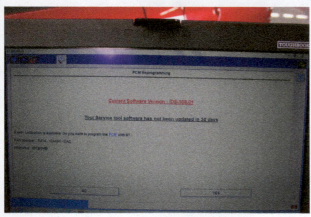

9 Start the program (in this case the Ford IDS).

SUMMARY

1. The programming of the electronically erasable programmable read only memory was a requirement for OBD-II.

2. The J2534 standard supports programming of the EEPROM in modules responsible for emission control with a pass-through device on all vehicles 2004 and newer.

3. EEPROM programming can be performed on-board the vehicle, off-board, or remotely with the proper equipment.

4. When reprogramming a module, it is important to use a battery maintainer so the vehicle's system voltage does not drop below the minimum level.

5. Many aftermarket programmers or "tuners" are designed to take the vehicle out of emission compliance and therefore are illegal for on- or off- road use.

REVIEW QUESTIONS

1. Why did the manufacturers begin using EEPROM in 1996?

2. What is the SAE J2534 standard used for?

3. What are the differences between on-board, off-board, and remote programming?

4. Why is it important to use a battery maintainer when reprogramming a module?

5. Why do some aftermarket programmers or "tuners" cause a failure at the emission test lane?

CHAPTER QUIZ

1. Technician A says that reprogramming an engine control module using the J2534 system requires a factory scan tool. Technician B says that reprogramming an engine control module using the J2534 system requires Internet access. Which technician is correct?
   a. Technician A only
   b. Technician B only
   c. Both Technician A and Technician B
   d. Neither Technician A nor Technician B

2. Which method can be used to reprogram an engine control module?
   a. On-Board
   b. Off-Board
   c. Remote
   d. Any of the above

3. A battery maintainer is used during reprogramming to _____.
   a. make sure the OBDII data is not lost
   b. make sure the customer's radio stations are not lost
   c. make sure the system voltage does not drop during the reprogramming event.
   d. All of the above

4. What is *not* required to reprogram a vehicles engine control module?
   a. A good Internet connection
   b. A manufacturer's scan tool
   c. A pass-through device
   d. A computer that meets the minimum specifications.

5. SAE J2534 is a mandated specification to all automakers who sell vehicles in the United States after 2004 to _____
   a. have standard data link connectors
   b. support reprogramming of the EEPROM
   c. make service information available to all who service vehicle emissions
   d. All of the above

6. How was programming updated before 1996?
   a. A new computer had to be installed
   b. A replaceable PROM was used
   c. The control cable was replaced
   d. The instrument panel cluster (IPC) was updated

7. Why is a special battery charger specified when programming?
   a. Must be a low-voltage, high amperage charger
   b. Must use a battery charger that produces little, if any, voltage fluctuations
   c. To be able to communicate with the J2534 unit
   d. Needs to be OBD/CARB approved

8. What organization created the J2534 standard?
   a. EPA
   b. CARB
   c. SAE
   d. OBD

9. What does a pass-through device do?
   a. Used between the vehicle and the scan tool
   b. Passes data between the Internet and the computer used to program a vehicle
   c. Used only for off-board programming only
   d. Used to monitor the data being transferred

10. Aftermarket programmers may create an issue of _____
    a. noncompliance
    b. excessive cost to the vehicle owner
    c. not being certified by EPA/CARB
    d. Both a and c

chapter 29
SYMPTOM-BASED DIAGNOSIS

INTRODUCTION

About 80% of problems can be solved using a systematic approach. However, for the remaining 20%, it is the skill and experience of the service technician that will help narrow the problem to the root cause.

This chapter is different from the previous chapters in this textbook, as it will be devoted to providing:

- Lists for common causes of problems based on their symptoms
- Lists of symptoms that a particular component could cause if it were defective
- Typical causes of a too rich or too lean condition that are included to help find those exhaust emission testing failures

This chapter is similar to having an experienced service technician next to you while you are working on a problem that seems difficult to solve. Enjoy.

ENGINE HESITATES, SAGS, OR STUMBLES DURING ACCELERATION

Hesitation means a delay in the operation of the engine when the accelerator pedal is depressed. Sometimes hesitation is described as **sag** or "lack of response" as the accelerator is pushed down.

The most common cause of hesitation is a too lean air–fuel mixture being delivered to the engine during the time the accelerator is depressed. When the accelerator pedal is depressed, additional air can quickly flow into the engine. Gasoline is heavier than air and cannot flow as fast into the engine as the air. As a result, the engine normally would hesitate until the correct amount of gasoline flow matches the increased amount of air entering the engine. Fuel systems are designed to compensate for this lag or hesitation by providing an additional shot or squirt of fuel into the intake manifold or cylinder just as the accelerator pedal is depressed.

- Carbon buildup on the backside of the intake valves absorbs gasoline vapors and can cause a hesitation, especially when the engine is cold. ● **SEE FIGURE 29–1.**
- A throttle-position (TP) sensor is used on electronic fuel-injection systems to signal the computer to provide an extra pulse to the fuel injector(s) just as the accelerator pedal is depressed to prevent a hesitation (● **SEE FIGURE 29–2**).

FIGURE 29–1 Carbon deposits on the intake valves can cause hesitation during acceleration, especially if the engine is cold.

FREQUENTLY ASKED QUESTION

What Is the Best Way to Find the Cause of Intermittent Problems?

Intermittent driveability problems are usually difficult to find. Most experts recommend the following procedures that have successfully been used to locate those hard-to-find faults.

1. With the engine running or the component operating, start wiggling the wires, connectors, and hoses. Watch for any change in the operation of the engine or components being moved.
2. Use a water spray bottle that has a little salt added and spray all the electrical wiring and wiring connections. The small amount of salt in the water helps make the water more electrically conductive. Watch for any change in the operation of the engine or component while spraying.
3. Unplug all the electrical connectors and look for rust or corrosion. If possible, use a male metal terminal of the correct size and try mating it with the female terminal, checking to see if the terminal may be too loose to make proper contact. This test is called the "drag test," also referred to as a "pull test."

IDLE AIR CONTROL (IAC)

MASS AIRFLOW (MAF) SENSOR

THROTTLE POSITION (TP) SENSOR

FIGURE 29–2 Typical throttle-position (TP) sensor.

Possible Cause	Reason
Throttle-position (TP) sensor	• The TP sensor voltage should be within the specified range at idle. If too high or too low, the computer may not provide a strong enough extra pulse to prevent a hesitation. • An open or short in the TP sensor can result in hesitation because the computer would not be receiving correct information regarding the position of the throttle.
Throttle-plate deposit buildup (port fuel-injected engines)	• An air flow restriction at the throttle plates creates not only less air reaching the engine but also swirling air due to the deposits. This swirling or uneven air flow can cause an uneven air–fuel mixture being supplied to the engine, causing poor idle quality and a sag or hesitation during acceleration.
Manifold absolute pressure (MAP) sensor fault	• The MAP sensor detects changes in engine load and signals to the computer to increase the amount of fuel needed for proper operation. Check the vacuum hose and the sensor itself for proper operation.
Check the throttle linkage for binding	• A kinked throttle cable or cruise (speed) control cable can cause the accelerator pedal to bind.

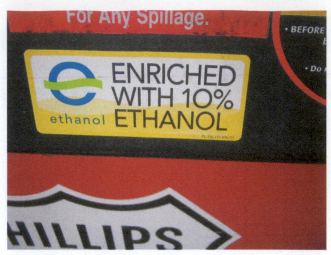

FIGURE 29–3 Many areas of the country use gasoline that is blended with up to 10% ethanol (ethyl alcohol). Sometimes too much alcohol can cause driveability problems.

Contaminated fuel	• Fuel contaminated with excessive amounts of alcohol or water can cause a hesitation or sag during acceleration.

NOTE: To easily check for the presence of alcohol in gasoline, simply get a sample of the fuel and place it in a clean container. Add some water and shake. If no alcohol is in the gasoline, the water will settle to the bottom and be clear. If there is alcohol in the gasoline, the alcohol will absorb the water. The alcohol-water combination will settle to the bottom of the container, but will be cloudy rather than clear. ● SEE FIGURE 29–3.

Clogged, shorted, or leaking fuel injectors	Any injector problem that results in less than an ideal amount of fuel being delivered to the cylinders can result in a hesitation, a sag, or **stumble** during acceleration.
Spark plugs or spark plug wires	Any fault in the ignition system such as a defective spark plug wire or cracked spark plug can cause hesitation, a sag, or stumble during acceleration. At higher engine speeds, a defective spark plug wire is not as noticeable as it is at lower speeds, especially in vehicles equipped with a V-8 engine.
EGR valve operation	• Hesitation, a sag, or stumble can occur if the EGR valve opens too soon or is stuck partially open.
False air	• A loose or cracked intake hose between the MAF sensor and the throttle plate can be the cause.

FIGURE 29-4 The deposits on the back (engine) side of the throttle plate can cause rough idle or stalling due to lack of proper air flow into the engine.

ROUGH IDLE OR STALLING

Rough (or **unstable**) **idle** is a common occurrence because many different systems have a direct effect on idle quality. If the engine **stalls** (stops running), most customers are very concerned because it can be a safety-related malfunction. For the engine to idle correctly, each cylinder has to have the same (or nearly the same) compression, air–fuel mixture, ignition timing, and quality of spark.

Possible Cause	Reason
Vacuum leak	• A vacuum leak (also called an air leak) allows extra air to enter the intake manifold or an individual cylinder, thereby leaning the air–fuel mixture to one or more cylinders. Because the cylinder(s) is not receiving the *same* air–fuel mixture, the engine will not run smoothly and a rough idle can result.
	• In some cases, a vacuum leak can cause a higher-than-normal idle speed or even cause the engine to stall.
Dirty throttle plate(s) (port fuel-injected engines)	• Dirty throttle plates can restrict the amount of air entering the engine. ● **SEE FIGURE 29–4**. This is especially noticeable when the engine is idling. Often, the idle air control valve can offset the effect of the dirty throttle by increasing the amount of air that bypasses the throttle plate. Although this may restore the proper idle speed, idle quality may still be poor.
	• In severe cases, dirty throttle plates can cause stalling, especially when coasting to a stop.
Clogged, shorted, or leaking fuel injectors	• A clogged or inoperative fuel injector causes the cylinder or cylinders affected to be leaner than usual. Because all cylinders are not receiving the same amount of fuel, the engine will run roughly and may even stall.
	• If an injector is leaking and not shutting off when power is removed from the injector, the injector will cause excessive amounts of fuel to be drawn into the affected cylinder or cylinders.
	• If an injector is electrically shorted, excessive current will flow through the windings of the injector coil. Two situations can occur: (1) The shorted injector may operate, but will draw current from another injector that shares the same injector driver inside the computer. In this case, the injector that is shorted will work okay, but the "good" injector will not work. (2) The shorted injector may work depending on how badly the injector is shorted and how the injector driver circuit inside the computer controls (limits) the current flow through the injector.
Ignition system fault	• Defective spark plug wires can cause a rough running or idling engine, and in severe cases can cause the engine to stall.
	• Dirty, cracked, unevenly gapped, or excessively worn spark plugs can cause poor engine operation, a rough idle, or even stalling.
	• Weak ignition may result from a shorted ignition coil, defective ignition module (igniter), or defective pickup coil or crankshaft position sensor.

Possible Cause	Reason
Exhaust gas recirculation (EGR) valve stuck open	• An open EGR valve allows inert exhaust gases to be mixed with the proper air–fuel mixture. The exhaust gases cannot burn and the EGR being open at idle is likely to cause a rough idle or stalling. • At higher engine speeds, exhaust gases can be introduced into the cylinder as is normally done; therefore, the engine runs okay above idle speed.
Positive crankcase ventilation (PCV) systems fault	• About 20% of the air going into the engine at idle comes from the PCV system. • Check that a replacement PCV valve may not be correctly calibrated for the engine (wrong PCV valve application during a previous service). • All vacuum hoses should be carefully inspected for cracks. • All vacuum passages should be carefully inspected for obstructions such as carbon buildup in manifold ports where the PCV hose attaches to the manifold.
Secondary air injection system malfunction	• Inspect the one-way check valves. A hole in a check valve can cause exhaust gases to flow into the air pump system and into the intake manifold, greatly affecting the air–fuel mixture.
Idle air control (IAC) problems	• If the IAC is stuck, the valve cannot provide the correct idle speed. Usually, this results in too high an idle speed, but it can result in a too low idle speed, causing the engine to idle roughly and, in severe cases, even stall. • Restricted IAC passages can limit the amount of air going into the engine at idle.
Manifold absolute pressure (MAP) or mass airflow (MAF) sensor fault	• A MAP sensor vacuum hose, either split open or collapsed, can greatly affect the operation of the MAP sensor. An incorrect MAP sensor signal to the computer can cause the computer to supply either a too rich or too lean command. • A defective MAP or MAF sensor can also cause a rough idle or stalling.
Malfunction or misadjusted park-neutral switch	• The computer will not command the proper air–fuel mixture if the gear selection is in drive or reverse, yet the computer "thinks" that the gear selector is still in park or neutral. • The idle speed is affected by the park-neutral switch and the engine may idle roughly or even stall.

SPARK KNOCK (PING OR DETONATION)

Spark knock (also called **detonation** or **ping**) is most noticeable during acceleration. Spark knock is usually due to excessively lean air–fuel mixtures or excessively hot engine operation. The noise or knock is a result of a secondary rapid burning of the last 3% to 5% of the gases inside the combustion chamber. When this secondary flame front hits the primary spark-ignited flame front, two situations occur:

1. Temperature greatly increases at the instant the two flame fronts collide.

2. Pressure greatly increases at the same time due to the temperature rise.

These two factors combine to cause the piston to "ring" like a bell, creating the characteristic sound of spark knock.

Possible Cause	Reason
Vacuum leak	Causes a leaner-than-normal air–fuel mixture.
Defective EGR valve/system	Exhaust gas recirculation (EGR) system uses inert gases to slow the burning process. If not enough exhaust gas is recirculated spark knock can occur.
Low coolant level	Could cause the engine to operate too hot.
Contaminated O_2 sensor	Causes the computer to deliver a too lean air–fuel mixture.
Electric cooling fan inoperative	Can cause the engine to operate at too high a temperature.
Too low fuel pressure	Can cause the engine to operate with a too lean air–fuel mixture.
Too advanced ignition timing	Causes excessive pressure buildup in the combustion chamber.
Knock sensor or system is not operating	If the knock sensor (KS) system is not operating, the ignition timing will not be retarded when spark knock is detected.
Park-neutral switch	The computer is not seeing a drive gear and the EGR is not commanded on if the vehicle is not in a drive gear (drive or reverse).
Defective valve stem seals	• Causes excessive carbon buildup inside the combustion chamber, creating higher-than-normal compression. • Defective valve stem seals are sources of carbon that can glow, which could be an ignition source that ignites the air–fuel mixture before the spark plug fires, causing preignition.

Possible Cause	Reason
Engine mechanical faults	Incorrect engine parts such as pistons, camshaft, or cylinder heads that can cause excessive compression.
PROM	An updated PROM (programmable read-only memory) may have been released that changes the ignition timing or air–fuel mixture to solve a spark knock concern.

ENGINE CRANKS OKAY, BUT IS HARD TO START

In order for engines to start, the correct air–fuel ratio must be delivered to the cylinders and a strong spark must be present to ignite the mixture. Worn engine parts can also cause an engine to not have enough compression or to have the valves open and close at the proper time and duration.

Possible Cause	Reason
Weak spark to the spark plugs	A weak spark caused by faults in the ignition coil(s), secondary spark plug wires, or distributor cap or rotor (if so equipped) can prevent the air–fuel mixture from igniting when the cylinder is under compression when the engine is being cranked.
Low fuel pressure	Low fuel pressure due to a weak fuel pump or defective fuel-pressure regulator can cause a lack of fuel being supplied to the engine. A defective check valve in the fuel pump can also cause the fuel pressure to drop to zero and can cause a long cranking period to occur before starting.
Contaminated or stale gasoline	Gasoline with excessive amounts of alcohol can cause hard starting, especially in cold weather. Stale gasoline is gasoline that has been stored for a long time (several months) and the light ends have evaporated, leaving the heavier portions of the gasoline that are hard to ignite.
Leaking, clogged, or inoperative fuel injectors	• If a fuel injector were to stick open, an excessive amount of fuel would fill the cylinder, causing the spark plug(s) to foul and make starting difficult. • If an injector were clogged or inoperative, a lack of fuel would cause the cylinder to be too lean, and hard starting (or no starting) may occur.

FIGURE 29–5 A vacuum gauge is an excellent and low-cost tool to use to make sure that the engine is functioning normally.

Low cranking vacuum	• Low cranking vacuum (lower than 2.5 in. Hg) can result from an idle air control (IAC) being stuck open or from an excessively worn engine. • Another cause of low cranking vacuum is the installation of a high-performance camshaft with too much duration. ● SEE FIGURE 29–5.
Excessively advanced or retarded ignition timing	• Excessively advanced ignition timing causes the spark to occur too soon while the piston(s) is coming up at the end of the compression stroke. This overadvanced timing usually causes the engine to crank slowly and unevenly. • Excessively retarded ignition timing causes the spark to occur near or after the piston reaches top dead center (TDC). This causes the engine to have to crank a long time before starting.
Excessively advanced or retarded valve timing	• Incorrect valve timing can occur due to wear (stretching) of the timing chain. • Incorrect installation of a replacement timing chain or timing belt may have occurred. Look for evidence of a previous timing belt or chain repair or replacement.

FIGURE 29–6 This meter indicates a cranking voltage of 10.32 volts, which is within specifications (above 9.6 V during cranking).

ENGINE DOES NOT CRANK OR CRANKS SLOWLY

The starter motor is designed to crank the engine between 80 and 250 revolutions per minute (RPM) to permit proper intake of a combustible air–fuel mixture to start. If the engine does not crank, then the fault is in the cranking circuit, which consists of the following components:

- Battery
- Starter motor
- Starter solenoid
- Ignition switch
- Park-neutral or clutch safety switch
- Cables, wires, and connectors

A fault in any of these components can cause slow cranking or no cranking of the engine when the ignition switch is turned to the Start position.

Possible Cause	Reason
Weak or discharged battery	The battery should be at least 75% charged with at least 12.4 volts for proper operation of the starter. ● SEE FIGURE 29–6.
Loose or dirty battery connections at the battery	Loose or corroded connections can cause an excessive voltage drop, resulting in lower voltage across the starter motor.
Defective or misadjusted park-neutral safety switch	The safety switch (either park-neutral with an automatic transmission or the clutch with a manual transmission) may cause an open circuit to the starter solenoid. With no voltage to the solenoid, a no-crank condition occurs.
Defective or misadjusted ignition switch	A defective or misadjusted ignition switch may cause an open circuit to the starter solenoid. With no voltage to the solenoid, a no-crank condition is noticed.
Blown fuse or fusible link	Most circuits are protected by a fuse and a fusible link. If either is blown or defective, no voltage can reach the starter solenoid; therefore, no cranking of the engine is possible.

DIESELING OR RUN-ON

Dieseling or **run-on** is a term used to describe the engine continuing to run after the ignition is turned off. A diesel engine operates by ignition of the fuel by heat of compression without the need for a spark to occur. Therefore, if the engine continues to run, an ignition source and fuel must be available. The ignition source is usually hot carbon deposits inside the combustion chamber.

Possible Cause	Reason
Leaking injectors	For the engine to continue to run with the key off, a source of fuel is necessary. An injector(s) that is leaking can provide the fuel, and the carbon deposit inside the combustion chamber can provide the ignition source.
Defective fuel-pressure regulator	A hole in the rubber diaphragm can provide a source of fuel after the ignition is turned off.

BACKFIRE

A **backfire** is the burning of fuel in the intake manifold or in the exhaust system. It is accompanied by a loud popping noise.

Possible Cause	Reason
Vacuum leak	A vacuum leak causes a leaner-than-normal air–fuel mixture. A lean mixture burns hotter and slower than the correct mixture. This slow burning mixture can continue burning throughout the exhaust stroke and can ignite the incoming air–fuel mixture when the intake valve opens at the end of the exhaust stroke. This burning of the intake charge in the intake manifold causes a backfire.

Possible Cause	Reason
Low fuel pressure	Causes a leaner-than-normal air–fuel mixture.
Clogged or inoperative fuel injector	Causes a leaner-than-normal air–fuel mixture.
• **Incorrect ignition timing** • **Crossed spark plug wire** • **Incorrect ignition timing** • **Crossed spark plug wire** • **Crossfire between two cylinders side-by-side** • **Cracked or carbon-tracked distributor cap** • **Defective or worn spark plugs** • **Worn camshaft** • **Fault in the valve train that could prevent proper valve opening and closing**	If the ignition timing is incorrect, either too advanced or retarded, the spark will not occur when it should. Due to the time it takes for the air–fuel mixture to burn (about 3 ms), it may cause the mixture to be burning in the exhaust system or into the intake manifold when the intake valve opens at the end of the exhaust stroke. If the valves do not open fully and close fully at the proper time, a backfire can occur. If the intake valve does not open as far as it should, a leaner-than-normal air–fuel mixture will be in the cylinder when the spark plug fires. This can cause the fuel to still be burning when the intake valve opens at the end of the exhaust stroke. A leaking valve can cause the burning air–fuel mixture to escape and can cause a backfire.
Exhaust gas recirculation (EGR) valve open all the time or defective EGR valve gasket	Exhaust gases are inert and do not react chemically with the air–fuel mixture. The purpose and function of the EGR system are to slow down the rate of burning of the air–fuel mixture by introducing a metered amount of exhaust gas into the cylinders. Too much EGR can drastically slow the burning of the fuel. This slowing down of the burning of the air–fuel mixture can cause the burning of the fuel to continue as the intake valve opens at the end of the exhaust stroke, which causes a backfire.

Possible Cause	Reason
Air pump fault such as a defective switching valve	Air pump operation injects extra air into the exhaust manifold or catalytic converter, depending on engine temperature and other factors. To prevent a backfire, the air pump output should be directed to the atmosphere or air cleaner during deceleration when the intake manifold vacuum is high.
Hole in the exhaust	An exhaust leak can cause excessive noise, which could be interpreted by the owner as a backfire.

CUTS OUT OR MISFIRES

When an engine **misfires**, it jerks or pulsates and is usually more noticeable when the engine is accelerated. Because the engine is not running smoothly, the cause of the misfire is usually due to faults in one or more cylinders, either with a lack of spark, fuel, or compression.

Possible Cause	Reason
Spark plugs and/or spark plug wires	Any fault in the secondary ignition system results in uneven firing of the cylinders, causing the engine to miss or cut out.
Engine mechanical faults such as: • **Worn camshaft** • **Bent pushrod** • **Broken valve spring** • **Lack of compression**	Any malfunction in the valve train would cause an uneven firing of the cylinders.

LACK OF POWER

A lack of power may also be noticeable as *sluggish* or *spongy* performance. This means that the engine delivers less-than-expected power and the vehicle speed does not increase as desired when the accelerator pedal is depressed.

Possible Cause	Reason
Retarded ignition timing	If the spark occurs later than normal, a decrease in power is the result. For example, the ignition timing is retarded if the spark occurs at 2 degrees before top dead center (BTDC) rather than at the specification of 10 degrees BTDC.
Retarded camshaft timing	A stretched timing chain or incorrect installation of a timing chain or belt can cause low power at low engine speeds. When the engine speed increases, however, the engine will perform correctly because the air–fuel mixture is better able to get into and out of the engine at a higher speed if the camshaft timing is retarded.
Exhaust system restriction	A restricted exhaust system can cause low power because some of the burned exhaust is still in the cylinder at the end of the exhaust stroke. This causes a less-than-ideal air–fuel mixture to be drawn into the cylinder on the next intake stroke. Check the following for possible restriction: • Exhaust system for collapsed or damaged sections. • Inspect and pound on the catalytic converter(s) and muffler(s) by hand to check for possible broken internal baffles. • Use a fitting that takes the place of the oxygen sensor and measure the amount of back pressure with the engine running using a pressure/ vacuum gauge. Most vehicle manufacturers specify a reading of less than 2.5 PSI at 2500 engine RPM.
Weak ignition coil or worn spark plugs	The ignition output of the coil should be capable of providing a high enough voltage to fire a spark tester that has a minimum required voltage of 25,000 volts (25 kV). A weak coil or an excessively worn spark plug can prevent the proper burning of the air–fuel mixture inside the cylinder. If the air–fuel mixture is not ignited, a lack of power results.
Restricted fuel filter, low fuel pump pressure, or contaminated gasoline	A lack of clean fuel at the proper pressure can cause the engine to produce less-than-normal power. A lack of fuel causes a lean air–fuel mixture that can also cause spark knock (ping or detonation), backfire, hesitation, and related problems.

Possible Cause	Reason
Excessive knock sensor activity	If an engine knock is detected, the computer retards the ignition timing to reduce or eliminate the spark knock. When the ignition timing is retarded, the engine produces less-than-normal power. Excessive spark knock activity can result from one or more of the following: • Too low octane-rated gasoline • Too lean air–fuel mixture • Excessive carbon buildup inside the combustion chamber • Engine mechanical or accessory drive belt faults causing a vibration or noise that is being sensed by the knock sensor as being caused by spark knock.
Engine mechanical faults	If the engine has a worn camshaft or low compression, it cannot produce normal power.
Accelerator pedal not opening the throttle all the way	If the mechanical linkage is out of adjustment or the interior carpet or mat prevents the throttle from opening all the way, a loss of power will be noticed. Have an assistant check that the throttle opens all the way when the accelerator pedal is depressed from inside the vehicle.

SURGES

A **surge** is a change in engine power under steady throttle conditions. A driver may feel a surge as if the vehicle was speeding up and slowing down with no change in the accelerator pedal. A lean air–fuel mixture is the most common cause of this condition.

Possible Cause	Reason
Lean air–fuel mixture	• A false rich condition caused by a contaminated oxygen sensor could cause the computer to reduce the amount of fuel delivered to the cylinders. • A restricted fuel line or fuel filter can cause a lean condition.
Excessive exhaust gas recirculation	A defective EGR valve or solenoid can cause an excessive amount of exhaust gas to enter the combustion chamber, resulting in a less-than-efficient mixture.

Possible Cause	Reason
Weak spark	A weak ignition coil, worn spark plugs, or defective spark plug wires can cause an ignition misfire, resulting in a lack of power that could be intermittent and cause a surge.
A clogged or defective fuel injector	Proper engine operation depends on each cylinder receiving the same amount of clean fuel at the proper pressure.

POOR FUEL ECONOMY

Poor **fuel economy** means lower-than-usual miles per gallon (or liters per 100 km in the metric system) as determined by an actual road test. The test procedure should include the following steps:

1. Fill the fuel tank (DO NOT overfill) and record the mileage (e.g. 52,168 miles).

2. Drive the vehicle normally for 100 to 200 miles or more.

3. Fill the tank again. Record the gallons of fuel used and the ending mileage (e.g., 10.6 gallons and 52,406 miles).

4. Calculate the miles per gallon:

$$52,406 - 52,168 = 238 \text{ miles}$$
$$238 \text{ miles} \div 10.6 \text{ gallons of fuel} = 22.4 \text{ MPG}$$

Fuel efficiency is determined by many factors including:

- Proper air–fuel mixture
- Proper ignition timing
- Proper gear ratio (this ensures as low a piston speed as practical while cruising in high gear)
- Mechanically sound engine including proper valve timing components
- Engine operating at its most efficient coolant temperature
- Proper operation of the exhaust emissions and fuel evaporative control systems
- Whether the vehicle has been operating with the A/C or defrost on all the time (This can reduce fuel economy.)

Possible Cause	Reason
The engine is not operating at the proper coolant temperature	• A defective or stuck-open thermostat can cause the engine to operate less efficiently. Using a lower-than-specified temperature thermostat can also reduce fuel economy. The temperature of the thermostat represents the opening temperature, and the thermostat is fully open 20°F higher than the opening temperature. For example: (1) a 180°F thermostat starts to open at 180°F and is fully open at 200°F. (2) A 195°F thermostat opens at 195°F and is fully open at 215°F. ● **SEE FIGURE 29–7** for an example of a stuck-open thermostat.

- Inoperative torque converter clutch (lockup torque converter). When a vehicle equipped with an automatic transmission/transaxle with a lockup converter reaches cruising speed, the torque converter clutch is applied, reducing the normal slippage that occurs inside a torque converter. When the torque converter clutch applies, the engine speed drops 150 to 250 RPM and increases fuel economy. Use a scan tool or tachometer to monitor the engine speed (RPM). The engine speed should drop as soon as the computer commands the torque converter clutch to apply.

- Check the evaporative emission control system for proper operation. A hole in the vacuum diaphragm can cause liquid gasoline to be drawn from the fuel tank directly into the engine, greatly reducing fuel economy. Use a hand-operated vacuum pump to check all charcoal canister vacuum diaphragms.

- Check the following engine-related systems: (1) ignition timing, (2) vacuum leaks, (3) dirty (clogged) air filter or air intake, and (4) exhaust system for restrictions.

FIGURE 29–7 This stuck-open thermostat caused the engine to fail to reach normal operating temperature. As a result, the fuel economy was much lower than normal and it failed a state vehicle exhaust emission test due to excessive hydrocarbons (HC).

RICH EXHAUST

A rich exhaust can be determined by a variety of methods, including:

- High CO exhaust readings (over 0.5%)
- Exhaust smell
- Poor fuel economy
- High O2S readings (consistently over 700 mV)
- More than –20% long-term fuel trim (LTFT)
- Black exhaust smoke

Although the oxygen sensor should provide a rich signal (O2S high) to the computer and the computer should restore proper operation, many faults in the engine management system can cause the engine to operate too rich, including:

1. Oxygen sensor skewed low or defective
2. False lean signals to the oxygen sensor caused by:
   - Ignition misfire (defective spark plug wires or fouled plugs)
   - Exhaust leak upstream of O2S such as a cracked exhaust manifold or leaking crossover pipe connections
3. Defective fuel-pressure regulator—a hole in the diaphragm can allow gasoline to flow from the fuel line directly into the intake manifold

LEAN EXHAUST

A lean exhaust can be determined by a variety of methods including:

- High O_2 exhaust readings (over 2%).
- Engine hesitates, bucks, jerks, or backfires through the air inlet.
- Low O2S reading (consistently less than 200 mV).
- High block lean numbers (more than 150 or more than a +20% long-term fuel-trim correction factor).

Although the oxygen sensor should provide a lean signal (O2S low) to the computer and the computer should restore proper operation, many faults in the engine management system can cause the engine to operate too lean, including:

1. Oxygen sensor skewed high or defective
2. False rich signal from O2S caused by silicon-contaminated or coated oxygen sensor

3. Large intake manifold or vacuum hose leak
4. Broken intake valve spring causing large internal vacuum (air) leak
5. Low fuel-pump pressure
6. Low voltage to the injectors
7. Poor computer ground causing improper opening of the injectors

TECH TIP

The Lighter Fluid Trick

A vacuum (air) leak is often difficult to find. A common technique is to use lighter fluid and carefully squirt along the intake manifold gasket and other possible sources of a leak. The small nozzle of the lighter fluid container makes it easy to find even a small leak. For hard-to-reach areas, attach a straw to the nozzle of the container to direct the lighter fluid. Propane also can be used effectively to locate vacuum leaks.

SYMPTOMS OF A DEFECTIVE COMPONENT

It is a good idea to know what **symptoms** a particular part or component will cause if defective. In this section, a component part or sensor is listed with typical symptoms the part or sensor could cause if defective.

NOTE: Many symptoms are similar for more than one component part or sensor. This section should *not* be used for diagnosis of an engine performance problem.

Engine Part or Sensor	Problem If Defective
Ignition coil	• No start or hard to start • Misfire under load • Intermittent missing/stalling • Cuts out at high engine speeds

Engine Part or Sensor	Problem If Defective
Manifold absolute pressure (MAP) sensor	• A MAP sensor is used to measure atmospheric pressure (altitude) when the ignition key is first turned on and to signal engine vacuum, which is a measure of engine load, to the computer. • Light load—less fuel, more ignition timing is possible. • Heavy load—more fuel, less ignition timing is possible. • Therefore, a fault in the MAP sensor can have a major effect on the air–fuel mixture supplied to the engine. • Some characteristic symptoms include: Rough idle and stalling Poor fuel economy Hesitates on acceleration Failed exhaust emissions tests for excessive HC and CO
Oxygen sensor	• Poor fuel economy, rough running, stalling, and excessive exhaust emissions (high HC and CO likely) can occur.

NOTE: The engine will usually operate correctly at or near wide-open throttle (WOT) because the computer ignores the oxygen sensor during these conditions and simply supplies the engine with a rich mixture needed for maximum acceleration.

	• Oxygen sensors usually fail low, meaning that the computer gases appear leaner than they actually are and, therefore, the computer will command a richer-than-needed amount of fuel. This is another reason why a defective oxygen sensor is not noticed during rapid acceleration.
Spark plug wires	• Engine misfire (especially in wet weather) • Loss of power

CAUTION: If a spark plug wire is defective, high voltage can cause a carbon track in the distributor cap or rotor (if equipped) or cause the ignition coil to become tracked (ruining the coil and requiring replacement).

Throttle-position (TP) sensor	• The TP sensor signals the computer regarding not only the position of the throttle, but also the rate of change (speed) at which the throttle is being depressed or released. The TP sensor is an important input device for the torque converter clutch (TCC). The TP voltage has to be greater than a certain percentage (usually about 10%) and less than a certain percentage (usually about 80%).

EXCESSIVE CO EXHAUST EMISSIONS

The chemical abbreviation CO stands for carbon monoxide, which is formed during the combustion process inside the engine by combining the carbon (C) from the gasoline (HC) and the oxygen (O) from the air. An efficient engine should produce very little CO if there is enough oxygen in the cylinder to create CO_2. However, if the air–fuel mixture is too rich, an excessive amount of CO emissions will be created. Therefore, CO is called the *rich indicator* exhaust gas.

Possible Cause	Reason
Clogged or restricted positive crankcase ventilation (PCV) system including the valve itself, the rubber hose, or the manifold vacuum port	Because about 20% of the air needed comes from the PCV system, a restriction in the system reduces the amount of air and increases the amount of CO produced by the engine.
Defective fuel-pressure regulator	A fuel-pressure regulator uses a spring-loaded rubber diaphragm to control fuel pressure. The strength of the spring determines the fuel pressure. On most port fuel-injected engines, a vacuum hose from the intake manifold attaches above the rubber diaphragm which changes the fuel pressure in relation to manifold vacuum. A hole in the rubber diaphragm can draw fuel from the fuel rail directly into the intake manifold. This extra fuel can cause the engine to run too rich and produce excessive CO exhaust emissions.
Too high fuel pressure	A restricted fuel return line or defective regulator can cause excessive fuel pressure. This excessive fuel pressure often results in excessively rich air–fuel mixture and excessive CO emissions.
Degraded catalytic converter	A degraded catalytic converter can cause the vehicle to fail an emission test for excessive CO emissions.

EXCESSIVE HC EXHAUST EMISSIONS

The chemical abbreviation for hydrocarbons (gasoline) is HC. Excessive HC exhaust emissions mean that the gasoline is not being properly burned inside the engine. Because the ignition system is used to ignite the air–fuel mixture, any malfunction in this system can result in higher-than-normal HC exhaust emissions.

Possible Cause	Reason
Ignition system faults	Allows unburned fuel to exit the engine. The entire ignition system should be inspected and tested, including: • Spark plugs. • Spark plug wires. • Distributor cap and rotor (if so equipped). ● **SEE FIGURE 29–8.** • Ignition timing.
Excessively lean air–fuel mixture	A very lean air–fuel mixture is often too lean to ignite. As a result, this unburned fuel is pushed out of the engine during the exhaust stroke. This is called a **lean misfire**.
Thermostat inoperative (stuck open) or opening temperature too low	An engine operating colder than normal causes a greater-than-normal amount of fuel to condense on the cylinder walls. Because liquid fuel cannot burn without oxygen, this layer of unburned fuel (HC) is pushed out of the exhaust system by the piston on the exhaust stroke. Using the specified-temperature thermostat reduces the amount of this quenched fuel, reduces HC emissions, and improves fuel economy.
Degraded catalytic converter	A degraded catalytic converter can cause a vehicle to fail an emission test for excessive HC emissions.

EXCESSIVE NO_X EXHAUST EMISSIONS

The chemical abbreviation for oxides of nitrogen is NO_X. Both nitrogen (N) and oxygen (O_2) are normally part of our atmosphere. It requires heat and/or pressure to combine them to form oxides of nitrogen. Excessive NO_X emissions, therefore, mean that the engine combustion chamber temperatures are too high or the chamber has excessive compression.

FIGURE 29–8 This corroded coil terminal on a waste spark-type ignition system caused a random misfire DTC to set (P0300) and it affected both cylinders and not just the one than had the corroded terminal.

FIGURE 29–9 This badly eroded water (coolant) pump caused the engine to overheat.

Possible Cause	Reason
Inoperative or restricted flow EGR valve	The purpose and function of the exhaust gas recirculation system are to introduce inert burned exhaust gases into the combustion chamber to reduce the peak temperatures to reduce NO_X emissions.
Cooling system fault such as low coolant level, clogged radiator, restricted air flow through the radiator	Any fault in the cooling system can cause an increase in engine operating temperatures, and therefore cause the engine to create excessive NO_X emissions. ● **SEE FIGURE 29–9.**

Possible Cause	Reason
Too far advanced ignition timing	Advanced ignition timing causes the spark to occur too soon while the piston is coming up on the compression stroke. As a result, the temperature and pressures inside the combustion chamber are increased, which increases the formation of NO_x.
Too low octane-rated fuel	Using a gasoline with an octane rating lower than specified by the vehicle manufacturer can cause the engine to spark knock (ping).
	Spark knock or ping is caused by a secondary explosion inside the combustion chamber, which causes a rapid pressure and temperature rise to occur. Therefore, if an engine is spark knocking (pinging), it is also emitting an excessive amount of NO_x.
Degraded catalytic converter	A degraded catalytic converter can cause a vehicle to fail an emission test for excessive NO_x emissions.

SUMMARY

1. A lean air–fuel mixture is the usual cause of hesitation or stumble during acceleration.
2. A vacuum leak and lean air–fuel mixture can cause a rough idle or stalling.
3. Spark knock (ping or detonation) is often caused by a too lean air–fuel mixture, or if the engine operating temperature is too high.
4. A hard-start problem is often due to a lack of fuel.
5. A slowly cranking engine is usually due to low battery voltage. A no-crank condition is usually due to an open circuit in the cranking circuit.
6. Poor fuel economy is usually due to an excessively rich air–fuel mixture.
7. A lean air–fuel mixture is usually due to a vacuum leak.
8. A rich air–fuel mixture can be caused by a defective oxygen sensor or the engine getting fuel from another source not controlled by the computer or fuel system.

REVIEW QUESTIONS

1. What are the five engine performance faults that can occur if a vacuum (air) leak occurs?
2. What symptom(s) may occur if the EGR valve is inoperative (never opens)?
3. What four items that can cause excessive CO exhaust emissions?
4. What four items that can cause excessive HC exhaust emissions?
5. What four items that can cause excessive NO_x exhaust emissions?

1. Technician A says that a partially stuck-open EGR valve can cause ping (spark knock) during wide-open throttle engine operation. Technician B says that the partially stuck-open EGR valve could cause the engine to stall while operating at idle speed. Which technician is correct?
   a. Technician A only
   b. Technician B only
   c. Both Technicians A and B
   d. Neither Technician A nor B

2. Technician A says that a too rich air–fuel mixture can be caused by a defective fuel-pressure regulator. Technician B says that a defective pressure regulator can cause a too lean air–fuel mixture. Which technician is correct?
   a. Technician A only
   b. Technician B only
   c. Both Technicians A and B
   d. Neither Technician A nor B

3. Technician A says that excessive NO_x exhaust emissions can be due to a defective PCV valve. Technician B says that a too lean air–fuel mixture can cause excessive NO_x exhaust emissions. Which technician is correct?
   a. Technician A only
   b. Technician B only
   c. Both Technicians A and B
   d. Neither Technician A nor B

4. Technician A says a defective TP sensor can cause the engine to hesitate during acceleration. Technician B says that dirty throttle plate(s) on a port-injected engine could cause a hesitation during acceleration. Which technician is correct?
   a. Technician A only
   b. Technician B only
   c. Both Technicians A and B
   d. Neither Technician A nor B

5. Technician A says that defective spark plug wires can cause the engine to misfire. Technician B says a fouled spark plug can cause the engine to misfire. Which technician is correct?
   a. Technician A only
   b. Technician B only
   c. Both Technicians A and B
   d. Neither Technician A nor B

6. Technician A says a rough idle on a fuel-injected engine can be caused by dirty throttle plates. Technician B says the wrong PCV valve could cause the engine to idle roughly. Which technician is correct?
   a. Technician A only
   b. Technician B only
   c. Both Technicians A and B
   d. Neither Technician A nor B

7. Technician A says that spark knock (ping or detonation) can be caused by a lean air–fuel mixture. Technician B says an inoperative cooling fan could cause the engine to spark knock. Which technician is correct?
   a. Technician A only
   b. Technician B only
   c. Both Technicians A and B
   d. Neither Technician A nor B

8. Technician A says that a stretched (worn) timing chain can cause the engine to lack power at slow speeds. Technician B says a clogged exhaust system can cause the engine to lack power at high speeds. Which technician is correct?
   a. Technician A only
   b. Technician B only
   c. Both Technicians A and B
   d. Neither Technician A nor B

9. Technician A says that poor fuel economy can be caused by a defective thermostat. Technician B says a defective evaporative charcoal canister can cause poor or reduced fuel economy. Which technician is correct?
   a. Technician A only
   b. Technician B only
   c. Both Technicians A and B
   d. Neither Technician A nor B

10. Which of the following symptoms could be caused by a failing ignition coil?
    a. Misfire under a load
    b. Intermittent stalling
    c. No start condition
    d. Any of the above

appendix 1
SAMPLE ADVANCED ENGINE PERFORMANCE (L1) CERTIFICATION-TYPE TEST

Content Area	Questions in Test	Percentage of Test (%)
A. General Powertrain Diagnosis	6	12
B. Computerized Powertrain Controls Diagnosis (including OBD II)	14	28
C. Ignition System Diagnosis	6	12
D. Fuel Systems and Air Induction Systems Diagnosis	7	14
E. Emission Control Systems Diagnosis	9	18
F. I/M Failure Diagnosis	8	16
Total	50	100

A. General Powertrain Diagnosis (6 questions)

1. A port fuel-injected OBD I-equipped V-6 engine with a MAF sensor has a rough idle and no diagnostic trouble codes (DTCs). Technician A says that the wrong PCV valve could have been installed during a previous service. Technician B says that a missing oil filler cap could be the cause. Which technician is correct?
   a. Technician A only
   b. Technician B only
   c. Both Technicians A and B
   d. Neither Technician A nor B

2. A P0300 (random misfire) DTC is being diagnosed. What service information is needed to be able to perform an effective diagnosis?
   a. Spark plug wire resistance specifications
   b. VIN
   c. Engine code
   d. All of the above

3. Which of the following data stream information is the least likely to be helpful during the diagnosis of a hard starting problem?
   a. O2S   c. CMP
   b. ECT   d. CKP

4. A vehicle failed a loaded I/M emission test for excessive NO_x and experienced spark knock (also called ping or detonation) during acceleration. Which is the least likely cause?
   a. Partially clogged radiator
   b. Lean air–fuel mixture
   c. Partially clogged catalytic converter
   d. Carbon deposits in the cylinder

5. The owner of a sport utility vehicle installed larger wheels and tires than specified. Technician A says that the vehicle will likely accelerate slower than before the change. Technician B says that the fuel economy (gas mileage) will be lower than before the change. Which technician is correct?
   a. Technician A only
   b. Technician B only
   c. Both Technicians A and B
   d. Neither Technician A nor B

6. A restricted exhaust system could be best diagnosed by which test?
   a. Vacuum test at idle
   b. Vacuum at 2500 RPM
   c. Cylinder leak down rate
   d. Running compression test

B. Computerized Powertrain Controls Diagnosis (including OBD II) (14 Questions)

7. Which item listed is not needed to know for an accurate diagnosis of an engine performance concern?
   a. Gasoline grade being used
   b. When and where the problem occurs
   c. The brand of oil used
   d. Stored or pending DTCs

8. The following scan data was retrieved from a vehicle that had two stored DTCs for low O2S voltage (bank #1 and bank #2). What is the most likely cause based on the following scan tool data?

   HO2S1 = 0.093 to 0.110 V   ECT = 212 degrees F
   HO2S2 = 0.004 to 0.209 V   (100 degrees C)
   STFT = +2%   IAT = 72 degrees F
   LTFT = +24%   (22 degrees C)
   MAF = 2.7 g/s   MAP = 1.41 V

   a. A defective fuel pump
   b. A partially clogged PCV valve or hose
   c. Partially clogged EGR ports
   d. An EVAP purge valve stuck open

9. A P0740 (torque converter clutch system problem) DTC is set. The freeze frame indicated the following parameters were present when the DTC was set. What is the most likely cause?

   Vehicle speed = 50 mph (80 km/h)
   ECT = 208°F (98°C)
   IAT = 75°F (24°C)
   TCC = on

EGR = 43%
Injector pulse width = 8.3 ms
IAC = 67 counts
TP = 1.97 V
Brake switch = off
Transmission gear = 4th (OD)
MAP = 2.48 V
Purge duty cycle = 28%

  a. A worn (defective) torque converter clutch
  b. A defective or misadjusted TP sensor
  c. A defective thermostat
  d. Excessive EGR flow

10. Which scan tool parameter is the most important to check when diagnosing a no-start condition?
  a. ECT
  b. CKP
  c. IAT
  d. HO2S

11. Which scan tool parameter is the most important to check when diagnosing a random misfire DTC (P0300)?
  a. HO2S
  b. Misfire counter
  c. MAF
  d. MAP

12. An engine lacks power and there are no stored DTCs. Which of the following scan tool readings at idle is the most likely to indicate the cause?
  a. HO2S1 = 0.088 to 0.917 V
  b. MAF = 3.8 g/s
  c. Injector pulse width = 3.3 ms
  d. MAP = 2.01 V

13. A technician is using a DMM set to read DC volts and attaches one test lead to the negative (–) post of the battery and the other lead to the back probed ground terminal of the TP sensor with the key on, engine off. The meter reads 0.55 volt. What condition does this reading indicate?
  a. TP sensor signal voltage reading
  b. Excessive computer ground voltage drop
  c. A discharged battery
  d. Reference voltage from the PCM

14. A fuel pump circuit is being diagnosed. The battery voltage is 12.6 volts but the voltage at the connector near the pump reads 12.4 volts. What is the most likely condition?
  a. A defective fuel pump relay
  b. Corrosion at the connector or wiring
  c. A defective fuel pump
  d. This is a normal reading

15. A P0401 DTC (exhaust gas recirculation flow insufficient detected) is being diagnosed using a bidirectional scan tool. The technician commands the EGR valve 100% on and the engine speed drops and starts to idle roughly but does not stall. Technician A says that this test shows that the EGR system is functioning and the problem must be with the EGR flow detection sensor (MAP or O2S) circuits. Technician B says that the DTC is likely a false code and should be erased and the vehicle driven to see if the code sets again. Which technician is correct?
  a. Technician A only
  b. Technician B only
  c. Both Technicians A and B
  d. Neither Technician A nor B

16. A high O2S voltage could be due to _____.
  a. a rich exhaust
  b. a lean exhaust
  c. a defective spark plug wire
  d. Both a and c

17. A low O2S voltage could be due to _____.
  a. a rich exhaust
  b. a lean exhaust
  c. a defective spark plug wire
  d. Both b and c

18. A technician is working on a vehicle equipped with a port fuel injection. After connecting the vehicle to a scan tool, the technician finds it has a long-term fuel trim of +20%. Technician A says that an exhaust leak in front of the oxygen sensor could cause this. Technician B says that a defective plug wire could cause this. Which technician is correct?
  a. Technician A only
  b. Technician B only
  c. Both Technicians A and B
  d. Neither Technician A nor B

19. A fuel-injected engine has a long-term fuel trim of +19% at idle and a long-term fuel trim of 0% at 2500 RPM. The most likely cause is:
  a. A small vacuum leak
  b. A defective MAF
  c. A defective fuel pressure regulator
  d. A faulty IAC

20. The O2S is being tested on a fuel-injected 4-cylinder engine. The reading is relatively steady ranging from 0.388 to 0.460 volt. Adding propane increases the voltage to 0.687 volt and creating a vacuum leak lowers the voltage to 0.312 volt. Technician A says the O2S may be defective. Technician B says there could be a crack in the exhaust manifold allowing outside air to enter the exhaust system upstream from the O2S. Which technician is correct?
  a. Technician A only
  b. Technician B only
  c. Both Technicians A and B
  d. Neither Technician A nor B

C. Ignition System Diagnosis (6 Questions)

21. An engine misfire is being diagnosed. One spark plug was discovered to be excessively worn and snow white while the others appear slightly worn and normal color. What is the most likely cause?
  a. A vacuum leak
  b. A loose spark plug
  c. A defective fuel pressure regulator
  d. A partially stuck open EGR valve

22. Where is the spark plug gap specification found on most vehicles?
  a. On the underhood decal
  b. In the owner's manual
  c. In the service manual (information)
  d. All of the above

23. An engine miss is being diagnosed on an engine equipped with a waste-spark-type electronic ignition (EI). Each plug wire is removed from the spark plug and a spark tester is installed one at a time, and then the engine is started. All but one of the cylinders fires the spark tester. Technician A says that the ignition module is the most likely cause. Technician B says that the coil is the most likely cause. Which technician is correct?
   a. Technician A only
   b. Technician B only
   c. Both Technicians A and B
   d. Neither Technician A nor B

24. The spark plug wires on a waste-spark-type electronic ignition were accidentally installed on the wrong terminal of the correct coil. The wire going to cylinder number 3, for example, was accidentally placed on the coil terminal to cylinder number 6 on a V-6 engine. Which is the most likely result?
   a. No change in engine operation will be noticed.
   b. The engine will miss and may set a misfire DTC.
   c. The engine will spark knock (ping) during acceleration.
   d. The engine will run smoothly, but will be sluggish and lack power.

Questions 25 and 26 require the use of the Composite Vehicle Type 4 Reference Booklet available for free at www.ASE.com

25. The MIL is flashing indicating a severe misfire has been detected by the PCM. Technician A says that a cracked spark plug could be the cause. Technician B says that an open at terminal "b" of ignition coil 6 could be the cause. Which technician is correct?
   a. Technician A only
   b. Technician B only
   c. Both Technicians A and B
   d. Neither Technician A nor B

26. A no-start condition is being diagnosed. The engine cranks normally but does not start. Technician A says a short-to-ground at terminal "b" of the camshaft position sensor could be the cause. Technician B says that a blown #3 fuse could be the cause. Which technician is correct?
   a. Technician A only
   b. Technician B only
   c. Both Technicians A and B
   d. Neither Technician A nor B

D. Fuel Systems and Air Induction Systems Diagnosis (7 Questions)

27. During routine service, it was noticed that the air filter was missing. Which other component could directly affect the engine operation as a result of the missing filter?
   a. MAF sensor
   b. MAP sensor
   c. Oxygen sensor
   d. IAT sensor

28. A lack of power is being diagnosed. The scan tool data (PID) at engine idle includes:

   ECT = 195°F
   IAT = 78°F
   IAC = 20
   MAF = 4.4 g/s
   MAP = 1.1 V
   Injector pulse width = 4.5 ms
   RPM = 750
   Vehicle speed = 0 mph
   HO2SI = 198 to 618 mV
   HO2S2 = 50 to 571 mV

   Which is the most likely fault?
   a. Contaminated oxygen sensors
   b. A clogged fuel filter or bad fuel pump
   c. A bad thermostat
   d. A stuck IAC

29. Long-term fuel trim is +2% at idle speed and +27% at 2500 RPM. Which is the most likely cause?
   a. A defective fuel pressure regulator
   b. An intake manifold leak
   c. A weak fuel pump
   d. A partially clogged catalytic converter

30. A P0132 (O2S circuit high voltage, bank 1 sensor 1) on a four-cylinder engine is being diagnosed. Technician A says that an intake manifold gasket leak (vacuum leak) could be the cause. Technician B says that a defective fuel pressure regulator could be the cause. Which technician is correct?
   a. Technician A only
   b. Technician B only
   c. Both Technicians A and B
   d. Neither Technician A nor B

31. A DTC P0101 (Mass or volume airflow circuit range or performance problem) is being diagnosed. Technician A says that a loose connection between the MAF sensor and the throttle body could be the cause. Technician B says the MAF sensor may be defective. Which technician is correct?
   a. Technician A only
   b. Technician B only
   c. Both Technicians A and B
   d. Neither Technician A nor B

32. A technician is working on an OBD-II V-8 engine equipped with port fuel injection. After connecting the vehicle to a scan tool, the technician finds it has a long-term fuel trim of +20% on bank 1. Bank 2 shows 0% fuel trim. Technician A says that an exhaust leak in front of the oxygen sensor on bank 1 could cause this. Technician B says that a defective plug wire on a cylinder on bank 2 could cause this. Which technician is correct?
   a. Technician A only
   b. Technician B only
   c. Both Technicians A and B
   d. Neither Technician A nor B

33. A fuel-injected engine has a long-term fuel trim of +18% at idle and a long-term fuel trim of 0% at 2500 RPM. The most likely cause is _____.
   a. a small vacuum leak
   b. a defective MAF
   c. a defective fuel pressure regulator
   d. a faulty IAC

D. Emission Control Systems Diagnosis (9 Questions)

34. A vehicle has had repeated EGR valve transducer failures. What is the most likely cause?
  a. A clogged catalytic converter
  b. A vacuum leak at the intake manifold gasket
  c. A partially clogged fuel injector
  d. Clogged EGR ports

35. The following scan data has been retrieved from a vehicle with a driveability problem.

LTFT = +2% @ idle
LTFT = +22% @ 2500 RPM
P0171 = bank 1 too lean
P0174 = bank 2 too lean

Which system is the most likely to be the cause of the problem?
  a. A fault in the exhaust system
  b. A fault in the induction system
  c. A fault in the emission control system
  d. A fault in the fuel delivery system

36. A vehicle fails an enhanced I/M test for excessive NO_x emissions. Technician A says that an excessively lean air–fuel mixture being supplied to the engine could be the cause. Technician B says that a defective cooling fan could be the cause. Which technician is correct?
  a. Technician A only
  b. Technician B only
  c. Both Technicians A and B
  d. Neither Technician A nor B

37. A vehicle fails for excessive NO_x emissions during an enhanced I/M test. Technician A says that a clogged EGR port(s) could be the cause. Technician B says that a partially clogged radiator could be the cause. Which technician is correct?
  a. Technician A only
  b. Technician B only
  c. Both Technicians A and B
  d. Neither Technician A nor B

38. A vehicle is being repaired for excessive NO_x emissions. Technician A says that a partially clogged PCV valve or hose could be the cause. Technician B says that a defective spark plug wire or worn spark plug could be the cause. Which technician is correct?
  a. Technician A only
  b. Technician B only
  c. Both Technicians A and B
  d. Neither Technician A nor B

39. A DTC P0442 evaporative emission control system leak is detected. Which is the most likely cause?
  a. A loose gas cap
  b. A clogged PCV hose
  c. A restricted carbon canister purge line
  d. A defective fuel tank pressure sensor

40. A vehicle is being diagnosed for failing an enhanced I/M emission test for excessive CO exhaust emissions. Which is the most likely cause?
  a. A clogged EVAP hose
  b. A lack of proper preconditioning
  c. A defective spark plug wire
  d. An inoperative EGR valve

41. Technician A says the catalytic converter must be replaced if it rattles when tapped. Technician B says a catalytic converter can be defective and not be working yet not be clogged. Which technician is correct?
  a. Technician A only
  b. Technician B only
  c. Both Technicians A and B
  d. Neither Technician A nor B

42. Used catalytic converters must be kept for possible inspection by the EPA for how long?
  a. 30 days
  b. 60 days
  c. 90 days
  d. 6 months

E. I/M Failure Diagnosis (8 Questions)

43. A vehicle fails a no-load I/M test for high CO. Technician A says that a hole in the exhaust downstream from the oxygen sensor could be the cause. Technician B says a defective (restricted) injector could be the cause. Which technician is correct?
  a. Technician A only
  b. Technician B only
  c. Both Technicians A and B
  d. Neither Technician A nor B

44. A fuel-injected vehicle is tested on a 4-gas exhaust analyzer.

HC = 102 PPM, CO = 0.3%, O2 = 6.3%, CO2 = 6.1%

Technician A says that everything is OK because the O2 and CO2 readings are about equal. Technician B says that the engine is running lean. Which technician is correct?
  a. Technician A only
  b. Technician B only
  c. Both Technicians A and B
  d. Neither Technician A nor B

45. A vacuum leak occurs when a small vacuum hose falls off a V-8 engine with port fuel injection. The owner then has the vehicle tested for exhaust emissions using a load-mode I/M test procedure. The most likely result will be _____.
  a. high HC reading
  b. normal readings
  c. high O2 reading
  d. high CO reading

46. A vehicle fails a load-mode I/M exhaust emission test for NO_x. Technician A says that decarbonization may help. Technician B says that the EGR passages may need to be cleaned. Which technician is correct?
  a. Technician A only
  b. Technician B only
  c. Both Technicians A and B
  d. Neither Technician A nor B

47. HC and CO_2 levels are high and CO and O_2 levels are low during a no-load I/M test. What is the most likely cause?
  a. Too rich
  b. A fault in the secondary ignition system
  c. Stuck closed EGR valve
  d. Lean misfire

48. Two technicians are discussing excessive HC exhaust emissions. Technician A says that a stuck open thermostat could be the cause. Technician B says that a lean misfire could be the cause. Which technician is correct?
   a. Technician A only
   b. Technician B only
   c. Both Technicians A and B
   d. Neither Technician A nor B

49. Technician A says an engine with the following test results is operating too rich. Technician B says the engine is running too lean causing a lean misfire. Which technician is correct?

   $HC = 287\,PPM, CO2 = 8.1\%, CO = 2.6\%,$
   $O2 = 0.1\%$

   a. Technician A only
   b. Technician B only
   c. Both Technicians A and B
   d. Neither Technician A nor B

50. Technician A says an engine with the following test results is operating too rich. Technician B says the engine is running too lean, causing a lean misfire. Which technician is correct?

   $HC = 13\,PPM, CO2 = 16.3\%, CO = 0.0\%, O2 = 0\%$

   a. Technician A only
   b. Technician B only
   c. Both Technicians A and B
   d. Neither Technician A nor B

ANSWERS

A. General Powertrain Diagnosis (6 Questions)

1. c	4. c
2. d	5. c
3. a	6. b

B. Computerized Powertrain Controls Diagnosis (including OBD II) (14 Questions)

7. c	14. d
8. a	15. d
9. a	16. a
10. b	17. d
11. b	18. c
12. d	19. a
13. b	20. a

C. Ignition System Diagnosis (6 Questions)

21. b	24. a
22. d	25. c
23. b	26. b

D. Fuel Systems and Air Induction Systems Diagnosis (7 Questions)

27. a	31. c
28. b	32. a
29. c	33. a
30. d	

E. Emission Control Systems Diagnosis (9 Questions)

34. a	39. a
35. d	40. b
36. c	41. c
37. c	42. b
38. d	

F. I/M Failure Diagnosis (8 Questions)

43. a	47. b
44. b	48. c
45. b	49. a
46. c	50. d

MLR—Maintenance & Light Repair
AST—Auto Service Technology (Includes MLR)
MAST—Master Auto Service Technology (Includes MLR and AST)

ENGINE PERFORMANCE (A8)

TASK	PRIORITY	MLR	AST	MAST	TEXT PAGE #	TASK PAGE #
A. GENERAL: ENGINE DIAGNOSIS						
1. Identify and interpret engine performance concerns; determine needed action.	P-1		✔	✔	2–8; 377–379	1
2. Research vehicle service information including, vehicle service history, service precautions, and technical service bulletins.	P-1	✔	✔	✔	3–7; 379–381	3–6, 24, 26, 35, 37, 38, 51, 52, 85, 95, 98,106
3. Diagnose abnormal engine noises or vibration concerns; determine needed action.	P-3		✔	✔	103–104	4, 5, 24
4. Diagnose the cause of excessive oil consumption, coolant consumption, unusual exhaust color, odor, and sound; determine needed action.	P-2		✔	✔	3–6; 90–91; 118–122; 132; 336-337	3, 28
5. Perform engine absolute manifold pressure tests (vacuum/boost); determine needed action.	P-1		✔	✔	128–131	31
6. Perform cylinder power balance test; determine needed action.	P-1		✔	✔	123–125	29
7. Perform cylinder cranking and running compression tests; determine needed action.	P-1		✔	✔	125–128	33
8. Perform cylinder leakage test; determine needed action.	P-1		✔	✔	128–129	34
9. Diagnose engine mechanical, electrical, electronic, fuel, and ignition concerns; determine needed action.	P-2		✔	✔	222–228	50
10. Verify engine operating temperature; determine needed action.	P-1		✔	✔	90	66
11. Verify correct camshaft timing including engines equipped with variable valve timing systems (VVT).	P-1	✔	✔	✔	92–93; 111–114	18

TASK	PRIORITY	MLR	AST	MAST	TEXT PAGE #	TASK PAGE #
B. COMPUTERIZED CONTROLS DIAGNOSIS AND REPAIR						
1. Retrieve and record diagnostic trouble codes (DTC), OBD monitor status, and freeze frame data; clear codes when applicable.	P-1		✔	✔	12–16; 157–164	99
2. Access and use service information to perform step-by-step (troubleshooting) diagnosis.	P-1		✔	✔	9–11; 19	2, 25, 36, 42, 47
3. Perform active tests of actuators using a scan tool; determine needed action.	P-1		✔	✔	16-17	25
4. Describe the use of OBD monitors for repair verification	P-1	✔	✔	✔	19–20; 160–164; 168-173	48
5. Diagnose the causes of emissions or drivability concerns with stored or active diagnostic trouble codes (DTC); obtain, graph, and interpret scan tool data.	P-1		✔	✔	12–16; 156–164	2, 39–41
6. Diagnose emissions or drivability concerns without stored diagnostic trouble codes; determine needed action.	P-1			✔	17–19; 168–173; 288–296	43–46, 48, 88,100
7. Inspect and test computerized engine control system sensors, powertrain/engine control module (PCM/ECM), actuators, and circuits using a graphing multimeter (GMM)/digital storage oscilloscope (DSO); perform needed action.	P-2			✔	50–57; 68–73; 232–236; 242–243; 251–252; 255–257; 274–279; 417–419	14, 63–84, 85–87
8. Diagnose drivability and emissions problems resulting from malfunctions of interrelated systems (cruise control, security alarms, suspension controls, traction controls, HVAC, automatic transmissions, non-OEM installed accessories, or similar systems); determine needed action.	P-2			✔	157–164; 176–177; 369–371	49, 85, 105
C. IGNITION SYSTEM DIAGNOSIS AND REPAIR						
1. Diagnose (troubleshoot) ignition system related problems such as no-starting, hard starting, engine misfire, poor drivability, spark knock, power loss, poor mileage, and emissions concerns; determine needed action.	P-2		✔	✔	176–184; 213–221	50, 54–57
2. Inspect and test crankshaft and camshaft position sensor(s); determine needed action.	P-1		✔	✔	215–216	60, 61
3. Inspect, test, and/or replace ignition control module, powertrain/engine control module; reprogram/initialize as needed.	P-3		✔	✔	214–215	51, 62
4. Remove and replace spark plugs; inspect secondary ignition components for wear and damage.	P-1	✔	✔	✔	219–221	58, 59
D. FUEL, AIR INDUCTION, AND EXHAUST SYSTEMS DIAGNOSIS AND REPAIR						
1. Diagnose (troubleshoot) hot or cold no-starting, hard starting, poor drivability, incorrect idle speed, poor idle, flooding, hesitation, surging, engine misfire, power loss, stalling, poor mileage, dieseling, and emissions problems; determine needed action.	P-2			✔	176–184; 189–199; 263–266; 288–296	49, 101
2. Check fuel for contaminants; determine needed action.	P-2		✔	✔	29–30	7

TASK	PRIORITY	MLR	AST	MAST	TEXT PAGE #	TASK PAGE #
3. Inspect and test fuel pumps and pump control systems for pressure, regulation, and volume; perform needed action.	P-1		✔	✔	308–314	89–93
4. Replace fuel filter(s) where applicable.	P-2	✔	✔	✔	308	94
5. Inspect, service, or replace air filters, filter housings, and intake duct work.	P-1	✔	✔	✔	256–257; 341–342; 349–352	97
6. Inspect throttle body, air induction system, intake manifold and gaskets for vacuum leaks and/or unmetered air.	P-2		✔	✔	91–92; 263–266	19, 97
7. Inspect test and/or replace fuel injectors.	P-2		✔	✔	337; 345–349	102–104
8. Verify idle control operation.	P-1		✔	✔	263–266	96
9. Inspect integrity of the exhaust manifold, exhaust pipes, muffler(s), catalytic converter(s), resonator(s), tail pipe(s), and heat shields; perform needed action.	P-1	✔	✔	✔	377	
10. Inspect condition of exhaust system hangers, brackets, clamps, and heat shields; determine needed action.	P-1	✔	✔	✔		
11. Perform exhaust system back-pressure test; determine needed action.	P-2			✔	130–132; 400–401	110
12. Check and refill diesel exhaust fluid (DEF).	P-2	✔	✔	✔		
13. Test the operation of turbocharger/supercharger systems; determine needed action.	P-2			✔	85–86	

E. EMISSIONS CONTROL SYSTEMS DIAGNOSIS AND REPAIR

TASK	PRIORITY	MLR	AST	MAST	TEXT PAGE #	TASK PAGE #
1. Diagnose oil leaks, emissions, and drivability concerns caused by the positive crankcase ventilation (PCV) system; determine needed action.	P-3		✔	✔	391–395	109, 111
2. Inspect, test, service and/or replace positive crankcase ventilation (PCV) filter/breather, valve, tubes, orifices, and hoses; perform needed action.	P-2	✔	✔	✔	391–395	111
3. Diagnose emissions and drivability concerns caused by the exhaust gas recirculation (EGR) system; inspect, and test, service and/or replace electrical/electronic sensors, controls, and wiring of exhaust gas recirculation (EGR) systems tubing, exhaust passages, vacuum/pressure controls, filters and hoses of exhaust gas recirculation (EGR) systems; determine needed action.	P-2		✔	✔	388–391	109, 112–114
4. Diagnose emissions and drivability concerns caused by the components and circuits of air injection systems; inspect, test, repair, and/or replace electrical/electronically-operated components and circuits of secondary air injection systems; determine needed action.	P-2		✔	✔	395–397	116
5. Diagnose emissions and drivability concerns caused by the evaporative emissions control (EVAP) system; determine needed action.	P-2			✔	407–410	117, 118
6. Diagnose emission and drivability concerns caused by catalytic converter system; determine needed action.	P-2			✔	397–403	115
7. Interpret diagnostic trouble codes (DTCs) and scan tool data related to the emissions control systems; determine needed action	P-3		✔	✔	391; 395; 397; 403; 410	109

ENGLISH GLOSSARY

AC coupling   A signal that passes the AC signal component to the meter, but blocks the DC component. Useful to observe an AC signal that is normally riding on a DC signal; for example, charging ripple.

AC/DC clamp-on DMM   A type of meter that has a clamp that is placed around the wire to measure current.

Accelerator pedal position (APP) sensor   A sensor that is used to monitor the position and rate of change of the accelerator pedal.

Accumulator   A temporary location for fluid under pressure.

Active fuel management (AFM)   A term used by General Motors to describe their variable displacement system. Previously called displacement on demand.

Actuator   An electromechanical device that performs mechanical movement as commanded by a controller.

Adaptive control   The PCM can learn how long a shift takes to complete and will command that the start the shift occurs sooner to allow time for the clutch to be fully engaged. The adjustment is called *adaptive learning*.

Adaptive learning   See Adaptive control

Adsorption   Attaches the fuel vapor molecules to the carbon surface.

AFV   Alternative fuel vehicle.

AIR   stands for air-injection reaction. Therefore, an AIR pump does pump air in a secondary air-injection system.

Air-fuel ratio   The ratio of air to fuel in an intake charge as measured by weight.

Air–fuel ratio sensor   A term used to describe a wide-band oxygen sensor.

Air reference chamber   This electrode is exposed to outside (ambient) air and is the signal electrode, also called the reference electrode or ambient air electrode.

AKI   Anti-knock index. The octane rating posted on a gas pump, which is the average of the RON and MON octane ratings.

Alpha   Alpha is the air-fuel ratio parameter displayed on Nissan/Infiniti vehicles.

100 = 14.7:1

Higher than 100 = PCM is adding fuel

Lower than 100 = PCM is subtracting fuel

Alpha is used as a single parameter that replaces both long-term fuel trim and short-term fuel trim.

Alternator   An electric generator that produces alternating current; also called an AC generator.

Ambient air electrode   This electrode is exposed to outside (ambient) air and is the signal electrode, also called the reference electrode or ambient air electrode.

Ambient side electrode   This electrode is exposed to outside (ambient) air and is the signal electrode, also called the reference electrode or ambient air electrode.

Analog-to-digital (AD) converter   An electronic circuit that converts analog signals into digital signals that can then be used by a computer.

Anhydrous ethanol   Ethanol that has no water content.

API gravity   An arbitrary scale expressing the gravity or density of liquid petroleum products devised jointly by the American Petroleum Institute and the National Bureau of Standards.

ASM   Acceleration simulation mode.

ASM 25/25 test   Places a 25% load on the vehicle while it is driven at a steady 25 mph. This represents 25% of the load required to simulate the FTP acceleration rate of 3.3 mph/sec.

ASM 50/15 test   Places a load of 50% on the vehicle at a steady 15 mph. This load represents 50% of the horsepower required to simulate the FTP acceleration rate of 3.3 mph/sec.

ASTM   American Society for Testing Materials.

B5   A blend of 5% biodiesel with 95% petroleum diesel.

B20   A blend of 20% biodiesel with 80% petroleum diesel.

Backfire   A backfire is the burning of fuel in the intake manifold or in the exhaust system. It is accompanied by a loud popping noise.

Back pressure   The exhaust system's resistance to flow. Measured in pounds per square inch (PSI).

Baffle   A plate or shield used to direct the flow of a liquid or gas.

Barometric manifold absolute pressure (BMAP) sensor   A sensor that measures both the barometric pressure and the absolute pressure in the intake manifold.

BARO sensor   A sensor used to measure barometric pressure.

Base pulse width   The base pulse width is the injector pulse width that is calculated by the PCM using information from sensors before the oxygen sensor (s) is operating and supplying air-fuel ratio information.

Battery   A chemical device that produces a voltage created by two dissimilar metals submerged in an electrolyte.

Battery electrical drain test   A test to determine if a component or circuit is draining the battery.

Bias voltage   In electrical terms, bias is the voltage applied to a device or component to establish the reference point for operation.

Binary   A computer system that uses a series of zeros and ones to represent to information.

Biodiesel   A renewable fuel manufactured from vegetable oils, animal fats, or recycled restaurant grease.

Biomass   Nonedible farm products, such as corn stalks, cereal straws, and plant wastes from industrial processes, such as sawdust and paper pulp used in making ethanol.

Blowby   Combustion gases that leak past the piston rings into the crankcase during the compression and combustion strokes of the engine.

Bore   The inside diameter of the cylinder in an engine.

Bottom dead center (BDC)   When the piston is at the bottom of the stroke.

Brake on/off (BOO)   Another name for the brake switch.

Break-out box (BOB)   An electrical tester that connects to a connector or controller and allows access to each terminal so testing can be performed using a meter or scope.

BTU   British thermal unit. A measure of heat energy. One BTU of heat will raise the temperature of one pound of water by one Fahrenheit degree.

Burn kV   Spark line voltage

BUS   A term used to describe a communication network.

Bypass ignition   A type of ignition system that uses the ignition control module to start the engine without the PCM but then switches to PCM control after the engine is running.

California Air Resources Board (CARB) A state of California state agency that regulates the air quality standards for the state.

CAN Controller area network. A type of serial data transmission.

CANP Canister purge.

Catalyst A catalyst is an element that starts a chemical reaction without becoming a part of, or being consumed in, the process.

Catalytic converter An emission control device located in the exhaust system that changes HC and CO into harmless H_2O and CO_2. If a three-way catalyst NO_x is also divided into harmless separate nitrogen (N_2) and Oxygen (O_2).

Catalytic cracking Breaking hydrocarbon chains using heat in the presence of a catalyst.

CCM Comprehensive Component Monitor.

Cellulose ethanol Ethanol produced from biomass feedstock such as agricultural and industrial plant wastes.

Cerium An element that can store oxygen.

Cetane number A diesel fuel rating that indicates how easily the fuel can be ignited.

Charging circuit Electrical components and connections necessary to keep a battery fully charged.

Charging rise time Using the digital storage oscilloscope and a current probe, a quick check can be made of the overall primary condition of the two most important parameters of the ignition circuit, the module current limits and the charging rise time of the circuit.

Check valve Contains a spring-type metallic disc or reed that closes the air line under exhaust backpressure.

Chrysler Collision Detection (CCD) The Chrysler Collision Detection (CCD) multiplex network is used for scan tool and module communications. It is a differential-type communication and uses a twisted pair of wires. The "collision" in the Chrysler Collision Detection BUS communications refers to the program that avoids conflicts of information exchange within the BUS and does not refer to airbags or other accident-related circuits of the vehicle.

CID Component identification.

Class 2 A type of BUS communication used in General Motors vehicles.

Clean Air Act Amendments (CAAA) Federal emission standards are set by the Clean Air Amendments (CAAA) of 1990 grouped by tier. All vehicles sold in the United States must meet Tier 1 standards that went into effect in 1994 and are the least stringent. Additional Tier 2 standards have been optional since 2001 and was fully phased in by 2009.

Clock generator A crystal that determines the speed of computer circuits.

Closed loop operation A phase of computer-controlled engine operation in which oxygen sensor feedback is used to calculate air/fuel mixture.

Cloud point The low-temperature point at which the waxes present in most diesel fuel tend to form wax crystals that clog the fuel filter.

Clutch volume index (CVI) Transmissions use input and an output speed sensors allowing the TCM to determine the gear ratio and how long it takes to make the shift. Chrysler refers to the adaptive control as the clutch volume index (CVI), which is the length of time it takes to fill the clutches with fluid.

Coal to liquid (CTL) A method used to make synthetic fuel.

CNG Compressed natural gas.

Coast-down stall A condition that results in the engine stalling when coasting to a stop.

Coil-on-plug ignition system An ignition system without a distributor, where each spark plug is integrated with an ignition coil.

Cold cranking amperes The rating of a battery's ability to provide battery voltage during cold-weather operation. CCA is the number of amperes that a battery can supply at 0°F (–18°C) for 30 seconds and still maintain a voltage of 1.2 V per cell (7.2 V for a 12-V battery).

Companion cylinder The cylinder that fires at the same time in a waste-spark-type ignition system.

Compressed natural gas (CNG) A type of alternative fuel.

Compression-sensing ignition A type of waste-spark ignition system that does not require the use of a camshaft position sensor to determine cylinder number.

Controller A term that is usually used to refer to a computer or an electronic control unit (ECU).

Controller Area Network (CAN) A type of serial data transmission.

COP ignition Coil-on-plug ignition. This term describes ignition systems where each spark plug has its own coil assembly mounted directly over top of it. Also known as coil-over-plug, coil-by-plug, or coil-near-plug ignition.

CPU Central processor unit.

Cracking A refinery process in which hydrocarbons with high boiling points are broken into hydrocarbons with low boiling points.

Cranking amperes A battery rating tested at 32°F (0°C).

Cranking circuit Electrical components and connections required to crank the engine to start. Includes starter motor, starter solenoid/relay, battery, neutral safety switch, ignition control switch, and connecting wires and cables.

Cranking compression test A engine diagnostic test that is performed by cranking the engine and measuring the cylinder pressure.

Cross counts Cross counts are the number of times an oxygen sensor changes voltage from high to low (from low to high voltage is not counted) in 1 second (or 1.25 second, depending on scan tool and computer speed).

CRT Cathode ray tube.

Cup design A design of an oxygen sensor that uses a shape like a cup or thimble.

Cycle A complete series of events that continually repeats.

Cylinder contribution test A cylinder contribution test, also called an injector power balance test, is an automated test that a scan tool performs by turning a fuel injector off to one cylinder at the time and monitors the drop, or increase in engine speed. This change in engine speed should be the same for all cylinders if all cylinders are working correctly.

Cylinder leakage test Fills the cylinder with compressed air, and the gauge indicates the percentage of leakage.

DC coupling A signal transmission that passes both AC and DC signal components to the meter. (See also AC coupling.)

Data link connector (DLC) The electrical connector where a scan tool is connected to access the computer of the vehicle.

DDS Demand delivery system.

Default (Limp in) A default (or limp-in) gear is the forward speed that is used if there is a failure in the electronic or computer system. If neither of two shift solenoids were engaged, then a default gear is actuated.

Default position The position of the throttle plate in an electronic throttle control without any signals from the controller.

Detonation A violent explosion in the combustion chamber created by uncontrolled burning of the air-fuel mixture; often causes a loud, audible knock. Also known as spark knock or ping.

DI   Distributor ignition.

Diagnostic executive   Software program designed to manage the operation of all OBD-II monitors by controlling the sequence of steps necessary to execute the diagnostic tests and monitors.

Dieseling   Dieseling, also called run-on, is a term used to describe the engine continuing to run after the ignition is turned off. A diesel engine operates by ignition of the fuel by heat of compression without the need for a spark to occur. Therefore, if the engine continues to run, an ignition source and fuel must be available. The ignition source is usually hot carbon deposits inside the combustion chamber.

Diesohol   Standard #2 diesel fuel combined with up to 15% ethanol.

Diffusion chamber   A section or part of a wide-band oxygen sensor that is exposed to exhaust gases.

Digital   A method of display that uses numbers instead of a needle or similar device.

DIS   Distributorless ignition system; also called direct-fire ignition system.

Displacement   The total volume displaced or swept by the cylinders in an internal combustion engine.

Displacement on demand (DOD)   A term used by General Motors to describe their variable displacement system.

Distillation   The process of purification through evaporation and then condensation of the desired liquid.

Distillation curve   A graph that plots the temperatures at which the various fractions of a fuel evaporate.

DMM   Digital multimeter. A digital multimeter is capable of measuring electrical current, resistance, and voltage.

DPFE sensor   Delta pressure feedback EGR sensor measures the pressure differential between two sides of a metered orifice positioned just below the EGR valve's exhaust side.

Drive-by-wire   A term used to describe an engine equipped with an electronic throttle control (ETC) system.

Drive cycle   Driving the vehicle under conditions that allow the PCM to conduct monitor tests.

DSO   Digital storage oscilloscope.

Dual cell   A design of a wide-band oxygen sensor that uses two cells.

Duty cycle   Refers to the percentage of on-time of the signal during one complete cycle.

DVOM   Digital volt-ohm-milliammeter.

Dwell   The amount of time, recorded on a dwell meter in degrees, that voltage passes through a closed switch.

Dynamic compression test   A compression test done with the engine running rather than during engine cranking, as is done in a regular compression test.

E10   A fuel blend of 10% ethanol and 90% gasoline.

E85   A fuel blend of 85% ethanol and 15% gasoline.

E & C   Entertainment and comfort.

EAC   Electronic air control.

ECA   Electronic control module. The name used by Ford to describe the computer used to control spark and fuel on older model vehicles.

ECM   Electronic control module on a vehicle.

ECT   Engine coolant temperature.

ECU   Electronic control unit on a vehicle.

E-Diesel   Standard #2 diesel fuel combined with up to 15% ethanol. Also known as diesohol.

EEPROM   Electronically erasable programmable read-only memory.

EGR   (Exhaust gas recirculation) An emission control device used to reduce NOx (oxides of nitrogen).

EI   Electronic ignition.

Electromagnetic induction   The generation of a current in a conductor that is moved through a magnetic field. Electromagnetic induction was discovered in 1831 by Michael Faraday.

Electromagnetic interference   An undesirable electronic signal. It is caused by a magnetic field building up and collapsing, creating unwanted electrical interference on a nearby circuit.

Electronic ignition   General term used to describe any of various types of ignition systems that use electronic instead of mechanical components, such as contact points.

Electronic pressure control (EPC)   A pulse-width-modulated solenoid used to control the transmission's hydraulic pump pressure regulator valve.

Electronic returnless fuel system   A fuel delivery system that does not return fuel to the tank.

Electronic spark timing   The computer controls spark timing advance.

Electronic throttle control (ETC)   A system that moves the throttle plate using an electric motor instead of a mechanical linkage from the accelerator pedal.

EMI   Electromagnetic interference. An undesirable electronic signal. It is caused by a magnetic field building up and collapsing, creating unwanted electrical interference on a nearby circuit.

Enable criteria   Operating condition requirements.

Engine mapping   A computer program that uses engine test data to determine the best fuel-air ratio and spark advance to use at each speed of the engine for best performance.

Equivalence ratio (ER)   The equivalence ratio (ER) is the inverse of lambda, with 1.0 equal to 1.0 lambda; however, 0.9 ER is equal to 1.1 lambda. Equivalence ratio (ER) = $1/\lambda$ (lambda), which is the inverse of lambda.

EREV   Extended range electric vehicle.

ERFS   Electronic returnless fuel system. A fuel delivery system that does not return fuel to the tank.

EST   Electronic spark timing.

ETBE   An octane enhancer for gasoline. It is also a fuel oxygenate that is manufactured by reacting isobutylene with ethanol. The resulting either is high octane and low volatility. ETBE can be added to gasoline up to a level of approximately 13 percent.

Ethanol   An octane enhancer added, at a rate of up to 10 percent, to gasoline; will increase the octane rating of the fuel by 2.5 to 3.0. Ethanol is a fuel oxygenate.

Ethyl alcohol   See definition for Ethanol.

EVP   A linear potentiometer on the top of the EGR valve stem indicates valve position for the computer.

EVRV   The computer pulses the solenoid to control the vacuum that regulates the operation of the EGR valve.

EWMA monitor   Exponentially weighted moving average monitor.

Exhaust gas recirculation   The process of passing a small, measured amount of exhaust gas back into the engine to reduce combustion temperatures and formation of NO_x (oxides of nitrogen).

Exhaust side-electrode   The electrode of a wide-band oxygen sensor that is exposed to the exhaust stream.

Exhaust valve   A valve through which burned gases from a cylinder escape into the exhaust manifold.

Exhaust valve cam phaser (EVCP) Spline phaser system of variable valve timing system.

External trigger When using an oscilloscope connecting when the scope is to be triggered or started is connected to another circuit when the one being measured.

Fail safe position A term used to describe the default position for the throttle plate in an electronic throttle control (ETC) system.

False air A term used to describe air that enters the engine without being measured by the mass air flow sensor.

False lean indication Occurs when an oxygen sensor reads low as a result of a factor besides a lean mixture.

False rich indication A high-oxygen sensor voltage reading that is not the result of a rich exhaust. Some common causes for this false rich indication include a contaminated oxygen sensor and having the signal wire close to a high-voltage source such as a spark plug wire.

FFV Flex-fuel vehicle. Flex-fuel vehicles are capable of running on straight gasoline or gasoline/ethanol blends.

Filter basket The final fuel filter in the fuel injection system located at the inlet of the fuel injector.

Finger design A design of an oxygen sensor that uses a shape like a cup or thimble.

Firing line The leftmost vertical (upward) line

Firing Order The order that the spark is distributed to the correct spark plug at the right time.

Fischer-Tropsch A refining process that converts coal, natural gas, or other petroleum products into synthetic motor fuels.

Flare An increase and then decrease in engine speed

Flare nut wrench A type of wrench used to remove brake lines.

Flash code retrieval a method used to retrieve diagnostic trouble codes that will cause the malfunction indicator light (MIL) to flash out the code sequence.

Flex fuel A term used to describe a vehicle that is capable of running on straight gasoline or gasoline–ethanol blends.

Four-stroke cycle An internal combustion engine design where four strokes of the piston (two crankshaft revolutions) are required to complete one cycle of events. The four strokes include intake, compression, power, and exhaust.

Fretting A condition that can destroy intake manifold gaskets and is caused by the unequal expansion and contraction of two different engine materials.

Freeze frame A snapshot of information.

Frequency The number of times a waveform repeats in one second, measured in Hertz (Hz), frequency band.

FTD Fischer-Tropsch diesel process. See Fischer-Tropsch.

FTP Federal test procedure.

Fuel compensation sensor A sensor used in flex-fuel vehicles that provides information to the PCM on the ethanol content and temperature of the fuel as it is flowing through the fuel delivery system.

Fuel rail A term used to describe the tube that delivers the fuel from the fuel line to the individual fuel injectors.

Fuel tank pressure (FTP) A sensor used to monitor the rate with which vacuum increases in the fuel tank.

Fuel trim A computer function that adjusts fuel delivery during closed-loop operation to bring the air-fuel mixture to as close to 14.7:1 as possible.

Fuel trim cells Most vehicles set aside different fuel trim cells for each combination of engine speed (RPM) and load. The computer can then correct for slight differences in fuel mixture separately for each cell.

Fungible A term used to describe a product, such as gasoline or electricity, that can be intermixed regardless of source because it is interchangeable and identical in physical properties.

Gang fired Pulsing injectors in groups.

Gasoline Refined petroleum product that is used primarily in a gasoline engine.

Gasoline direct injection A fuel injection system design in which gasoline is injected directly into the combustion chamber.

Generic OBD II See Global OBD II.

Gerotor A type of positive displacement pump that is often used in engine oil pumps. It uses the meshing of internal and external gear teeth to pressurize the fuel.

Global OBD II Is the standardized format of on-board diagnostics that is the same for all vehicles, following SAE standard J1962. Global OBD II was designed for engineers and when OBD II was first introduced, it was not intended to be used by service technicians.

GMLAN GM local area network. A type of serial data transmission by General Motors.

GMM Graphing multimeter.

Grain Alcohol See Ethanol.

Graticule The series of squares on the face of a scope. Usually 8 by 10 on a screen.

GTL Gas-to-liquid. A refining process in which natural gas is converted into liquid fuel.

Hall effect to come

Hall-effect switch A semiconductor moving relative to a magnetic field, creating a variable voltage output. Used to determine position. A type of electromagnetic sensor used in electronic ignition and other systems. Named for Edwin H. Hall, who discovered the Hall effect in 1879.

Hertz A unit of measurement of frequency. One Hertz is one cycle per second, abbreviated Hz. Named for Heinrich R. Hertz, a 19th-century German physicist.

Hesitation Hesitation means a delay in the operation of the engine when the accelerator pedal is depressed.

HEV Hybrid electric vehicle. Describes any vehicle that uses more than one source of propulsion, such as an internal combustion engine (ICE) and electric motor(s).

High energy ignition The brand name for the electronic ignition used in General Motors vehicles.

High impedance test meter A digital meter that has at least 10 million ohms of internal resistance as measure between the test leads with the meter set to read volts.

High voltage (HV) Applies to any voltage above 50 volts.

HSD High side driver.

HO2S Heated oxygen sensor.

Hybrid electric vehicle Describes any vehicle that uses more than one source of propulsion, such as internal combustion engine (ICE) and electric motor(s).

Homogeneous mode A mode of operation in a gasoline direct injection system where the air- fuel mixture is the same throughout the cylinder.

Hydrocracking A refinery process that converts hydrocarbons with a high boiling point into ones with low boiling points.

Hydrokinetic pump This design of pump rapidly moves the fuel to create pressure.

I/M 240 test It is a portion of the 505-second FTP test used by the manufacturers to certify their new vehicles. The "240" stands for 240 seconds of drive time on a dynamometer.

IAC Idle air control.

IC Ignition control.

ICM Ignition control module.

Idle air control (IAC) counts The commanded position of a typical idle air control valve

Idle speed control (ISC) motor A motor, usually a stepper motor, used to move a pintle that allows more or less air past the throttle plate thereby controlling idle speed.

Idle stop A condition when the engine stops when a hybrid electric vehicle comes to a stop.

IEC International Electrotechnical Commission.

Ignition coil An electrical device consists of two separate coils of wire: a primary and a secondary winding. The purpose of an ignition is to produce a high-voltage (20,000 to 40,000 V), low-amperage (about 80 mA) current necessary for spark ignition.

Ignition Off Draw A Chrysler term used to describe battery electrical drain or parasitic draw.

Ignition timing The exact point of ignition in relation to piston position.

Impeller The mechanism in a water pump that rotates to produce coolant flow.

Inches of Mercury A measurement of vacuum; pressure below atmospheric pressure.

Inductive ammeter A type of ammeter that is used a Hall Effect senor in a clamp that is used around a conductor carrying a current.

Inductive reactance An opposing current created in a conductor whenever there is a charging current flow in a conductor.

Inert Chemically inactive; not able to chemically combine with any other chemical.

Inertia switch Turns off the electric fuel pump in an accident.

Infrared thermometer (pyrometer) Measures the inlet and the outlet temperatures.

Input conditioning What the computer does to the input signals to make them useful; usually includes an analog to digital converter and other electronic circuits that eliminate electrical noise.

Input speed sensor (ISS) The sensor that measures the speed of the input shaft which is the same or almost the same as the engine speed. This is also called *turbine speed sensor (TSS)* because it is used to determine the speed of the turbine shaft.

Intake valve The valve that is open during the intake stroke and allows air to entire the cylinder.

Ion-sensing ignition An electronic ignition system that uses the spark plug as a sensor to determine camshaft position, misfire, and knock.

Iridium spark plugs Use a small amount of iridium welded onto the tip of a small center electrode 0.0015 to 0.002 inch (0.4 to 0.6 mm) in diameter. The small diameter reduces the voltage required to jump the gap between the center and the side electrode, thereby reducing possible misfires. The ground or side electrode is usually tipped with platinum to help reduce electrode sap wear.

ISC Idle speed control.

KAM Keep alive memory.

Key fob A decorative unit attached to keys. Often includes a remote control to unlock/lock vehicles.

Keyword A type of network communication used in many General Motors vehicles.

Kilo Means 1000; abbreviated k or K.

Knock sensor A sensor that can detect engine spark knock.

Lambda It is the Greek letter that represents ratio, as in air-fuel ratio.

Lambda Sensor Oxygen sensor or O_2 sensor. Lambda is the Greek letter that represents ratio, as in air-fuel ratio.

LDP Leak detection pump.

Lean air–fuel (LAF) sensor A term used to describe a wide-band oxygen sensor.

Lean indicator The higher the oxygen (O_2) levels in the exhaust the leaner the air–fuel mixture.

Lean misfire A very lean air–fuel mixture is often too lean to ignite. As a result, this unburned fuel is pushed out of the engine during the exhaust stroke.

LED test light Uses an LED instead of a standard automotive bulb for a visual indication of voltage.

Light-off temperature The catalytic converter does not work when cold and it must be heated to its light-off temperature of close to 500°F (260°C) before it starts working at 50% effectiveness.

Light-off time (LOT) The time it takes for an oxygen sensor to be start to work.

Linear EGR Contains a solenoid to precisely regulate exhaust gas flow and a feedback potentiometer that signals the computer regarding the actual position of the valve.

LOC Light-off converter.

Logic probe A type of tester that can detect either power or ground. Most testers can detect voltage but most of the others cannot detect if a ground is present without further testing.

Long-term fuel trim (LTFT) Long-term fuel trim (LTFT) is designed to add or subtract fuel for a longer amount of time than short-term fuel trim.

Low voltage Low voltage triggers the ignition control module (ICM) by the use of the rotating distributor shaft.

LPG Liquefied petroleum gas. Another term for propane.

LSD Low side driver.

M85 Internal combustion engine fuel containing 85% methanol and 15% gasoline.

Magnetic sensor A type of sensor that uses a magnet wrapped with a coil of wire.

Malfunction indicator lamp This amber dash board warning light may be labeled check engine or service engine soon.

Manifold absolute pressure Sensor used to measure the pressure inside the intake manifold compared to a perfect vacuum.

Mass air flow (MAF) sensor Measures the density and amount of air flowing into the engine, which results in accurate engine control.

MCA Marine cranking amps. A battery specification.

MDS Multiple displacement system. A Chrysler term used to describe their variable displacement system.

Mechanical returnless fuel system A returnless fuel delivery system design that uses a mechanical pressure regulator located in the fuel tank.

Mega Million. Used when writing larger numbers or measuring large amount of resistance.

Meter accuracy The accuracy of a meter measured in percent.

Meter resolution The specification of meter that indicates how small or fine a measurement the meter can detect and display.

Methanol Typically manufactured from natural gas. Methanol content, including co-solvents, in unleaded gasoline is limited by law to 5 percent.

Methanol to gasoline (MTG) A process of creating gasoline from methanol.

Methyl alcohol See Methanol.

Micro One-millionth of a volt or ampere.

MID Monitor Identification.

Milli One thousandth of a volt or ampere.

Millisecond(ms) sweep The scope will sweep only that portion of the pattern that can be shown during a 5- or 25-ms setting.

Mini converter A small, quick heating oxidation converter.

Misfire An engine misfire is when a cylinder does not fire or fire well enough to contribute to the operation of the engine. When the engine is running properly, each cylinder contributes equally and the engine speed is consistent.

Mode $06 Mode $06 is used to monitor all of the tests of the system and components. Mode $06 allows the service technician to view what the computer is doing and see the results of all of the tests that are being performed.

Module current limits Using the digital storage oscilloscope and a current probe, a quick check can be made of the overall primary condition of the two most important parameters of the ignition circuit, the module current limits and the charging rise time of the circuit.

MTBE Methyl tertiary butyl ether. MTBE is an oxygenated fuel that is used as a gasoline additive to enhance its burning characteristics being phased out due to ground water contamination concerns.

MTHF Methyltetrahydrofuron. A component of P-series nonpetroleum-based fuels.

Multiplexing A process of sending multiple signals of information at the same time over a signal wire.

Mutual Induction The generation of an electric current due to a changing magnetic field of an adjacent coil.

Negative backpressure On each exhaust stroke, the engine emits an exhaust "pulse." Each pulse represents a positive pressure. Behind each pulse is a small area of low pressure. Some EGR valves react to this low-pressure area by closing a small internal valve, which allows the EGR valve to be opened by vacuum.

Nernst cell Another name for a conventional oxygen sensor. The Nernst cell is named for Walther Nernst, 1864–1941, a German physicist known for his work in electrochemistry.

Network A communications system used to link multiple computers or modules.

Neutral position A term used to describe the home or the default position of the throttle plate in an electronic throttle control system.

NGV Natural gas vehicle.

NMHC Non-methane hydrocarbon.

Node A module and computer that is part of a communications network.

Nonchecking Some General Motors throttle-body units that do not hold pressure.

Nonvolatile RAM Computer memory capability that is not lost when power is removed.

Noid light Designed to electrically replace the injector in the circuit and to flash if the injector circuit is working correctly.

NOx Oxides of nitrogen; when combined with HC and sunlight, form smog.

NTC Usually used in reference to a temperature sensor (coolant or air temperature). As the temperature increases, the resistance of the sensor decreases.

Octane rating The measurement of a gasoline's ability to resist engine knock. The higher the octane rating, the less prone the gasoline is to cause engine knock (detonation).

Oil control valve (OCV) The camshaft position actuator oil control valve (OCV) directs oil from the oil feed in the head to the appropriate camshaft position actuator oil passages.

Oil gallery An oil pump which is driven by the engine, forces the oil through the oil filter and then into passages in the crankshaft and block.

OL Overload or over limit

Open circuit Any circuit that is not complete and in which no current flows.

Open loop operation A phase of computer-controlled engine operation where air/fuel mixture is calculated in the absence of oxygen sensor signals. During open loop, calculations are based primarily on throttle position, engine RPM, and engine coolant temperature.

Optical sensors Use light from a LED and a phototransistor to signal the computer.

Organic A term used to describe anything that was alive at one time.

ORVR Onboard refueling vapor recovery.

OSC Oxygen storage capacity.

Oscilloscope A visual display of electrical waves on a fluorescent screen or cathode ray tube.

Output speed sensor (OSS) This speed sensor, also called the vehicle speed (VS) sensor, is used by the PCM for speedometer and cruise control operation as well as for transmission/transaxle operation and shift-related fault detection.

Oxygenated fuels Fuels such as ETBE or MTBE that contain extra oxygen molecules to promote cleaner burning. Oxygenated fuels are used as gasoline additives to reduce CO emissions.

Oxygen sensor (O2S) A sensor in the exhaust system to measure the oxygen content of the exhaust.

Ozone Oxygen rich (O_3) gas created by sunlight reaction with unburned hydrocarbons (HC) and oxides of nitrogen (NO_x); also called smog.

Paired cylinders Another name used to describe companion cylinders in a waste-spark-type ignition system.

Palladium An element that acts as a catalyst.

Paper test Hold a piece of paper or a 3 × 5 index card (even a dollar bill works) within 1 inch (2.5 cm) of the tailpipe with the engine running at idle. The paper should blow out evenly without "puffing." If the paper is drawn toward the tailpipe at times, the exhaust valves in one or more cylinders could be burned.

PCV Positive crankcase ventilation.

Peak-and-hold injector A type of injector driver that uses full battery voltage to the injector and the ground side is controlled through the computer. The computer provides a high initial current flow (about 4 amperes) to flow through the injector windings to open the injector core. Then the computer reduces the current to a lower level (about 1 ampere).

Pending code A code(s) that is displayed on a scan tool when the MIL is not on. Because the MIL is not on, this indicates that the fault has not repeated to cause the PCM to turn on the MIL.

Petrodiesel Another term for petroleum diesel, which is ordinary diesel fuel refined from crude oil.

Petroleum   Another term for crude oil. The literal meaning of petroleum is "rock oil."

PFE   Pressure feedback EGR.

Pickup coil   An ignition electronic triggering device in the magnetic pulse generator system.

Piezoresistivity   Change in resistance due to strain.

Ping   Secondary rapid burning of the last 3 to 5% of the air-fuel mixture in the combustion chamber causes a second flame front that collides with the first flame front causing a knock noise. Also called detonation or spark knock.

Piston stroke   Is a one-way piston movement between the top and bottom of the cylinder.

Planar design   A design of oxygen sensor where the elements including the zirconia electrolyte and the two electrodes and heater are stacked together in a flat type design.

Plastic optical fiber (POF)   The material used to transmit data over the byte flight BUS used in safety critical systems, such as airbags, and uses the time division multiple access (TDMA) protocol, which operates at 10 million bps.

Platinum   An element that acts as a catalyst.

Platinum spark plugs   Spark plugs that have a small amount of the precious metal platinum included on the end of the center electrode, as well as on the ground or side electrode.

Polarity   The condition of being positive or negative in relation to a magnetic pole.

Port fuel-injection   Uses a nozzle for each cylinder and the fuel is squirted into the intake manifold about 2 to 3 inches (70 to 100 mm) from the intake valve.

Positive backpressure   At low engine speeds and light engine loads, the EGR system is not needed, and the backpressure in it is also low.

Potentiometer   A 3-terminal variable resistor that varies the voltage drop in a circuit.

Power balance test   A test to determine if all cylinders are contributing power equally.

Powertrain control module   The on-board computer that controls both the engine management and transmission functions of the vehicle.

Preconverter   See Mini Converter.

Pressure control solenoid (PCS)   A computer-controlled solenoid that maintains the proper pressure in the hydraulic system of an electronically controlled automatic transmission. Also called a *variable force solenoid or force motor*.

Pressure control valve (PCV)   A valve used to control the fuel system pressure on a demand delivery-type fuel system.

Pressure differential   A difference in pressure from one brake circuit to another.

Pressure transducer   A pressure transducer can be used in the low- and/or high-pressure refrigerant line. The transducer converts the system pressure into an electrical signal that allows the ECM to monitor pressure.

Pressure vent valve   A valve located in the fuel tank to prevent overpressure due to the thermal expansion of the fuel.

Primary winding   The coil winding that is controlled by the electronic ignition control module or PCM.

Programmable controller interface (PCI)   A type of network communications protocol used in Chrysler brand vehicles.

PROM   Programmable read-only memory.

Propane   See LPG.

Protocol   A protocol is set of rules or a standard used between computers or electronic control modules. Protocols include the type of electrical connectors, voltage levels, and frequency of the transmitted messages. Protocols, therefore, include both the hardware and the software needed to communicate between modules.

Pulse generator   An electromagnetic unit that generates a voltage signal used to trigger the ignition control module that controls (turns on and off) the primary ignition current of an electronic ignition system.

Pulse train   A DC voltage that turns on and off in a series of pulses.

Pulse width   The amount of "on" time of an electronic fuel injector.

Pump cell   A pump cell is the area above the Nernst cell which is another zirconia layer with two electrodes. The two cells share a common ground, which is called the reference.

Pup converter   A small catalytic converter that is used upstream from the main converter.

PWM   Pulse-width modulation. The control of a device by varying the on-time of the current flowing through the device.

Radio frequency identification (RFID)   Most security systems today use a radio frequency identification (RFID) security system.

RAM   A nonpermanent type of computer memory used to store and retrieve information.

Rationality   Refers to a PCM comparison of input value to values.

Read-only memory   A permanent type of computer memory programmed by the computer manufacturer to store the operating instructions and parameters of the computer.

Reference electrode   This electrode is exposed to outside (ambient) air and is the signal electrode, also called the reference electrode or ambient air electrode.

Reference voltage   In a conventional zirconia oxygen sensor, a bias or reference voltage can be applied to the two platinum electrodes, and then oxygen ions can be forced (pumped) from the ambient reference air side to the exhaust side of the sensor.

Remote keyless entry (RKE)   The part of the key fob has a battery to power the transmitter, which is used to lock and unlock a vehicle door(s) by remote control.

Reserve capacity   The number of minutes a battery can produce 25 A and still maintain a battery voltage of 1.75 V per cell (10.5 V for a 12 V battery).

Residual or rest pressure   Prevents vapor lock and hot-start problems on these systems.

RFG   Reformulated gasoline. RFG has oxygenated additives and is refined to reduce both the lightest and heaviest hydrocarbon content from gasoline in order to promote cleaner burning.

Rhodium   An element that acts as a catalyst.

Rich indicator   CO is the rich indicator. The higher the CO reading, the richer the air–fuel mixture. High concentrations of CO indicate that not enough oxygen was available for the amount of fuel.

RMS   Root mean square.

Roller cell   Vane pump.

Rotary vane pump   The pump consists of a central impeller disk, several rollers or vanes that ride in notches in the impeller, and a pump housing that is offset from the impeller centerline.

Rough (unstable) idle   Rough (or unstable) idle is a common occurrence because many different systems have a direct effect on idle quality. If the engine stalls (stops running), most customers are very concerned because it can be a safety-related malfunction. For the engine to idle correctly, each cylinder has to have the same (or nearly the same) compression, air–fuel mixture, ignition timing, and quality of spark.

Running compression test The running compression test can inform a technician of the relative compression of all the cylinders.

Run-on A term used to describe the engine continuing to run after the ignition is turned off. Also called dieseling. A diesel engine operates by ignition of the fuel by heat of compression without the need for a spark to occur. Therefore, if the engine continues to run, an ignition source and fuel must be available. The ignition source is usually hot carbon deposits inside the combustion chamber.

RVP Reid vapor pressure. A measure of the volatility at exactly 100 degrees F.

Sag means a delay in the operation of the engine when the accelerator pedal is depressed. Also called a hesitation.

Saturation The point of maximum magnetic field strength of a coil.

Scan tool An electronic test device that can communicate with the vehicle's control module and determine operational data.

Schmitt trigger Converts the analog signal into a digital signal.

Secondary winding A winding that has about 100 times the number of turns of the primary winding, referred to as the turns ratio (approximately 100:1).

Self-Induction The generation of an electric current in the wires of a coil created when the current if first connected or disconnected.

Servomotor An electric motor that moves an actuator such as the throttle plate in an electronic throttle control system.

Sequential fuel injection A fuel injection system in which injectors are pulsed individually in sequence with the firing order.

Serial communication interface (SCI) Serial Communication Interface, a type of serial data transmission used by Chrysler.

Serial data Data that is transmitted by a series of rapidly changing voltage signals

SHED test Sealed housing for evaporative determination test.

Short-term fuel trim (STFT) Short-term fuel trim (STFT) is a percentage measurement of the amount the computer is adding or subtracting from a calculated value.

SIDI Spark ignition direct injection.

Side-channel pump Turbine pump

Signal electrode This electrode is exposed to outside (ambient) air and is the signal electrode, also called the reference electrode or ambient air electrode.

Single cell A type of wide-band oxygen sensor that uses one cell using four wires; two for the heater and two cell wires.

SIP State implementation plan.

Skewed Inaccurate information such as a skewed sensor that does not show the value of the conditions to the PCM accurately.

Slip ring end The end of a generator (alternator) that has the brushes and the slip rings.

Smog The term used to describe a combination of smoke and fog. Formed by NO_x and HC with sunlight.

Smog pump Pulls fresh air in through an external filter and pumps the air under slight pressure to each exhaust port through connecting hoses or a manifold.

Smoke machine A machine that generates smoke under a slight pressure which can be used to find leaks. Usually used to find leaks in the EVAP system.

Society of automotive engineers (SAE) A professional organization made up of automotive engineers and designers that establishes standards and conducts testing for many automotive-related functions.

Spark knock Secondary rapid burning of the last 3 to 5% of the air-fuel mixture in the combustion chamber. Causes a second flame front that collides with the first flame front causing a knock noise.

Spark line A short horizontal line immediately after the firing line.

Spark tester Looks like a spark plug except it has a recessed center electrode and no side electrode. The tester commonly has an alligator clip attached to the shell so that it can be clamped on a good ground connection on the engine.

Splice pack A central point where many serial data lines jam together, often abbreviated SP.

Spline phaser A type of variable valve timing actuator that uses a piston inside the cam phaser and rides along the helical splines, which compresses a coil spring. This movement causes the cam phaser gear and the camshaft to move in an opposite direction.

SPOUT The term used by Ford to describe the "spark out" signal from the ICM to the PCM.

Stall An engine that stops running.

Standard corporate protocol (SCP) A network communications protocol used by Ford.

Stumble a hesitation, or sag, during acceleration.

State-of-health (SOH) A signal sent by modules to all of the other modules in the network indicating that it is well and able to transmit.

Stoichiometric An air-fuel ratio of exactly 14.7:1. At this specific rate, all the gasoline is fully oxidized by all the available oxygen.

Straight vegetable oil (SVO) A term used to describe vegetable oil which is a triglyceride with a glycerin component.

Stratified mode A mode of engine operation where the air–fuel mixture is richer around the spark plug than it is in the rest of the cylinder.

Stroke The distance the piston travels in the cylinder of an engine.

Surge A surge is a change in engine power under steady throttle conditions. A driver may feel a surge as if the vehicle was speeding up and slowing down with no change in the accelerator pedal. A lean air–fuel mixture is the most common cause of this condition.

SWCAN Abbreviation for single wire CAN (controller area network).

Switchgrass A feedstock for ethanol production that requires very little energy or fertilizer to cultivate.

Switching Turning on and off of the primary circuit.

Syn-gas Synthesis gas generated by a reaction between coal and steam. Syn-gas is made up of mostly hydrogen and carbon monoxide and is used to make methanol. Syn-gas is also known as town gas.

Syncrude Crude oil generated from coal or natural gas through synthetic processes such as Fischer-Tropsch.

Synthetic fuel Fuels generated through synthetic processes such as Fischer-Tropsch.

TAME Tertiary amyl methyl ether. TAME is an oxygenating fuel and is used as a gasoline additive similar to ETBE or MTBE.

Tap test Involves tapping (not pounding) on the catalytic converter using a rubber mallet.

Task manager A term Chrysler uses to describe the software program that is designed to manage the operation of all OBD-II monitors by controlling the sequence of steps necessary to execute the diagnostic tests and monitors.

TBI Throttle body injection.

Technical service bulletin (TSB) Special papers that describe certain repair operations for specific vehicles.

TEL Tetra ethyl lead. TEL was used as an antiknock additive in gasoline, but has been phased out in favor of more benign additives such as ethanol.

Terminating resistor Resistors placed at the end of a high-speed serial data circuit to help reduce electromagnetic interference.

Test light A light used to test for voltage. Contains a light bulb with a ground wire at one end and a pointed tip at the other end.

Thermactor pump See Smog pump.

Thimble design A design of an oxygen sensor that uses a shape like a cup or thimble.

Throttle position sensor Signals the computer as to the position of the throttle.

TID Task identification.

Time base The setting of the amount of time per division when adjusting a scope.

Top dead center (TDC) The highest point in the cylinder that the piston can travel. The measurement from bottom dead center (BDC) to TDC determines the stroke length of the crankshaft.

Torque management The program inside the powertrain control module that controls shift timing and quality to provide a smoother driving experience.

Transceiver A transceiver functions as both a reviewer and a transmitter. The transceiver is usually mounted on the steering column assembly. The antenna for the transceiver is a coil of wire mounted within the plastic ring that mounts around the lock cylinder.

Transponder The transponder is mounted in the key or the body of the key fob. A transponder has an antenna, which consists of a coil of wire as well as a circuit board containing the processing electronics and data memory

Transistor A semiconductor device that can operate as an amplifier or an electrical switch.

Transmission adapt pressure (TAP) The General Motor's term for which manages oil pressure to control clutch fill rates to allow for adaptive control and which compensates for clutch pack wear.

Transmission control module (TCM) The term given to the computer that controls An automatic transmission and called a *transmission control unit (TCU)*.

Transmission range (TR) switch The transmission switch, also called the manual lever position (MLP) sensor, is used as an input to the PCM/TCM which indicates the driver request for which drive range is being requested.

Trigger A trigger is a device that signals the switching of the coil on and off. A trigger is typically a pickup coil in some distributor-type ignitions and a crankshaft position sensor (CKP) on electronic systems (waste spark and coil on plug).

Trigger level The voltage level that a waveform must reach to start display.

Trigger slope The voltage direction that a waveform must have to start display. A positive slope requires the voltage to be increasing as it crosses the trigger level; a negative slope requires the voltage to be decreasing.

Trip The vehicle must be driven under a variety of operating conditions for all active tests to be performed. A trip is defined as an engine-operating drive cycle that contains the necessary conditions for a particular test to be performed.

Turbine pump Turns at higher speeds and is quieter than the other electric pumps.

Turbine speed sensor (TSS) The sensor that measures the speed of the input shaft that is the same or almost the same as the engine speed. This is also called input speed sensor (ISS).

Turns ratio The ratio between the number of turns in the primary and number of turns in the secondary winding of an ignition coil.

TWC Three-way catalytic converter, all three exhaust emissions (NO_x, HC, and CO) are converted to carbon dioxide (CO_2) and water (H_2O).

Twisted pair A pair of wires that are twisted together from 9 to 16 turns per foot of length. Most are twisted once every inch (12 per foot) to help reduce electromagnetic interference from being induced in the wires as one wire would tend to cancel out any interference pickup up by the other wire.

UART Universal asynchronous receive/transmit, a type of serial data transmission.

UBP UART-based protocol

UCG Underground coal gasification.

ULSD Ultra-low-sulfur Diesel. Diesel fuel with a maximum sulfur content of 15 parts per million.

Up-integrated ignition A type of ignition system that does use a separate ignition control module. All functions of the ignition are included inside the PCM.

Vacuum lock Fuel tanks must be vented to prevent a vacuum lock as fuel is drawn from the tank. As fuel is used and its level drops in the tank, the space above the fuel increases. As the air in the tank expands to fill this greater space, its pressure drops. Without a vent, the air pressure inside the tank would drop below atmospheric pressure, developing a vacuum which prevents the flow of fuel.

Vane airflow (VAF) sensor Older engine systems use a movable vane in the intake stream called a vane airflow (VAF) sensor. The vane is part of the vane airflow (VAF) sensor. The vane is deflected by intake airflow.

Vane phaser A vane phaser is an actuator used in most variable valve timing systems and uses a rotor with four vanes, which is connected to the end of the camshaft. The rotor is located inside the stator, which is bolted to the cam sprocket. The stator and rotor are not connected. Oil pressure is controlled on both sides of the vanes of the rotor, which creates a hydraulic link between the two parts. The oil control valve varies the balance of pressure on either side of the vanes and thereby controls the position of the camshaft. A return spring is used under the reluctor of the phaser to help return it to the home or zero degrees position.

Vapor lock A lean condition caused by vaporized fuel in the fuel system.

Variable displacement system A term used to describe a system where some cylinders are deactivated to reduce fuel consumption.

Variable fuel sensor See definition for compensation sensor.

Vehicle speed (VS) sensor A sensor that measures the speed of vehicle. It can use the output speed sensor or the wheel speed sensor depending on the vehicle.

V-FFV Virtual flexible fuel vehicle. This fuel system design does not use a fuel compensation sensor and instead uses the vehicle's oxygen sensor to adjust for different fuel compositions.

Volatile Volatile RAM memory is lost whenever the ignition is turned off.

Volatile organic compound These compounds include gases emitted from paints, solvents, glass, and many other products.

Volatility A measurement of the tendency of a liquid to change to vapor. Volatility is measured using RVP, or Reid vapor pressure.

Voltage drop Voltage loss across a wire, connector, or any other conductor. Voltage drop equals resistance in ohms times current in amperes (Ohm's law).

Volumetric efficiency The ratio between the amount of air-fuel mixture that actually enters the cylinder and the amount that could enter under ideal conditions expressed in percent.

VTEC Variable valve timing and lift electronic control. A term used by Honda/ Acura to describe their variable timing and lift system.

VVT Variable valve timing

Washcoat A porous aluminum material

Waste vegetable oil (WVO) Oil that is used and can include animal or fish oils from the cooking process.

Wet compression test When oil is used to help seal around the piston rings.

Wood alcohol See Methanol.

WWFC World wide fuel charter. A fuel quality standard developed by vehicle and engine manufacturers in 2002.

INDEX